2004

ATTORNEY-CLIENT PRIVILEGE IN CIVIL LITIGATION

PROTECTING AND DEFENDING CONFIDENTIALITY

VINCENT S. WALKOWIAK, EDITOR

SHEARMAN & STERLING LLP
801 Pennsylvania Ave., N.W., Suite 900
Washington, DC 20004-2604

Defending Liberty
Pursuing Justice

Cover design by ABA Publishing

08 07 06 05 04   5 4 3 2 1

Cataloging in Publication data is on file with the Library of Congress.

Walkowiak, Vincent S., 1946– .
The attorney-client privilege in civil litigation / Vincent S. Walkowiak, editor
    Includes index.
    ISBN 1-59031-394-1 (pbk.)

Discounts are available for books ordered in bulk. Special consideration is given to state bars, CLE programs, and other bar-related organizations. Inquire at Book Publishing, ABA Publishing, American Bar Association, 321 North Clark Street, Chicago, Illinois 60610.

www.ababooks.org

Contents

CHAPTER 9
**A Second Look at Privilege and Confidentiality in the
Reinsurance Arena   149**
John W. Thornton
Jane Thornton Mastrucci
Cynthia Harrison Ruiz

CHAPTER 10
**Attorney-Client and Work-Product Doctrines in Environmental
Coverage Litigation   217**
Margaret E. Wetherald
Deborah Dowd

CHAPTER 11
**Preserving the Confidentiality of Investigations by In-House and
Outside Counsel   223**
Aimee B. Anderson

CHAPTER 12

**Applying the Attorney-Client Privilege to Investigations Involving
Attorneys: What Is Fair Game in Discovery?   245**

David E. Bland
Scott G. Johnson
Elisabeth M. Will

CHAPTER 13
Conflict Between the Permissive Scope of Fact Witness Investigation and Protection of Attorney-Client Communication   283
Vincent S. Walkowiak

CHAPTER 14
Discovery of the In-House Expert Assigned to Litigation   303
Joseph C. Kearfott

CHAPTER 22
Beyond the Labor and Employment Lawyer's Looking Glass: Who Is My Client?   441

Jeffrey S. Goldman
Philip F. Ackerman

Preface

The Third Edition of *The Attorney-Client Privilege in Civil Litigation* (originally published as *The Attorney-Client Privilege Under Siege*) is the product of the hard work of the numerous authors who contributed chapters to it. When the book was first published in 1989, it was perceived that the attorney-client privilege had been coming under increasing attack. Recent developments, culminating in the debate that surrounded passage of the Sarbanes-Oxley Act and proposals to alter the confidentiality obligations of attorneys, have contributed to the perception that the attorney-client privilege is under continuing attack.

We hope that this volume of related works will contribute to understanding the appropriate parameters of this most important evidentiary privilege.

While the work of the authors is pivotal to the volume, there have been unrecognized contributors. I would like to thank Kevin Miles, our law librarian, for assisting in last-minute cite checks. The largest unrecognized contributor has been my secretary, Janice Hoffman. Aside from having typed and retyped many of the chapters, she coordinated receipt of the chapters, contacted many of the authors numerous times, and assisted in editing a number of the chapters. More than once she caught editing problems that had escaped my initial attention. Her assistance was invaluable.

Vincent S. Walkowiak
Fulbright & Jaworski L.L.P.
Dallas, Texas
2004

About the Editor

Vince Walkowiak is a partner in the Dallas office of Fulbright & Jaworski L.L.P. and is the co-head of the firm's product liability litigation practice group. Mr. Walkowiak has extensive experience in tort and commercial litigation, including the defense of products liability, extra-contractual liability, and lender liability issues. He is a former law professor who has represented several European and Asian companies transacting business in the United States and has authored or edited more than 11 books on product liability or attorney-client privilege topics.

Mr. Walkowiak is an experienced trial attorney, having represented clients in both federal and state courts as well as in alternative dispute resolution forums, including arbitrations and mediations. In addition, he has been counsel before the United States Consumer Product Safety Commission, representing clients' interests in matters involving product recall issues.

Mr. Walkowiak is a member of the Defense Research Institute, the International Association of Defense Counsel, the National Institute of Trial Advocacy, the Texas Association of Defense Counsel, and the College of the State Bar. He is a sustaining member of the Product Liability Advisory Council. He is a fellow of the Dallas and Texas Bar Foundations and a member of the Minnesota State, Illinois State, and American Bar Associations, as well as the State Bar of Texas. He is currently on the Board of Directors of the Texas General Counsel Practices Forum. He has held numerous offices in the American Bar Association and was the 1998-1999 Chair of the Civil Procedure & Evidence Committee of the Tort and Insurance Practice Section of the ABA.

Mr. Walkowiak has written numerous law review articles and book chapters and has edited books on products liability and trial practice. A former law professor, he often addresses legal education groups and has been a faculty member of the National Institute of Trial Advocacy since 1979.

Mr. Walkowiak received a B.A. in 1968 and a J.D. in 1971 from the University of Illinois.

About the Authors

Philip F. Ackerman
Philip Ackerman is a litigation associate at Sonnenschein, Nath & Rosenthal, L.L.P. After law school, he worked at Altheimer & Gray until 2003. Prior to law school, he worked at The Northern Trust Company. He has a B.B.A. from the University of Wisconsin-Madison and a J.D. from Tulane Law School.

Aimee B. Anderson
Aimee Anderson is a partner at Wildman, Harrold, Allen & Dixon L.L.P. and concentrates her practice in the areas of product liability defense, local governmental liability, and civil rights litigation. Ms. Anderson was formerly a senior counsel in the police policy section of the City of Chicago Law Department and has served on committees of the American Bar and Chicago Bar Associations, as well as the Illinois Law Enforcement Training & Standards Board. She has written and lectured extensively to bar associations and law enforcement agencies on topics such as discovery and trial practice in civil litigation, racial profiling, and civil rights litigation.

David E. Bland
David Bland is a partner at Robins, Kaplan, Miller & Ciresi, L.L.P., practicing in the firm's Los Angeles and Minneapolis offices. He received his B.A. in 1975 from the University of Minnesota and his J.D., cum laude, in 1979 from William Mitchell College of Law. His practice focuses on property and liability insurance coverage litigation, directors' and officers' coverage litigation, crime and fidelity claim evaluation and litigation, environmental litigation, construction litigation, national coordination of claim defense, drafting of policy language and endorsements to insurance policies, intellectual property litigation, and general commercial litigation. He also has an active appellate practice.

Jeffery J. Carlson
Jeffery Carlson, a 1974 graduate of UCLA School of Law, is the managing partner at Carlson, Messer & Turner, L.L.P., a general civil litigation defense firm specializing in product liability, toxic tort litigation, professional malpractice, insurance, and employment law. Mr. Carlson has authored and co-authored many articles and lectured on numerous continuing education panels and seminars on such diverse topics as product liability law, toxic torts, trial technique, evidentiary matters, expert witnesses, and *Daubert*. He is a member of the American Bar Association, Association of Defense Trial Attorneys, Defense Research Institute (Drug & Medical Device Steering Committee), Federation of Defense and Corporate Counsel, and Product Liability Advisory Committee.

Harva Dockery
Harva Dockery, has been a partner with Fulbright & Jaworski, L.L.P. in Dallas, Texas, since 1989 and has extensive experience in corporate and securities law, mergers and acquisitions, oil and gas limited partnership offerings, and master limited partnerships. In addition, Ms. Dockery handles public and private securities offerings, tender offers, proxy solicitations, going-private transactions, joint ventures, loan transactions, workouts, and conversions of agricultural cooperatives into business corporations. She has also handled corporate and securities matters for various constituencies in bankruptcy and workout contexts. She received a B.A. in 1975 and a J.D. in 1980 from the University of Texas, where she was a member of the *Texas Law Review.*

Deborah Dowd
Deborah Dowd is a solo practitioner in Seattle, Washington. Her practice emphasizes coverage issues for insurers on the national level. She graduated from Washington & Lee University School of Law in 1976.

Brien Flanagan
Brien Flanagan is an associate in Schwabe, Williamson & Wyatt's Environmental Law Department, Portland, Oregon. Mr. Flanagan's practice centers on federal and state remediation, cost recovery, and contribution actions. In addition, he handles litigation matters in bankruptcy and commercial litigation, antitrust, and mass torts cases. Mr. Flanagan has experience consulting with small and medium-sized businesses on compliance and mitigation measures to avoid or minimize potential liability.

Arthur H. Garwin
Arthur H. Garwin is ABA's Professionalism Counsel and director of Publications and Conference Planning for the ABA Center for Professional Responsibility. He has served as staff counsel to the ABA Standing Committee on Professionalism and to the ABA Commission on Multidisciplinary Practice and has written numerous articles on professional responsibility, including 39 ethics columns for the *ABA Journal.* He also has served for 10 years as editor of *The Professional Lawyer.* Mr. Garwin has B.S. and J.D. degrees from the University of Illinois and an M.B.A. from Northwestern University. He practiced law for 15 years before coming to the ABA in 1990.

Jeffrey S. Goldman
Mr. Goldman is a partner in Sonnenschein's Labor and Employment Group in Chicago, Illinois. His practice involves labor law, management rights and responsibilities, and the defense of disparate business practices. In recent years he has defended the wage classification systems of white-collar employers in financial services across the country. He represents businesses throughout the country in labor, employment, and civil rights litigation, equal opportunity matters, and discriminatory business practices issues. He graduated from Brown University with an A.B. in history and earned his J.D. from the University of Chicago Law School.

Kenneth A. Hindman

Kenneth A. Hindman is Of Counsel to Fellows, Johnson & LaBriola in Atlanta, Georgia. His practice is concentrated on litigation of business and insurance matters and on appellate practice. He earned a B.A. with distinction from the University of Virginia and also received his J.D. from that school, where he was an Echols Scholar and a DuPont Regional Scholar.

Neal Hueske

Neal Hueske is a partner in the Bend, Oregon, office of Schwabe, Williamson & Wyatt, LLC. Since joining the firm in 1991, Mr. Hueske has focused his practice on both judicial and administrative environmental matters, as well as on general civil litigation. Specific areas of expertise include air quality, wetlands, water rights, remediation of contaminated property, and litigation over species protection. He is a former adjunct professor at Northwestern School of Law, Lewis & Clark College.

Allan Kanner

Allan Kanner is a member of Allan Kanner & Associates, P.L.L.C., with offices in New Orleans, Louisiana, where he specializes in environmental, toxic tort, class action, and complex business litigation. He is a member of the bars of Louisiana, New Jersey, Pennsylvania, California, the District of Columbia, and Puerto Rico (Federal). Since 1990, he has been an Adjunct Professor of Law at the Tulane Law School. In 2004, he is a Visiting Lecturer at the Duke Law School and Boalt Hall. Previously he was a Visiting Professor at Yale Law School and the University of Texas Law Schools. He earned an A.B. from the University of Pennsylvania and a J.D. from Harvard Law School.

Joseph C. Kearfott

Joseph Kearfott is with Hunton & Williams, L.L.P., Richmond, Virginia, and has been a lecturer on civil litigation at the University of Virginia-Georgetown and T.C. Williams School of Law, at the Washington and Lee Trial Advocacy Course, and at various courses sponsored by the ALI-ABA, American and Richmond Bar Associations, and Virginia CLE. He is co-author of *Virginia Evidentiary Foundations*. He earned a B.A. from Davidson College and a J.D. from the University of Virginia.

Eileen C. Kennelly

Eileen Kennelly is an associate in the New York office of LeBoeuf, Lamb, Greene & MacRae, L.L.P. Ms. Kennelly practices in the area of commercial litigation and arbitration with a concentration on insurance and reinsurance matters.

Michael A. Knoerzer

Michael Knoerzer is a partner in the New York office of LeBoeuf, Lamb, Greene & MacRae, L.L.P., where he practices in the area of commercial litigation and arbitration with an emphasis on oil insurance and reinsurance disputes. Mr. Knoerzer has been a speaker and author on oil reinsurance topics for Mealey's, ARIAS-U.S., the Practising Law Institute, and the American Bar Association. He also serves as mediator in the Alternative Dispute Resolution Program of the New York State Supreme Court.

Scott G. Johnson

Scott Johnson is a partner in Robins, Kaplan, Miller & Ciresi, L.L.P., practicing in the firm's Los Angeles and Minneapolis offices. He received his B.S., magna cum laude, in 1982 from Winona State University and his J.D., magna cum laude, in 1986 from William Mitchell College of Law. His practice focuses primarily on property and liability insurance coverage litigation, subrogation, and general commercial litigation.

Thomas J. Leach

Thomas Leach is professor of law and director of the Center for Legal Advocacy at the University of the Pacific-McGeorge School of Law in Sacramento, California, where he teaches trial advocacy. From 1978 to 1996 he was a trial attorney with the Philadelphia firm of Drinker, Dibble & Reath, practicing construction law, franchising, and products liability. Mr. Leach holds a J.D. from the University of Pennsylvania, an M.A. in teaching from Wesleyan University (1969), and a B.A. from Cornell University (1967). He has taught in numerous deposition and trial advocacy training programs for the National Institute for Trial Advocacy and currently directs its Western Deposition and Western Regional Programs.

Sarah Elizabeth Lemons

Sarah Lemons is a litigation associate with the Dallas, Texas, office of Fulbright & Jaworski, L.L.P. She received her B.A., cum laude, in 2000 and her J.D. in 2003 from Vanderbilt University, where she was the executive editor of the *Vanderbilt Journal of Entertainment Law & Practice.*

Alan J. Martin

Alan Martin has been with the Chicago, Illinois, law firm of Mayer, Brown, Rowe & Maw L.L.P. since 1987 and has been a partner since 1993. His primary practice area encompasses representation in complex insurance coverages, general commercial litigation, and arbitration, both as counsel and as an arbitrator.

Jane Thornton Mastrucci

Jane Thornton Mastrucci is a partner at Quintairos, Prieto, Wood & Boyer, P.A. and practices from the firm's Miami, Florida, office. Her areas of practice are nursing home, hospital, insurance, and medical malpractice defense litigation. She is also one of only a handful of lawyers in Florida who specialize in nursing home administrative law. She graduated magna cum laude from the University of Notre Dame and earned a J.D. from Notre Dame Law School in 1978. She co-authored four articles with her father, John W. Thornton, Sr., and has given numerous presentations in the nursing home and healthcare fields. She is a former vice chairman of the American Bar Association's TIPS Excess, Surplus & Reinsurance Law Committee and a member of A.I.D.A.'s Reinsurance and Insurance Arbitration Society and the Defense Research Institute.

Demetrios G. Metropoulos

Demetrios Metropoulos is a partner at Mayer, Brown & Platt in Chicago, Illinois. His primary practice area is commercial litigation. Metropoulos is a graduate of the University of Michigan and Stanford Law School, where he served as senior editor of the *Stanford Law Review* and earned membership in the Order of the Coif. Prior to joining Mayer, Brown & Platt, he worked for Coopers & Lybrand, and in 1993 he clerked for the Honorable Joseph T. Sneed on the U.S. Court of Appeals for the Ninth Circuit.

Tibor Nagy

Tibor Nagy is currently clerking for the Honorable Melinda Harmon in the U.S. District Court for the Southern District of Texas. He received his B.A. from Dartmouth College and his J.D. from Yale Law School. Mr. Nagy was the 2003 National Trial Competition Northeastern Region Champion and plans to pursue a career as a trial lawyer.

Kirk Pasich

Kirk Pasich is a partner in the Los Angeles law firm of Pasich & Kornfeld, L.L.P. He has been named by *American Lawyer* as one of the top 45 lawyers in the country under the age of 45, by *California Law Business* to its "Legal Dream Team" as one of California's top 25 litigators, and by *Chambers USA: America's Leading Business Lawyers 2003-2004* as "the market leader for policy-holder representation in California." Kirk is the author, co-author, or editor of several books and more than 300 articles.

Michael F. Pezzulli

Michael F. Pezzulli has been practicing law for more than 25 years, having commenced his legal career by being selected to be a law clerk to the Honorable John A. Field, Jr., senior circuit judge for the United States Court of Appeals for the Fourth Circuit. He is a veteran trial lawyer, having tried cases throughout the United States in both federal and state courts. He is board certified in civil trial law by the Texas Board of Legal Specialization and an associate of the American Board of Trial Advocates. He has presented numerous papers for such varied organizations as the American Bar Association, the State Bar of Texas, the Defense Research Institute, and numerous law schools.

Cynthia Harrison Ruiz is an associate at Quintairos, Prieto, Wood & Boyer, P.A. and practices from the firm's Miami, Florida, office. Her areas of practice are insurance defense litigation, medical malpractice and nursing home defense litigation, and nursing home administrative law. She graduated magna cum laude with a B.A. from the University of Colorado and earned a J.D. from the National Law Center at George Washington University. Ms. Ruiz practiced law at Spears Barnes, et al. in Durham, North Carolina, for five years before relocating to Florida.

Veronica L. Spicer

Veronica Spicer is an associate at Mayer, Brown, Rowe & Maw L.L.P., Chicago, Illinois, and a graduate of the University of Chicago Law School. Prior to joining the firm, she clerked for the Hon. Kathryn H. Vratil, District Court of Kansas, and the Hon. Terence T. Evans, Seventh Circuit Court of Appeals. She is a member of the Kansas and Illinois State Bars.

John W. Thornton
Mr. Thornton served as the Legislative and Administrative Code Representative on Hospital Risk Managers' Qualifications, Rules, and Liability; acted as the legislative attorney for the Florida School Board Association; and represented the Dade County School Board. He served on the Planning Committee for the National Institute on "Reinsurance Recoverables" held in June 1988 and served on the ABA/TIPS programs for more than two decades. He has spoken and written on a wide range of topics, including insurance, products liability, medical mediation and malpractice, and nursing home litigation and pre-suit procedures. He graduated magna cum laude from Notre Dame and earned a J.D. from Notre Dame Law School.

Steven A. Wagner
Steven Wagner is an associate at Berman Fink Van Horn, P.C. in Atlanta, Georgia. He graduated from the State University of New York College at Buffalo (B.A., cum laude) and earned his law degree from Emory University School of Law.

Margie Wetherald
Margie Wetherald's practice with Keller Rorhback, L.L.P., focuses on insurance litigation, coverage analysis, and bad faith. She is experienced in handling a wide range of first- and third-party commercial coverage issues on behalf of insurance companies. She regularly advises clients and litigates coverage matters involving environmental, first-party property, advertising injury, personal injury, construction defect, product, and toxic tort claims. Margie has 17 years of experience in analysis and litigation of issues arising from complex, multi-year insurance programs and long-tail claims. She received her B.A. cum laude from Mount Holyoke College in Massachusetts in 1980 and her J.D. from Cornell Law School in 1983. She is admitted to practice in Washington, the U.S. district courts for the Eastern and Western Districts of Washington, the Ninth Circuit Court of Appeals, and the United States Supreme Court.

Elisabeth M. Will
Elisabeth Will is an associate in the Minneapolis, Minnesota, office of Robins, Kaplan, Miller & Ciresi, L.L.P., where her practice focuses on property and liability insurance coverage and subrogation litigation. She is a 2000 magna cum laude graduate of Southwest Minnesota State University and a 2003 graduate of the University of Iowa Law School with distinction, where she was managing editor of the *Iowa Law Review* (2002-2003).

Table of Cases

CHAPTER 1

An Overview of the Attorney-Client Privilege When the Client Is a Corporation

VINCENT S. WALKOWIAK

In recent years the attorney-client privilege has come under increasing attack as claims arose that the security provided by this rule of evidence fostered the actions of some corporate officers, and attorneys, whose greed, ignorance or outright larceny permitted major corporations to fail and millions of investors to lose all or large portions of their investments. Wrongdoers will continue to ply their trade, and frequently to ply it in secrecy. The solution to these problems is not to eliminate valid evidentiary privileges in an effort to frustrate future malefactors. It is not the confidentiality inherent in the attorney-client privilege that is at fault, and any contributions to secrecy are justified by the inherent value of the privilege. Recent changes to the privilege notwithstanding, the need for confidential communication in the corporate setting is as great, if not greater, than it ever was.

The purpose of the attorney-client privilege, established long ago, is to promote the free flow of information between attorneys and their clients while removing the fear that the details of those communications will be revealed to outsiders.[1] It is presumed that the attorney will be able to render accurate advice by ensuring that the information he or she receives and provides will remain confidential. The client is encouraged, therefore, to provide full disclosure even of facts that, if disclosed, could adversely affect the client. It is frequently the most harmful information that the attorney needs most in order to provide accurate counsel to a client.

The attorney-client privilege is one of the oldest evidentiary privileges in Anglo-American Law.[2] This chapter represents an overview of federal and state law regarding the attorney-client privilege as an evidentiary privilege and the procedures that relate to it, especially as they apply to communications by attorneys representing corporations.

Many of the situations selected for inclusion in this chapter involve the assertion of this privilege by corporate in-house or general counsel. Although every court recognizes that these attorneys fully qualify for the privilege, the rules as they have been applied to the claims of privilege by in-house counsel are frequently more exacting. In many respects the in-house attorney, much like Caesar's wife, must be free of any taint before some courts will allow in-house counsel to effectively assert the privilege. While this position may not be legally warranted, it is nevertheless the position that many courts take, and to ignore that fact is to ignore the reality within which rules of law are interpreted. The position taken by those courts is consistent with the liberal interpretation that applies to many discovery rules, the suspicions that surround in-house counsel's role in the corporation, and the consequent narrow interpretation to which many evidentiary privileges are currently subject.

The Attorney-Client Privilege: First Principles

The attorney-client privilege is the evidentiary rule that is designed to encourage (by protecting) the free flow of information between an attorney and his or her client. The underlying assumption is that our legal system is more civilized and efficient because we recognize the attorney-client privilege. This premise is an unverifiable postulate of felicific calculus. However, it is believed that without broadly interpreting and enforcing the privilege, the potential benefit to our legal system becomes more elusive because the protected client must, as a threshold matter, determine whether confidential disclosures to his or her attorney may be disclosed to a party with opposing legal interests. Undoubtedly, this risk can "chill" the full disclosure that otherwise might have been made. Thus, it is advanced that the legal system is harmed because the attorney's advice was not based upon full disclosure. Because it may have been rendered without all of the underlying facts, the advice itself may be incorrect. It is believed that only by encouraging full disclosure without fear that it will be used against the client can our adversary legal system "encourage" full disclosure. It is important to understand the rationale underlying this legal doctrine because the potential damage to the attorney-client privilege's policy and objectives should always be argued when attempting to establish this privilege, regardless of the context in which the privilege is being defended.

Free flow of information between attorney and client is as important within a corporation as it is outside the corporation. Some might even argue that it is more important for in-house counsel to obtain full disclosure unfettered by the fear of having to reveal those confidences in order to properly satisfy their obligations to provide accurate legal counsel to their corporate clients. As one court phrased the matter, legal "advice does not spring from a lawyer's head as Athena did from the brow of Zeus."[3] Phrased differently, the attorney-client privilege "rests on the need for the advocate and the counselor to know *all* that relates to the client's reasons for seeking representation if the professional mission is to be carried out."[4]

The attorney-client privilege is traditionally and historically a product of the common law but it has been codified in many states. In some states, the statute merely restates the common law,[5] while other states, like Arizona and Texas, specifically set forth not only the privilege but also many of the procedural rules regarding its use.[6] A good working definition of the privilege is contained in the Texas Rule of Civil Evidence 503(b), which defends the attorney-client privilege as follows:

> A client has a privilege to refuse to disclose and to prevent any other person from disclosing confidential communications made for the purpose of facilitating the rendition of professional legal services to the client.[7]

Establishing the Privilege

Generally, a party seeking to protect privileged communication from discovery must, at some stage:

1. Affirmatively and specifically plead or assert the attorney-client privilege;
2. Produce evidence concerning the applicability of the attorney-client privilege; and
3. For written material, allow the trial court to determine whether an in camera inspection is necessary to determine if the privilege applies.

If the trial court orders an in camera inspection, the party asserting the privilege should segregate and produce to the court those materials the court seeks to inspect to determine if the privilege applies. Failure to follow this procedure may waive any complaint of the trial court's action regarding the privilege.[8]

Thus, the party resisting discovery of the material that is claimed to be privileged must specifically claim the privilege relied on and establish the justification for its imposition. In written discovery, the discovery response must identify the privilege and identify each document to which the privilege applies. General objections will generally not suffice. Simply listing documents under the heading "Attorney-Client/Attorney Work-Product" is generally insufficient to protect documents from discovery. A global claim that a list of documents is protected by one or more privileges is also too general to prevent their discovery. And while often called an absolute privilege, the attorney-client privilege is subject in every jurisdiction to exceptions for which the privilege may not be asserted.[9]

The parameters of the attorney-client privilege in federal court were fully set forth in *United States v. United Shoe Machinery Corp.*,[10] a frequently cited case from 1950, in which the court stated that:

> The privilege applies only if (1) the asserted holder of the privilege is or sought to become a client; (2) the person to whom the communication was made (a) is a member of the bar of a court, or his subordinate and (b) in connection with this communication is acting as a lawyer; (3) the communication relates to a fact of which the attorney was informed (a) by his client (b) without the presence of strangers (c) for the purpose of securing primarily either (i) an opinion of law or (ii) legal services or (iii) assistance in some legal proceeding, and not (d) for the purpose of committing a crime or tort; and (4) the privilege has been (a) claimed and (b) not waived by the client.[11]

It is well established that the attorney-client privilege applies to the corporate client,[12] although even this principle has not gone unchallenged, and at least one court, subsequently reversed, held that the attorney-client privilege could not be claimed by a corporation.[13] However, while the prerequisites for asserting the attorney-client privilege set forth above are rather straightforward when applied to an individual, they are not so simple when the client is a corporation. The most obvious difference is that the corporate entity speaks through the many voices of its employees, agents, and representatives. Thus, when a corporation asserts the attorney-client privilege, there are questions about: (1) which natural persons' communications are protected, (2) who within the corporation may assert the privilege, and (3) who within the corporation may waive the privilege.

Not surprisingly, there is no uniform answer to these questions either among the states or between state and federal law. In the area of who may claim that their communications are privileged, courts have adopted and applied two general tests: (1) the control group test, and (2) the subject matter test. The determination of which test applies depends upon the forum in which one finds oneself and both the jurisdiction's substantive evidence law of privilege and the conflicts of law rules which that jurisdiction has adopted. Since the rule applied may be affected by various factors, it is important for an attorney representing a corporation to understand both tests. It is not enough just to know the test that is applied in the state in which the communication took place, since corporate litigation frequently involves parties from different states, and the likelihood that a corporation may be sued in a state in which it is not a resident is evident.

Determining the Rule of Privilege: Control Group v. Subject Matter

There are principally two approaches that have been advanced to resolve the question of which corporate representatives may engage in confidential communications with attorneys representing the corporation.[14] The first, or "control group test," provides that the client may be an entity and have confidential communications *only if* the corporate representative can act on the legal advice rendered or if the corporate representative has authority to obtain legal representation on behalf of the corporation.[15]

The control group test for determining what communications by a corporate employee are protected by the attorney-client privilege originated with *City of Pennsylvania v. Westinghouse Electric Corp.*[16] In this case, the defendant, Westinghouse, asserted the attorney-client privilege in order to prevent disclosure of an employee's statement to Westinghouse's general counsel. In rejecting the application of the attorney-client privilege to this communication, the court adopted the following definition of the scope of the attorney-client privilege in the corporate setting:

> [I]f the employee making the communication, of whatever rank he may be, is in a position to control or even to take a substantial part in a decision about any action which the corporation may take upon the advice of the attorney, or if he is an authorized member of a body or group which has that authority, then, in effect, he is (or personifies) the corporation when he makes his disclosure to the lawyer and the privilege would apply. In all

other cases the employee would be merely giving information to the lawyer to enable the latter to advise those in the corporation having the authority to act or refrain from acting on the advice.[17]

While these are the primary elements of the control group test, some states have expanded the control group to include, for example, advisors to top management if management relies upon those advisors' communications in making legal decisions.[18]

It is obvious that the control group test is extremely narrow in scope. Although it is evident to everyone that low-level employees frequently possess information that may be vital to a corporation's management when management of the corporation is seeking legal advice, the control group test provides the protection of the attorney-client privilege *only* to the communications of the top management. And while the limited protection afforded by the work-product doctrine might be available when litigation is anticipated, communications such as those by a non-management group employee in the absence of anticipated litigation may not be protected. Despite this very narrow application, however, a number of states continue to follow the control group test for corporations asserting the attorney-client privilege.[19]

In 1993, the Texas Supreme Court, in *National Tank Co. v. Brotherton*,[20] addressed the scope of the attorney-client privilege under Texas state law in circumstances when the client was a corporation. In a plurality opinion (which was effectively joined by all other justices on this issue), Chief Justice Phillips held that the Texas Rules of Evidence, Rule 503 had in effect adopted the "control group test" by virtue of its definition of "representative of the client"—that is, "one having authority to obtain professional legal services, or to act on advice rendered pursuant thereto, on behalf of the client."[21] Thus, even if legal matters were discussed between attorneys and employees, the failure to have an appropriate corporate representative involved was fatal to the creation of a privileged communication. For this and other reasons, the subject matter test was criticized.[22] However, the subject matter test defined the scope of the attorney-client privilege in Texas until 1998, when the Texas Rules of Evidence were amended by the court to include the subject matter test in addition to the control group test for communications to attorneys. In Texas, the attorney-client privilege may now be asserted by:

(A) a person having authority to obtain professional legal services, or to act on advice thereby rendered, on behalf of the client, or

(B) any other person who, for the purpose of effectuating legal representation for the client, makes or receives a confidential communication while acting in the scope of employment for the client.[23]

As the Texas Supreme Court did in amending its rule for the attorney-client privilege in the corporate context, the Seventh Circuit Court of Appeals, some years earlier in the leading case of *Harper & Row Publishers, Inc. v. Decker*,[24] adopted the subject matter test to define the persons whose communications were covered by the attorney-client privilege. The Seventh Circuit recognized that an employee, while not a member of the control group, is sufficiently identified with the corporation so that his communication to the corporation's attorney should be privileged when the employee makes that communication at the direction of his supervisors. However, the court imposed the additional condition that the subject matter upon which the attorney's advice was being sought by the corporation and dealt with in the communication by the employee should involve the performance by the employee of the duties of his employment.[25]

The principles expressed by the court in *Harper & Row v. Decker*,[26] while generally accepted, were viewed by some courts as too broad. Thus, the court in *Diversified Indus., Inc. v. Meredith*[27] adopted what became known as the modified subject matter test. This test set forth five elements that needed to be satisfied in order to determine whether a corporate employee's communications with counsel were privileged. These five elements are:

1. The communication must be made for the purpose of securing legal advice;
2. The employee making the communication should be doing so at the direction of his corporate supervisor;
3. The employee's superior made the request for the communication in order for the corporation to secure legal advice;
4. The subject matter of the communication was within the scope of the employee's corporate duties; and
5. The communication was not disseminated beyond those persons who, because of the corporate structure, needed to know its contents.[28]

These principles ultimately gained acceptance by the United States Supreme Court, and although the Supreme Court declined to establish a rule of privilege to govern all conceivable future questions in which the question of the applicable scope of the attorney-client privilege would be addressed in the corporate context, it essentially approved the modified subject matter test. In *Upjohn Co. v. United States*,[29] the United States Supreme Court rejected the "control group" test and held that the attorney-client privilege protected communication between corporate counsel and lower-level corporate employees under certain circumstances. This is now often referred to just as the "subject matter" test and is employed in federal courts in non-diversity cases. In reaching its decision, the Court reasoned that:

> In the case of the individual client, the provider of information and the person who acts on the lawyer's advice are one and the same. In the corporate context, however, it will frequently be employees beyond the control group as defined by the court below—"officers and agents . . . responsible for directing [the company's] action in response to legal advice"—who will possess the information needed by the corporation's lawyers. Middle-level—and indeed lower-level—employees can, by actions within the scope of their employment, embroil the corporation in serious legal difficulties, and it is only natural that these employees would have the relevant information needed by corporate counsel if he is adequately to advise the client with respect to such actual or potential difficulties.[30]

While the *Upjohn* Court limited its holding to the facts before it and expressly declined to lay down a broad rule, the issue of the availability of the privilege to corporations in litigation in federal court governed by this rule is, for all practical purposes, now settled. The holding clearly states that confidential communications by corporate employees about matters within the scope of their employment, and made for the purpose of enabling counsel to provide legal advice to the corporation, fall within the scope of the attorney-client privilege. Still, because the attorney-client privilege suppresses information, it is obstructive to the truth-finding process and is narrowly construed.

Case law seems to indicate that the perceived need for a narrow construction is more likely to occur when a corporate entity seeks to invoke the privilege to protect communications of or to in-house counsel. Because in-house counsel may play a dual role of legal advisor and business advisor, the privilege applies only if the communication's purpose is to gain or provide legal assistance. The varied scope of responsibility of some in-house counsel within a corporation may suggest that the issue of the role being performed by in-house counsel when they have communications will no doubt continue to receive strict scrutiny in order to determine whether those communications are privileged.

Since *Upjohn*, in addition to Texas, at least some variation of the subject matter test has been adopted by the majority of the states having considered the rule as well as having been cited formally by a number of states that have not adopted a specific rule.[31]

Since the privilege belongs to the client, the claim of privilege must be made by or on behalf of the client.[32] In the case of a corporation, the representative of the corporation may assert the privilege on behalf of the corporation.

The privilege attaches early in the attorney-client relationship. For example, the Texas Rules of Civil Evidence define "client" as someone who consults a lawyer *"with a view* to obtaining professional legal services from him."[33] Once created, the privilege continues.[34] In the corporate setting, it is generally held that the privilege may be asserted only by an authorized corporate representative on behalf of the corporation.[35] The attorney for the corporation is the representative generally in the best position to assert the privilege, whether at a deposition, responding to written discovery, or at trial. Thus, although the privilege belongs to the client, the lawyer may claim the privilege on behalf of the client and is presumed to have that authority to assert the attorney-client privilege in the absence of evidence to the contrary.[36]

Conflict of Laws—Application of the Proper Test

It stands to reason that the determination of what jurisdiction's law should govern the attorney-client privilege may determine whether a particular communication is privileged. Although the United States Supreme Court, in *Upjohn*, addressed the issue of this evidentiary privilege, the determination of the scope of the privilege was made on evidentiary grounds, and consequently there is no guarantee that a particular court will apply the subject matter test to corporate communications of non-control group personnel even in federal court outside those circumstances specifically defined by the Court as requiring its application.

The decision of the United States Supreme Court was made on evidentiary grounds consequently, the scope of the privilege in litigation in federal court is governed by the Federal Rules of Evidence. While *Upjohn* establishes that actions in federal court that are based upon federal statutes or federal claims require the application of the subject matter test to corporate communications between agents of the corporation and its attorneys, the Federal Rules of Evidence adopt a policy in keeping with the limits of federal court authority in diversity cases. The Federal Rules of Evidence provide that:

> [T]he (attorney-client) privilege of a witness [or] person . . . shall be gov-
> erned by the principles of the common law as they may be interpreted by
> the courts of the United States in the light of reason and experience. How-
> ever, in civil actions and proceedings, with respect to an element of a claim
> or defense as to which state law supplies the rule of decision, the privilege
> of a witness [or] person . . . shall be determined in accordance with state
> law.[37]

The incongruity of this principle has not been lost upon some commentators who have pointed out that a single corporation might be involved in two cases in the same federal court before the same judge, one based upon diversity and one based upon a federal claim, in which that judge would be expected to apply the subject matter test to the corporate communications in the case based upon federal law under *Upjohn*, while the diversity case could require the application of the particular forum state's privilege rule, which could easily be the control group test. This incongruity alone, while perhaps a little far-fetched, does dictate a cautionary note, and relying upon traditional conflicts rules offers little comfort. The *Restatement (Second) of Conflicts* favors the forum's laws, which will more likely hold that the communication is *unpro-tected* by the privilege.[38] Consequently, a jurisdiction that follows the subject matter test and the *Restatements'* view of conflicts might find itself in the awkward position of being asked to substitute its own rules regarding the attorney-client privilege and apply the control group test of another jurisdiction, and find that a communication that would be privileged under its interpretation of the attorney-client privilege is not privileged in the particular litigation, since its conflict rules dictate the imposition of the more narrow approach. Even if this is not the result of this scenario, the possibility alone suggests that a forum selection clause and choice of law clause should be a standard provision in any contract where the parties may be able to control which standard will apply.

In-House Attorney as Executive

Regardless of which rule the particular jurisdiction applies, as has been noted earlier, in-house counsel face additional problems in asserting the attorney-client privilege to communications they have with corporate employees. This position is not unprec-edented.To begin with, outside of the United States, an attorney who is also an em-ployee of a corporation is not entitled to assert that his communications are privileged.[39] Even though it is well settled that the attorney-client privilege applies to corpora-tions and that a corporation may be a "client" of in-house counsel as contemplated by the privilege, there are still areas of concern. In some corporate settings, corporate counsel is asked to serve only as the corporation's attorney, managing litigation or otherwise performing purely legal works. In many corporations, especially those that engage a single in-house counsel, the range of responsibilities is much broader. Corporate counsel has been described as a person who advises the corporation on compliance with a myriad of regulations and business practices.[40] Because of their legal training they have been asked to conduct internal investigations, chair committees, serve on the board of directors, and become de facto human resources managers, among other responsibilities. As such, the corporate attorney may be expected to give advice of a business or legal nature, or a combination of both. The attorney-client privilege, however, attaches *only* to communications between attorneys and clients made for the purpose of giving or securing legal advice. It is the commingling of this legal and business advice that creates the greatest problems for courts asked to define the scope of a particular communication. Even the most well-meaning and conscientious court can be excused if it too broadly interprets the scope of discovery and too narrowly restricts the scope of the privilege under these circumstances.

With the broad nature of in-house counsel's responsibilities and the type of advice frequently requested of them, the communications of in-house counsel are thus given greater scrutiny when privilege protection is sought. Basically, the courts look to whether counsel was acting in the capacity of an attorney when receiving the communication or giving the advice. The fact that corporate counsel is an attorney does not render as privileged all communications with employees of the corporation.[41] Counsel must be acting in the capacity of an attorney when receiving or making a communication, and therefore must be communicating with the corporate employees, officers or retained counsel for the purpose of formulating legal opinions or advice. The corporation, for this reason, cannot merely pass questionable documents through the law department for review and thereby have them declared protected from outside scrutiny, just as it could not provide such documents to its outside counsel in order to protect them from disclosure.

As the courts continue to struggle with whether particular communications were made to corporate counsel in their business or legal capacity, the federal courts have been reluctant to protect the communications of in-house counsel who prepare client tax returns, patent viability reports, or investigative reports that are solely for internal use.[42] If in-house counsel cannot limit their work to solely legal work, the next best safeguard is for in-house counsel desiring to protect privileged communication to develop internal procedures that clearly indicate when they are acting as an attorney. This will distinguish their legal work, which is privileged, from the work they must perform when they are acting as an "executive" within the company. In addition, it is worthwhile for in-house counsel to be able to establish their role as an attorney. And while joining a bar association or even being a member of the particular state's bar may not be a prerequisite for asserting the attorney-client privilege, they are worthwhile efforts, as they support the proposition that corporate counsel is first and foremost an attorney. The importance of these precautions can be illustrated best when examined in the context of whether internal reports are privileged. These reports can be the most difficult of the documents prepared by in-house counsel to have found privileged.

Internal reports can present an especially difficult problem for in-house counsel to protect. In *Simon v. G.D. Searle & Co.*,[43] a diversity action, the court applied Minnesota law regarding the attorney-client privilege as it was required to do pursuant to the Federal Rules of Evidence.[44] In *Simon*, the defendant's risk management department had developed aggregate risk statements from individual case loss information statements prepared by in-house counsel. The district court held that the individual case loss materials were privileged, on the basis that Minnesota law protects statements made by a client to the attorney, as well as the attorney's advice given to the client in response to the client's inquiry.[45] An Eighth Circuit standard was next applied to the communications. This standard provided that "[w]hen a client acts on privileged information from his attorney, the results are protected from discovery to the extent that they disclose the privileged matter, directly or inferentially."[46] The privilege claim, however, was denied to the documents in their entirety when the court determined that the individual figures, which were prepared by an attorney and privileged, lost their identity as privileged communications when they were given to the client and combined by the client in order to create the aggregate information. The aggregate figures were not direct compilations of the individual figures. Rather, the court found that the individual figures were factored by variables such as inflation. and thus were so changed as to be untraceable to the privileged communication.

The conclusion is inescapable that the issue of whether an in-house counsel's communications are privileged is exacerbated when the counsel provides business advice in addition to legal advice to his or her corporate client. It has been presumed that communications with outside counsel are for the purpose of seeking legal advice.[47] This presumption is not given to in-house counsel, because in-house counsel is perceived as being equally capable of having provided business as well as legal advice. This is evidenced by the frequency with which courts cite to the fact that in-house lawyers provide both types of service to their clients.[48] Consequently, the risk is great that if the communication is made in order for the in-house counsel to render business advice, even to a small degree, the protection afforded by the attorney-client privilege may be unavailable to that communication.

Even when courts do recognize that communication by corporate employees with in-house counsel are entitled to the protection of the attorney-client privilege, they seem to apply a heightened standard in determining when that privilege applies. As articulated by one judge when presented with the issue of whether the attorney-client privilege protected the communication of an in-house attorney who also served as the company's vice president, the burden upon the company was clear:

> We are mindful, however, that [in-house counsel] was a company vice president, and had certain responsibilities outside the lawyer's sphere. The company can shelter [in-house counsel's] advice only upon a *clear showing* that [in-house counsel] gave it in a professional legal capacity.[49]

In this instance, the heightened standard that the communication was made for legal and not business reasons meant that the proponent of the privilege was required to show by affidavit the precise facts that existed to support the claim of privilege.[50] A few precautions beforehand could assist in meeting even this heightened standard.

To help establish that the privilege applies, if communication between an employee and in-house counsel is oral, the employee should be instructed that it is for a legal purpose and the privilege explained to the employee. If the communication is written, the document should expressly state that it is for a legal purpose and should expressly state that there are no business aspects to the communications.[51] The communication should also include the other elements of the privilege. The document should state that it is requested by the employee's superior, that it is confidential, and that it is addressed to in-house counsel in his or her capacity as in-house counsel.

In-House Counsel as a Witness

In-house counsel is most frequently exposed to the risk of being called as a witness when the attorney signs or verifies a pleading, responds to discovery, or signs an affidavit, although there are other circumstances when it may occur. The simple guideline to follow that will most frequently prevent the corporation's lawyer from being noticed for deposition is to make sure that all attesting matters are performed by a corporate officer, not in-house counsel.

Attorneys who perform corporate functions beyond representation of the corporate client invite their own deposition. Admittedly, in some instances this is unavoidable. In *Johnston Dev. Group v. Carpenters Local 1578,*[52] a RICO action brought by a contractor against various labor unions, plaintiff's in-house counsel also served as the vice president. In that dual capacity, she was the sole person to take notes at important meetings between the parties before the litigation began, and she was the sole witness to certain pre-litigation conversations of which highly disputed accounts had been given. The court was somewhat receptive to limiting the practice of deposing opposing counsel, but acknowledged that they were forced to allow a limited examination of the in-house counsel/vice president because she had witnessed the crucial conversations that were in controversy in the litigation.

Again, the signally important procedure that will lessen the likelihood of in-house counsel being deposed is to witness or attest to as few documents or purely business transactions as possible. That is, in-house counsel should *not* sign affidavits of discovery compliance if a corporate official can do so. Also, in-house counsel should not get involved with the mechanics of discovery, such as searching files, as this merely increases the likelihood of becoming a fact witness when the scope of that discovery compliance is at issue.

The Shelton Doctrine: Noticing the Opposing Counsel's Deposition

Parties typically attempt to notice the deposition of opposing counsel, including in-house counsel, for several reasons. First, it can be a shortcut to information available through more traditional and legitimate methods of discovery. Second, it may create grounds for the disqualification of opposing counsel under the ethical rule forbidding attorneys to serve both as advocate and as witness in the same trial. Third, it may be used as an inappropriate means of harassing the opposing party.

Recognizing the existence of these illegitimate motives, the important policies at issue, and the general demeaning of the legal profession that such a practice causes, courts have begun to exercise their responsibility to prevent such depositions from taking place. Although the reasons that an inquiring party can muster for deposing the opposing counsel are unique to each case, the clear trend, since being first addressed at the federal circuit level in *Shelton v. American Motors Corp.,*[53] is to grant a protective order against the taking of an opposing party's counsel. As a practical matter, because of *Shelton,* the law on this issue seems to be moving toward a position where courts generally will permit the deposition of opposing counsel only upon a showing of substantial need and only after alternate discovery avenues have been exhausted or proven impractical.

The attorney is not permitted to testify (and may therefore refuse to answer questions) as to communications made to him or her by the client unless the client consents. However, the right to refuse to testify exists only if:

1. The holder of the privilege is a client (or a potential client);
2. The person to whom the communication was made is a lawyer;
3. The communication relates to a fact of which the attorney was informed:
   (a) by the client;
   (b) not in the presence of strangers; and
   (c) for the purpose of receiving a legal service;
4. The privilege has been asserted and has not been waived by the client.[54]

If these elements are not satisfied, the privilege has not been established. If, on the other hand, all the requirements are satisfied, the privilege exists but can still be waived. When the deposition of counsel has been noticed, and not quashed, use of the *Shelton* policy arguments set out below should be advanced in order to have the privilege upheld:

1. The deposition will inevitably hinder the attorney-client relationship and inhibit counsel's preparation of the client's case;
2. It is unlikely counsel has any more non-privileged information than is available from other sources;
3. Routine attempts to depose counsel will inevitably tie up the court's time with disputes over the scope of privilege and related matters; and
4. There should be no interrogation of an attorney to impeach discovery unless prior substantial evidence shows that a significant violation of the discovery obligation has occurred.

In some instances, the need for the deposition of counsel can be obviated by stipulating that certain witnesses will not be called and that certain issues will not be raised at trial. For example, in *Perry v. Jeep Eagle Corp.,*[55] the defendants avoided the deposition of their in-house counsel by arguing that the information sought was not relevant to plaintiffs' claims and by stipulating that the study that plaintiffs sought to question the attorney about would not be offered in evidence during the trial. The court recognized that where a matter is not put at issue, there is no need to pursue information about it through deposition of the in-house counsel.

Another method of finding constructive alternatives to deposing counsel is through a discovery conference. A discovery conference provides counsel with the opportunity to ask the court to require the opponent to demonstrate why the depositions he or she seeks are necessary to the preparation of their case. The purpose is to focus the court's attention on the opponent's overall discovery plan instead of the mere discovery details. This permits the court to learn that the opponent can obtain the necessary information on the real areas of dispute without deposing in-house counsel.

In federal court, as in many states, a discovery conference can be convened upon a motion to the court if counsel has "attempted without success to effect with opposing counsel a reasonable program or plan for discovery."[56] Such a motion should include a statement of the issue of the case, a proposed discovery plan (including all proposed orders affecting discovery), and a "statement showing that the attorney making the motion has made a reasonable effort to reach agreement with opposing attorneys on matters set forth in the motion."[57]

Once the motion has been filed, the court "shall" conduct such a conference and then enter an order establishing a discovery plan and setting limitations on discovery. The Advisory Notes to Rule 26(f) specify that this is not to be done "routinely," but if attempts at informal conferences fail, this may be the only alternative to filing a motion to quash the deposition.

An attorney employed by a corporation is not entitled to immunity from a deposition.[58] Where opposing parties have been aggressive enough to pursue an objection, the courts have agreed that counsel must provide the specific information necessary to determine whether the protection of the attorney-client privilege or the work-product doctrine is justified. For example, in *In re Shopping Carts Antitrust Litigation*[59] the court stated that a party seeking to assert the privilege must provide information from which the court could reasonably conclude that the communications (1) concerned the seeking of legal advice; (2) was between a client and an attorney acting *in his professional* capacity; (3) was related to legal matters; and (4) was and is, at the client's insistence, permanently protected.[60] The defendants in the *Shopping Carts* litigation failed to provide the requisite information, although specific instructions in the plaintiffs' interrogatories had requested the basis for any claim of privilege.

The "Joint Defense" Scenario

Joint defense principles arise when there has been sharing of information between or among parties with the same legal interests. This sharing, if conducted in accordance with the discussion below, should not result in the waiver of the attorney-client privilege.[61] There are, however, pitfalls that may be encountered when relying upon the joint defense privilege. Increasingly, depositions of counsel (including in-house counsel) are being noticed in an attempt to discover information about *other* manufacturers' defenses on the grounds that waiver of the privilege occurred by sharing information with an attorney representing a different client. To minimize the risk of waiver, if information is going to be shared with other defense counsel, a signed writing (letter or formal agreement) from other counsel should be obtained that states the following:

1. The information transmitted contains confidential, privileged attorney-client communications;
2. It is being sent only to counsel for other defendants in the pending matter;
3. The disclosure is only to further common defenses;

4. The information will not be furnished to any other person, either through copying of letter or disclosure of its contents, in whole or part;
5. All signatories to the document voluntarily waive on behalf of their client any actions they may have at any time against any or all signatories; and
6. All parties agree that no protective orders ban disclosure of such information

A variation of the joint defense privilege is the "pooled information" situation.[62] Parties may assert the attorney-client privilege even when they pooled information if they can establish that they are:

1. Parties in the same lawsuit;
2. Parties who are about to be in the same lawsuit, making the communications in anticipation of litigation; or
3. Parties with common defenses against a plaintiff.

The rule does not apply to situations where there is no common interest to be promoted by a joint consultation, and where the parties meet on a purely adversary basis. From the wording of this principle, the privilege also does not apply to matters not relevant to the pending litigation or to communications with other parties themselves.[63] The principle applies only to communications with a party's lawyer or a lawyer's representative.

Self-Critical Analysis Privilege

During the past 20 years, a qualified privilege for self-critical analysis has slowly evolved in some jurisdictions. It is closely related to the attorney-client privilege, though it has not been widely recognized, and has in fact been rejected in many jurisdictions in most instances.

This privilege was first explicitly recognized in *Bredice v. Doctors Hospital, Inc.,*[64] and is based upon strong public policy considerations. In *Bredice,* a malpractice action, the plaintiff sought production of the minutes and reports of the defendant hospital board concerning the death of a patient. The court denied the discovery requests on the grounds that "[t]here is an overwhelming public interest in having those staff meetings held on a confidential basis so that the flow of ideas and advice can continue unimpeded."[65] The court also stated that "[t]he purpose of these staff meetings is the improvement, through self-analysis, of the efficiency of medical procedures and techniques . . . and that the value of discussions involving construc-tive criticism would be destroyed if the meetings were opened to the process of discovery."[66] This privilege for health care providers has been codified in some states and protects from disclosure medical committee or peer review reports of the medi-cal staff of a health care facility.[67]

The self-critical analysis has been recently defined as including the following criteria: (1) the information must result from an internal investigation or review conducted to improve or evaluate the products or products or procedures of a party; (2) the party must have originally intended that the information remain confidential and must demonstrate a strong interest in preserving the free flow of that type of information; and (3) the information must be of a type whose flow would be curtailed if discovery were allowed.

The self-critical analysis privilege has been considered in products liability cases as well. In *Lloyd v. Cessna Aircraft Co.,*[68] during a deposition, plaintiff's counsel sought information regarding a "top ten list" of confidential memoranda from staff meetings "designed to review, analyze, and evaluate operations for the continued self-improvement in the quality of their respective product."[69] Cessna objected to the request, alleging that the information sought was protected under a qualified privilege.

The court, after noting that the plaintiff was not seeking actual production of the list, permitted questioning of the Cessna witness. In reaching its holding, however, the court noted that "[w]ere the government seeking herein to obtain copies of the minutes of other reports of the actual discussions of Cessna's top ten meetings, this court might be inclined to follow the principles enunciated in the afore-cited [self-critical analysis] cases; under such circumstances the court would feel obligated to apply a balancing approach before allowing the wholesale disclosure of the specific details of any such meetings."[70]

In a more recent application of the privilege in a products liability case, the court, in *Bradley v. Melroe Company,*[71] limited the discovery of in-house investigative files of previous accidents to the factual data contained in those files. Applying a standard similar to the one required under the work-product exclusion, the court held that the defendant manufacturer could redact all mental impressions, opinions, evaluations, recommendations, and theories. In reaching its holding, the court noted that "in many instances, and it certainly appears to be so in this case, manufacturers study reports of accidents involving their products for the purpose of ascertaining if preventive measures can be taken to avoid future accidents."

> In such cases, courts have recognized a privilege of self-critical analysis precluding the discovery of impressions, opinions and evaluations but allowing the discovery of factual data. The reasoning behind this approach is that the ultimate benefit to others from this critical analysis of the product or event far outweighs any benefits from disclosure.[72]

Some courts have applied the self-critical analysis privilege in the context of mandatory reports prepared by a defendant manufacturer for filing with governmental regulatory agencies. The central problem raised by requests for information relating to such reports is the clash between highly valued interests in disclosure that will contribute to full and fair determination of all facts relevant to the plaintiff's claims against the need for confidentiality to (a) assure fairness to persons who have been required by law to engage in self-evaluation, and (b) to make the self-evaluation process more effective by creating an incentive structure rewarding candid and unconstrained self-evaluation. Thus, when faced with the request for such information, defense counsel must raise strenuous opposition on grounds that the consuming public's interest in a reporting scheme that encourages full and frank disclosure to governmental agencies greatly outweighs the plaintiff's need for the information. Clearly, if the contents of government-compelled self-evaluations are subject to disclosure in private lawsuits, the success of the particular reporting scheme is certain to suffer adverse consequences.

Losing the Privilege: From Brinksmanship to Outright Disaster

Although the rules of the privilege are relatively easy to state, it is the implementation of them that is multi-faceted and sometimes extremely complex. The talisman steering most unsuccessful assertions is the ultimate conclusion that the statement or disclosure, as the case may be, is beyond the intended scope of the privilege, or the communication was not between an attorney, acting as attorney, and his or her client. When an entity's practices outpace the theory justifying the suppression of otherwise relevant information, the party asserting this privilege, and seeking the protection of the court, will be denied the benefits of the privilege. Additionally, the privileged communication may be disclosed if the privilege is waived.

Failing to Consistently Assert the Privilege

There are a number of procedural mistakes that can lead to waiver. Ordinarily, the privilege is waived by the failure to assert it when a question is asked about a confidential communication. Voluntary production of a document during discovery or trial can also waive an objection based on the privilege.[73] Thus, in *West v. Solito,*[74] the court stated that neither a motion in limine nor an objection at trial will prevent the admission into evidence of privileged information that was disclosed without objection in a deposition. The court held that even though the trial court ordered that privilege objections be reserved for trial, "once the matter has been disclosed, it cannot be retracted or otherwise protected."[75] Therefore, the conclusion here is ob-vious. An attorney whose client is asked for privileged information in a deposition or a trial must object and instruct the client not to answer in order to protect the privilege, and, if privileged documents have been produced, must attempt to regain custody of those documents.

The Selected Disclosure Problem

Even though the privilege has attached to a particular communication, the privilege may be waived. Texas Rule of Civil Evidence 511 provides a representative definition of the principles of waiver. One waives a privilege if, while the holder of the privilege, he "voluntarily discloses or consents to disclosure of any significant part of the privileged matter unless such disclosure itself is privileged. . . ."[76] For example, in *Axelson, Inc. v. McIlhaney,*[77] the court found that a company waived the attorney-client privilege concerning information relating to the company's internal investigation of kickbacks to its employees. The company's investigation information was the subject of the trial of a federal action brought by the company, and the information was revealed to federal law enforcement agencies as well as a national publication.

Some of the more frequently encountered "high-risk" areas for waiving the privilege by selective disclosure of information may occur in the following situations:

1. Responding to a government investigation
2. Information supplied to government agency
3. Insurance renewals
4. Auditor or accountant inquiry
5. Public financial disclosure documents (SEC forms)

6. Any disclosure to third parties not working under the attorney, or not at the attorney's direction, or for non-legal purposes.

Waiver

Assertion of the privilege, discussed previously, is a relatively clear-cut doctrine as compared to waiver of the privilege. As noted earlier, in order to preserve the attorney-client privilege, not only must the privilege be claimed, it must also be established that the privilege has not been waived. In many instances, the issue of waiver is not present; however, determining who can waive the privilege may be a matter of some concern for the attorney representing a corporation.

It has been held that an employee of a corporation, whose communications have been claimed as privileged under the attorney-client privilege on behalf of the corporation, may waive that privilege.[78] Most courts, however, follow the principles of the *Re-statement (Third) of the Law Governing Lawyers,* which provides that only an authorized agent of the corporation may waive the privilege of the corporation. Accordingly, it is the general rule that a corporation's privileged communication protected by the attorney-client privilege cannot be waived by the unauthorized disclosure by either a current or former employee. Corporate counsel should, of course, be proactive rather than reactive in this area. Rarely does privileged information that has been disclosed by a current or former corporate employee in an unauthorized fashion have a positive consequence, regardless of whether a court subsequently affirms that a waiver was ineffective. The attorney should, therefore, instruct employees with whom he communicates that the communication is confidential. In addition, the attorney should be aware that there is the possibility of a waiver occurring at an employee's deposition. The attorney should be wary and prepared to object and instruct the employee not to answer a question that calls for the disclosure of privileged attorney-client communications at a deposition. If necessary the attorney should be prepared to contact the court for instructions, terminate the deposition, and seek a protective order from the court.[79] The failure to take these measures may be construed by the court as waiver of the privilege.[80]

Waiver by Inadvertent Disclosure

Texas Rule of Civil Evidence 511 is representative of the general rule and provides that a "voluntary disclosure" of a privileged communication waives the privilege. Occasionally, particularly in large document productions, and sometimes despite substantial safeguards and precautions, a party will inadvertently produce a few privileged documents to the opposing party. The question is whether such an inadvertent production constitutes "voluntary disclosure" that waives the privilege, perhaps extending to all communications relating to the subject matter of the disclosed documents.

The Texas Supreme Court first addressed this issue in *Granada Corp. v. Honorable First Court of Appeals.*[81] The court reasoned that, depending upon the facts, an inadvertent production of a privileged document could be either "voluntary" or "involuntary." Only a voluntary production would constitute a waiver of the privilege. In *Granada*, the court held that the producing party carries the burden of showing specific circumstances confirming the involuntary nature of an inadvertent disclosure of a privileged document.[82]

The *Granada* court identified the following factors as relevant to whether a particular inadvertent disclosure is voluntary and therefore results in waiver:

(a) whether "precautionary measures" were taken ("efforts reasonably calculated to prevent the disclosure");
(b) whether there was "delay in rectifying the error";
(c) the "extent of any inadvertent disclosure"; and
(d) the "scope of discovery."[83]

In light of case law such as this, the attorney responsible for a large document production should create a plan (preferably in writing) for the production of documents that will minimize the chances of an inadvertent production of a privileged document.

Attorneys who discover that they have inadvertently produced a privileged document should move quickly. They should immediately file the appropriate motion with the court (for example, a Motion to Compel Return of Privileged Documents Inadvertently Produced). Then they should familiarize themselves with the burdens that are faced under cases, and principles such as *Granada*; assemble by affidavit the evidence needed to sustain that burden; file the affidavits; and have the motion set for hearing. Interestingly, the Texas Supreme Court addressed this problem more directly by procedural rule simplifying, at least in Texas, the procedures that need to be followed for the recovery of inadvertently produced privileged materials. The Texas Rules of Civil Procedure now provide that:

> A party who produces material or information without intending to waive a claim of privilege does not waive that claim under these rules or the Rules of Evidence if—within ten days or a short time ordered by the court, after the producing party actually discovers that such production was made—the producing party amends the response, identifying the material or information produced and stating the privilege asserted. If the producing party thus amends the response to assert a privilege, the requesting party must promptly return the specified material or information and any copies pending any ruling by the court denying the privilege.[84]

Written client communications may also lose the protection of the attorney-client privilege if they are used at trial or in a deposition to refresh the witness's recollection.[85] The Federal Rules of Evidence provide that "if a witness uses a writing to refresh memory . . . for the purpose of testifying . . . an adverse party is entitled to have the writing produced at the hearing."[86] Accordingly, if the attorney uses an otherwise privileged document to refresh his client's memory on the witness stand, or in preparation for or at a deposition, waiver has occurred.[87] Although asserted, the work-product doctrine has been found to be adequate protection from disclosure when work product documents have been used to prepare a witness for depositions.[88] The courts have even followed the reasoning that disclosures of work product in these circumstances should be automatic and should not require a showing of substantial need or undue hardship.[89]

Offensive Use of the Privilege

The "offensive use" doctrine arises when privileged material is used as a "sword" rather than as a "shield." For example, if the client claims that "my former attorney didn't tell me I had a claim until the statute of limitations had expired," then the former attorney may be deposed on this topic to prevent "manifest unfairness.[90] Whether the client was aware of a fact is now relevant and relates to the heart of the claim. For this reason, if there is information that would reveal that a fact was made known to the client by the attorney, then the adversary may discover this information. The assertion of the attorney-client privilege in this setting goes well beyond the intended purposes of the attorney-client privilege, and consequently the privilege is unavailable to protect this type of communication. It is the pursuit of this type of claim that makes otherwise protected discussions and conversations discoverable and is analogous to an unintentional waiver.

Similarly, using the communications of an attorney to pursue a claim offensively may also lead to a claim of waiver of privileges that might otherwise be available if they were raised defensively. Placing at issue matters with which the attorney is involved will greatly increase the likelihood that the party opposing the privilege will subsequently notice the deposition of this attorney and seek the disclosure of otherwise protected communications. In *U.S. v. Pepper's Steel & Alloys, Inc.,*[91] the defendant, in response to a Rule 30(b)(6) notice, produced the supervising examiner for the defendant's liability division. While the defendant did not contest the taking of the attorney's deposition, the attorneys for the produced witness repeatedly objected to questions on the grounds that the information was protected as work product. Pointing out that the defendant chose the witness for examination, the court was unsympathetic to the defendant's claims of privilege.

The "Good Cause" Exception

One of the most troubling instances of waiver for the in-house counsel is the "good cause" exception.

The good cause exception is invoked when concerns of countervailing policy dictate that the attorney-client privilege or the work-product doctrine should be ignored. In shareholder suits, for example, courts have reasoned that the corporate attorney's true client is the shareholder and, accordingly, that communications with corporate executives cannot be privileged in those suits when the substance of the conversation is at issue. Such an analysis puts in peril many communications between in-house counsel and corporate executives, because a privilege-negating shareholder suit is always possible. But, in the case of closely held corporations, one state has held the attorney's duty is owed to the corporation itself, and not to the shareholders or directors.[92] Suffice it to say, this is a dynamic area.[93]

A leading case in which the "good cause" waiver was almost successfully argued by a party seeking the discovery of privileged documents is *Sporck v. Peil.*[94] In *Sporck,* the court denied the plaintiff's motion to compel the production of documents that the defendant acknowledged had been provided to him by his attorney in preparation for his deposition. The defendant claimed that the selection of documents was protected from disclosure by the work-product doctrine, a less restrictive rule against non-disclosure than the attorney-client privilege. Stressing that defendant's counsel had culled these select documents from the hundreds of thousands produced by defendants, the court found that the process of sifting relevant documents from the mass of produced documents was protected as attorney work product:

> We believe that the selection and compilation of documents by counsel in this case in preparation for pretrial discovery falls within the highly-protected category of opinion work product . . . . Rule 26(b)(3) placed an obligation on the trial court to protect against unjustified disclosure of defense counsel's selection process.[95]

Noteworthy is the fact that the court engaged in an analysis to determine whether there was "good cause" to compel production or whether the attorney-client privilege and work-product information should be respected.

There are important points to bear in mind while performing various tasks, such as making decisions or providing advice, which involve the creation of documents or conversations that are intended to be confidential. Counsel should periodically conjure up the mental image of an adversarial proceeding in which he or she is attempting to establish the privilege against an aggressive opponent. This will inevitably result in closer attention being paid to observing the necessary formalities to preserve the privilege.

In addition to the principles articulated earlier in this chapter, to further lay a foundation for prevailing on claims of privilege in the future, the attorney should consistently and judiciously follow the formalities associated with the privilege, such as:

1. Follow or refer to the *Upjohn* factors in letters and memoranda.
2. Mark all appropriate documents as "privileged" and "prepared as confidential communications at request of counsel."
3. Ensure that memos seeking information identify counsel by title as "counsel," and in legal opinions state that they are "in my opinion as counsel."
4. Keep circulation and distribution of *legal* memos severely limited to "control group" personnel.

Thus, to maintain the attorney-client privilege, a company should specify on reports prepared by employees that the report was prepared for counsel regarding legal services. Also, the signature of counsel and statements that the report is to be confidential will help ensure that the document is protected.

Distinguishing the Attorney Work-Product Doctrine from the Attorney-Client Privilege

The Attorney-Work Product Doctrine

The attorney-client privilege must be distinguished from the attorney work-product doctrine, especially when the client is a corporation. Although the principles are similar, "the work product doctrine is distinct from and broader than the attorney-client privilege."[96] This greater scope is, however, met by a concomitant reduction in the strength of protection offered by the *doctrine*, as opposed to the *privilege*. The attorney-client privilege covers communications made by the client to the attorney or communications by the attorney to the client that incorporate or are based upon the clients' communications. Once properly invoked, the attorney-client privilege is virtually inviolate. The attorney work-product doctrine is a qualified protection for certain materials prepared by or for an attorney "acting for his client in anticipation of litigation."[97] Work product–protected materials may be ordered to be produced on a showing of "substantial need" of the documents and the opponents' ability to establish that they are "unable without undue hardship to obtain the substantial equivalent of the materials by other means."[98] Therefore, even though the mental impressions of the attorney will be protected when work-product materials are ordered produced, it is important for attorneys seeking the most inviolate level of protection to establish that the attorney-client privilege applies to documents or other discovery that contains attorney-client communications.

An attorney's work product is protected because it would be patently unfair and contrary to the adversarial nature of the law to permit discovery of materials that contain an attorney's mental impressions, conclusions, opinions or legal theories that have been created in preparation for trial.[99] For material to be considered prepared in anticipation of litigation, the prospect of litigation must be identifiable even if the litigation was not already begun.[100] Thus, a party may not simply claim that materials have been prepared in anticipation of litigation, but may be required to identify the basis for his or her belief.[101] This doctrine is a rule of procedure that limits the discovery of non-privileged but protected materials.

Work-product materials include different kinds of information. They include legal memoranda, witness statements, documents collected by counsel to provide an understanding of the claims or defenses, memoranda or reports from outside consultants, and statistical data compiled electronically as a result of (or to evaluate) a claim or lawsuit as well as the identity of confidential consultants. Other, similar materials may be protected (and, in many instances, rendered absolutely non-discoverable) by the attorney-client privilege, which is limited to confidential communications made by a client to his counsel for the purpose of securing legal advice. Not surprisingly, items otherwise subject to work-product protection lose that status by being sent to testifying experts to review.[102]

Limits of the Work-Product Doctrine

While Rule 34 of the Federal Rules of Procedure makes material such as a computerized data support system discoverable, Rule 26(b)(3) of the Federal Rules of Civil Procedure protects against discovery a computerized litigation support system prepared "in anticipation of litigation." Rule 26(b)(3) provides:

> [A] party may obtain discovery of documents and tangible things otherwise discoverable . . . and prepared in anticipation of litigation or for trial by or for another party or by or for that other party's representative (including the other party's attorney, consultant, surety, indemnitor, insurer, or agent) only upon a showing that the party seeking discovery, has substantial need of the materials in preparation of the party's case and that the party is unable without undue hardship to obtain the substantial equivalent of the materials by

other means. In ordering discovery of such materials when the required showing has been made, the court shall protect against disclosure of the mental
impressions, conclusions, opinions, or legal theories of an attorney or other
representative of a party concerning the litigation.

Therefore, discovery of documents and tangible things prepared in anticipation of
litigation are protected unless the party seeking such discovery shows substantial need
and is unable to obtain such documents and/or tangible things without "undue hardship." However, even if the party requesting a computerized system can show a substantial need for the system or undue hardship in obtaining the substantial equivalent,
Rule 26(b)(3) virtually prohibits discovery of the lawyer's mental impressions and
opinions concerning the litigation.

Not only does Federal Rule 26(b)(3) extend to the protection of materials prepared by lawyers, but it also protects those materials, mental impressions or opinions
of other representatives of the party who are acting on behalf of the party to the litigation, including consultants and the system specialist who may have designed the computer litigation support system. The emphasis is on whether the discovery of the
computer support system would disclose the subjective opinions, mental impressions
and trial strategy of the party or its representatives in the lawsuit. Clearly, Rule 26(b)(3)
extends the work-product protection to computerized litigation support systems that
are prepared in anticipation of litigation. It is important, however, to note that documents that are merely kept in the ordinary course of business will not be protected,
even though they are stored in a computerized litigation support system.

Asserting the Work-Product Privilege in Successive Litigation

As noted in the above-quoted portion of Rule 26, some items protected by "work
product" immunity can be made subject to discovery if a sufficient showing of substantial need and undue hardship is made by the discovering party. It would be unwise
to assume that this showing will be more difficult for a plaintiff in an already closed
case. Indeed, because of the passage of time, the work-product-protected data held by
corporate counsel may be the only source of pertinent information, and therefore a
court may find that the substantial need/undue hardship test is met.

In this regard, *Shelton v. AMC*[103] was a close decision. Plaintiffs had filed notices
to take the depositions of several individuals, including Rita Burns, a staff attorney for
American Motors Corporation. Ms. Burns was the supervising in-house counsel on
certain Jeep "rollover" cases. She was deposed, but refused to answer many questions
on the basis of work-product and attorney-client privilege. These questions primarily
involved the existence or nonexistence of various documents regarding the model
Jeep involved in the case at hand. The work-product privilege was for materials prepared "in anticipation" of previous litigation. Ms. Burns's standard reply was as follows:

Any information I have concerning documents which might possibly be
responsive to your questioning, I've acquired solely through my capacity
as an attorney for American Motors and my efforts to find information

which would assist me in defending the company in litigation, and therefore I decline to respond to the question.[104]

In its opinion, the lower court noted that the mere fact that documents or knowledge of documents came to an attorney while acting for a client was not sufficient to invoke the attorney-client privilege.[105] In addition, the court held that the work-product doctrine from past cases did not protect discovery of the existence or nonexistence of documents.[106] Ultimately, the district court entered a default judgment against AMC as a sanction for Ms. Burns's repeated refusals to answer the deposition questions. The limited issue on appeal to the Eighth Circuit was whether a deponent's mere acknowledgment of the existence of corporate documents was protected by the work-product or attorney-client privileges. In the course of its opinion, the Eighth Circuit acknowledged that the boundaries of discovery had expanded and that the practice of taking the depositions of opposing counsel was becoming increasingly popular. The court stressed, however, that opposing counsel's depositions should be taken only when the party seeking to take the deposition can show that "(1) no other means exist to obtain the information than to depose opposing counsel . . . ; (2) the information sought is relevant and not privileged; and (3) the information is crucial to the preparation of the case."[107] This foundation had not been laid by the plaintiffs.

Conclusion

Although the attorney-client privilege is an ancient one, it is frequently still the subject of attack in litigation. This is not so much the result of a direct assault upon the privilege, but rather upon its application to new and evolving circumstances. By careful preparation and adherence to the rules that define and set the parameters of the attorney-client privilege, attorneys working for corporations can establish the viability and necessity of this oldest of evidentiary privileges.

Notes

1. *See e.g.,* Commodity Futures Trading Comm. v. Weintraub, 471 U.S. 343, 348 (1985); Safeway Ins. Co. v. Superior Court, 181 Ariz. 378, 891 P.2d 246 (Ariz. App. 1995); West v. Solito, 563 S.W.2d 240, 245 (Tex. 1978).

2. *See* Annesley v. Anglesea, 17 How. St. Tr. 1139 (1743); Hunt v. Blackburn, 128 U.S. 464 (1888).

3. *In re* Sealed Case, 737 F.2d 94,99 (D.C. Cir. 1984).

4. Trammel v. United States, 445 U.S. 40, 51 (1980) (emphasis supplied).

5. *See* Colo. Rev. Stat. § 13-90-107()v)(b) (2003); Ga. Code Ann. § 24-9-24 (2002); Nev. Rev. Stat. Ann. § 49.095 (2003); Tenn. Code Ann. § 22-3-105 (2003).

6. *See, e.g.,* Ariz. Rev. Stat. § 12-2234; Tex. R. Civ. Evid. 503.

7. Tex. R. Civ. Evid. 503(a)(2).

8. *See* People v. Agado, 964 P.2d 565 (Colo. App. 1998); Cacamo v. Liberty Mut. Fire Ins. Co., 798 So. 2d 1210 (La. App. 2001); Loftin v. Martin, 776 S.W.2d 145 (Tex. 1989); Weissel Enters., Inc. v. Curry, 718 S.W.2d 56 (Tex. 1986) (per curiam).

9. Thus, the Texas Rules of Evidence set forth the following categories of situations in which the attorney-client privilege does not exist:

(1) Furtherance of crime or fraud. If the services of the lawyer were sought or obtained to

enable or aid anyone to commit or plan to commit what the client knew or reasonably should have known to be a crime or fraud;

(2) Claimants through same deceased client. As to a communication relevant to an issue between parties who claim through the same deceased client, regardless of whether the claims are by testate or intestate succession or by inter vivos transactions;

(3) Breach of duty by a lawyer or client. As to a communication relevant to an issue of breach of duty by a lawyer to the client or by a client to the lawyer;

(4) Document attested by a lawyer. As to a communication relevant to an issue concerning an attested document to which the lawyer is an attesting witness; or

(5) Joint clients. As to a communication relevant to a matter of common interest between or among two or more clients if the communication was made by any of them to a lawyer retained or consulted in common, when offered in an action between or among any of the clients.

Tex. R. Evid. 403(d). *See also* Ky. R. Evid. 403(d); La. Code Evid. art. 506(c). Florida sets forth the following situations in which the privilege does not apply:

(a) The services of the lawyer were sought or obtained to enable or aid anyone to commit or plan to commit what the client knew was a crime or fraud.

(b) A communication is relevant to an issue between parties who claim through the same deceased client.

(c) A communication is relevant to an issue of breach of duty by the lawyer to the client or by the client to the lawyer, arising from the lawyer–client relationship.

(d) A communication is relevant to an issue concerning the intention or competence of a client executing an attested document to which the lawyer is an attesting witness, or concerning the execution or attestation of the document.

(e) A communication is relevant to a matter of common interest between two or more clients, or their successors in interest, if the communication was made by them to a lawyer retained or consulted in common when offered in a civil action between the clients or their successors in interest.

Fla. Stat. § 09.502(4)(2003). It has likewise been held that statutory construction of a sunshine law preempts assertion of the attorney-client privilege in circumstances where it could otherwise have been asserted. State *ex rel* Reno v. Neu, 434 So. 2d 1035 (Fla. Ct. App. 1983); McKay v. Board of County Comm'r, 103 Nev. 490, 746 P.2d 124 (1987). *But see* Dodson v. Floyd, 529 F. Supp. 1056 (N.D. Ga. 1981).

10. United States v. United Shoe Machinery Corp., 89 F. Supp. 357 (D. Mass. 1950).

11. *Id.* at 358-59.

12. *See, e.g.,* United States v. Louisville & Nashville R.R., 236 U.S. 318 (1915); A. v. District Court, 191 Colo. 10, 550 P.2d 315 (1976), *cert den.,* 429 U.S. 1040 (1977); Marriott Corp. v. American Academy of Psychotherapists, Inc., 157 Ga. App. 497, 277 S.E.2d 785 (1981). *See generally* Annot., *What Corporate Communications Are Entitled to Attorney-Client Privilege–Modern Cases,* 27 A.L.R. 5th 76 (1995); Kahl v. Minnesota Wood Specialty, Inc., 277 N.W.2d 395 (Minn.1979).

13. *See* Radiant Burners, Inc. v. American Gas Ass'n., 207 F. Supp. 771 (N.D. Ill. 1962), *rev'd* 320 F.2d 314 (7th Cir. 1963).

14. Because of ambiguities surrounding choice of law issues, if the stricter "control group" test is followed, then the communication will always qualify for protection if it involves only control group personnel.

15. The "control group test" is discussed in *In re* Grand Jury Investigation, 599 F.2d 1224 (3d Cir. 1978).

16. 210 F. Supp. 483 (F. Supp. 1962). *See also* Hercules, Inc. v. Exxon Corp., 434 F. Supp. 136 (D. Del. 1977).

17. *Id.* at 485.

18. Consolidation Coal Co. v. Bucyrus-Erie Co., 89 Ill. App. 3d 103, 432 N.E.2d 250 (1982).

19. *See, e.g.,*

Alaska	ALASKA R. EVID. 503(a)(2)
Hawaii	HAWAI I R. EVID. 503(a)(2)
Illinois	Consolidation Coal Co. v. Bucyrus-Erie Co., 89 Ill. App. 3d 103, 432 N.E.2d 250 (1982)
Maine	MAINE R. EVID. 502(a)(2)
New Hampshire	N.H. R. EVID. 502(a)(2)
Oklahoma	12 OKLA. STAT. § 2502(A)(4) (2003)

See generally Hamilton, *Conflict Disparity and Indecision: The Unsettled Corporate Attorney-Client Privilege,* 1997 Ann Surv. Am. L. 629; Note, *Attorney-Client Privilege for Corporate Clients: The Control Group Test,* 84 HARV. L. REV. 424 (1970).

20. 851 S.W.2d 193 (Tex. 1993).

21. *Id.* at 197 (quoting then prevailing Tex. R. Civ. Evid. 503(1)(2)).

22. *See, e.g.,* Godfrey, *The Revised Attorney-Client Privilege for Texas,* 3 TEXAS TECH L. REV. 139 (1999).

23. TEX. R. EVID. 503(a)(2).

24. 423 F.2d 487 (7th Cir. 1970), *aff'd* 400 U.S. 348 (1971).

25. 423 F.2d at 491-92.

26. 423 F.2d 487 (7th Cir. 1970), *aff'd* 400 U.S. 348 (1976).

27. 572 F.2d 596 (8th Cir. 1977).

28. *Id.* at 609.

29. 449 U.S. 383 (1981).

30. 449 U.S. at 391; *see also* Southern Bell Tel. & Tel. Co. v. Deason, 632 So. 2d 1377 (Fla. 1994).

31.

Alabama	ALA. R. EVID. 502(a)(2).
Arizona	ARIZ. REV. STAT. § 12-2234 (2003).
Arkansas	Courteau v. St. Paul Fire & Marine Ins. Co., 307 Ark. 513, 821 S.W.2d 45 (1991)
California	D.I. Chadbourne, Inc. v. Superior Court, 60 Cal. 2d 7823, 36 Cal. Rptr. 468 (1964)
Colorado	Denver Post Corp. v. Univ. of Colorado, 739 P.2d 874 (Colo. App. 1987)
Connecticut	Shew v. Freedom of Information, 245 Conn. 149, 714 A.2d 664 (1998)
Florida	Southern Bell Tel. & Tel. Co. v. Deason, 632 So. 2d 1377 (Fla. 1994)
Georgia	Marriott Corp. v. American Acad. of Psychotherapists, Inc., 157 Ga. App. 497, 277 S.E.2d 785 (1981)
Kentucky	KY. R. EVID. 503(A)(2)
Louisiana	LA. CODE EVID. art. 506(A)(2).
Massachusetts	National Employment Service Corp. v. Liberty Mutual Insurance Co., 1994 Westlaw 878920 (Mass. Super. Ct. 1994)
Michigan	Fruehauf Trailer Corp. v. Hagelthorn, 208 Mich. App. 447, 528 N.W.2d 778, appeal den. 543 N.W. 2d 314 (Mich. 1995).
Mississippi	MISS. R. EVID. 502(a)(2)
Missouri	Delaporte v. Robey Building Supply, Inc., 812 S.W.2d 526 (Mo. App. 1991)

Nevada	Worleigh v. Second Judicial Dist. Court, et al, 111 Nev. 345, 891 P.2d 1180 (1995)
North Dakota	N.D. R. Evid. 502(a)(2)
Oregon	ORE. REV. STAT. 40.225 Rule 503(1)(d) (2001)
Tennessee	Union Planters Nat'l Bank v. ABC Records, Inc., 82 F.R.D. 472 (W.D. Tenn. 1979) (predicting Tennessee would adopt the subject matter test by construing TENN. CODE ANN. § 29-305)
Texas	TEX. R. EVID. 501
Utah	UTAH R. EVID. 504(a)(4)
Vermont	Baisley v. Missiquoi Cemetery Ass'n, 167 Vt. 473, 708 A.2d 924 (1998).

32. *See* Sikes v. Segers, 266 Ark. 654, 587 S.W.2d 554 (1979); West v. Solito, 563 S.W.2d 240 (Tex. 1978).

33. ALA. R. EVID. 502(A)(1); TEX. R. EVID. 503(a)(1); *see also* State v. Talley, 102 Ala. 25, 15 So.722 (1894).

34. It has been held that the privilege remains after the death of the client. Wesp v. Everson, 33 P.3d 191 (Colo. 2001); Collins v. Utley, 332 Ill. App. 258, 75 N.E.2d 36 (Ill. App. 1947); Eloise Bauer & Assocs. v. Electronic Realty Assocs., 621 S.W.2d 200, 204 (Tex. Civ. App.–Texarkana 1981, *writ ref'd* n.r.e.).

35. In a context similar to that of the corporate world, it was held that White House lawyers could not claim that their conversations with the First Lady were privileged from disclosure in an investigation in which the President and First Lady were being investigated, since the attorneys represented the White House and not the First Lady or the President. *In re* Grand Jury Subpoena Duces Tecum, 112 F.3d 910 (8th Cir. 1997). *See also In re* Grand Jury Investigation, 599 F.2d 1224 (3d Cir. 1979).

36. *See, e.g.,* ALA. R. EVID. 502(c). *See also* TEX. R. EVID.503(c) "The person who was the lawyer or the lawyer's representative at the time of the communication is presumed to have authority to claim the privilege but only on behalf of the client." This point was also made in *Cole v. Gabriel,* 822 S.W.2d 296 (Tex. App.–Ft. Worth 1991, orig. proceeding) in a slightly different way when it was held that a lawyer had no standing to assert the attorney-client privilege in his individual capacity. *See also* Fisher v. United States, 425 U.S. 391 (1976); Klitzman, Klitzman & Gallagher v. Krut, 744 F.2d 955 (3d Cir. 1984).

37. FED. R. EVID. 501.

38. RESTATEMENT (SECOND) OF CONFLICTS § 139. *See also* Atlantic Coast Line R.R. v. Daugherty, 111 Ga. App. 144, 141 S.E.2d 112 (1965) for the proposition that the privilege should be narrowly construed to permit liberal discovery. *See also* Knoff v. American Crystal Sugar Co., 380 N.W.2d 313 (N.D. 1986).

39. *See generally* Hill, *A Problem of Privilege: In-House Counsel and the Attorney-Client Privilege in the United States and the European Community,* 27 CASE W. RES. J. INT'L L. 145 (1995).

40. Upjohn Co. v. United States, 449 U.S. 383 (1981).

41. This statement presupposes that corporate counsel will be an attorney admitted to the bar of a state, not necessarily the bar of the state in which the corporation is located, in order to assert the privilege. *See* Paper Converting Mach. Co. v. FMC Corp., 215 F. Supp. 249 (E.D. Wis. 1963); Georgia-Pacific Plywood Co. v. United States Plywood Corp., 18 F.R.D. 463 (S.D.N.Y. 1956). Failure to be a member of the bar may be fatal to the claim of privilege. It has been held that communications with an unlicensed in-house counsel are not privileged. Financial Technologies International, Inc. v. Smith, 247 F. Supp. 2d 397 (S.D.N.Y. 2000). *But see* Hawes v. State, 88 Ala.37, 7 So. 302 (1890).

42. This doctrine that the communication must be for legal advice is longstanding, even in the noncorporate context. *See ,e.g.,* State v. Marshall, 8 Ala. 240 (1845). *See* G&S Invs. v. Belman, 145

Ariz. 258, 700 P.2d 1358 (Ariz. App. 1984); Spence v. State, 252 Ga. 338, 313 S.E. 2d 475 (1984). *See also* Colton v. United States, 306 F.2d 633 (2d Cir. 1962); United States v. Lawless, 709 F.2d 485 (7th Cir. 1987); Munoz v. State Farm Mut. Auto Ins. Co., 968 P.2d 126 (Colo. App. 1998).

43. 816 F.2d 397 (8th Cir. 1987).

44. Fed. R. of Evid. 501

45. Minn. Stat. Ann. § 595.023, subd. 1(b) (West Supp. 1987).

46. 816 F.2d 397, at 403 n.6.

47. Diversified Indus., Inc. v. Meredith, 572 F.2d 596, 610 (8th Cir. 1977).

48. *See, e.g., In re* Sealed Case, 737 F.2d 94, 99 (D.C. Cir. 1984); McLaugherty v. S. Ffermann, 132 F.R.D. 234 (N.D. Cal. 1990); *see generally* Giesel, *The Legal Advice Requirement of the Attorney-Client Privilege: A Special Problem for Attorneys Representing Corporation*s, 48 Mercer L.rev. 1169 (1997).

49. *In re* Sealed Case, 737 F.2d 94, 99 (D.C. Cir. 1984).

50. *See also* No. Carolina Electric Membership Corp. v. Carolina Power & Light Co., 110 F.R.D. 511 (M.D.N.C. 1986); Borase v. M/A Comm. Inc. 171 F.R.D. 10 (D. Mass 1997). *See generally* Southern Bell Tel. & Tel. Co. v. Deason, 632 So. 2d 1377 (Fla. 1994) for the proposition that the attorney-client privilege will be subject to a higher level of scrutiny when asserted by a corporation.

51. Malco Mfg. Co. v. Elco Corp., 45 F.R.D. 24 (D. Minn. 1968).

52. 130 F.R.D. 348 (D.N.J. 1990).

53. 805 F.2d 1323 (9th Cir. 1986).

54. United States v. United Shoe Machinery Corp., 89 F. Supp. 357, 358-59 (1950).

55. 126 F.R.D. 542 (S.D.N.Y. 1989).

56. 1980 Notes of Advisory Committee on Rules for Rule 26(f).

57. Fed. R. Civ. P. 26(f).

58. *See, e.g.,* Munn v. Bristol Bay Housing Auth., 777 P.2d 188 (Alaska 1989).

59. 95 F.R.D. 299 (S.D.N.Y. 1982).

60. *Id.* at 305-06 (emphasis supplied).

61. For a more complete discussion of the Joint Defense Privilege *see* Chapter 19 *infra*.

62. *See* Ryals v. Canales, 767 S.W.2d 226, 228 (Tex. App.–Dallas 1989, orig. proceeding) (citing H. Wendorf & D. Schleueter, Texas Rules of Evidence Manual 601-02 (2d Ed. 1988).

63. Tex. R. Civ. Evid. 503(b) provides:

> A client has a privilege to refuse to disclose and to prevent any other person from disclosing confidential communications made for the purpose of facilitating the rendition of professional legal services to the client [and made:]. . . (3) by him or his representative or his lawyer or a representative of the lawyer to a lawyer, or a representative of a lawyer representing another party in a pending action and concerning a matter of common interest therein.

64. 50 F.R.D. 249 (D.D.C. 1970). *See also* 4 Moore, Federal Practice ¶ 26.22(2) at 1287 (2d ed. 1969).

65. 50 F.R.D. 249.

66. *Id.* at 250.

67. In Texas, the Occupation Code protects from disclosure the evaluation of a medical review or peer review committee. Tex. Occ. Code § 160.007(e). The Medical Committee records and proceedings of a medical organization are also privileged (excluding business records). Tex. Health & Safety Code § 161.032. *See In re* University of Texas Health Center, 33 S.W.3d 822 (Tex. 2000); Brownwood Hosp. v. 11th Court of Appeals, 927 S.W.2d 24 (Tex. 1996); Irving Healthcare Sys. v. Brooks, 827 S.W.2d 12 (Tex. 1996); Memorial Hosp. v. McCown, 927 S.W.2d (Tex. 1996). *See generally* Friend, *The New Rules of Show & Tell: Identifying and Protecting the Peer Review and Medical Committee Privileges*, 49 BAYLOR L. REV. 607 (1997).

68. 74 F.R.D. 510, 510-22 (E.D. Tenn. 1977).

69. *Id.* at 520.

70. *Id.* at 522.

71. 141 F.R.D. 1 (D.D.C. 1992).

72. *Id.* at 2.

73. See the discussion regarding the loss of the attorney-client privilege through inadvertent disclosure of privileged documents in this volume.

74. 563 S.W.2d 240 (Tex. 1978).

75. *Id.* at 245.

76. TEX. R. EVID. R. 511(i).

77. 755 S.W.2d 170 (Tex. App.–Amarillo 1988, orig. proceeding).

78. Jonathan Corp. v. Prime Computer, Inc., 114 F.R.D. 693 (W.D. Va. 1987).

79. *E.g.,* FED. R. CIV. P. 26.

80. Perignon v. Bergen Brunswick Corp., 77 F.R.D. 455 (N.D. Cal. 1978).

81. 844 SW.2d 223 (Tex. 1992) (orig. proc.).

82. *Id.* at 226.

83. *See* Floyd v. Coors Brewing Co., 952 P.2d 797 (Colo. App. 1997) for a similar discussion and holding. *See also* Abamor Hous. & Dev. v. Lisa Daly Lady Decor, 698 So. 2d 276 (Fla. App. 1997), *rev. den.,* 704 So. 2d 520 (Fla. 1997).

84. Tex. R. Civ. P. 193.3(d).

85. FED. R. EVID. 612.

86. *Id.*

87. *See, e.g.,* Hannon v. St. Joseph's Hosp. & Med. Ctr., 318 N.J. Super. 22, 722 A.2d 971 (1999).

88. *See* FED. R. EVID. 612. *See generally* Shipes v. BIC Corp., 154 F.R.D. 301 (M.D. Ga. 1994); Nutramax Lab. Inc. v. Twin Lab., Inc., 183 F.R.D. 458 (D. Md. 1998); Margaret Hall Found. v. Strong, 121 F.R.D. 141 (D. Mass. 1988); Redvanly v. NYNEX Corp., 152 F.R.D. 460 (S.D.N.Y. 1993); Begner v. State Ethics Comm'n, 250 Ga. App. 327, 552 S.E.2d 431 (2001).

89. *See* Berkey Photo, Inc. v. Eastman Kodak Co., 74 F.R.D. 613 (S.D.N.Y. 1977) (although the court did not order disclosure in *Berkey,* it stated, "To put the point succinctly, there will be hereafter powerful reasons to hold that materials considered work product should be withheld from prospective witnesses if they are to be withheld from opposing parties." 74 F.R.D. at 617.

90. Conkling v. Turner, 883 F.2d 431 (5th Cir. 1989).

91. 132 F.R.D. 695 (S.D. Fla. 1990).

92. Michigan State Bar Comm. on Prof. and Judicial Ethics, Opinion (CI-1178, 1/18/88).

93. *See* discussion at note 35 *supra* for a related matter.

94. 759 F.2d 312 (3d Cir. 1985).

95. *Id.* at 316.

96. United States v. Nobles, 422 U.S. 225, 238 n.11 (1975).

97. *Id.* at 237-38.

98. *See* FED. R. CIV. P. 26(b)(3); TEX. R. CIV. P. 192.5(b)(2).

99. *See* Hickman v. Taylor, 329 U.S. 495, 511 (1947).

100. *See* Toledo Edison Co. v. G.A. Technologies, Inc. Torrey Pines Tech. Div., 847 F.2d 335, 339-40 (6th Cir. 1988) (party need only show anticipation of litigation and need not establish the identities, positions, and responsibilities of the persons creating the materials with respect to the litigation expected); *see also* Simon v. G.D. Searle & Co., 816 F.2d 397, 401 (8th Cir. 1987) (risk management and aggregate records were discoverable, as they were not prepared in anticipation of any particular litigation).

101. *See* Resolution Trust Corp. v. Diamond, 773 F. Supp. 597, 603 (S.D.N.Y. 1991).

102. *See* Gray v. Dist. Court, 994 P.2d 296 (Colo. 1994).

103. 805 F.2d 1333 (8th Cir. 1986).

104. *Id.* at 1323.
105. *Id.* at 1326.
106. *Id.* at 1327.
107. *Id.*

CHAPTER 2

Confidentiality and Its Relationship to the Attorney-Client Privilege

ARTHUR GARWIN[*]

Introduction

Confidentiality and attorney-client privilege are related but distinct concepts that are frequently confused. The attorney-client privilege applies "in judicial and other proceedings in which a lawyer may be called as a witness or otherwise required to produce evidence concerning a client."[1] This privilege "protects only against *compelled* disclosure, and only against disclosure of information *communicated* between client and lawyer."[2] Compelled disclosure might occur in a deposition, for example, or in response to a subpoena. If a lawyer is asked a question in a deposition or at a trial that arguably calls for an answer containing privileged information, the lawyer is obligated to refuse to answer (unless the client agrees to waive the privilege) and force a ruling by the court. If the court agrees that the testimony would be privileged, the court will sustain the objection and effectively order the lawyer not to answer.

Confidentiality is a principle of legal ethics that governs whether a lawyer may reveal information related to a client representation. Confidentiality rules are not limited to judicial or other proceedings, but rather apply in all representational contexts.[3] In addition, confidentiality applies to all information related to a representation,[4] whatever its source, and not merely to client communications.[5] The exceptions are drawn narrowly and the scope of confidentiality is applied expansively.[6] Since confidential-

---

* This chapter could not have been written in the short time available without the help and encouragement of William Hodes, an ABA Center for Professional Responsibility member from Indiana. Mr. Hodes is president of The William Hodes Professional Corporation, and Professor Emeritus of Law at Indiana University.

ity is an ethics rule, the ramification of a breach by the lawyer of the lawyer's duty of confidentiality is a possible disciplinary action and sanction against the lawyer.

Everything that is privileged is also protected by the confidentiality principle but the converse is not true.[7] The confidentiality rule covers far more than communications between a client and a lawyer. Not everything that is protected by the confidentiality rule is protected by the attorney-client privilege. "Attorney-client privilege has numerous exceptions, which courts apply liberally. Much of what would be confidential ultimately proves to be subject to discovery or production in court."[8]

Moreover, the privilege protects only the communications themselves, not underlying facts, the disclosure of which may be compelled from those who communicated them to the attorney.[9] Thus, the other side can ask your client: "Is X true?" and demand an answer (in a formal proceeding), unless something like the Fifth Amendment applies. But they cannot ask the client: "Did you tell your lawyer whether X is true?" Furthermore, as explained in the example in Information versus Communication, infra, even a lawyer could be compelled to testify about the facts if he or she gained knowledge of them without a communication from the client.

Information versus Communication

The distinction between information about a client and communication about that information leads to a further distinction between observations and communicative acts. For example, a lawyer's observations about a client's physical condition are not privileged, even though the lawyer presumably would not have been in a position to make the observations absent a relationship of confidentiality and trust. At the same time, and conversely, a genuine communication from a client to a lawyer retains its privileged character, even if it is made demonstratively, through body language or gestures, rather than with words. Thus, as explained in illustrations accompanying Restatement of the Law Governing Lawyers § 69, Comment *e*, if a client—in response to his attorney's question—silently rolls up his sleeve to reveal a tattoo, the lawyer could not be compelled to testify about the tattoo. But the opposite would be true if the same client visited his lawyer's office wearing a short-sleeve shirt, and the lawyer noticed the tattoo.[10] [footnote omitted]

Model Rule 1.6—Confidentiality of Information

The Model Rules of Professional Conduct were adopted by the ABA in 1983, replacing the Model Code of Professional Responsibility. Since that time, almost all the states have adopted the Model Rules format and Model Rule 1.6 or some modified version of it. Model Rule 1.6, as originally adopted, contained only two exceptions— current (b)(5) and a less permissive version of (b)(1). In 2002, the ABA added current (b)(4) and (b)(6). Then, in 2003, the ABA added (b)(2) and (b)(3) (see further discussion about the context of these additions under Crime-Fraud Exception, infra). Many states already had adopted or are now considering adopting versions of those exceptions.

ABA Model Rule 1.6: Confidentiality of Information

(a) A lawyer shall not reveal information relating to the representation of a client unless the client gives informed consent, the disclosure is impliedly authorized in order to carry out the representation or the disclosure is permitted by paragraph (b).

(b) A lawyer may reveal information relating to the representation of a client to the extent the lawyer reasonably believes necessary:

(1) to prevent reasonably certain death or substantial bodily harm;

(2) to prevent the client from committing a crime or fraud that is reasonably certain to result in substantial injury to the financial interests or property of another and in furtherance of which the client has used or is using the lawyer's services;

(3) to prevent, mitigate or rectify substantial injury to the financial interests or property of another that is reasonably certain to result or has resulted from the client's commission of a crime or fraud in furtherance of which the client has used the lawyer's services;

(4) to secure legal advice about the lawyer's compliance with these Rules;

(5) to establish a claim or defense on behalf of the lawyer in a controversy between the lawyer and the client, to establish a defense to a criminal charge or civil claim against the lawyer based upon conduct in which the client was involved, or to respond to allegations in any proceeding concerning the lawyer's representation of the client; or

(6) to comply with other law or a court order.

In general, as discussed above, a lawyer has a duty to keep confidential information relating to the representation of a client. However, this duty is subject to several exceptions. In the case of each exception, the disclosure is permitted only to the extent the lawyer reasonably believes necessary.

Public Information

The Restatement of the Law Governing Lawyers states that "[t]he law generally provides that a client communication cannot become public and still remain protected by the attorney-client privilege. . . . The scant case authority is divided on the question whether the definition of confidential client information includes publicly available information. . . ."[11]

This question of confidentiality of public information is particularly relevant in the context of the conflicts rules, where, for example, information protected by Model Rule 1.6 figures in the equation of whether a duty to a former client under Model Rule 1.9(b) prohibits representation.[12] In discussing disqualification of lawyers due to conflicts with duties owed to former clients, the Comment to Model Rule 1.9 states that:

Information that has been disclosed to the public or to other parties adverse to the former client ordinarily will not be disqualifying. . . .[13] The absence of a similarly limiting provision in ABA Model Rule 1.8(b), which applies to ongoing representations, is not inconsistent. Any such lawyer use would be impermissible on the broad ground (see ABA Model Rule

1.7) that a lawyer may not use even publicly known information to the detriment of a current client, whether to further a personal interest of the lawyer or to further the interest of another client. Revealing client information adversely in a way that is gratuitous or negligent would violate the duty to take all reasonably available steps to advance the client's lawful objectives."[14] [citations omitted]

However, this conclusion derives from the duty of loyalty, not confidentiality.[15] Model Rule 1.6 does not put generally known information outside the boundaries of confidentiality. Though the duty that would be violated would be that of loyalty to the client, rather than confidentiality, the result is the same, and the duties are inextricably bound in this context. However, Hazard and Hodes, in *The Law of Lawyering*, criticize what they perceive to be the too broad nature of the confidentiality rule in regard to public information.

[R]ead literally and in isolation, the rule is so stringent as to approach the unworkable and the unrealistic. . . . [It] . . . does not exclude information "relating to a client" that happens to be in the public domain or generally known. Thus, unless this commonsense limitation is read in to Rule 1.6(a), a lawyer could be disciplined merely for writing about a client's case, revealing only material that was in the trial transcript or other public documents.

. . . [T]he overinclusion of too much material within the universe of protected confidential information can have awkward consequences. If a lawyer is charged with disclosing information that is technically protected by Rule 1.6, but would not be protected under a sensible reading of the rule, there will be inevitable pressure to force the situation into one of the other recognized exceptions to reach the proper result. Over the long run, this could harm the basically well-balanced regime of limited and narrow exceptions.[16] [endnotes omitted]

Paragraph (a) Impliedly Authorized Disclosures

Model Rule 1.6(a) specifically permits disclosure of client information when "impliedly authorized in order to carry out the representation." The Comment states that "[e]xcept to the extent that the client's instructions or special circumstances limit that authority . . . a lawyer may be "impliedly authorized" to admit a fact that cannot properly be disputed or to make a disclosure that facilitates a satisfactory conclusion to a matter."[17] Thus, for example, the Disciplinary Board of the Hawaii Supreme Court has stated that "if an attorney reasonably and in good faith determines that confidentiality should be waived in order to effectuate the deceased clients' intended estate plan, the attorney would be permitted and obligated to make such disclosure."[18] The ABA Standing Committee on Ethics and Professional Responsibility has said that a lawyer hired by an insurance company to defend an insured "may disclose the insured's confidential information . . . to the insurer if the lawyer reasonably believes that doing so will advance the interests of the insured" and will not "affect a material interest of the insured adversely."[19] On the other hand, the Committee also has stated that "[a] lawyer should not, absent informed client consent, reveal to a judge the limits of the lawyer's settlement authority or the lawyer's advice to the client regarding settlement."[20]

Authorized Disclosures

As paragraph (a) of the Rule indicates, if disclosure is not impliedly authorized or otherwise permitted by the Rule's exceptions (see below), then client consent is required. That consent must be informed, which means that "the lawyer has communicated adequate information and explanation about the material risks of and reasonably available alternatives to the proposed course of conduct."[21]

What is adequate information and explanation in the context of Rule 1.6? "[R]elevant issues include whether disclosure could result in the attorney-client privilege being waived, or the information being disclosed to others or used to the client's disadvantage."[22]

Paragraph (b) Exceptions

Physical Harm

Paragraph (b)(1) was amended in February 2002, pursuant to the Report with Recommendation of the Commission on Evaluation of the Rules of Professional Conduct ("Ethics 2000 Commission"). Prior to the amendment, the rule permitted disclosure "to prevent the client from committing a criminal act that the lawyer believes is likely to result in imminent death or substantial bodily harm." The exception was broadened in three ways. First, the word "imminent" was replaced with "reasonably certain." Thus, "the exception now authorizes disclosure to prevent serious physical harm that may occur at a later date. . . ."[23] For example, "a lawyer who knows that a client has accidentally discharged toxic waste into a town's water supply may reveal this information to the authorities if there is a present and substantial risk that a person who drinks the water will contract a life-threatening or debilitating disease and the lawyer's disclosure is necessary to eliminate the threat or reduce the number of victims."[24]

Second, there is no longer a requirement that it be the client who will cause this level of harm. It could be the client's uncle or business partner whom the client would prefer to protect. Third, the criminal act requirement was removed.

The hypothetical often used to illustrate perceived problems related to this exception prior to the 2003 rule change was derived from the case of *Spaulding v. Zimmerman.*[25]

> In that celebrated case, lawyers were defending the driver in a civil suit arising out of a serious automobile accident. The defendant's doctor examined the plaintiff and discovered a life-threatening aortic aneurysm that was probably—but not certainly—caused by the accident. The plaintiff's own doctor had not discovered the aneurysm, and plaintiff's lawyers had (mistakenly) not requested the defense team's medical reports. A settlement agreement was worked out and approved by the court, while the plaintiff and his lawyers were still in the dark about plaintiff's true medical condition.[26]
>
> . . .

No confidentiality issue was presented in the actual case, because the lawyers unilaterally decided not to disclose, but it is certainly possible that even if the clients had been told about the aneurysm, they would have embargoed the information. In that event, the ultimate question would have to be faced: would the lawyers have discretion to disclose against the wishes of their clients in this extraordinary circumstance, or would they be prohibited by the rules of ethics from doing what is morally right? [endnote omitted][27]

Under the current rule, the lawyers would have the discretion to disclose.

Crime-Fraud Exception

Paragraphs (b)(2) and (b)(3) of Model Rule 1.6 were adopted by the ABA House of Delegates and added to the rule in August 2003 pursuant to the Report with Recommendation of the ABA Task Force on Corporate Responsibility.[28] These changes, which were driven by the "issues relating to corporate responsibility arising out of the unexpected and traumatic bankruptcy of Enron and other Enron-like situations,"[29] were consistent with the existing rules in many states.

Paragraph (b)(2) addresses preventing a client's action that is going to cause harm, whereas paragraph (b)(3) addresses preventing, mitigating or rectifying harm resulting from an action by the client that has already occurred. In both instances, the exception applies only when the lawyer's services have been or are being used in furtherance of the crime or fraud. So, if a client merely tells his lawyer that he is about to commit a crime or fraud (presumably one that would not result in reasonably certain death or substantial bodily harm and thus be covered under paragraph (b)(1)), paragraph (b)(2) does not provide a vehicle for the lawyer to reveal that confidential information. Likewise, if the client "confesses" to the lawyer about his completed crime or fraud, the lawyer cannot reveal information in order to prevent, rectify or mitigate the financial harm if the lawyer's services have not been used in furtherance thereof.

While these exceptions are discretionary in form, it can be argued that the reality is that lawyers will convert "may reveal" into "must reveal," because, when faced with clients involved in fraud, the lawyers are going to disclose the information to avoid getting sued or prosecuted later themselves. In addition, Model Rule 4.1(b) provides that "in the course of representing a client, a lawyer shall not knowingly fail to disclose a material fact when disclosure is necessary to avoid assisting a criminal or fraudulent act by a client, unless disclosure is prohibited by Rule 1.6." Thus, if it is permissive to reveal under Rule 1.6, it becomes mandatory under Rule 4.1 if the information to be revealed is material and the disclosure is necessary to avoid assisting the client's criminal or fraudulent act. This assumes, of course, that the lawyer's participation was "innocent," because otherwise the lawyer would have been an accessory to the crime or fraud and would have violated Rule 1.2(d) (which states that "a lawyer shall not counsel a client to engage, or assist a client, in conduct that the lawyer knows is criminal or fraudulent") at the time the lawyer provided the services, and violated Rule 1.16(a) by not withdrawing.

The crime-fraud exception to the confidentiality rule is similar to but not the same as the crime-fraud exception to the attorney-client privilege. The confidentiality exception applies only when the likelihood of financial loss is great and the lawyer reasonably believes that use or revelation is necessary to prevent the crime or fraud or to prevent, rectify, or mitigate the loss it causes. . . . In contrast, the crime-fraud exception to the attorney-client privilege . . . applies without regard to the consequences of the intended act so long as the act itself is a crime or fraud. That exception to the attorney-client privilege applies only when a client consults a lawyer with intention to obtain assistance to commit a crime or fraud or so uses the lawyer's services, whereas the [confidentiality exception] applies regardless of the client's intention at the time of consultation. . . . Finally, [the confidentiality exception] is limited to client acts in which a lawyer's services are employed; the crime-fraud exception [to the attorney-client privilege] applies whether or not the lawyer's services are so employed. Due to the several differences . . . a finding that a lawyer permissibly used or disclosed confidential client information . . . and a determination whether [the exception to the attorney-client privilege] applies must be made independently.[30]

Two examples from the Restatement of the Law Governing Lawyers illustrate how these exceptions operate.

In the first instance, a lawyer prepares an opinion letter on behalf of a client. The lawyer later receives information that gives him reason to believe that the transaction for which he wrote the letter was criminal or fraudulent, a fact that the lawyer did not know at the time he wrote the letter. Because the lawyer's services were used, the lawyer has discretion to disclose the information in order to prevent, mitigate or rectify any substantial injury to the financial interests or property of another that is reasonably certain to result or has resulted from the transaction.[31]

In the second instance, a client seeks assistance from a lawyer in defending against charges by a regulatory agency of participation in a scheme to defraud. The loss to the victim has already occurred. Though the lawyer comes to believe that the client's acts were fraudulent and caused the harm, the lawyer does not have discretion to disclose the client's confidential information because the lawyer's services were not used in furtherance of the fraud.[32]

Ethics Advice

Paragraph (b)(4) of Model Rule 1.6 was added in February 2002 pursuant to the Report with Recommendation of the Ethics 2000 Commission. "Although disclosure to secure ethics advice is often impliedly authorized,[33] Rule 1.6(b)(4) permits disclosure even when this is not the case 'because of the importance of a lawyer's compliance with the Rules of Professional Conduct.'"[34] "Moreover, clients are adequately protected by the requirement that such disclosures be made only when protected by the attorney-client evidentiary privilege."[35] This is so because the person consulted will also be a lawyer, who will establish a new attorney-client privilege with the inquiring lawyer. The second lawyer also will be subject to a new confidentiality obligation vis-à-vis the inquiring lawyer under Rule 1.6.

The following illustration from *The Law of Lawyering* provides a good example of how this exception operates.

Lawyer L is representing a client in a difficult matter involving novel and complex legal issues. Opposing counsel has also threatened—informally so far—to move to disqualify L, claiming that L violated the rules of professional conduct. L retains another lawyer to provide himself with legal advice about handling the legal issues in the underlying case. Shortly thereafter, L informally consults [a professional responsibility] expert . . . about the ethical issues that have arisen.

. . .

The disclosures L must make to the consulting lawyer are in furtherance of the main representation, and are accordingly "impliedly authorized" under Rule 1.6(a), even when the consultation is not revealed to the client. . . .

The analysis does not change merely because the consultation with the legal ethics expert is an informal one. The law professor probably needs to be given some client information in order to be able to respond properly, and the law professor—being a lawyer as well—must also abide by normal confidentiality and conflict of interest rules. The consultation and attendant disclosures are again "impliedly authorized" in the sense of Rule 1.6(a), because disqualification of L would adversely affect the client. However, out of an abundance of caution, L should reveal only such details as are necessary to a full understanding of the issues involved. L should not reveal the identity of his client unless it is germane.[36]

Claim or Defense

Paragraph (b)(5) contains the only exception to the Rule that has not been either recently added or amended (although it was renumbered). Perhaps the most common use of this exception is to allow a lawyer to reveal confidential information to collect a fee.[37] However, "[t]his right to use confidences . . . does not create a right to blackmail the client. The lawyer may not state to the client: 'Pay the fee or I will reveal to your employer your income tax problems.'" The lawyer may only exercise the right to reveal client information to the extent that it is reasonably necessary to establish or collect the fee. There must not be any extortion or unnecessary disclosure."[38] [footnote omitted]

The exception also applies to other kinds of claims. For example, the ABA Standing Committee on Ethics and Professional Responsibility has concluded "that a retaliatory discharge or similar claim by a former in-house lawyer against her employer is a 'claim' under Rule 1.6 (b)."[39]

The self-defense portion of the exception permits disclosure to defend claims brought against the lawyer by clients or third parties. The "exception applies even if the client attacks the lawyer's work in a proceeding to which the lawyer is not a party. The self-defense exception also applies when a third party makes a claim based upon the lawyer's representation of the client."[40]

"The lawyer's right to respond arises when an assertion of such complicity has been made. Paragraph (b)(5) does not require the lawyer to await the commencement of an action or proceeding that charges such complicity, so that the defense may be established by responding directly to a third party who has made such an assertion."[41]

Other Law or Court Order

Paragraph (b)(6) was added in February 2002 pursuant to the Report with Recommendation of the Ethics 2000 Commission.

"Prior to the amendment, the Rule did not address whether lawyers are permitted or required to disclose information when such disclosure is required by other law or a court order. Former Comment [20], however, stated that a lawyer must comply with the final orders of a court or other tribunal requiring the lawyer to give information about the client, and former Comment [21] referred to other law that may supersede Rule 1.6. The Commission recommended that the text of Rule 1.6 be amended to explicitly permit, but not require, disclosure to comply with law or court orders. No change in substance was intended. See also Comments [12] and [13]."[42]

However, similar to the crime-fraud exceptions above, this exception, while discretionary in form, in practice converts "may reveal" into "must reveal" because of the "other law" or "court order" that applies. For example, in the case of a court order, the conversion may take place as follows. Someone demands that a lawyer provide information about a client. The lawyer's first response, instinctually, is: "Sorry, it's privileged." Only after a court rules that there is no privilege does the lawyer retreat to: "Okay, but it's still confidential." However, then the court says: "Fine. It may be confidential, so you can't reveal the information to your wife or your golfing buddies—but I'm ordering you to answer anyway, because we're in court, and in court only the evidence rules apply. And by the way, even though it's confidential, there's an exception that allows you to disclose in situations just like this one." Then the lawyer says (to himself): "I think that 'may disclose' just turned into "must disclose," because the judge is going to hold me in contempt if I don't comply. And I won't get into trouble with the lawyer disciplinary authorities if I do testify, because of the permission given me under the court order exception to the confidentiality rule."

Other Laws

The Annotated Model Rules of Professional Conduct provides the following examples of this exception:

> [T]he Internal Revenue Code, 26 U.S.C. § 6050, compels lawyers to disclose, through IRS Form 8300, the identities of clients and the amounts and payment dates of all cash fees in excess of $10,000.
>
> . . .
>
> The issue also arises in connection with statutes requiring that child abuse be reported. *See, e.g.*, N.Y. City Ethics Op. 1997-2 (1997) (lawyer employed by social service agency may disclose information relating to abuse of minor client to social service agency if required by law).[43]

And, even though the other law may require disclosure, the lawyer "must discuss the matter with the client to the extent required by Rule 1.4."[44]

Court Orders

Although a determination of whether a lawyer must reveal client information in an adversarial proceeding will turn on rules of evidence rather than rules of ethics, the lawyer's ethical duty of confidentiality nevertheless plays a role.[45]. . . Absent informed consent of the client to do otherwise, the lawyer should assert on behalf of the client all nonfrivolous claims that the order is not authorized by law or that the information sought is protected against disclosure by the attorney-client privilege or other applicable law.[46]

If the lawyer is ordered to disclose the information, the lawyer's ethical obligations mandate that the disclosure be limited to that required by the court.[47]

Legal Ethics: The Lawyer's Deskbook on Professional Responsibility provides an example of how the limitation upon this exception might work in practice. In the course of representing a client regarding a business proposal, a lawyer uncovers information from third parties that relates to the representation. Pursuant to a criminal investigation, a court later orders the lawyer to reveal this information to a grand jury on the grounds that it is not protected by the evidentiary privilege, having not been the result of a communication between the client and the lawyer. The lawyer obeys the court order. Later, reporters ask him whether he complied. He answers: "Yes." Then they ask him what he said to the grand jury. If the lawyer tells them, he will commit a disciplinary violation by revealing information relating to the representation that remains protected by the confidentiality rule.[48]

Notes

1. MODEL RULES OF PROF'L CONDUCT R. 1.6 cmt. [3] (2004).

2. GEOFFREY C. HAZARD, JR. & W. WILLIAM HODES, THE LAW OF LAWYERING, 3d ed., 2003 Supplement, § 9.2, p. 9-6 [hereinafter HAZARD & HODES].

3. *See* X Corp. v. Doe, 805 F. Supp. 1298 (E.D. Va. 1992) (Whereas "the attorney client-privilege is . . . applied in the litigation context by judges, not lawyers, for the purpose of deciding whether to compel the disclosure of putatively privileged material . . . the . . . standard for disclosure of confidential information is one that is applied in the first instance by lawyers, not judges, as they struggle with the decision whether voluntarily to disclose certain confidential information they believe reflects an ongoing or future fraud. Judges apply the . . . standard in the second instance only to review post hoc whether a voluntary disclosure was ethically appropriate or, as here, to decide whether to enjoin a potential voluntary disclosure. . . ."). *See also* Zacharias, *Harmonizing Privilege and Confidentiality*, 41 S. TEX. L. REV. 69 (Winter 1999) for a discussion of why confidentiality rules developed so broadly, *and* Zacharias, *Rethinking Confidentiality*, 74 IOWA L. REV. 351 (1989) for a discussion of why the client-protective basis for this broad development may be misplaced.

4. "[M]any jurisdictions . . . have adopted versions of Rule 1.6 that continue to use the phrasing of the Model Code, protecting clients' 'confidences and secrets,' rather than 'information relating to the representation of a client.' The Model Code defined a 'confidence' as 'information protected by the attorney-client privilege.' Thus, if information available from other sources or disclosed by the client is not protected by the attorney-client privilege, it would not be protected as a *confidence* by Rule 1.6 in such jurisdictions. . . . However, the information could be protected as a secret." ANNO-

TATED MODEL RULES OF PROF'L CONDUCT, 5th ed., at 91 [hereinafter AMR]. The choice of the word "confidence" to represent "privilege" in this context adds to the confusion between the concepts. *Also see* Zacharias, *The Fallacy That Attorney-Client Privilege Has Been Eroded: Ramifications and Lessons for the Bar*, PROF. LAW., 1999 SYMPOSIUM ISSUE 39.

5. *See* Model Rule 1.6 *infra. Also see* RESTATEMENT (THIRD) OF THE LAW GOVERNING LAWYERS, § 59 (2000) [hereinafter RESTATEMENT]. The attorney-client privilege and the rule of confidentiality also apply to prospective clients. *See* Model Rule 1.18(b) (regarding confidentiality and prospective clients) and RESTATEMENT § 70 (2000) (regarding the attorney-client privilege and prospective clients). For purposes of this discussion, references will be made only to current or former clients.

6. Zacharias, *Harmonizing Privilege and Confidentiality*, 41 S. TEX L. REV. 69, 73 (Winter 1999). *See also* RESTATEMENT, § 59 cmt. b (2000) ("The expansive definition of client information not protected by the attorney-client privilege that nonetheless a lawyer is obliged to keep confidential comes primarily from the law of agency and rules of professional regulation.") and ROTUNDA, LEGAL ETHICS: THE LAWYER'S DESKBOOK ON PROFESSIONAL RESPONSIBILITY § 7.1 (2002-2003) [hereinafter ROTUNDA] ("The attorney is the agent of her client, who is the principal. It is a general rule of agency law that the agent must neither use nor disclose 'information confidentially given to him by the principal or acquired by him during the course of or on account of his agency. . . .' Restatement of the Law of Agency, Second, § 395.")

7. "The confidentiality rule . . . applies not only to matters communicated in confidence by the client but also to all information relating to the representation, whatever its source." MODEL RULES OF PROF'L CONDUCT, R. 1.6 cmt. [3] (2004).

8. Zacharias, *supra* note 6. ("[A]ttorney-client privilege rules are products of lawsuits. Courts and legislators make the rules. Whoever adopts the rules initially, it is judges who interpret them and flesh them out. Because privilege applies only when one client attempts to prevent the other side's access to potentially probative evidence in litigation, courts implementing privilege are cognizant of secrecy's negative attributes. Thus, judges tend to interpret attorney-client privilege narrowly.")

9. *See* Upjohn Co. v. United States, 449 U.S. 383, 395, 101 S. Ct. 677, 685 (1981).

10. HAZARD & HODES, 2003 Supplement, § 9.7, at 9-24.

11. RESTATEMENT, § 59 cmt. d (2000).

12. MODEL RULES OF PROF'L CONDUCT R. 1.9 (2004)

> (b) A lawyer shall not knowingly represent a person in the same or a substantially related matter in which a firm with which the lawyer formerly was associated had previously represented a client
> (1) whose interests are materially adverse to that person; and
> (2) about whom the lawyer had acquired information protected by Rules 1.6 and 1.9(c) that is material to the matter; . . .

13. MODEL RULES OF PROF'L CONDUCT R. 1.9 cmt. [3] (2004).

14. RESTATEMENT, § 59 cmt. d (2000).

15. "Loyalty and independent judgment are essential elements in the lawyer's relationship to a client." MODEL RULES OF PROF'L CONDUCT R. 1.7 cmt. [1] (2004).

16. HAZARD & HODES, *supra* note 2, § 9.15 at 9-53.

17. MODEL RULES OF PROF'L CONDUCT R. 1.6 cmt. [5] (2004).

18. Haw. Ethics Op. 38 (1999). *See also* Kan. Ethics Op. LEO 01-01 (2001).

19. ABA Formal Ethics Op. 01-421 (2001). *See generally* RESTATEMENT, § 61 (2000) (permitting disclosure that advances client's interests). *See also* ABA Informal Ethics Op. 86-1518 (1986) (interpreting exception for disclosures impliedly authorized as permitting lawyer to disclose to opposing counsel, without client consultation, inadvertent omission of contract provision).

20. ABA Formal Ethics Op. 93-370 (1993).

21. MODEL RULES OF PROF'L CONDUCT R. 1.0(e) (2004).

22. AMR, *supra* note 4 at 93, *citing* ABA Formal Ethics Op. 01-421 (2001) *and* Banner v. City of Flint, 136 F. Supp. 2d 678 (E.D. Mich. 2000) (lawyer who obtained confidences from initial consultation with prospective client violated Rule when he deposed her in another matter without explaining to her the availability of attorney-client privilege).

23. AMR, *supra* note 4 at 95.

24. MODEL RULES OF PROF'L CONDUCT R. 1.6 cmt. [6] (2004).

25. Spaulding v. Zimmerman, 116 N.W.2d 704 (Minn. 1962).

26. HAZARD & HODES, 2003 Supplement, § 9.20.

27. *Id. See also* Roger Cramton & Lori Knowles, *Professional Secrecy and Its Exceptions*: Spaulding v. Zimmerman *Revisited*, 83 MINN. L. REV. 63 (1998) for a thorough examination of this case, including interviews with some of the historical characters.

28. *See* http://www.abanet.org/buslaw/corporateresponsibility/final_report.pdf. The ABA House of Delegates had previously rejected the same recommendation made by the Ethics 2000 Commission two years earlier.

29. *Id.,* quoting Robert Hirshon, President of the American Bar Association, Charge to ABA Task Force on Corporate Responsibility, March 28, 2002.

30. RESTATEMENT, § 67 at 507 (2000).

31. *Id.* at 508.

32. *Id.* at 508-09.

33. See discussion *supra* regarding impliedly authorized disclosure.

34. AMR at 96, quoting MODEL RULES OF PROF'L CONDUCT R. 1.6 cmt. [9] (2003).

35. *Reporter's Explanation of Changes*, Ethics 2000 Commission, *available at* http://www.abanet.org/cpr/e2k-rule16rem.html.

36. HAZARD & HODES, 2003 Supplement, § 9.17 at 9-63.

37. "This aspect of the rule expresses the principle that the beneficiary of a fiduciary relationship may not exploit it to the detriment of the fiduciary." MODEL RULES OF PROF'L CONDUCT R. 1.6 cmt. [11] (2004).

38. ROTUNDA, *supra* note 6 at § 7-11.3 (2002-2003).

39. ABA Standing Committee on Ethics and Professional Responsibility, Op. 01-424 (2001): "Whether, and to what extent, former in-house counsel may sue their former employers for employment-related matters varies among jurisdictions. Some jurisdictions permit such actions provided they can be maintained without violating client confidences." AMR at 97.

40. AMR at 96.

41. MODEL RULES OF PROF'L CONDUCT R. 1.6 cmt. [10] (2004). *See also* HAZARD & HODES, § 9.23, DISCLOSURE OF CLIENT CONFIDENCES AS A MATTER OF PREEMPTIVE SELF-DEFENSE.

42. *Reporter's Explanation of Changes*, Ethics 2000 Commission, *available at* http://www.abanet.org/cpr/e2k-rule16rem.html.

43. AMR, *supra* note 4 at 99-100.

44. MODEL RULES OF PROF'L CONDUCT R. 1.6 cmt. [12] (2004).

45. AMR, *supra* note 4 at 88.

46. MODEL RULES OF PROF'L CONDUCT R. 1.6 cmt. [13] (2004).

47. AMR, *supra* note 4 at 88, *citing* "Ariz. Ethics Op. 2000-11 (2000) (lawyer called as witness in legal proceeding must invoke attorney-client privilege regarding communication with client *and* Rule 1.6 concerning all other information relating to representation, but lawyer must comply with final order of court in matter); R.I. Ethics Op. 2000-8 (2000) (lawyer questioned at deposition about matters relating to representation of deceased client is required by Rule 1.6 to invoke lawyer-client privilege, ethical duty of confidentiality, and, if applicable, work-product doctrine; lawyer must comply with final orders of court requiring disclosure)."

48. ROTUNDA, *supra* note 6 at § 7-1 (2002-2003).

CHAPTER 3

The Attorney-Client Privilege and the Sarbanes-Oxley Act of 2002

HARVA R. DOCKERY

Since June 30, 2002, no discussion of the attorney-client privilege (among many other legal concepts) would be complete without consideration of some aspects of the Sarbanes-Oxley Act of 2002.[1] That was when Congress enacted the unprecedented statute to "protect investors by improving the accuracy and reliability of corporate disclosures made pursuant to the securities laws, and for other purposes."[2] Section 307 of the act gave the Securities and Exchange Commission, for the first time, express authority to issue rules establishing "standards of professional conduct for attorneys appearing and practicing before the Commission."[3] Section 307 specifies that these rules must require attorneys to report any material violation of securities laws, breach of fiduciary duty or similar violation by a publicly held or other specified company or its agents to certain officers of the company and, if those officers do not appropriately respond, to report the violation or breach to the company's audit committee or board of directors.[4]

In November 2002, the Commission issued its proposed rules under Section 307 of the Sarbanes-Oxley Act and solicited comments on them.[5] The proposed rules contained the reporting obligations specifically required by Section 307 (the "reporting up" rules), but also contained other provisions, including a requirement that an attorney withdraw from representation of a company and report the withdrawal to the Commission if the company's management fails to respond appropriately to the attorney's report of certain violations or breaches. This latter aspect of the proposed rules, the "noisy withdrawal" requirements, proved controversial. In January 2003, the Commission adopted the proposed reporting up rules, with some adjustments, but deferred adoption of any noisy withdrawal or other "reporting out" rules pending further consideration and comment.[6] As of this writing, no noisy withdrawal or other reporting out rules have been adopted.

Both the adopted reporting up rules and the proposed reporting out rules raise issues relating to the attorney-client privilege.

The Adopted Attorney Conduct Rules

The reporting up and related rules are embodied in new Part 205 of the Code of Federal Regulations.[7] They became effective on August 5, 2003.[8] Following is a brief restatement of some relevant aspects of these rules.

Basic Premises

The rules set forth some basic premises. First, the standards contained in the rules are the minimum standards of professional conduct for attorneys[9] appearing and practicing before the Commission[10] in the representation[11] of an issuer.[12] These standards are intended to supplement the standards of professional conduct applicable to an attorney in any jurisdiction in which the attorney is admitted to practice law. The Commission's standards are not intended to limit the ability of any jurisdiction to impose additional obligations on attorneys, as long as those obligations are consistent with the Commission's standards. However, the Commission's standards will govern if the standards of a state or other U.S. jurisdiction conflict with the Commission's standards.[13]

Second, an attorney appearing and practicing before the Commission in the representation of an issuer owes his or her professional and ethical duties to the issuer as an organization. Working with an issuer's officers, directors, and employees in the course of representing the issuer does not make those individuals clients.[14]

Third, an attorney appearing and practicing before the Commission in the representation of an issuer may reveal to the Commission, without the issuer's consent, confidential information related to the representation to the extent the attorney reasonably believes[15] necessary:

- To prevent the issuer from committing a material violation[16] that is likely to cause substantial injury to the financial interest or property of the issuer or investors;
- To prevent the issuer, in a Commission investigation or administrative proceeding, from suborning perjury or committing an act that is likely to perpetrate a fraud on the Commission;[17] or
- To rectify the consequences of a material violation by an issuer that has caused or may cause substantial injury to the financial interest or property of the issuer or investors in the furtherance of which the attorney's services were used.[18]

Reporting Up Requirements

The rules also mandate specific reporting requirements in certain instances. If an attorney appearing and practicing before the Commission in the representation of an issuer becomes aware of evidence of a material violation[19] by the issuer or by any officer, director, employee or agent of the issuer, the attorney must forthwith report[20] that evidence to the issuer's chief legal officer (or equivalent) or to both the issuer's chief legal officer and the issuer's chief executive officer (or equivalents).[21] The attorney may instead choose to go directly to the issuer's audit or other specified committee or to the board of directors if the attorney believes it would be futile to report the evidence of the material violation to those officers.[22] Alternatively, the attorney may report the material violation to a qualified legal compliance committee.[23]

The chief legal officer (or equivalent) must then make an appropriate inquiry into the evidence reported by the attorney to determine whether the reported material violation has occurred, is ongoing or is about to occur. If the officer determines that no material violation has occurred, is ongoing or is about to occur, the officer must so notify the reporting attorney. Unless the officer reasonably believes that no material violation has occurred, is ongoing or is about to occur, he or she must take all reasonable steps to cause the issuer to adopt an appropriate response[24] and must so advise the reporting attorney.[25]

If the reporting attorney does not reasonably believe that the chief legal officer (or equivalent) or the chief executive officer (or equivalent) has provided an appropriate response to the attorney's report within a reasonable time, the attorney must report the evidence of the material violation to the issuer's audit committee, or, if there is no audit committee, to an independent committee of the issuer's board of directors, or, if there is no such committee, to the issuer's board of directors.[26]

If the reporting attorney believes that an appropriate and timely response to the report has been made (whether by the specified officers, the specified committee or the board of directors), he is not required to take any other action. If, however, the reporting attorney does not believe that an appropriate and timely response to the report has been made, he must communicate this belief, with an explanation, to the officers and directors to whom he made the report.[27]

Supervisory attorneys[28] are required to make reasonable efforts to ensure that subordinate attorneys[29] under their supervision comply with the rules. If a subordinate attorney reports evidence of a material violation to a supervisory attorney, the supervisory attorney is responsible for complying with the reporting requirements and the subordinate attorney is deemed to have complied with the reporting rules.[30] If a subordinate attorney has reported evidence of a material violation to a supervisory attorney and reasonably believes that the supervisory attorney has failed to comply with the reporting rules, then the subordinate attorney may comply with the reporting rules without the intervention of the supervisory attorney.[31]

Enforcement

The authority to enforce the Commission's rules is vested solely in the Commission.[32] If an attorney appearing and practicing before the Commission violates the rules, he is subject to civil penalties and remedies available to the Commission for violations of federal securities laws.[33] The violating attorney may also be subject to a Commission administrative disciplinary proceeding, which could result in the attorney's censure or denial of the privilege of appearing and practicing before the Commission. These remedies are in addition to any remedies in a jurisdiction where the attorney is admitted to practice or practices. If an attorney complies with the Commission's rules, she will not be subject to disciplinary action or other remedies under any inconsistent standards imposed by any state or other U.S. jurisdiction.[34]

An attorney may use a report of a material violation under the rules and the responses to the report in connection with any investigation, proceeding or litigation in which her compliance with the rules is an issue.[35]

Attorney-Client Privilege Issues Raised by the Adopted Rules

The adopted rules are grounded in the widely accepted doctrine that the client of an attorney retained by an organization is the organization, and not any of its agents or other constituents.[36] Because an organization can act only through its agents, no one agent or other constituent should have the expectation that his or her communication with the organization's attorney should carry with it any special privilege or other protection as against an authorized officer or director of the organization.[37] It follows that if any of the organization's officers, directors, agents or other constituents disclose to the organization's attorney information that may be confidential, then the attorney's discussing that information with authorized officers or directors of the organization cannot breach the confidential or privileged nature of the communication.

It is also well-recognized that any privilege or other protection to be conferred on the communication between an organization's attorney and its agents and other constituents belongs to the organization (that is, to the client) and not to the organization's agents or other constituents.[38] Because an organization can act only through its agents, the attorney-client privilege may only be asserted by the appropriate agents of the organization, but they do so on behalf of the organization.[39]

The Commission's reporting up rules are consistent with these principles. The rules recognize that an attorney appearing and practicing before the Commission in the representation of an issuer owes his or her duties to the issuer.[40] The rules also require only that the attorney report evidence of a material violation within the issuer (that is, only to specified officers of the issuer or to the issuer's board of directors or a committee of the board of directors).[41]

The more controversial aspect of the adopted rules[42] is the statement that an attorney appearing and practicing before the Commission in the representation of an issuer *may* disclose confidential information to the Commission without the issuer's consent for specified purposes, including preventing the issuer's commission of, or rectifying the consequences of, a material violation that is likely to cause, or has caused, substantial injury to the financial interest or property of the issuer or its investors, and preventing the issuer from suborning perjury or committing an act likely to perpetrate a fraud on the Commission.[43] The concern regarding this permissive disclosure rule is its erosive effect on the attorney-client privilege.

In adopting the permissive disclosure rule, the Commission noted that most, but not all, states have adopted analogous rules of professional conduct.[44] Based on the experiences of states that have these kinds of rules, the Commission found that there is no evidence that the state rules have interfered with the attorney-client relationship and that the public interest outweighs concerns about the attorney-client relationship in the limited instances in which the Commission's permissive disclosure rule applies.[45] In addressing concerns that the Commission has no authority to adopt permissive disclosure rules that preempt state rules having a lesser obligation, the

Commission apparently reasoned that it has that authority because the Commerce Clause of the Constitution grants the federal government the right to regulate the securities industry, the Sarbanes-Oxley Act specifically requires the Commission to establish rules delineating standards of professional conduct, and under the Supremacy Clause of the Constitution, valid rules of the Commission may preempt conflicting state rules.[46] Even in light of the Commission's reasoning, there are at least three concerns about the permissive disclosure rule's effect on the attorney-client privilege.

First, that the permissive disclosure rule does not mandate any disclosure may ameliorate concerns about its negative effect on the principle underlying the attorney-client privilege—to promote unhindered and complete communication between the attorney and the client. Those attorneys who are not comfortable with disclosing information to the Commission pursuant to the Commission's rules because the laws of the jurisdictions in which they practice do not permit disclosure will, at least, have the option of refraining from such disclosure. Others may argue that because the Commission's adopted rules permit disclosure of information that may not be disclosed under the attorney-client privilege or other confidentiality requirements in a particular state, the right to disclose that information granted by the Commission's rules preempts the state's prohibition of the disclosure, and therefore an attorney practicing in that state may disclose the information without violating the state's preempted rules.[47] Thus, the Commission's adopted permissive disclosure rule abrogates the protections afforded by the attorney-client privilege in some states.

Second, state laws permitting disclosure in particular circumstances are not necessarily equivalent to the Commission's permitted disclosure rules.[48] Many of those laws speak in terms of "fraud" by a client, and do not refer to "material violations" that would meet the Commission's definition of that term.[49] It may be difficult for any attorney to fit the disclosure granted by the Commission's permissive disclosure rule within the parameters of other requirements with which the attorney must comply. Thus, even attorneys practicing in states that do permit disclosure of privileged information under circumstances analogous to those contained in the Commission's rule may risk violating the attorney-client privilege under state law if they assume that the preemptive supremacy of the Commission's permissive disclosure rule is valid.[50]

Finally, the attorney-client privilege belongs to the issuer, who has the right to make the decision as to whether to waive the privilege, and not to the attorney, who, under the permitted disclosure provisions of the Commission's adopted rules, has the right to determine whether disclosure is appropriate.[51] Giving this discretion to attorneys, even in the limited circumstances described in the rules, further endangers the protections afforded by the attorney-client privilege.

The Commission's adopted rules are new. As best practices develop and judicial and other interpretations regarding the rules are rendered, the appropriate application and validity of the Commission's adopted permitted disclosure rule will become clearer. It was the Commission's proposed rules, discussed below, mandating an attorney's withdrawal from representation and reporting on that withdrawal that has caused greater concerns in the context of the attorney-client privilege.

The Proposed Reporting Out Rules

The Commission has proposed two alternative rules to address what actions must (or may) be taken if an attorney who has reported evidence of a material violation under the reporting up rules does not receive an appropriate and timely response. The first proposal was made in November 2002 and was included with the proposed reporting up rules.[52] The alternative proposal was made in January 2003, in response to comments made on the first proposal.[53] It is impossible to predict whether any final rule will be one of the two proposed rules or some variation on them.

Neither of the proposed rules is required by the Sarbanes-Oxley Act, but the Commission believes that they are "potentially important minimum standards for attorneys appearing and practicing before the Commission in the representation of issuers."[54] Both of the proposed rules raise issues regarding the attorney-client relationship and, more specifically, the attorney-client privilege. To put the proposed rules in the appropriate context, a brief restatement of each alternative is provided below.

The First Proposed Rule

Under the first proposal, if an attorney has reported evidence of a material violation in accordance with the reporting up rules, has not received an appropriate response or a timely response, believes a material violation *is ongoing or is about to occur*, and believes that the material violation is likely to result in substantial injury to the financial interest or property of the issuer or of investors, then the attorney *must* take specified actions.[55] First, if the attorney is retained (as opposed to employed) by the issuer, he or she must withdraw from representing the issuer, notify the Commission of the withdrawal, and disaffirm to the Commission any opinion, document, affirmation, representation or characterization contained in a document filed with or submitted to the Commission that the attorney has prepared or assisted in preparing and that the attorney reasonably believes is or may be materially false or misleading.[56] Second, if the attorney is employed by the issuer, he or she *must* notify the Commission of his or her intention to disaffirm, and promptly disaffirm, any part of a document filed with or submitted to the Commission, if he or she has prepared or assisted in the preparation of the document and reasonably believes that part of the document may be materially false or misleading.[57]

Also under the first proposal, if an attorney has reported evidence of a material violation, has not received an appropriate and timely response, believes that a material violation has occurred, and believes that the material violation is likely to have resulted in substantial injury to the financial interest or property of the issuer or of investors but is not ongoing, then the attorney *may* take the actions described above.[58]

In either of these cases, the issuer's chief legal officer (or equivalent) must inform any attorney who replaces the withdrawing attorney that the previous attorney withdrew for professional considerations.[59]

Finally, the first proposed rule states that giving any notice under the proposed rule will not breach the attorney-client privilege.[60]

The Second Proposed Rule

Under the second proposal, if an attorney has reported evidence of a material violation in accordance with the reporting up rules, has not received an appropriate and timely response, and reasonably concludes there is substantial evidence of a material violation that *is ongoing or about to occur* and that is likely to cause substantial injury to the financial interest or property of the issuer or of investors, then the attorney *must* take specified actions.[61] First, if the attorney is retained by the issuer, he or she must withdraw from representing the issuer and so notify the issuer.[62] Second, if the attorney is employed by the issuer, he or she must cease any participation in any matter concerning the violation and notify the issuer that it has not provided an appropriate and timely response to the attorney's report.[63] An attorney who is prohibited from taking the required actions, by order or rule of a court, administrative body or other authority having jurisdiction over the attorney, will not be required to do so if he or she has sought leave to withdraw from the representation or to cease participation in the matter. In this case, the attorney must notify the issuer that he or she would have taken these actions but for the prohibition.[64] Third, if an attorney believes that he or she has been discharged by the issuer for reporting evidence of a material violation under the reporting up rules, the attorney must notify the issuer's chief legal officer (or equivalent).[65]

The issuer's chief legal officer (or equivalent) must inform any attorney who replaces the attorney who has given a notice of withdrawal, suspension of participation in a matter or wrongful discharge to the issuer under the proposed rule that the previous attorney withdraw, ceased to participate in the matter or gave notice of discharge pursuant to the proposed rule.[66]

Finally, if an attorney has given a notice required by the proposed rule, then the issuer must report the notice and related circumstances in a current report on Form 8-K filed with the Commission.[67] If the issuer fails to file this report, the attorney may inform the Commission that a notice was given to the issuer as required by the proposed rule.[68]

Attorney-Client Privilege Issues Raised by the Proposed Reporting Out Rules

Both of the proposed rules require notices or disclosures to the Commission or to the public in specified circumstances. Under these circumstances, the first proposed rule requires a non-employee attorney to notify the Commission of his or her withdrawal under the proposed rule, and requires an employee attorney to notify the Commission of any intention to disaffirm a document filed with or furnished to the Commission.[69] Under the second proposed rule, the issuer is required to report on the circumstances in a publicly available document (by means of a current report on Form 8-K) if a non-employee attorney has given the issuer a notice of withdrawal, if an employee attorney has given the issuer a notice of suspension of participation in a matter, or if any attorney has given the issuer a notice of wrongful discharge under the requirements of the proposed rule.[70]

In either case, these requirements could have a chilling effect on the free flow of communications between the attorney and the client. This is because an issuer's officers and directors may be reluctant to seek an attorney's advice knowing that it could lead to a required withdrawal and notice by the attorney and the attendant adverse consequences to the issuer, even if the issuer's position is reasonable.[71] Because the free exchange of information is the cornerstone of the attorney-client privilege,[72] the requirements of the proposed rules could erode the scope of the benefits that the attorney-client privilege is intended to provide.

The first proposed rule states that the required notifications to the Commission will not breach the attorney-client privilege.[73] According to the Commission, this "restates what is largely settled law" and is in line with the professional conduct rules of the majority of states, which generally permit an attorney's disclosure of confidential information to prevent or rectify the consequences of a criminal or fraudulent act.[74] The proposed rule expands the scope of these state professional conduct rules, first because a material violation, as defined in the rule, is not necessarily a criminal or fraudulent act, even if it may result in substantial injury, and second because most of the state professional conduct rules only permit disclosure of confidential information and do not require it.[75] While it is true that the attorney is required to state in the notice only that the withdrawal is for professional considerations,[76] the fact that the attorney has withdrawn for professional considerations is likely to imply that something is wrong and thus, arguably, breaches the attorney-client privilege.[77]

The second proposed rule requires that the issuer, rather than the attorney, disclose information about the attorney's withdrawal from representation, suspension of participation in a matter, and wrongful discharge.[78] Although it may appear that an issuer's disclosure of these matters should be less problematic than the attorney's disclosure of them, this premise is not logical. First, the information that the issuer must disclose still may entail privileged attorney-client content. Second, unlike the first proposed rule, the second proposed rule requires information about the circumstances related to a withdrawal, not just the fact that it occurred because of professional considerations. Third, the public nature of the disclosure is more likely than the notice to the Commission to negatively affect the market for the issuer's securities and the issuer's relationships with others, including its customers, suppliers, and employees, even if this result is unwarranted.[79]

The second proposed rule exempts an attorney from withdrawing or suspending participation in a matter if doing so is prohibited by another authority having jurisdiction over the attorney.[80] This exemption is helpful in aligning the proposed reporting out rules with state laws designed to protect the attorney-client privilege, but it requires the attorney seeking the protection of the exemption to take extraordinary measures that may be impracticable—that is, to obtain a determination by a court or other administrative authority that the attorney is prohibited from complying with the proposed rule.[81]

Finally, the second proposed rule permits an attorney to inform the Commission if the issuer fails to file a current report on Form 8-K required by the proposed rule upon notice of withdrawal, suspension of participation in a matter or wrongful discharge.[82] This permissive disclosure raises some of the same issues in connection with the attorney-client privilege as the adopted rules' permissive disclosure by attorneys of certain events to the Commission.[83] Any newly mandated disclosure of information protected by the attorney-client privilege erodes the privilege.

The Commission has proposed these rules because it wants to "further the purposes of the up-the-ladder requirements, enhance investor confidence in the financial reporting process . . . deter instances of attorney and issuer misconduct and . . . reduce its impact on issuers and their shareholders."[84] The Commission also wants to preserve zealous advocacy of attorneys on behalf of their clients and "does not want to discourage issuers from seeking and obtaining appropriate and effective legal advice."[85] In deciding what additional attorney conduct rules to adopt, the Commission has a tough job in meeting all of these goals. At the very least, any new rules mandating the reporting of the withdrawal or non-participation of an attorney under the circumstances described in the proposed rules will likely adversely affect the attorney-client privilege as we knew it before Sarbanes-Oxley.

Notes

1. Sarbanes-Oxley Act of 2002, Pub. L. No. 107-204, 116 Stat. 745 (codified as amended in scattered sections of 15 U.S.C.).

2. *Id.*

3. 15 U.S.C. § 7245 (2003); *see* Implementation of Standards of Professional Conduct for Attorneys, Securities Act Release No. 8150 [2002-2003 Transfer Binder], Fed. Sec. L. Rep. (CCH) ¶ 186,802 at 86,513 (Nov. 21, 2002). In 1935, the Commission adopted Rule 2(e), later redesignated as Rule 102(e), as part of its rules of practice. This rule permits the Commission to censure, suspend or disbar professionals, including attorneys, practicing before it if they have engaged in improper conduct or do not meet certain standards, but it does not establish standards of conduct and was not specifically mandated by statute. *See* Securities Act Release No. 8150 at 86,516.

Other provisions of the Sarbanes-Oxley Act may affect the professional conduct of lawyers, including certification requirements for an issuer's chief executive officer and chief financial officer (Section 302 of the act), prohibitions on improperly influencing auditors (Section 303 of the act), document destruction limitations (Sections 802 and 1102 of the act), whistle-blower protection (Sections 806 and 1107 of the act), and specific statutory authority for censoring, suspending, and disbarring attorneys practicing before the Commission (Section 602 of the act). *See* ATTORNEYS' LIABILITY ASSURANCE SOCIETY, INC., SARBANES-OXLEY: A GUIDE FOR LAWYERS 24-32 (2004). While all of these sections of the act could bring into issue various aspects of the attorney-client privilege, Section 307, together with rules adopted, or to be adopted, under that section, is clearly the provision of the act that has the most significant potential for affecting the attorney-client privilege.

4. Section 307 reads, in its entirety, as follows:

> Not later than 180 days after the date of enactment of this Act, the Commission shall issue rules, in the public interest and for the protection of investors, setting forth minimum standards of professional conduct for attorneys appearing and practicing before the Commission in any way in the representation of issuers, including a rule—
>
> (1) requiring an attorney to report evidence of a material violation of securities law or breach of fiduciary duty or similar violation by the company or any agent thereof, to the chief legal counsel or the chief executive officer of the company (or the equivalent thereof); and
>
> (2) if the counsel or officer does not appropriately respond to the evidence (adopting, as necessary, appropriate remedial measures or sanctions with respect to the violation), requiring the attorney to report the evidence to the audit committee of the board of directors of the issuer or to another committee of the board of directors comprised solely of directors not employed directly or indirectly by the issuer, or to the board of directors.

See 15 U.S.C. § 7245.

5. Securities Act Release No. 8150, *supra* note 3.

6. Implementation of Standards of Professional Conduct for Attorneys, Securities Act Release No. 8185 [2002-2003 Transfer Binder], Fed. Sec. L. Rep. (CCH) ¶ 186,823 at 87,069 (Aug. 5, 2003).

7. Standards of Professional Conduct for Attorneys Appearing and Practicing Before the Commission in the Representation of an Issuer, 17 C.F.R. § 205 (2003).

8. Securities Act Release No. 8185, *supra* note 6.

9. "Attorney" means any person who is admitted, licensed or otherwise qualified to practice law in any jurisdiction, domestic or foreign, or who holds himself or herself out as admitted, licensed or otherwise qualified to practice law. 17 C.F.R. § 205.2(c).

10. "Appearing and practicing before the Commission" means:

(i) Transacting any business with the Commission, including communications in any form;

(ii) Representing an issuer in a Commission administrative proceeding or in any Commission investigation, inquiry, information request or subpoena;

(iii) Providing advice on U.S. securities laws or the Commission's rules or regulations under those laws regarding any document that the attorney has notice will be filed with or submitted to, or incorporated in any document that will be filed with or submitted to, the Commission, including the provision of advice in the context of preparing, or participating in the preparation of, the document; or

(iv) Advising an issuer as to whether information or a statement, opinion or other writing is required under U.S. securities laws or the Commission's rules or regulations under those laws to be filed with or submitted to, or incorporated into any document that will be filed with, or submitted to, the Commission.

"Appearing and practicing before the Commission" does not include an attorney who:

(i) Conducts the activities described above outside of the context of providing legal services to an issuer with whom the attorney has an attorney-client relationship; or

(ii) Is a non-appearing foreign attorney.

A "non-appearing foreign attorney" is an attorney admitted to practice law in a non-U.S. jurisdiction; who does not hold himself or herself out as practicing, and does not give legal advice regarding, U.S. federal or state securities or other laws; and who (i) conducts activities that would constitute appearing and practicing before the Commission only incidentally to, and in the ordinary course of, the practice of law in a jurisdiction outside the United States or (ii) is appearing and practicing before the Commission only in consultation with counsel, other than a non-appearing foreign attorney, admitted or licensed to practice in a state or other United States jurisdiction.

Id. at § 205.2(a).

In its release adopting the rules, the Commission noted that it is possible to have an attorney-client relationship within the meaning of the definition of "appearing and practicing before the Commission," even though the attorney-client privilege may not be available for communications between the attorney and the client. Securities Act Release No. 8185, *supra* note 6, at 87,072.

11. "In the representation of an issuer" means providing legal services as an attorney for an issuer, regardless of whether the attorney is employed or retained by the issuer. Standards of Professional Conduct for Attorneys, *supra* note 7, at § 205.2(g).

12. "Issuer" means an issuer (as defined in section 3 of the Securities Exchange Act of 1934 (15 U.S.C. § 78c)—generally, any entity that issues securities) whose securities are registered under section 12 of that act (15 U.S.C. § 78l), which is required to file reports under section 15(d) of that act (15 U.S.C. § 78o(d), or which files or has filed an unwithdrawn registration statement that has not yet become effective under the Securities Act of 1933 (15 U.S.C. § 77a *et seq.),* but does not

include a foreign government issuer. The term "issuer" includes any person controlled by an issuer, if an attorney provides legal services to that controlled person on behalf of, at the behest of or for the benefit of the issuer, regardless of whether the attorney is employed or retained by the issuer. *Id.* at § 205.2(h). The inclusion of an issuer's subsidiaries in this definition is consistent with arrangements under which an attorney may represent both a parent company and its subsidiaries, with the right to invoke the attorney-client privilege with respect to the attorney's communications with any of them. Securities Act Release No. 8185, *supra* note 6, at 87,080.

13.   Standards of Professional Conduct for Attorneys, *supra* note 7, at § 205.1 *See* text accompanying notes 44-47, *infra.*

14.   *Id.* at § 205.3(a). *See also infra* note 37.

15.   "Reasonably believes" means that an attorney believes the matter in question and that the circumstances are such that the belief is not unreasonable. *Id.* at § 205.2(m). "Reasonable" or "reasonably" denotes, with respect to the actions of an attorney, conduct that would not be unreasonable for a prudent and competent attorney. *Id.* at § 205.2(1).

16.   "Material violation" means a material violation of an applicable U.S. federal or state securities law, a material breach of fiduciary duty arising under U.S. federal or state law, or a similar material violation of any U.S. federal or state law. *Id.* at § 205.2(i). "Breach of fiduciary duty" refers to any breach of fiduciary or similar duty to the issuer recognized under an applicable federal or state statute or at common law, including misfeasance, nonfeasance, abdication of duty, abuse of trust, and approval of unlawful transactions. Id. at § 205.2(d).

17.   The term "perpetrate a fraud" includes a knowing misrepresentation of a material fact to, or the concealment of a material fact from, the Commission with the intent to induce the Commission to take, or to refrain from taking, a particular action. *See* Securities Act Release No. 8185, *supra* note 6, at 87,092. The kinds of acts referred to include concealing material facts; making materially false representations; using a writing or document, knowing that it contains a materially false statement; committing perjury; or suborning perjury. *See* 18 U.S.C. §§ 1001, 1621, 1622 (2003).

18.   *See* Standards of Professional Conduct for Attorneys, supra note 7, at § 205.3(d)(2)(i).

19.   "Evidence of a material violations" means credible evidence, based on which it would be unreasonable, under the circumstances, for a prudent and competent attorney not to conclude that it is reasonably likely that a material violation has occurred, is ongoing or is about to occur. *Id.* at § 205.2(e).

20.   "Report" means to make known to directly, either in person, by telephone, by e-mail, electronically or in writing. *Id.* at § 205.2(n).

21.   *Id.* at § 205.3(b)(1).

22.   *Id.*

23.   The rules provide for an alternative reporting procedure for attorneys representing issuers that have established a qualified legal compliance committee. If the attorney chooses to make the report to the qualified legal compliance committee rather than to the chief legal officer and chief executive officer, then the attorney has satisfied his or her obligation to report that evidence and will not be required to take any further action, including any determination of whether the issuer's response to the attorney's report is adequate. *Id.* at § 2053(c)(1).

A qualified legal compliance committee is, generally, a committee of the board of directors consisting of at least three members who are independent (one of whom is a member of the issuer's audit committee or, if there is no audit committee, a member of an equivalent committee of independent directors); that has adopted written procedures for the confidential receipt, retention, and consideration of any report under the rules; and that has been given the authority to inform the issuer's chief legal officer and chief executive officer (or equivalents) of any such report, to determine whether an investigation is necessary regarding the report, to take certain actions in connection with the report and the investigation, to recommend appropriate responses to the report, and to take all other appropriate action in connection with the report, including the authority to notify the Commission if the issuer fails in any material way to implement the response that the qualified legal compliance committee has recommended. *Id.* at § 205.3(c); *see also* Securities Act Release No. 8185, *supra* note 6, at 87,081.

24. "Appropriate response" means a response to an attorney regarding reported evidence of a material violation as a result of which the attorney reasonably believes:

> (i) That no material violation has occurred, is ongoing or is about to occur;
>
> (ii) That the issuer has adopted appropriate remedial measures, including appropriate steps or sanctions to stop any material violations that are ongoing, to prevent any material violation that has yet to occur, and to remedy or otherwise appropriately address any material violation that has already occurred and minimize the likelihood of its recurrence; or
>
> (iii) That the issuer, with the consent of its board of directors, a committee of its board of directors to whom a report could be made pursuant to the rules, or a qualified legal compliance committee, has retained or directed an attorney to review the reported evidence of a material violation and either:
>
> (a) Has substantially implemented any remedial recommendations made by the attorney after a reasonable investigation and evaluation of the reported evidence; or
>
> (b) Has been advised that the attorney may, consistent with his or her professional obligations, assert a colorable defense on behalf of the issuer (or the issuer's officer, director, employee or agent, as the case may be) in any investigation or judicial or administrative proceeding relating to the reported evidence of a material violation.

Id. at 205.2(b). *See* Securities Act Release No. 8185, *supra* note 6, at 87,073.

25. Standards of Professional Conduct for Attorneys, *supra* note 7, at § 205.3(b)(2).

26. *Id.* at § 205.3(b)(3).

27. *Id.* at § 205.3(b)(9).

28. A "supervisory attorney" is "an attorney supervising or directing another attorney who is appearing and practicing before the Commission in the representation of an issuer." *Id.* at § 205.4(a). The chief legal officer of an issuer is, by definition, a supervisory attorney. *Id.* If a subordinate attorney appears and practices before the Commission in the representation of an issuer, then the subordinate attorney's supervisory attorneys, by definition, appear and practice before the Commission. *Id.* at § 205.4(b).

29. A "subordinate attorney" is an attorney who appears and practices before the Commission in the representation of an issuer on a matter under the supervision or direction of another attorney (other than under the direct supervision or direction of the issuer's chief legal officer). *Id.* at § 205.5(a).

30. *Id.* at § 205.5(c).

31. *Id.* at § 205.5(d).

32. *Id.* at § 205-07.

33. *Id.* at § 205.6(a).

34. *Id.* at § 205.6(c). Regarding the Commission's authority to exonerate noncompliance with a state's rules under a pre-emption theory, *see* text accompanying notes 44-47, *infra*.

35. *Id.* at § 205.3(d)(1). The right to use the report belongs to the attorney. Securities Act Release No. 8185, *supra* note 6, at 87,090. This comports with state law as well. *See, e.g.,* TEX. DISCIPLINARY R. PROF'L CONDUCT 1.05(c)-(d), reprinted in TEX. GOV'T CODE ANN., tit. 2, subtit. G, app. A (Vernon's Supp. 2004) (TEX. STATE BAR R. art. X, § 9) (permitting a lawyer to reveal both privileged and unprivileged confidential information in specified cases relating to the lawyer's need to defend himself or herself).

36. *See* MODEL R. PROF'L CONDUCT 1.13 (2003); TEX. DISCIPLINARY R. PROF'L CONDUCT 1.12.

37. *See* Securities Act Release No. 8185, *supra* note 6, at 87,083-084; ATTORNEY-CLIENT PRIVILEGE IN CIVIL LITIGATION: PROTECTING AND DEFENDING CONFIDENTIALITY 5 (Vincent S. Walkowiak ed., 2d ed. 1997).

Rule 205.3(b)(1) specifically states that "communicating [evidence of a material violation] to the issuer's officers or directors does not [constitute disclosure of privileged or protected information regarding] the attorney's representation of the issuer." Standards of Professional Conduct for Attorneys, supra note 7, at § 205.3(b)(1).

38. Walkowiak, *supra* note 37, at 5.

39. *Id.*

40. Standards of Professional Conduct for Attorneys, *supra* note 7, at § 205.3(a).

41. *Id.* at § 205.3(b).

42. A second controversial aspect of the originally proposed rules was excluded from the adopted rules, but provides some insight into the analysis of the adopted rules as they relate to the attorney-client privilege. The originally proposed rules contained a statement that an attorney's sharing information regarding a material violation to the Commission would not constitute a waiver of any applicable privilege as to other persons. Many commentors expressed concern that the Commission did not have the authority to promulgate a rule preserving the attorney-client privilege or work-product protection, a protection that many believe can only be granted by law or court interpretation. The proposed rule regarding waiver of privilege or protection was therefore withdrawn by the Commission, citing the risk that attorneys relying on the proposed rule could suffer adverse consequences under the laws of other jurisdictions by disclosing information to the Commission in reliance on the proposed rule. The Commission, however, said that it would continue to follow its policy of entering into confidentiality agreements to obtain otherwise privileged or protected information from issuers and, in such cases, would continue to argue that disclosure of information under those confidentiality agreements does not waive any privilege or protection. *See* Securities Act Release No. 8185, *supra* note 6, at 87,085.

43. Standards of Professional Conduct for Attorneys, *supra* note 7, at § 205.3(d)(2). *See* text accompanying notes 15-18, *supra*.

44. *See generally* Securities Act Release No. 8185, *supra* note 6, at 87,090-093; *see also* MODEL RULES OF PROF'L CONDUCT R. 1.6(b).

45. *See* Securities Act Release No. 8185, *supra* note 6, at 87,093; text accompanying notes 15-18, *supra*.

46. *See id.* at 87,071; *see also infra* notes 47-48.

47. *See, e.g.*, Public Statement by SEC Official: Letter Regarding Washington State Bar Association's Proposed Opinion on the Effect of the SEC's Attorney Conduct Rules from Giovanni P. Prezioso, General Counsel, Securities and Exchange Commission, to J. Richard Manning, President, Washington State Bar Association, and David W. Savage, President-Elect, Washington State Bar Association (July 23, 2003), *available at* http://www.sec.gov/news/speech/spch072303gpp.htm.

48. *See, e.g.*, CAL. R. PROF'L CONDUCT 3-600 and 3-700 (limiting an attorney's response to an organization's violation of law to reporting the violation within the organization and withdrawal from the representation); WASH. ST. CT. R. PROF'L CONDUCT 1.6 (permitting disclosure of confidential information only (i) to prevent the client from committing a crime; (ii) in connection with a controversy involving the attorney's conduct; or (iii) to disclose breaches of fiduciary responsibilities. *Cf.* MODEL RULES OF PROF'L CONDUCT R. 1.6(b) (as recently amended in an effort to comport with the Commission's new attorney conduct rules, permitting disclosure of confidential information (i) to prevent death or substantial bodily harm; (ii) to prevent a client from committing a crime or fraud resulting in injury to the financial interest or property of another; (iii) to prevent, mitigate, or rectify the substantial injury to the financial interest or property or another; (iv) to secure legal advice about compliance with rules of professional conduct; (v) in connection with a controversy involving the attorney's conduct; or (vi) to comply with other law or court order).

49. *See, e.g.*, TEX. DISCIPLINARY R. PROF'L CONDUCT 1.05(c)(7)-(8) (permitting disclosure of confidential information if it is necessary to prevent a client's commission of a criminal or fraudulent act or to rectify the consequences of a client's criminal or fraudulent act).

50. *See* text accompanying note 47, *supra*.

51. *See* Walkowiak, *supra* note 37, at 5.

52. *See* Securities Act Release No. 8150, *supra* note 3, at 86,539-540.

53. *See* Securities Act Release No. 8186 [2002-2003 Transfer Binder], Fed. Sec. L. Rep. (CCH) 186,824, at 87,111 (Jan. 29, 2003).

54. *Id.* at 87,112.

55. Securities Act Release No. 8150, *supra* note 3, at 86,520, 86,537.

56. *Id.* at 86,541.

57. *Id.*

58. *Id.* at 86,542.

59, *Id.* at 86,541, 86,543.

60. *Id.* at 86,544.

61. Securities Act Release No. 8186, *supra* note 53, at 87,117.

62. *Id.*

63. *Id.* at 87,117-118.

64. *Id.* at 87,118.

65. *Id.*

66. *Id.*

67. *Id.* at 87,119.

68. *Id.* at 87,120.

69. *See* Securities Act Release No. 8150, *supra* note 3, at 86,541; text accompanying notes 55-57, *supra*.

70. *See* Securities Act Release No. 8186, *supra* note 53, at 87,119; text accompanying notes 58-68, *supra*.

71. *See id.* at 87,112-113.

72. Walkowiak, *supra* note 37, at 3.

73. *See* Securities Act Release No. 8150, *supra* note 3, at 86,544.

74. *See id.*

75. *See id.* See text accompanying notes 36-50, *supra*.

76. *See id.* at 86,542.

77. *See* Letter from 79 Law Firms to Jonathan G. Katz, Secretary, Securities and Exchange Commission 2 (Apr. 7, 2003), *available at* http://www.sec.izov/rules/proposed/s74502/79lawfirmsl.htm.

78. *See* Securities Act Release No. 8186, *supra* note 53, at 87,119.

79. *See* Letter from 79 Law Firms, *supra* note 77, at 5.

80. *See* Securities Act Release No. 8186, *supra* note 53, at 87,118.

81. *See* text accompanying note 64, *supra*.

82. *See id.* at 87,120.

83. *See* Securities Act Release No. 8185, *supra* note 6, at 87,091; text accompanying notes 47-51, *supra*.

84. *See* Securities Act Release No. 8186, *supra* note 53, at 87,114.

85. *Id.*

CHAPTER 4

The Attorney-Client Privilege and Corporate Communications: What's Still Confidential?

MICHAEL A. KNOERZER
EILEEN C. KENNELLY

Introduction

The attorney-client privilege applies to corporate communications, although differently, and perhaps less readily, than it once did. In the wake of corporate scandals involving some of the largest and best-regarded companies in the United States, public advocacy groups, shareholders, legislatures, and regulators have demanded that corporate transactions be more transparent to the investing public. Assertions of privilege—which by their nature tend to aid in the concealment of facts and reduce transparency—are subject to greater scrutiny than ever before.

At the same time, corporate attorneys have been assigned broader responsibility in managing the affairs of their employers, including matters that may not fall within the ordinary ambit of the attorney-client relationship. Well before the recent wave of corporate failures, courts had already become keenly aware that corporate attorneys were performing numerous tasks that were not deserving of the protection of the attorney-client privilege. Courts now perform searching inquiries of the communications made by corporate attorneys in order to determine whether the communications are made for the purpose of obtaining legal advice, and therefore are privileged, or whether the communications are made in the ordinary course of business, and therefore are not privileged.

In light of concerns regarding corporate responsibility, the American Bar Association has modified its Model Rules to permit lawyers to report corporate wrongdoing. Corporate attorneys, and those outside counsel working for corporate enterprises, also find themselves subject to the federally mandated Sarbanes-Oxley reporting requirements that require potential corporate wrongdoing to be reported to management, or an independent audit committee, with little regard for whether a privileged communication may be compromised. These new disclosure requirements raise fresh concerns regarding whether corporate attorneys and their clients will continue to enjoy—in any meaningful way—the protections afforded by the attorney-client privilege. This commentary attempts to address some of the questions raised by the changing approach of courts and legislatures toward corporate communications.

The Attorney-Client Privilege Generally

The attorney-client privilege exists to "encourage full and frank communication between attorneys and their clients and thereby promote broader public interests in the observance of law and administration of justice."[1] The privilege is intended to protect communications between attorneys and clients that "include legal advice or reflect information provided by the client in confidence."[2] The attorney-client privilege applies only if:

> (1) the asserted holder of the privilege is or sought to become a client; (2) the person to whom the communication was made (a) is a member of the bar of a court, or his subordinate and (b) in connection with this communication is acting as a lawyer, (3) the communication relates to a fact of which the attorney was informed (a) by his client (b) without the presence of strangers (c) for the purpose of securing primarily either (i) an opinion on law or (ii) legal services or (iii) assistance in some legal proceeding, and not (d) for the purpose of committing a crime or tort; and (4) the privilege has been (a) claimed and (b) not waived, by the client.[3]

Courts have declared that the attorney-client privilege is to be narrowly applied, because it is inconsistent with the general rule favoring liberal discovery in order to get at the truth.[4] The burden of establishing the attorney-client privilege rests upon the party claiming it.[5]

Application of the Attorney-Client Privilege to Corporations

Since the United States Supreme Court's landmark 1981 decision in *Upjohn v. United States*, it has been well-settled under federal law that a corporation is entitled to assert the attorney-client privilege with regard to its communications with its in-house counsel.[6] *Upjohn*, however, is not always the controlling authority. In cases where state law controls, state courts—and federal courts sitting in diversity—apply state law to determine the applicability of the privilege.[7] However, state courts have typically followed *Upjohn*, ruling that the attorney-client privilege applies to "[a] corporation's communications with counsel, no less than the communications of other clients with counsel."[8]

Although it is well-settled that the attorney-client privilege applies to corporate clients, the assertion of the privilege presents "nettlesome questions"[9] and "special problems"[10] when the communication is between a corporation and its counsel. These questions and problems can be addressed by reference to the elements of the attorney-client privilege.

The Asserted Holder of the Privilege Is, or Sought to Become, a Client

The client, not the attorney, owns attorney-client privilege. In representations concerning private persons, it is relatively easy to determine the identity of the client. In the corporate context, the aforementioned "nettlesome questions" arise. Generally speaking, the "client" is the corporate entity itself.[11] But a corporation is, in essence, a legal fiction populated by, and managed by, individual persons. Are all of these people "the client"?

A somewhat discredited line of authority limited protections of the attorney-client privilege to only those "clients" who were part of a "control group" of managers working in the corporation.[12] A more enlightened approach is to declare that the attorney-client privilege applies to an attorney's communications with employees at any level in the corporation.[13] This approach reflects the fact that, in many corporations today, significant responsibility is decentralized, and spread, among employees of all levels: "The attorney-client privilege . . . extends to communications between and among non-lawyer employees of the client, who make inquiries at the attorney's direction or relay the attorney's advice on legal, as opposed to business, issues to other employees."[14] In corporations run in a decentralized fashion, employees at all levels of the corporation may have need for legal advice: "'This follows from the recognition that since the decision-making power over the corporate client may be diffused among several employees, the dissemination of confidential communications to such persons does not defeat the privilege.'"[15] Moreover, because courts have recognized that the modern trend is toward employee mobility, the attorney-client privilege has been upheld to protect against disclosure of communications between the corporation's counsel and a former employee.[16] Thus, the former employee remains a "client."

Not surprisingly, a corporation's Board of Directors is also the client. In *In re: Grand Jury 90-1*,[17] the court considered whether a legal opinion letter, which was requested by and written to the president of a company by outside counsel, retained its privileged status when the president forwarded the letter to the company's board of directors. The court found that because the client was the company and not the president, relaying the legal information to the board of directors was merely making advice available to another part of the "inanimate entity" and was, therefore, protected by the attorney-client privilege.[18]

The Person to Whom the Communication Is Made Is a Member of the Bar of a Court or the Bar Member's Subordinate

The attorney-client privilege will apply to communications between a client and a (1) lawyer, (2) paralegal working for the lawyer, or (3) another employee in the lawyer's office, provided that in connection with the communication the subordinate is acting as a lawyer. The lawyer need not be a member of the bar in the state in which the communication occurred.

Since *Upjohn*, there has been little debate that a lawyer working as an employee of a corporation enjoys the benefits of the attorney-client privilege. There is a difference, however, in how courts approach privilege questions when corporate counsel are involved. Although an attorney's status as in-house counsel "neither dilutes nor waives the privilege,"[19] corporations face a higher burden of proof when they assert the attorney-client privilege with respect to in-house counsel "lest the mere participation of an attorney be used to seal off disclosure."[20] Courts maintain a stricter standard for determining whether communications between corporate clients and in-house counsel are privileged because an in-house attorney is an employee of his client, his livelihood depends on that single client, and—as in-house counsel—he is more likely to combine legal and non-legal functions.[21] In *United States v. Chevron Corp.*, the court noted that while it is logical to apply a presumption that communications with outside counsel are for the purpose of obtaining legal advice, the presumption should not apply to communications with in-house counsel because of in-house counsel's frequent involvement in the corporation's business decisions.[22]

The Attorney-Client Privilege Protects Communications, Not Facts

The attorney-client privilege only protects against disclosure of "communications." The facts that form the basis of the communication cannot be withheld on the grounds of the attorney-client privilege unless such disclosure would reveal confidential communications.[23] Thus, a client cannot prevent discovery of underlying facts by funneling those facts through its attorney. However, the attorney-client privilege will protect documents summarizing factual information if it is "sufficiently clear that the [documents] would not have been created had plaintiff not needed the assistance of counsel."[24] As set forth in greater detail below, this element of the attorney-client privilege is applied with equal force to corporations: if an in-house attorney is simply memorializing facts, no privilege will apply to that effort.[25]

The Communication Must Be Confidential

The burden of establishing the attorney-client privilege rests upon the party claiming it.[26] To successfully assert the attorney-client privilege, the party seeking the protection of the privilege must take appropriate action to preserve the confidentiality of the documents that are claimed to be privileged.[27] Nevertheless, most courts hold that an "unintended and erroneous disclosure of a document containing privileged material does not constitute a waiver of the privilege if the attorney and client have taken 'reasonable precautions to ensure confidentiality.'"[28] Of course, voluntary disclosure of documents otherwise protected as attorney-client communications will affect a waiver of the privilege.[29] The attorney-client privilege protects only communications that were intended to be held in confidence and does not attach to communications that were intended to be or are disclosed to third parties.[30] The client may disclose an otherwise privileged communication without the consent of the attorney. However, as an agent of the client, an attorney may cause a waiver of the privilege.[31]

Even if an attorney-client communication is widely distributed within a company, it may retain its privileged status so long as the communication was intended to be confidential. In *Exxon Corp. v. Department of Conservation & Natural Resources*, the Supreme Court of Alabama reversed a jury award on the state's breach of contract and fraud claims of $87.7 million in compensatory damages and $3.42 billion in punitive damages because the trial court erred in admitting into evidence a privileged letter prepared by in-house counsel.[32] The letter in question was authored by Exxon's in-house counsel in the mid-1990s when an Exxon manager asked counsel for a legal analysis of the royalty provisions of an oil lease agreement between the company and the state. The letter offered three different interpretations of the royalty provisions of the lease agreement and evaluated the likelihood of success of each interpretation should litigation ensue. Exxon officials adopted one of the three proposed interpretations and proceeded with oil production at the leasehold site. The state later audited Exxon's royalty payments and a dispute arose regarding the royalties due under the lease agreement. At trial, the court admitted the attorney's letter, reasoning that the company had waived the privilege because the letter had been widely distributed within the company and speculating that the letter "probably went out to other companies as well."[33] Finding Exxon made a prima facie showing that the company intended to keep the attorney's communication confidential, the Supreme Court of Alabama found that the state failed to prove that the letter was not a confidential communication and found no evidence in the record that the letter had been distributed outside the company.[34] The court reversed the judgment, finding the letter to be a confidential communication conveying a legal opinion, prepared by an Exxon attorney on behalf of the corporation, and pertaining to the very issues before the jury at trial.[35]

For corporate attorneys, the challenge is to keep legal advice separate from business advice, and to limit dissemination of the legal advice to only those individuals who are on a "need to know" basis. This is harder than it sounds. Corporate attorneys working to facilitate a complex transaction for their corporate clients rarely work alone. Instead, corporate attorneys work closely with consultants, experts, accountants, and other advisors necessary to the transaction. In this context, corporate attorneys are often called upon to make facts and other information available to outside professionals who are not employees of the company. Corporate attorneys must be mindful that communications with other professionals will most likely not be privileged unless it can be demonstrated that the communication was for the express purpose of rendering legal advice back to the corporation. The strong possibility exists, however, that the purpose of the communication will be declared by a court to be to advance a business purpose of the corporation. In that case, communications with outside professionals will not be deemed privileged. Corporate counsel must take extra care to preserve the confidentiality of their communications with the client by not including outside advisors in the communication of otherwise confidential legal advice.[36] As the Southern District of New York recently stated, "[n]othing in the policy of the privilege suggests that . . . attorneys, simply by placing accountants, scientists, or investigators on their payrolls and maintaining them in their offices, should be able to invest all communications by clients to such persons with a privilege the law has not seen fit to extend when the latter are operating under their own steam."[37]

The Touchstone for the Privilege: Legal Advice

Of all the "nettlesome questions" presented by the application of the attorney-client privilege to corporate lawyers, none has caused more ink to be spilled than the issue of whether the corporate attorney is rendering legal advice or business advice. "The cornerstone of the [attorney-client] privilege has always rested on the notion that the communication must be for the purpose of securing or rendering legal advice."[38] If the attorney is simply asked to give business advice, and not legal advice, all or part of the communication between the attorney and the client may not be protected.[39] "Although on occasion seamlessly intertwined, there is nevertheless a sharp distinction between legal and business advice; the privilege protects only the former, and not the latter."[40]

Whether a corporate attorney is acting in a legal capacity or a business capacity is often a difficult and fact-intensive question.[41] Consistent with the burden of proving the privilege overall, it is the corporation's burden to prove that the conduct in question was a legal matter and not a business matter: "Because an in-house attorney, particularly one who holds an executive position in the company, often is involved in business matters, in order to demonstrate that the communication in question is privileged, the company bears the burden of 'clearly showing' that the in-house attorney gave advice in her legal capacity, not in her capacity as business advisor."[42] This can be a challenging goal, because, as courts have recognized, the lines between in-house counsel's legal and business roles have blurred and evaluation of these blurred lines requires close scrutiny: "Due to the increasing role of in-house counsel as business strategist, courts have begun to more closely scrutinize the attorney-client privilege as it applies to corporate counsel."[43]

Even communications made while an attorney is acting partly in a legal capacity may be discoverable if the communication encompasses a significant business purpose. To successfully assert that the attorney-client privilege applies to its communications, the corporation must make a clear showing that in-house counsel's advice was given in a legal capacity[44] and is primarily of a legal character.[45] A communication is "primarily legal" if the corporation can show that it "would not have been made but for the [corporation]'s need for legal advice or services."[46] "The critical inquiry is whether, viewing the lawyer's communication in its full content and context, it was made in order to render legal advice or services to the client."[47] Courts have recognized that "[t]he overlap between 'business' advice and 'legal' advice requires a pragmatic approach" and, therefore, "'[t]he mere fact that business advice is given or solicited does not . . . automatically render the privilege lost: where the advice given is predominantly legal, as opposed to business, in nature the privilege will still attach.'"[48]

Examples of legal advice include all communications related to litigation, including interview notes with witnesses in preparation for potential litigation,[49] internal legal memoranda[50] or communications regarding litigation strategy.[51] As two recent cases demonstrate, other types of in-house counsel communications are less clearly privileged.

As part of the World Trade Center litigation, the United States District Court for the Southern District of New York recently addressed the distinction between an in-house attorney's legal role and business role in *SR Int'l Business Ins. Co. Ltd. v. World Trade Center Properties LLC*.[52] *WTC Properties* involved a coverage dispute between the leaseholder of the World Trade Center (the "Silverstein Parties") and its insurer, Swiss Re. In July 2001, GMAC Commercial Mortgage Corporation (GMAC) loaned the Silverstein Parties $563 million to finance the World Trade Center leasehold. GMAC thereafter securitized the loan by selling mortgaged-backed securities to a number of institutional investors. In connection with this transaction, GMAC retained the Harbor Group, Ltd. (Harbor Group) as its insurance advisor to assist in determining the amount of insurance coverage that GMAC would require the Silverstein Parties to obtain to insure the World Trade Center.[53]

After the 9/11 loss, Swiss Re sought documents and testimony of employees of GMAC and its insurance advisors, the Harbor Group. Asserting the attorney-client privilege and attorney work-product doctrine, GMAC declined to produce various documents containing written communications allegedly made at the request of in-house counsel. Swiss Re moved to compel.

The first group of documents withheld by GMAC involved drafts of documents, notes, and written and oral communications between and among GMAC employees, Harbor Group employees, and GMAC in-house counsel relating to communications with investors. According to GMAC's counsel, after learning of the destruction of the World Trade Center, she recognized the possibility of litigation with the investors. In light of this concern, she directed GMAC employees to work with the insurance consultants at the Harbor Group to collect information necessary to respond to investors' inquiries. GMAC contended that, in light of in-house counsel's involvement, production of these documents and communications was protected by the attorney work-product doctrine and the attorney-client privilege.

As an initial matter, the court rejected GMAC's contention that the communications were made in anticipation of litigation and therefore constituted attorney work product. Based upon deposition testimony and other evidence in the record, the Court concluded that the communications at issue were made not in anticipation of litigation, but merely to avoid potential, but not yet anticipated, litigation. According to the court, an effort merely to avoid litigation is not a basis to assert that work was performed in anticipation of litigation.[54]

The court next addressed whether the documents and communications created to respond to investors' concerns were attendant to the normal conduct of GMAC's business and would have occurred with or without involvement of in-house counsel. The court found that GMAC would, in the normal course of business, be required to answer investor concerns—with or without input from in-house counsel—and that therefore the effort in collecting that information and preparing responses to investors constituted a non-privileged business communication.[55]

The court did uphold GMAC's assertion of privilege to communications between its in-house counsel and GMAC employees made for the purpose of seeking or obtaining legal advice (as opposed to business advice). However, the court rejected extension of the privilege to communications between GMAC attorneys and the Harbor Group consultants. The court reasoned that in the absence of any showing that the Harbor Group employees were the functional equivalent of GMAC employees, or that the Harbor Group and GMAC shared a common interest, no privilege could be extended. The court rejected GMAC's argument that its designation of the Harbor Group as "litigation consultants" created a basis for claiming a common interest privilege, particularly where the retention letter made no reference to litigation, and the letter was not addressed to, or authored by, GMAC counsel.

With reference to notes of a September 14, 2001 meeting involving parties that represented competing interests in the adjustment of the loss, GMAC argued that because its non-attorney employees and consultants took notes at the direction of, and in the stead of, in-house counsel, those notes were privileged. The court rejected this assertion, pointing out that notes that merely set forth facts, without revealing an attorney's thought processes, are not subject to work-product protection, even if an attorney had prepared those notes.[56]

The court last addressed GMAC's refusal to produce documents related to the underlying insurance coverage secured by the leaseholders. In regard to insurance-related transaction documents that predated September 11, the court ordered production, reasoning that "[i]n the context of the preparation of disclosure documents relating to a private placement, statements of the client to the lawyer are generally made with an understanding that the information will be disclosed to others. In that context, such communications are not protected by the attorney-client privilege."[57]

Electronic Data Systems Corporation v. Steingraber

In *Electronic Data Systems Corporation v. Steingraber*, 2003 U.S. Dist. LEXIS 11818 (E.D. Tex. July 9, 2003), the Eastern District of Texas examined the assertion of attorney-client privilege by Electronic Data Systems Corporation (EDS). EDS had retained outside counsel to investigate an alleged fraud by an employee and subsequently terminated the employee for cause based upon the investigation findings. The terminated employee brought an action against EDS and sought to discover communications between EDS and its counsel relating to the investigation, arguing that the communications were made to facilitate a business decision—i.e., termination of an employee—rather than the rendition of privileged legal services.[58] The court, however, found that because outside counsel was "hired . . . to contribute its legal expertise to the investigation," including interpreting contracts, evaluating litigation risk, interviewing witnesses, and weighing the value of evidence, the communications between the attorneys and the corporation were for the rendition of legal services and, thus, protected by the attorney-client privilege under Texas law.[59]

Miscellaneous Conduct by In-house Counsel

Many communications between attorneys and their corporate clients are not privileged, such as advising a client of the date of trial;[60] providing an attorney with information for the purpose of preparing a tax return;[61] and communications arising out of an investigation undertaken for the purpose of making business recommendations to the corporation.[62] These decisions hinge upon the principle that, for the attorney-client privilege to apply, the client's "confidential communication must be for the *primary* purpose of soliciting legal, rather than business, advice" (emphasis added).[63]

However, the fact that a communication refers to non-legal matters does not, in and of itself, forfeit the privilege.[64] In addition, the absence of any apparent legal research in an attorney's communication is not fatal as long as the communication reflects the attorney's professional skills and judgment.[65] Courts have recognized that an in-house counsel's memorandum is privileged if it "concerns legal rights and obligations and where it evidences other professional skills such as a lawyer's judgment and recommended legal strategies."[66]

Contract Negotiations by In-House Counsel

The line between legal advice and business advice is perhaps at its haziest when in-house counsel is involved in negotiating contracts. For example, in *Note Funding Corp. v. Bobian Investment Co., N.V.,*[67] the plaintiff sought discovery of communications regarding business negotiations and analyses that were "handled in whole or part" by the attorneys for the corporation. In considering whether the attorney-client privilege applies when an attorney is engaged in negotiations on behalf of the corporation, the court noted that:

> Assessment of this argument requires the court to tread an occasionally blurry line. In pursuing large and complex financial transactions, commercial entities often seek the assistance of attorneys who are well equipped both by training and by experience to assess the risks and advantages in alternative business strategies. When providing this assistance, counsel are not limited to offering their client purely abstract advice as to the rules of law that may apply to their situation. Of necessity, counsel will often be required to assess specific tactics in putting together transactions or shaping the terms of commercial agreements, and their evaluation of alternative approaches may well take into account not only the potential impact of applicable legal norms, but also the commercial needs of their client and the financial benefits or risks of these alternative strategies.[68]

The court noted that the "fact that an attorney's advice encompasses commercial as well as legal considerations does not vitiate the privilege."[69] According to the court, the key distinction is "whether the attorney's performance depends principally on his knowledge of or application of legal requirements or principles, rather than his expertise in matters of commercial practice."[70]

Applying these principles, the court held that documents that included discussions of commercial strategy and tactics "in a context that [made] it evident that the attorney [was] presenting the issues and analyzing the choices on the basis of his legal expertise and with an obvious eye to the constraints imposed by applicable law" were privileged.[71]

A contrary result was reached with respect to in-house counsel's involvement in negotiations in *Georgia-Pacific Corp. v. GAF Roofing Manufacturing Corp.*[72] GAF's in-house environmental attorney acted as GAF's negotiator with respect to environmental provisions in an asset purchase agreement between Georgia-Pacific and GAF. GAF asked its in-house attorney to review the proposed agreement and related documents and to advise management of environmental issues raised by the agreement. In connection with this assignment, he recommended changes to the contract and engaged in negotiations with respect to environmental provisions.[73] After GAF terminated the agreement because of concerns about environmental risks, Georgia-Pacific commenced a breach of contract action and sought to depose GAF's in-house counsel. Georgia-Pacific moved for an order compelling the in-house counsel to testify regarding: (1) recommendations made by counsel regarding changing the proposed environmental provisions and the impact of such changes; (2) recommendations made by counsel regarding alternative negotiating strategies; and (3) whether GAF's management instructed counsel to cancel further negotiations.[74]

The District Court for the Southern District of New York held that communications between GAF's in-house environmental attorney and management were not undertaken as a legal advisor for the corporation. Rather, they were undertaken "[a]s a negotiator on behalf of management." Thus, the court found that the attorney was acting in a business capacity.[75]

Similarly, *Cooper-Rutter Associates, Inc. v. Anchor National Life Insurance Co.*[76] concerned two handwritten memoranda that were "prepared by an individual who was both in-house counsel and corporate secretary to one of the defendants."[77] The court found that the documents "concern[ed] both the business and legal aspects of the defendants' ongoing negotiations with the plaintiff" regarding the business transaction out of which the lawsuit arose.[78] Based upon this finding, New York's Appellate Division, Second Department, ruled that "the documents were not primarily of legal character, but expressed substantial non-legal concerns," and therefore were not privileged.[79] Interestingly, the court apparently did not protect from discovery those portions of the memoranda that did contain legal advice.

The Impact of New Reporting Requirements upon the Attorney-Client Privilege

The Sarbanes-Oxley Act

Although attorneys have largely been untarnished in the corporate scandals of recent vintage, there has been a growing recognition that corporate attorneys are uniquely able to learn of corporate misdeeds because of their role as corporate advisors and confidantes. In these roles, corporate attorneys have sometimes been placed in the position of approving arguably improper positions. For example, in the wake of Enron's collapse, a special investigative committee (the Powers Committee) found in February 2002 that Enron's flawed financial disclosures, which concealed the company's improper transactions, had been approved by Enron's in-house and outside counsel.[80] Since Enron, there has been a growing sense among some commentators that the public interest would be benefited if corporate attorneys were required to report corporate misdeeds to regulators or criminal authorities.

Much has been written about the Sarbanes-Oxley Act of 2002, which creates new reporting obligations for corporate attorneys. Section 307 of Sarbanes-Oxley required the Securities and Exchange Commission (SEC) to promulgate rules establishing minimum standards of conduct for attorneys.[81] Pursuant to Section 307, the SEC promulgated Rule 205, which imposes a reporting requirement on attorneys appearing and practicing before the SEC in the representation of an issuer.[82] Attorneys subject to this rule must report evidence of material violations of securities laws and breaches of fiduciary duty "up-the-ladder" within the corporation.[83] Ultimately, if the officer or counsel does not respond "appropriately," the attorney must report the evidence to an audit committee, another committee of independent directors, or the full board of directors of the corporation.[84]

The SEC had also proposed a "noisy withdrawal" provision, which would address an attorney's notification to the Commission once the attorney reports a material violation up-the-ladder and reasonably believes an issuer's directors either made no response (within a reasonable time) or failed to make an appropriate response.[85] When the SEC promulgated Rule 205, it extended the comment period regarding the "noisy withdrawal" provision and proposed alternatives.[86] As of the time of this writing, no final "noisy withdrawal" rule has been promulgated.

Rule 205's reporting requirements raise serious questions regarding the application of the attorney-client privilege to communications between attorneys and the directors, officers, and employees of their corporate clients. Those in favor of the new regulations contend that Section 307 and Rule 205 do not impair the attorney-client privilege because the corporation, rather than the individuals employed by the corporation, is the client.[87] According to this line of thinking, by reporting the misconduct of individuals within the corporation, the attorney is only protecting the interests of the client and not revealing client confidences.

The countervailing argument is that a corporation acts and communicates with its counsel only through the individuals employed to act on its behalf. Some commentators argue that the new reporting obligations will have a direct and chilling effect on the privilege and on the role of attorneys within corporations:

> [T]he interaction between the attorney and the entity is a fiction. The attorney is hired by the directors or executives of the entity. If an attorney is dependant on the client for his or her livelihood, it is more difficult to report on that client. Essentially the attorney would discuss certain business with a CEO and, at the conclusion of the conversation, inform this person that the attorney will now report these confidential discussions up-the-ladder. . . . Rule 205 risks chilling the confidential communications historically viewed as central to the attorney-client relationship.[88]

If an attorney is obligated to report the conduct of others, "either internally to the board or externally to the SEC, [that reporting requirement] could limit the attorney's inclusion in and exposure to sensitive corporate matters."[89] To exclude the corporate attorney from sensitive or confidential corporate matters would severely impair his or her ability to help the corporation steer clear of trouble. Counsel would be excluded from the very matters on which his or her advice is most needed.

The Association of The Bar of the City of New York, in comments filed with the SEC prior to its promulgation of Rule 205, predicted the SEC's reporting requirements would erode the privilege afforded to communications between corporations and their attorneys and would diminish the value of the corporate attorney-client relationship:

> A likely consequence of this erosion of privilege is that corporate officers or employees may not turn to lawyers for advice in situations where legal advice may, if obtained, have benefited the corporation and its shareholders. Another likely consequence is that, when a corporation turns to a lawyer for advice, it may, in light of the lawyer's new obligation to report the client's transgressions, limit the information it provides to its counsel upon which to formulate such advice. This chilling of communications between

attorneys and clients, causing issuers to act without legal advice or to act upon legal advice rendered upon more limited information, will likely undermine the attorney's ability to gather the relevant facts and advise the issuer as to appropriate conduct . . . .[90]

It is difficult to dispute the logic of this argument. The very feature that makes corporate counsel the beneficiary of confidential and sensitive information—the attorney-client privilege—is being compromised. The result may be that corporate management is no longer quite so willing to share confidences with its counsel.

The American Bar Association's Model Rules

While the SEC ventured for the first time into the uncharted waters of regulating attorney conduct, the American Bar Association, which establishes Model Rules of Conduct to guide the individual states in the regulation of attorneys, also turned its attention to the corporate attorney-client relationship. At its annual meeting in August 2003, the American Bar Association's delegates approved changes to the ABA's Model Rules that permit attorneys to report corporate fraud. The first change, which passed by a narrow 17-vote margin, adds an exception to the attorney-client privilege under Rule 1.6, permitting—but not requiring—a lawyer to reveal information relating to the representation of a client to the extent the lawyer reasonably believes necessary either (1) "to prevent the client from committing a crime or fraud that is reasonably certain to result in substantial injury to the financial interests or property of another and in furtherance of which the client has used or is using the lawyer's services" or (2) "to prevent, mitigate or rectify substantial injury to the financial interests or property of another that is reasonably certain to result or has resulted from the client's commission of a crime or fraud in furtherance of which the client has used the lawyer's services."[91] Before the addition of these provisions, the Model Rules permitted an attorney to reveal confidential information only to prevent a reasonably certain death or substantial bodily harm, to secure legal advice about compliance with the rules, in connection with a dispute between the attorney and client, or to comply with a court order.[92]

The second change to the Model Rules approved by the ABA would require an attorney to report fraud up the corporate ladder and, if the company's "highest authority" fails to address the fraud, would permit—but not require—the attorney to reveal confidential information if he or she reasonably believes that the violation is reasonably certain to result in substantial injury to the organization.[93] It has been reported that the ABA hopes its mandatory "reporting-up" and voluntary "reporting-out" provisions will serve to guide the SEC in its consideration of the proposed "noisy withdrawal" provisions.[94]

ABA delegates opposing the rule changes echoed the concerns raised by critics of the Sarbanes-Oxley reporting requirements, arguing that the new Model Rules could result in "the exclusion of lawyers from corporate boardrooms when questionable conduct is being considered."[95] Supporters of the changes, however, cited the fact that 42 states had already approved a financial harm exception to the attorney-client privilege and argued that there had been no evidence that attorneys in those states consequently were excluded from the corporate decision-making process.[96] At least one commentator has noted that while the ABA's new rules do not *obligate* lawyers to report corporate malfeasance, "the mere softening of the once-inviolate privilege is a significant development in the nation's legal climate and evidence of the scandals' historic impact."[97]

Conclusion

We begin as we started, by stating that the attorney-client privilege still applies to corporate communications, although differently, and less readily, than it once did. It is still not clear just how Sarbanes-Oxley and its implementing rules or the ABA's new Model Rules will affect either the role of in-house counsel or the continued application of the attorney-client privilege to communications between corporations and their counsel. The choice of whether a corporate attorney should either reveal a corporate confidence or be deemed a wrongdoer himself is perhaps not a fair choice. As new laws develop and are interpreted, corporate counsel will be required to be keenly aware of new responsibilities that may be not only difficult to fulfill while keeping your job, but also are repugnant to what lawyers once deemed were their ethical responsibilities.

Notes

1. Upjohn Co. v. United States, 449 U.S. 383, 389 (1981).
2. Fine v. Facet Aerospace Prods. Co., 133 F.R.D. 439, 444 (S.D.N.Y. 1990).
3. United States v. United Shoe Mach. Corp., 89 F. Supp. 357, 358-59 (D. Mass. 1950); *see also In re* Pfohl Bros. Landfill Litig., 1997 U.S. Dist. LEXIS 10709, at *18-19 (W.D.N.Y. March 14, 1997); *accord.* United States v. White, 950 F.2d 426, 430 (7th Cir. 1991); American Standard, Inc. v. Pfizer, Inc., 828 F.2d 734 (Fed. Cir. 1987).
4. It is important to distinguish two other privileges also commonly employed by corporations: the attorney work-product doctrine and the self-critical analysis privilege.

Unlike the attorney-client privilege, the work-product doctrine does not apply to client communications, and therefore is not a true privilege. Instead, the work-product doctrine is more akin to a discovery rule, as is suggested by its classification at Rule 26(b)(3) of the Federal Rules of Civil Procedure:

> [A] party may obtain discovery of documents and tangible things otherwise discoverable . . . and prepared in anticipation of litigation or for trial or for another party or by or for that party's representative . . . only upon a showing that the party . . . is unable without undue hardship to obtain the substantial equivalent of the materials by other means. In ordering discovery of such materials . . . the court shall protect against disclosure of the mental impressions, conclusions, opinions, or legal theories of an attorney or other representative of a party concerning the litigation.

Fed. R. Civ. P. 26(b)(3).

The purpose of the work-product doctrine is to ensure that, in the absence of undue hardship, the legal work one client pays for need not be shared with that client's opponents. *See* Gundacker v. Unisys Corp., 151 F.3d 842, 848 (8th Cir. 1998); Pittman v. Frazer, 129 F.3d 983, 988 (8th Cir. 1997). "Ordinarily, the work-product doctrine should only be applied after it is decided that the attorney-client privilege does not apply." Electronic Data Sys. Corp. v. Steingraber, 2003 U.S. Dist. LEXIS 11818, at *4 (E.D. Tex. July 9, 2003) (citing Upjohn Co. v. United States, 449 U.S. 383, 397 (1981).

The self-critical analysis privilege is a judicially created protection that was more prominent in the 1970s and 1980s than it appears today. The privilege prevents the disclosure of a corporation's internal investigations or evaluations in order to encourage entities to conduct such evaluations in the public interest. *See* Etienne v. Mitre Corp., 146 F.R.D. 145, 147 (E.D. Va. 1993); Wylie v. Mills, 195 N.J. Super. 332, 338 (Law Div. 1984); Roberts v. National Detroit Corp., 87 F.R.D. 30 (E.D. Mich. 1980); Gillman v. United States, 53 F.R.D. 316 (S.D.N.Y. 1971). Like work product, the self-critical evaluation privilege is qualified in that it can be overcome by a showing of substantial need. *See* Banks v. Lockheed-Georgia Co., 53 F.R.D. 283 (N.D. Ga. 1971); Rosario v. New York Times Co., 84 F.R.D. 626 (S.D.N.Y. 1979).

There are three criteria for the self-critical evaluation to apply: (1) the information that is the subject of a production request must be the criticisms or evaluations or the products of an evaluation or critique conducted by the party opposing the production; (2) the public need for confidentiality of such analysis must be such that the unfettered internal availability of such information should be encouraged as a matter of public policy; and (3) the analysis or evaluation must be of the character that would result in the termination of such self-evaluative inquiries or critical input in future situations if the information was subject to disclosure. *See* CPC Int'l, Inc. v. Hartford Accident & Indem. Co., 262 N.J. Super. 191, 195 (Law Div. 1992) (refusing to apply self-critical analysis privilege to protect plaintiff's environmental compliance audits from insurers in a coverage dispute matter); *see also* Dowling v. American Hawaii Cruises, Inc., 971 F.2d 423, 426 (9th Cir. 1992), *on remand*, 869 F. Supp. 806 (D. Haw. 1994) (quoting Note, *The Privilege of Self-Critical Analysis*, 96 HARV. L. REV. 1083, 1086 (1983).

5. United States v. Int'l Bhd. of Teamsters, 119 F.3d 210, 214 (2d Cir. 1997); United States v. Adlman, 68 F.3d 1495, 1500 (2d Cir. 1995), *vacated on remand*, 134 F.3d 1194 (2d Cir. 1998).

6. *See* Upjohn v. United States, 449 U.S. at 390.

7. Georgia-Pacific Corp. v. GAF Roofing Mfg. Corp., No. 93 Civ. 5125, 1996 U.S. Dist. LEXIS 671, at *7 (S.D.N.Y. Jan. 25, 1996); *see also* FED. R. CIV. P. 501, which provides that privileges are governed by state common law in civil diversity cases.

8. Rossi v. Blue Cross & Blue Shield, 73 N.Y.2d 588, 592, 542 N.Y.S.2d 508 (1989). The application of the attorney-client privilege to corporations was accepted as a matter of law before *Upjohn* in several jurisdictions. *See, e.g.*, United States v. Louisville & N.R. Co., 236 U.S. 318, 35 S. Ct. 363, 59 L. Ed. 598 (1915); Seaboard S. R.R. v. Interstate Commerce Comm., 827 F.2d 699 (11th Cir. 1987); People v. Belge, 59 A.D.2d 307, 308, 399 N.Y.S.2d 539 (4th Dep't 1977).

9. *Rossi*, *supra* note 8, at 592.

10. *International Bhd.*, *supra* note 5, at 214.

11. *See* First Fed. Sav. Bank of Hegewisch v. United States, 55 Fed. Cl. at 266 (explaining that the privilege is not restricted to individuals, but may be invoked by a corporate entity) (citing *Upjohn*, 449 U.S. at 390).

12. *See* Barr Marine Prods. Co. v. Borg-Warner Corp., 84 F.R.D. 631, 636-37 (E.D. Pa. 1979).

13. *In re* John Doe Corp., 675 F.2d 482, 488 (2d Cir. 1982).

14. *SR Int'l Bus. Ins. Co. Ltd.*, 2002 U.S. Dist. LEXIS 11949 at *12; National Educ. Training Group, Inc. v. Skillsoft Corp., 1999 U.S. Dist. LEXIS 8680, at *9 (S.D.N.Y. June 10, 1999) ("Courts have also recognized that intra-corporate distribution of legal advice received from counsel does not necessarily vitiate the privilege, even though the legal advice is relayed indirectly from counsel through corporate personnel.").

15. Baltimore Scrap Corp. v. David J. Joseph Co., 1996 U.S. Dist. LEXIS 18617, at *17 (D. Md. Sept. 17, 1996).

16. *See* Radovic v. City of New York, 168 Misc. 2d 58, 642 N.Y.S.2d 1015 (Sup. Ct. N.Y. County 1996) (once the privilege attaches, it is not dissolved by the termination of the employment relationship).

17. 758 F. Supp. 1411, 1413 (D. Col. 1991).

18. *Id.*

19. Ferko v. Nat'l Ass'n for Stock Car Auto Racing, Inc., 218 F.R.D. 125, 139 (E.D. Tex. 2003).

20. *Rossi, supra* note 8, at 593 (citations omitted).

21. *See* Bank Brussels Lambert v. Credit Lyonnais (Suisse), S.A, 220 F. Supp. 2d 283, 286 (S.D.N.Y 2002).

22. United States v. Chevron Corp., 1996 U.S. Dist. LEXIS 4154, at *8-9 (N.D. Cal. March 12, 1996); SEC v. Gulf & Western Indus., Inc., 518 F. Supp. 675 (D.D.C. 1981); *see also Rossi, supra* note 8, at 592-93 (noting that unlike outside counsel, staff attorneys' "day-to-day involvement in their employers' affairs may blur the line between legal and nonlegal communications; and their advice may originate not in response to the client's consultation about a particular problem but with them, as part of an ongoing, permanent relationship with the organization").

23. Electronic Data Systems Corp. v. Steingraber, 2003 U.S. Dist. LEXIS 11818, at *6-7 (applying Texas law); *In re* Pfohl Bros., 1997 U.S. Dist. LEXIS 10709, at *17-18 (applying New York law); Hardy v. New York News, Inc., 114 F.R.D. 633, 644 (S.D.N.Y. 1987).

24. *In re Grand Jury Proceedings*, 2001 U.S. Dist. LEXIS 15646, at *98 (quoting AFP Imaging Corp. v. Philips Medizin Sys., 1993 U.S. Dist. LEXIS 18234, at *5 (S.D.N.Y. Dec. 28, 1993)).

25. SR Int'l Business Ins. Co. Ltd. v. World Trade Center Props. LLC, 2002 U.S. Dist. LEXIS 11949 at *10 (S.D.N.Y. July 3, 2002).

26. Fisher v. United States, 425 U.S. 391 (1976); Fox v. California Sierra Financial Services, 120 F.R.D. 520 (N.D. Cal. 1988); *In re*: Grand Jury Subpoenas dated March 19, 2002 and August 2, 2002, 318 F.3d 379, 384 (2d Cir. 2003).

27. *In re* Horowitz, 482 F.2d 72 (2d Cir.), *cert. denied*, 414 U.S. 867 (1973); *see also* Perrignon v. Bergen Brunswig Corp., 77 F.R.D. 455 (N.D. Cal. 1978).

28. Note Funding Corp. v. Bobian Inv. Co., No. 93 Civ. 7427, 1995 U.S. Dist. LEXIS 16605, at *14-15 (S.D.N.Y. Nov. 9, 1995) (quoting *In re* Grand Jury Proceedings Involving Berkley & Co., 466 F. Supp 863, 869 (D. Minn. 1979)).

29. *See* Thomas v. Pansy Ellen Products, Inc., 672 F. Supp. 237, 243 (W.D.N.C. 1987); United States v. Aronoff, 466 F. Supp. 855, 862 (S.D.N.Y. 1979); I.B.M. v. Sperry Rand Corp., 44 F.R.D. 10, 13 (D. Del. 1968); *see also In re* Columbia/HCA Healthcare Corp. Billing Prac. Litig., 293 F.3d 289 (6th Cir. 2002) (rejecting the notion that a party may "selectively" waive the privilege).

30. SR Int'l Bus. Ins. Co. Ltd. v. World Trade Ctr. Props. LLC, 2002 U.S. Dist. LEXIS 11949, at *29 (S.D.N.Y. July 3, 2002); *In re* Grand Jury Subpoena, 482 F.2d 72, 81-82 (2d Cir. 1973) (stating that "it is vital to a claim of privilege that the communications between client and attorney were made in confidence and have been maintained in confidence").

31. Long-Term Capital Holdings v. United States, 2002 U.S. Dist. LEXIS 23224, at *n.14 (U.S. Dist. 2002).

32. Exxon Corp. v. Dep't of Conservation & Natural Resources, 859 So. 2d 1096 (Ala. 2002).

33. *Id.* at 1104.

34. *Id.* at 1105.

35. *Id.* at 1108.

36. *See* SR Int'l Business Ins. Co. Ltd. v. World Trade Center Props. LLC, 2002 U.S. Dist. LEXIS 11949 at *13-14 (defendant lender's communications with insurance advisors following Sept. 11 not protected); Black & Decker Corp. v. United States, 2003 U.S. Dist. LEXIS 20110 (D. Md. 2003) (communications with accountants not protected).

37. *Id.* at *14 (quoting *In re* Grand Jury Matter, 147 F.R.D. 82, 84 (E.D. Pa. 1992)).

38. First Fed. Sav. Bank of Hegewisch v. United States, 55 Fed. Cl. 263, 267 (Ct. Fed. Cl. 2003).

39. *See* Boca Inveserlings P'ship v. United States, 31 F. Supp. 2d 9 (D.D.C. 1998) (holding that communications made by and to in-house counsel by corporate client seeking and obtaining legal advice is protected by the attorney-client privilege, but communications made by and to in-house counsel with respect to business matters, management decisions or business advice are not); Hardy

v. New York News, Inc., 114 F.R.D. 633 (S.D.N.Y. 1987) (holding that communication with in-house attorney was not privileged because the attorney was not acting in the role of attorney but in the role of director of employee or labor relations); *Note Funding*, 1995 U.S. Dist. LEXIS 16605, at *5; People v. Belge, 59 A.D.2d 307, 309, 399 N.Y.S.2d 539, 540 (4th Dep't 1977).

40. First Fed. Sav. Bank of Hegewisch v. United States, 55 Fed. Cl. at 268.

41. *See* Breneisen v. Motorola, Inc., 2003 U.S. Dist. LEXIS 11485, at *10-11(N.D. Ill. 2003) ("Generally, there is a presumption that a lawyer in the legal department of the corporation is giving legal advice, and an opposite presumption for a lawyer who works on the business or management side. However, the lawyer's position in the corporation is not necessarily dispositive.").

42. Ames v. Black Entm't Television, 1998 U.S. Dist. LEXIS 18053, at *20 (S.D.N.Y. Nov. 18, 1998).

43. Alan S. Naar & Gary K. Wolinetz, *Applying the Attorney-Client Privilege to In-house Counsel*, The Metropolitan Corporate Counsel, Nov. 1995.

44. *See In re* Grand Jury Subpoena, 599 F.2d 504, 510 (2d Cir. 1979).

45. *Rossi, supra* note 8, at 594.

46. First Chicago Int'l v. United Exch. Co., 125 F.R.D. 55, 57 (S.D.N.Y. 1989).

47. Spectrum Sys. v. Chemical Bank, 78 N.Y.2d at 379, 371 (1991).

48. ABB Kent-Taylor, Inc. v. Stallings and Co., Inc., 172 F.R.D. 53, 57 (W.D.N.Y. 1996) (quoting United States v. Davis, 131 F.R.D. 391, 401 (S.D.N.Y. 1990)); *see also In re* Currency Conversion Fee Antitrust Litig., 2002 U.S. Dist. LEXIS 21196 at *6 (Nov. 4, 2002) (finding document entitled to attorney-client privilege even if some portion could be considered business advice where the document predominantly provided legal advice).

49. *See* Peterson v. Wallace Computer Servs., Inc., 984 F. Supp. 821, 824 (D. Vt. 1997) (notes and memoranda of witness interviews conducted in anticipation of litigation).

50. *See Rossi, supra* note 8, at 590 (internal memorandum regarding company form that was subject of imminent lawsuit).

51. See Radovic v. City of New York, 168 Misc. 2d 58, 642 N.Y.S.2d 1015, 1017 (discussions with witness in preparation for trial privileged).

52. 2002 U.S. Dist. LEXIS 11949 (S.D.N.Y. July 3, 2002). In a separate opinion, the Southern District addressed the scope of the attorney-client privilege's application to agents and/or those who share a common interest privilege in *SR Int'l Business Ins. Co., Ltd. v. World Trade Center Props., LLC*, 2002 U.S. Dist. LEXIS 10919 (S.D.N.Y. June 19, 2002).

53. 2002 U.S. Dist. LEXIS 11949 at *2.

54. *World Trade Center Props. LLC*, 2002 U.S. Dist. LEXIS 11949 at *9. The Court cited with favor the decision in *Grand Jury Proceedings*, No. M-11-189, 2001 U.S. Dist. 15646 *49-50 (S.D.N.Y. Oct. 3, 2001) ("[I]t is not enough that the document was created after the threat of litigation is real—it is 'also necessary that the motivation for creating that document be the litigation.'").

55. *Id.* at *11-12.

56. *Id.* at *22-23.

57. *Id.* at *29-30.

58. *See* Electronic Data Systems Corp. v. Steingraber, 2003 U.S. Dist. LEXIS at *7.

59. *Id.* at 8-9.

60. United States v. Uptain, 552 F.2d 1108, 1109 (5th Cir. 1977).

61. *In re* Grand Jury Investigation, 842 F.2d 1223, 1224-25 (11th Cir. 1987).

62. Diversified Indus., Inc. v. Meredith, 572 F.2d 596, 603 (8th Cir. 1977).

63. North Carolina Elec. Membership Corp. v. Carolina Power & Light Co., 110 F.R.D. 511, 514 (M.D.N.C. 1986).

64. Spectrum Sys. v. Chemical Bank, 78 N.Y.2d at 380; *Rossi, supra* note 8, at 594.

65. *Rossi, supra* note 8, at 594.

66. *Id.*

67. 1995 U.S. Dist. LEXIS 16605 (S.D.N.Y. Nov. 9, 1995).

68. *Note Funding*, 1995 U.S. Dist. LEXIS 16605, at *6-7.

69. *Id.* at *7.

70. *Id.* at *8.

71. *Id.* at *8-9.

72. Georgia-Pacific Corp. v. GAF Roofing Mfg. Corp., 1996 U.S. Dist. LEXIS 671 (S.D.N.Y. Jan. 24, 1996).

73. *Id.* at *2.

74. *Id.* at *6-7.

75. *Id.* at *12.

76. Cooper-Rutter Assocs., Inc. v. Anchor Nat'l Life Ins. Co., 168 A.D.2d 663, 563 N.Y.S.2d 491 (2d Dep't 1990).

77. *Id.*

78. *Id.*

79. *Id.*

80. Chi Soo Kim and Elizabeth Laffitte, Note, *The Potential Effects of SEC Regulation of Attorney Conduct Under the Sarbanes-Oxley Act*, 16 GEO. J. LEGAL ETHICS 707 (Summer 2003) (citing Report from the Special Investigative Committee on Enron to the Enron Board of Directors (February 1, 2002), *available at* http://news.findlaw.com/wp/docs/enron/specinv020102rpt.pdf (Powers Report)).

81. The full text of Section 307 reads:

> Not later than 180 days after the date of enactment of this Act [enacted July 30, 2002], the Commission shall issue rules, in the public interest and for the protection of investors, setting forth minimum standards of **professional conduct** for **attorneys** appearing and practicing before the Commission in any way in the representation of issuers, including a rule —
>
> (1) requiring an **attorney** to report evidence of a material violation of securities law or breach of fiduciary duty or similar violation by the company or any agent thereof, to the chief legal counsel or the chief executive officer of the company (or the equivalent thereof); and
>
> (2) if the counsel or officer does not appropriately respond to the evidence (adopting, as necessary, appropriate remedial measures or sanctions with respect to the violation), requiring the **attorney** to report the evidence to the audit committee of the board of directors of the issuer or to another committee of the board of directors comprised solely of directors not employed directly or indirectly by the issuer, or to the board of directors.

15 U.S.C.S. § 7245 (2003).

82. Rule 205 defines an "issuer" by reference to the definition of "issuer" in the Securities and Exchange Act of 1934. *See* 17 C.F.R. § 205.

83. *See* 17 C.F.R. § 205.3.

84. *See Id.*

85. *See Implementation of Standards of Professional Conduct for Attorneys*, 17 C.F.R. Parts 205, 240 and 249, Release Nos. 33-8186; 34-47282; IC-25920 (proposed January 29, 2003).

86. *Id.*

87. Robert A. Del Giorno, *Corporate Counsel as Government's Agent: The Holder Memorandum and Sarbanes-Oxley Section 307*, 27 CHAMPION 22, 26 (Nat'l Assn. of Criminal Defense Lawyers, Inc., August 2003).

88. *Id.* at 26.

89. Kim & Laffitte, *supra* note 80, at 723.

90. *Comments on Rules Implementing Section 307 of the Sarbanes-Oxley Act: Standards of Professional Conduct for Attorneys Practicing Before the SEC*, 58 THE RECORD 23, 50-51 (2003) (republishing comments filed by The Association of The Bar of the City of New York with the SEC on December 16, 2003).

91. Rule 1.6(b)(2)-(3), ABA MODEL RULES OF PROF'L CONDUCT (2003).

92. *See* Rule 1.6(b)(1)-(4), ABA MODEL RULES OF PROF'L CONDUCT (2002); Sue Reisinger, *The ABA Gets With the Program*, CORPORATE COUNSEL, October 2003.

93. Rule 1.13(c), ABA MODEL RULES OF PROFESSIONAL CONDUCT (2003).

94. *See, e.g.,* Sue Reisinger, *The ABA Gets with the Program*, CORPORATE COUNSEL, October 2003, at 19 (citing Alfred Carlton, the immediate past president of the ABA).

95. Jason Hopson, *ABA Delegates OK Changes in Confidentiality*, THE RECORDER, August 12, 2003.

96. *See id.; see also ABA Amends Rule on Client Confidentiality to Allow Lawyers to Disclose Financial Fraud*, BNA's BANKING REPORT, August 25, 2003, at 273-74.

97. Stephen Andersen, *Plaintiffs Chip Away at Attorney-Client Privilege; General Counsel Must Be Clear When Dishing Out Legal Advice*, CORPORATE LEGAL TIMES, October 2003, at 22.

CHAPTER 5

Communications Between Related Corporations and the Attorney-Client Privilege[*]

VINCENT S. WALKOWIAK

Direct Communications Between a Parent Corporation and Its Subsidiary

The purpose of the attorney-client privilege is to promote complete disclosure between attorney and client by protecting confidential communications between them.[1] However, the privilege "will not conceal everything said and done in connection with an attorney's legal representation of a client in a matter."[2] The privilege applies only if: (1) the asserted holder of the privilege is or sought to become a client; (2) the person to whom the communication was made is an attorney; and (3) the communication relates to a fact of which the attorney was informed by his client in confidence for the purpose of securing legal advice. The privilege shields communications by the client to the attorney or the attorney to the client.[3] The privilege does not apply if it has been waived or if the legal advice is sought for the purpose of committing fraud or a crime.[4]

Otherwise protected communications exchanged between related or similarly interested corporations have been held protected by the attorney-client privilege.[5] Courts have reached this conclusion by applying one of three tests: (1) the common ownership test illustrated in *United States v. United Shoe Machinery Corp.*;[6] (2) the "community of interest" test illustrated in *Duplan v. Deering*;[7] and (3) the "joint defense" test illustrated in *Weil Ceramics & Glass, Inc. v. Work.*[8]

---

 * This chapter is an update and rewrite in part of "The Availability of the Attorney-Client and Work-Product Privileges in Connection with Communications Between Related Corporations" published in the first edition of this book.

The Common Ownership Test

In the leading case of *United States v. United Shoe Machinery Corporation,*[9] the court held that the "client" for purposes of the attorney-client privilege is the parent corporation and all of its affiliates and subsidiaries. However, in *United Shoe,* all of the corporations used the same inside and outside counsel. While this might have created problems if this had been a suit to pierce the corporate veil, it simplified the matter of privilege for the court. It becomes more difficult to determine the limits of the attorney-client privilege when the parent and its subsidiaries and/or affiliates share confidential communications but nevertheless employ different counsel.

United Shoe was followed by the court in *American Telephone & Telegraph Co.,*[10] a complex antitrust action in which the court approved and adopted substantive and procedural guidelines relating to the law of privilege and its application to related corporations. In *American Telephone & Telegraph,* the court directed that the attorney-client privilege applied to communications between AT&T and its wholly owned subsidiaries considered collectively, citing the United States Supreme Court's opinion in *United States v. United Shoe Machinery Corp.*[11] However, the court in AT&T did not indicate whether the parent and its subsidiaries employed different counsel.

The "Community of Interest" Test

In *Duplan v. Deering,*[12] the court did address whether communications between a parent and subsidiary were privileged when those entities did not use a common attorney. In *Duplan,* a patent-antitrust case, the court held that there was a sufficient "community of interest" between a French corporation, which was a patent owner, and some of its subsidiaries for the attorney-client privilege to apply to communications made to or received by them.[13] In order for this court's interpretation of the scope of the privilege to apply, the interest must be an identical legal interest. As the court stated: "The key consideration is that the nature of the interest be identical, not similar, and be legal, not solely commercial. . ."[14] The court further stated:

> Although an interest of a third party corporation from a commercial standpoint would not establish a sufficient community of interest, the fact that the communications are among formally different corporate entities *which are under common ownership* or control leads this court to treat such interrelated corporate communications in the same manner as intra-corporate communications . . . . Thus, if a corporation with a legal interest in an attorney-client communication relays it to another related corporation, the attorney-client privilege is not thereby waived. If the communications were relayed to an unrelated third-party corporation, the privilege would be waived (emphasis added).[15]

Thus, the privilege was held applicable even though the parent and its subsidiary corporations each employed their own separate attorneys.

The court in *Roberts v. Carrier Corp.*[16] adopted the "community of interest" test first articulated in *Duplan* and extended it to apply to communications between related subsidiaries. In *Roberts,* the plaintiff brought suit for injuries suffered in a house fire allegedly caused by a Carrier-manufactured furnace. The plaintiff sought discovery pertaining to a valve that was manufactured by the Essex Group. The Essex Group, Carrier, and Hamilton were all wholly owned subsidiaries of United Technologies. The Essex Group claimed that the information that the plaintiff sought concerning the valve was in the possession of Hamilton. Specifically, the plaintiff sought to discover "all communications and/or agreements between Carrier Corporation and Hamilton concerning this lawsuit, whether written or not."[17] Hamilton and Carrier objected to the request on the basis of attorney-client privilege and the work-product doctrine.

The court found that existing case law extended the attorney-client privilege to communications between a parent and a subsidiary. The court then opined that: "The language of these cases . . . suggests that the privilege can extend further."[18] Accordingly, the court held that the two related subsidiaries, Carrier and Hamilton, had an identical legal interest based on the defense of the claim alleging malfunction of the valve.

While Hamilton is not a party to the Texas lawsuit, and thus technically is not defending a claim against it, it nevertheless has a significant interest in the outcome of [plaintiff's] case, given that it is now responsible (within the United Technologies family) for [the valve]. The legal consequences of this case will have an impact on other present or potential litigation involving [the valve], an impact to be directly felt by Hamilton. Thus, a concerted effort with Carrier is in Hamilton's immediate and long-range interest. Within the confines of this case, the identity of interest arises out of the valve itself and the defense of the claim involving it. Thus, interrelated corporate communications, as the *Duplan* court describes them, between Hamilton and Carrier do not waive the attorney-client privilege that each enjoys in consulting with its attorneys because of their relationship via United Technologies and the identical legal interest shared in defending a claim involving [the valve].[19]

Other courts have also found communications between related corporations to be protected by the attorney-client privilege. For instance, a California appellate court addressing the issue of whether direct communications disclosed to the parent are protected by the attorney-client privilege concluded that the privilege applies by reasoning that the communication was in furtherance of the subsidiary's interest.[20] In this case, GAF, an asbestos manufacturer, brought suit against INA Corporation, the parent holding company, and its wholly owned subsidiaries, Insurance Company of North America (Subsidiary One) and INA (Subsidiary Two). Subsidiary Two was GAF's products liability insurer. To investigate the extent of coverage of Subsidiary Two's products liability insurance policies with respect to asbestos-related claims against its insureds, it hired outside counsel. Outside counsel met with officers of Subsidiary Two to discuss these matters, and GAF sought to discover the memoranda, notes, and conversations connected with this meeting. Subsidiary Two asserted that the attorney-client privilege rendered such materials confidential. GAF responded by asserting that the privilege was inapplicable due to the presence at the meeting of the vice-president of the parent and the president of Subsidiary One.

The court examined California Evidence Code § 952 which defined a confidential communications as follows:

> [I]nformation transmitted between a client and his lawyer in the course of
> that relationship and in confidence by a means which, so far as the client is

aware, discloses the information to no third persons other than those who are present to further the interest of the client in the consultation or those to whom disclosure is reasonably necessary for the transmission of the information to the accomplishment of the purpose for which the lawyer is consulted, and includes a legal opinion formed and the advice given by the lawyer in the course of that relationship.[21]

The court then concluded that the officers were not outsiders at the meeting, as the vice president of Subsidiary Two was acting in the capacity of legal consultant and adviser to INA, and the president of Subsidiary One was a part-time expert consultant and adviser on reserve policies and sound actuarial practices.[22] Finding these functions necessary to further the interests of the client, Subsidiary Two, the court concluded that the communications were entitled to the protection afforded by the attorney-client privilege.

Addressing the general question of whether under California law an officer or employee of a holding or affiliated company can exchange otherwise protected communications with a wholly owned subsidiary or affiliate without destroying the confidentiality of the attorney-client communication, the court stated:

> The key concept here is need to know. While involvement of an unnecessary third person in attorney-client communications destroys confidentiality, involvement of third persons to whom disclosure is reasonably necessary to further the purpose of the legal consultation preserves confidentiality of communication.
>
> . . . INA was not a solitary island in a remote ocean but a member of a large archipelago of wholly-owned subsidiaries located in INA Corporation's inland sea. Basic policy and direction on critical problems would ultimately be determined by the parent company. As the court observed in *Duplan Corporation v. Deering Milliken,* 397 F. Supp. 1146, 1164 (D.S.C. 1975): 'The chain of command in military, business, government, and private societies is an accepted pattern of modern civilization.' Such being the case, simultaneous delivery of legal advice to a subsidiary client and a controlling parent company, a delivery which facilitates speedy and accurate determination of business policy by the parent, furthers the interest of the client in the consultation.[23]

Moreover, the court asserted that the protection provided by the attorney-client privilege is not limited to instances where a subsidiary's attorney-client consultation is attended by the president of the holding company but:

> [A]pplies equally to other representatives of the holding company and its affiliates who are present for good business reasons to further the interest of the client. *Absent some conflict of interest or some evidence of antagonism among entities,* disclosure of counsel's legal opinion to holding company and affiliated company officers and employees who need to know this information in order to properly perform their duties is a disclosure

which is reasonably necessary to accomplish the purpose for which counsel have been consulted. Hence it is privileged (emphasis added).[24]

In another case interpreting an attorney-client privilege statute, *Scott Paper Co. v. Ceilcote Co., Inc.,*[25] an employee of Defendant Ceilcote sent a letter to its parent corporation's in-house counsel and plaintiff sought discovery of the letter. The court applied Maine's Rule of Evidence 502(b), which provided:

A client has a privilege to refuse to disclose and to prevent any other person from disclosing confidential communications made for the purpose of facilitating the rendition of professional legal services *to the client between himself or his representative* and his lawyer or his lawyer's representative (emphasis added).[26]

Finding that the letter at issue was written by a "representative" of the client, contained information regarding the subject matter of this litigation, and requested legal advice, the court concluded that the letter was protected by the attorney-client privilege.

The "Joint Defense" Test

Communications between a related corporation may also be protected by the attorney-client privilege under the theory that they are conducting a "joint defense." This defense protects confidential communications between potential co-defendants and jointly retained counsel against disclosure from third parties.[27] Waiver of the privilege requires consent of all co-defendants except litigation adversaries.[28]

For example, in *Weil Ceramics & Glass, Inc. v. Work,*[29] related subsidiaries were shielded by the attorney-client privilege because they were co-defendants. *Weil* involved three related corporations: Lladro, S.A., which manufactured porcelain products, Disenos Artisticos Industriales (DAISA), which designed the products, and Weil Ceramic & Glass, Inc., which distributed the products. All three corporations were wholly owned by Sodigei, which in turn was owned by the Lladro Brothers. DAISA filed suit against Karen-Leslie Co. and two of its affiliates. Karen-Leslie was a company engaged in the acquisition and sale of hard goods, including these products. The suit charged copyright infringement. Weil also filed suit against the same defendants claiming trademark violations. The defendants then interposed a counterclaim that all three corporations violated the antitrust laws.

In the course of discovery, DAISA and Weil refused to produce a number of documents, asserting the attorney-client privilege and the work-product doctrine to correspondence between the attorneys for Lladro, DAISA, and DAISA and Weil. The court sustained the application of the attorney-client privilege to the exchange of information between the attorneys for the related subsidiaries on three separate grounds. First, the court found that the "joint defense" rule was applicable because all three of the corporations were named as co-defendants and co-conspirators. The "joint defense" rule according to this court allowed counsel for co-defendants to share privileged information without fear of waiver. Second, the court found that all three corporations satisfied the "community of interest" rule articulated in *Duplan v. Deering.*[30] Finally, the court sustained the claim of privilege on the ground that the corporations were commonly owned and thus should be considered a single client for attorney-client privilege purposes, citing *United Shoe.*

The "joint defense" theory has covered the communications of unrelated corporations whose privileged communications have been protected by the attorney-client privilege.[31] In *Transmirra Products Corporation v. Monsanto Chemical Co.,*[32] a patent infringement case, communications between the attorneys for corporations who were sued by a common plaintiff were at issue. Addressing the attorney-client privilege, the court stated: "[P]ersons represented by different attorneys but conducting a joint defense may pool information without waiving (the attorney client) privilege."[33] In undertaking to apply the attorney-client privilege to these communications, the court cited with approval to *Schmitt v. Emory,*[34] in which the joint defense privilege was previously recognized.

In *Schmitt* the court had held that:

> Where an attorney furnished a copy of a document entrusted to him by his client to an attorney who is engaged in maintaining substantially the same cause on behalf of other parties in the same litigation, without an express understanding that the recipient shall not communicate the contents thereof to others, the communication is made not for the purpose of allowing unlimited publication and use, but in confidence, for the limited and restricted purpose to assist in asserting their common claims. The copy is given and accepted under the privilege between the attorney furnishing it and his client. For the occasion, the recipient of the copy stands under the same restraints arising from the privileged character of the document as the counsel who furnished it, and consequently he has no right, and cannot be compelled, to produce or disclose its contents.[35]

Transmirra applied the work-product doctrine to the communication in order to determine if the communication was privileged, because the defendant did not raise the attorney-client privilege as a basis for the confidentiality of the document. However, the reasoning employed in *Transmirra* has been applied to cases dealing with the attorney-client privilege. For example, in the *Matter of Grand Jury Subpoena, Nov. 16, 1974,*[36] the discoverability of certain notations and memoranda recording interviews and discussions between independently represented defendants in a securities fraud action were involved. The court held that the documents memorializing the meetings between prospective co-defendants were protected by the attorney-client privilege because the defendants were participants in a common defense.[37] Moreover, the court rejected the contention that in order to establish this defense of a joint defense, the statement needed to be made by an interested party in the presence of his own attorney.[38]

Similarly, in *Continental Oil Co. v. United States,*[39] memoranda exchanged between two unrelated corporations were held to be protected by the attorney-client privilege based on the joint defense doctrine. The corporations, Standard Oil and Continental Oil, had interviewed their own employees in connection with a grand jury proceeding. The parties exchanged memoranda recording these interviews "in order to apprise each other as to the nature and scope of the inquiry proceeding before the Grand Jury."[40] Upholding the defendants' assertion of privilege, the court noted that it was irrelevant that an indictment had not yet been returned and that the parties were not yet actual joint defendants.[41]

Privilege Denied

Not all communications made between corporations asserting a common defense will be protected by the attorney-client privilege. For example, in *Magna Leasing, Inc. v. Staten Island Mall,*[42] the plaintiff sought discovery of a settlement agreement between the defendant and a third party, Chase Manhattan Mortgage and Realty Trust. The court rejected the defendant's claim that a settlement agreement was privileged because it contained communications concerning joint defenses. The court emphasized that the communications at issue must relate to the joint defense:

> Communications among the attorneys for co-defendants are privileged only *if the communications are designed to further a joint or common defense . . .*
>
> In the instant case, the settlement agreement insofar as we have ordered disclosure relates merely to the transfer of assets between defendants and Chase. The relevant portions embody no communications concerning the manner or substance of parties' joint or common defense of the actions brought by the other tenants (emphasis added).[43]

Thus, at least in the view of this court, in order to claim the protection of the attorney-client privilege the documents must relate to the joint defense.

In short, the attorney-client privilege may be asserted by a corporation when it shares otherwise confidential communications with a related corporation if: (1) the corporations are considered a "single client" because of their common ownership; (2) the corporations share an identical legal interest in the litigation; or (3) the corporations are co-defendants or potential co-defendants.

The Work Product Doctrine as It Applies to Communications Between Related Corporations

The Supreme Court has recognized qualified protection for materials prepared by an attorney acting for his client in anticipation of litigation.[44] This privilege has been extended to include the work of agents of the attorney.[45] Documents protected by the work-product doctrine are generally discoverable only upon a showing of substantial need and that the party seeking the information is unable without undue hardship to obtain the substantial equivalent of the materials by other means.[46] There is generally no work-product immunity for documents that were prepared in the regular course of business prior to the onset of litigation[47] or for other non-litigation purposes.[48]

The work-product doctrine covers oral communications as well as tangible materials such as documents.[49] As the court in *Transmirra* stated: "There should be no essential difference between written legal memoranda or opinions developed during conversations or conferences."[50]

The issue of whether the work-product doctrine attaches to communications between related corporations is important because the work product is broader than the attorney-client privilege. Moreover, any waiver of attorney-client privilege does not affect the protection granted to an attorney's work product.[51]

In *Duplan v. Deering*,[52] the court held that the work-product privilege may attach to joint consultations between a parent and subsidiary if the communications were for purposes of gathering evidence during preparation for litigation. "The sharing of information between counsel for parties having common interests does not destroy the work-product privilege during the course of litigation."[53]

Similarly, other cases involving non-related corporations have found that the work-product privilege applies to shared information when the corporations have a "community of interest" in potential or actual litigation. For instance, in *Transmirra Products Corporation v. Monsanto Chemical Co.*,[54] discussed previously, the plaintiff sought discovery of information regarding legal assistance rendered to a third party whom the plaintiff had previously charged with infringement of the same patent. Holding the communications between the former defendant and the present defendant protected by the work-product doctrine, the court relied on the "community of interest" between the two defendants in the litigation.

"One could not deny the advantages of, and even the necessity for, an exchange or pooling of information between attorneys representing parties sharing such a common interest in litigation, actual or prospective."[55]

Similarly, in *Burlington Industries v. Exxon Corp.*,[56] the court held that the exchange of information between joint licensees that have a mutual interest in a patent action is protected by the work-product doctrine:

> Upon a proper showing of the existence of such joint licensing program, documents prepared by attorneys in anticipation of litigation involving their clients, and exchanged in confidence between attorneys representing the joint licensors, will not lose the protection of the work product doctrine.[57]

The court stated that the party with whom the claimant of the privilege shares a "community of interest" need not be a party to the litigation.[58]

In addition to documents and communications exchanged between related corporations, interviews of potential witnesses conducted by counsel for a parent corporation when the subsidiary is being sued should also be protected, as it is clear that interviews of witnesses in anticipation of litigation are entitled to the protection of the privilege.[59] Caution is the key word here, however, as a number of jurisdictions have specifically made witnesses' statements discoverable and in some instances have excluded witness statement from the protection afforded by the work-product doctrine.[60] Thus, even though it was a witness statement that gave rise to the recognition of the attorney work-product doctrine, witness statements are no longer protected from disclosure in Texas and states that follow a similar rule. In those jurisdictions that still recognize that the work-product doctrine protects witness statements, the reasoning of *Duplan v. Decker*[61] may apply. In those jurisdictions, the exchange of information between counsel for parties entitled to assert a common work-product doctrine will apply to a corporation's interviews of witnesses connected with the litigation. Under these circumstances, these interviews would be protected by the work-product doctrine.

Thus, it has generally been held that the work-product doctrine will protect communications between related corporations that share a "community of interest" in litigation.

Most of the cases that have held the attorney-client privilege or work-product doctrine applicable to communications between parent and subsidiaries have not discussed the effect of the extent of the parent's stock ownership.[62] However, in *American Tel. & Tel.,*[63] the court addressed the issue of whether the percentage of ownership of the subsidiary should affect whether a parent and its subsidiaries are treated as a single client for purposes of the attorney-client privilege. This court held that only the parent's wholly owned subsidiaries and majority-owned subsidiaries should be considered a single client for attorney-client privilege purposes. The court excluded minority-owned companies from the rule, explaining:

> The cases referring to parent, subsidiary, and affiliate corporations in regard to the attorney-client privilege simply reach the conclusion that there was a single client without examining this question. Perhaps the conclusion to be reached may well depend on where one begins. If analysis begins with the proposition that corporations under unified control are "one," even though comprised of components held in varying degrees of ownership, then a minority-owned company can be assimilated to one in which substantial, although not majority, ownership is held. On the other hand, if analysis begins with the proposition that formerly distinct corporations are separate persons except as specific legal purpose warrants treating them as one, then a different conclusion is reached.[64]

The court rejected the prospect that minority-owned subsidiaries and their parents could be considered a "single client" within the attorney-client privilege because a minority-owned company is a distinct corporation with independent stockholders. However, the court stated, "[W]e found no cases in which there was a consideration of the degree of ownership required to give rise to the parent, subsidiary, or affiliate relationship."[65]

When a parent corporation sells a subsidiary, an issue is raised regarding which corporation now controls the attorney-client privilege as to communications between the two entities before the sale. In *Commodity Futures Trading Commission v. Weintraub,*[66] the Supreme Court recognized that new managers of a corporation may waive the attorney-client privilege as to communications by former officers and directors. In *Weintraub,* the Supreme Court held that the trustee of a corporation in bankruptcy has the power to waive the debtor corporation's attorney-client privilege with respect to communications that occurred before the filing for bankruptcy. The Court noted that, for solvent corporations, the power to waive the privilege is exercised by officers and directors consistently with their fiduciary duty to act in the best interest of the corporation. The Court further stated:

> When control of a corporation passes to new management, the authority to
> assert and waive the corporation's attorney-client privilege passes as well.
> New management installed as a result of a takeover, merger, loss of confi-
> dence by shareholders, or simply normal succession, may waive the attor-
> ney-client privilege with respect to communications made by former officers
> and directors. Displaced managers may not assert the privilege over the
> wishes of current managers. . . .[67]

The reasoning in *Weintraub* has been extended to cases involving the sale of a
subsidiary.[68] *In re Sealed Case*[69] addressed the issue of who controls the attorney-
client privilege of a corporate subsidiary after it is sold with respect to confidential
communications between the subsidiary and parent prior to the sale. In *Sealed Case,*
the parent corporation sold all of the stock of the subsidiary corporation to the purchaser. After the sale, the purchaser filed a securities fraud lawsuit against the parent
seller. The purchaser moved to compel production of certain documents that the parent corporation claimed were privileged as attorney-client communications. The subsidiary (now controlled by the purchaser) waived its attorney-client privilege in favor
of the purchaser. The documents at issue fell into two categories: (1) memoranda
between subsidiary officers and employees and in-house counsel in the parent's legal
department who handled legal matters for both the parent and the subsidiary, and (2)
documents relating to a lawsuit in which subsidiary and seller were both defendants
and represented by the same counsel.

As to the first set of documents, the court relied on the principle stated in *Weintraub*
"that a normal consequence of a succession of corporate management, with or without a change in ownership, is that the new management has the authority to assert or
waive the corporation's privilege based on their determination of the best interests of
the corporation."[70] Thus, the court concluded that the parties to a subsidiary divestiture by sale of stock should be treated as having contracted on the assumption that
after the sale, the management of the divested corporation will control its attorney-
client privilege. It ordered the documents produced. However, the court noted that the
parties are free to vary this rule by agreement. Moreover, the court opined in dicta that
confidentiality can be protected by employing separate counsel for the subsidiary.

As to the second set of documents, the court concluded that the privilege that
attached to the joint defense material could not be waived by the subsidiary in favor of
the subsidiary's purchaser without the parent seller's consent. Where the subsidiary
seeks access of joint defense material "for the benefit of its new owner, particularly
where its new owner is a litigation adversary of its former parent, the argument for
applying the special waiver rule of the joint defense cases is strong."[71]

In *Medcom Holding Company v. Baxter Travenol Laboratories, Inc.,*[72] the court
adopted reasoning similar to that in *Sealed Case,* holding that an acquiring company
controlled the subsidiary's attorney-client privilege with respect to communications
between the subsidiary and the former parent occurring prior to, and relating to the
sale of, the subsidiary. In *Medcom,* Baxter, the parent, sold Medcom, Inc., its subsidiary, to Medcom Holding. Medcom Holding sought to compel production of communications between officers and employees of Medcom, Inc. and attorneys in Baxter's
legal department that related to the sale of Medcom, Inc. Baxter's in-house counsel

handled matters for both Baxter and its subsidiaries. Affirming the lower court's determination that parties who negotiate a corporate acquisition should expect that the privileges of the acquired corporation are incidents of the sale, the court stated:

> In issue here . . . is Medcom, Inc.'s right to control its own privilege rights after divestiture from Baxter. Although both Medcom, Inc. and Baxter are entitled to assert the attorney-client privilege with respect to communications made on their behalf, either may waive it. A client may waive a privilege by voluntary disclosure to a third party; the disclosure breaches the confidentiality of the attorney-client relationship and, therefore, waives the privilege. (citations omitted) Medcom, Inc. has elected to voluntarily disclose the privileged information to its current sole shareholder Medcom Holding; this waives the privilege.[73]

Like *Sealed Case, Medcom* also involved confidential communications between the former parent and its former subsidiary as co-defendants. Similarly, the *Medcom* court held that the subsidiary, Medcom, Inc., could not unilaterally waive its joint defense privilege in favor of Medcom Holding, its purchaser.

New management may not control the attorney-client privilege with respect to communications between a subsidiary's officers and its own independent counsel where these communications were a violation of the fiduciary duty owed to the parent.[74] Thus, in *In re Diasonics Securities Litigation,*[75] the court held that after divestiture of a subsidiary, the attorney-client privilege remained with the parent. However, *Diasonics* involved unique facts. In that case, Diasonics acquired Fischer Corp. Two stockholders of Fischer continued in their capacity as officers of the subsidiary and additionally became officers of Diasonics.

Thereafter, these officers sought rescission of the acquisition, and after rescission, they resigned their positions with the parent. Subsequently, Diasonics was sued by its stockholders, who claimed misrepresentations in connection with a public offering of Diasonics common stock. Plaintiffs sought discovery of documents regarding the Fischer transaction. Fischer claimed that the attorney-client privilege protected notes made by the officers during their employment by both Diasonics and Fischer concerning their consultations with an attorney regarding the possible rescission.

Rejecting this contention, the court held that the officers had breached their fiduciary duty to the shareholders of Diasonics and thus could not raise the privilege:

> The attorney-client communications were made when the two individuals had a fiduciary responsibility to the board of directors and shareholders of Diasonics and not to the presently existing board and shareholders of Fischer; therefore, if any· right existed in the corporation to raise the attorney-client privilege, it remained with Diasonics and with Fischer after it had separated from Diasonics.[76]

Moreover, the court stated that the officers' actions in seeking the exception to the attorney-client privilege was applicable.

Diasonics was distinguished by both the *Sealed Case* court and the *Medcom* court because it involved breach of fiduciary duty and fraud. As the *Diasonics* court itself stated: "[A] fiduciary cannot hide behind the attorney-client privilege to avoid discovery of his wrongdoing."[77]

Unlike a sale of stock, the right to assert the attorney-client privilege does not pass upon a sale of assets of a corporation. In *Sobol v. E.P. Dutton, Inc.,*[78] plaintiff sued defendant Dutton for breach of contract. Dutton had purchased the rights to plaintiff's book from Nelson. Plaintiff sought discovery of correspondence between employees of Nelson and Nelson's outside counsel. Dutton averred that the attorney-client privilege that attached to these communications passed to Dutton when Dutton purchased the rights from Nelson. Distinguishing *Weintraub,* the court pointed out that Dutton was not the new management of Nelson, holding that the right to assert the attorney-client privilege was unavailable. The court stated:

> Neither *Weintraub* nor any other case cited by Dutton holds that the attorney-client privilege is an incident of the sale of a portion of tangible assets of a corporation and is transferred upon sale. Dutton did not purchase all of Nelson, but only a portion of its assets. Dutton and Nelson engaged in an ordinary commercial transaction in which Dutton purchased contractual rights previously assigned to Nelson by the plaintiff. This transaction has nothing to do with the attorney-client relationship between Nelson and its counsel.[79]

Conclusion

Otherwise protected communications shared between related corporations have been held to be protected by the attorney-client privilege under three tests: (1) the corporations constitute a single client for purposes of the attorney-client privilege; (2) the corporations share a "community of interest" and (3) the corporations are engaged in a joint defense to litigation. Communications that constitute work product independent of the attorney-client privilegemay remain protected by the qualified privilege despite the fact that they were shared with a related corporation if the corporations share a "community of interest."

Additionally, when a parent corporation and subsidiary share otherwise protected attorney-client communications, and the parent later sells the subsidiary, the courts have held that the attorney-client privilege is controlled by the subsidiary's new management.

Notes

1. 8 WIGMORE, EVIDENCE § 2291 (1961).

2. *In re* Fischel, 557 F.2d 209, 212 (9th Cir. 1977).

3. *See* Georgia-Pacific Plywood Co. v. United States Plywood Corp., 18 F.R.P. 463 (S.D.N.Y. 1956) ("Since communications by the attorney to the client might reveal the substance of a client's communication, they are also within the privilege.").

4. *See* United States v. United Shoe Machinery Corp., 89 F. Supp. 357, 358 (D. Mass. 1950).

5. *See, e.g.,* United States v. American Telephone & Telegraph Co., 86 F.R.D. 603, 616-18

(D.D.C. 1979); *see also In re* Sealed Case, 120 F.R.D. 66-70 (N.D. Ill. 1988) (legal advice provided jointly to multiple corporate clients is generally privileged against third parties).

6. 89 F. Supp. 357, 358 (D. Mass. 1950).

7. 397 F. Supp. 1146, 1184-85 (D.S.C. 1974).

8. 110 F.R.D. 500 (E.D.N.Y. 1986).

9. 89 F. Supp. 357, 359 (D. Mass. 1950).

10. 86 F.R.D. at 603, 616 (D.D.C. 1980).

11. 89 F. Supp. 357 (D. Mass 1950); 86 F.R.D. at 616.

12. 397 F. Supp. 1146, 1184-85 (D.S.C. 1974).

13. *Id.* at 1184-85.

14. *Id.* at 1172. *See also* Bank Brussels Lambert v. Credit Lyonnais, 160 F.R.D. 437 (S.D.N.Y. 1995).

15. 397 F. Supp. at 1172; Shamis v. Ambassador Factors Corp., 24 F. Supp. 2d 879 (S.D.N.Y. 1999) (no privilege for unrelated third-party corporation).

16. 107 F.R.D. 678, 687-88 (N.D. Ind. 1985) (applying Indiana law).

17. *Id.* at 681.

18. *Id.* at 688.

19. *Id.*

20. *See* Insurance Co. of North America v. Superior Court of Los Angeles, 108 Cal. App. 3d 758, 166 Cal. Rptr. 880 (1980).

21. *Id.* at 763, 166 Cal. Rptr. at 883.

22. *Id.* at 765, 166 Cal. Rptr. at 884.

23. *Id.* at 768, 166 Cal. Rptr. at 886.

24. *Id.* at 769, 166 Cal. Rptr. at 887. *See also* George v. Siemens Indus. Automation, 182 F.R.D. 134 (D.N.J. 1998); Bank Brussels Lambert v. Credit Lyonnais, S.A., 160 F.R.D. 437 (S.D.N.Y. 1995) for the proposition that the privilege applies to corporations with similar legal interests.

25. 103 F.R.D. 591, 597 (D. Maine 1984).

26. *Id.* at 597.

27. *In re* Grand Jury Subpoena Duces Tecum dated Nov. 16, 1974, 406 F. Supp 381 (S.D.N.Y. 1975).

28. *See* Medcom Holding v. Baxter Travenol Laboratories, Inc., 689 F. Supp. 841, 845 (N.D. Ill. 1988).

29. 110 F.R.D. 500 (E.D.N.Y. 1986).

30. 397 F. Supp. 1146 (D.S.C. 1974).

31. Continental Oil Co. v. United States, 330 F.2d 347 (9th Cir. 1964). *See also* Transmirra Products Corp. v. Monsanto Chemical Co., 26 F.R.D. 572 (S.D.N.Y. 1960).

32. 26 F.R.D. 572 (S.D.N.Y. 1960).

33. *Id.* at 576.

34. 211 Minn. 547, 2 N.W.2d 413, 414 (1942), *overruled on other grounds*, Leer v. Chicago Railway Co., 308 N.W. 2d 305 (1981) (privilege sustained where joint interest in excluding particular evidence is present).

35 2 N.W.2d at 413, 417 (1942).

36. 406 F. Supp. 381 (1975).

37. *Id.* at 391.

38. *Id.* at 391. *But see* Schachar v. American Academy of Ophthalmology, Inc., 106 F.R.D. 193 (N.D. Ill. 1985) (attorney must be a party to the communication for privilege to attach).

39. 330 F.2d 347 (9th Cir. 1964).

40. *Id.* at 348.

41. *Id.* at 350.

42. 76 F.R.D. 559 (S.D.N.Y. 1977).

43. *Id.* at 564.

44. Hickman v. Taylor, 329 U.S. 495 (1947).

45. United States v. Nobles, 422 U.S. 225 (1975). *See generally* Annotation, 35 A.L.R.3d 412 (1971).

46. *See* FED. R. CIV. P. 26(b)(3). *See also In re* Joint Eastern and Southern District Asbestos Litig., 119 F.R.D. 4 (E.D.N.Y. 1988) (product book, containing photographs of asbestos products, that constituted attorney work product was discoverable upon showing of substantial need).

47. *See, e.g.,* Hardy v. New York News, Inc., 114 F.R.D. 633 (S.D.N.Y. 1987) (fact that documents prepared for business purpose were also determined to be of potential use in pending litigation does not turn those documents into attorney work product).

48. *See* United States v. El Paso Co., 682 F.2d 530, 542 (5th Cir. 1982), *cert. denied*, 466 U.S. 944 (1984) (materials assembled pursuant to public requirements unrelated to litigation are not protected by work-product doctrine qualified immunity).

49. Delco Wire & Cable, Inc. v. Weinberger, 109 F.R.D. 680, 691 (E.D. Pa. 1986) (principles announced in *Hickman* concerning attorney work product protects, although the federal rule applies only to tangibles).

50. 105 F.R.D. at 579. *See also In re* Grand Jury Subpoena Dated November 8, 1979, 622 F.2d 933 (6th Cir. 1980) (work product consists of the tangible and intangible material).

51. *See, e.g.,* Transmirra Products Corp. v. Monsanto Chemical Co., 26 F.R.D. 572, 578 discussed *supra*.

52. 397 F. Supp. 1146 at 1172.

53. *Id.* at 1172. *See also Amer. Tel. & Tel.,* 86 F.R.D. at 634 (a party does not lose the trial preparation material privilege by disclosing material to a person aligned in interest against a common adversary).

54. 26 F.R.D. 572 (S.D.N.Y. 1960).

55. *Id.* at 579.

56. 65 F.R.D. 26, 45 (D. Md. 1974).

57. *Id.* at 45.

58. *Id.* at 43. *See also* Stanley Works v. Haeger Potteries, Inc., 35 F.R.D. 551, 555 (N.D. Ill. 1964) ("Where attorneys for parties having a mutual interest in litigation exchange their work product, it remain protected by a qualified privilege.").

59. Hickman v. Taylor, 329 U.S. 495, 505 (1947). *See also* Schuler v. United States, 113 F.R.D. 518 (W.D. Mich. 1986).

60. Thus, the Texas Rules of Civil Procedure define the permissible scope of discovery regarding witness statements in the following manner:

> A party may obtain discovery of the statement of any person with knowledge of relevant facts—a "witness statement"—regardless of when the statement was made.

TEX. R. CIV. P. 192.3(h). Addressing specifically the possible assertion of the work-product doctrine to attempt to exclude such statements, the rules state:

> Even if made or prepared in anticipation of litigation or for trial, the following is not work product protected from discovery:
> (1) information discoverable under Rule 192.3 concerning experts, trial witness, witness statements and contentions.

TEX. R. CIV. P. 192.5(c). *See In re* Team Transport, Inc., 996 S.W.2d 256 (Tex. App.–Houston [14th Dist] 1999, orig. proceeding) in which an employee who had witnessed an accident had sent a letter to the insurance carrier for her employer describing the accident. The letter was discoverable. *Id.* at 259. *See also In re* Jiminez, 4 S.W.3d 894 (Tex. App. Houston–[1st Dist] 1999, orig. proceeding); *In re* W&G Trucking, 990 S.W.2d 473 (Tex. App.–Beaumont 1999, orig. proceeding). However, while witness statements are not protected, notes taken during a conversation or interview with a witness are defined as not being a witness statement and consequently may be privileged. TEX. R. CIV. P. 192.3. An attorney may still interview a witness and preserve the notes that are taken under the attorney work-product doctrine, but if he or she attempts to memorialize these comments by having the witness sign a statement, or transcribes those notes in virtually any manner, that transcription may represent a statement of the witness and be discoverable.

Statements of witnesses may still be privileged if they are attorney-client privileged statements. *See* TEX. R. CIV. P. 192, cmt. 9. *In re* Fontenot, 13 S.W.3d 111 (Tex. App.–Ft. Worth 2000, orig. proceeding).

61. 397 F. Supp. 1146 (D.S.C. 1974).

62. *See, e.g.,* Duplan v. Deering, 397 F. Supp. at 1184-85 (emphasizing that community of interest between the corporations must be legal, not commercial); United States v. United Shoe Machinery Corp., 89 F. Supp. 357 at 359 (D.S.C. 1930) (court relied upon fact that the corporations all used same counsel and their legal affairs were closely related); Insurance Co. of North America v. Superior Court of Los Angeles, 108 Cal. App. 3d 758 at 768, 166 Cal. Rptr. at 880 (although subsidiaries were wholly owned by parent, court did not rely on this fact in its reasoning).

63. 86 F.R.D. at 603, 616-17.

64. *Id.*

65. *Id.*

66. 471 U.S. 343 (1985).

67. *Id.* at 378.

68. *See* O'Leary v. Purcell Co., 108 F.R.D. 641, 644 (D.N.C. 1985) (surviving corporation from a merger has standing to assert attorney-client privilege with respect to documents produced by merged subsidiary).

69. 12 F.R.D. 66 (N.D. Ill. 1988).

70. *Id.* at 70.

71. 120 F.R.D. at 72.

72. 689 F. Supp. 841 (N.D. Ill. 1988).

73. *Id.* at 844.

74. *See In re* Diasonics Securities Litigation, 110 F.R.D. 570 (D. Colo. 1986).

75. *Id.*

76. *Id.* at 574.

77. *Id.* at 576.

78. 112 F.R.D. 99 (S.D.N.Y. 1986).

79. *Id.* at 103.

CHAPTER 6

Privilege of Manufacturer Product Safety Quality Assurance Reviews

ROSEWELL PAGE III

Introduction

It is a reality of modern business that corporations of every size reach business and legal decisions only after extensive discussions by the board of directors or some other group or committee of the organization. Often these discussions and the decisions resulting from them are memorialized in the form of minutes or a report. For example, in the product liability areas, corporate board members, legal counsel, management and even lower-level employees will participate in discussions and decisions relating to the sale of a particular product with or without some arguable safer feature. Legitimate differences of opinion concerning the safety of the product, design alternatives, or preferred materials are recorded.

In product litigation, plaintiffs will seek to discover the content of these discussions, either by requests for production of the minutes or the report of the committee or by deposing one or more of the participants. Whether the corporation can protect such information on the basis of privilege is the subject of this chapter.

The scope of discovery in civil trials today is quite broad. By rule, a party can discover "any matter relevant to the subject matter involved in the action."[1] The information is discoverable even if it would be inadmissible at trial as long as the request appears "reasonably calculated to lead to the discovery of admissible evidence."[2] Under today's rules, even the once forbidden "fishing expedition" is frequently permitted. Thus, the only meaningful limitation on the scope of discovery is privilege.

Evidentiary privileges are matters of both state and federal law. In some jurisdictions, privileges are governed by statutory provisions; in others, including federal, common law principles control. For this reason, there may be differences between the jurisdictions regarding the scope of a particular privilege.

In the context of corporate discussions and decision-making, two privileges potentially arise: the attorney-client privilege and the critical self-evaluation privilege. This chapter examines how these privileges arise in the corporate setting where discussions take place at various levels. Such discussions can be structured so that confidentiality can best be protected in ensuing litigation. Particular emphasis will be on discussions at various levels of the corporation regarding product safety.

Attorney-Client Privilege

The attorney-client privilege is universally recognized. For this reason, it provides the best protection for internal discussions regarding product safety. Since the 1950s, the attorney-client privilege has expressly applied to the corporate client.[3] The American Law Institute states the rationale for privilege as follows:

> In a society as complicated in structure as ours and governed by laws as complex and detailed as those upon us, expert legal advice is essential. To the furnishing of such advice the fullest freedom and honesty of communication of pertinent facts is a prerequisite. To induce clients to make such communications, the privilege to prevent their later disclosure is said by courts and commentators to be a necessity. The social good derived from the proper performance of the functions of lawyers acting for their clients is believed to outweigh the harm that may come from the suppression of the evidence in specific cases.[4]

An additional basis for recognizing the attorney-client privilege in the context of the corporation is to encourage open discussion of potentially harmful aspects of its products in the hope that such discussions will improve the product and thus benefit the consumer and society as a whole. The task is to structure discussions of product safety to come within the scope of the attorney-client privilege.

Though the courts lack uniformity on the precise wording, the generally accepted elements of a privileged attorney-client communication are: (1) a communication (2) from a client (3) to an attorney (or vice versa) (4) that concerns the rendering of legal advice (5) that is intended to remain confidential, and (6) that in fact does remain confidential. The party asserting the attorney-client privilege has the burden of proving that it exists; therefore, the corporation should be prepared to demonstrate each of these elements if it hopes to successfully assert the privilege as a defense to discovery of internal corporate discussions.

Communication

Establishing that a communication has taken place should not be difficult. Any oral or written statement, question or opinion disclosed to another is communication. It is conceivable, however, that a client might communicate with counsel by other than words or writing. For example, a corporate client might perform a demonstration or experiment for counsel during the course of a consultation. Even though the experiment is not an oral or written communication, it would be protected if it was intended by the client to be confidential.[5]

Client

Proving that the communication has taken place between an attorney and client is more difficult. In the corporate context, identifying the "client" can be a difficult task. Until 1980, when the Supreme Court decided *Upjohn Co. v. United States,*[6] two basic tests prevailed for determining which employees of the corporation should be considered the client. One test was the so-called "control group" test wherein the corporate client consisted of those employees, regardless of their position in the company, who were directly involved in the subject matter of the legal advice sought. In *Upjohn,* the Court expressly rejected the control group test as being too limiting, but at the same time did not approve the subject matter test. Instead, the Court advocated a case-by-case analysis and implied by its analysis of the facts of *Upjohn* that the following factors were significant:

1. That the communication between lower-level employees and counsel take place at the direction of corporate supervisors.
2. That the communication take place in order to secure legal advice from counsel.
3. That the information sought from lower-level employees be needed to supply a basis for legal advice.
4. That the communication involve matters within the scope of the employees' corporate duties.
5. That the employees themselves be aware that the purpose of the communication is for the corporation to obtain legal advice.
6. That the communication take place with the understanding that it would remain confidential.[7] Essentially this is a modified version of the subject matter test announced by the Eighth Circuit in *Diversified Industries, Inc. v. Meredith.*[8]

Under the *Upjohn* modified subject matter test, a product safety committee comprised of lower-level design engineers, product testing engineers, management representatives or other personnel could constitute the "client" for purposes of the attorney-client privilege. Counsel should be added to this committee as should some responsible representative from upper-level management. The committee should be expressly charged by resolution of the board of directors or a directive from management with the exclusive purpose of discussing products and their safety features *with counsel* so that counsel can advise management of the corporation's exposure to liability from an accident involving the product. The committee's standing rules should emphasize the necessity of confidentiality. The management representative should instruct lower-level members of the committee that the reason for their inclusion on the committee is to provide information essential for counsel to render legal advice.

Counsel *must* be present, or there is no communication to counsel. Lower-level members of the committee must be instructed as to their role, or they may not be the client. Counsel must be consulted for the purpose of rendering *legal* advice, such as the corporation's exposure to liability from the sale of a particular product. Otherwise, he may not act in his role as a lawyer. The discussions must take place with the understanding that they will remain confidential, or no privilege attaches. The *substance* of the discussions must remain confidential, otherwise any protection afforded by the attorney-client privilege may be waived. This does not mean, however, that conclusions reached as a result of discussion must remain confidential.

Lawyer Consulted as Lawyer

Determining whether an attorney is consulted in his capacity as the corporation's lawyer or for some other purpose is not always easy. One problem frequently encountered in the corporate setting, particularly with in-house counsel, is that a lawyer may perform more than one role within the company. For example, counsel may also serve as an officer or as a member of the board of directors. However, counsel's participation in board or committee meetings does not automatically subject discussions at these meetings to the attorney-client privilege. A corporate attorney may act as a business advisor, labor negotiator, investigator, accountant, tax preparer, etc. There is no test that clearly delineates between lawyering and some other activity.

A number of factors have been identified as relevant in drawing this line. One factor is whether the same service could have been performed for the corporation by a non-lawyer. This determination, in turn, depends not just on what the lawyer is actually doing, but on why he is doing it. For example, by simply gathering facts, the lawyer acts only in his role as investigator—something a non-lawyer can do quite easily. However, if the investigation is done for the purpose of gathering the necessary facts so that accurate legal advice can be given, the lawyer acts as a lawyer.

In *Upjohn*, one of the primary factors influencing the Court to find that the attorney-client privilege had attached was the fact that counsel for *Upjohn* had conducted an internal investigation into questionable overseas payments not for the purpose of restructuring overseas operations (business advice), but to advise corporate management of the *legal* implications of such conduct. As the Court noted, "[t]he first step in the resolution of any legal problem is ascertaining the factual background and sifting through the facts with an eye to the legally relevant."[9]

The courts' treatment of the attorney-client privilege in patent advice situations is instructive on whether the lawyer is acting as a lawyer when he is involved in product safety evaluation, since communications to a patent lawyer contain much technical data. As one court notes, the domain of the patent lawyer is highly technical and necessarily requires analysis of specific aspects of a particular invention.[10] The patent lawyer cannot give proper legal advice without such technical analysis.

By analogy, the domain of the product liability lawyer is equally technical. Counsel for a corporation selling consumer products must also engage in fact-finding and analysis of the technical aspects of a product before he can render appropriate legal advice about the product's potential for exposing the company to liability. It is, however, important to establish and record that the purpose of the lawyer's involvement in the technical aspects of product safety evaluation is to gather all the information relevant to rendering a *legal* opinion on the company's potential for liability. This creates an evidentiary foundation for the privilege.

Another factor to consider is how the client treats the relationship. For example, in *Diversified Industries*, *supra*, there was evidence that the board of directors hired outside counsel solely to perform an investigation, not to render legal advice. The majority ultimately determined that the law firm was acting in a legal capacity. However, a strong dissent emphasized the fact that the "client" did not view the relationship with the law firm as an attorney-client relationship. By carefully documenting the role of the lawyers, both in-house and outside, the corporation can establish a proper and provable foundation.

Courts also will look to how the attorney treats his work for the client. The lawyer who serves the corporation in multiple capacities—officer, board member, shareholder, business advisor, and tax preparer as well as general counsel—should carefully document when he is acting as director, officer, shareholder, etc., and when he is acting as general counsel. When an attorney drafts a document regarding minutes of a meeting, he should sign in the capacity in which he served. For example, John Doe, Counsel for XYZ, Inc., John Doe, Director, XYZ, Inc. or John Doe, Treasurer, XYZ, Inc.

Moreover, the tone of the report given by the lawyer should indicate that the lawyer undertook to give legal advice. For example, if the report merely recites facts, the inference may be that the lawyer was acting solely as an investigator. However, if the report suggests the potential legal consequences of that set of facts, then it suggests that the lawyer was present to render legal advice. The minutes of meetings should reflect that the lawyer was requested to attend for the purpose of giving legal advice. Those portions of the minutes that are sensitive might be recorded separately and noted as being confidential communications to the attending lawyer.

Legal Advice

Once it is determined whether the lawyer was acting in his role as a lawyer, it must be determined whether the communication between the lawyer and client involved the securing of legal advice. Frequently, advice has both legal and non-legal aspects. As the court noted in *United States v. United Shoe Machinery Corp.*:[11]

> The modern lawyer almost invariably advises his client upon not only what is permissible but also what is desirable. And it is in the time [sic] public interest that the lawyer should regard himself as more than predicter of legal consequences. His duty to society as well as to his client involves many relevant social, economic, political, and philosophical considerations. And the privilege of nondisclosure is not lost merely because relevant non-legal considerations are expressly stated in a communication which also includes legal advice.[12]

For example, advice given by a lawyer to the corporation regarding product safety contains legal advice about the legal consequences, if any, of an accident involving a product, and business advice concerning whether the product could be modified for sale. While the courts are split on whether the privilege attaches at all where the lawyer's advice is a mixture of legal and business advice, the majority position is that the privilege attaches where the legal advice predominates.[13] The problem then is to determine when the communication is predominantly legal.

The more closely the legal and non-legal advice are related, the more likely it is that the legal advice is the dominant reason for the communication and vice versa. Also, the timing of the communication should be consistent with the need for legal advice. Finally, advice is predominantly legal when the ultimate decision to be made by the corporation *requires* the legal advice rather than the non-legal advice.

For example, in *Henson v. Wyeth Laboratories, Inc.*,[14] the court determined that the company's request for in-house counsel's advice regarding the company's decision to enter into a contract with a chemical supplier was not *primarily* concerned with legal advice. It emphasized that the attorney involved also served as the secretary of the corporation, that nothing in the involved memoranda contained "specific requests" for legal services, and that the memoranda as a whole were essentially a "recordation of technical data" prepared with a view more toward the *desirability* of doing business with the supplier and using the trademark involved than the *legality* of doing so.[15] Thus, the ultimate decision required only the business advice.

Confidentiality

The final element necessary for the creation of the privilege is confidentiality. Whether a particular communication was confidential when it occurred depends primarily on the expectation of the client. The circumstances surrounding the communication, such as the presence of a non-corporate outsider, compliance with in-house formalities, and the place where the communication took place, all must be consistent with the expectation of confidentiality. Moreover, designating certain documents as confidential helps establish the expectation, unless the client routinely designates certain things as confidential. Overzealous designation of communications as confidential may lessen the likelihood that truly confidential communication will be treated as confidential.

Moreover, once confidentiality has been established at the initiation of the communication, such confidentiality must be maintained. Wide circulation of a document or communication may be deemed evidence of waiver. The more widely the communication is circulated throughout the organization, the less likely that the client intended the communication to remain confidential. If confidentiality is to be maintained, disclosure should be limited to those employees of the corporation with need to know, either to ensure that the attorney is obtaining both full and accurate information or to allow those employees to take appropriate action on the advice given.

Critical Self-Evaluation Privilege

Critical self-evaluation may be a more accurate characterization of what typically happens in meetings held to discuss product safety. For this reason, where such a privilege is recognized, the critical self-evaluation privilege may be an appropriate vehicle for maintaining the confidentiality of internal product safety discussions. This privilege may also make more sense financially to smaller businesses that do not have the resources to involve a lawyer in everyday decisions.

The self-evaluation privilege evolved in the context of hospital peer review activity and has been applied narrowly in other contexts. The privilege exists to preserve the confidentiality of self-critical in-house investigations. It was initially designed to provide incentives to corporate management to investigate internal affairs and take whatever corrective action is necessary to prevent harmful or illegal conduct. Without such a privilege, the threat of disclosure could cause management to avoid aggressive, self-regulating action, thereby increasing the chance that harmful, illegal or inefficient conduct could continue unbeknownst to top-level corporate management or the consumer of the company's service or product. However, the privilege has witnessed an erosion in its applicability.

Development

The first case recognizing the existence of the self-evaluation privilege was *Bredice v. Doctors Hospital, Inc.*[16] *Bredice* involved a request for the minutes of monthly hospital peer review committee meetings where the hospital staff discussed potential problems in patient care, typically in response to allegations of malpractice. The case established three generally recognized requirements for the self-evaluation privilege: (1) that the investigation be intended to be and remain confidential; (2) that the investigation be designed to evaluate the company's liability or exposure rather than to determine the facts underlying the potential liability or exposure; and (3) that the inquiry involve a matter of the public interest.[17]

The *Bredice* court found the peer review committee had endeavored to preserve the confidentiality of its reports, and held that "[c]onfidentiality is essential to effective functioning of these staff meetings; and these meetings are essential to the continued improvement and the care and treatment of patients. . . . To subject these discussions and deliberations to the discovery process, without a showing of exceptional necessity, would result in terminating such deliberations."[18] The court then found that the sole objective of the committee meetings was to find ways to improve patient care, not to conduct a fact-finding mission into the underlying malpractice action.

Finally, the court noted that the work of the committee served an important public interest—improving the quality of patient care. The *Bredice* court concluded that a breach in the confidentiality of the hospital's in-house investigative report would have a "chilling effect" on the candidness of those questioned.

The position taken in *Bredice* now commands the approval of a majority of jurisdictions with respect to hospital peer review and it is codified in many states. However, the analysis used in *Bredice* to protect hospital peer review reports has not been extended generally into other areas.

Civil Rights Litigation

One area that has seen extensive claims for the self-evaluation privilege is civil rights litigation. Using the rationale of the *Bredice* line of decisions, some courts have found that disclosure of confidential reports about a company's efforts to comply with EEOC requirements would discourage candid self-criticism and evaluation of affirmative action plans and, therefore, would be contrary to the important public policy implicit in EEOC requirements.[19]

Courts have diluted the effectiveness of the self-evaluation privilege in the civil rights context by allowing discovery of the statistical and objective data used by the internal investigative team. However, those courts consistently have protected subjective material, including evaluative statements or opinions and recommendations concerning future employment practices.[20] As with hospital peer review committees, some courts have found that a strong public interest is promoted by maintaining the confidentiality of such reports, since the primary purpose of Title VII is to foster candid reflection and internal evaluation of minority employment practices.[21] That purpose would be destroyed if employers feared disclosure of their comments.[22]

However, since 1990, the effectiveness of the self-evaluation privilege has been weakened in civil rights litigation in light of the Supreme Court's decision in *University of Pennsylvania v. EEOC*.[23] This case involved an Asian-American woman claiming that she had been denied tenure by the university because of her ethnicity and her gender.[24] During discovery she requested to see her tenure review file and the files of five male faculty members who were granted tenure.[25] The university resisted this request, claiming these documents were privileged as "confidential peer review materials" and should not be subject to discovery.[26] The Supreme Court held that the university was not entitled to this privilege and, furthermore, that the confidential peer review privilege did not exist.[27] The Court reasoned that Congress had addressed peer review materials in Title VII legislation, but had not extended this privilege to that material.[28] Therefore, the Supreme Court declined to create a new evidentiary privilege in the context of Title VII.[29]

Courts that have followed *University of Pennsylvania* have done so only in the context of Title VII discrimination litigation. In *Tharp v. Sivyer Steel Corp.*,[30] the court declined to recognize the self-evaluative privilege because: (1) the "chilling" effect disclosure will have on employers is not outweighed by the need potential plaintiffs have; (2) the number of equal employment forms that are filed will not diminish, because employers are already required to file the forms regardless of any danger of disclosure; (3) employers will not be less candid on equal employment reports because of the potential threat of disclosure; (4) Title VII's mission in eradicating employment discrimination would be diminished if this privilege were allowed, and (5) the Supreme Court found no historical, traditional, or textual reason to allow a "confidential peer review privilege" in Title VII litigation.[31] Other federal courts have lodged criticism of the self-evaluative privilege in Title VII actions. Ultimately, however, this difference rests on the idea that defendants may be hesitant to be critical of themselves, thus hampering a potentially positive exercise, in contrast to a plaintiff's need in observing the defendant-employer's documents. Therefore, until the Supreme Court definitively sets forth the applicability of the self-critical analysis privilege in other contexts, the federal courts will most likely remain in conflict.

Safety Evaluations

A clear mandate from early cases on the self-evaluation privilege is that the report sought to be protected must be truly self-evaluative. Corporations will not be allowed to protect the discovery of the objective facts that happen to be contained in a confidential report. The reason for the strict requirement of subjectivity is the very reason underlying the privilege: that is, to provide an incentive for corporate management to identify, discuss, evaluate, and correct problems by removing the fear that such proceedings will form the basis of a lawsuit against them. In this respect, the self-evaluation privilege is analogous to the familiar evidentiary rule precluding use of subsequent remedial measures to prove the negligence.[32]

An excellent example of a case employing the self-evaluation privilege as the exclusive reason for maintaining the confidentiality of an internal safety evaluation is *Wylie v. Mills*.[33] in this case, the company investigated an accident involving an employee using a company truck. The admitted purpose of the investigation was to consider the need for changes in company safety policies and procedures to avoid injuries to employees in the future.

The court concluded that the public interest in improving safety, combined with the probability that self-critical evaluations designed to discuss safety options would not take place unless the discussion would remain confidential, required that the individual's request for disclosure be denied. As the court notes:

> Valuable criticism can neither be sought nor obtained nor generated in the shadow of potential or even possible public disclosure. It is not realistic to expect candid expressions of opinion or suggestions as to future policy or procedures in an air of apprehension that such statements may well be used against one's colleague or employer in a subsequent litigated matter.
>
> The purpose of an investigation intended to seek criticism, opinion or suggestion and form the basis of criticism of then existing policy or procedure is self-improvement. The value of the investigation is questionable if the input is not reliable. It is clear that the reliability of the input in this situation varies inversely with the risk of disclosure of the input or resulting criticisms.
>
> * * * *
>
> Unless confidential safety investigations are encouraged, safety improvements in the workplace and in general will be stifled.[34]

The task is to structure the work of the product safety committee to provide the appropriate evidentiary basis and thereby increase the likelihood that the court will uphold the privilege against discovery of the committee's confidential reports and minutes.

However, the Ninth Circuit narrowed the privilege afforded safety committees in *Dowling v. American Hawaii Cruises, Inc.*[35] In *Dowling*, the plaintiff, an employee of the defendant, sued the cruise line for not repairing an oil leak on which he slipped and was injured.[36] During discovery, the plaintiff sought the minutes of the internal safety review committee.[37] The defendant resisted these requests and claimed that they were protected under the "self-critical analysis" privilege.[38] However, the court held that this privilege would not protect routine internal corporate reviews of matters related to safety concerns for three reasons.[39] First, the "chilling effect" will not occur because companies do not want a public reputation as unsafe. Second, such reviews are not always performed with the expectation that they will be confidential. Finally, the "fairness rationale offered to justify application of the privilege to documents that a party has been legally required to prepare [such as reviews mandated by the federal government] is inapplicable to voluntarily conducted safety reviews."[40]

Additionally, the *Dowling* court made the distinction between voluntary pre-accident and post-accident reports. The court reasoned that post-accident reports are protected by the privilege because important candid discussion, which may help prevent future accidents, would be stifled if there was a threat of disclosure.[41] Therefore, in the context of voluntary safety reviews, in contrast to those mandated by the government, pre-accident reports may not be afforded the privilege, while post-accident reports may.

Establishing the Self-Evaluative Privilege

The corporate client must establish the confidentiality of the meetings from start to finish. In this regard, reference to the corporate bylaws, resolutions or management directives which authorized the meetings and evaluations will be helpful. Also helpful would be references in minutes of board or committee meetings as to their confidentiality. The minutes and any reports, either preliminary or final, must be circulated only to a limited group of people, be marked confidential, and remain confidential.

In order to establish the self-evaluation privilege, the corporation must demonstrate that the purpose of the evaluation is not to conduct a general fact-finding mission, but to examine critically the company's products and, in particular, safety features in the context of improvement. The product evaluation process must be designed to invoke the subjective analysis of the committee as to the potential problems with the product, and what the company can do to correct those problems. Whatever factual data is included in the evaluation will be discoverable—the privilege protects only the subjective analysis of the product safety committee. In addition, a company should be aware that the Ninth Circuit will not protect even a self-critical evaluative review if it is prepared before an accident actually occurs. Unfortunately, the Circuit's reasoning, while supportive of plaintiffs' rights, will suppress candid review by a safety committee because a company will always be aware of potential litigation in the wake of accidents. However, the Ninth Circuit narrowly tailored its holding to pre-accident voluntary safety reviews, so a corporation should still follow the previous guidelines when undergoing other types of self-critical analysis.

Policy of the Self-Evaluative Privilege

The policy arguments that support the self-evaluation privilege in other areas are also present in the work of a product safety committee: the privilege prevents the product liability plaintiffs from taking advantage of the manufacturer's self-evaluation of its products. The manufacturer may have to provide the pieces of the puzzle, but it should not be forced to put together the plaintiff's case for him. The plaintiff should not get a free ride on the work of the manufacturer's product safety committee.

Further, the court should consider the impact of a rule denying the privilege: in-house investigations and product evaluations are increasingly common in today's corporate world. Frequently those investigations are not instigated by counsel. Sophistication in the business world has developed so that counsel are not required for each and every legal problem faced by a corporation. A rule allowing discovery of confidential in-house investigations conducted and reported in the absence of an attorney would inhibit the ability and desire of corporate management to solicit complete and candid cooperation from its employees.

The self-evaluation privilege is essentially identical to the work-product privilege except that instead of *anticipating* litigation, the company is trying to avoid it.[42] In *Hickman v. Taylor*,[43] the Supreme Court warned that "[w]ere such materials open to opposing counsel on mere demand, much of what is now put down in writing would remain unwritten. . . . Inefficiency, unfairness and sharp practices would inevitably develop . . . in the preparation of cases for trial. The effect on the legal profession would be demoralizing. And the interests of the clients and the cause of justice would be poorly served."[44] The same could be said if a corporation's critical self-evaluation were discoverable.

Application of the Privilege on Documents Prepared for the Government

Some courts also have concluded that critical self-evaluation reports and documents that are prepared pursuant to a government mandate are privileged from discovery. In *Bredice v. Doctors Hospital, Inc.*,[45] for example, privileged documents are prepared by a hospital committee established pursuant to the Joint Commission on Accreditation of Hospitals. Also, in *Banks v. Lockheed-Georgia Co.*,[46] an unemployment discrimination suit, privileged reports were prepared for the Department of Defense Contracts Compliance Office. Similarly, in *Shipes v. BIC Corp.*,[47] the court found that the self-critical analysis would protect from disclosure material prepared in accordance with the Consumer Product Safety Commission if the material is subjective and evaluative, rather than material otherwise available from original sources.[48]

However, preparation pursuant to a government agency's mandate will not necessarily protect documents. For example, in *Roberts v. Carrier Corp.*,[49] a products liability suit, the court permitted discovery of documents produced pursuant to an investigation by the Consumer Product Safety Commission. Although those documents were given to the Commission pursuant to governmental requirements, they were not produced solely for the Commission's investigation. Rather, the reports were prepared in the regular course of business and later turned over to the government. The court feared that a less restrictive interpretation of the government mandate requirement might result in the defendant's manipulation of privilege. For example, a defendant could protect all of its internal documents from discovery by claiming that they were turned over to a governmental agency. Again the court focused on the primary value in the privilege—ensuring that investigations are conducted in the best interest of the public, rather than in the best interests of the company.[50]

Recent Developments—A Discouraging Trend

Since the *Bredice* Court first recognized the critical self-evaluation privilege, some courts expanded the privilege to cases involving railroad accident investigations,[51] product safety assessments,[52] and general products liability.[53] While some state courts have recognized the critical self-evaluation privilege,[54] a majority of others have not.[55] In general, most courts have disapproved of use of the critical self-evaluation privilege, and that trend continues today.[56] Even those courts that apply that critical self-evaluation privilege do so narrowly.[57] Counsel should be wary in relying on the privilege.

Conclusion

Both the attorney-client privilege and the critical self-evaluation privilege will potentially protect discovery of a company's internal products safety evaluations. Both have advantages and drawbacks. The attorney-client privilege has the advantages of universal recognition and absolute protection, and the disadvantages of uncertain application to the corporate client. Similarly, the self-critical analysis privilege has recently become an uncertainty in the corporate setting, but more damaging is that its recognition has come under attack. The proceedings of product safety committees ought to remain protected if there has been appropriate preparation and attention to the elements of each privilege given the policies supporting them. However, it is unfortunate that many federal and state courts will not permit the self-critical analysis privilege to apply to many sensitive situations when it appears the privilege is most warranted.

Notes

1. Fed. R. Civ. P. 26(b)(1).
2. *Id.*
3. Radiant Burners, Inc. v. American Gas Ass'n, 320 F.2d 314 (7th Cir.), *cert. denied,* 375 U.S. 929 (1963).
4. Model Code of Evidence, R. 210 cmt. a.
5. *See* San Francisco v. Superior Court, 231 P.2d 26 (Cal. 1951).
6. Upjohn Co. v. United States, 449 U.S. 383 (1981).
7. *Id.* at 394-95.
8. Diversified Indus., Inc. v. Meredith, 572 F.2d 596 (8th Cir. 1978).
9. Upjohn *supra* note 6, at 390-91.
10. Cuno, Inc. v. Pall Corp., 121 F.R.D. 198, 202 (E.D.N.Y. 1988); *see also* Knogo Corp. v. United States, 213 U.S.P.Q. 936 (Ct. Cl. 1980).
11. United States v. United Shoe Machinery Corp., 89 F. Supp. 357 (D. Mass. 1950).
12. *Id.* at 359.
13. *See, e.g.,* Eutectic Corp. v. Metco, Inc., 61 F.R.D. 35 (E.D.N.Y. 1973).
14. Henson v. Wyeth Labs., Inc., 118 F.R.D. 584 (W.D. Va. 1987).
15. *Id.* at 587.
16. Bredice v. Doctors Hosp., Inc., 50 F.R.D. 249 (D.D.C. 1970), *aff'd* without opinion, 479 F.2d 920 (D.C. Cir. 1973).
17. *See also* Robert J. Bush, *Stimulating Corporate Self-Regulation—the Corporate Self-Evaluative Privilege: Paradigmatic Preferentialism or Pragmatic Panacea,* 87 Nw. U. L. Rev. 597, 605 (1993) ("[F]irst, the information sought to be protected must result from a critical self-analysis; second, the free flow of this type of information must advance some public interest; and third, absence of confidentiality must curtail the free flow of this type of information.").
18. Bredice v. Doctors Hosp. Inc., 50 F.R.D. at 250.
19. *See, e.g.,* Banks v. Lockheed-Georgia Co., 53 F.R.D. 283 (N.D. Ga. 1971).
20. *See, e.g.,* Webb v. Westinghouse Elec. Corp., 81 F.R.D. 431 (E.D. Pa. 1978); Gillman v. United States, 53 F.R.D. 316 (S.D.N.Y. 1971).
21. Keyes v. Lenoir Rhyne College, 552 F.2d 579 (4th Cir.), *cert. denied,* 434 U.S. 904 (1977).
22. Wylie v. Mills, 478 A.2d 1273 (N.J. Super. Ct. Law Div. 1984).
23. University of Pa. v. EEOC, 493 U.S. 182 (1990).
24. *Id.* at 185.
25. *Id.* at 186.
26. *Id.* at 188.
27. *Id.* at 189.
28. *Id.*
29. *Id.*
30. Tharp v. Sivyer Steel Corp., 149 F.R.D. 177 (S.D. Iowa 1993).

31. *Id.* at 182-84; *see* Aramburu. v. Boeing Co., 885 F. Supp. 1434, 1440-41 (D. Kan. 1995) (embracing a similar rationale as *Tharp* by not extending the self-critical analysis to peer review materials); *see also* Harding v. Dana Transport, Inc., 914 F. Supp. 1084, 1099-1101 (D.N.J. 1996) (rejecting application of self-critical analysis privilege to attorney's investigative report reviewing individual Title VII complaints rather than company's overall employment policies).

32. *See* Sheppard v. Consolidated Edison Co., 893 F. Supp. 6, 8 (E.D.N.Y. 1995) (allowing a defendant to maintain the self-critical analysis privilege on evaluative, not objective, material in a Title VII action).

33. Wylie v. Mills, 478 A.2d 1273 (N.J. Super. Ct. Law Div. 1984).

34. *Id.* at 1277-78.

35. Dowling v. American Haw. Cruises, Inc., 971 F.2d 423 (9th Cir. 1992).

36. *Id.* at 424.

37. *Id.*

38. *Id.*

39. *Id.* at 425.

40. *Id.* at 426.

41. *Id.* at 427; *see* FED. R. EVID. 407, advisory committee's note (encouraging people to take, or at least not discouraging them from taking, steps in furtherance of added safety).

42. *But see Dowling*, 971 F.2d at 427 (holding that voluntary pre-accident safety reviews are not protected by the privilege).

43. Hickman v. Taylor, 329 U.S. 495 (1947).

44. *Id.* at 511.

45. Bredice v. Doctors Hosp., Inc., 53 F.R.D. at 249-50.

46. Banks v. Lockheed-Georgia Co., 53 F.R.D. 283 (N.D. Ga. 1971).

47. Shipes v. BIC Corp., 154 F.R.D. 301 (M.D. Ga. 1994).

48. *Id.* at 307.

49. Roberts v. Carrier Corp., 107 F.R.D. 678 (N.D. Ind. 1985).

50. *See also* Scroggins v. Uniden Corp. of Am., 506 N.E.2d 83 (Ind. Ct. App. 1987) (stating that the self-critical analysis privilege does not protect any documents mandated by the government, because the state legislature has not recognized such a privilege); Lamitie v. Emerson Elec. Co., 535 N.Y.S.2d 650 (N.Y. 1988) (holding that the self-critical analysis does not exist in New York to protect against disclosure of documents prepared for the Consumer Product Safety Commission).

51. Granger v. Nat'l R.R. Corp., 116 F.R.D. 507 (E.D. Pa. 1987).

52. Lloyd v. Cessna Aircraft Co., 74 F.R.D. 518 (E.D. Tenn. 1977).

53. Bradley v. Melroe Co., 141 F.R.D. 1 (D.D.C. 1991).

54. Kansas Gas & Elec. v. Eye, 789 P.2d 1161 (Kan. 1990) (discussing Berst v. Chapman, 653 P.2d 107 (Kan. 1982), in which the Kansas Supreme Court recognized the self-critical analysis privilege); Anderson v. Hahnemann Med. Coll., 1985 WL 47218 (Pa. Commw. Ct.).

55. Harris-Lewis v. Mudge, 1999 WL 98589 (Mass. Super. 1999); Grimes v. DSC Comm. Corp., 724 A.2d 561 (Del. Ch. 1998); Payton v. New Jersey Turnpike Auth., 691 A.2d 321 (N.J. 1997) (self-critical analysis does not exist in common law but court may consider it in balancing need for discovery against prejudice to party resisting it); Cloud v. Superior Court (Litton Indus. Inc.), 58 Cal. Rptr. 2d 365 (Cal. App. 1996) (self-critical analysis privilege not in state evidence code, thus does not exist in California); Office of Consumer Council v. Dep't of Pub. Util. Control, 665 A.2d 921 (Conn. Super. 1994); Combined Communications Corp. v. Pub. Serv. Co. of Colorado, 865 P.2d 893 (Colo. App. 1993) (self-critical analysis privilege does not exist in Colorado); Univ. of Ky. v. Courier-Journal & Louisville Times Co., 830 S.W.2d 373 (Ky. 1992); Southern Bell Tel. & Tel. Co. v. Beard, 597 So. 2d 873 (Fla. App. 1992) (all privileges in Florida are statutory, thus no common law privilege for self-critical analysis exists); Limite v. Emerson Electric Co.-White Rodgers Division, 535 N.Y.S. 2d 650 (App. Div. 3d Dep't 1988), *leave to appeal dismissed*, 74 N.Y.2d 650

(1989) ("critical self analysis privilege" inapplicable inasmuch as no New York court has applied such a privilege); Scroggins v. Uniden Corp. of America, 506 N.E.2d 83 (Ind. App. 1987) (Indiana courts recognize only statutory privileges).

56.   Arthur Ganious v. Apache Clearwater Operations, Inc., et al., 2004 U.S. Dist. LEXIS 2043 (E.D. La. 2004) (refusing to apply critical self-evaluation privilege in oil rig accident); Lawson v. Fisher-Price, Inc., 191 F.R.D. 381 (D. Vt. 1999) (applying Vermont law and refusing to apply the critical self-evaluation privilege where the records in question are generated and retained by businesses in compliance with government regulation); Franzon v. Massena Memorial Hospital, 189 F.R.D. 220 (N.D.N.Y. 1999) (refusing to apply critical self-evaluation privilege to medical review boards, files and records); *In re* July 5, 1999 Explosion at Kaiser Aluminum & Chemical Co., 1999 U.S. Dist. LEXIS 14107 (E.D. La. 1999), *cert. denied sub nom*, 532 U.S. 919 (2001) (refusing to apply the critical self-evaluation privilege to documents related to an explosion at a chemical plant); Limite v. Emerson Electric Co.-White Rodgers Division, 535 N.Y.S.2d 650 (1988) (refusing to apply critical self-evaluation privilege to documents related to propane gas explosion allegedly caused by defective water heater); Lloyd v. Cessna Aircraft Co., 74 F.R.D. 518 (E.D. Tenn. 1977) (refusing to apply critical self-evaluation privilege to documents regarding the manufacture of a private aircraft).

57.   Granger v. National Railroad Passenger Corp., 116 F.R.D. 507 (E.D. Pa. 1987) (applying the critical self-evaluation privilege to certain documents because production of those documents would "tend to hamper honest, candid self-evaluation geared towards the prevention of future accidents," but refusing to apply the privilege to other documents related to the cause of the accident because such documents were at the heart of plaintiff's action).

CHAPTER 7

Communications Between Attorneys and Putative Class Members

ALLAN KANNER
TIBOR NAGY

Introduction

The traditional view of disputes in our legal system is that they are discrete events. A stockbroker defrauded an investor. A phone company breached its contract with a customer. A boss fired a worker. The resulting lawsuit in any of these cases was traditionally a one-on-one fight, what Professor Chayes has referred to as the "bipolar mode of litigation."[1] Today we might look for patterns or group wrongs in those same events. For example, in the boss firing a worker hypothetical, we may look, in appropriate circumstances, for patterns of discrimination or harassment.

Group litigation, in particular the use of class actions, has emerged as a superior alternative to the traditional bipolar suit in many areas of the law. This changing conception about the nature and role of litigation in addressing root causes, moreover, has materially altered our view of how an attorney can and should communicate with potential clients. The civil rights and labor movements in particular taught us that it is not only proper but often desirable for an informed lawyer to share information with lay people, including potential clients, about their rights. This recognition of the need for the targeted dissemination of information has moved into other substantive areas in which systemic wrongs occur, and traditional restraints on lawyer advertising and solicitation have accordingly weakened.

In this chapter we examine the modern case law governing attorney contact with potential clients in the class action setting. Part II examines the rules restricting communications between lawyers and non-clients generally, in particular the rules against solicitation and contact with represented parties, and discusses how these rules apply in the class action setting. The traditional model of no-comment rules is examined, as

105

is the modern framework that replaced that model with the Supreme Court's decision in *Gulf Oil Co. v. Bernard*.[2] In Part III we examine communications between class counsel and putative class members in the three stages of a class action: (1) pre-certification; (2) post-certification but before the end of the opt-out period; and (3) post-certification, post-opt-out period. Particular attention is given to when such communications may be prohibited and when courts will conclude that an attorney-client relationship exists between class counsel and putative class members. Part IV examines how the involvement of an organization that putative class members belong to, for example a labor union, affects the analyses discussed in Part III. Finally, Part V discusses communications with putative class members in opt-*in* class actions, such as cases brought under the Fair Labor Standards Act.[3]

Communications with Non-Clients Generally

Rules Against Solicitation, Contact with Represented Parties, and Misleading Statements

When dealing with non-clients, lawyers must observe the various rules that govern communications with potential clients and opposing parties. The most important rules with respect to potential clients are states' ethical rules against solicitation. Most states have rules that prohibit in-person and direct telephone solicitation, as well as restrictions on solicitation and advertisements by mail. The goal of such rules is to avoid exploitation of potential clients, especially those in vulnerable situations, and to prevent activities that would undermine the public view of the profession. Model Rule 7.3, which is representative of the rules actually adopted in most jurisdictions, states the following:

> (a) A lawyer shall not by in-person, live telephone or real-time electronic contact solicit professional employment from a prospective client when a significant motive for the lawyer's doing so is the lawyer's pecuniary gain, unless the person contacted: (1) is a lawyer; or (2) has a family, close personal, or prior professional relationship with the lawyer. (b) A lawyer shall not solicit professional employment from a prospective client by written, recorded or electronic communication or by in-person, telephone or real-time electronic contact even when not otherwise prohibited by paragraph (a), if: (1) the prospective client has made known to the lawyer a desire not to be solicited by the lawyer; or (2) the solicitation involves coercion, duress or harassment.[4]

Although there is undoubtedly a right to communicate with non-clients, rules such as these must be strictly followed. That said, abuses likely occur at country clubs and in hospitals every day.

With respect to communications with opposing parties, the most important rules are those barring contacts with parties represented by counsel. Model Rule 4.2 is followed in most jurisdictions:

> In representing a client, a lawyer shall not communicate about the subject of the representation with a person the lawyer knows to be represented by

another lawyer in the matter, unless the lawyer has the consent of the other lawyer or is authorized to do so by law or a court order.[5]

The rule is meant to prevent undue influence by lawyers on opposing parties.[6] When the opposing party is a corporation, the rule generally applies to management and to any other employees who may have privileged information. In the corporate context, the rule may also apply to former employees.[7]

Both solicitation rules and rules against contact with represented parties of course apply to class actions. In the class action context, however, these rules can be more difficult to interpret and apply, for at least two major reasons. First, many class actions are about matters in the public interest and so raise First Amendment issues. Second, courts have been somewhat sloppy in describing the status of putative class actions prior to their actual certification. Thus, in the early stages of a class action, for example, the precise status of putative class members is often unclear. During the precertification and opt-out periods, it can be difficult to determine whether putative class members are actual or potential clients, or whether they are represented parties or non-parties. Plaintiff's counsel, wanting to disseminate information or conduct discovery related to certification, may risk charges of solicitation, especially with respect to class members who have retained other counsel. Defense counsel, wanting to settle claims or investigate the scope of liability, may risk violating Model Rule 4.2. Furthermore, because class actions have a public law aspect to them and because the stakes involved are often very high, courts have been particularly sensitive to the potential for misleading and self-serving communications by both plaintiffs' and defense counsel. Plaintiff's counsel, for example, might attempt to "drum up" litigation, or convey a misleading sense of urgency about joining a class.[8] Defense counsel, on the other hand, might mislead class members into opting out, or might otherwise misrepresent class members' rights.[9]

The Traditional Model: No-Comment Local Rules

To deal with the problem of communications with putative class members, many courts, following the first edition of the *Manual for Complex Litigation*, initially adopted a prophylactic approach in which the district court adopted a "no-comment" local rule or individual judges issued "gag orders."[10] Many federal district courts, for example, had local rules that stated something like the following:

> In every case sought to be maintained by any party as a class action, all parties thereto and their counsel are hereby forbidden, directly or indirectly, orally or in writing, to communicate concerning such actions with any potential or actual class member, not a formal party to the case, without approval by the Court.[11]

The same result, in jurisdictions that did not have a no-comment local rule, was often achieved by individual judges' use of blanket protective orders.[12]

No-comment rules have numerous flaws. As an initial matter, they are overly broad prior restraints on speech that almost certainly violate attorneys' First Amendment rights.[13] In addition, the rules often operate to harm the interests of putative class members, preventing them from obtaining much-needed legal advice and hindering the efficient operation of group litigation. In the late 1970s, as class actions became increasingly common, courts began to recognize the problems posed by no-comment rules.[14] In 1981, in *Gulf Oil Co. v. Bernard*,[15] the Supreme Court struck down the use of such rules in the federal courts.

In April 1976 Gulf Oil Company and the Equal Employment Opportunity Commission (EEOC) entered into a conciliation agreement involving alleged discrimination against black and female employees at the company's Port Arthur refinery. Gulf agreed to cease various allegedly discriminatory practices, to undertake an affirmative action program covering hiring and promotion, and to offer back pay to alleged victims of discrimination based on a set formula. Gulf began to send notices to the 643 employees eligible for back pay, stating the exact amount available to each person in return for execution within 30 days of a full release of all discrimination claims dating from the relevant time period.

Shortly thereafter, a class action was filed on behalf of all current and former African-American employees, alleging racial discrimination in employment and seeking injunctive, declaratory, and monetary relief. Gulf promptly filed a motion for an order limiting communications by parties and their counsel with potential class members. An accompanying brief described the EEOC conciliation agreement, asserting that 452 of the 643 employees entitled to back pay under that agreement had signed releases and been paid by the time the class action was filed. Furthermore, Gulf claimed that one of the attorneys for the class had recently attended a meeting of 75 class members, where he had discussed the case and recommended that the employees not sign the releases sent under the conciliation agreement. The attorney allegedly advised employees to return checks they already had received, since they could receive at least double the amounts involved through the class action. The district court, without making any findings of fact, entered a temporary order prohibiting all communications concerning the case from parties or their counsel to potential or actual class members. The court later issued a modified order that imposed a complete ban on all communications concerning the class action between parties or their counsel and any actual or potential class member who was not a formal party, without the court's prior approval. The modified order exempted communications from Gulf describing the EEOC conciliation agreement and making settlement offers to class members. On appeal from a subsequent final order, respondents argued that the limitations on communications imposed by the district court were beyond the power granted the court in Federal Rule of Civil Procedure 23(d) and were unconstitutional under the First Amendment. A divided panel of the Fifth Circuit affirmed the district court, but on rehearing en banc that decision was reversed, and the district court order was held to be an unconstitutional prior restraint on expression.[16]

The Supreme Court affirmed, though limited its decision to a holding that the district court abused its discretion under Rule 23(d). The Court agreed that "[b]ecause of the potential for abuse, a district court has both the duty and the broad authority to exercise control over a class action and to enter appropriate orders governing the conduct of counsel and parties."[17] Nevertheless, district courts' discretion is "not unlimited." The Court, in a passage that is particularly helpful for determining the scope of district courts' authority to limit communications between class counsel and putative class members, stated the following:

> The order interfered with their efforts to inform potential class members of the existence of this lawsuit, and may have been particularly injurious—not only to respondents but to the class as a whole—because the employees at that time were being pressed to decide whether to accept a backpay offer from Gulf that required them to sign a full release of all liability for discriminatory acts. In addition, the order made it more difficult for respondents, as the class representatives, to obtain information about the merits of the case from the persons they sought to represent.
>
> Because of these potential problems, an order limiting communications between parties and potential class members should be based on a clear record and specific findings that reflect a weighing of the need for a limitation and the potential interference with the rights of the parties. Only such a determination can ensure that the court is furthering, rather than hindering, the policies embodied in the Federal Rules of Civil Procedure, especially Rule 23. In addition, such a weighing—identifying the potential abuses being addressed—should result in a carefully drawn order that limits speech as little as possible, consistent with the rights of the parties under the circumstances.[18]

The Court therefore held that blanket prohibitions on communications with potential class members exceeded district courts' authority under Rule 23. Both unfounded protective orders, like the one in *Gulf Oil*, and "no-comment" local rules, like those found in many districts at the time, could no longer be used to manage communications with class members. Notably, the Court also identified particular communications between class counsel and putative class members that *were* appropriate in the pre-certification setting: informing potential class members of the existence of the lawsuit; advising them to obtain legal advice before signing releases with the defendant; and generally "obtain[ing] information about the merits of the case."[19] The Court thus recognized the fundamental importance of pre-certification communications with putative class members.

The Modern Model: Case Management

Blanket restraints on communications with putative class members are therefore no longer tolerated by most federal courts.[20] In the federal system, *Gulf Oil* makes clear that such restraints violate Rule 23. In state courts, such restraints not only violate public policy and the efficient administration of group litigation, but are also probably unconstitutional.[21]

The void left by the erosion of no-comment rules, however, has not been filled by a new, coherent model of how courts should govern communications with putative class members. Instead, courts and leading authorities continue to disagree about what types of communications are appropriate in different circumstances.[22] In a sense this, and not some particular set of rules, is what the *Gulf Oil* court envisioned: decisions to restrict communications between attorneys and putative class members are supposed to be fact-specific, case-by-case determinations. Although more flexible, this new model is often hard to navigate, and a consideration of what courts typically do in generally applicable situations is therefore useful.

Communications with Putative Class Members

Three situations applicable to all class actions are the stages of the certification process: (1) pre-certification; (2) the opt-out period (i.e., post-certification but before the end of the opt-out period); and (3) post-certification and post-opt-out period. The extent to which a party may communicate directly with potential class members is determined, in large part, by which stage the class action has reached. We consider each stage in turn.

Pre-certification

In a traditional lawsuit, when an attorney files a complaint on a client's behalf, the existence of an attorney-client relationship is unquestioned. In a class action, the same is true of class counsel and the class representatives. There is, however, no such clarity with respect to the relationship between class counsel and unnamed class members. The majority view in the federal courts is that an attorney-client relationship does not exist between class counsel and putative class members until the district court certifies the class.[23] In state courts the predominant view is less clear, with one authority suggesting that an attorney-client relationship is created "as of the time the complaint is filed with the court,"[24] while many states' courts seems to disagree.[25] Whatever court one is in, it is clear that even if no formal attorney-client relationship exists between class counsel and putative class members, unnamed members of the class are *not* mere third parties to the litigation. Instead, they have a unique status in the case that warrants careful treatment by plaintiffs' and defense counsel alike. The *Manual for Complex Litigation*, for example, states that "there is at least an incipient fiduciary relationship between class counsel and the class he or she is seeking to represent."[26] Newberg opines that defense counsel can communicate with putative class members "only in the ordinary course of business" and only if "they do not infringe on what some courts have characterized as the *constructive attorney-client relationship* that exists between counsel for class representatives and the members of the class."[27] The key variable is likely to be the nature and purpose of the subject communication.

As a general rule, then, both plaintiffs' and defense counsel are free to communicate with putative class members prior to certification, but these communications are limited. Class counsel are typically free to provide additional information, respond to inquiries, and seek information needed to represent the class.[28] Defense counsel are typically free to make communications in the ordinary course of business and to discuss settlement offers with individual class members, though they must take care not to give false or misleading information or attempt to influence class members in making their decision whether to remain in the class.[29] As the cases discussed below illustrate, however, because of the contentiousness of class action litigation—as well as the fact that a number of courts still have no-comment local rules—pre-certification communications with putative class members often end up being governed by a court order.

Jackson v. Motel 6 Multipurpose, Inc. and Abdallah v. Coca-Cola Company
In *Jackson v. Motel 6 Multipurpose, Inc.,* the Eleventh Circuit granted a writ of mandamus vacating a district court's order allowing certain communications between plaintiffs' counsel and putative class members.[30] Two class actions, later consolidated, had been filed against Motel 6, alleging racial discrimination against employees and customers. Because the district court had a no-comment local rule,[31] plaintiffs' counsel moved for an order allowing relief from the rule, and specifically requesting that they be allowed to do the following:

1. Establish a 1-800 number to which potential class members may call;
2. Publish notices of the ongoing litigation in publications nationwide and solicit information about potential class members and their alleged experiences with discrimination at Motel 6 motels;
3. Respond to requests for information from those who respond to the advertisements or call the 1-800 number;
4. Distribute mass mailings to Motel 6 employees soliciting information regarding the plaintiffs' allegations of discrimination at Motel 6 motels; and
5. Further communicate ex parte with any "persons who may have knowledge of" the alleged discrimination, except for current Motel 6 management or supervisory employees.[32]

The district court, which had not yet ruled on the motions for class certification, granted the order.

By the time Motel 6's second petition for mandamus was heard, the district court had certified one of the classes, the *Jackson* class, and referred the certification decision of the other class, the *Petaccia* class, to the magistrate. The Eleventh Circuit held that the *Jackson* class was erroneously certified and concluded that "the communications order was an abuse of discretion from the beginning." In a less than convincing opinion, the court focused on the fact that the district court entered the communications order long before it ruled on certification and on the danger to Motel 6's reputation in concluding that the order was an abuse of discretion:

> The communications order was entered months prior to any decision regarding whether either of the two proposed classes would in fact be certified. While we cannot say that orders authorizing communication with potential class members may never precede class certification, district courts must strive to avoid authorizing injurious class communications that might later prove unnecessary. An order authorizing class communications prior to class certification is likely to be an abuse of discretion when (1) the communication authorized by the order is widespread and clearly injurious and (2) a certification decision is not imminent or it is unlikely that a class will in fact be certified. In such circumstances, the danger of abuse that always attends class communications—the possibility that plaintiffs might use widespread publication of their claims, disguised as class communications, to coerce defendants into settlement—is not outweighed by any need for immediate communications.

The advertisements and mass mailings allowed by the order at issue in the instant petition are nationwide in scope and are surely causing serious and irreparable harm to Motel 6's reputation and to its relationship with its employees. . . . Moreover, the order was entered almost six months prior to the court's decision to certify the *Jackson* class and to refer the *Petaccia* plaintiffs' motion for class certification to a magistrate judge.[33]

The court did make an exception for the mass mailings:

We note, however, that insofar as the district court's February 21 order authorizes the *Petaccia* plaintiffs to conduct mass mailings to Motel 6 employees, it authorizes inquiries and communications that would be allowable as a normal discovery matter, whether the *Petaccia* class is certified or not.[34]

The *Motel 6* decision is likely wrongly decided for two reasons. First, and most importantly, it adopts precisely the posture of ruling on communications orders struck down in *Gulf Oil*: communications between class counsel and putative class members were *presumed* inappropriate unless class counsel could make a showing otherwise. Indeed, the district court's local rule, the lawfulness of which the Eleventh Circuit did not directly address, said exactly that.[35] *Gulf Oil*, however, makes clear that communications between class counsel and putative class members, at least with respect to district courts' authority to interfere with such communications under Rule 23(d), are presumptively valid. District courts should not *authorize* communications prior to certification but rather, based on specific facts in the record, should only *limit* them, and should do that in as narrowly tailored a manner as possible.

Second, it is error to assume, as the Eleventh Circuit clearly did, that an "order authorizing class communications prior to class certification is likely to be an abuse of discretion when . . . a certification decision is not imminent or it is unlikely that a class will in fact be certified."[36] *Gulf Oil* makes clear that the imminence of a district court's decision on certification is not nearly as significant as the *Motel 6* court suggests. Not only had the district court in *Gulf Oil not* ruled on certification, it had initially dismissed the plaintiffs' complaint as untimely.[37] The Supreme Court, in an opinion that was explicitly meant to "determine the scope of a district court's authority to limit communications from named plaintiffs and their counsel to prospective class members,"[38] said *nothing* about the imminence of a decision on certification. Moreover, the Court's conclusion that the no-comment order in the *Gulf Oil* case was improper was specifically based on reasons that make clear that the imminence of a decision on certification is irrelevant:

The order interfered with their efforts to inform potential class members of the existence of this lawsuit, and may have been particularly injurious— not only to respondents but to the class as a whole—because the employees at that time were being pressed to decide whether to accept a backpay offer from Gulf that required them to sign a full release of all liability for discriminatory acts. In addition, the order made it more difficult for respondents, as the class representatives, to obtain information about the merits of the case from the persons they sought to represent.[39]

Both informing putative class members of the existence of a class action and obtaining information about the merits of the case from them—communications that are indisputably legitimate under *Gulf Oil*—frequently and often necessarily occur long before the district courts' decision on certification.

Despite its flaws, class counsel must be familiar with *Motel 6* in order to meet defense counsel's likely reliance on it. In *Abdallah v. Coca-Cola Co.*,[40] a widely publicized case filed shortly after *Motel 6*, for example, defendants relied centrally on *Motel 6* in seeking an order to limit class counsel's contact with putative class members. A racial discrimination class action was filed on behalf of employees of Coca-Cola, and, again because of a no-comment local rule in the district court, plaintiffs' counsel moved for an order allowing certain communications. Relying specifically on *Motel 6* and the fact that "the certification decision will not be made at any time in the near future," the district court limited class counsel's ability to communicate with putative class members to responding to unsolicited inquiries. According to the court, "[s]uch communications, when initiated by potential class members and not Plaintiffs' counsel, are neither widespread nor injurious." Because of the *Motel 6* "widespread and injurious" standard, however, the court ordered plaintiffs' counsel to remove the class action complaint from a website on which it had been posted subsequent to the filing of the suit.[41]

Notably, the *Abdallah* court made two rulings that were not based on *Motel 6*. Because of the "inherent danger" that communications by an employer could "deter potential class members from participating in the suit," the court prohibited Coca-Cola "from discussing this lawsuit directly with potential class members, except to the extent it needs to speak with managerial employees to investigate the acts, omissions, and statements they committed that may expose Coca-Cola to liability in this action."[42] Furthermore, the court denied Coca-Cola's request that plaintiffs' counsel be prohibited from contacting employees "deemed to be represented by the Company's counsel," which the company claimed included: (1) supervisory and managerial employees; (2) any employees whose acts or admissions could be attributed to Coca-Cola; (3) employees involved in defending the action; and (4) those likely to have privileged information. Though it recognized that the state's ethical rules prohibited ex parte contacts with opposing parties, the court concluded that "upper-level employees of CocaCola have a right to bring a discrimination claim against their employer. Therefore, to the extent that these employees wish to pursue employment claims against CocaCola, they may communicate freely with Plaintiffs and their counsel."[43]

The *Abdallah* court's decision to allow employees "deemed to be represented by the Company's counsel" to contact and communicate freely with class plaintiffs and their counsel is undoubtedly correct under the Model Rules. There is no question, in short, that employees have a right to sue their employer, and that in doing so they can retain and communicate with their own counsel. It is worth noting, however, that courts sometimes rely on the principle that no attorney-client relationship exists between class counsel and putative class members until a class is certified to erroneously conclude that class counsel should not be allowed to engage in pre-certification, ex parte communications with managerial employees who are potential class members, even if the communication relates solely to the development of the class action and does not implicate the corporation's privileged information. This was precisely the court's ruling in *Hammond v. City of Junction City*,[44] in which the district court held that class counsel's contact with the defendant's Director of Human Relations was not only not privileged, since it occurred before certification and therefore before there was an attorney-client relationship, but also violated the ethical prohibition against contacting a party represented by counsel. To avoid such a restraint on pre-certification communications with putative class members, counsel should emphasize that (1) *Gulf Oil* makes clear that pre-certification contacts with putative class members are perfectly appropriate and are often essential to the development of a class action,[45] and (2) should directly address any concerns regarding privileged information that corporate employees may have and take specific precautions with respect to such information during any ex parte contacts.[46]

The Opt-Out Period

Once a class has been certified, most courts hold that the rules governing communications apply as though each class member is a client of class counsel.[47] Under those rules, in particular Model Rule 4.2, defendants and their counsel ordinarily may communicate with class members or putative class members only through class counsel for plaintiffs.[48] This is so even in opt-out class actions, where many putative class members may elect to opt-out before the end of the opt-out period.[49] Thus attorneys other than class counsel, in particular defense counsel and objectors, must take care not to engage in inappropriate communications with the class.

The classic case concerning inappropriate communications by defense counsel at this stage of a class action is *Kleiner v. First National Bank of Atlanta*.[50] *Kleiner* involved what Judge Vance called "a ground-breaking class action against the First National Bank of Atlanta . . . sounding in fraud, RICO and breach of contract."[51] Several weeks after the trial judge certified the class under Rule 23(b)(3), but before the end of the opt-out period, defense counsel sought to obtain discovery from a number of putative class members. Class counsel moved for a protective order, arguing that discovery and unilateral contacts by the bank before the close of the exclusion period would intimidate potential class members and discourage them from participating in the suit. The court granted the order prohibiting the bank's requested discovery, but specifically took the broader question of unsupervised contacts between the bank and class members under advisement pending further briefing.

Several weeks later the bank "seized upon the idea of soliciting class exclusion requests as a means to reducing its potential liability and quelling the adverse publicity the lawsuit had spawned."[52] Furthermore, defense counsel decided that phone calls would be better than letters, given the danger that people would disregard letters as more "junk mail." Because the putative class consisted of bank customers, the bank had access to class members' contact information, and indeed its loan officers had developed relationships with many of the potential plaintiffs. The bank officers were told to "do the best selling job they had ever done," and the telephone campaign soliciting opt-outs took place, not coincidentally, during the district judge's two-week vacation. The campaign proved very successful: the bank's officers obtained opt-out commitments from 2,800 of the 3,000 putative class members contacted, representing a sum total of $694,997,218 in past or present loans. The district judge, however, was not pleased. Upon returning from her vacation, she held a hearing on the matter and declared the solicitation scheme illegal under Model Rule 4.2 and the district court's local rule banning solicitation of opt-outs. Defense counsel was held to have knowingly participated in the scheme and to have given legal advice in bad faith. He was sanctioned $50,000; was ordered to pay, along with his firm and the bank, all legal fees associated with the hearing and costs for curative notice; and was disqualified from further representation in the case. As a final measure, the district court ruled that the exclusion requests would be voidable following entry of judgment.

The Fifth Circuit affirmed the district court's ruling that the solicitation scheme violated Model Rule 4.2, and further held that the scheme violated the court's protective order.[53] Thus, even though the opt-out period had not ended and many of the bank's customers may very well have elected to opt-out, the court of appeals confirmed that class counsel and the putative class members should be treated as though they had an attorney-client relationship. In a cogent discussion of the proper role of trial judges in policing communications with putative class members, Judge Vance went on to discuss the authority of district courts to ban opt-out solicitations under Rule 23. Addressing solicitation requests generally, the court stated:

> When confronted with claims pressed by a plaintiff class, it is obviously in defendants' interest to diminish the size of the class and thus the range of potential liability by soliciting exclusion requests. Such conduct reduces the effectiveness of the 23(b)(3) class action for no reason except to undermine the purposes of the rule. A unilateral communications scheme, moreover, is rife with potential for coercion. If the class and the class opponent are involved in an ongoing business relationship, communications from the class opponent to the class may be coercive. . . . Unsupervised, unilateral communications with the plaintiff class sabotage the goal of informed consent by urging exclusion on the basis of a one-sided presentation of the facts, without opportunity for rebuttal. The damage from misstatements could well be irreparable.[54]

With respect to the specific solicitation scheme in *Kleiner*, the court stated:

> In view of the tension between the preference for class adjudication and the individual autonomy afforded by exclusion, it is critical that the class receive accurate and impartial information regarding the status, purposes and effects of the class action. . . . In this case, the carefully constructed edifice of check and countercheck, notice and reply, was obliterated when the telephones were lifted from their cradles. The Bank's actions obstructed the district court in the discharge of its duty to "protect both the absent class and the integrity of the judicial process by monitoring the actions before it." The Bank's subterfuge and subversion constituted an intolerable affront to the authority of the district court to police class member

contacts. Accordingly, we hold that the trial court had ample discretion under Rules 23(b)(3) and 23(d) to prohibit the Bank's overtures.[55]

The *Kleiner* court went beyond its holding that an attorney-client relationship exists between class counsel and putative class members after certification and emphasized that "it is critical that the class receive accurate and impartial information." Although mindful of *Gulf Oil*, *Kleiner* firmly establishes "the authority of the district court to police class member contacts" when misleading information or other improper influence on putative class members is threatened.

As *Kleiner* illustrated, class counsel and putative class members are generally held to have an attorney-client relationship during the opt-out period, despite the fact that a number of potential class members may elect to opt-out. Typically, then, inappropriate communications with putative class members are not likely to come from class counsel during the opt-out period—though they may, as in *Kleiner*, come from defense counsel. One source of potential communications problems, however, is objectors. After a class has been certified and, as is typically the case, a settlement has been proposed, objecting counsel have a strong incentive to encourage putative class members to opt-out. A leading case illustrating this problem is *Georgine v. Amchem Products, Inc.*[56]

In *Georgine*, a massive class of asbestos-exposure victims had been certified by the district court.[57] During the opt-out period, dozens of objectors began a campaign of soliciting opt-outs, primarily through the mass-mailing of letters to putative class members. These letters reached over 650,000 potential class members, 236,323 of whom ultimately elected to opt-out of the class settlement. Class counsel and the defendants (the "settling parties") in the case filed a joint motion requesting that the court remedy the adverse effects of the opt-out solicitation campaign. In particular, the settling parties sought: (1) the negation of all exclusion requests; (2) the creation of a second notice and opt-out period for class members who timely requested exclusion from the class; and (3) the issuance of an injunction requiring that all communications by asbestos plaintiffs' attorneys that concern the class action or settlement bear a "Disclosure Statement."[58]

The court began its analysis by discussing the harm caused by misleading communications to putative class members, and by examining the allegedly misleading communications sent by the objectors:

> Misleading communications to class members concerning litigation pose a serious threat to the fairness of the litigation process, the adequacy of representation and the administration of justice generally. . . . Here, I find that unilateral communications with class members by various attorneys were misleading and made it unlikely that class members, who received these communications or were informed of their contents, made an informed choice to exclude themselves from the class. . . . Many of the letters and advertisements were misleading because they (1) made statements regarding the terms of the settlement that created false impressions about the effect of the settlement on the recipient, e.g., the false statement that

opting out is the only way to secure future compensation; asbestos companies can back out of the settlement at any time; and (2) did not reveal the
personal interests of the drafters of the letters and advertisements. Moreover, because these communications contained only one-sided attacks on
the terms of the settlement without any discussion of the settlement benefits or the existence of the Court-approved notice materials, the effect of
the misleading aspects of the communications was compounded.[59]

The court then discussed several of the most misleading of the objectors' letters.
The single most misleading letter, according to the court, was a mailing sent by the
law firm of Baron & Budd. This letter stated that "[t]he only way to protect your rights
to future compensation is to sign the enclosed 'opt out' form immediately" and that
"[i]f you do not send in this form immediately, YOU WILL LOSE VALUABLE RIGHTS
IN THE EVENT YOU DEVELOP AN ASBESTOS-RELATED DISEASE IN THE
FUTURE."[60] Although it was true that some of the recipients of the letter might not
have qualified for compensation under the terms of the settlement, the court concluded that "the letter creates the impression to all readers, both those who will be
eligible to receive compensation in the future and those who will not, that the only
way to obtain future compensation is to sign the enclosed opt-out form. That simply is
incorrect."[61] Furthermore, the court criticized the letter for failing to explain any of the
benefits of the settlement and for "encourag[ing] recipients to make decisions to opt
out of the class without the benefit of the Court-approved notice materials."[62] Finally,
the court observed that "the most disturbing aspect of the letter is that it fails to mention that Baron & Budd represents class members who are objecting to the settlement
and, therefore, are not neutral observers." After examining numerous similar communications, the court granted the settling parties' request for the negation of all exclusion requests and the creation of a second notice and opt-out period.

Georgine illustrates a principled, well-reasoned application of *Gulf Oil*. The court
engaged in a thorough review of the record, and decided upon a remedy specifically
tailored to remedy the identified harm caused by the misleading communications.
Although recognizing the inherent bias on the part of objectors, the court did not
attempt to impose any blanket restriction on their communication with putative class
members. Indeed, the court seemed legitimately open to the use of forthright communications by objectors: "this Court encourages the free flow of ideas relating to the
advantages and disadvantages of the settlement, in order to evaluate the relative merits of conflicting arguments."[63] It is worth noting that of all the misleading characteristics of the contested letters the one that bothered the court the most was the failure of
the objectors to identify their biases: "In the instant case, because none of the communications at issue revealed to the recipient that the drafter had a financial motive to
obtain additional optouts, the recipient was not on notice to closely scrutinize the
substance of the communications."[64] While objections to proposed settlements are
sometimes in the best interests of the class, objectors have no legitimate reason to hide
their financial interest in soliciting class members' opt-outs. Courts can and most likely
will use their "broad authority to exercise control over a class action" to remedy the
effects of any misleading communications.

Post-Certification, Post-Opt-Out Period

Once a class has been certified and the opt-out period has closed, it is clear that an attorney-client relationship exists between class counsel and all class members who have not opted out.[65] Thus, subject to the requirement of court approval for settlement or dismissal of the suit, class counsel can freely communicate with class members. Moreover, in keeping with the rule against communications with represented parties, defense counsel are barred from communicating with class members, other than through class counsel.

The Role of Class Members' Organizations

An advocacy group and its agents, such as a union concerned about workplace health hazards, have broad First Amendment rights of speech and association that include the right to help their members protect themselves through the legal system,[66] to hire attorneys to act as personal counsel for members,[67] and to advise injured members to seek legal advice and even refer them to specific outside attorneys for assistance in personal injury litigation.[68] In *United Transportation Union v. State Bar of Michigan*,[69] for example, the U.S. Supreme Court held that a state court injunction restraining a railroad union from giving or furnishing legal advice to its members or their families violated the First Amendment. The Court, reflecting on the line of cases that required this result, stated the following:

> In the context of this case we deal with a cooperative union of workers seeking to assist its members in effectively asserting claims under the FELA. But the principle here involved cannot be limited to the facts of this case. At issue is the basic right to group legal action, a right first asserted in this Court by an association of Negroes seeking the protection of freedoms guaranteed by the Constitution. The common thread running through our decisions in *NAACP v. Button, Trainmen,* and *United Mine Workers* is that collective activity undertaken to obtain meaningful access to the courts is a fundamental right within the protection of the First Amendment. However, that right would be a hollow promise if courts could deny associations of workers or others the means of enabling their members to meet the costs of legal representation.[70]

An association, therefore, has a well established First Amendment right to communicate with its members for the purpose of providing or aiding in the provision of legal aid. This interest intersects with the law regarding communications with putative class members when an association is a named party and class representative in a class action in which its members are putative class members. For example, a union and several workers may bring suit on behalf of all members of the union.[71] Similarly, a civil rights group[72] or a state optometric association[73] might seek to bring class actions on behalf of their members. In these scenarios, does the *United Transportation Union* line of cases give the association—either directly or through class counsel—a broader right to communicate with putative class members than would be the case for ordinary, individual class representatives?

In theory, it seems the answer to this question is no. This is not, however, because associations do not have broad First Amendment rights to communicate with their members, but rather is because *Gulf Oil* makes clear that ordinary, individual class representatives and their class counsel have broad rights to communicate with putative class members, too: "an order limiting communications between parties and potential class members should be based on a clear record and specific findings that reflect a weighing of the need for a limitation and the potential interference with the rights of the parties."[74] However, as we have seen, federal courts have not uniformly applied the *Gulf Oil* standard, and in those situations the fact that an association is a class representative can provide a second basis for challenging a restraint on communications with putative class members. Although there appear to be no published cases dealing with this precise issue, the First Amendment rights of associations and their members under the *United Transportation Union* line of cases is well established, and courts that have certified class actions with associations as class representatives have recognized that the associations (typically unions or civil rights groups) would use their greater, collective resources to furnish legal services to their members.[75] Unfettered communications with the associations' members, therefore, is arguably implicit.

Opt-In Class Actions

Section 216(b) of the Fair Labor Standards Act[76] (FLSA) provides a private right of action for employees to recover unpaid minimum wages and overtime compensation; to redress retaliatory discharges; and to enforce the terms of the Age Discrimination in Employment Act (ADEA). Actions under section 216(b) can be brought individually or as collective actions. Unlike modern class actions, however, section 216(b) actions operate as "spurious" or "opt-in" class actions: "No employee shall be a party plaintiff to any such action unless he gives his consent in writing to become such a party and such consent is filed in the court in which such action is brought."[77] The role of notice in these opt-in actions, therefore, is different and arguably even more important than notice in opt-out actions: without notice of the suit and of one's right to opt-in, a potential plaintiff literally *cannot* participate in the litigation.

While individual notice is required in opt-out class actions under Rule 23, the federal courts were long divided on the issue of whether a district court even had the authority to facilitate the joinder of section 216(b) class members by approving the sending of notice in opt-in actions brought under FLSA. Some courts held that notice of a proposed action under section 216(b) was neither required nor authorized, and that a district court lacked authority to direct notice to potential class members.[78] Other courts held that such notice was improper solicitation of litigation.[79] On the other hand, several courts concluded that the right to bring a representative action carried with it the right to notify those persons whom the plaintiff wished to represent, and thus approved notification of potential class members.[80]

The split in the lower courts was resolved by the Supreme Court in *Hoffman La-Roche, Inc. v. Sperling*,[81] an action brought under ADEA in which plaintiffs sought court-approved notice under section 216(b). Stressing the "wisdom and necessity" of "judicial intervention in the management of litigation" and noting that the rationale of

Gulf Oil applied in section 216(b) actions, the Court held that "district courts have *discretion*, in appropriate cases, to implement 29 U.S.C. section 216(b) . . . by facilitating notice to potential plaintiffs."[82] The Court, however, specifically refused to examine the details of the notice at issue in the case, and emphasized that it was "confirm[ing] the existence of the trial court's discretion, not the details of its exercise."[83] Furthermore, the Court stated, "We do not address any conflicts between court-authorized notice and communications with potential plaintiffs by counsel."[84] Thus, the Court specifically left open the possibility that a district court could refuse to approve or otherwise facilitate notice to potential plaintiffs in a section 216(b) action, and that notice would have to be accomplished by "communications with potential plaintiffs by counsel" that did not involve the court.

Several pre-*Hoffman* opinions that refused to issue or allow notice under section 216(b) illustrate how courts conceive of the nature and scope of these direct communications between class counsel and potential plaintiffs. In *Dolan v. Project Construction Corporation*,[85] for example, the Court of Appeals for the Tenth Circuit affirmed an order of the district court refusing to issue court-approved notice under section 216(b) and, further, granting a protective order with respect to discovery plaintiffs had sought in order to learn the names and addresses of potential plaintiffs. Although it concluded that court-approved notice was inappropriate, the *Dolan* court expected that plaintiffs' counsel would seek out and contact potential plaintiffs on their own:

> However, recent United States Supreme Court cases regarding legal communication dictate the allowance of a level of reasonable communication by the plaintiff and counsel with those parties he can discover without judicial assistance . . . . Additionally, "an order limiting communications between parties and potential class members should be based on a clear record and specific findings that reflect a weighing of the need for a limitation and the potential interference with the rights of the parties." *Gulf Oil Co. v. Bernard,* 452 U.S. 89, 101 (1981). Although *Gulf Oil* is a case involving a Rule 23 action, the principle of law is applicable to all representative actions.[86]

Thus, under *Dolan*, even if a district court refuses to facilitate notice under section 216(b), it should not interfere with plaintiffs' attorneys' attempts to inform potential class members of the suit, unless such interference is consistent with *Gulf Oil*.

The Seventh Circuit, in another pre-*Hoffman* case, took a different approach. In *Woods v. New York Life Insurance*,[87] the court held that district courts could review and approve communications between section 216(b) plaintiffs and potential class members but could not send out notice that was on judicial letterhead or that was signed by a judicial officer. The court addressed the concern, shared by many plaintiffs' attorneys bringing actions under section 216(b), that the judicial imprimatur on the notice was necessary in order to avoid potential solicitation complaints under state law:

> At oral argument the plaintiffs' counsel stated that he wanted the imprimatur in order to shield himself from a possible complaint under state law that he was trying to stir up litigation; but if the notice is approved by a

federal court under the authority that we hold it has by virtue of section 16(b) of the Fair Labor Standards Act, any effort by the state to punish the lawyer who mails the notice would violate the supremacy clause of the United States Constitution. It is the court's order, not its letterhead or its clerk's signature, that provides the lawyer with immunity from a state's efforts to prevent communications authorized by section 16(b). Indeed the order may be unnecessary; section 16(b) of its own force may preempt state laws that operate to prevent the representative plaintiff or his counsel from communicating with other (actual or potential) class members; such laws could even raise First Amendment problems.[88]

Notably, however, the *Woods* court did *not* believe that class counsel could freely contact potential plaintiffs, even if the content of the communications was perfectly appropriate. Instead, the court envisioned the following procedure, at least in section 216(b) actions:

> Before this suit was filed, Woods had sent invitations to other members of the class to join with him, and New York Life does not challenge his right to do this. After suit was filed, however, we do not think it would have been proper for Woods or his counsel to have sent out such invitations without first communicating to the defendant's counsel his intention to do so, so that the defendant's counsel would have an opportunity to verify the accuracy of the notice and, if he wished, to move for an order amending the notice or limiting its distribution in an appropriate manner. We cannot find any express basis in rule or statute for inferring either the duty of the plaintiff's counsel to notify the defendant's counsel in this manner or the power of the district court to regulate the content and distribution of the notice to potential class members; but we think both the duty and the power may fairly be inferred from section 16(b) itself and from Rule 83 of the Federal Rules of Civil Procedure, which provides that "in all cases not provided for by rule, the district courts may regulate their practice in any manner not inconsistent with" the Federal Rules. Once a section 16(b) action is commenced, the defendant has a vital interest in, and the court a managerial responsibility regarding, the joinder of additional parties plaintiff, and these concerns support the modest duty and power that we infer.[89]

While the *Woods* court recognized the right of class counsel to communicate with potential class members, as well as the potential "First Amendment problems" with state laws interfering with such communications, the court invented a procedure under section 216(b) that, in effect, requires class counsel to obtain approval by either defense counsel or the court before sending out notice to potential class members. Such a requirement is arguably inconsistent with *Gulf Oil*, which the Court has explicitly held applies to actions under § 216(b).[90]

Finally, in *Goerke v. Commercial Contractors & Supply Co.*,[91] the district court for the Northern District of Georgia adopted the reasoning of the Tenth Circuit in *Dolan* in holding that it had no power under FLSA to authorize notice to potential class members. Because plaintiffs' counsel, like the plaintiffs' attorneys in *Wood*, expressed concern about violating the rules of the State Bar of Georgia, the court specifically addressed the alternative to court-approved notice under section 216(b):

> The denial of this motion, however, does not preclude the plaintiff engaging in protected communication with other potential plaintiffs who can be discovered without intervention by the court . . . . As the Supreme Court has held in *Gulf Oil Company vs. Bernard,* an order limiting communications between parties and potential class members "should be based on a clear record and specific findings that reflect a weighing of the need for limitation and the potential interference with the rights of the parties." There is no question that *Bernard* dealt with a Rule 23 class action, and was based upon the standards of the *Federal Rules of Civil Procedure.* However . . . the rationale behind *Bernard* was equally applicable to a representative action under 216(b). Thus, although this court has found that it has no power to approve and authorize the dissemination of a notice to potential class members, there are forms of protected communication in which plaintiff's counsel can engage with potential class members. As regards plaintiff's fears, expressed in the brief in support of this motion, plaintiff need only make certain that any communications in which he engages are directed toward the provision of *notice,* rather than toward active solicitation of individuals to join in the present litigation.[92]

Thus, the *Goerke* court specifically held that in the absence of court-approved notice, class counsel in a section 216(b) action could communicate with potential class members and such communications would be governed by the principles set forth in *Gulf Oil*.

Conclusion

As the Supreme Court made clear in *Gulf Oil*, communications between class counsel and putative class members are critical to the prosecution of class actions. Thus, while district courts have broad authority to police these communications, their decision to do so must be based on a clear record and specific findings that reflect a weighing of the need for the limitation and the potential for interference with the rights of the parties. Only such a determination, as the Court itself has stated, "can ensure that the [district] court is furthering, rather than hindering, the policies embodied in the Federal Rules of Civil Procedure, especially Rule 23."[93] Furthermore, the analysis in *Gulf Oil* applies with, if anything, even more force in the other class action contexts discussed in this essay. When a union or civil rights group is a named plaintiff in a class action, for example, the groups' First Amendment rights to communicate with and provide legal assistance to their members provides an additional argument against interference with class counsel's contacts with the putative class. In opt-in class actions under FLSA, furthermore, it is now clear that district courts have the authority to issue notice to putative class members. The fact that class members will not be able to participate in the suit unless they affirmatively opt in strongly suggests that courts should approve and issue notice. At the very least, they should not hinder class counsel from communicating with putative class members.

Notes

1. Chayes, *The Role of the Judge in Public Law Litigation*, 89 HARV. L. REV. 1281 (1976) (nature of dispute impacts on procedure); *see also* Rosenberg, *The Causal Connection in Mass Exposure Cases: A "Public Law" Vision of the Tort System*, 97 HARV. L. REV. 851 (1984) (role of class action).

2. 452 U.S. 89 (1981).

3. 29 U.S.C. § 201 *et seq.*

4. ABA MODEL RULES OF PROF'L CONDUCT (2002 ed.) R. 7.3.

5. ABA MODEL RULES OF PROF'L CONDUCT (2002 ed.) R. 4.2.

6. Dubois v. Gradco Systems, Inc., 136 F.R.D. 341, 344 (D. Conn. 1991), *citing* G. HAZARD & W. HODES, THE LAW OF LAWYERING: A HANDBOOK ON THE MODEL RULES OF PROFESSIONAL CONDUCT 436 (1988 Supp.).

7. *See* ALLAN KANNER & TIBOR NAGY, PERSPECTIVES ON THE ATTORNEY-CLIENT PRIVILEGE AND WORK PRODUCT DOCTRINE §§ II.A & V.

8. *See, e.g., In re* McKesson HBOC, Inc. Securities Litig., 126 F. Supp. 2d 1239, 1245 (N.D. Cal. 2000) (counsel's solicitations to potential class members improper because they communicated "a gratuitous sense of urgency").

9. *See, e.g.,* Kleiner v. First National Bank of Atlanta, 751 F.2d 1193 (5th Cir. 1985) (affirming imposition of substantial sanctions upon defense counsel who had participated in campaign of seeking opt-outs from putative class members).

10. Pamela Mathy, *The Validity of Class Action No-Comment Rules*, 13 RUTGERS L.J. 285, 285 (1982); *see also* Gulf Oil Co. v. Bernard, 619 F.2d 459, 464 n.3 (5th Cir. 1980) (en banc) (noting that both the 1973 and 1977 editions of the MANUAL FOR COMPLEX LITIGATION advocated this approach).

11. Middle District of Florida's Local Rule 4.04(e).

12. *See, e.g.,* Gulf Oil Co. v. Bernard, 452 U.S. 89 (1981).

13. Gulf Oil Co. v. Bernard, 619 F.2d 459 (5th Cir. 1980) (en banc).

14. *See, e.g.,* Rodgers v. United States Steel Corp., 508 F.2d 152 (3d Cir. 1975); Gulf Oil Co. v. Bernard, 619 F.2d 459 (5th Cir. 1980) (en banc).

15. 452 U.S. 89 (1981).

16. 619 F.2d 459 (5th Cir. 1980) (en banc).

17. 452 U.S. at 100.

18. *Id.* at 101-02.

19. *Id.* at 101.

20. *See, e.g.,* Gates v. Cook, 234 F.3d 221, 227 (5th Cir. 2000); Wiginton v. Ellis, 2003 WL 22232907 at *3, slip op. (N.D. Ill., Sept. 16, 2003). However, a number of federal district courts, notably the Middle District of Florida and the Northern District of Georgia, still have no-comment local rules. *See infra* discussion of Jackson v. Motel 6 Multipurpose, Inc., 130 F.3d 999 (11th. Cir. 1997) *and* Abdallah v. Coca-Cola Co., 186 F.R.D. 672 (N.D. Ga. 1999).

21. Gulf Oil Co. v. Bernard, 619 F.2d 459 (5th Cir. 1980) (en banc).

22. *See* MANUAL FOR COMPLEX LITIGATION § 30.2 ("Communication with the class is a major concern in the management of class actions. The court and counsel will need to develop appropriate means for providing information to, and obtaining it from, members of the class, and for handling inquiries from potential or actual class members while avoiding communications that may interfere with the conduct of the litigation. The law provides little definitive guidance in this area, so much is left to the court's judgment."). *Compare, e.g.,* THOMAS A. DICKERSON, CLASS ACTIONS: THE LAW OF 50

States § 4.06[2], at 457 (2001) ("The members of the purported class on whose behalf a class action is instituted are deemed represented by counsel for the class representatives as of the time the complaint is filed with the court."), *with Atari, Inc. v. Super. Ct.*, 212 Cal. Rptr. 773, 776 (Ct. App. 1985) ("We cannot accept the suggestion that a potential (but as yet unapproached) class member should be deemed 'a party . . . represented by counsel' even before the class is certified . . . .").

23. Manual for Complex Litigation § 30.24 ("no formal attorney-client relationship exists between class counsel and the putative members of the class prior to class certification").

24. Thomas A. Dickerson, Class Actions: The Law of 50 States § 4.06[2], at 457 (2001) ("The members of the purported class on whose behalf a class action is instituted are deemed represented by counsel for the class representatives as of the time the complaint is filed with the court.").

25. *See, e.g.*, Atari, Inc. v. Super. Ct., *supra* note 22; Lewis v. Bayer A.G., 2002 WL 1472339 (Pa. Com. Pl., June 12, 2002) (holding, without addressing question of whether putative class members were deemed represented by class counsel prior to certification, that defendant was allowed to contact putative class members regarding adverse drug reactions).

26. Manual for Complex Litigation § 30.24.

27. 3 Newberg & Conte, Newberg on Class Actions 3d § 15.14 at 1541 (1992).

28. *See* Gulf Oil Co. v. Bernard, 452 U.S. 89 (1981); Oppenheimer Fund, Inc., v. Sanders, 437 U.S. 340, 354 n.20 (1978); *see also* Manual for Complex Litigation § 30.24.

29. *See* Kleiner v. First National Bank of Atlanta, 751 F.2d 1193 (5th Cir. 1985); *see also* Manual for Complex Litigation § 30.24.

30. 130 F.3d 999 (11th. Cir. 1997).

31. The Middle District of Florida's Local Rule 4.04(e), which provides that: "In every case sought to be maintained by any party as a class action, all parties thereto and their counsel are hereby forbidden, directly or indirectly, orally or in writing, to communicate concerning such actions with any potential or actual class member, not a formal party to the case, without approval by the Court."

32. Jackson v. Motel 6 Multipurpose, Inc., 130 F.3d at 1002.

33. *Id.* at 1004.

34. *Id.* at 1008 n.19.

35. *See supra* note 31.

36. Jackson v. Motel 6 Multipurpose, Inc., 130 F.3d 1004.

37. Gulf Oil Co. v. Bernard, 452 U.S. 89, 97 n.8 (1981).

38. *Id.* at 91.

39. *Id.* at 101.

40. 186 F.R.D. 672 (N.D. Ga. 1999).

41. *Id.* at 678.

42. *Id.* at 679.

43. *Id.* at 677. *See also* Spratley v. State Farm Mut. Auto. Ins. Co., 78 P.3d 603, 609 (Utah 2003) (holding that attorneys who resigned from State Farm claiming that demands of their jobs would force them to violate attorney ethics rules could, in suit for constructive discharge and retaliation, disclose privileged and confidential information to the extent "reasonably necessary to establish their claim against State Farm").

44. 2002 WL 169370 (D. Kan. 2002).

45. *See supra* text accompanying note 38.

46. *See, e.g.,* Benjamin J. Vernia, *Right of Attorney to Conduct Ex Parte Interviews with Former Corporate Employees*, 57 A.L.R. 5th 633 (1998) (suggesting that attorneys should "establish a script of statements and questions to be followed in all initial contacts with former employees").

47. *See* Manual for Complex Litigation § 30.24 ("Once a class is certified, the rules governing communications apply as though each class member is a client of class counsel. Under accepted ethical principles, defendants and their attorneys may communicate on matters regarding the litigation with class members who have not opted out, but only through class counsel.").

48. *But see* Roberts v. Weim, 130 F.R.D. 416 (N.D. Cal. 1988) (denying plaintiff's request for an order requiring prior approval of any communications by defense counsel to putative class members during opt-out period).

49. Newberg suggests the possibility of a less absolute view, premised on the likelihood that at least some putative class members will opt out of the litigation after certification and before the exclusion period expires. *See* 3 NEWBERG & CONTE, NEWBERG ON CLASS ACTIONS 3d § 15.15 at 1543 to 1544 (1992). Under that view, post-certification communications may still be permissible (albeit potentially hazardous if the court disagrees) on grounds that the putative class member being communicated with retains an independent right to make his or her own decisions until the end of the exclusion period.

50. 751 F.2d 1193 (5th Cir. 1985).

51. *Id.* at 1196.

52. *Id.* at 1197.

53. *Id.* at 1200 n.15.

54. *Id.* at 1202-03.

55. *Id.* at 1203.

56. 160 F.R.D. 478 (E.D. Pa. 1995). Another potential source of trouble is competing counsel in securities class actions. See *In re* Worldcom, Inc. Securities Litig., 2003 WL 22701241 (S.D.N.Y. Nov. 17, 2003) (discussing misleading letters sent by securities class action firm to absent class members and ordering curative notice).

57. For an extensive discussion of the history of this litigation, *see* Georgine v. Amchem Products, Inc., 157 F.R.D. 246, 257 61 (E.D. Pa. 1994).

58. *Id.* at 489. Notably, the settling parties elected not to seek an order banning all potentially misleading communications by objectors with putative class members during the second opt-out period. Class counsel specifically informed the court that while they supported the inclusion of a disclosure statement on all future communications, they could not support "any order that would restrain attorney-client communications in any manner." *Id.* at n.11.

59. *Id.* at 490.

60. *Id.* at 491.

61. *Id.*

62. *Id.* at 490.

63. *Id.* at 495.

64. *Id.* at 496.

65. *See* 3 NEWBERG & CONTE, NEWBERG ON CLASS ACTIONS 3d § 15.18 at 1549 (1992).

66. Mozzochi v. Borden, 959 F.2d 1174, 1180 (2d Cir. 1992); NACCP v. Button, 371 U.S. 415, 432-33 (1963) (enforcement of barratry statute may be invalid if it prohibits privileged exercise of First Amendment rights "whether or not . . . the petitioner has engaged in privileged conduct"); United States v. Spock, 416 F.2d 165 (1st Cir. 1969) (conspiracy law held not enforceable against protected advocacy of opposition to Vietnam War).

67. United Mine Workers v. Illinois Bar, 389 U.S. 217, 221-22 (1967).

68. Brotherhood of Railroad Trainmen v. Virginia *ex rel.* Virginia State Bar, 377 U.S. 1 (1964). *See also* United Mine Workers v. Illinois Bar Ass'n, 389 U.S. 217, 223-25 (1967) (governmental interference violates associational rights, as well as First and Fourteenth Amendment concerns, even if it is justified by a legitimate objective, such as the avoidance of conflicts of interest in attorney-client relationships, unless government shows that a serious impairment of the objective would clearly occur absent the challenged interference, and that no less intrusive regulation could prevent such impairment).

69. 401 U.S. 576.

70. *Id.* at 585-86 (1971).

71. *See, e.g.,* International Woodworkers of America v. Georgia-Pacific Corp., 568 F.2d 64, 67 (8th Cir. 1977); Social Services Union, Local 535, etc. v. County of Santa Clara, 609 F.2d 944 (9th Cir. 1979); National Ass'n of Letter Carriers v. United States Civil Service Comm., 346 F. Supp. 578 (D.D.C.), *rev'd on other grounds,* 413 U.S. 548 (1972); Glass, Molders, Pottery Plastics, and Allied Workers Int'l Union, et al. v. Wickes Cos., Inc., No. L-06023-88 (Sup. Ct., Camden Cty., N.J. Feb. 24, 1992).

72. Hispanics United of DuPage County v. Village of Addison, Ill., 160 F.R.D. 681 (N.D. Ill. 1995); Alliance to End Repression v. Rochford, 565 F.2d 975 (7th Cir. 1977); League of United Latin American Citizens v. Salinas Fire Dept., 88 F.R.D. 533, 543 (N.D. Cal. 1980); Women's Committee for Equal Employment Opportunity v. National Broadcasting Co., 71 F.R.D. 666 (S.D.N.Y. 1976).

73. Alabama Optometric Ass'n v. Alabama State Board of Health, 379 F. Supp. 1332 (M.D. Ala. 1974).

74. Gulf Oil Co. v. Bernard, 452 U.S. at 102.

75. Social Services Union, Local 535, etc. v. County of Santa Clara, 609 F.2d 944, 946 (9th Cir. 1979) ("It is now clear that unions may maintain actions under Title VII on behalf of their members. Indeed, policy considerations weigh strongly in favor of affording standing to unions which file suit to end discriminatory employment practices. The financial backing and legal expertise that unions can provide would materially advance the type of private enforcement essential to the effectiveness of Title VII."); League of United Latin American Citizens v. Salinas Fire Dept., 88 F.R.D. 533, 543 (N.D. Cal. 1980) ("Organizations dedicated to the eradication of prejudice and bias and to the promotion of equal opportunity for their members are . . . [even] more suited to class representation than the union [in Social Services Union]"); International Woodworkers of America, etc. v. Chesapeake Bay Plywood Corp. 659 F.2d 1259, 1268 (4th Cir. 1981) ("[T]he Union, as a class representative with standing under Article III to raise its members' claims, is seeking to redress injuries suffered by its members. Here it acts merely as a conduit for the vindication of its members' rights to be free of discrimination in their employment.").

76. 29 U.S.C. § 201 *et seq.*

77. *Id.* at 216(b).

78. *See* Baker v. Michie Co., 93 F.R.D. 494 (W.D. Va. 1982); McKenna v. Champion Int'l Corp., 747 F.2d 1211 (8th Cir. 1984).

79. Baker v. Michie Co. 93 F.R.D. 494 (W.D. Va. 1982); Roshto v. Chrysler Corp., 67 F.R.D. 28 (E.D. La 1975).

80. Braunstein v. Eastern Photographic Labs., Inc., 600 F.2d 335 (2d Cir. 1978); Woods v. New York Life Ins. Co., 686 F.2d 578 (7th Cir. 1982); Riojas v. Seal Produce, Inc., 82 F.R.D. 613 (S.D. Tex. 1979).

81. 493 U.S. 165 (1989).

82. *Id.* at 169 (emphasis added).

83. *Id.* at 171.

84. *Id.* at 171 n.2.

85. 725 F.2d 1263 (10th Cir. 1984).

86. *Id.* at 1269.

87. 686 F.2d 578 (7th Cir. 1982).

88. *Id.* at 581.

89. *Id.* at 580.

90. Hoffman LaRoche, Inc. v. Sperling, 493 U.S. at 171.

91. 600 F. Supp. 1155 (N.D. Ga. 1984).

92. *Id.* at 1161 (citations omitted).

93. Gulf Oil Co. v. Bernard, 452 U.S. at 101-02.

CHAPTER 8

The Application of the Attorney-Client Privilege and the Work-Product Doctrine to Communications Between Insureds and Insurance Carriers

KIRK A. PASICH

Introduction

When there has been an accident, an occurrence, a claim made, or some other event that may be covered by insurance, an insured typically communicates with its insurance carrier. This initial communication is typically followed by additional communications, by the transmittal of information, and even by the carrier interviewing employees and potential witnesses. There are often at least two purposes behind these communications. First, the insured typically communicates with its carriers so that it may obtain the benefit of the insurance coverage it purchased. This obviously includes a defense against and indemnification for any claims. Second, the carrier may want to investigate the claim and related events to determine whether the claim is covered and whether its obligations are excused because of the insured's conduct or because of an exclusion.

Upon receiving notice of an actual or potential claim, the carrier has a duty to investigate. This duty extends not only to the facts regarding the claim and the insured's potential exposure, but also to the facts that support coverage for the claim. As the California Supreme Court has explained:

> [I]t is essential that an insurer fully inquire into possible bases that might support the insured's claim . . . . [A]n insurer cannot reasonably and in good faith deny payments to its insured without thoroughly investigating the foundation for its denial.[1]

During its investigation, the carrier may create and compile various documents relating to the defense against the claim and to its coverage determination. These often include documents relating to the substantive merits of the claim asserted against the insured and to coverage defenses the carrier may wish to assert, such as the defense that the insured expected and intended to inflict the injury claimed by the underlying plaintiff. The investigatory documents may include witness statements, post-accident reports, assessments by claims adjusters, or advice letters from in-house or outside counsel, and communications from attorneys defending the insured against the claim.

When the insured and the insurance carrier are working together to defend a claim, neither will want its own communications or the results of the carrier's investigation revealed to third parties, the underlying claimant, or potential claimants. In this case, the attorney work-product doctrine may offer the parties some protection from disclosure.

Likewise, when the insured and an insurance carrier are embroiled in a coverage dispute, neither usually wants third parties to have access to its documents, but both want and claim a right to access the other's documents. For example, the insured often will seek to discover all information the carrier may have in its claims file in order to determine why the carrier denied coverage and if that denial was in bad faith.

In turn, the carrier may want access to documents found in the underlying defense counsel's files and to documents that might show that there is no coverage because the insured intended to inflict injury—the very documents the underlying plaintiff will want to use to establish the insured's liability. In this situation, there is a real tension between the parties' efforts to litigate their coverage dispute and the need to avoid creating the very liability for which the insured is seeking a defense from the carrier. To the extent possible, this issue should be avoided because an insurance carrier should not be able to create the very liability it is supposed to be defending its insured against by attempting to establish that it has no duty to indemnify the insured.[2]

However, regardless of how or when a coverage dispute is resolved, there frequently are questions over who has access to what information. Generally speaking, these questions include the following:

- Is information gathered by an insurance carrier in its investigation of a claim protected from discovery by a third-party claimant?
- Is information gathered by an insurance carrier in its investigation of a claim protected from discovery by the insured?
- Are the underlying defense files protected from disclosure to a carrier?
- Are communications between insurance carriers and insureds protected from disclosure to third-party claimants?

There typically is no privilege known as the "insured-carrier" privilege.[3] However, most states recognize that communications between an insured and an insurance carrier are protected by the attorney-client privilege, at least to the extent the communication relates to the defense of the claim. A minority of the states and at least some federal courts have reached a contrary conclusion, holding that such communications are *not* protected by the attorney-client privilege.[4]

Application of the Attorney-Client Privilege

The Majority View

As noted above, the majority view is that an insured's communications to its insurance carriers regarding a possible claim or other event potentially covered by insurance may be covered by the attorney-client privilege. Courts following the majority view typically hold that an insured's communications to its carriers generally are protected from disclosure by the attorney-client privilege. This means that communications about potentially covered events are protected by the privilege against disclosure to third parties, including potential claimants.[5]

This approach is premised on the theory that communications from an insured to a carrier are primarily made so that the information communicated can be relayed to the attorney retained by the carrier to defend the insured. As the Illinois Supreme Court explained in the leading decision supporting the broad approach:

> [B]y the terms of the common liability insurance contract, the insured effectively delegates to the insurer the selection of an attorney and the conduct of the defense of any civil litigation. The insured is ordinarily not represented by counsel of his own choosing either at the time of making the communication or during the course of litigation. Under such circumstances we believe that the insured may properly assume that the communication is made to the insurer as an agent for the dominant purpose of transmitting it to an attorney for the protection of the interests of the insured.[6]

Even under the majority view, not necessarily all communications to insurance-related entities are protected. For example, in *Shere v. Marshall Field & Co.,*[7] the insured's safety director prepared a claim report on a form supplied by an independent adjusting service retained by the insured and one of its carriers. When the injured claimant sought to compel production of the report in the lawsuit against the insured, the insured was ordered to produce the report. The insured's attorney was subsequently held in contempt for refusing to produce the report. The Illinois Appellate Court affirmed, stating:

> In the instant case the statement was given by the Director of Safety to Safety and Claims Service. Safety and Claims Service is an independent contractor retained by both defendant and by defendant's excess public-liability insurer to investigate and adjust claims. However, it is not an insurer. The attorney-client privilege has never been extended to cover communications to such third parties. There was no contractual obligation on the part of Safety and Claims Service to defend as there was in the *Ryan* case, and there is no reason to assume that it was an agent for the defendant's attorneys. We therefore find no reason to extend the privilege to the instant independent investigating and adjusting service.[8]

Furthermore, even under the majority view many courts recognize that the attorney-client privilege does not apply just because there is a communication between an insured and a carrier relating to the defense against a possible claim. Many courts hold that the attorney-client privilege protects communications only if (1) the *dominant purpose* of those communications relates to the defense of the insured by counsel retained by the carrier and (2) the insured had a reasonable expectation of confidentiality.[9]

The leading decision is *Gene Compton's Corp. v. Superior Court.*[10] In this case, the California Court of Appeal considered whether the privilege attached to an accident report prepared by one of the insured's employees, which was subsequently given to the carrier and thereafter given to an attorney first appointed by the insurer *after* the time the insured gave the report to the carrier. The court noted that the evidence demonstrated that the communication was made for the predominant purpose of transmittal to the attorney selected to defend the insured and that the information was intended to be confidential. Based on these findings, the court held that this constituted a privileged communication, stating:

> [I]n such circumstances as are here involved the transmission of a privileged communication to the attorney through the agency of an insurance carrier does not destroy the privilege.[11]

The California Supreme Court subsequently disapproved the implication in *Gene Compton's* that communications from an insured to an insurance carrier are privileged as a matter of law.[12] Hence, California law is clear that communications may be privileged if the trier of fact decides that the primary purpose for the communications was for transmittal to an attorney at some point during the course of professional employment.[13]

A similar approach was taken in *State v. Pavin.*[14] In *Pavin,* the insured was involved in an automobile accident. Ten days after the accident, he was interviewed in the hospital by an insurance adjuster, who prepared a statement. The insured refused to sign the statement, noting that his mother had been advised by an attorney that he should not do so. Subsequently, the insured was convicted of the crime of fourth-degree death by automobile. One of the key items of evidence admitted against him was the unsigned statement prepared by the insurance adjuster. On appeal, the insured argued that the statement was protected by the attorney-client privilege and had been erroneously admitted into evidence.

The New Jersey Superior Court, Appellate Division, rejected this argument. In doing so, the court considered the various approaches taken by other courts, citing to decisions in many other states. The court rejected the notion of a per se privilege, instead finding a fact-based inquiry to be the "better approach."[15] It summarized the support for that approach as follows:

> Those cases that have concluded that communications between an insured and his adjuster are not per se privileged note that an insurance carrier has the right to review and consider an insured's statement for any legitimate purpose connected with the company's business, such as coverage, cooperation, or renewal. The statement is ordinarily used by the insurer to determine whether and on what basis adjustment of the claim could be

attempted. Only if adjustment is not effected and a claim is pursued, will the information be turned over to counsel for use in litigation. If the insured gives a false statement, or a statement that supplies facts regarding some other defense against the insurer's liability under the policy, the insurer can make use of those facts to the detriment of the insured. Thus these cases say that the relationship is not automatically comparable at all stages to that of attorney and client, since it is not at all clear that the insured's interests are being protected by the insurance carrier.[16]

With this reasoning in mind, the court considered the facts before it. The court first noted that the adjuster interviewed the insured within a few days after the accident and before any claim was filed. The court then noted that there was no evidence that the adjuster was acting on instructions of any attorney or that an attorney had even been retained by the carrier. Finally, the court noted that the insured's "expectation of privacy was nonexistent" because he did not think of the adjuster as his legal adviser, refusing to sign the prepared statement on the advice of his mother's attorney.[17]

Another court employed the same methodology. In *Lectrolarm Custom Systems, Inc. v. Pelco Sales, Inc.*,[18] the court found that even when an insurance carrier has reserved its rights to deny coverage, there is a "common interest" between the insured and the carrier and that, therefore, "disclosure of privileged information by [the insured] to [the carrier] does not waive the attorney-client privilege or the work product doctrine."[19] The court explained as follows:

> [T]he attorney-client privilege is not automatically waived if an otherwise privileged document is disclosed to a third party. The most common situation in which disclosure occurs without waiver is where parties have a common interest. The existence of a common defense allows the parties and counsel allied in that defense to disclose privileged information to each other without destroying the privileged nature of those communications. This "common defense doctrine" also referred to as the "joint defense privilege" expands the application of the privileges to circumstances in which parties are represented by separate counsel but engage in a common legal enterprise.[20]

The court also reasoned that "the threat of production" to a claimant of information shared between an insured and its carrier would "create[] a wedge between the insured and their insurance carrier which is not in the best interests of any of the parties in this or any other litigation."[21]

Thus, under the majority view, communications between insureds and their insurance carriers will be protected because the communications are inherently deemed to be privileged or because they were made for the dominant purpose of protecting the insured's rights, with a reasonable expectation of confidentiality, and/or regarding a subject of common interest (that is, the insured's potential exposure). Therefore, the following questions should be answered affirmatively in order for the communications to be protected from disclosure to third parties (such as governmental agencies and private claimants):

1. Was the communication made for the dominant purpose of protecting the insured's rights?
2. Was the communication made with a reasonable expectation of confidentiality?
3. Was there a "common interest in the matter to which the communication relates?

The Minority View

Some courts have held that communications between insureds and carriers are not protected by the attorney-client privilege.[22] These courts base their decisions on the theory that communications between an insured and a carrier are unlike communications between a client and an attorney because an insurer may use information it obtains from an insured for purposes that are contrary to the insured's interests. As the Wisconsin Supreme Court has explained:

> When the insured makes such a statement he is ordinarily fulfilling a condition of his policy, requiring him to notify the insurer of the occurrence and circumstances of the accident and to co-operate with the insurer. If the statement be false, the insurer may use it against the insured as foundation for a claim of non-cooperation. If the statement discloses facts giving rise to some other defense against the insurer's liability under the policy, the insurer is doubtless free to make use of those facts.[23]

The most recent decision adopting the minority view is *Langdon v. Champion*.[24] In this case, the Alaska Supreme Court addressed the applicability of the attorney-client privilege to information compiled in an insurer's files. The court first compared the majority and minority views:

> A shrinking majority of states prohibit discovery of statements made by an insured to his insurer. Most of these courts base their decision on provisions in the insurance policy which require the insurer to defend the insured and the insured to cooperate in the investigation. . . .
>
> A substantial and growing minority of state courts, on the other hand, have concluded that statements made to an insurer by the insured are generally not protected by the attorney-client privilege. . . . The federal rule is likewise . . . .
>
> Courts adopting this view reason that communications between insured and insurer are not in the same class as communications between client and attorney, because the insurer may use its information for purposes inimical to the interests of the insured.[25]

The court then concluded as follows:

> We find the growing minority and federal rule most persuasive. In our opinion, the cases according protection to statements between insurers and insureds have extended the attorney-client privilege into areas in which it

was never intended to apply. Moreover, the minority rule is more in line with our policy favoring liberal discovery. . . .

We therefore hold that the attorney-client privilege does not extend to statements made by an insured to his insurer, except in those cases where it can be shown that the adjustor received the communication at the express direction of counsel for the insured. Only in the latter instance do we think it can fairly be said that the adjustor is acting as "one employed to assist the lawyer in the rendition of professional legal services," thus making him a "representative of the lawyer" within the meaning of [Alaska] Evidence Rule 503(a) (4).[26]

Witness Interviews by Carriers or Their Counsel

Even if the attorney-client privilege applies to a particular communication, another question commonly encountered is whether the privilege applies to witness interviews conducted by an insurance carrier or its counsel. As a general rule, the privilege only protects interviews with the "corporation" or certain of its employees. Interviews with non-employee witnesses typically will *not* be protected.[27] Therefore, interviews by insurers of non-employee witnesses will not be protected by the attorney-client privilege.

However, some courts have recognized that the privilege should apply to interviews of the insured's employees. In *D.I. Chadbourne, Inc. v. Superior Court,*[28] the California Supreme Court set forth the rules to be applied in California when an employee communicates with the employer's carrier.[29] The applicability of the various rules turned on the status of the employee in the corporation or in the litigation.[30] According to the court, the attorney-client privilege does not apply in the following situations:

1. When an employer directs an employee, at the request of its carrier, to make a statement to the carrier to be communicated to the employer's attorney *if* the carrier has not advised the employer that the employee's statement is to be obtained and used in such a manner;[31]
2. When an employee of a defendant corporation is not a co-defendant or a person who may be charged with liability, except for a situation where the employee is the natural person to be speaking for the corporation;[32]
3. When "an employee has been a witness to matters which require communication to the corporate employer's attorney, and the employee has no connection with those matters other than as a witness," even though his employer required him to make the statement;[33] and
4. When an employee "has not been expressly directed by his employer to make a statement, [and the employee] does not know that his statement is sought on a confidential basis (or knowing that fact does not intend [the statement] to be confidential.[34]

However, the *Chadbourne* court held that the privilege does apply in several situations, including:

1. When an employee makes a report as part of his/her normal duties or if the employer requests a report to be made and the dominant purpose of the request is confidential transmission of the report to an attorney;[35] and
2. When an employee is a defendant in his own right or is a person who may be charged with liability.[36]

These guidelines make sense, given that California follows the "dominant purpose" approach to applying the attorney-client privilege to insured/carrier communications.[37] They also make sense under the broader approach because they do not unnecessarily interfere with the liberal discovery policy utilized in most jurisdictions. Of course, in the minority of states that do not protect insured/carrier communications with the attorney-client privilege, the privilege would not apply to witness interviews.

The Impact of a Carrier's Reservation of Rights or Declination on the Applicability of the Attorney-Client Privilege

The impact of an insurance carrier's reservation of rights or declination on the applicability of the attorney-client privilege to an insured's communications with its carriers has seldom been addressed. However, there are decisions that provide some guidance.

In *Dixie Manufacturing Co. v. Ricks*,[38] the insured's president met with counsel employed by its carrier regarding a lawsuit brought against the insured by an employee. At trial, the attorney was permitted to testify over the insured's objection. The Georgia Supreme Court affirmed on appeal. In doing so, the court emphasized that the attorney had, before meeting with the insured, informed the insured that the carrier was not liable under its policy and that the attorney did not, and would not, represent the insured. In light of these facts, the court concluded that it did "not see how the evidence objected to can be regarded as privileged communications between an attorney and his client."[39]

In *State ex rel. L.Y. v. Davis*,[40] the carrier denied coverage for a potential claim against its insured after receiving from its insured information regarding the claim. When the claimant sued, he requested production of this information, arguing that the carrier's denial of coverage meant that there was no insured-insurer relationship with respect to this claim. The court disagreed, stating:

> If communications between insured and insurer are to be privileged only if the insurer ultimately admits coverage, there is no incentive for the insured to make full disclosure to his insurer. In fact, it may be impossible and, at best, difficult for the insurer to determine whether coverage exists without the insured making a full explanation of the circumstance surrounding the claim.[41]

Therefore, the court concluded that claims need not actually be covered by an insurance policy.

Thus, it seems that at least until such time as the insurance carrier makes it clear to the insured that it will not provide a defense and will not be retaining counsel for the insured, the attorney-client privilege should apply if the dominant purpose of the communications is for transmittal to an attorney. Likewise, if the insured communicates with the carrier knowing that the carrier will not provide a defense, it seems the communications arguably would not be privileged because the requirements of the dominant purpose test would not be met.

As for the impact of reservations of rights, the analysis employed in *State ex rel. L.Y.* is even more applicable. With a reservation of rights, the carrier typically assumes the defense against the claim. Thus, there is no reason to treat communications from an insured relating to the defense of the claim any differently than they would be treated if the carrier assumed the defense without a reservation of rights. In fact, such a result is consistent with the *Restatement of the Law Governing Lawyers*. As noted above, the *Restatement* recognizes that communications between the defense lawyer and the carrier's representatives "should be regarded as privileged and otherwise immune from discovery by the claimant or another party to the proceeding."[42]

California had addressed this issue at least in part by statute. California Civil Code section 2860, which governs an insured's right to select counsel when there is a conflict of interest between insured and carrier, requires that the insured disclose to the carrier all information concerning the action except privileged materials relevant to coverage disputes.[43] Section 2860(d) provides that "[a]ny information disclosed [to the carrier] by the insured or by independent counsel is not a waiver of the privilege as to any other party."[44] Thus, in California, a carrier's declination or reservation should not affect the applicability of the attorney-client privilege.

Application of the Work-Product Doctrine

The work-product doctrine may offer some protection to communications between an insured and an insurance carrier and also may prevent discovery by third parties of information contained in the carrier's claims files. The purpose of the doctrine is to assure the lawyer the "opportunity to work 'with a certain degree of privacy, free from unnecessary intrusion by opposing parties and their counsel.'"[45] Under this doctrine, an attorney's mental impressions and work product, at least to the extent generated in anticipation of litigation, will be discoverable only upon a showing of "good cause."[46] "Fact" work product, which includes "non-legal opinions and thoughts about the facts [of the claim]" is discoverable upon the moving party's showing of substantial need and undue hardship. Conversely, "opinion" work product may be more difficult to discover. Opinion work product consists of the attorney's "mental impressions, conclusions, opinions or legal theories."[47] Consequently, the claims adjusters' and counsel's thoughts regarding a claim should be insulated from third-party discovery. Thus, if a claims adjuster has a law degree or if claims assessment is performed by either in-house or outside counsel, the insured and/or its insurance carriers can seek to invoke the doctrine.

The Federal Rules of Civil Procedure state that materials prepared in "anticipation of litigation" are not discoverable unless the moving party has "substantial need of the materials" and "is unable without undue hardship to obtain the substantial equivalent of the materials by other means."[48] This rule applies to documents prepared by a party's representative, including its insurer.[49] It even can extend to documents prepared by a non-lawyer.[50] Thus, if the material was not prepared in anticipation of litigation, but instead was prepared as part of the ordinary course of business, the work-product doctrine will not protect it from discovery. Whether documents have been prepared in anticipation of litigation or in the ordinary course of business will be determined on a case-by-case basis.[51] Further, many courts have held that the privilege must be asserted on a document-by-document basis, as opposed to asserting the privilege over all the materials at issue.[52]

However, there is no bright-line standard delineating the scope of the work-product doctrine. Jurisdictions following the federal rule have adopted both majority and minority views, while other jurisdictions, including California, have developed their own standards.[53] Consequently, whether the doctrine applies to protect documents from disclosure can be determined only by reference to the applicable standard in the particular jurisdiction.

The Majority View: Information in an Insurance Carrier's Claim Files Is Collected in the Ordinary Course of Business

If the documents at issue were not prepared or collected in anticipation of litigation, then the work-product doctrine will not apply and the documents will be discoverable upon a showing of relevance.[54]

Among the states that follow the federal rule, the majority view recognizes that a significant part of an insurance carrier's business is to investigate and assess claims. As the Colorado Supreme Court explained:

> Because a substantial part of an insurance company's business is to investigate claims made by an insured against the company or by some other party against an insured, it must be presumed that such investigations are part of the normal business activity of the company and that reports and witness' statements compiled by or on behalf of the insurer in the course of such investigations are ordinary business records as distinguished from trial preparation materials.[55]

Based on this rationale, these courts hold that unless the carrier's investigation was performed at the request of or under the direction of counsel, all materials resulting from the investigation are "conclusively presumed to have been made in the ordinary course of business and not in anticipation of litigation."[56] However, the federal courts following the majority rule offer no clear guidelines regarding the level of certainty needed to transform investigative material from work performed in the ordinary course of business to work performed in anticipation of litigation. Some courts note that the "[m]ere likelihood of litigation in the future is insufficient for invoking the privilege. Rather, the probability of litigation must be substantial and the commencement of litigation imminent."[57] For these courts, "[t]he mere contingency that litigation may result is not determinative . . . While litigation need not be imminent, the primary motivating purpose behind the creation of a document or investigative report must be to aid in possible future litigation."[58]

Other courts have focused not on the pendency of litigation, but rather on the document itself. "[T]he test should be whether, in light of the nature of the document and the factual situation in the particular case, the document can fairly be said to have been prepared or obtained because of the prospect of litigation."[59]

Thus, under the majority federal view, information in an insurance carrier's claim files should not be deemed to be work product unless the carrier proves, on a document-by-document basis, that the information was prepared in anticipation of litigation.

The Minority View: Information in an Insurance Carrier's Claim File Is Collected in Anticipation of Litigation

Under the minority federal view, courts accept that all insurance carriers' investigations generally are undertaken in anticipation of litigation. As the Iowa Supreme Court observed:

> In our litigious society, when an insured reports to his insurer that he has been involved in an incident involving another person, the insurer can reasonably anticipate that some action will be taken by the other party. The seeds of prospective litigation have been sown, and the prudent party, anticipating this fact, will begin to prepare his case. Although a claim may be settled short of the instigation of legal action, there is an ever-present possibility of a claim's ending in litigation. The recognition of this possibility provides, in any given case, the impetus for the insurer to garner information regarding the circumstances of a claim.[60]

Based on this rationale, these courts conclude that most information in an insurance carrier's claim files is protected from discovery by the work-product doctrine.[61]

While the minority view may not permit the insured to discover certain claim documents in coverage litigation against a carrier, it does protect the insured and the carrier from being forced to disclose potentially damaging documents to an underlying claimant. Furthermore, the protection afforded under the minority view may vary, depending upon who is seeking access to the material in question. As one court explained:

> When the party seeking the work product does not have a special relationship with the insurer, different considerations may apply. For example, in investigations of an accident, because of potential claims by the third party against the insured, the possibility of litigation might arise at an earlier time. However, when the claim is made by its insured, an insurance company cannot in good faith contend that there is a reasonable possibility of litigation with respect to every claim submitted to it.[62]

In jurisdictions that follow the federal rule but have not adopted a position on the question of whether an insurance carrier's claim files constitute "work product," the majority rule should be adopted. As the Alaska Supreme Court reasoned in rejecting the minority view:

> The minority rule, we believe, is flawed because it presumes too much. Simply because an event has occurred which may require an insurer to provide

payments under its contract with an insured does not automatically transform an insurer's activities into preparation for litigation. An insurance company routinely investigates possible claims whether or not there is any
possibility of litigation, and we do not believe that [the work product doc-
trine] was intended to insulate insurers from discovery merely because they
regularly deal with potential claims. The minority rule also improperly re-
lieves insurers and their insureds of a substantial portion of the obligations
of discovery imposed on parties generally . . . . Indeed, under the minority
rule, hardly any document authorized by or for an insurer is discoverable
without the showing of substantial need and undue hardship . . . .[63]

The California View

Not all jurisdictions follow the federal statute. California, for example, has a statute
protecting work product from disclosure that is broader than the federal rule. In California, work product is not discoverable unless denial "will unfairly prejudice the
party seeking discovery," and in no event may a "writing that reflects an attorney's
impressions, conclusions, opinions, or legal research or theories" be discovered.[64]

The California rule protects work product in all legal contexts rather than merely
protecting work performed in anticipation of litigation.[65] However, like the federal
rule, opinion work product also enjoys absolute immunity in California.[66]

Furthermore, the policy behind the privilege in California is essentially the same
as the federal policy. The privilege is intended to preserve the rights of attorneys to
prepare for trial with a certain amount of privacy and to prevent attorneys from reap-
ing the benefits of their opponents' work.[67]

The Application of the Work Product Doctrine to Defense Materials

In many insurance coverage cases, there are questions as to the timing of occurrences
and the extent of any damage or injury involved. This is particularly true in environmental coverage litigation. As a result, insurance carriers often seek to discover reports by outside consultants in connection with any underlying litigation. In jurisdictions
following the federal rule, the discoverability of these reports will depend upon which
view of "anticipation of litigation" the jurisdiction follows. Even if such reports are
"work product" in the underlying litigation, they may be discoverable in the coverage
litigation. Courts differ as to whether the work-product protection lapses once litigation or anticipation of litigation has ended or whether it offers "perpetual protection,"
thereby preventing discovery of the material in later proceedings.[68]

The Limited Protection View

Some courts hold that the protection extends only to documents prepared in anticipation of the specific litigation before the court. "Thus, documents prepared for one case
are freely discoverable in another case."[69]

Moreover, one court following the limited protection view has required not only
that the documents be prepared in preparation for the specific action before the court
but also that the parties be adversaries in order for the privilege to apply.

Here, the sought-after materials were . . . prepared for the mutual benefit of insureds and insurers against a third-party adversary. Insurers were not the adversary from whom the attorney's trial strategies and opinions required protection. Insurers and insureds have only become adversarial since the termination of the primary litigation. While the work-product materials, had they been requested by the third-party opponent in the underlying lawsuit, would have been entitled to protection, the same protection is not warranted here.[70]

The Broad Protection View

However, both the Fourth and Eighth Circuits have held that reports prepared in previous litigation are not discoverable in the current litigation.[71] In *In re Murphy*,[72] the court held that the work-product doctrine protects documents prepared in anticipation of unrelated, terminated litigation. The court reasoned that this protection was consistent with the purpose of the work-product doctrine as announced by the United States Supreme Court in *Hickman v. Taylor*,[73] which recognized the attorney's need for enough privacy to perform his duties responsibly and effectively.[74] According to the *Murphy* court,

> [w]hat is needed, if we are to remain faithful to the articulated policies of Hickman, is a perpetual protection for work product, one that extends beyond the termination of the litigation for which the documents were prepared. Any less protection would generate the very evils that the Court in Hickman attempted to avoid.[75]

California also appears to follow the Fourth and Eighth Circuit's view of broad protection.[76]

The Intermediate View

A third approach was recognized in *Levingston v. Allis-Chalmers Corp.*[77] In *Levingston,* the court held that the work-product doctrine applies only when the two suits are related.[78] Thus, to the extent that the underlying litigation and coverage litigation are deemed to be closely related—as they should be—the underlying defense files should be treated as work product and should not be discoverable in the coverage litigation.[79]

Waiver of the Work Product Doctrine

Even if documents qualify as work product, the protection against discovery may be waived. However, determining when the doctrine has been waived may not be easy.

Waiver Under Federal Law

Federal courts are split on what represents a waiver of the attorney work-product doctrine. The majority of federal courts hold that conduct that might constitute a waiver of the attorney-client privilege will not necessarily result in a waiver of the work-product protection. As one court stated:

> We do not consider the strict standard of waiver in the attorney-client privilege context . . . to be appropriate for work product cases. . . . The purpose of the work product doctrine is to protect information against opposing parties, rather than against all others outside a particular confidential relationship, in order to encourage effective trial preparation . . . . A disclosure made in the pursuit of such trial preparation, and not inconsistent with maintaining secrecy against opponents, should be allowed without waiver of the privilege.[80]

This led the court to conclude that "while the mere showing of a voluntary disclosure to a third person will generally suffice to show waiver of the attorney-client privilege, it should not suffice in itself for waiver of the work product privilege."[81]

In contrast, a minority of courts hold that the standard for waiver of the work-product protection is the same as the standard for waiver of the attorney-client privilege—that is, the disclosure or consent to disclosure of work product material by the holder of the privilege waives it.[82]

Whichever standard is used to determine waiver, most federal courts agree that disclosure to an allied party will not waive the privilege.[83] As stated in *In re Crazy Eddie Securities Litigation*,[84] "[c]ounsel may therefore share work product, including ideas, opinions, and legal theories, with those having similar interests in fully preparing litigation against a common adversary."[85]

This should mean that when an insurance carrier is defending its insured against a "common adversary," disclosure to the insured of any information in the claims file and disclosure to the carrier of defense files should not waive the work-product protection as to third parties, including the underlying claimants.[86] Where the insured and insurer are co-parties, this "allied party" or "common adversary" exception to the waiver doctrine protects the insured from disclosing a claims file or insured-insurer communications to third-party claimants.

Waiver Under California Law

There is no waiver provision in California Code of Civil Procedure section 2018, the California statute stating the work-product doctrine. As a result, California courts have not reached a consensus on what standard is to be used to determine if the protection has been waived.

In *Williamson v. Superior Court*,[87] the California Supreme Court held that the fact that parties may be co-defendants does not assure that they are not adversaries. The court specifically recognized that on the facts before it, the sharing of information among co-defendants is not necessarily the sharing of information among allied parties. As the court noted, "[e]ach codefendant seeks to disclaim any responsibility for the alleged injuries, and argues that if there is responsibility for the alleged injuries it is due to the failure of the other. Certainly, there exists that relationship which suggests a conflict of interest."[88]

Thus, as one commentator has suggested, *Williamson* implies that California would follow the federal minority rule and hold that disclosure to anyone, even a co-defendant, could constitute waiver of the privilege.[89]

However, in *Fellows v. Superior Court,*[90] the court seemed to follow the rule followed by a majority of federal courts. In *Fellows,* the claimants had brought a bad faith action against an insurance carrier for failure to settle their uninsured motorist claims after the issue of coverage had been resolved by an arbitrator. The carrier sought production of the files of the claimants' former attorney. The court held that although the attorney had turned the file over to the claimants, this did not constitute waiver of the work product doctrine.[91] The court also held that initiation of a civil action by the claimants against the carrier did not waive the protection:

> [A]uthorization by the attorney to his client to waive the privilege cannot be construed as a waiver in and of itself. Nor can the action of an attorney in disclosing the contents of his file to his client be construed as a waiver by disclosure of the privileged material *since the disclosure is not to a disinterested person . . .* but to the client whose interest in nondisclosure is supported by the policy reasons which underlie the creation of the privilege.[92]

Thus, Fellows indicates that, like the majority of federal courts, California recognizes that disclosure of work product to persons with a common interest or a common adversary should not waive the work-product privilege.

Safeguards an Insured May Employ to Protect the Attorney-Client Privilege and the Work-Product Doctrine

In those jurisdictions that do not recognize the applicability of the attorney-client privilege and/or work-product doctrine to an insured's communications with its carriers, there is little an insured can do to protect communications other than to carefully screen the contents of the communications to minimize any damage should the communications be used by a claimant. However, in jurisdictions that recognize that such communications or the information conveyed may be protected by the privilege and/or the doctrine, an insured can take steps to maximize the likely application of those protections. Those steps include the following:

1. Make sure the predominant purpose of the communication relates to a defense against the claim. Because a court might conduct an in camera examination of any communications, it is probably a good idea to include appropriate language in any communication, such as "This letter provides information that may assist the counsel retained to defend us against the claim . . . ."
2. Make sure that the communication is made with the expectation of confidentiality. It is useful in this regard to instruct (preferably in writing, to create a "paper trail") anyone communicating with insurers about claims that all communications are to be regarded as confidential and for the purpose of assisting counsel in defending against a claim.
3. Make sure that any communication is actually sent to the counsel selected to defend the insured.
4. If the carrier wants to interview the insured's employees, determine in advance the purpose of the interviews. If the purpose is to learn when, for ex-

ample, the insured first knew that chemicals were leaking into groundwater, that may relate not only to the defense against a claim, but also to the carrier's determination of whether the claim is covered (e.g., was the damage "expected and intended" by the insured or was the problem a "known risk" that should have been disclosed in the policy application?). If there is more than one possible reason for the interview, a court might conclude that the dominant purpose did not relate to the defense of the claims.

5. Keep in mind that if an insured is represented by its own counsel (for example, coverage counsel) in its communications and meetings with its carriers, the appearance is created that the insured is not looking to its carrier as a legal advisor. This could lead a court to conclude that there was no attorney-client relationship between the insured and the carrier (as agent for the defense counsel ultimately selected), which means that even in jurisdictions following the most favorable approach, the attorney-client privilege might not apply to the communications.

6. Consider asking the carrier to select counsel before there are any substantive communications or witness interviews. The attorney could then request the communications and interviews, which might improve the chances of the work-product doctrine being applied. Furthermore, if counsel are retained before communications, this eliminates an argument accepted by some courts in rejecting the applicability of the privilege—that counsel had not been retained at the time of the communication.

7. Carefully monitor any discussions with carriers of coverage issues. Under even the broadest views, these discussions might not be protected from discovery because they do not relate to the defense of the claim.

8. Know which jurisdiction's law will apply and what that law is with respect to an insured's communications with carriers *before* the communications occur, if possible.

Conclusion

As the above demonstrates, all communications between an insured and an insurer should be carefully monitored to ensure, to the extent possible, that the protections afforded by the attorney-client privilege and the work-product doctrine will apply. To the extent there is any doubt, insureds should err on the side of caution insofar as the specifics of what is communicated to insurance carriers (but without violating the duty to cooperate imposed by most insurance policies). Of course, carriers also have reason to tread carefully in this area. After all, if a communication from an insured to a carrier turns out to be the evidence that a claimant uses to establish the insured's liability, it may be the carrier who bears the financial burden, at least to the extent of the aggregate limits of its insurance policy.

Notes

1. Egan v. Mut. of Omaha Ins. Co., 24 Cal. 3d 809, 819, 620 P.2d 141, 169 Cal. Rptr. 691 (1979), *cert. denied and appeal dismissed*, 445 U.S. 912 (1980). *See also* ALLAN D. WINDT, INSURANCE CLAIMS AND DISPUTES, § 2.5, at 66 (4th ed. 2001) ("The implied covenant of good faith and fair

dealing in the policy should necessarily require the insurer to conduct any necessary investigation in a timely fashion and to conduct a reasonable investigation before denying coverage.").

2. *See* Tews Funeral Home, Inc. v. Ohio Cas. Ins. Co., 832 F.2d 1037, 1046 (7th Cir. 1987) (a determination of the duty to indemnify "is premature while the underlying action is pending if the indemnity decision would require a court to adjudicate facts in the underlying dispute"); Montrose Chem. Corp. v. Superior Court, 6 Cal. 4th 287, 301, 861 P.2d 1153, 24 Cal. Rptr. 2d 467 (1993) ("To eliminate the risk of inconsistent factual determinations that could prejudice the insured, a stay of the declaratory relief action pending resolution of the third party suit is appropriate when the coverage action turns on facts to be litigated in the underlying action."); Cal-Farm Ins. Co. v. TAC Exterminators, Inc., 172 Cal. App. 3d 564, 572, 218 Cal. Rptr. 407 (1985) (when underlying action has not yet been tried, "the resolution of coverage must be determined by accepting as true all the allegations contained in the complaint in the underlying action").

3. *See* Lectrolarm Custom Sys., Inc. v. Pelco Sales, Inc., 212 F.R.D. 567, 566 (E.D. Cal. 2002) ("Federal courts have never recognized a blanket privilege regarding insured-insurer communications.").

4. *Cf.* Cutchin v. State, 143 Md. App. 81, 90-91, 792 A.2d 359 (2002) (acknowledging two views, but noting that the decisions involved "turn on their facts and few, if any, truly stand for the proposition that all insured-liability or indemnity insurer communications are privileged, or the proposition that none are privileged").

5. *See, e.g.*, Metroflight, Inc. v. Argonaut Ins. Co., 403 F. Supp. 1195, 1197-98 (N.D. Tex. 1975) (there is a privilege for communications from insured to carrier regarding facts of claim when intended to assist counsel in defense); Bellmann v. District Court, 187 Colo. 350, 531 P.2d 632 (1975), *overruled on other grounds*, Kay Labs., Inc. v. District Court, 653 P.2d 721 (Colo. 1982); Grand Union Co. v. Patrick, 247 So. 2d 474 (Fla. Dist. Ct. App. 1971); People v. Ryan, 30 Ill. 2d 456, 197 N.E.2d 15 (1964); State *ex rel.* Cain v. Barker, 540 S.W.2d 50 (Mo. 1976); Heidebrink v. Moriwaki, 104 Wash. 2d 392, 706 P.2d 212 (1985).

6. People v. Ryan, 30 Ill. 2d 456, 197 N.E.2d 15, 17 (1964). *See* also Scripps Health v. Superior Court, 109 Cal. App. 4th 529, 535, 135 Cal. Rptr. 2d 126 (2003) ("It has long been recognized that communications made by an insured to his 'liability insurance company, concerning an event which may be made the basis of a claim against him covered by the policy, is a privileged communication, as being between attorney and client, if the policy requires the company to defend him through its attorney, and the communication is intended for the information or assistance of the attorney in so defending him.'"); Bellmann v. District Court, 187 Colo. 350, 531 P.2d 632, 634 (1975) ("Since control of [the insured's] defense rested entirely with [the carrier] and counsel retained by [it], we hold that the insurance investigator who took the [insured's] statement was, in effect, an agent of the attorneys for the purpose of acquiring and transmitting this information to them."); Grand Union Co. v. Patrick, 247 So. 2d 474 (Fla. Dist. Ct. App. 1971) (communication of accident report to carrier protected by attorney-client privilege because communication was, in essence, a communication between insured and counsel to benefit the defense of the case); Braglia v. Cephus, 146 Ill. App. 3d 241, 496 N.E.2d 1171, 1176 (1986) (following *Ryan*); Martin v. Clark, 92 Ill. App. 3d 518, 415 N.E.2d 30, 32 (1980) (following *Ryan* and holding that statement given by insured to carrier "was protected by the attorney-client privilege and . . . should not have been subject to discovery"); 81 AM. JUR. 2d, *Witnesses,* § 194, at 228 (1976) (under the broad approach, the carrier "is regarded as a mere intermediate agent to transmit the communications to the attorneys of its claims department or to an eventual trial attorney if an action is brought"); 55 A.L.R.4th 336, 342 (1987). In fact, the *Restatement of the Law Governing Lawyers* recognizes this broad approach. The *Restatement* states:

> [C]ommunications between the lawyer and representatives of the insurer concerning such matters as progress reports, case evaluations, and settlement should be regarded as privileged and otherwise immune from discovery by the claimant or another party to

the proceedings. Similarly, communications between counsel retained by an insurer to coordinate the efforts of multiple counsel for insureds in multiple suits and such coordinating counsel are subject to privilege.

RESTATEMENT (THIRD) OF THE LAW GOVERNING LAWYERS § 134 cmt. f (2000). The *Restatement* also provides:

> The privilege applies to communications to and from the client disclosed to persons who hire the lawyer as an incident of the lawyer's engagement. Thus, the privilege covers communications by a client-insured to an insurance-company investigator who is to convey the facts to the client's lawyer designated by the insurer, as well as communications from the lawyer for the insured to the insurer in providing a progress report or discussing litigation strategy or settlement . . . .

Id., § 70 cmt. f, illus. 5.

7. 26 Ill. App. 3d 728, 327 N.E.2d 92 (1974).

8. *Id.* at 94. *See also* RESTATEMENT (THIRD) OF THE LAW GOVERNING LAWYERS, § 70 cmt. f., illus. 5 (2000) (recognizing that privilege does not apply to "communications by an insured to an insurance investigator who will report to the company"). *But see* D.I. Chadbourne, Inc. v. Superior Court, 60 Cal. 2d 723, 727, 388 P.2d 700, 36 Cal. Rptr. 468 (1964) (question of fact as to whether privilege attaches when communication from insured's employee to independent contractor employed by carrier for subsequent transmittal to carrier and then to counsel selected by insurer); Gene Compton's Corp. v. Superior Court, 205 Cal. App. 2d 365, 366, 23 Cal. Rptr. 250 (1962) (insured's communication to insurance broker for transmission to carrier privileged), *disapproved on other grounds,* D.I. Chadbourne, Inc. v. Superior Court, 60 Cal. 2d 723, 388 P.2d 700, 36 Cal. Rptr. 468 (1964).

9. *See, e.g.,* State v. Anderson, 247 Minn. 469, 78 N.W.2d 320 (1956) (statements by insured to carrier not privileged because not shown that statements made for exclusive use in insured's defense and in confidence); Jacobi v. Podevels, 23 Wis. 2d 152, 127 N.W.2d 73 (1964) (statements by insured to insurance adjuster not privileged because no action pending or threatened and no counsel retained for insured).

10. 205 Cal. App. 2d 365, 23 Cal. Rptr. 250 (1962).

11. *Id.* at 379.

12. *See* D.I. Chadbourne, Inc. v. Superior Court, 60 Cal. 2d 723, 731, 388 P.2d 700, 36 Cal. Rptr. 468 (1964). However, the court approved of the "dominant purpose" test and "left intact Gene Compton's . . . ." Travelers Ins. Cos. v. Superior Court, 143 Cal. App. 3d 436, 451, 191 Cal. Rptr. 871 (1983).

13. *Id. See also* Heffron v. Los Angeles Transit Lines, 170 Cal. App. 2d 709, 718, 339 P.2d 567 (1959) (communication privileged "if the policy requires the company to defend [the insured] through its attorney, and the communication is intended for the information or assistance of the attorney in so defending him").

14. 202 N.J. Super. 255, 494 A.2d 834 (1985).

15. 494 A.2d at 837.

16. *Id.*

17. *Id.* at 838.

18. 212 F.R.D. 567 (E.D. Cal. 2002).

19. *Id.* at 572.

20. *Id.* (citations omitted)

21. *Id.* at 573.

22. *See, e.g.,* Rogers v. Aetna Cas. & Sur. Co., 601 F.2d 840, 845 (5th Cir. 1979); Jackson v. Kroblin Refrigerated Xpress, Inc., 49 F.R.D. 134, 136-37 (N.D. W.Va. 1970); Gottlieb v. Bresler, 24 F.R.D. 371, 372 (D.D.C. 1959) ("[A] communication received by a liability insurance company from one of its insureds concerning a matter covered by the insurance policy is not a privileged

communication."); Longs Drug Stores v. Howe, 657 P.2d 412, 415-16 (Ariz. 1983); Conley v. Graybeal, 315 A.2d 609, 610 (Del. Super. 1974); DiCenzo v. Izawa, 723 P.2d 171, 176-78 (Haw. 1986).

23. Jacobi v. Podevels, 127 N.W.2d 73, 76 (Wis. 1964).

24. 752 P.2d 999 (Alaska 1988).

25. *Id.* at 1002-03.

26. *Id.* at 1003-04.

27. *See, e.g.,* Van Alen v. Anchorage Ski Club, 536 P.2d 784, 787 (Alaska 1975) ("eyewitness" statements taken by insurers not protected by work-product doctrine); D.I. Chadbourne, Inc. v. Superior Court, 60 Cal. 2d 723, 734, 388 P.2d 700, 36 Cal. Rptr. 468 (1964) (attorney-client privilege does not attach to statement by a witness who is not an employee of the client corporation). *See also* Trade Center Properties, Inc. v. Superior Court, 185 Cal. App. 2d 409, 411, 8 Cal. Rptr. 345 (1960).

28. 60 Cal. 2d 723, 388 P.2d 700, 36 Cal. Rptr. 468 (1964).

29. 60 Cal. 2d at 736-38.

30. *Id.*

31. *Id.* at 737-38 (employer's intent controls as to whether privilege applies, and if carrier has not advised employer that statement will be obtained for attorney, "it cannot be said that the corporation intended the statement to be made as a confidential communication from client to attorney").

32. *Id.* at 736-37.

33. *Id.* at 737. *See also* Alpha Beta Co. v. Superior Court, 157 Cal. App. 3d 818, 827, 203 Cal. Rptr. 752 (1984) (following *Chadbourne* in holding not privileged some information obtained from an employee who had no connection with the litigation other than as a witness).

34. 60 Cal. 2d at 737-38.

35. *Id.* at 737.

36. *Id.* at 736. *See* Sierra Vista Hospital v. Superior Court, 248 Cal. App. 2d 359, 365, 56 Cal. Rptr. 387 (1967) (privilege applies to report made by hospital administrator whose duties were those of a general business manager and included protection of the employer hospital from "legal action or liability").

37. *See* Scripps Health v. Superior Court, 109 Cal. App. 4th 529, 533-34, 135 Cal. Rptr. 2d 126 (2003) ("When the corporate employer has more than one purpose in requiring the report, the dominant purpose will control"; report held privileged when one purpose was quality assurance/ peer review because "dominant purpose" was attorney review in anticipation of possible litigation).

38. 153 Ga. 364, 112 S.E. 370 (1922).

39. *Id.* at 370.

40. 723 S.W.2d 74 (Mo. Ct. App. 1986).

41. *Id.* at 75.

42. RESTATEMENT (THIRD) OF THE LAW GOVERNING LAWYERS, § 134 cmt. f (2000). *See* Lectrolarm Custom Sys., Inc. v. Pelco Sales, Inc., 212 F.R.D. 567, 571-73 (E.D. Cal. 2002) (rejecting underlying plaintiff's request for production of documents from carrier even though carrier had reserved rights, noting that "common defense doctrine" preserved attorney-client privilege); Heffron v. Los Angeles Transit Lines, 170 Cal. App. 2d 709, 718, 339 P.2d 567 (1959) (communication privilege "if the policy requires the company to defend [the insured] through its attorney, and the communication is intended for the information or assistance of the attorney in so defending him"); Sawyer v. Southwest Airlines, 2002 U.S. Dist. LEXIS 25111 (D. Kan. Dec. 23, 2002) (underlying plaintiff's motion to compel production of documents exchanged between insured and carrier denied because an insured and carrier, who had duty to defend, "have an interest in common . . . that [is] of a legal and not commercial nature").

43. CAL. CIV. CODE § 2860.

44. *Id.*

45. Connecticut Mut. Life Ins. Co. v. Shields, 16 F.R.D. 5, 8 (S.D.N.Y. 1954).

46. *See* Hickman v. Taylor, 329 U.S. 495, 510 (1947).

47. FED. R. CIV. PROC. 26 (b)(3). Duplan Corp. v. Moulinage et Retorderie de Chavanoz, 509 F.2d 730 (4th Cir. 1974), *cert. denied,* 420 U.S. 997 (1975). *See also In re* Murphy, 560 F.2d 326 (8th Cir. 1977).

48. FED. R. CIV. PROC. 26(b)(3).

49. *Id.*

50. Diversified Indus., Inc. v. Meredith, 572 F.2d 596, 603 (8th Cir. 1977).

51. *See* Pete Rinaldi's Fast Foods, Inc. v. Great Am. Ins. Cos., 123 F.R.D. 198 (M.D.N.C. 1988); Upjohn v. United States, 449 U.S. 383, 396-97 (1981).

52. *See, e.g.,* Auto-Owners Ins. Co. v. Totaltape, Inc., 135 F.R.D. 199, 202 (M.D. Fla. 1990) ("[t]he trend in lower federal courts is to analyze work product claims concerning insurance files on a case by case basis"); Burr v. United Farm Bureau Mut. Inc. Co., 560 N.E.2d 1250, 1256 (Ind. Ct. App. 1990) ("the privilege must be asserted on a document by document basis and with the utmost clarity").

53. *See* BP Alaska Exploration, Inc. v. Superior Court, 199 Cal. App. 3d 1240, 1250 (1988) ("federal law is not controlling in California").

54. Thomas Organ Co. v. Jadranska Slobodna Plovidba, 54 F.R.D. 367, 370 (N.D. Ill. 1972).

55. Hawkins v. District Court, 638 P.2d 1372, 1378 (Colo. 1982).

56. Henry Enters., Inc. v. Smith, 592 P.2d 915, 920 (Kan. 1979). *Accord,* Harper v. Auto-Owners Ins. Co., 138 F.R.D. 655, 663 (S.D. Ind. 1991) ("[A] document or thing produced or used by an insurer to evaluate an insured's claim in order to arrive at a claims decision in the ordinary and regular course of business is not work product . . . ."); Western Nat'l Bank v. Employers Ins., 109 F.R.D. 55 (D. Colo. 1985); APL v. Aetna Cas. & Sur. Co., 91 F.R.D. 10, 17 (D. Md. 1980) ("[W]hile litigation often results from an insurance company's denial of a claim, it cannot be said that any document prepared by an insurance company after such a claim has arisen is prepared in anticipation of litigation within the meaning of Rule 26(b)(3)."); Benton v. Brookfield Props. Corp., 2003 U.S. Dist. LEXIS 13020 *7 (S.D.N.Y. July 29, 2003) ("An insurance company's decision whether to afford coverage is part of its normal business decision-making and does not constitute work-product even though the insurance company may face the prospect that if coverage is denied, the insured will commence litigation against it."); Langdon v. Champion, 752 P.2d 999, 1007 (Alaska 1988) ("An insurance company routinely investigates possible claims whether or not there is any possibility of litigation, and we do not believe that [the work-product doctrine] was intended to insulate insurers from discovery merely because they regularly deal with potential claims."); in fact, even if the carrier retains a law firm to perform the claims assessment, this will not necessarily protect the claims file information from discovery. *See* Mission Nat'l Ins. Co. v. Lilly, 112 F.R.D. 160 (D. Minn. 1986).

57. Stauffer Chem. Co. v. Monsanto Corp., 623 F. Supp 148, 152 (E.D. Mo. 1985).

58. Janicker v. George Washington Univ., 94 F.R.D. 648, 650 (D.D.C. 1982).

59. APL v. Aetna Cas. & Sur. Co., 91 F.R.D. 10, 15 (D. Md. 1980) (citation omitted). *See* Amica Mut. Ins. Co. v. W.C. Bradley Co., 217 F.R.D. 79, 83 (D. Mass. 2003) ("Coverage investigations by insurance companies are not per se conducted in anticipation of litigation, and a determination as to whether documents generated during such investigations were prepared in anticipation of litigation, as opposed to in the ordinary course of business, should be made on a case-by-case basis."); Henderson v. Zurn Indus., Inc., 131 F.R.D. 560 (S.D. Ind. 1990).

60. Ashmead v. Harris, 336 N.W.2d 197, 201 (Iowa 1983) (quoting Fireman's Fund Ins. Co. v. McAlpine, 391 A.2d 84, 89-90 (R.I. 1978)).

61. *See* Almaguer v. Chicago, R.I.&P.R. Co., 55 F.R.D. 147, 148 (D. Neb. 1972).

62. Pete Rinaldi's Fast Foods, Inc. v. Great Am. Ins. Cas., 123 F.R.D. 198, 202 (M.D.N.C. 1988). *See also* Henderson v. Zurn Indus., Inc., 131 F.R.D. 560, 571 n.11 (S.D. Ind. 1990) (court acknowl-

edged a difference between third-party claims against a carrier and direct first-party claims; "one would expect there to be more litigation on third-party claims than on direct first-party contract actions, with a resultant increased anticipation of such litigation in the third-party context").

63. Langdon v. Champion, 752 P.2d 999, 1006-07 (Alaska 1988).

64. CAL. CODE CIV. PROC. § 2018(c).

65. *Id.*; Rumac, Inc. v. Bottomley, 143 Cal. App. 3d 810, 192 Cal. Rptr. 104 (1983).

66. *See* BP Alaska Exploration, Inc. v. Superior Court, 199 Cal. App. 3d 1240, 245 Cal. Rptr. 682 (1988).

67. *See* CAL. CODE CIV. PROC. § 2018(a).

68. *See* Levingston v. Allis-Chalmers Corp., 109 F.R.D. 546 (S.D. Miss. 1985); Federal Trade Commission v. Grolier, Inc., 462 U.S. 19 (1983).

69. Levingston v. Allis-Chalmers Corp., 109 F.R.D. 546 at 552. *See* United States v. Internat'l Business Machines Corp., 66 F.R.D. 154, 178 (S.D.N.Y. 1974) (documents must be prepared in anticipation of the litigation in which special immunity accorded to such material is sought); Honeywell, Inc. v. Piper Aircraft Corp., 50 F.R.D. 117, 119 (M.D. Pa. 1970) (same); Hanover Shoe, Inc. v. United Shoe Mach. Corp., 207 F. Supp. 407, 410 (M.D. Pa. 1962) (materials must be prepared for case at bar).

70. Waste Management, Inc. v. International Surplus Lines Ins. Co., No. 70958 (Ill. 1991).

71. *See* Duplan Corp. v. Moulinage et Retorderie de Chavanoz, 509 F.2d 730 (4th Cir. 1974), *cert. denied*, 420 U.S. 997 (1975); *In re* Murphy, 560 F.2d 326 (8th Cir. 1977).

72. 560 F.2d 326 (8th Cir. 1977).

73. 329 U.S. 495 (1947).

74. 560 F.2d at 333.

75. *Id.* at 334.

76. *See* Fellows v. Superior Court, 108 Cal. App. 3d 55, 62, 166 Cal. Rptr. 274 (1980) ("[T]he attorney's work product privilege . . . survives the termination of the litigation or matter in which the work product is prepared and may be claimed in subsequent litigation—whether related or unrelated to the prior matter—to preclude disclosure of the attorney's work product.").

77. 109 F.R.D. 546 (S.D. Miss. 1985).

78. *Id.* at 552. *Accord,* Hercules, Inc. v. Exxon Corp., 434 F. Supp. 136, 153 (D. Del. 1977) ("[T]his Court accepts the 'sounder view' that the documents prepared for one case have the same protection in a second case where the two cases are closely related in parties or subject matter."); Republic Gear Co. v. Borg-Warner Corp., 381 F.2d 551, 557 (2d Cir. 1967); Midland Inv. Co. v. Van Alstyne, Noel & Co., 59 F.R.D. 134, 138 (S.D.N.Y. 1973).

79. *See* Special Magistrate's Report and Recommendation No. 2, *In re* Texas Eastern Transmission Corp. PCB Contamination Ins. Coverage Litig., MDL Docket No. 764 (E.D. Pa. Apr. 8, 1991), *reprinted in* 5 *Mealey's Litigation Reports—Insurance,* No. 23, § C (Apr. 16, 1991).

80. United States v. Am. Tel. & Tel. Co., 642 F.2d 1285, 1299 (D.C. Cir. 1980) (citation omitted).

81. *Id.* (emphasis omitted).

82. *See* D'Ippolito v. Cities Serv. Co., 39 F.R.D. 610 (S.D.N.Y. 1965).

83. Continental Oil Co. v. United States, 330 F.2d 347 (9th Cir. 1964).

84. 131 F.R.D. 374, 379 (E.D.N.Y. 1990).

85. *Id.* at 379.

86. *See* Bovis Lend Lease, LMB, Inc. v. Seasons Contracting Corp., 2002 U.S. Dist. LEXIS 23322, *14, 17 (S.D.N.Y. Dec. 5, 2002) ("certainly, documents created after litigation has already commenced, when the claims handlers' work has plainly shifted from investigating the initial claim to assisting in the defense of the pending litigation and evaluating litigation exposure, are likely to be covered by the work product doctrine. . . . Similarly, correspondence between an insured and its liability insurer, written 'as a consequence of pending litigation for the purpose of mounting a defense to the claim' is entitled to work product protection."). *See also* Niagara Mohawk Power

Corp. v. Stone & Webster Eng'g Corp., 125 F.R.D. 578, 587 (N.D.N.Y. 1989) ("sharing work product material with a friendly party does not waive the work product protection as it applies to an adverse third party").

87. 21 Cal. 3d 829, 582 P.2d 126, 148 Cal. Rptr. 39 (1978).

88. 21 Cal. 3d at 836 (quoting Gorman Rupp Indus., Inc. v. Superior Court, 20 Cal. App. 3d 28, 31, 97 Cal. Rptr. 377 (1971)).

89. *See* Greg Kopta, *Applying the Attorney-Client and Work Product Privileges to Allied Party Exchange of Information in California,* 36 UCLA L. Rev. 151 (1988).

90. 108 Cal. App. 3d 55, 166 Cal. Rptr. 274 (1980).

91. 108 Cal. App. 3d at 65-66.

92. *Id.* (emphasis added)

CHAPTER 9

A Second Look at Privilege and Confidentiality in the Reinsurance Arena[*]

JOHN W. THORNTON
JANE THORNTON MASTRUCCI
CYNTHIA HARRISON RUIZ

Litigation, Reinsurance Policies, and the New Millenium

In recent years, there has been an explosion of litigation directly and indirectly involving reinsurance scenarios. Because of the unique nature of reinsurance agreements, the communications between insurer and reinsurer are more "open" than would otherwise be the case in a traditional contractual scenario. This in turn creates a number of interesting problems relating to confidentiality and the discoverability of communications and information shared with the reinsurer. Before these issues can be considered, however, the unique nature of reinsurance must be briefly explored.

Reinsurance: A Brief Primer

A reinsurance contract involves an agreement under which one insurer transfers, or "cedes," a portion of its risk to another insurance company in return for a percentage of the premium.[1] Reinsurance differs from direct insurance in that there is no liability running from the reinsurer to the original insured.[2] Rather, a reinsurance contract is a contract of indemnity, and liability does not attach until the reinsured has actually made payment on the underlying claim.[3] Put differently, a reinsurance agreement indemnifies against loss rather than against liability.[4]

---

[*]This chapter is dedicated to the memory of John W. Thornton, Sr., the original author, who passed away November 21, 2003. He was a great lawyer, scholar, and person, and his legacy will live on through the countless colleagues, friends, and family members touched and inspired by his life.

The goal of reinsurance is to diversify the risk of loss, which then reduces not only the risk, but also the capital reserves that must be held by the ceding company.[5] Moreover, reinsurance serves a number of important corporate and societal interests, such as (1) increasing a carrier's ability to accept new risks and allowing it to accept larger risks that might otherwise exceed its capacity, (2) increasing stability for the ceding company, (3) allowing catastrophic risks to be spread across the industry, and (4) promoting competition among insurers.[6] When a reinsurance company transfers a part of its risk, the transaction is termed a "retrocessional agreement," with the transferring reinsurer referred to as the "retrocedent" and the reinsurer assuming the risk referred to as the "retrocessionaire."[7]

Reinsurance agreements fall into one of two broad, general categories: "facultative" reinsurance and "treaty" or "automatic" reinsurance.[8] In "facultative" reinsurance scenarios, the agreement relates to all or part of a single insurance policy.[9] As a facultative agreement covers all or a part of a particular, identifiable risk, the reinsurer is free to accept or reject each particular risk offered.[10] In contrast, in a "treaty" or "automatic" reinsurance scenario, the reinsurance policy concerns a specific group or class of policies issued by the ceding insurer, such as earthquake insurance.[11] As the reinsurer is accepting a type of risk as opposed to a specific identifiable risk, the reinsurer is obligated to accept the class of risks covered by the agreement, including those as yet unwritten.[12] Stated slightly differently, in treaty reinsurance, the ceding company is trying to reduce its risk of loss from either a class of customers or an industry, rather than those relating to a specific policy.[13]

Both facultative and treaty reinsurance agreements can also be further classified as either "proportional reinsurance" or "excess of loss reinsurance." In a proportional or pro rata agreement, coverage is typically provided on a pro rata, or percentage, basis for each of the coverages placed with the reinsurance company by the underlying insurer. In contrast, in excess of loss scenarios, coverage is not triggered until or unless the loss reaches a certain predetermined threshold.[14]

A reinsurance agreement needs to be distinguished from "assumption" insurance, in which policies already issued by insurance carriers are purchased outright, and the second company then stands in the shoes of the original insurer, with obligations running directly to the insured.[15] In the traditional reinsurance scenario, there is no liability running directly between the reinsurer and the underlying insured. However, in some reinsurance agreements, the parties negotiate what is called a "cut through" clause. When this clause is present, the insured entity can seek coverage directly from the reinsurer.[16] Such an agreement would become quite valuable to an insured if the original insurance carrier were to become insolvent: this would allow the covered entity to avoid the pitfalls posed by insolvency proceedings and instead look to the reinsurer directly for reimbursement of loss. Similarly, if the reinsurance money had already been paid to the cedent prior to bankruptcy, such a "cut through" clause would give the underlying insured priority to the reinsurance proceeds in many jurisdictions.[17]

"Follow the Fortunes" Clauses in General

A relatively central tenet of reinsurance law is that the reinsurer must "follow the fortunes" of the ceding company. What this means is that the reinsurer is responsible for the payment of the loss as determined by the original, underlying policy. The reinsurer may not "second-guess" a decision made by the ceding company. "Follow the fortunes" clauses or, as John Thornton liked to call them, "follow the misfortunes" clauses, were originally intended to provide that the reinsurer repay the ceding company for a loss the ceding company was obligated to pay under the terms of its policy, even if such was reformed by the courts. Thus, if the ceding company were obligated to pay its insured, or make a payment on behalf of its insured as a result of the company's liability for loss under the policy of insurance, then the reinsurer in turn would be liable under its contract of reinsurance to the ceding company.

The American Heritage Dictionary defines the word "fortune" as "a hypothetical, often personified force or power that favorably or unfavorably governs the events of one's life." The Concise Oxford Dictionary defines "fortune" as "luck, good or bad." Some reinsurers prefer to use the phrase "technical insurance fortunes," meaning only those exposures that are related to, and which flow from, the underwriting of a particular risk. Some prefer to use the term "underwriting fortunes." However, the "follow the fortunes" clause may be construed without resort to such confusing terms. More simply, it can be read as "follow the liability." In more complete but complex terms, it can be thought of as "subject in all respects to all the general and special stipulations, clauses, etc., of the company's policy."

Until the early '60s, these clauses were prevalent in the industry. However, developing case law during that period made it apparent that the presence of such clauses in reinsurance contracts was becoming problematic; such clauses were being construed to expose reinsurers on such contracts to direct action lawsuits by third parties in the event of insolvency, even though it was contrary to the generally accepted principle that a person not a party to a contract cannot derive any benefits therefrom. Many reinsurers consequently made Herculean efforts to avoid the use of this clause in contracts. However, if the clause could not be eliminated, it was mandated that the following sentence be added to the clause for protection against potential third-party exposure: "Nothing herein shall in any manner create any obligations or establish any rights against the Reinsurer in favor of any third parties or any persons not parties to the agreement."

Another important issue involved the potential exposure that arose for a reinsurer in contracts where *excess judgments* were not explicitly considered in "follow the fortunes" clauses. In the landmark case of *Peerless Ins. Co. v. Inland Mutual Ins. Co.*,[18] an insurer who held a $15,000 automobile liability policy reinsured $10,000 of the policy under a reinsurance agreement including a "follow the fortunes" clause. The insurer affirmatively decided not to settle the case, and a verdict was rendered for $75,000. The insured then brought a negligent failure to settle action against the insurer, which it settled for $27,500. The court ruled that the "follow the fortunes" wording rendered the reinsurer liable for two-thirds of the total settlement amount, as that clause expanded the reinsurer's liability to include excess judgments. After this decision was handed down, reinsurers became acutely aware of the fact that if they were unable to *delete* the "follow the fortunes" clause, they had better specifically exclude those exposures they were not prepared to assume. Moreover, with the surge of bad-faith actions and punitive awards, the *Peerless* decision makes it all the more important to be aware of the ramifications of the "follow the fortunes" clause.

It should be noted that the "follow the fortunes" clause does not prevent the reinsurer from raising the defense that the underlying claim did not fall within the policy coverage.[19] This is true even if the ceding company makes a reasonable, good-faith decision that coverage was owed.[20]

Recent Developments in Reinsurance and "Follow the Fortunes" Case Law

A topic that has received a significant amount of attention in recent years is the liability of the reinsurer for the insurer's defense costs incurred in connection with litigating the subject loss. In *Bellefonte Reinsurance Co. v. Aetna Cas. and Sur. Co.*,[21] the court of appeals held that a "follow the fortunes" clause did not operate to make the reinsurers liable for the insurer's defense costs above and beyond the limits of liability set forth in the reinsurance certificate; rather, the clause subjected the reinsurer to the direct risks borne by the insurer under the policy. However, this was recently called into question in *TIG Premier Ins. Co. v. Hartford Acc. & Indem. Co.*,[22] which held that there was a genuine issue of material fact relating to the meaning of the policy language pertaining to reimbursement of costs. Expert testimony was offered that the reinsurance industry's standard practice was to assess the reinsurer with the percentage of the defense costs corresponding to the percentage of liability reinsured. Hence, a reinsurer with 20 percent of the underlying obligation would also be responsible for 20 percent of the related defense costs.

In *British Int'l Ins. Co. Ltd. v. Seguros La Republica, S.A.*,[23] the court noted that the "follow the fortunes" doctrine has become associated with the duty on the part of the reinsurer to accept without challenge a settlement negotiated by the insurer on the underlying claim. In a related action in the same dispute,[24] the court rendered a decision on another topical issue: reimbursement for *costs* expended by the insurer in a declaratory judgment action. The court held that the fact that one or some reinsurers reimburse the ceding insurer for declaratory judgment expenses does not make the practice so "notorious" that it has become an implied term in a reinsurance contract.[25]

The Duty of "Utmost Good Faith"

The duty of utmost good faith, or *uberrima fides*, is considered by many to be the "flip side" of the follow the fortunes doctrine in reinsurance. The etiology of the two doctrines are inextricably tied together: the reinsurance carrier must defer to the ceding company as relates to the claim investigation, attempts at settlement, and most matters relating to the claim itself; however, the ceding company in turn is required to act with the "utmost good faith" in its disclosures to and treatment of the reinsurer. This existence of the duty of utmost good faith dates back to the Supreme Court decision of *Sun Mutual Ins. Co. v. Ocean Ins. Co.*[26] In that case, the Supreme Court held that the insurance carrier ceding coverage had an absolute duty to disclose all of the underlying facts that had any bearing on issuance of the coverage, and that the failure to do so voided the contract for reinsurance. This doctrine has matured over the years and is now generally accepted to require disclosure of the information that is material to the decision to underwrite the risk, such as frequency of loss, nature of the business, existence of excess or other insurance on the risk.[27]

There exists a duty of good faith and fair dealing between the reinsured and the reinsurer in connection with every reinsurance contract.[28] The consequences of a breach of that duty can be severe: in *Reliance Ins. Co., et al v. Certain Member Companies, et al.,*[29] the reinsurer succeeded in having the reinsurance binder declared void, as both the cedent and its broker breached their duties of utmost good faith relating to disclosure.

Recent Example Involving Reinsurance Scenario and Duty of Good Faith

Some of the myriad issues relating to "bad faith" or, at the very least, the absence of the "utmost good faith" in connection with reinsurance contract litigation are illustrated in the relatively recent case of *Commercial Union Ins. Co. v. Seven Provinces Ins.*[30] The landscape in the reinsurance arena has been slowly changing over the years, and reinsurance is gradually transforming itself from a "Gentleman's Agreement" to a quasi-normal insurance contract, fraught with dangers and uncertainties. This case helps to underscore some of the growing pains associated with that transformation.

Knowledge of the underlying facts and circumstances of this dispute is essential to an understanding of the legal (ramifications of this decision. In *Commercial Union,* a reinsurance arrangement was entered into in the early 1960s between Employers' Surplus Lines Insurance Company (ESLIC) and defendant Seven Provinces Insurance Company, Ltd. (Seven Provinces). ESLIC wrote a number of different insurance policies for Teledyne, a California-based manufacturing company. In 1963, ESLIC ceded a portion of this risk to Seven Provinces in a facultative reinsurance agreement.

Environmental contamination was discovered at a number of different Teledyne sites in 1982, and the company faced cleanup claims brought by the Environmental Protection Agency (EPA) extending into the millions of dollars, along with numerous third-party liability claims. Claims were submitted to Teledyne's insurance carriers, including Commercial Union (CU), ESLIC's successor in interest, and litigation was required to determine CU's obligations to Teledyne under the numerous policies relating to Teledyne's numerous manufacturing sites. A settlement was eventually reached, in which CU paid Teledyne $2.2 million and Teledyne released CU from all existing and potential future liability relating to environmental claims.

During the settlement negotiations, quite a bit of attention was focused on one site, the "semiconductor site"; the site had been in operation since 1962, and the cleanup costs for this location were estimated at $20.93 million. The insurance agreement between Teledyne and ESLIC / CU was a general liability policy covering losses greater than $50,000 and up to $1.95 million, and spanned a one-year period, from 7/1/1963 to 7/1/1964. CU determined that $843,000 of the total $2.2 million settlement should be allocated to that site, and its reinsurers were so notified. Losses exceeding $500,000 were reimbursed by a carrier not involved in the suit. The other $450,000 in liability was billed as follows: $225,000—or one half—was billed to Seven Provinces, then $180,000 of CU's remaining half was billed to a pool of treaty reinsurers, which resulted in CU being ultimately responsible for $45,000 of the original loss amount. Suit was ultimately brought by CU to recover the $225,000 from Seven Provinces, along with costs and attorney's fees.

The first defense raised by Seven Provinces was the "net retention" claim, relating to and based upon a clause in the original reinsurance agreement. The pertinent clause read as follows:

> (1) [1] Being a reinsurance of and warranted same NETT rate, terms and conditions as and to follow the settlements of the (ESLIC) and that the local office of the said Company retains during the currency of this insurance at least $225,000.00 being 50 percent of $450,000 excess, $50,000.00 combined single limit [2] subject to reduction by any general excess loss or excess catastrophe reinsurance whether effected by the head office or local office of the Company [3] on the identical subject matter and risk and in identically the same proportion on each separate part thereof, but [4] in the event of the retained line being less than as above, Underwriter's lines to be proportionally reduced.

(Bracketed numbers were inserted by the Court, and were not in the original text of the agreement. Also note that NETT is the British term for retention.) Seven Provinces argued that this clause required ESLIC/CU to retain the entirety of the $225,000 risk, and that its proportionate share of the reinsured risk must be reduced under the language of the agreement, since CU reinsured $180,000, or 80 percent, of its $225,000 risk. The court found the language to be ambiguous, and expert testimony was taken from both sides on the issue. After weighing the evidence, the court found that the clause required Seven Provinces liability to be proportionately reduced only if ESLIC obtained facultative reinsurance on its retained portion, and did not relate to treaty reinsurance; Seven Provinces liability was *not* to be reduced by the CU treaty reinsurance pool that was put in place by the head office (not the local office) of the company, and which did not amount to reinsurance on the identical subject matter.

Seven Provinces' next challenge related to CU's allocation of $843,000 of the $2.2 million settlement amount to the Teledyne semiconductor site for the 1963-1964 coverage year. CU offered testimony showing the rationale behind the allocation decision to illustrate that it was done in good faith, in accordance with its normal allocation procedures relating to hazardous waste claims. Seven Provinces, however, alleged that it was somehow unreasonable or done in bad faith. The court recognized that the interplay between two well-recognized reinsurance doctrines must be considered in this situation; the "follow the fortunes" doctrine and the "follow the settlements" doctrine. Under the follow the fortunes doctrine, Seven Provinces was bound by the reinsured's good-faith determination that the loss was in fact covered by the policy. Under the related "follow the settlements" doctrine, the reinsurer must "abide by a reinsured's good-faith decision to settle, rather than litigate, claims on that policy. . . the reinsurer must go along with however the reinsured settles the claim."[31] To require otherwise would allow the reinsurer to challenge each settlement, attacking one possible choice by the reinsured among a number of reasonable settlement alternatives, which would act as a significant deterrent to settlement. The court found as a matter of law that the allocation was reasonable, and that Seven Provinces had not produced any evidence that it was made in bad faith. Seven Provinces' allegations that the allocation was made so as to maximize reinsurance recovery was not supported by the evidence. Furthermore, the court specifically held that there was no evidence to support the claim that the settlement was an *ex gratia* payment (made as a favor rather than pursuant to a legal obligation) made to obtain the release of future claims rather than to compensate for actual damages incurred.

The most interesting analysis came in deciding CU's claim for attorneys' fees and costs for being forced to litigate Seven Provinces' responsibility to pay a valid and outstanding claim. This claim was being brought under a Massachusetts statute and was hence somewhat language-specific. However, the underlying logic is still quite valuable. The court reviewed the lengthy and somewhat convoluted history behind the presentation of the claim—it was legitimately confused by missing reinsurance certificates and other documentation problems. However, the claim was originally presented in August of 1993. The reinsurance certificate was undisputedly located and in the hands of Seven Provinces as of August 1995. Rather than paying the sum due at that time, Seven Provinces continued to raise other, unrelated issues as barriers to payment—while at the same time trying to negotiate some type of compromise on the claim. The Court noted that "Seven Provinces' behavior was particularly egregious when seen in the context of the mores of the reinsurance industry, an industry which has operated for centuries on the principle of 'utmost good faith' (*uberrimae fidei*)."[32] The court went on to note that:

> (2) . . . these traditions of trust and mutual reliance came under strain in the 1980s. Because of high interest rates . . . insurers paid less attention to the risks they insured, and the quality of the underwriting began to suffer. At the same time, environmental and asbestos liability began to upset the calculations on which many insurance relationships had been founded. See *Compagnie de Reassurance*, 944 F. Supp at 993. Trade publications are beginning to note the change in tone, speaking of the 'death of the handshake'. Michael J. Brady and Lawrence O. Monin, *Reinsurance Disputes: Death of the Handshake*, 61 Def. Couns. J. 529 (1994). Seven Provinces' conduct is more in keeping with this new climate.[33]

The court held that Seven Provinces had acted in breach of its duty of utmost good faith, and entered judgment in favor of CU in the amount of $450,000—double the amount owed pursuant to a Massachusetts statutory multiplier—plus attorneys fees since August 1995 (the date of discovery of the certificate) plus costs.

How Discovery, Privilege, and Confidentiality Relate to Reinsurance

In the relatively recent past, the majority of reinsurance disputes took the form of arbitration, and reinsurance was a little-discussed topic, especially in actions between a policyholder and an insurance carrier. Simply put, reinsurance and discovery from reinsurers was just not mainstream consideration. However, with the recent growth in large tort actions, such as toxic torts and environmental cleanup cases from contamination, reinsurance has become the subject of more interest at all levels of business and litigation. The issue of the discoverability of reinsurance-related information typically arises in one of two scenarios: a) a dispute between an insured and an insurer, in which information about reinsurance is sought by the policyholder to bolster some element of the underlying case, or b) a dispute between the ceding company and the reinsurer relating to the transaction itself or reinsurance coverage for a particular loss.

The attorney-client and work-product privileges take on a new significance in modern litigations involving large corporate entities with many joint or overlapping issues. For example, communication is essential in a large corporation with numerous far-flung operations, but any communication carries with it the risk of divulgence. Conversations between in-house counsel and corporate employees are protected.[34] However, the following criteria must be met for corporate employee-attorney privilege to attach:

- The communication would not have been made but for the contemplation of legal services;
- The employee making the communication did so at the direction of his or her corporate superior;
- The superior made the request of the employee as part of the corporation's effort to secure legal advice or services;
- The content of the communication relates to the legal services being rendered, and the subject matter of the communications within the scope of the employee's duties;
- The communication is not disseminated beyond those persons who, because of the corporate structure, need to know its contents.

This protects select communication within the entity, but what about between entities? It has been held that if an insured agreed with its excess insurer that it would open its books and records to the excess insurer, then such items, including its attorney reports, were discoverable by the excess insurer.[35] Similarly, if a ceding company voluntarily submits attorney-client privileged information to another reinsurer in the normal course of business negotiations, it waives the privilege as to any reinsurer's requests.[36] However, what occurs in a bad-faith action? It has been held that the files of an attorney hired by an insurer to investigate claims made by the insured are privileged in a subsequent action brought by that insured against the carrier for bad faith.[37] The application of the doctrine in insurance and reinsurance scenarios is rarely simple or straightforward.

The very nature of the reinsurance relationship makes the issue of discovery sought by a policyholder from a reinsurer especially troublesome. The ceding company has a clearly imposed duty to disclose all pertinent information to the reinsurer; this is the essential element of the duty of utmost good faith, and depending upon the nature of the reinsurance agreement, it could include disclosure of such information as the ceding carrier's attorney's assessment of the risks and merits of the underlying suit, which is clearly privileged. If the courts then decide that the reinsurer must turn all of that information over to the policyholder, this could put the ceding company at a serious disadvantage. Even more important, it could and would staunch the free flow of information between the ceding and reinsuring carriers, which is an essential element of reinsurance.

Discovery of Reinsurance Information by Policyholder in Action Against the Insurance Company

Discoverability of the Reinsurance Policy Itself

Whether or not reinsurance information is discoverable depends upon what is being sought, along with the posture of the underlying action. Historically, there was some dispute regarding whether or not the reinsurance policy itself was or should be discoverable in litigation between the insured and the insurance company. Some courts have held that Rule 26 permitted the insured to obtain its insurer's reinsurance agreements as a matter of course because such agreements constituted an "insurance agreement" as defined by Rule 26(a)(1)(2).[38] However, other courts drew a number of distinctions, and allowed exceptions to the basic rule of production.[39] More recently, in *MedMarc Casualty Ins. Co. v. Arrow International, Inc.,*[40] the successor court to *Rhone-Poulenc* decided that a reinsurer had to produce the reinsurance policy in response to a subpoena served by the insured in an underlying declaratory judgment action against the insurer; however, other reinsurance materials were irrelevant, as they had no bearing on the interpretation of an unambiguous policy provision in the primary liability insurance policy. This articulates what has become the general rule: the policy itself may be obtained, but additional information is much more fact-specific.

The statutory scheme in the particular state should be referenced by the prudent practitioner. Many states have specific statutes that mandate disclosure of certain insurance information. For example, Florida Statute Annotated section 627.4137 (formerly FSA 627.7264) provides:

1. Each insurer which does or may provide liability insurance coverage to pay all or a portion of any claim which might be made shall provide, within 30 days of the written request of the claimant, a statement, under oath, of a corporate officer or the insurer's claims manager or superintendent setting forth the following information with regard to each known policy of insurance, including excess or umbrella insurance:
   a. the name of the insurer
   b. the name of each insured
   c. the limits of the liability coverage
   d. a statement of any policy or coverage defense which such insurer reasonable believes is available to such insurer at the time of filing such statement
   e. a copy of the policy.
   In addition, the insured, or his insurance agent, upon written request of the claimant of the claimant's attorney, shall disclose the name and coverage of each known insurer to the claimant and shall forward such request for information as required by this subsection to all affected insurers. The insurer shall then supply the information required in this subsection to the claimant within 30 days of receipt of such request.
2. The statement required by subsection (1) shall be amended immediately upon discovery of facts calling for an amendment to such statement.

However, FSA section 627.401, which delineates the scope of the chapter, specifically exempts reinsurance from the mandates of FSA section 627.4137. In Florida, reinsurance information is privileged from the viewpoint of original claimant.[41]

Broader Discovery of Other Reinsurance Information

The insured may argue that communications between the ceding insurer (the reinsured) and reinsurer are relevant to the issue of policy interpretation inasmuch as such communications could reveal admissions from the ceding company interpreting its own policy language to cover the claims at issue.[42] In addition, the insured could contend that the information maintained by the reinsurer with respect to the claims at issue may also be relevant to when the ceding company received notice for each individual claim (potentially reflected in correspondence or notice to the reinsurer) and is also relevant to the issue of whether the ceding company conducted an adequate investigation prior to declining coverage for the claims.[43] The insured may contend that the reinsurance information it seeks may also bear on the issue of whether the ceding company was prejudiced in any fashion by the timing of the insured's notice of the claims at issue.

There are reported cases that support the position that the reinsurance documents sought by the insured may not be relevant or otherwise subject to production in a declaratory judgment action. For example, in *Leski Inc. v. Federal Ins. Co.*,[44] the court sustained the insurer's objection to the relevancy of documents and information regarding reinsurance in the pending declaratory judgment action as "very tenuous" because the insured's decision to obtain reinsurance and communicate with its reinsurers is and was based upon "business considerations and not questions of policy interpretation."[45]

Any information regarding reinsurance is, at best, evidence of the undisclosed, unilateral intentions by the insurer, which are not material to the interpretation of an insurance contract between the insurer and the insured.[46] The court in *Rhone-Poulenc v. Home Indemnity Co.*[47] recognized that the issue of reinsurance does not even potentially become relevant until the court makes the specific finding that there is an ambiguity in the policy at issue that requires the consideration of extrinsic evidence. Under this logic, the appropriateness of discovery regarding reinsurance in an action between the insured and the insurer should not even be considered unless and until there has been a finding by the district court that one or more of the provisions of the policies at issue is ambiguous.

It has been clearly held that where the Retrocession Agreement was unambiguous on its face, parol evidence was inadmissible to explain its terms.[48] Similarly, in *In re Texas Eastern Transmission Corp.*,[49] the court held that there must first be a holding that a policy is ambiguous and therefore subject to the admission of extrinsic evidence of intent before reinsurance information is even arguably relevant. Finding no allegations or evidence of ambiguity in the action before it, the court precluded the disclosure of "any information as to the amount of any reinsurance or the identity of any reinsurer or even the fact of reinsurance."[50] The various states have decided these discovery issues a number of different ways, and the body of case law for each jurisdiction needs to be reviewed prior to proceeding in a state court action. For example, courts in Florida have clearly held that the reinsurance contract is irrelevant to the original claims in an action between an insured and an insurer.[51]

In reviewing Rule 45, the court may quash or modify a subpoena that requires the "disclosure of privileged or other protected matter to which no exception or waiver applies"[52] or "requires disclosure of a trade secret or other confidential research, development or commercial information."[53] As to this aspect of Rule 45, some courts have recognized a proprietary information/trade secret privilege in connection with certain reinsurance information.[54] The court in *Rhone-Poulenc* supported its decision to preclude the production of reinsurance information on the basis that:

> (3) Reinsurance materials contain confidential business information regarding the pricing and coverage of reinsurance policies, which, if you reveal to competitors could damage the insurance carrier's ability to compete in the reinsurance market as well as our present business relationships with reinsurers.

Thus, the reinsurer can object to the production of its reinsurance materials as proprietary business information. However, the court may simply require that the proprietary documents of information with which the reinsurer is concerned be produced subject to in camera review, a confidentiality agreement, or a protective order prohibiting the insured from using the produced documents or information outside the limited scope of the declaratory judgment proceeding.[55]

With respect to the disclosure of documents regarding the ceding company's reserves, most courts have been persuaded that reserve calculations are of tenuous probative value, as such calculations assume the likelihood of an adverse verdict, and typically such estimates do not entail an evaluation of coverage "based upon a thorough factual and legal consideration. . . ."[56] Accordingly, the reinsurer possibly will be able to avoid production of the ceding company's reserve information.[57]

Responding to a Third-Party Subpoena for Reinsurance Documents under Rule 45 of the Federal Rules of Civil Procedure

Rule 45 of the Federal Rules of Civil Procedure authorizes the insured's attorney to issue a subpoena directly to the reinsurer, under the auspices of the United States District Court for the district in which the subpoena seeks to compel the production of documents.[58] The reinsurer is entitled to respond with a Motion to Quash or modify the subpoena. Upon a hearing thereof, even if the court finds that some documents are responsive and should be produced, the court can modify or restrict the subpoena to protect the reinsurer "from significant expense (or burden) resulting from the inspection and copying commanded."[59] Under those circumstances, most courts would likely extend the time for the reinsurer to object and respond to the subpoena rather than quash the subpoena outright.

Attorney-Client Privilege and the "Common Interest" Rule as Applies to Subpoenas
The strength of the objection that the subpoena requests information and documents
protected by the attorney-client privilege and work-product doctrine is somewhat fact-
specific. This objection may or may not be available to reinsurers when seeking to prevent the disclosure of information and materials prepared by counsel to the ceding
company that happen to end up in the reinsurer's files.[60] However, the attorney-client
privilege extends to communications from the ceding company to its reinsurer based on
the "community of interest" between the ceding company and its reinsurer.[61] In *Durham,*
the court held that where the insurer/ceding company and the reinsurer share in the risk
of potential liability on claims, there is a conformity of interest which serves as a sufficient basis to support the reinsurer's objection to produce materials obtained from the
ceding company on the basis of the attorney-client privilege. Thus, the reinsurer may be
able to shield documents that reveal attorney-client communications between the ceding
company and its coverage counsel from production to the insured in the declaratory
judgment action.[62]

More recently, in *Travelers Cas. and Sur. Co. v. Excess Ins. Co. Ltd.,.*[63] the court
strongly reaffirmed the rule that the "common interest" or "joint defense" doctrine would
apply to shield communications and notes exchanged in conferences between reinsurers
as being protected by the attorney-client privilege. However, as with any privilege, the
attorney-client privilege and/or the work-product privilege can be waived by voluntary
disclosure of the information to others.[64] Moreover, while privileges must be recognized, they must be limited to the scope required to effectuate the underlying purpose of
the privilege.[65]

It must be remembered that failure to make any objection to this subpoena (even if
you intend to negotiate with the insurance counsel) may waive your right to withhold
production of the requested materials.[66] However, the simple act of filing one or more
objections to the subpoena will shift the burden of securing compliance with the subpoena back on the insured, which must then request that the court order the reinsurer to
comply with the terms of the subpoena. Fed. R. Civ. P. 45(c)(2)(B). Should you take the
more extreme measures by responding to the subpoena through an immediate motion
for a protective order pursuant to Rule 26(c), you will bear the burden of demonstrating
"good cause" entitling you to such an order. Fed. R. Civ. P. 26(c).

Additional Privilege Issues That Arise in Reinsurance Litigation Situations

Samaritan Foundation, et al. v. Superior Court of the State of Arizona[67] highlights an
interesting "twist" in the analysis of the role of attorney-client and work-product privilege in the context of statements of corporate employees. Third party Samaritan appealed an order that required disclosure of summaries of interviews of corporate
employees—operating room nurses—which were prepared by a nurse paralegal in anticipation of litigation, after those summaries had been edited by the court during an in
camera inspection. The court affirmed that the interviews were work product, and protected by the attorney-client privilege, as they had been prepared by a properly super-
vised nurse paralegal acting under the direction of the attorney. However, in determining
the applicability of the corporate attorney-client privilege, the court adopted the reasoning of the Supreme Court of Illinois and split corporate employees into two different

classes: control and non-control employees.[68] The "control group" was defined as those who "personify the corporation by their managerial or advisory authority to shape corporate decisions in response to the corporate lawyer's advice.[69]

In *Consolidated Coal Company v. Bucyrus-Erie Company,*[70] the court addressed the discoverability of a metallurgical report prepared by an engineer employee of the company. The subject report contained a large amount of data which the court held did *not* constitute attorney work product; the court further found that the engineer-employee was not a member of the "control group." The *Consolidated* court went on to hold that the attorney's notes and memoranda were discoverable only if a party seeking disclosure conclusively demonstrates the absolute impossibility of securing similar information from other sources. As stated above it must be recalled that the individual engineer was merely supplying information, and was not within the control group. The court also performed an in camera examination of the attorney's notes.

In adopting the "control group" theory, the *Samaritan* court distinguished its scenario from that found in the contemporaneous Supreme Court decision of *Upjohn Co. v. United States.*[71] In *Upjohn*, the general counsel of Upjohn began an investigation internally to determine if there had been any incidents in which corporate employees appeared to have bribed foreign officials. Questionnaires were sent to foreign affiliates regarding payments, and interviews were held with corporate officers and employees. The IRS demanded production of the questionnaires *as answered*, along with the general counsel's notes taken during the interviews. Such production was objected to based on attorney-client privilege and work product/preparation in anticipation of litigation. The *Upjohn* Court held that all of the requested material was protected by the attorney-client privilege; this privilege must extend to all corporate employees, not just those recognized as "controlling" the corporation. Moreover, the work product of the attorney—the notes taken of the conversations—was protected even though the plaintiff demonstrated both substantial need and an inability to obtain the equivalent without undue hardship, as is required under Rule 26. The conferences with the attorney had been held at the direction of management, to investigate the conduct or proposed conduct that fell within the scope of employment. Moreover, the attorney was authorized by management to inquire into the subject and was seeking information to assist counsel in evaluating whether an employee's conduct had bound, or would bind, the corporation, and assessing the legal consequences, if any, of that conduct, along with formulating appropriate legal responses to actions that had been or may be taken by others with regard to that conduct. Production of such notes would reveal the "mental impressions" of the attorney, which are entitled to special protection. However, the attorney-client privilege does not protect disclosure of the *underlying facts* by those who communicated with the attorney. It is the communication that is protected, not the underlying facts.

Justice Burger wrote a separate concurring opinion also condemning the "control group" test. However, he went one step further, and set forth a "standard" to be used for the future to determine if communication between an employee or former employee speaking with an attorney relating to conduct within the scope of employment and at the direction of corporate management is privileged.

(4) The attorney must be one authorized by the management to inquire into the subject and must be seeking information to assist counsel in perform-

ing any of the following functions: (a) evaluating whether the employee's conduct has bound or would bind the corporation; (b) assessing the legal consequences, if any, of that conduct; or (c) formulating appropriate legal responses to actions that have been or may be taken by others with regard to that conduct.[72]

It must be noted that this test was *not* adopted in the majority opinion. Rather, the majority opinion noted that:

(5) Middle-level—and indeed lower-level—employees can, by actions within the scope of their employment, embroil the corporation in serious legal difficulties, and it is only natural that these employees would have the relevant information needed by corporate counsel if he is adequately to advise the client with respect to such actual or potential difficulties.[73]

The *Upjohn* decision recognizes the existence of a privilege based on a confidential relationship, but indicated that the application of the privilege should be determined on a case-by-case basis, citing Federal Rules of Evidence.[74]

The *Samaritan* court distinguished *Upjohn* on three separate bases. First, *Upjohn* creates a *federal* evidentiary standard and is not binding on the states. Second, scholars have found much fault with *Upjohn*, describing its characterization as overbroad. Third, *Upjohn* was intended, by the very language of its decision, to be limited to its facts. The plaintiff in that action (the IRS) had not demonstrated that it could not obtain the same material from alternative sources, hence it was not significantly prejudiced by application of the privilege.

The *Samaritan* court noted that the substantial need for the information by the plaintiff outweighed the corporate interest in maintaining confidentiality and ordered production of some of the summaries to the plaintiff, despite the fact that the summaries were categorized as work product and not attorney-client privileged. The trial court, during an in camera review, found and excised some privileged material; the remainder was ordered to be produced as functional equivalent of witness statements. (There was no peer review privilege asserted). The court compared witness deposition testimony with the summaries and found that the inability of the witnesses on deposition to remember certain facts constituted a substantial need.[75]

As soon as the underlying incident occurred, the hospital signed up its employees as clients of the hospital's legal department. This had *not* occurred in the *Upjohn* matter. The original interview summaries were therefore directly blocked from production. The Arizona Court of Appeals created a qualified discovery immunity for material prepared in anticipation of litigation, thereby separating out from each document the privileged mental impressions of the lawyer or the paralegal, and allowed discovery of the facts themselves. The court stated that, under Arizona statutes, corporations are protected by the attorney-client privilege; however, the qualifying line for application of that privilege must be drawn to promote the flow of lawyer-client communication but at the same time be a complete block to external access of internal corporate witnesses and facts. The court further distinguished the Illinois Supreme Court's *Consolidated Coal* case, as Illinois had limited the privilege to communications with the "control group" employees.[76]

The *Samaritan* court also discussed Vincent C. Alexander, *The Corporate Attorney-Client Privilege: A Study of the Participants*.[77] The court noted that as a general rule, communication is privileged at least when, as here, an employee or former employee speaks with an attorney at the direction of management, and regarding conduct or proposed conduct that fell or would fall within the scope of that person's employment. The court adopted the "qualified privilege" discussed by Alexander, in which the privilege can be overcome in limited circumstance involving special need. The court stated that this appropriately balanced the need for confidentiality with the opponent's need for information from "non-control group members." The *Samaritan* court preferred this approach to that explained in *Upjohn*, noting that adherence to *Upjohn* preserves too broad a zone of silence and would frustrate the state's discovery policies, which are geared to the ultimate ascertainment of the truth.[78]

Privilege and Confidentiality in Disputes Between the Ceding Company and the Reinsurer

Disputes between the ceding company and the reinsurer can take a number of forms and involve a number of different issues. However, two typical litigation scenarios might be: (1) Reinsurer asserts underlying claim was poorly handled—by, for example, not giving the reinsurer timely notice of the claim—so the "follow the fortunes" doctrine should not apply; and (2) Reinsurer alleges that coverage should not be afforded because ceding company did not disclose all of the relevant risk information.

Reinsurer's Defense of Late Notice of Claim: Actual Prejudice versus Bad Faith

One potential defense to coverage that can be raised by a reinsurer is late notice of the underlying claim for which reinsurance is being invoked. The viability of this defense will depend upon the law of the particular state in which the action is being brought. However, in a growing number of jurisdictions, either actual prejudice or bad faith needs to be proven to support the viability of this defense. A landmark case in this area is *Unigard Security Ins. Co. Inc. v. North River Ins. Co.*[79] In *Unigard*, the reinsurer instituted a declaratory judgment. Regarding whether the ceding insurer's failure to timely notify it of the signing of an intercompany agreement (the "Wellington Agreement") establishing asbestos claims liabilty would support a late notice defense to claims under the reinsurance policy. Despite the fact that reinsurance agreements are "insurance contracts," the Unigard court noted as a preliminary matter that the general rule that any ambiguous policy language will be construed against the insurer does *not* apply, as reinsurance contracts represent an "arm's length" transaction between two equal, quite sophisticated parties.[80] The canons of construction developed to protect individual purchasers of original insurance policies do not apply in reinsurance scenarios.

In analyzing the viability of the late notice defense, the Second Circuit first reaffirmed much of the basic law relating to reinsurance agreements, primary of which is that the reinsurer is not directly liable to the original insured. Rather, reinsurance involves indemnity as opposed to liability, and reinsurers accordingly do not examine risks, receive notice of loss from the original insured, or investigate claims. Rather, the reinsurers are dependent on their ceding insurers for prompt and full disclosure of information concerning pertinent risks to determine whether to associate in the defense of a claim. As a result, the Second Circuit noted that the relationship between the reinsurer and the ceding company is and must be one of "utmost good faith." It also must be kept in mind that there are two different types of reinsurance agreements: in "facultative reinsurance," the reinsurer is covering a part or all of a single insurance policy; in contrast, in "treaty reinsurance," the reinsurer is covering specified classes of the ceding insurance company's policies.[81] The reinsurance agreement between North River and Unigard was a facultative reinsurance agreement.

The rationale underlying the notice provision was explained by the *Unigard* court to be threefold: (1) to apprise the reinsurer of potential liabilities to enable it to set reserves; (2) to enable the reinsurer to associate in defense and control of the underlying claims; and (3) to assist the reinsurer in determining whether and at what price to renew reinsurance coverage.[82] The court noted that the reinsurance agreement itself provided that "prompt notice shall be given by the [ceding insurer] to the Underwriting Managers on behalf of the Reinsurers of any occurrence or accident which appears likely to involve this reinsurance. . . ."[83] The *Unigard* court also noted that "being an insurance company, the [ceding insurer] is held to a high degree of compliance with policy provisions which require prompt notice to the reinsurer. . . ."[84]

The court determined that North River *did not* give adequate notice of the Agreement to the reinsurer, Unigard. The Wellington Agreement recited that it was the sole agent, and that it had exclusive authority and discretion to administer, evaluate, settle, pay and defend all asbestos-related claims. North River did not give Unigard timely notice of the Wellington Agreement (notice was given 5 months late) and thus breached the notice clause of the facultative reinsurance certificate in question, or of any facultative certificates. The only notice that was given was to the reinsurer's agent, which handled any and all treaty reinsurance agreements. The Second Circuit clarified *Christiana, supra*, on requiring a reasonable time after the duty to give notice to the reinsurer has arisen: All that is required is a reasonable possibility of such a happening, based upon an objective assessment of the information available, and that such a possibility may exist even though the ceding company may find "there are some factors that tend to suggest the opposite."[85]

However, the Second Circuit went on to note that Unigard was required to show that it was prejudiced by the lack of notice—and the definition of "prejudice" in the context of reinsurance was quite unclear. *Id.* at 1067. Courts have typically examined the loss of the "right of association" that comes from a lack of notice in determining the existence of prejudice. For example, in *Fortress Re, Inc. v. Central Nat'l Ins. Co.,*[86] the court held that not only must the reinsurer show that it would have "associated" if given proper notice, but it also must show that this would have resulted in a more favorable outcome. An even greater burden was placed on the reinsurer in *Insurance Co. of Pa. v. Associated Int'l Ins. Co.,*[87] when it was required to prove that there was a "substantial likelihood" that it could have defeated the claim or settled it for a smaller sum. Some older cases have placed less of a burden on the reinsurer; however, the trend seems to require a significant showing of "prejudice" in the form of tangible economic injury—loss of the contractual right of association alone is insufficient. The *Unigard* court ultimately held that the reinsurer did not demonstrate that sufficient prejudice resulted from the "late notice," hence the defense to coverage was denied.

However, any "bad faith" on the part of the ceding company to the reinsurer in not giving prompt notice may supplant the requirement of proof of actual, significant prejudice. The duty of good faith requires the ceding insurer to place the reinsurer "in the same [situation] as himself [and] to give to him the same means and opportunity of judging the value of the risks."[88] The Second Circuit therefore queried what "good faith" requires of a ceding insurer in the notice context. The court held that:

> (6) we [thus] think that the proper minimum standard for bad faith should be gross negligence or recklessness. If a ceding insurer deliberately deceives a reinsurer, that deception is of course bad faith. However, if a ceding insurer has implemented routine practices and control to ensure notification to reinsurers but inadvertence causes a lapse, the insurer has not acted in bad faith. But if a ceding insurer does not implement such practices and controls, then it has willfully disregarded the risk to reinsurers and is guilty of gross negligence. A reinsurer, dependent on its ceding insurer for information, should be able to expect at least this level of protection, and, if a ceding insurer fails to provide it, the reinsurer's late loss notice defense should succeed.

In the recent New Jersey case *British Ins. Co. of Cayman v. Safety National Casualty,*[89] the Circuit Court held that under New Jersey law, a reinsurer can prevail on a "late notice" defense only if it can demonstrate significant prejudice. The court noted that "prejudice in a late notice defense is determined by examining (1) whether substantial rights have been irretrievably lost and (2) the likelihood of success of the insurer in defending against the victim's claim."[90] Similarly, in *Newcap Ins. Co. v. Employers Reinsurance Corp.,*[91] the district court noted that untimely notice from the insured to the reinsurer excuses performance only where there is actual prejudice resulting from the late notice. Further, in a reinsurance scenario, it must be shown that the reinsurer's participation in the defense would have altered the result of the trial in order for "substantial prejudice" to be found.[92]

"Common Interest Rule" as Arises in Litigation Between Reinsurer and Ceding Company

The relationship between these doctrines is well explained in the matter of *North River Ins. Co. v. Philadelphia Reinsurance Corp.*[93] As part of its discovery efforts in the reinsurance litigation, CIGNA Re sought attorney-client communications between North River and the coverage counsel who had represented it in the arbitration with Owens-Corning. CIGNA Re was interested in documents that bore on North River's decision to abandon its appeal of the arbitrator's decision against it. A federal magistrate denied CIGNA Re's discovery request, and the district court upheld the denial.

CIGNA Re first argued that the communications between North River and its counsel were discoverable under what it termed the "common interest" doctrine, which is an exception to the rule relating to attorney-client privilege. The doctrine provides that, when multiple parties are represented by the same attorney, communications between the attorney and the parties are *not* privileged if the parties later sue one another. In a typical litigation claim, for example, counsel may represent both the insured and the insurer in defending the claim, and his communications with either side would be unprotected should the insured or the carrier later sue the other.

This argument is *not* applicable to the relationship between the ceding company and the reinsurer. As the North River court noted, the ceding carrier and the reinsurer may have a common interest, but the ceding company's counsel does not have an attorney-client relationship with the reinsurer. Without such a relationship, there is no "common interest" exception to the attorney-client privilege, and communications between the ceding company and its counsel remain protected:

> (7) "As a matter of general privilege law, there is no automatic waiver of the attorney-client privilege merely because an insured and its insurers have a "common interest" in the outcome of a particular issue. That waiver may be found only when there has been a dual representation of both parties. . . . Thus, although Judge Pisano (the magistrate) analyzed the issue in a different way, he reached the correct result in finding that the "common interest" doctrine did not require North River to produce its attorney-client documents to CIGNA Re.[94]

CIGNA Re then argued that the "cooperation" clause of the reinsurance certificate waived North River's attorney-client privilege. The cooperation clause, using standard language, provided that North River "shall make available for inspection and place at the disposal of the reinsurer at reasonable times any of its records related to this reinsurance or claims in connection therewith. . . ."[95] However, the North River court found that the cooperation clause was not specific enough to provide a blanket waiver of the attorney-client privilege held by the ceding insurer. The court wrote:

> (9) Although a reinsured may contractually be bound to provide its reinsurer with all documents or information in its possession that may be relevant to the underlying claim adjustment and coverage determination, absent more explicit language, it does not through a cooperation clause give up wholesale its right to preserve the confidentiality of any consultation it may have with its attorney concerning the underlying claim and its Coverage determination." 797 F. Supp. at 369.

CIGNA Re next contended that North River had no reasonable expectation that the attorney-client communications would be confidential because industry custom dictated that reinsurers have access to such documents. The court concluded, however, that industry custom was not enough to impose a waiver of the attorney-client privilege on North River; rather, only clear and explicit language in the reinsurance certificate could create such a waiver.[96]

CIGNA Re then argued that North River was under a fiduciary obligation of full disclosure. The court quickly rejected this idea because a reinsurer did not have "sufficient influence and control" over the ceding company to create a fiduciary relationship:

(11) "The presence of sufficient influence and control over the affairs of another necessary to give rise to fiduciary responsibilities is absent between reinsured and reinsurer. The reinsurer's "right to associate" gives it adequate means by which to keep informed of events that may give rise to coverage under its agreement, and also provides a sufficient means to protect its own interests. Reinsurance agreements are negotiated at arm's-length between equally sophisticated parties. Reinsurers are well aware of the risks inherent in reinsurance obligations and are adequately situated to protect their interests."[97]

Finally, CIGNA Re argued that North River had waived the attorney-client privilege by putting "in issue" the communications with its lawyers. The court rejected this idea as well, stressing that the "in issue" exception to the attorney-client privilege "should be construed narrowly to create an implied wavier of the privilege only when the party puts in issue the contents of an attorney-client communication. . . . This will occur only when the party has asserted the claim or defense that he intends to prove by disclosure of an attorney-client communication."[98] Such a defense might include advice of counsel, which sometimes is used in bad-faith cases. The court noted that North River had represented it had no intention of relying on an attorney-client communication in proving its case. The court dismissed the notion that the ceding company raised the attorney-client privilege merely by "placing the broad question of coverage in issue. . . ."[99] It upheld the magistrate's finding that the privilege applied, and North River could protect its communications with coverage counsel.

The North River case clarifies some of the confusing issues involving the relationship between reinsurers and ceding carriers. That relationship is not a fiduciary one, and therefore is not subject to the strict disclosure rules that exist in fiduciary situations. A ceding company can turn to coverage counsel for advice on difficult claims, and can reasonably expect that the advice it receives will be protected from discovery in later disputes with its reinsurers. Under the logic of this case, reinsurers seeking to make the case that a claim is not covered under the ceding company's policy will have to argue that position on the merits, rather than rely on possible "smoking guns" in the files of coverage counsel.

Other Major Issues Involving Privilege and Confidentiality That Arise in Reinsurance Scenarios

Arbitration, Privilege, and Reinsurance

Some reinsurers have deleted arbitration clauses from standard contract language, but most reinsurance contracts still mandate arbitration. It must be noted that arbitration can be waived by not asserting the right immediately.[100] One feature of arbitration (and other alternative dispute resolution mechanisms) often deemed attractive is the heightened level of confidentiality presumed to be available. In the context of reinsurance disputes, confidentiality may be deemed especially critical due to the multifaceted interrelationships so often involved.

Reinsurance contracts often contain a confidentiality provision in the arbitration clause. This inclusion parallels the clear expressions favoring confidentiality in arbitration rules and guidelines promulgated for more general purposes. For example, the Center for Public Resources, a recognized leader in dispute resolution, has adopted the *Rules for Non-Administered Arbitration of Business Disputes,* which provided, in Rule 16, that "the parties and the arbitrators shall treat the proceedings, any related discovery and the decisions of the Tribunal as confidential, except in connection with a judicial . . . [to the award or its enforcement] and unless otherwise required by law." Similarly, the *Code of Ethics for Arbitrators in Commercial Disputes,* Canon VI, provides that "(u)nless otherwise agreed by the parties, or required by applicable rules of law, an arbitrator should keep confidential all matters relating to the arbitration."

It has been explained that "privacy is a respected hallmark of arbitration, safeguarded by the courts, cherished by the participants in the arbitration, and honored by third parties."[101] It is unlikely that the author of those words would be willing to offer such a sweeping generalization in 2004. While arbitration participants may genuinely cherish "privacy" in arbitration, to say the "privacy" (or more precisely, "confidentiality") has been "safeguarded" by the courts and "honored by third parties" would be a serious overstatement. When dealing with assertions of confidentiality in situations where discovery rules mandate disclosure, courts are faced with a tension between the confidentiality bargained for in contract and urged by the parties and what is suggested to be the public's "right to every man's evidence."[102] In other words, the disclosure "required by applicable rules of law" can deal a heavy blow to expectations of confidentiality in arbitration.

The reported cases dealing with attempts to intrude upon the confidentiality of the arbitration process most often have involved attempts to depose an arbitrator. Courts routinely have refused to allow a party "to depose an arbitrator for the purpose of impeaching or clarifying his decision."[103] Even when a party tries to undermine the finality of the arbitrator's decision with claims of bias or interest, the questioning of arbitrators, when allowed at all, is conducted under judicial supervision and only in cases where clear evidence of impropriety has been presented.[104]

Courts have rarely analyzed, in confidentiality terms, a third party's request for the discovery of records of arbitration proceedings, perhaps because discovery rules on their face would seem to mandate such disclosure in the absence of an identifiable privilege.[105] In *Milone v. General Motors Corp.,*[106] General Motors, the defendant in a products liability action, sought to discover from the plaintiff's insurer documents relating to a no-fault arbitration with the insurer in connection with the accident. The court conducted a traditional privilege inquiry and found that the documents were not prepared in connection with any common interest shared between the insurer and the adversarial plaintiff.[107] Further, since the documents were developed in preparation for the earlier arbitration and not for the pending litigation, no work-product privilege attached.[108] In a similar vein, in an action involving a dispute in the construction industry, a North Carolina court of appeals allowed discovery by a third-party contractor of the transcripts of an arbitration proceeding between a contracting university and a prime contractor on the same job.[109] The recent case of *Security Ins. Co. of Hartford v. Trustmark Ins. Co.*[110] involved a suit between two reinsurers relating to a retrocession agreement. One of the reinsurers requested and was granted production of documents reflecting past disputes relating to that same agreement, despite the fact that arbitration was ongoing relating to some aspects of disputes in United Kingdom; any confidentiality concerns that might exist relating to documents created for the purposes of arbitration have no bearing on the actual business transaction that was the basis for the dispute being arbitrated.

The Impact of Rule 408 of the Federal Rules of Evidence

Rule 408, stated broadly, provides that evidence of offering or accepting settlements is not admissible in order to prove liability. It further states that "evidence of conduct or statements made in compromise negotiations is likewise not admissible." However, the rule does not require exclusion of evidence that is otherwise discoverable. While Rule 408 explicitly addresses the "admissibility" of settlement discussions (as distinguished from "discoverability"), a few courts have extended Rule 408 to apply to the *discoverability* of settlement proceedings, as well as their admissibility.[111]

The *Bottaro* rationale has been explicitly rejected by one court. In *Bennett v. La Pere*,[112] the court explained that it thought that *Bottaro* had misconceived the policy rationale underlying Rule 408. It said that Rule 408 was meant to guard against allowing settlement discussions to "unimpededly creep into evidence at trial": however, after a settlement is obtained, parties no longer have that fear, since the matter is postsettlement. Hence, the *Bottaro* court concluded that the concept that discovery should be prevented so as not to discourage negotiations was misconceived. Other courts have held that Rule 408 applies only to the *admissibility* of settlement discussions, and not to their *discoverability*.[113]

The Florida statute is even more limited. It addresses only the confidentiality of the arbitration panel's award. It provides, in pertinent part:

> FSA 684.19. *Awards.*
> (1) A written statement of the reasons for an award shall be issued only if all parties agree to the issuance thereof or the tribunal determines that a failure to do so could prejudice recognition or enforcement of the award.
> An award may be made public by the tribunal or by a party only if:
> (a) All parties to the arbitration consent thereto in writing;
> (b) Disclosure is required by law; or
> (c) Disclosure is necessary in connection with any judicial or other official proceeding concerning the award.[114]

If the phrase "required by law" were to be interpreted to cover discovery requests pursuant to rules of procedure, the statutory protections would essentially be illusory.

Ethical Considerations in Connection with Privilege and Confidentiality

There are a number of extremely important ethical considerations that come into play when dealing with complex litigations such as those found in insurance and reinsurance scenarios, each of which both requires and deserves separate consideration.

1. Communication with Person Represented by Counsel

This issue is specifically addressed in Rule 4.2 of the American Bar Association Annotated Model Rules of Professional Conduct, 5th Edition (June 2003), which provides:

> In representing a client, a lawyer shall not communicate about the subject of the representation with a party the lawyer knows to be represented by another lawyer in the matter, unless the lawyer has the consent of the other lawyer or is authorized by law to do so.

In the comment to this rule, it is specifically noted that it does not prohibit communication with a party, or an employer or agent of a party, concerning matters *outside* the representation. For example, the existence of a controversy between a government agency and a private party, or between two organizations, does not prohibit a lawyer for either from communicating with non-lawyer representatives of the other regarding a separate matter. Also, parties to a matter may communicate directly with each other, and a lawyer having independent justification for communicating with the other party is permitted to do so. Communications authorized by law include, for example, the right of a party to a controversy with a government agency to speak with government officials about that matter.

The Comment to the rule, which was adopted from the ABA rules, states in part:

> In the case of an organization, this rule prohibits communications by a lawyer for one party concerning the matter in representation with persons having a managerial responsibility on behalf of the organization and with any other person, whose act or omission in connection with that matter may be imputed to the organization for purposes of civil or criminal liability or whose statement may constitute an admission on the part of the organization.

If an agent or employee of the organization is represented in the matter by his or her own counsel, the consent by that counsel to a communication will be sufficient for purposes of this rule. The rule also covers any person, whether or not a party to a formal proceeding, who is represented by counsel concerning the matter in question.

Rule 4.2 continues the traditional prohibition against communicating with a person known to be represented by another lawyer without that lawyer's consent. The provision is substantially identical to DR7-104(A)(1) of the predecessor Model Code of Professional Responsibility.[115]

Purpose of the Rule against Contact

The purpose of Rule 4.2 is to prevent lawyers from taking advantage of uncounselled lay persons and to preserve the integrity of the lawyer-client relationship.[116]

Opposing Parties May Speak to Each Other

As the Comment to Rule 4.2 states, the parties to a matter may voluntarily speak to each other without their lawyer's consent, and lawyers are not obligated to dissuade their clients from doing so.[117]

Can a Lawyer Advise a Client to Communicate with a Represented Party Directly?

A lawyer does not have an obligation to actively dissuade a client from communicating with another party. However, Rule 8.4(a) makes it unethical and improper for a lawyer knowingly to assist or induce another to violate the rules, and, therefore, could be construed to prohibit the lawyer from directing or advising a client to communicate with a represented party.[118]

There are a number of additional specific topics that are directly addressed in the comments/annotations to Rule 4.2, which are quite pertinent to this discussion. These include the following.

Using a Third Person to Communicate with a Represented Party

Rules 8.4 and 5.4(c) would also prohibit a lawyer from circumventing Rule 4.2 through the use of a third person. Thus, a lawyer may not advise or permit another to communicate in a manner that would be impermissible if engaged in by the lawyer.[119]

However, the distinction must be drawn between contact that is caused or directed by the lawyer and contact that occurs independently, and not at the lawyer's behest. In *Hayes v. Commonwealth,* 25 S.W.3d 463 (Ky. 2000), a detective who interviewed an indicted defendant without the prosecutor's knowledge was not considered an "agent" of the prosecutor for purposes of Rule 4.2. However, in *Commonwealth v. Louhisdon,* No. Civ. A-01-201-B, 2001 WL 360047 (Mass. Super. Ct. 2001), a district attorney specifically directed a psychiatrist to meet with a represented inmate in order to submit a report to the court; this was determined to be in violation of Rule 4.2.

Communication Need Not Be Intentional

Communication with the represented party can be an ethical violation even though it was not intentional.[120] Moreover, in *In re Howes,*[121] a prosecutor was found in violation of Rule 4.2 by simply listening to a criminal defendant discuss the case without knowledge of the defense counsel, despite the fact that no questions were asked.

Is the Represented Person a "Party" to the Matter?

There are several conditions that must be met before a Rule 4.2 violation can be established. First, the represented person with whom the lawyer is communicating must be a "party" to the matter. However, as the Comment to Rule 4.2 states, the term "party" is not limited to formal parties in litigation.[122]

When the Represented Party Is an Organization

When an organization, such as a corporation, is the represented party, certain other persons will be treated as parties as well. The Comment to Rule 4.2 provides a test for determining whether a person such as an employee is a party for purposes of the rule, known as the "managing-speaking" test. Stated simply, informal contact is prohibited with any person within the organization who was a "manager" of the company or who could speak on behalf of the company. For example, in *Palmer v. Pioneer Inn Assocs. Ltd.,*[123] the court articulated that "under the managing-speaking test, ex parte interviews are barred for employees holding managerial positions giving the authority to speak for and bind the corporation." Conversely, in *NAACP v. Florida Dep't of Corr.,*[124] the court reasoned that a plaintiff's attorney could interview "rank and file" prison employees, as it was quite "unlikely" that any statements made by those persons could bind the employer, or that their actions could be imputed to the employer.

The distinction drawn by the courts revolves around the status of the employee as an "alter ego" of the corporation, which includes consideration of the relationship between the person and the corporation's lawyers.[125]

However, there have been cases that have gone against this prevailing rule. For example, in *Morrison v. Brandeis University*,[126] the plaintiff's attorney was permitted interviews with members of the university faculty committee that had passed on plaintiff's eligibility for tenure, even though members might personify defendant university and speak for it with respect to the lawsuit. Moreover, some states rely heavily on the distinction between employees or managers and the individuals in the "litigation control group."[127]

Former Employee of a Corporate Party Opponent

The ABA Committee on Ethics and Professional Responsibility states that former employees of a corporation may be contacted without consulting the corporation's counsel, as they are no longer in positions of authority and, therefore, cannot bind the corporation.[128] This general rule is well enunciated in *Estate of Schwartz v. H.B.A. Mgmt., Inc.*,[129] in which the court held that the rules do not prohibit a lawyer from contacting a former employee of the corporation who has not consented to representation in the matter by the corporate counsel or who had not assisted counsel in the discovery process, Even if the negligence of that former employee could be imputed to the corporation.[130]

These rules, and the comments thereto, are in accord with *Upjohn v. United States, supra.* The Second District Court of Appeals of Florida also followed this logic in *Barfuss v. Diversicare Corp. of America*,[131] where it stated that former employees who participated in the care of the nursing home plaintiffs could not be contacted concerning the care provided, but distinguished employees as "merely witnesses" to the plaintiff's care, and thus not likely to possess privileged information. As such, their testimony or admissions would not be considered statements or admissions of the corporate defendant and could not be used to impute liability. It distinguished its earlier decision of *Manor Care of Dunedin, Inc. v. Keiser.*,[132] in which it had ruled that both the plaintiff and the defendant nursing home were entitled to conduct ex parte interviews of the defendant's former employees.

In *Keiser*, the lower court had decided that Rule 4-4.2, prohibiting ex parte contact with unrepresented employees of a represented corporation, does not apply once the employees leave the corporation. On review, the court of appeals remanded the case to the trial court to allow the defendant nursing home to renew its Motion for Protective Order to prohibit ex parte interviews of former employees who were specifically identified as belonging to the "managerial group" during their tenure with the defendant corporation. The *Barfuss* court appears to have assumed that all former employees who participated in the care of the plaintiff would have privileged information, or that their testimony would impute liability to the defendant or that their admissions would bind the defendant. (*Upjohn* assumes the same.) In *Barfuss*, the court ruled that the trial judge's order requiring the plaintiff to provide the defendant with copies of statements given by the former employees, excluding their attorney's impressions, did not depart from the essential requirements of the law.

In *Reynoso v. Greynolds Park Manor Inc.*,[133] the Florida Third District Court of Appeals expressly departed from the Second District's more restricted view as espoused in *Barfuss*. In *Reynoso*, the court held that Rule 4-4.2 of the Rules of Professional Conduct does not bar the plaintiff from conducting ex parte interviews, either directly or through an investigator, with 60 former employees of the defendant nursing home who had formerly provided care to the plaintiff's ward, but with restrictions to avoid inquiring into matters subject to attorney-client privilege, and to strictly adhere to the ethical prescriptions for dealing with unrepresented parties. However, no notice of intent to invoke the jurisdiction of the Florida Supreme Court was ever filed, and thus the conflict between *Reynoso* and *Barfuss* was never subject to review.

The ABA opinion cited in *Reynoso* showed concern about dealing with former employees of a corporate party, because an organizational party necessarily acts through others, and liability may survive the termination of the employment relationship.[134]

> (2) In the case of an organization, this rule prohibits Communications by a lawyer for one party concerning the matter in representation with persons having a managerial responsibility on behalf of the organization and with any other person whose act or omission in connection with that matter may be imputed to the organization for purposes of civil or criminal liability or whose statement may constitute an admission on the part of the organization.

It further noted that the purpose of the rule was to preserve the proper functioning of the legal system and shield the adverse party from improper approaches.[135] The 1991 opinion further stated "the rule against communicating with the opposing party without consent of that party's lawyer is not admissible of any exceptions or communications with sophisticated parties. . . ." It further pointed out that the Comment addresses "persons" and not "employees," and that the rule presumably also governs independent contractors whose relationship with the organization may have placed them in the factual position contemplated by the Comment. The Comment went on to state that although it is not specifically discussed, the adversary attorney seeking to communicate with a former employee must be careful not to seek to induce the former employee to violate the privilege attaching to attorney-client communications to the extent his or her communications as a former employee with his or her former employer's counsel are protected by the privilege (the privilege not belonging to or for the benefit of the former employee, but rather the former employer). Such an attempt could violate Rule 4.4, which requires respect for the rights of third persons.

Florida Bar Committee on Professional Ethics, Opinion #88-14, March 7, 1989, recited that a former manager or employee is no longer in a position to speak for the corporation. Further, under both the Federal and Florida Rules of Evidence, statements that might be made by the former manager or other former employees during an ex parte interview would not be admissible against the corporation, citing Rule 801(d)(2)(D), Federal Rules of Evidence (contra the annotated cases thereunder) and section 90.803(18)(d), Florida Evidence Code, which provides that a statement by an agent or servant of a party is admissible against the party if it concerns a matter within the scope of the agency or employment and is made during the existence of the agency or employment relationship. Admissibility is not the real issue: the issue is the confidentiality and ethics issues prohibiting such contact in the first place.

The "tug-of-war" sparked by the issue of the whether Rule 4-4.2 of the Rules of Professional Conduct extends to former employees of an organizational party is illustrated by the case law history in the U.S. District Court, Middle District of Florida. In *Rentclub, Inc. v. TransAmerica Rental Finance Corp.*,[136] *affirmed* 43 F.3d 1439 (11th Cir. 1995), the *Rentclub* court adopted the restricted view of *Barfuss* and *Keiser*. In *Rentclub*, the former managerial employee of the corporate defendant had been retained by the opposing party as a "trial consultant" and also testified against his former employer as a fact witness. The U.S. District Court found that ex parte communications with a former employee created the appearance of impropriety and were prohibited because of the likelihood that the former employee possessed privileged information. This former managerial-level employee testified against his former employer on factual matters that involved managerial practices, strategies, and other specialized information acquired during his tenure with the defendant corporation. The payment by the opposing attorney's law firm to that person created the appearance of professional impropriety. The court held that by its payment to the consultant, it created an inference that it had induced the consultant to breach the confidences acquired during his employment with the corporate party, so the court disqualified the law firm from further representation of its client in that matter. The U.S. District Court placed particular emphasis on the likelihood that the former employee had become aware of "confidential . . . proprietary information and . . . confidential and business documents" belonging to his former corporate employer, and noted that he had even "engaged in intra-office communications relating to litigation which was substantially related to the case."[137]

In *Lang v. Reedy Creek Improvement District*,[138] suit was brought by current and former female firefighters based on sex discrimination and civil rights violations. In considering whether or not to permit contact with former employees of the defendant, the court "recognizes but declines to apply *Rentclub*'s blanket prohibition on ex parte communications with all former employees to the facts in the case at bar."[139] Rather, the court reviewed the treatment of this issue by other jurisdictions, and permitted ex parte communications with former employees, but with the following limitations:

1. Upon contacting any former employee, Plaintiffs' counsel shall immediately identify herself as the attorney representing Plaintiffs in the instant suit and specify the purpose of the contact.
2. Plaintiffs' counsel shall ascertain whether the former employee is associated with either Defendant or is represented by counsel. If so, the contact must terminate immediately.
3. Plaintiffs' counsel shall advise the former employee that (a) participation in the interview is not mandatory and that (b) he or she may choose not to participate or to participate only in the presence of personal counsel or counsel for the Defendants. Counsel must immediately terminate the interview of the former employee if she or he does not wish to participate.

4. Plaintiffs' counsel shall advise the former employee to avoid disclosure of privileged materials. In the course of the interview, Plaintiffs' counsel shall not attempt to solicit privileged information and shall terminate the conversation should it appear that the interviewee may reveal privileged matters.

5. Plaintiffs shall create and preserve a list of all former employees contacted and the date(s) of contact(s) and shall maintain and preserve any and all statements or notes resulting from such contacts, whether by phone or in person. Defendants are entitled to review the lists and notes within seven (7) days of demand subject to the protections of work product.

6. Should the Defendants have reason to believe that a violation of either the ethical rules or this Court's Order has occurred, the Defendants shall file an appropriate motion with this Court. Appropriate sanctions or remedial measures will be imposed if a violation is found by the Court. If the violation is revealed at trial, the Defendants shall make such a motion in open Court, and the Court will take the matter under advisement at that time.[140]

As these cases show, interviews with former employees are conducted at one's own risk, and Courts have not been averse to becoming actively involved in setting limits on such contacts. A prudent practitioner should tread lightly to avoid the distinct possibility of engaging in an unwitting ethics violation, to the detriment of himself, his firm, and possibly his client.

Discussions with Former Corporate Employees: The Confidentiality Problem

The subject matter of the discussion, however, may be protected by the attorney-client privilege.[141] A corporate employee who is a party for purposes of the attorney-client privilege is not necessarily a party for the purposes of Rule 4.2.[142]

Witnesses

Rule 4.2 does not preclude a lawyer from interviewing the intended witnesses of another party.[143]

Members of a Class Action

Members of a class action suit are "parties" within the meaning of Rule 4.2.[144]

Is the Party "Represented?"

A second requirement for a Rule 4.2 violation is that the party with whom the lawyer has the "communication" must be represented by counsel.[145]

Is the Party Represented in the Matter Being Discussed?

A third requirement for a Rule 4.2 violation is that the party with whom the lawyer is communicating must be represented in connection with the matter being discussed. Thus, a lawyer representing a client against a represented party in one matter may nonetheless communicate with the represented party concerning a wholly unrelated matter for which the client does not have representation as long as the lawyer has an independent justification for doing so. In this context, the client would not be a represented party for the purposes of Rule 4.2.[146]

This rule does not prohibit communication with a party, or an employee or agent of a party, concerning matters outside the representation, For example, the existence of a controversy between a government agency and a private party or between two organizations does not prohibit a lawyer for either from communicating with nonlawyer representatives of the other regarding a separate matter. Also, parties to a matter may communicate directly with each other, and a lawyer having independent justification for communicating with the other party is permitted to do so. Communications authorized by law include, for example, the right of a party to a controversy with a government agency to speak with government officials about the matter.

In the case of an organization, this rule prohibits communications by a lawyer for one party concerning the matter in representation with persons having a managerial responsibility on behalf of the organization and with any other person whose act or omission in connection with that matter may be imputed to the organization for purposes of civil or criminal liability or whose statement may constitute an admission on the part of the organization. If an agent or employee of the organization is represented in the matter by his own counsel, the consent by that counsel to a communication will be sufficient for purposes of this rule.[147] This rule also covers any person, whether or not a party to a formal proceeding, who is represented by counsel concerning the matter in question.

Is the Communication Made in Connection with the Representation of a Client?
A Rule 4.2 violation cannot occur unless the lawyer was communicating with the represented party in connection with the representation of a client or on behalf of a client.[148]

Consent by Opposing Lawyer
Rule 4.2 permits communications with a represented party when the consent of the party's lawyer is obtained.[149]

Direct Settlement Negotiations with Opposing Party
The anti-contact prohibition of Rule 4.2 applies to direct settlement negotiations with an opposing party.[150] However, as is reflected in C.W. Wolfram, *Modern Legal Ethics* section 11.6, at 613 (1986), some have suggested that an exception to this rule against contact with the opposing party should exist when opposing counsel refuses to convey settlement offers.

The Anti-contact Rule in Domestic Relations Litigation
The anti-contact rule is frequently implicated in domestic relations litigation.[151]

When a Governmental Agency Is the Represented Party
When a governmental agency is the represented party, the Comment to Rule 4.2 indicates that communications with government officials are permitted as "authorized by law." Courts interpreting DR 7-104(A) of the predecessor Model Code similarly supported broad access to government employees.[152]

Prosecutors Communicating with Represented Criminal Defendants

In the context of criminal proceedings, Rule 4.2 prohibits prosecutors and their agents from speaking with a represented criminal defendant without notice to the defendant's lawyer and either a reasonable opportunity to be present or consent.[153]

However, communications with represented criminal suspects prior to the initiation of formal judicial proceedings as part of a non-custodial investigation by government agents or with informants generally are not considered subject to the anti-contact rule. The rationale is usually that the rule is coextensive with the accused's Sixth Amendment right to counsel, and that the contact is within the "authorized by law" exception.[154]

Federal Prosecutors

In 1988 a sharp debate arose between the American Bar Association and the United States Attorney General as to the applicability of Rule 4.2 to federal prosecutors conducting criminal investigations. The Justice Department, in response to the decision in *United States v. Hammad,*[155] which suppressed evidence a prosecutor obtained by violating DR 7-I04(A)(1), the anti-contact provision of the predecessor Model Code, took the position that federal prosecutors cannot be sanctioned for violating the ethical rule barring contacts with a defendant "in the course of authorized law enforcement activity." The position, which has generated great controversy, is based on the Supremacy Clause and on the "authorized by law" exception to the ethical rule.[156]

The American Bar Association responded with a resolution rejecting the Justice Department's position and "oppos(ing) any attempt by the Justice Department unilaterally to exempt its lawyers from the professional conduct rules that apply to all lawyers under applicable rules of the jurisdictions in which they practice."[157]

One court has dismissed an indictment based upon the prosecutor's direct contacts with the defendant in an effort to arrange a guilty plea.[158] Although the defendant had asked for the discussions and a federal magistrate had approved them, the judge ruled that the contacts had effectively deprived the defendant of the lawyer of his choice.

Violation of Rule 4.2

A lawyer who has violated Rule 4.2 may be disqualified from representing his or her client.[159]

2. Fairness to Opposing Party and Counsel

This issue is specifically addressed in Rule 3.4 of the *American Bar Association Annotated Model Rules of Professional Conduct*, 5th Edition (June 2003), which provides:

> A lawyer shall not:

> (a)unlawfully obstruct another's party's access to evidence or unlawfully alter, destroy or conceal a document or other material having potential evidentiary value. A lawyer shall not counsel or assist another person to do any such act;

(b) falsify evidence, counsel or assist a witness to testify falsely, or offer an inducement to a witness that is prohibited by law;

(c) knowingly disobey an obligation under the rules of a tribunal, except for an open refusal based on an assertion that no valid obligation exists;

(d) in pretrial procedure, make a frivolous discovery request or fail to make reasonably diligent effort to comply with a legally proper discovery request by an opposing party;

(e) in trial, allude to any matter that the lawyer does not reasonably believe is relevant or that will not be supported by admissible evidence, assert personal knowledge of facts in issue except when testifying as a witness, or state a personal opinion as to the justness of a cause, the credibility of a witness, the culpability of a civil litigant or the guilt or innocence of an accused; or

(f) request a person other than a client to refrain from voluntarily giving relevant information to another party unless:

(1) the person is a relative or an employee or other agent of a client; and

(2) the lawyer reasonably believes that the person's interests will not be adversely affected by refraining from giving such information.

COMMENT

The procedure of the adversary system contemplates that the evidence in a case is to be marshaled competitively by the contending parties. Fair competition in the adversary system is secured by prohibitions against destruction or concealment of evidence, improperly influencing witnesses, obstructive tactics in discovery procedure, and the like.

(2) Documents and other items of evidence are often essential to establish a claim or defense. Subject to evidentiary privileges, the right of an opposing party, including the government, to obtain evidence through discovery or subpoena is an important procedural right. The exercise of that right can be frustrated if relevant material is altered, concealed or destroyed. Applicable law in many jurisdictions makes it an offense to destroy material for purposes of impairing its availability in a pending proceeding or one whose commencement can be foreseen. Falsifying evidence is also generally a criminal offense. Paragraph (a) applies to evidentiary material generally, including computerized information. Applicable law may permit a lawyer to take temporary possession of physical evidence of client crimes for the purpose of conducting a limited examination that will not alter or destroy material characteristics of the evidence. In such a case, applicable law may require the lawyer to turn the evidence over to the police or other prosecuting authority, depending on the circumstances.

(3) With regard to paragraph (b), it is not improper to pay a witness's expenses or to compensate an expert witness on terms permitted by law. The common-law rule in most jurisdictions is that it is improper to pay an occurrence witness any fee for testifying and that it is improper to pay an expert witness a contingent fee.

(4) Paragraph (f) permits a lawyer to advise employees of a client to refrain from giving information to another party, for the employees may identify their interests with those of the client.[160]

Alteration, destruction or concealment of evidence is a potential problem area in large, multiparty litigations such as reinsurance scenarios.[161] Under this rule, procuring the absence of a witness is treated as obstruction of evidence.[162]

3. Dealing with an Unrepresented Person

This issue is specifically addressed in Rule 4.3 of the *American Bar Association Annotated Model Rules of Professional Conduct,* 5th Edition (June 2003), which provides:

> In dealing on behalf of a client with a person who is not represented by counsel, a lawyer shall not state or imply that the lawyer is disinterested. When the lawyer knows or reasonably should know that the unrepresented person misunderstands the lawyer's role in the matter, the lawyer shall make reasonable efforts to correct the misunderstanding. The lawyer shall not give legal advice to an unrepresented person, other than the advice to secure counsel, if the lawyer knows or reasonably should know that the interests of such a person are or have a reasonably possibility of being in conflict with the interests of the client.

COMMENT

An unrepresented person, particularly one not experienced in dealing with legal matters, might assume that a lawyer is not interested in loyalties or is a disinterested authority on the law even when the lawyer represents a client. In order to avoid a misunderstanding, a lawyer will typically need to identify his or her client and, where necessary, explain that the client has interests opposed to those of the unrepresented person. For misunderstandings that sometimes arise when a lawyer for an organization deals with an unrepresented constituent:[163]

> (5) The Rule distinguishes between situations involving unrepresented persons whose interests may be adverse to those of the lawyer's client and those in which the person's interests are not in conflict with the client's. In the former situation, the possibility that the lawyer will compromise the unrepresented person's interest is so great that the Rule prohibits the giving of any advice, apart from the advice to obtain counsel. Whether a lawyer is giving impermissible advice may depend on the experience and sophistication of the unrepresented person, as well as the setting in which the behavior and comments occur. This Rule does not prohibit a lawyer from negotiating the terms of a transaction or settling a dispute with an unrepresented person. So long as the lawyer has explained that the lawyer represents an adverse party and is not representing the person, the lawyer may inform the person of the terms on which the lawyer's client will enter into an agreement or settle a matter, prepare documents that require the

person's signature and explain the lawyers' own view of the meaning of the document or the lawyer's view of the underlying legal obligations.

This rule was amended in 2002 to add the last sentence of the Rule prohibiting an attorney from "giving advice" to an unrepresented person, in an attempt to discourage overreaching in negotiations.[164]

The interplay between Rules 4.2 and 4.3 was discussed in *Reynoso v. Greynolds Park Manor Inc.*,[165] which adopted the *ABA Lawyer's Manual on Professional Conduct* on Rule 4.2. It does not cover former employees who may be sued, or have liability insurance to cover their acts or omissions, but the comments on Rule 4-4.2 prohibit a liability interview without a corporate counsel's permission.[166]

4. Respect for Rights of Third Persons

This issue is specifically addressed in Rule 4.4 of the *American Bar Association Annotated Model Rules of Professional Conduct*, 5th Edition (June 2003), which provides:

> (b) In representing a client, a lawyer shall not use means that have no substantial purpose other than to embarrass, delay, or burden a third person, or use methods of obtaining evidence that violate the legal rights of such a person.
>
> (c) A lawyer who receives a document relating to the representation of the lawyer's client and knows or reasonably should know that the document was inadvertently sent shall promptly notify the sender.

COMMENT

> (1) Responsibility to a client requires a lawyer to subordinate the interests of others to those of the client, but that responsibility does not imply that a lawyer may disregard the rights of third persons. It is impractical to catalogue all such rights, but they include legal restrictions on methods of obtaining evidence from third persons and unwarranted intrusions into privileged relationships, such as the client-lawyer relationship.
>
> (2) Paragraph (b) recognizes that lawyers sometimes receive documents that were mistakenly sent or produced by opposing parties or their lawyers. If a lawyer knows or reasonably should know that such a document was sent inadvertently, then this Rule requires the lawyer to promptly notify the sender in order to permit that person to take protective measures. Whether the lawyer is required to take additional steps, such as returning the original document, is a matter of law beyond the scope of these Rules, as is the question of whether the privileged status of the document has been waived. Similarly, this Rule does not address the legal duties of a lawyer who receives a document that the lawyer knows or reasonably should know may have been wrongfully obtained by the sending person. For purposes of this Rule, "document" includes e-mail or other electronic modes of transmission subject to being read or put into readable form.

(3) Some lawyers may choose to return a document unread, for example, when the lawyer learns before receiving the document that it was inadvertently sent to the wrong address. Where a lawyer is not required by applicable law to do so, the decision to voluntarily return such a document is a matter of professional judgment ordinarily reserved to the lawyer.[167]

Listing of Related Topics and Supplemental Authority

Privilege in general
- The privilege between insured and insurer.[168]
- Prosecution's privilege against disclosure of an informer.[169]
- For the rights and duties of the attorney in a criminal prosecution (Civil RICO/ Criminal) when client informs him of intent to present perjured testimony.[170]
- As to testimony by in-house corporate counsel, the test is the client's intent—to reveal or not to reveal to a third party or to the public.[171]

Work-product and attorney-client privilege
- No attorney-client privilege by attorney or client in connection with the underlying suit or relating to bad faith of the insurer and negligence of the defense attorney.[172]
- Discovery regarding the reinsurer's liability for the primary insurer's failure to compromise or settle.[173]
- Work-product privilege as applying to material prepared for terminated litigation or for claims that did not result in litigation.[174]
- Florida requires the attorney to testify on contemplated or actual civil fraud (including absconding with funds) by his client, dating back to *Kneale v. Williams*.[175]
- Attorney work-product privileges as applicable to documents prepared in anticipation of terminated litigation.[176]
- Inadvertent disclosure of privileged documents does not waive the attorney-client privilege in New Jersey.[177]
- Deposition of corporate general counsel can seek disclosure of underlying facts only on which he relied to instruct co-counsel to threaten opposing counsel with sanctions; however, beyond discovery of these facts, corporate client is entitled to attorney-client privilege.[178]
- *Safeway Ins. Co. v. Superior Court of the State of Arizona*[179] held that plaintiff in a wrongful death suit may not depose an employee of Safeway regarding communications with the Safeway company attorney *or* obtain documents from their claim file protected by attorney-client privilege. There was no claim made of the fraud exception to the attorney-client privilege, and hence there was no need for an in camera review.[180]
- The attorney-client privilege may be asserted as to an existing client or as to one seeking to become a client.[181]
- The statement to an opposing attorney that "strong and valid defenses are available" is at most a legal conclusion and not a waiver of the attorney-client privi-

lege; in contrast, selective disclosure of documents to counsel's benefit may be a total waiver.[182]

- The attorney-client privilege and attorney work-product privilege are perverted if used to further illegal activities.[183]
- If the client is deceased, the attorney-client privilege can be waived only by the express consent of the executor, administrator of the estate or surviving spouse. *State v. McDermott,* 598 N.E.2d 147 (Ohio App. 1991).
- Defendant's notes taken in preparation for consultation with a lawyer were protected.[184]
- Party being questioned about the errata sheet changes on his prior deposition can state that he consulted his lawyer, but content of the communications with his lawyer are privileged.[185]
- What to do if conspiratorial intent is disclosed by the client.[186]
- When an independent auditor was hired by the insurer to audit insured's books, the information was considered material prepared in preparation for litigation and was privileged.[187]

Disqualification of law firm—issues

- Disqualification of the law firm from representing a party in a federal civil suit involving a former client of that firm.[188]

Accountant-client privilege and related communications

Privilege for communications in general:[189]

- *Dees v. Scott*[190] held the statutory privilege was between client and his public accountant or certified public accountant; otherwise, the corporate accountant not so privileged could testify.[191] Further, the corporate attorney could testify if the client intended the information to be revealed to a third party or the public; otherwise, the information could not be disclosed.[192]
- However, a statute creating an accountant-client privilege may specifically exclude any information a CPA might have obtained relative to or in connection with the examination or audit or report of any financial statement, books or records.[193]
- Conspiracy between a client and an accountant not privileged.[194]
- Accountant-client privilege may be waived.[195]
- Discovery and liability of the independent accountant to the shareholder or investor.[196]
- Preparer of tax returns testimony privileged in federal tax prosecution.[197]
- What to do if conspiratorial intent is disclosed to accountant by the client.[198]

Reinsurance and insurance issues

- Both the reinsurer and the excess insurer have the right to question the dates of loss used in establishing the underlying or the ceding coverage, so as to determine proper exhaustion of limits or proper reinsurance claim by the ceding company.[199]
- The reinsurer did not unreasonably withhold payment of reinsurance proceeds under the reinsurance certificate by reserving its rights and filing a declaratory judgment action.[200]

- Insurance and Reinsurance Disputes, *Defense Counsel Journal,* July 1988.
- Fishing for Reinsurance Proceeds, *Defense Counsel Journal*, January 1988.
- Liability in Excess of Policy Limits; Bad Faith; Insurance Excess and Reinsurance Coverage Disputes. 1986.
- Discovery of an Insurer's File: Now you See It, Now You Don't, *The Forum,* Fall 1984.
- Work Product Discovery in Insurance Litigation, *Indiana Law Review*, Vol. 18, No. 2, 1985.
- Discovery, *Insurance Law and Practice*, Section 12080 (1982).
- Discovery of Reserve and Reinsurance Information—An Update: Vol. 44, No. 3, Spring 1994, *Federation of Insurance and Corporate Council Quarterly.*
- *See*: The Professional Responsibilities of Insurance Defense Lawyers, Fall 1995, *Duke Law Journal*—on the Tripartite Relationship.

Excess insurance issues
- An underlying insurer should honor its duty to an excess insurer to enter into reasonable settlements within the limits of the primary coverage.[201]
- The duty of good faith and fair dealing between the primary carrier and the excess carrier includes a duty to reasonably assign dates of loss so as to result in a fair and appropriate allocation of loss between the underlying and excess carriers.[202]
- There is also a duty placed on the underlying carrier to accept a reasonable settlement offer within the underlying limits, to in effect protect the excess carrier.[203]

In *Continental Casualty Co. v. United States Fidelity & Guaranty Co.*,[204] U.S. Fidelity had primary coverage of $200,000 and Continental wrote an excess policy of $1 million. Prior to trial, plaintiff made a demand of $320,000 with U.S. Fidelity to pay its limit of $200,000 and the insured to pay $120,000 (at that point plaintiff was unaware of the excess coverage). U.S. Fidelity refused to settle and a verdict was rendered in the amount of $743,895. Continental then sued U.S. Fidelity to recover the $513,859 paid under its excess policy. The court held that U.S. Fidelity breached its duty of good faith and fair dealing, even though the lowest settlement demand exceeded its $200,000 policy limit. The court further found that once a breach of the duty of good faith and fair dealing is found, the plaintiff excess carrier need only show the amount of the demand to establish a prima facie case for recovery of the amounts paid by the excess.

Issues of privilege in connection with corporations and corporate bankruptcies
- Who can disclose who has possession of various corporate books and records—subsidiaries, branches and/or affiliates?[205]
- Who has possession, custody or control of corporate books or records for purposes of order to produce?[206]
- The trustee in bankruptcy (receiver in insolvency) has the power to waive the privilege of communications available to the bankrupt (insolvent).[207] No testimony in the bankruptcy proceedings is available for use in the criminal pro-

ceedings against him.[208] For insolvency proceedings, see 7 A.L.R. 4th 16 § 1l(b); 30 A.L.R. 4th 1110, § 10.

- Similarly, directors of a corporation have the power to waive the privilege of confidentiality of communications.[209]
- Corporate attorney's privilege in controversy between corporation, and officer/director/stockholder.[210]
- For a corporation's claim of privilege for agent or employee's communication to the corporate attorney.[211]
- In international trade cases, access to confidential matter as privileged. See 29 U.S. Code Ann. § 151 6(a)(b)(2)(B); 73 A.L.R. Fed. 247.
- For confidential clerk or stenographer's testimony as privileged.[212]
- Affiliated or subsidiary corporation's books and records—the issue of compelling a party to disclose information that is in the hands of an affiliate or subsidiary corporation, or an independent contractor who was not made a party to the suit.[213]
- Individual officer, director or agent of the corporation or unincorporated association's right to assert personal privilege against self-incrimination with respect to production of corporate books and records.[214]
- Computerized business records produced.[215]
- Rehabilitator's documents are not public records under the Kentucky Open Records Act.[216] Thus, the rehabilitator is not synonymous with commissioner. The legislature did not intend to convert companies such as Kentucky Central into a public agency through the Rehabilitation Act. Similarly, in New York, the superintendent of insurance as liquidator was not an "agency" of the state under the Freedom of Information Act of New York.[217]
- What constitutes an "invasion of privacy?"
- Right to privacy vs. exchange among insurers of medical information concerning applicant or insured.[218]
- Public disclosure of a person's indebtedness as invasion of privacy. 33 A.L.R. 3d 154.
- Oral declarations as invasion of right of privacy.[219]
- Investigations and surveillance, shadowing or trailing as invasions of privacy.[220]
- Privileged reports/communications between liability or indemnity insurer and the insured.[221]
- Freedom of Information Act,[222] exempting from disclosure personnel and medical files; exempting "confidential source,"[223] government attorney exemption.[224]
- For filing documents in a motion in limine for the court to review.[225]
- For open court refusal by a party to permit introduction of privileged testimony as being prejudicial.[226]

Privilege and confidentiality issues in connection with electronic surveillance, eavesdropping, and wiretapping:
- Sound recordings—admissibility into evidence in spite of privileged nature.[227]

Issues involving bad faith in general
- Bad faith on the part of the insurer in failing to pay, or in delaying payment of insured's claims, versus insured's misrepresentations of bad faith.[228]
- Attorney-client and work-product privileges may be lost by insurers in bad-faith cases.[229]
- A statutory bad-faith claim in Florida[230] should be held in abatement pending the outcome of the underlying contractual dispute.[231]
- "Person" under FSA 624.155 includes third parties (such as injured plaintiffs), and such persons can also bring suit for bad faith under this statute.[232]

Related issues
- Privileged communications between the insurer and its agents and adjusters in actions for libel or slander of its own agents or third party.[233]
- There is no attorney-client privilege where the insurer directs the defense attorney to write to a third party or where the insured directs his attorney to write to an insurer.[234]
- The federal court sitting in diversity jurisdiction will follow the law of the forum.[235]
- Subpoena duces tecum power and objections.[236]
- Protective orders—statements of witnesses to be produced.[237]
- Advertisements, brochures, and/or catalogues by a litigant containing admissions contrary to a position now taken by him.[238]

General Background: Statutory and Common-Law Privileges and Confidentialities

A. Rules of Civil Procedure
There are a number of Federal Rules of Civil Procedure that shape the privilege and confidentiality issues one may encounter in the course of litigation of primary, excess, umbrella, and reinsurer cases. These will be repeated herein for convenience.

1. Federal Rules of Civil Procedure
RULE 26: GENERAL PROVISIONS GOVERNING DISCOVERY; DUTY OF DISCLOSURE

(a) Required Disclosures; Methods to Discover Additional Matter.

(1) Initial Disclosures. "Except in categories of proceedings specified in Rule 26(a)(1) (E), or to the extent otherwise stipulated or directed by order, a party must, without awaiting a discovery request, provide to other parties:

(A) the name and, if known, the address and telephone number of each individual likely to have discoverable information that the disclosing party may use to support its claims or defenses, unless solely for impeachment, identifying the subjects of the information;

(B) a copy of, or a description by category and location of, all documents, data, compilations, and tangible things that are in the possession, custody, or control of the party and that the disclosing party may use to support its claims or defenses, unless solely for impeachment;

(C) a computation of any category of damages claimed by the disclosing party, making available for inspection and copying as under Rule 34 the documents or other evidentiary material, not privileged or protected from disclosure, on which such computation is based, including material bearing on the nature and extent of injuries suffered; and

(D) for inspection and copying as under Rule 34 any insurance agreement under which any person carrying on an insurance business may be liable to satisfy part or all of a judgment which may be entered in the action or to indemnify or reimburse for payments made to satisfy the judgment."

(E) The following categories of proceedings are exempt from initial disclosure under Rule 26(a)(1):

(i) an action for review of an administrative record;

(ii) a petition for habeas corpus or other proceeding to challenge a criminal conviction or sentence;

(iii) an action brought without counsel by a person in custody of the United States, a state, or a state subdivision;

(iv) an action to enforce or quash an administrative summons or subpoena;

(v) an action by the United States to recover benefit payments;

(vi) an action by the United States to collect on a student loan guaranteed by the United States;

(vii) a proceeding ancillary to proceedings in other courts; and

(viii) an action to enforce an arbitration award.

These disclosures must be made at or within 14 days after the Rule 26(F) conference unless a different time is set by stipulation or court order, or unless a party objects during the conference that initial disclosures are not appropriate in the circumstances of the action and states the objection in the Rule 26(f) discovery plan. In ruling on the objection, the court must determine what disclosures—if any—are to be made and set the time for disclosure. Any party first served or otherwise joined after the Rule 26(f) conference must make these disclosures within 30 days after being served or joined unless a different time is set by stipulation or court order. A party must make its initial disclosures based on the information then reasonably available to it and is not excused from making its disclosures because it has not fully completed its investigation of the case or because it challenges the sufficiency of another party's disclosures or because another party has not made its disclosures.

(2) Disclosure of Expert Testimony.

(A) In addition to the disclosures required by paragraph (1), a party shall disclose to other parties the identity of any person who may be used at trial to present evidence under Rules 702, 703, or 706 of the Federal Rules of Evidence.

(B) Except as otherwise stipulated or directed by the court, this disclosure shall, with respect to a witness who is retained or specially employed to provide expert testimony in the case or whose duties as an employee of the party regularly involve giving expert testimony, be accompanied by a written report prepared and signed by the witness. The report shall contain a complete statement of all opinions to be expressed and the basis and reasons therefor; the data or other information considered by the witness in forming the opinions; any exhibits to be used as a summary of or support for the opinions; the qualifications of the witness, including a list of all publications authored by the witness within the preceding ten years; the compensation to be paid for the study and testimony; and a listing of any other cases in which the witness had testified as an expert at trial or by deposition within the preceding four years.

(C) These disclosures shall be made at the times and in the sequence directed by the court. In the absence of other directions from the court or stipulation by the parties, the disclosures shall be made at least 90 days before the trial date or the date the case is to be ready for trial or, if the evidence is intended solely to contradict or rebut evidence on the same subject matter identified by another party under paragraph (2)(B), within 30 days after the disclosure made by the other party. The parties shall supplement these disclosures when required under subdivision (e)(1).

(3) Pretrial Disclosures. In addition to the disclosures required in the preceding paragraphs, a party shall provide to other parties the following information regarding the evidence that it may present at trial other than solely for impeachment purposes:

(A) the name and, if not previously provided, the address and telephone number of each witness, separately identifying those whom the party expects to present and those whom the party may call if the need arises;

(B) the designation of those witnesses whose testimony is expected to be presented by means of a deposition and, if not taken stenographically, a transcript of the pertinent portions of the deposition testimony; and

(C) an appropriate identification of each document or other exhibit, including summaries of other evidence, separately identifying those which the Party expects to offer and those which the party may offer if the need arises.

Unless otherwise directed by the court, these disclosures shall be made at least 30 days before trial. Within 14 days thereafter, unless a different time is specified by the court, a party may serve and file a list disclosing (i) any objections to the issue under Rule 32(a) of a deposition designated by another party under Rule 26(a)(3)(B) and (ii) any objection, together with the grounds therefor, that may be made to the admissibility of materials identified under Rule 26(a)(3)(C). Objections not so disclosed, other than objections under Rule 402 and 403 of the Federal Rules of Evidence, are waived unless excused by the court for good cause.

(4) Form of Disclosures. Unless the court orders otherwise, all disclosures under Rules 26(a)(1) through (3) must be made in writing, signed, and served.

(5) Methods to Discover Additional Matter. Parties may obtain discovery by one or more of the following methods: depositions upon oral examination or written questions; written interrogatories; production of documents or things or permission to enter upon land or other property under Rule 34 or 45(a)(1)(C), for inspection and other purposes; physical and mental examinations; and requests for admission.

(b) Discovery Scope and Limits. Unless otherwise limited by order of the court in accordance with these rules, the scope of discovery is as follows:

(1) In General. Parties may obtain discovery regarding any matter, not privileged, which is relevant to the claim or defense of any party, including the existence, description, nature, custody, condition, and location of any books, documents, or other tangible things and the identity and location of persons having knowledge of any discoverable matter. For good cause, the court may order discovery of any matter relevant to the subject matter involved in the action. Relevant information need not be admissible at the trial if the discovery appears reasonably calculated to lead to the discovery of admissible evidence. All discovery is subject to the limitations imposed by Rule 26(b)(2)(i), (ii), and (iii).

(2) *Limitations.* By order, the court may alter the limits in these rules on the number of depositions and interrogatories or the length of depositions under Rule 30. By order or local rule, the court may also limit the number of requests under Rule 36. The frequency or extent of use of the discovery methods otherwise permitted under these rules and by any local rule shall be limited by the court if it determines that: (i) the discovery sought is unreasonable, cumulative or duplicative, or is obtainable from some other source that is more convenient, less burdensome, or less expensive; (ii) the party seeking discovery has had ample opportunity by discovery in the action to obtain the information sought; or (iii) the burden or expense of the proposed discovery outweighs its likely benefits, taking into account the needs of the case, the amount in controversy, the parties' resources, the importance of the issues at stake in the litigation, and the importance of the proposed discovery in resolving the issues. The court may act upon its own initiative after reasonable notice or pursuant to a motion under Rule 26(c).

(3) *Trial Preparation: Materials.* Subject to the provisions of subdivision (b)(4) of this rule, a party may obtain discovery of documents and tangible things otherwise discoverable under subdivision (b)(l) of this rule and prepared in anticipation of litigation or for trial by or for another party or by or for that other party's representative (including the other party's attorney, consultant, surety, indemnitor, insurer, or agent) only upon a showing that the party seeking discovery has

substantial need of the materials in the preparation of the party's case and that the party is unable without undue hardship to obtain the substantial equivalent of the materials by other means. In ordering discovery of such materials when the required showing has been made, the court shall protect against disclosure of the mental impressions, conclusions, opinions, or legal theories of an attorney or other representative of a party concerning the litigation.

A party may obtain without the required showing a statement concerning the action or its subject matter previously made by the party. Upon request, a person not a party may obtain without the required showing a statement concerning the action or its subject matter previously made by that person. If the request is refused, the person may move for a court order. The provisions of Rule 37(a)(4) apply to the award of expenses incurred in relation to the motion. For purposes of this paragraph, a statement previously made is (A) a written statement signed or otherwise adopted or approved by the person making it, or (B) a stenographic, mechanical, electrical, or other recording, or a transcription thereof, which is a substantially verbatim recital of an oral statement by the person making it and contemporaneously recorded.

(4) Trial Preparation: Experts.

(A) A party may depose any person who has been identified as an expert whose opinions may be presented at trial. If a report from the expert is required under subdivision (a)(2)(B), the deposition shall not be conducted until after the report is provided.

(B) A party may, through interrogatories or by deposition, discover facts known or opinions held by an expert who has been retained or specially employed by another party in anticipation of litigation or preparation for trial and who is not expected to be called as a witness at trial only as provided in Rule 35(b) or upon a showing of exceptional circumstances under which it is impracticable for the party seeking discovery to obtain facts or opinions on the same subject by other means.

(C) Unless manifest injustice would result, (i) the court shall require that the party seeking discovery pay the expert a reasonable fee for time spent in responding to discovery under this subdivision; and (ii) with respect to discovery obtained under subdivision (b)(4)(B) of this rule, the court shall require the party seeking discovery to pay the other party a fair portion of the fees and expenses reasonably incurred by the latter party in obtaining facts and opinions from the expert.

(5) *Claims of Privilege or Protection of Trial Preparation Materials.* When a party withholds information otherwise discoverable under these rules by claiming that it is privileged or subject to protection as trial preparation material, the party shall make the claim expressly and shall describe the nature of the documents, communications, or things not produced or disclosed in a manner that, without revealing information itself privileged or protected, will enable other parties to assess the applicability of the privilege or protection.

(d) Protective Orders. Upon motion by a party or by the person from whom discovery is sought, accompanied by a certification that the movant has in good faith conferred or attempted to confer with other affected parties in an effort to resolve the dispute without court action, and for good cause shown, the court in which the action is pending or, alternatively, on matters relating to a deposition, the court in the district where the deposition is to be taken may make any order which justice requires to protect a party or person from annoyance, embarrassment, oppression, or undue burden or expense, including one or more of the following:

(1) that the discovery not be had;

(2) that the disclosure or discovery may be had only on specified terms and conditions, including a designation of the time or place;

(3) that the discovery may be had only by a method of discovery other than that selected by the party seeking discovery;

(4) that certain matters not be inquired into, or that the scope of the discovery be limited to certain matters;

(5) that discovery be conducted with no one present except persons designated by the court;

(6) that a deposition, after being sealed, be opened only by order of the court;

(7) that a trade secret or other confidential research, development, or commercial information not be revealed or be revealed only in a designated way; and

(8) that the parties simultaneously file specified documents or information enclosed in sealed envelopes to be opened as directed by the court.

If the motion for protective order is denied in whole or in part, the court may, on such terms and conditions as are just, order that any party or person provide or permit discovery. The provisions of Rule 37(a)(4) apply to the award of expenses incurred in relation to the motion.

(d) Timing and Sequence of Discovery. Except in categories of proceedings exempted from initial disclosure under Rule 26(a)(1)(E), or when authorized under these rules or by order or agreement of the parties, a party may not seek discovery from any source before the parties have conferred as required by Rule 26(f). Unless the court upon motion, for the convenience of parties and witnesses and in the interests of justice, orders otherwise, methods of discovery may be used in any sequence, and the fact that a party is conducting discovery, whether by deposition or otherwise, does not operate to delay any other party's discovery.

(e) Supplementation of Disclosures and Responses. A party who has made a disclosure under subdivision (a) or responded to a request for discovery with a disclosure or response is under a duty to supplement or correct the disclosure or response to include information thereafter acquired if ordered by the court or in the following circumstances:

(1) A party is under a duty to supplement at appropriate intervals its disclosures under subdivision (a) if the party learns that in some material respect the information disclosed is incomplete or incorrect and if the additional or corrective information has not otherwise been made known to the other parties during the discovery process or in writing. With respect to testimony of an expert from whom a report is required under subdivision (a)(2)(B), the duty extends both to information contained in the report and to information provided through a deposition of the expert, and any additions or changes to this information shall be disclosed by the time the party's disclosures under Rule 26(a)(3) are due.

(2) A party is under a duty reasonably to amend a prior response to an interrogatory, request for production, or request for admission if the party learns that the response is in some material respect incomplete or incorrect and if the additional or corrective information has not otherwise been made known to the other parties during the discovery process or in writing.

[Subparagraphs (f) and (g) of Rule 26 are omitted.]

Rule 30: DEPOSITIONS UPON ORAL EXAMINATION

[Subparagraph (a) is omitted in its entirety.]

Notice of Examination: General Requirements; Method of Recording; Production of Documents and Things; Deposition of Organization; Deposition by Telephone.

(1) A party desiring to take the deposition of any person upon oral examination shall give reasonable notice in writing to every other party to the action. The notice shall state the time and place for taking the deposition and the name and address of each person to be examined, if known, and, if the name is not known, a general description sufficient to identify the person or the particular class or group to which the person belongs. If a subpoena duces tecum is to be served on the person to be examined, the designation of the material to be produced as set forth in the subpoena shall be attached to or included in the notice.

[Subparagraphs (b)(2) through (7) are omitted.]

(c) Examination and Cross-Examination; Record of Examination; Oath; Objections.

Examination and cross-examination of witnesses may proceed as permitted at the trial under the provisions of the Federal Rules of Evidence except Rules 103 and 615. The officer before whom the deposition is to be taken shall put the witness on oath or affirmation and shall personally, or by someone acting under the officer's direction and in the officer's presence, record the testimony of the witness. The testimony shall be taken stenographically or recorded by any other method authorized by subdivision (b)(2) of this rule. All objections made at the time of the examination to the qualification of the officer taking the deposition, to the manner of taking it, to the evidence presented, to the conduct of any party, or to any other aspect of the proceeding shall be noted by the officer upon the record of the deposition; but the examination shall proceed, with the testimony being taken subject to the objections. In lieu of participating in the oral examination, parties may serve written questions in a sealed envelope on the party taking the deposition and the party taking the deposition shall transmit them to the officer, who shall propound them to the witness and record the answers verbatim.

[Subparagraphs (d) through (g) omitted.]

Rule 34: PRODUCTION OF DOCUMENTS AND THINGS AND ENTRY UPON LAND FOR INSPECTION AND OTHER PURPOSES

(a) Scope. Any party may serve on any other party a request (1) to produce and permit the party making the request, or someone acting on the requestor's behalf, to inspect and copy any designated documents (including writings, drawings, graphs, charts, photographs, phonorecords, and other data compilations from which information can be obtained, translated, if necessary, by the respondent through detection devices into reasonable usable form), or to inspect and copy, test, or sample any tangible things which constitute or contain matters within the scope of Rule 26(b) and which are in the possession, custody or control of the party upon whom the request is served; or (2) to permit entry upon designated land or other property in the possession or control of the party upon whom the request is served for the purposes of inspection and measuring, surveying, photographing, testing, or sampling the property or any designated object or operation thereon, within the scope of Rule 26(b).

[Subparagraphs (b) and (c) omitted.]

A number of the Federal Rules of Evidence are also quite pertinent, specifically Rules 401, 402, 403, 501, 801, and 803.

Rule 401. DEFINITION OF "RELEVANT EVIDENCE"

"Relevant evidence" means evidence having any tendency to make the existence of any fact that is of consequence to the determination of the action more probable or less probable than it would be without the evidence.

Rule 402. RELEVANT EVIDENCE GENERALLY ADMISSIBLE; IRRELEVANT EVIDENCE INADMISSIBLE

All relevant evidence is admissible, except as otherwise provided by the Constitution of the United States, by Act of Congress, by these rules, or by other rules prescribed by the Supreme Court pursuant to statutory authority. Evidence which is not relevant is not admissible.

Rule 403. EXCLUSION OF RELEVANT EVIDENCE ON GROUNDS OF PREJUDICE, CONFUSION, OR WASTE OF TIME

Although relevant, evidence may be excluded if its probative value is substantially outweighed by the danger of unfair prejudice, confusion of the issues, or misleading the jury, or by considerations of undue delay, waste of time, or needless presentation of cumulative evidence.

Rule 501: PRIVILEGES—GENERAL RULE

Except as otherwise required by the Constitution of the United States or provided by Act of Congress or in rules prescribed by the Supreme Court pursuant to statutory authority, the privilege of a witness, person, government, State, or political subdivision thereof shall be governed by the principles of the common law as they may be interpreted by the courts of the United States in the light of reason and experience. However, in civil actions and proceedings, with respect to an element of a claim or defense as to which State law supplies the rule of decision, the privilege of a witness, person, government, State, or political subdivision thereof shall be determined in accordance with State law.

Rule 801: DEFINITIONS

Statements Which Are Not Hearsay. A statement is not hearsay if—

Prior Statement by Witness. The declarant testifies at the trial or hearing and is subject to cross-examination concerning the statement, and the statement is (A) inconsistent with the declarant's testimony, and was given under oath subject to the penalty of perjury at a trial, hearing, or other proceeding, or in a deposition, or (B) consistent with the declarant's testimony and is offered to rebut an express or implied charge against the declarant of recent fabrication or improper influence or motive, or (C) one of identification of a person made after perceiving the person; or

Admission by Party-Opponent. The statement is offered against a party and is (A) the party's own statement, in either an individual or a representative capacity, or (B) a statement of which the party has manifested an adoption or belief in its truth, or (C) a statement by a person authorized by the party to make a statement concerning the subject, or (D) a statement by the party's agent or servant concerning a matter within the scope of the agency or employment made during the existence of the relationship, or (E) a statement by a coconspirator of a party during the course and in furtherance of the conspiracy. The contents of the statement shall be considered but are not alone sufficient to establish the declarant's authority under subdivision (C), the agency or employment relationship and scope thereof under subdivision (D), or the existence of the conspiracy and the participation therein of the declarant and the party against whom the statement is offered under subdivision (E).

Rule 803. HEARSAY EXCEPTIONS; AVAILABILITY OF DECLARANT IMMATERIAL

Records of Regularly Conducted Activity. A memorandum, report, record, or data compilation, in any form, of acts, events, conditions, opinions, or diagnoses, made at or near the time by, or from information transmitted by, a person with knowledge, if kept in the course of a regularly conducted business activity, and if it was the regular practice of that business activity to make the memorandum, report, record or data compilation, all as shown by the testimony of the custodian or other qualified witness, or by certification that complies with Rule 902(11), Rule 902(12), or a statute permitting certification, unless the source of information or the method or circumstances of preparation indicate lack of trustworthiness. The term "business" as used in this paragraph includes business, institution, association, profession, occupation, and calling of every kind, whether or not conducted for profit.

(8) Public Records and Reports. Records, reports, statements or data compilations, in any form, of public offices or agencies, setting forth (A) the activities of the office or agency, or (B) matters observed pursuant to duty imposed by law as to which matters there was a duty to report, excluding, however, in criminal cases matters observed by police officers and other law enforcement personnel, or (C) in civil actions and proceedings and against the Government in criminal cases, factual findings resulting from an investigation made pursuant to authority granted by law, unless the sources of information or other circumstances indicate lack of trustworthiness.

SOME SAMPLE REINSURANCE POLICY LANGUAGE

Examining Specific Policy Language Considerations:

A.   Article 1 - Business Covered

This Agreement, subject to the terms and conditions herein contained, is to indemnify the reinsured in respect of the net excess liability as herein provided and specified which may occur during the term of this Agreement arising out of any and all binders, policies, and contracts of insurance or reinsurance heretofore or hereafter issued or renewed by the reinsured and classified by the reinsured as Casualty.

B.   Article 4 - Exclusions

This Agreement does not cover business classified by the reinsured as:

(a) Automobile Liability other than Hired car and Auto Non-Ownership liability when issued with a multi-peril policy;

(b) Umbrella business;

(c) Credit Insurance and Financial Guarantee and Insolvency;

(d) Pools, Associations and Syndicates, as per Clause attached. This exclusion shall not apply to those associations that obtain insurance from the reinsured directly or through a mass marketing arrangement.

(e) Assumed Obligatory Reinsurance;

(f) War Risks;

(g) Nuclear incidents as provided in the Nuclear Incident Exclusion clauses - Liability-Reinsurance, as per attached clause.

C.   Article 5 - Net Retained Lines

This agreement applies only to that portion of any insurance or reinsurances covered by this Agreement which the Reinsured retains net for its own account and in calculating the amount of any loss hereunder and also in computing the amount in excess of which this Agreement attaches, only loss or losses in respect of that portion of any insurance or reinsurance which the Reinsured retains net for its own account shall be included. It is understood and agreed that the amount of the Reinsurer's liability hereunder in respect of any loss or losses shall not be increased by reason of the inability of the Reinsured to collect from any other reinsurers, whether specific or general, any amounts which may have become due from them, whether such inability arises from the insolvency of such other reinsurers or otherwise.

D.   Article 6 - Limit and Retention

No claim shall be made upon the Reinsurer for any loss under this section of the Agreement unless and until the Reinsured shall have first sustained an ultimate net loss in excess of $500,000 in respect of each such loss occurrence. The limit of liability of the Reinsurer in respect of any one such loss occurrence shall be $500,000.

E.   Article 7 - Ultimate Net Loss (Arbitration Clause)

The term "ultimate net loss" shall be the sum actually paid or to be paid by the Reinsured in settlement of losses or liability including any Extra Contractual Obligations after making deduction for all recoveries, all salvages, and all claims upon other reinsurance whether collected or not, and shall include all adjustment expenses arising from the settlement of claims other than the salaries of employees and the office expense of the Reinsured. Nothing in this clause, however, shall be construed to mean that losses are not recoverable from the Reinsurer until the ultimate net loss to the Reinsured has been ascertained.

All salvages, recoveries or payments recovered or received subsequent to a loss settlement under this Agreement shall be applied as if recovered or received prior to the aforesaid settlement and all necessary adjustments shall be made by the parties hereto.

F.   Article 8 - Definitions

The Reinsured shall be the sole judge of what constitutes one risk.

The term "loss occurrence" as used herein shall be understood to mean "each and every accident or occurrence or series of accidents or occurrences arising out of any one event."

G.   Article II - Notice of Loss and Loss Settlements

In the event of a loss hereunder, or a happening likely to give rise to a loss hereunder, prompt notice shall be given to the Reinsurer.

The Reinsured shall submit to the Reinsurer promptly an individual notice of each claim or loss which, in the opinion of the Reinsured, involves or is likely to involve the Reinsurer. The Reinsured shall advise the Reinsurer of the amount of gross claims or loss reserve and gross adjustment expense reserve the Reinsured is carrying on each such claim or loss and of any subsequent change(s) in such reserves.

Any loss settlements made by the Reinsured shall be unconditionally binding upon the Reinsurer and the Reinsurer shall benefit proportionately in all salvages and recoveries.

H.   Article 12 - Expiration During Loss

If this Agreement should terminate while a loss occurrence is in progress, it is understood and agreed that the Reinsurer is responsible, subject to the other conditions of this Agreement, for its proportion of the entire loss or damage resulting from such loss occurrence.

I.   Article 13 - Access to Records

The Reinsurer, by its duly appointed representatives, shall have the right, at any reasonable time, to examine all papers in possession of the Reinsured referring to business affected hereunder.

J.   Article 14 - Statistics

The Reinsured shall furnish the Reinsurer such quarterly and annual statistics as may be necessary to comply with statutory requirements and in such form as may be mutually agreed upon.

K. Article 15 - Errors and Omissions

Any inadvertent delay, omission or error shall not be held to relieve either party hereto from any liability which would attach to it hereunder if such delay, omission or error had not been made. Such delay, omission or error shall be rectified immediately upon discovery.

L.   Article 16 - Arbitration

As a precedent to any right of action hereunder, if any dispute shall arise between the Reinsured and the Reinsurers with reference to the interpretation of this Agreement or their rights with respect to any transaction involved, whether such dispute arises before or after termination of this Agreement, such dispute, upon the written request of either party, shall be submitted to three arbitrators, one to be chosen by each party and the third by the two so chosen. If either party refuses or neglects to appoint an arbitrator within thirty days after the receipt of written notice from the other party requesting it to do so, the requesting party may appoint two arbitrators. If the two arbitrators fail to agree in the selection of a third arbitrator within thirty days of their appointment, each of them shall name two, of whom the other shall decline one, and the decision shall be made by drawing lots. All arbitrators shall be executive officers of insurance or reinsurance companies or underwriters at Lloyd's, London not under control of either party to this Agreement.

The arbitrators shall interpret this Agreement as an honorable engagement and not as merely a legal obligation; they are relieved of all judicial formalities and may abstain from following the strict rules of law, and they shall make their award with a view to effecting the general purpose of this Agreement in a reasonable manner rather than in accordance with a literal interpretation of the language.

The decision in writing of any two arbitrators, when filed with the parties hereto, shall be final and binding on both parties. Judgment may be entered upon the final decision of the arbitrators in any court having jurisdiction. Each party shall bear the expense of its own arbitrator and shall jointly and equally bear with the other party the expense of the third arbitrator and of the arbitration. Said arbitration shall take place in Marshall, Michigan, unless some other place is mutually agreed upon by the Reinsured and the Reinsurers

M. Article 17 - Insolvency

In the event of the insolvency of the Reinsured, this reinsurance shall be payable directly to the Reinsured, or to its liquidator, receiver, conservator or statutory successor on the basis of the insolvency of the Reinsured or because the liquidator, receiver, conservator or statutory successor of the Reinsured has failed to pay all or a portion of any claim. It is agreed, however, that the liquidator, receiver, conservator or statutory successor of the Reinsured shall give written notice to the Reinsurers of the pendency of a claim against the Reinsured indicating the policy or bond reinsured which claim would involve a possible liability on the part of the Reinsurers within a reasonable time after such claim is filed in the conservation or liquidation proceeding or in the receivership, and that during the pendency of such claim, the Reinsurers may investigate such claim and interpose, at their own expense, in the proceeding where such claim is to be adjudicated any defense or defenses that they may deem available to the Reinsured or its liquidator, receiver, conservator or statutory successor. The expense thus incurred by the Reinsurers shall be chargeable, subject to the approval of the court, against the Reinsured as part of the expense of conservation or liquidation to the extent of a pro rata share of the benefit which may accrue to the Reinsured solely as a result of the defense undertaken by the Reinsurers.

Where two or more Reinsurers are involved in the same claim, and a majority in interest elect to interpose defense to such claim, the expense shall be apportioned in accordance with the terms of the reinsurance Agreement as though such expense had been incurred by the Reinsured.

The reinsurance shall be payable by the Reinsurers to the Reinsured or to its liquidator, receiver, conservator or statutory successor, except as provided by Section 315 of the New York Insurance Law or except (a) where the Agreement specifically provides another payee of such reinsurance in the event of the insolvency of the Reinsured, and (b) where the Reinsurers with the consent of the direct insured or insureds have assumed such policy obligations of the Reinsured as direct obligations of the

Reinsurers to the payees under such policies and in substitution for the obligations of the Reinsured to such payees.

N. Article 18 - Intermediary ("Intermediary" Clauses)

(Intermediary) is hereby recognized as the intermediary through whom all communications relating hereto (including but not limited to notice, statements, premiums, return premiums, commissions, taxes, losses, loss adjustment expense, salvage and loss settlement) shall be transmitted to both parties. It is understood, as regards remittances due either party hereunder, that payment by the Reinsured to (Intermediary) shall constitute payment to the Reinsured to the extent such payments are actually received by the Reinsured.

O. Article 19 - Extra Contractual Obligations ("ECO" Clauses)

This Agreement shall protect the Reinsured within the limits hereof, where the ultimate net loss includes any Extra Contractual Obligations.

"Extra Contractual Obligations" are defined as those liabilities not covered under any other provision of this Agreement and which arise from the handling of any claim on business covered hereunder, such liabilities arising because of, but not limited to, the following: Failure by the Reinsured to settle within the policy limit, by reason of alleged or actual negligence, fraud or bad faith in rejecting an offer of settlement or in the preparation or prosecution of an appeal consequent upon such action.

The date on which an Extra Contractual Obligation is incurred by the Reinsured shall be deemed, in all circumstances, to be the date of the original accident, casualty, disaster or loss occurrence.

However, this Article shall not apply where the loss has been incurred due to fraud of a member of the Board of Directors or a corporate officer of the Reinsured acting individually or collectively or in collusion with any individual or corporation or any other organization or party involved in the presentation, defense or settlement of any claim covered hereunder.

Using Policy Language as a Guide to Discovery:

Policy language will often provide a guide and indicate that certain items will likely be present in the insurer's and insured's underwriting, audit and claim files, as well as in their intermediaries' files. The following provisions (taken from Excess Liability policies) give some examples of such items:

B. Inspection and Audit

Underwriters shall be permitted but not obligated to inspect the Insured's property and operations at any time. Neither the Underwriters' right to make inspections nor the making thereof nor any report thereon shall constitute an undertaking on behalf of or for the benefit of the Insured or others, to determine or warrant that such property or operations are safe.

D. Reporting of Claims

The Insured shall immediately give notice, in writing, to Underwriters' representative, as set forth in Item 5 of the Declarations, of any claim or claims to which this Policy applies which may exceed 25 percent of the applicable amount set forth in the attached Schedule of Underlying Amounts.

E. Assistance and Cooperation

Underwriters shall not be called upon to assume charge of the settlement or defense of any claim made or suit brought or proceeding instituted against the Insured, but Underwriters shall have the right and shall be given the opportunity to associate with the Insured in the defense and control of any claim, suit or proceeding relative to any Loss either hereunder or within the Underlying Amounts, in which event the Insured and Underwriters shall cooperate in all things in the defense of such claim, suit or proceeding and the Insured shall make available to Underwriters such information and access to records as Underwriters may require.

F. Service of Suit Clause

It is agreed that in the event of the failure of Underwriters hereon to pay amount claimed to be due hereunder, Underwriters hereon, at the request of the Insured, will submit to the jurisdiction of any court of competent jurisdiction within the United States and will comply with all requirements necessary to give such court jurisdiction and all matters arising hereunder shall be determined in accordance with the law and practice of such court.

It is further agreed that service of process in such suit may be made upon the person(s) or firm named in Item 9 of the Declarations and that, in any suit instituted against any one of them upon this Policy, Underwriters will abide by the final decision of such court or of any Appellate court in the event of an appeal. The person(s) or firm named in Item 9 of the Declarations are authorized and directed to accept service of process on behalf of Underwriters in any such suit and/or upon the request of the Insured to give a written undertaking to the Insured that they will enter a general appearance on Underwriters' behalf in the event such a suit shall be instituted.

Further, pursuant to any statute of any state, territory or district of the United States which makes provision therefore, Underwriters hereon hereby designate the Superintendent, Commissioner or Director of Insurance or other officer specified for that purpose in the statute, or his successor or successors in office, as their true and lawful attorney upon whom may be served any lawful process in any action, suit or proceeding instituted by or on behalf of the insured or any beneficiary hereunder arising out of this Policy of insurance, and hereby designate the person(s) or firm named in Item 9 of the Declarations as the person to whom the said officer is authorized to mail such process or true copy thereof.

G. Insolvency

In the event of the insolvency of the Insured or upon takeover of the Insured's business by any State or Federal Official or Agency, or by any Receiver or Liquidator, acting or appointed for this purpose, this Policy shall be cancelled immediately without the necessity of Underwriters or Underwriters' representative giving notice of such cancellation and as a consequence this Policy will terminate immediately. In the event of such cancellation Underwriters will refund to the Receiver or Liquidator the unearned premium or pro rata of the premium paid hereon, whichever is the lesser. The insolvency of the Insured or the takeover of the Insured's business by any State or Federal Official or Agency or by any Receiver or Liquidator shall not reduce or eliminate the underlying amounts.

Consideration of Offset Clauses and Funding Clauses:

Examination should also be made of the offset clauses and funding provisions present in the policy language:

OFFSET CLAUSE—One possible version

Each party hereto shall have, and may exercise at any time, and from time to time, the right to offset any balance or balances, whether on account of premiums or on account of losses or otherwise, due from such party to the other (or, if more than one, any other party hereto under this Agreement or under any other reinsurance agreement heretofore or hereafter entered into by and between them) and may offset the same against any balance or balances due or to become due to the former from the latter under the same; or any other reinsurance agreement between them; and the party asserting the right of offset shall have and may exercise such right whether the balance or balances due or to become due to such party from the other are on account of premiums or on account of losses or otherwise and regardless of the capacity, whether as assuming insurer or as ceding insurer, in which each party acted under the agreement or, if more than one, the different agreements involved, provided, however, that, in the event of the insolvency of a party hereto, offsets shall only be allowed in accordance with the provisions of the Insurance Law of the State of New York.

OFFSET CLAUSE—Alternative version

Each party hereto shall have, and may exercise at any time and from time to time, the right to offset any balance or balances, whether on account of premiums or on account of losses or otherwise, due from such party to the other (or, if more than one, any other) party hereto under this Agreement and may offset the same against any balance or balances due or to become due to the former from the latter under the same; and the party asserting the right of offset shall have and may exercise such right whether the balance or balances due or to become due to such party from the other are on account of premiums or on account of losses or otherwise and regardless of the capacity, whether as assuming insurer or as ceding insurer, in which each party acted under the agreement involved, provided, however, that, in the event of the insolvency of a party hereto, offsets shall only be allowed in accordance with the provisions of the Insurance Law of the State of New York.

FUNDING CLAUSE

(This clause is only applicable to those Reinsurer(s)who cannot qualify for credit by the State having jurisdiction over the Company's loss reserves.)

a.   As regards policies or bonds issued by the Company coming within the scope of this Agreement, the Company agrees that, when it shall file with the Insurance Department or set up on its books reserves for losses covered hereunder which it shall be required by law to set up, it will forward to the Reinsurer a statement showing the proportion of such loss reserves which is applicable to the Reinsurer. The Reinsurer hereby agrees that it will apply for and secure delivery to the Company of a clean, irrevocable and unconditional Letter of Credit, issued by a bank which is acceptable to the regulatory authority(ies) having jurisdiction over the Company's loss reserves in an amount equal to the Reinsurer's proportion of reserves in respect of known outstanding losses that have been reported to the Reinsurer and allocated loss expenses relating thereto as shown in the statement prepared by the Company. Under no circumstances shall any amount relating to reserves in respect of Incurred But Not Reported Losses be included in the amount of the Letter of Credit.

b.   The Letter of Credit shall be issued for a period of not less than one year, and shall automatically extend for one year from its date of expiration or any future expiration date, unless thirty (30) days prior to any expiration date the issuing bank shall notify the Company by registered mail that the bank elects not to consider the Letter of Credit extended for any additional period. An issuing bank, not a member of the Federal Reserve System or not chartered in New York State, shall provide sixty (60) days notice to the Company prior to any expiration in the event of non-extension.

c.   Notwithstanding any other provision of this Agreement, the Company or its successors in interest may draw upon such credit at any time without diminution because of the insolvency of the Company or of the Reinsurer for one or more of the following purposes only:

1. To pay the Reinsurer's share or to reimburse the Company for the Reinsurer's share of any loss reinsured by this Agreement, the payment of which has been agreed by the reinsurer and which has not been otherwise paid;

2. To make refund of any sum which is in excess of the actual amount required to pay the Reinsurer's share of any liability reinsured by this Agreement; or

3. In the event of expiration of the Letter of Credit as provided for above, to establish deposit of the Reinsurer's share of known and reported outstanding losses and allocated expenses relating thereto under this Agreement. Such cash deposit shall be held in an interest-bearing account separate from the Company's other assets, and interest thereon shall accrue to the benefit of the Reinsurer.

d.   The issuing bank shall have no responsibility whatsoever in connection with the propriety of withdrawals made by the Company or the disposition of funds withdrawn, except to ensure that withdrawals are made only upon the order of properly authorized representatives of the Company.

e.   At annual intervals, or more frequently as agreed but never more frequently than quarterly, the Company shall prepare a specific statement, for the sole purpose of amending the Letter of Credit, of the Reinsurer's share of known and reported outstanding losses and allocated expenses relating thereto. If the statement shows that the Reinsurer's share of such losses and allocated loss expenses exceeds the balance of credit as of the statement date, the Reinsurer shall, within thirty (30) days after receipt of notice of such excess, secure delivery to the Company of amendment of the Letter of Credit increasing the amount of credit by the amount of such difference. If, however, the statement shows that the Reinsurer's share of known and reported outstanding losses plus allocated loss expenses relating thereto is less than the balance of credit as of the statement date, the Company shall, within thirty (30) days after receipt of written request from the Reinsurer, release such excess credit by agreeing to secure an amendment to the Letter of Credit reducing the amount of credit available by the amount of such excess credit.

APPLICATION LANGUAGE—EXCESS LIABILITY POLICY

APPLICATION FOR EXCESS LIABILITY POLICY

The completion for and submission to Underwriters of this application does not constitute a binder or insurance nor any insurance coverage whatsoever nor do underwriters undertake to offer any terms or coverage.

<u>Application for Excess Liability Policy (London 85)</u>
(Applicants are advised to read the form before completing this application.)

1. Full name of Applicant (including all companies to be insured):
   Notes: (a) Give details of any operations for which coverage is not required;
   (b) If the companies to be insured are not the Parent Company, please give name of the Parent Company.

2. Description of all Operations.

3. Describe all the products manufactured, handled, distributed or sold under the following classifications:

Classification	*Description*	*Annual Sales*
(a) Aircraft and/or Aerospace Products or any material or substance supplied to or for use by the Aircraft and/or Aerospace Industry		
(b) Pharmaceutical, Chemicals, Petrochemicals and Nuclear Energy		
(c) Any other products		

4. (a) Give details of any insurance the Applicant intends to purchase as respects the Underlying Amounts and details of any insurance that may be in force that would act in the same manner.

   (b) Give details of any non-standard exclusions contained therein.

5. State loss records during the past ten years specifying:
   (a) Full details of all claims exclusive of expenses (whether insured or not) in excess of $10,000 (enter full amount for first dollar for each case) and specify amounts and date paid and amounts outstanding, showing separately the date of loss and the date claim was first made in writing against the Insured.

(b) In respect to Products Liability, the Aggregate amount, separately by the date of loss and the date the claim was first made in writing against the Insured, of losses (from first dollar) for each year and specify amounts paid and outstanding.

(c) The organization that has evaluated any outstanding amounts and the date of the said evaluation.

6.   Has the Applicant ever handled his own losses in any self-insured areas and if so, give details of such loss handling.

7.   The policy for which this Application is being made does require that the Insured self-insures the Underlying Amounts and as a consequence, gives details as to the Applicant's approach to loss handling.

NOTE: Please enclose with this Application the latest Annual Report and Interims. If these are not available or are not published or are not available, Underwriters may not consider this application unless adequate alternative information to Underwriters' satisfaction can be supplied.

We know of no other relevant facts which might affect Underwriters' judgment when considering this application.

Dated _____   Signed _____

Notes

1. *See, e.g., In re* Liquidation of Inter-American Ins. Co. of Illinois, 707 N.E.2d 617 (Ill. App. 1 Dist. 1999).
2. Travelers Cas. and Sur. Co. v. Certain Underwriters at Lloyd's of London, 760 N.E.2d 319 (N.Y. 2001).
3. Michigan Tp. Participating Plan v. Federal Ins. Co., 592 N.W.2d 760 (Mich. App. 1999); *Travelers, supra.*
4. Hollipeter v. Stuyvesant Ins. Co., 523 S.W.2d 595 (Mo. App. 1975).
5. American Bankers Ins. Co. of Florida v. Northwestern Nat. Ins. Co., 198 F.3d 1332 (11th Cir. 1999).
6. Donaldson v. United Community Ins. Co., 741 So. 2d 676 (La. App. 3d Cir. 1999).
7. John Hancock Property and Cas. Ins. Co. v. Universal Resinsurance Co., Ltd., 147 F.R.D. 40 (S.D.N.Y. 1993).
8. British Ins. Co. of Cayman v. Water Street Ins. Co., Ltd., 93 F. Supp. 2d 506 (S.D.N.Y. 2000).
9. American Employers' Ins. Co. v. Swiss Reinsurance America Corp., 2003 WL 21801639 (D. Mass. 2003).
10. British Ins. Co. of Cayman v. Safety Nat. Cas., 2003 WL 21536693 (3rd Cir. N.J. 2003).
11. *American Employers, supra* note 9.
12. *British Ins. Co., supra* note 10; North River Ins. Co. v. CIGNA Reinsurance Co., 52 F.3d 1194 (3rd Cir. N.J.) 1995).

13. Travelers Cas. & Sur. Co. v. Certain Underwriters at Lloyd's of London, 760 N.E.2d 319 (N.Y. 2001).

14. *See, e.g.,* Travelers Cas. & Sur. Co. v. Certain Underwriters, 734 N.Y.S.2d 531 (N.Y. 2001).

15. Merit Life Ins. Co. v. C.I.R., 853 F.2d 1435 (7th Cir. Ind. 1988).

16. *See, e.g.,* Allstate Ins. Co. v. Administratia Asigurarilor de Stat., 875 F. Supp. 1022, 1028 (S.D.N.Y. 1995); Credit Managers Ass'n v. Kennesaw Life & Accident Ins. Co., 809 F.2d 617, 623-24 (9th Cir. 1987).

17. Mitchell v. State of Florida, 233 So. 2d 792 (Fla. Ct. App. 1969); Clark & Co. Inc. v. Department of Ins. as Receiver of Eastern Ins. Co., 436 So. 2d 1013 (1st DCA 1983).

18. 251 F.2d 696 (1958).

19. American Ins. Co. v. North American Co., 697 F.2d 77 (2d Cir. 1982).

20. Christiana Gen. Ins. Corp. v. Great American Ins. Co., 979 F.2d 268, 280 (2d Cir. 1992) (reinsurer cannot dispute good-faith determinations relating to defense or settlement, but it is not obligated to provide coverage for payments clearly beyond the scope of the policy); North River Ins. Co. v. Cigna Reinsurance Co., 52 F.3d 1194 (3d Cir. 1995) (reinsurer obligated to reimburse for all good-faith payments, but retains the right to question if the underlying liability results from an insured loss); Aetna Cas. & Surety v. Home Ins. Co., 882 F. Supp. 1328 (S.D.N.Y. 1995) (reinsurer not obligated to follow settlement if loss paid is outside scope of coverage; bound by all good-faith determinations of ceding company except as to whether the loss is within the terms of the policy).

21. 903 F.2d 910 (2d Cir. 1990).

22. 35 F. Supp. 2d 348 (S.D.N.Y. 1999).

23. 2001 WL 897180 (S.D.N.Y. 2001).

24. 342 F.3d 78 (2d Cir. 2003).

25. *See also* Employers Reinsurance Corp. v. Mid-Continent Cas. Co., 202 F. Supp. 2d 1221 (D. Kan. 2002) (reinsurance agreement provided coverage for declaratory judgment fees and expenses reinsured incurred in connection with underlying action).

26. 1 S. Ct. 582, 107 U.S. 485 (1883).

27. *See, e.g.,* Security Mutual Casualty Co. v. Affiliated FM Ins. Co., 471 F.2d 238 (8th Cir. 1972); Calvert Fire Ins. Co. v. Unigard Mut. Ins. Co., 526 F. Supp. 623 (D. Neb. 1980), *aff'd,* 676 F.2d 707 (8th Cir. 1982).

28. Security Mutual Cas. Co. v. Transport Indemnity Co., 66 Cal. App. 3d 1009, 136 Cal. Rptr. 365 (1977); Northwestern Mutual Fire Ass'n v. Union Mutual Fire Ins. Co. of Providence, R.I., 144 F.2d 274 (9th Cir. 1944) (duty is of utmost good faith), Columbia Nat'l Fire Ins. Co. v. Pittsburgh Fire Ins. Co., 210 N.W. 158 (Mich.) (fiduciary relationship between reinsured and reinsurer); Mutuelle General Francoise Vie v. Life Ins. Co. of Pennsylvania, 688 F. Supp. 386 (N.D. Ill. 1988) (duty of utmost good faith).

29. 886 F. Supp. 1147 (S.D.N.Y. 1995).

30. 9 F. Supp. 2d 49 (D. Mass 1998).

31. *Id.* at 66. Under these doctrines, the reinsurer is bound unless there is evidence of gross negligence or recklessness (citing North River Ins. Co. v. CIGNA Reinsurance Co., 52 F.3d 1194 (3d Cir. 1995), or that the settlement was not even arguably within the realm of the reinsurance coverage (citing Mentor Ins. Co. (U.K.) v. Norges Brannkasse, 996 F.2d 506 (2d Cir. 1993)).

32. *Id.* at 69.

33. *Id.*

34. Shell Oil Co. v. Par Four Partnership, 638 So. 2d 1050 (Fla. Ct. App. 1994); Southern Bell Tel. & Tel. Co. v. Deason, 632 So. 2d 1377 (Fla. 1994).

35. Southeastern Pa. Transit Auth. v. Transit Cas. Co., 55 F.R.D. 553 (D.C. Pa. 1972).

36. North River Ins. Co. v. Columbia Casualty Co., No. 90 Civ. 2518, 1995 U.S. Dist. LEXIS 9570 (S.D.N.Y. 7/11/95).

37. The Aetna Cas. & Surety Co. v. Superior Court, 200 Cal. Rptr. 471, 153 Cal. App. 3d 467 (1st Dist. Ct. App. 1984).

38. *See* National Union Fire Ins. v. Continental Illinois Corp., 116 F.R.D. 78 (N.D. Ill. 1978) (reinsurance agreement is an "insurance agreement" for purposes of production in discovery).

39. *See* Rhone-Poulenc Rorer, Inc. v. Home Indemnity Co., 139 F.R.D. 609 (E.D. Pa. 1991) (Rule 26(b)(2)'s requirement that "insurance agreements" which would respond to any judgment be produced does not apply to reinsurance agreements unless the insured seeks actual damages against the insurer (rather than just a declaration of policy interpretation).

40. 2002 WL 1870452 (E.D. Pa. 2002).

41. McDonough Const. Corp. v. Pan American Surety Co., 190 So. 2d 617 (Fla. Dist. Ct. App. 1966).

42. *See* National Union Fire Ins. Co. v. Stouffer Chemical, 558 A.2d 1091 (Del. Super. Ct. 1989); The Potomac Elec. Power v. California Union Ins. Co., 136 F.R.D. 1 (D. D.C. 1990).

43. *See* Playtex, Inc. v. The Columbia Casualty Co., Del. Super. Ct., CA 88 C-MR-233 (Oct. 12, 1988 and Jan. 5, 1989).

44. 129 F.R.D. 99, 106 (D.N.J. 1989).

45. *Id.*

46. *See* Rhone-Poulenc Rorer, Inc. v. Home Indemnity Co., 139 F.R.D. 609, 611-12 (E.D. Pa. 1991).

47. 139 F.R.D. 609 (E.D. Pa.).

48. United Equitable Ins. Co. v. Reinsurance Co. of America, 510 N.E.2d 924 (Ill. App. 1987).

49. MDL 764 (E.D.Pa. July 26, 1989) (available in MEALEY'S LITIGATION REPORTS: INSURANCE, Aug. 8, 1989, Vol. 3 No. 19).

50. *See also* Occidental Chemical Corp. v. Hartford Accident & Indemnity Co., Index No. 4109/8 C. slip op. at 5 (N.Y. Sup. Ct., Niagara County, Dec. 4, 1990) (available in MEALEY'S LITIGATION REPORTS: INSURANCE, Jan. 15, 1991, Vol. 5 No. 10).

51. McDonough Const. Corp. v Pan American Surety, 190 So. 2d 617 (Fla. App. 1966).

52. FED. R. CIV. PROC. R. 45(c)(3)(A)(iii).

53. FED. R. CIV. PROC. R. 45(c)(3)(B)(i).

54. *See Potomac Electric*, 136 F.D.R. at 3 (court holds correspondence regarding underwriting or reinsurance agreements irrelevant and proprietary); Firemans Fund Ins. Co. v. Superior Court, 233 Cal. App. 3d 1138, 286 Cal. Rptr. 50, 51 (Cal. App. 1st Dist. 1991) (holding that trial court should have conducted an in camera review of claims communications between insurer and reinsurer for sensitive commercial information prior to disclosure to the insured).

55. *See* Employers Commercial Union Ins. Co. v. Browning-Ferris Indus. of Kansas City, Inc., 91-2161-JWL (April 5, 1993) (reported in MEALEY'S LITIGATION REPORTS: REINSURANCE, April 28, 1993, Vol. 3, No. 24).

56. *Rhone-Poulenc, supra* note 39 at 613-14.

57. *See, e.g.*, Union Carbide Corp. v. Travelers Indemnity Co., 61 F.R.D. 411 (W.D. Pa. 1973).

58. *See* FED. R. CIV. PROC. R. 45(a)(3).

59. FED. R. CIV. PROC. R. 45(c)(3)(A).

60. *See* Great American Surplus Lines Ins. v. Ace Oil Co., 120 F.R.D. 533 (E.D. Cal. 1988) (attorney-client privilege may be asserted, and waived, only by the insurer having the attorney-client relationship with counsel).

61. *See* Durham Indus. v. North River Ins. Co., 79 Civ. 1705 (S.D. N.Y. 1980).

62. *See also* International Ins. Co. v. Sargent & Lundy, No. 87 CH 10934, Cir. Ct. of Cook County, Ill., Ch. Div., transcript at 30-32 (April 5, 1989; Green, J.) (communications between an insurer and its reinsurer are privileged and a court should not compel the insurer or the reinsurer to divulge such privileged communications).

63. 197 F.R.D. 601 (S.D. Ohio 2000).

64. *See* Bank of America, N.A. v. Terra Nova Ins. Co., 212 F.R.D. 166 (S.D.N.Y. 2002).

65. Lintz v. American General Finance, Inc., 1999 WL 450197 (D. Kan. 1999).

66. *See* Deal v. Lutheran Hospitals and Homes, 127 F.R.D. 166 (D. Alaska 1989).

67. 844 P.2d 593 (Ariz. App. 1993).

68. Consolidation Coal Co. v. Bucyrus-Erie Co., 432 N.E.2d 250 (1982).

69. Samaritan Foundation, et al. v. Superior Court of the State of Arizona, 844 P.2d at 01.

70. 432 N.E. 2d 250 (Ill. 1982).

71. 449 U.S. 383, 390, 101 S. Ct. 677, 683, 66 L. Ed. 2d 584 (1981).

72. *Id.,* 101 S. Ct. at 689, *citing e.g.* Diversified Indus., Inc. v. Meredith, 572 F.2d 596, 609 (8th Cir. 1978) (en banc); Harper & Row Publishers, Inc. v. Decker, 423 F.2d 487, 491-92 (7th Cir. 2970), *aff'd by equally divided court,* 91 S. Ct. 479 (1971); Duplan Corp. v. Deering Milliken, Inc., 397 F. Supp. 1146, 1163-65 (D. S.C. 1984).

73. 449 U.S. at 391, 101 S. Ct. at 683.

74. 501, 449 U.S. at 396.

75. *Samaritan, supra* note 69 at 598.

76. *Consolidated Coal,* 432 N.E.2d at 257-58.

77. 63 ST. JOHN'S L. REV. 191, 381.

78. 844 P.2d at 602.

79. 4 F.3d 1149 (2d Cir. 1993) (applying the law of New York) (also discussed *supra* relating to the doctrine of utmost good faith).

80. *Id.* at 1064.

81. *Id.* at 1053-54 *citing* KLAUS GERATHEWOHL, REINSURANCE PRINCIPLES AND PRACTICE 64-128 (1980).

82. *Id.* at 1065 (citations omitted).

83. *Id.*

84. *Id., citing* CHRISTIANA GENERAL INS. CO. V. GREAT AMERICAN INS. CO., 979 F.2d 268, 278 (2d Cir. 1992) (quoting 19 GEORGE J. COUCH, CYCLOPEDIA OF INSURANCE LAW, § 80.71 (2d ed. 1983)).

85. Unigard Security lns. Co. Inc. v. North River lns. Co. at 1065.

86. 766 F.2d 163, 166-67 (4th Cir. 1985).

87. 922 F.2d 516 (9th Cir. 1990).

88. *Id.* at 1069.

89. 335 F.3d 205 (3d Cir. 2003).

90. *Id.* at 212, *citing* Baen v. Farmers Mut. Fire Ins., 381 N.J. 187, 712 A.2d 634, 644 (N.J. 1998).

91. 2003 WL 22955869 (D. Kan. Dec. 12, 2003).

92. *Id.*

93. 797 F. Supp. 303 (U.S. Dist. Ct. N.J. 1992).

94. 799 F. Supp. at 367-68.

95. *Id..* at 368.

96. *Id.* at 369.

97. *Id.* at 370.

98. *Id.* (emphasis added).

99. *Id.* at 370-71.

100. Menorah Ins. Co. Ltd. v. INX Reinsurance Corp., 72 F.3d 218 (lst Cir. 1995).

101. R. Page, *Privacy in Arbitration,* N.Y. L. J., June 14, 1979; *see also* M. DOMKE, DOMKE ON COMMERCIALARBITRATION, § 24.07 at 387 (1987).

102. *See* Branzburg v. Hayes, 408 U.S. 665, 688 (1972).

103. Sperry Int'l Trade, Inc. v. Government of Israel, 602 F. Supp. 1440, 1443 (S.D. N.Y. 1985); *see also* Woody v. General Teamsters Union, Local 406, 583 F. Supp. 1471 (W.D. Mich. 1984); Brownko Int'l v. Ogden Steel Co., 585 F. Supp. 1432 (S.D. N.Y. 1983); Reichman v. Creative Real Estate Consultants, Inc., 476 F. Supp. 1276 (S. D. N.Y. 1979).

104. *See, e.g.,* Andros Compania Maritima v. Marc Rich & Co., A.G., 579 F.2d 691, 702 (2d Cir. 1978); Sperry, *supra*, 602 F. Supp. at 1443.

105. *See* FED. R. CIV. P. 26(b).

106. 84 A.D.2d 921, 446 N.Y.S.2d 650 (1981).

107. 446 N.Y.2d at 651.

108. *Id.*

109. Industrotech Constr. Inc. v. Duke Univ., 67 N.C. App. 741, 314 S.E.2d 272 (1984).

110. 218 F.R.D. 18 (D. Conn. 2003).

111. *See, e.g.,* Weissman v. Fruchtman, 1986 WL 15669 (S.D.N.Y. 1986), *citing* Bottaro v. Hatton Assoc., 96 F.R.D. 158, 160 (E.D.N.Y. 1982) (Given the strong public policy of favoring settlements and the congressional intent to further that policy by insulating the bargaining table from unnecessary intrusions, we think the better rule is to require some particularized showing of a likelihood that admissible evidence will be generated by the dissemination of the terms of a settlement agreement.).

112. 112 F.R.D. 136, 139-40 (D.R.I. 1986).

113. *See, e.g., In re* General Motors Corp. v. Engine Interchange Litig., 594 F.2d 1106, 1124 n.20 (7th Cir. 1979), *cert. denied sub nom. See also* Oswald v. General Motors Corp., 444 U.S. 870 (1979); NAACP Legal Defense & Educ. Fund v. Dep't of Justice, 612 F. Supp. 1143, 1146 (D. D.C. 1985).

114. FLA. STAT. ANN. § 684.19 (West 1990).

115. *See generally* Kurlantzi, *The Prohibition on Communication with an Adverse Party,* 51 CONN. B.J. 136 (1977); Leubsdorf, *Communication With Another Lawyer's Client: The Lawyer's Veto and the Client's Interest,* 127 U. PA. L. REV. 683 (1979); Annotation, *Communication with Party Represented by Counsel as Ground for Disciplining Attorney,* 26 A.L.R. 4th 102 (1983).

116. *See* United States v. Batchelor, 484 F. Supp. 812 (E.D. Pa. 1980) (societal interest that lay persons not make decisions of major legal implication without advice of counsel); Frey v. Department of Health and Human Services, 106 F.R.D. 32 (E.D.N.Y. 1985) (noting courts and commentators have stated that provision is meant to prevent situations in which adverse counsel would take advantage of represented party); Carter v. Kamaras, 430 A.2d 1058 (R.I. 1981) (preserves proper functioning of judicial system); Wright v. Group Health Hosp., 103 Wash. 2d 192, 691 P.2d 564, 50 A.L.R. 4th 641 (1984) (presence of the party's attorney theoretically "neutralizes the contact" by opposing party's attorney); ABA Comm. on Ethics and Prof'l Responsibility, Informal Op. 83-1498 (1983) (prohibition is necessary to preserve the proper functioning of attorney-client relationship and to shield party from improper approaches); *see also* G.C. HAZARD, JR. & W.W. HODES, THE LAW OF LAWYERING, 730 (2d ed. 1990) (prevents lawyer from taking advantage of lay person to secure admission against interests or achieve unconscionable settlement of dispute); C.W. WOLFRAM, MODERN LEGAL ETHICS § 11.6, at 612, 613 (1986) (application of anticontact rule should be guided by its policy objective; unlikely that rule would prevent second lawyer from discussing with another lawyer's client suspected malpractice, excess fees, or possible client dissatisfaction).

117. *See, e.g.,* Lewis v. S.S. Baune, 534 F.2d 1115 (5th Cir. 1976) (dissolution of injunction enjoining parties from discussing settlement without counsel's consent); Wilson v. Brand S Corp., 27 Wash. App. 743, 621 P.2d 748 (1980) (lawyer's statement to client that client could not be prevented from making direct contact with represented opposing party was not proper basis on which to refuse admission of lawyer pro hac vice).

118. *See, e.g., In re* Marietta, 223 Kan. 11, 569 P.2d 921 (1977) (lawyer disciplined for causing client to communicate with opposing party).

119. *See, e.g.,* Schantz v. Eyman, 418 F.2d 11 (9th Cir. 1969) (prosecutor responsible for post-indictment questioning of accused by state psychiatrist), *cert. denied,* 397 U.S. 1021 (1970); Crane v. State Bar, 30 Cal. 3d 117, 635 P.2d 163, 177 Cal. Rptr. 670 (1981) (lawyer responsible for letters sent by lawyer's employees on letterhead over lawyer's purported signature); People v. Hobson, 39

N.Y.2d 479, 348 N.E.2d 894, 384 N.Y.S.2d 419 (1976) (statements elicited by police officers); *In re* Burrows, 291 Or. 135, 629 P.2d 820, 22 A.L.R.4th 906 (1981) (failure to obtain opposing counsel's consent not excused by delegating task to non-lawyers); *see also* ABA Comm. on Prof'l Ethics, Informal Op. 663 (1963) (lawyer cannot communicate through private investigator).

120. *See, e.g., In re* Industrial Gas Antitrust Litig. (unpublished), No. 80C3479 (N.D. Ill. Jan. 28, 1986), 1986 WL 1846, *reported in* ABA/BNA *Law. Manual on Prof'l Conduct,* 2 CURRENT REP. 71 (March 19, 1986) (lawyer's negligent failure to instruct investigator not to communicate with represented party); Crane v. State Bar of California, 30 Cal. 3d 117, 635 P.2d 163, 177 Cal. Rptr. 670 (1981) (negligent failure to prevent employees from contacting represented parties); Carter v. Kamaras, 430 A.2d 1058 (R.I. 1981) (immaterial whether direct contact is intentional or negligent violation); *In re* McCaffrey, 275 Or. 23, 549 P.2d 666 (1976) (immaterial whether communication is negligent or intentional).

121. 940 P.2d 159 (N.M. 1997).

122. *See* C.W. WOLFRAM, MODERN LEGAL ETHICS § 11.6.2, at 611 n.30 (1986) (term as used in Rule 4.2 evidently refers broadly to any person represented by a lawyer in a matter); *see also* United States v. Jamil, 546 F. Supp. 646 (E.D.N.Y. 1982) (person who retains counsel as protection against grand jury investigation is "represented party" for ethical purposes even if adversarial proceedings have not yet begun), *rev'd on other grounds,* 707 F.2d 638 (2d Cir. 1983); ABA Comm. on Prof'l Ethics, Informal Op. 1149 (1970) (in suit initiated by insurance company as subrogee to insured's claim, defense lawyer improperly communicated with insured, the named plaintiff, without obtaining consent of insurance company's lawyer, whose representation extended indirectly to insured as well). This issue of "person" versus "party" is considered in great depth in Hellman, *When "Ethics Rules" Don't Mean What They Say: The Implications of Strained ABA Ethics Opinions,* 10 GEO. J. LEGAL ETHICS 317 (1997).

123. 257 F.3d 999 (9th Cir. 2001).

124. 122 F. Supp. 2d 1335 (M.D. Fla 2000).

125. *In re* FMC Corp., 430 F. Supp. 1108 (S.D. W. Va. 1977) (denial of motion enjoining party's lawyer from communicating with all salaried employees of defendant without counsel's consent); Sobel v. Yeshiva Univ., 1981 WL 334, 28 Empl. Prac. Dec. (CCH ¶ 32-479 (S.D.N.Y. 1981) (practical approach adopted with respect to university employees; issue is whether person has sufficient authority to bind); Mills Land and Water Co. v. Golden West Refining Corp., 186 Cal. App. 3d 1016, 230 Cal. Rptr. 461 (1986) (communication by opposing counsel with current board director improper despite conflict of interest between corporation and director); Fair Automotive Repair, Inc. v. Car-X Service Systems, Inc., 128 Ill. App. 3d 763, 471 N.E.2d 554 (1984) (prohibition applicable to those in corporate "control" group); Niesig v. Team I, 76 N.Y.2d 363, 559 N.Y.S.2d 493, 558 N.E.2d 1030 (1990) (rule applies to corporate employees whose acts or omissions in matter at issue are binding on corporation or imputed to it for liability purposes, or who are implementing advice of corporate counsel); State v. Ciba-Geigy Corp., 247 N.J. Super. 314, 589 A.2d 180 (App. Div. 1991) (adopting *Niesig* rationale; corporate criminal defendant is entitled to order barring State from interrogating any of its employees whose acts or omissions State seeks to impute to corporate defendant); Wright v. Group Health Hosp., 103 Wash. 2d 192, 691 P.2d 564 (1984) (current . . . employees are parties if they have managerial authority sufficient to give them right to speak for and bind the corporation); Featherstone v. Schaerrer, 34 P.3d 194 (Utah 2001) (secretary-treasurer of defendant corporation deemed "represented person" because his statements could bind the company). *See also* ABA Comm. on Ethics and Prof'l Responsibility, Informal Op. 83-1489 (1983) (rationale for rule grounded in notion that certain employees are considered the alter ego of the corporation); ABA Comm. on Ethics and Prof'l Responsibility, Informal Op. 1410 (1978) (officers and employees who can commit corporation are parties); ABA Comm. on Ethics and Prof'l Responsibility, Informal Op. 1377 (1977) (municipal employee with power to commit municipal corporation is a party); *cf.* ABA Comm. on Professional Ethics and Grievances, Formal Op. 66

(1932) (not improper for attorney to communicate directly with president of adverse corporation concerning name of corporate officer most familiar with subject to be covered by deposition when corporate attorney failed to respond to such request).

126.   125 R.D. 14 (D. Mass. 1989).

127.   *See, e.g.*, Andrews v. Goodyear Tire & Rubber Co., Inc., 191 F.R.D. 59 (D.N.J. 2000) (manager of a represented company was deemed not to be in the litigation control group for the purposes of the anticontact rule, and could be contacted without violation of Rule 4.2). For a general discussion of this complicated topic, *see generally* Krulewich, *Ex Parte Communications with Corporate Parties: The Scope of the Limitations on Attorney Communications with One of Adverse Interest*, 82 NW. U. L. REV. 1274 (1988); Miller & Calfo, *Ex Parte Contact with Employees and Former Employees of a Corporate Adversary: Is It Ethical?* 42 BUS. LAW. 1053 (1987); Stahl, *Ex Parte Interviews with Enterprise Employees: A* Port-Upjohn *Analysis*, 44 WASH. & LEE L. REV. 1181 (1987) (recommending a functional approach: ". . . any present or former employee who is identified with an enterprise, either for purposes of resolving disputed issues or effective representation of the enterprise, [should be deemed] a party representative for discovery purposes); Annotation, *Right of Attorney to Conduct Ex Parte Interview with Corporate Party's Non-management Employees*, 50 A.L.R. 4th 652 (1985).

128.   ABA Comm. on Ethics and Prof'l Responsibility, Formal Op. 91-359 (1991).

129.   673 So. 2d 116 (Fla. 1996).

130.   *See also* Polycast Technology Corp. v. Uniroyal, Inc., 129 F.R.D. 621 (S.D.N.Y. 1990) (predecessor code provision does not bar contacts with former employees, at least absent a showing that employee possessed privileged information); Amarin Plastics, Inc. v. Maryland Cup Corp., 116 F.R.D. 36 (D. Mass. 1987) (motion for protective order to prevent ex parte communication with adverse corporation's former president denied where no showing that his acts or omissions could be imputed to corporation; situation where former employee's act was subject of litigation or where former employee had contract with corporation to assist in litigation distinguished); Bovele v. Valley Hilton Hotel, 199 Cal. App. 3d 708, 245 Cal. Rptr. 144 (1988) (former employees who were not members of control group are not "parties represented by counsel); Niesig v. Team 1, 76 N.Y.2d 363, 559 N.Y.S.2d 493, 558 N.E.2d 1030 (1990) (anticontact rule applies only to current employees, not to former employees); Wright v. Group Health Hosp., 103 Wash. 2d 196, 691 P.2d 564 (1984) (former employee cannot possibly speak for corporation). *See generally* Miller & Calfo, *Ex Parte Contact with Employees and Former Employees of a Corporate Adversary: Is It Ethical?*, 42 BUS. LAW. 1053 (1987) ([C]ourt authorization or opposing counsel's consent should be required if the former employee was highly placed in the company. . . , or if the former employee's actions are precisely those sought to be imputed to the corporation.).

131.   656 So. 2d 486 (Fla. App. 1995).

132.   611 So. 2d 1305.(Fla. App. 1992).

133.   659 So. 2d 1156 (Fla. App. 1995).

134.   *Id.* at 1160.

135.   (citing ABA Formal Opinion 108 (1934)).

136.   811 F. Supp. 651 (M.D. Fla. 1992).

137.   Norton v. Tallahassee Memorial Hospital, 689 F.2d 938 (11th Circuit 1982) (appearance of professional impropriety sufficient to warrant disqualification).

138.   888 F. Supp. 1143 (M.D. Fla. 1995).

139.   *Id.* at 1147.

140.   *Id.* at 1148-49.

141.   *See, e.g.*, Porter v. Arco Metals Co.., 642 F. Supp. 1116 (D. Mont. 1986) (ex parte contact with former employees proper as long as it does not concern a privileged matter).

142.   *Id.* (interview with former employees of defendant corporation by plaintiff's counsel presented no attorney-client privilege issue unless counsel asked employees to divulge confidential

communications); Sobel v. Yeshiva Univ., 1981 WL 334, 28 Empl. Prac. Dec. (CCH) ¶ 32,479 (S.D.N.Y. 1981) (interests protected by attorney-client privilege have no bearing when plaintiffs are employees of primary defendant and issue concerns internal corporate employee policies); Wright v. Group Health Hosp., 103 Wash. 2d 192, 691 P.2d 564 (198~) (policies represented by [Rules 4.2 and 1.6] are different); *cf.* Massa v. Eaton Corp. 109 F.R.D. 312 (W.D. Mich. 1985) (DR 7-104(A) of predecessor Model Code applies to communications with any managerial-level employee of corporate party) (citing Upjohn Corp. v. United States, 449 U.S. 383 (1981) (middle- and lower-level employees could be "clients" for purpose of attorney-client privilege if their communication with counsel is needed to advise corporate client); Bobele v. Valley Hilton Hotel, 199 Cal. App. 3d 708, 245 Cal. Rptr. 144 (1988) (under *Upjohn*, prohibition against ex parte contact with represented party extends to all corporate employees). For further discussion, *see* Stah., *Ex Parte Interviews with Enterprise Employees: A Post-*Upjohn *Analysis*, 44 WASH. & LEE L. REV. 1181 (1987) (recommending a functional approach: ". . . any present or former employee who is identified with an enterprise, either for purposes of resolving disputed issues or effective presentation of the enterprise, [should be deemed] a party representative for discovery purposes).

143. *See, e.g.*, Devlin v. Rosman, 205 So. 2d 346 (Fla. App. 1967) (dictum) (counsel free to interview other party's witness with or without consent of counsel); ABA Comm. on Prof'l Ethics and Grievances, Formal Op. 117 (1934) (communication with witness proper if there is no deception and the lawyer discloses role). However, special rules apply when the witness is also a party to the action, including the special scenarios involving corporate parties. *See* ABA Comm. on Prof'l Ethics and Grievances, Formal Op. 187 (1983) (anti-contact rule is applicable when witness is also a party).

144. *See, e.g., In re* Federal Skywalk Cases, 97 F.R.D. 370 (W.D. Mo. 1983) (communication with class members violated disciplinary rule; defendants held in contempt); Impervious Paint Indus., Inc. v. Ashland Oil Co., 508 F. Supp 720 (N.D. Ky. 1981) (plaintiff class members are to be treated as represented by plaintiff's counsel), *appeal dismissed*, 659 F.2d 1081 (6th Cir. 1981); *but see* Gulf Oil Co. v. Bernard, 452 U.S. 89 (1981) (recognition that ethics rules against communication with represented parties impose restraints on expression in context of class action).

145. *See, e.g.,* United States v. Jamit, 546 F. Supp. 646 (E.D.N.Y. 1982) (person who retains counsel as protection against grand jury investigation is "represented party" for ethical purposes even if adversarial proceedings have not yet begun), *rev'd on other grounds*, 707 F.2d 638 (2d Cir. 1983); Abeles v. State Bar, 9 Cal. 3d 603, 510 P.2d 719, 108 Cal. Rptr. 359 (1973) ("represented" includes party who has counsel of record, regardless of whether such counsel in fact is authorized to act for that party); *see also* ABA Comm. on Prof'l Ethics, Informal Op. 827 (1965) (under ABA Canons of Prof'l Ethics, Informal Op. 827 (1965)) (under ABA Canons of Professional Ethics, communication by plaintiff's lawyer with defendant in effort to collect judgment proper where legal relationship between defendant and his lawyer had *terminated*); ABA Comm. on Prof'l Ethics, Informal Op. 1149 (1970) (in suit initiated by insurance company as subrogee to insured's claim, defense lawyer improperly communicated with insured, the named plaintiff, without obtaining consent of insurance company's lawyer, whose representation extended indirectly to insured as well); Monceret v. Bd. of Prof'l Responsibility, 29 S.W.3d 455 (Tenn. 2000) ("party" not limited to named plaintiff or defendant; may include witnesses). *But see In re* Boothe, 303 Or. 643, 740 P.2d 785 (1987) (communication with person no longer represented not improper even though lawyer thought person was represented).

146. *See, e.g.*, United States v. Hammed, 858 F.2d 834 (2d Cir. 1988) (applicability of anti-contact rule should be limited to instances in which the suspect has retained counsel "specifically for representation in conjunction with criminal matter in which he or she is held suspect"), *cert. denied*, 111 S. Ct. 192 (1990); State v. Russell, 194 Neb. 64, 230 N.W.2d 196 (1975) (no violation occurred when prosecutor communicated directly with defendant unrepresented in matter being discussed even though prosecutor knew defendant was represented in different matter); *In re* Burrows, 291 Or.

135, 629 P.2d 820 (1981) (subject matter includes communication with defendant concerning undercover activities disclosed in hope of leniency). *But see* State v. Yatman, 320 So. 2d 401 (Fla. App. 1975) (client represented by lawyer in one case deemed represented in related case).

147. *Compare* Rule 403.4(1).

148. *See, e.g., In re* Mettler, 305 Or. 12, 748 P.2d 1010 (1988) (lawyer working as state securities examiner was not acting in the course of representation of client); *see also* ABA Comm. on Ethics and Prof'l Responsibility, Informal Op. 1193 (1971) (lawyer conducting investigation for bail bond program was not representing client).

149. State *ex rel.* Nebraska State Bar Ass'n v. Hollstein, 202 Neb. 40, 274 N.W.2d 508 (1979) (consent to further communication implied); *In re* Mauch, 107 Wis. 2d 557, 319 N.W.2d 877 (1982) (communication proper given ambiguous response from party's lawyer and initiation of contact by party). *But see In re* Murray, 287 Or. 633, 601 P.2d 780 (1979) (lawyer cannot delegate to client obligation to obtain consent of represented party's lawyer). Consent is required regardless of the party's legal sophistication. *See, e.g.*, Meat Price Investigators Ass'n v. Iowa Beef Processors, Inc., 448 F. Supp. 1 (S.D. Iowa 1977) (consent required despite fact that party was sophisticated business person), *aff'd*, 572 F.2d 163 (8th Cir. 1978). *See generally* Leubsdorf, *Communicating with Another Lawyer's Client: The Lawyer's Veto and the Client's Interest*, 127 U. Pa. L. Rev. 683 (1979) (argues for client's right to authorize communications).

150. *See, e.g.,* Waller v. Kotzen, 567 F. Supp. 424 (E.D. Pa. 1983) (settlement negotiated directly with liability insurance carrier improper), *appeal dismissed*, 734 F.2d 9 (3d Cir. 1984); Vafiades v. Sheppard Bus Serv., Inc., 192 N.J. Super. 301, 469 A.2d 971 (1983); Turner v. State Bar, 36 Cal. 2d 155, 222 P.2d 857 (1950) (lawyer's communication not excused even though parties independently arrived at settlement terms); *In re* Atwell, 232 Mo. App. 186, 115 S.W.2d 527 (1938) (lawyers conducted negotiations and obtained release from opposing party); *see also* ABA Comm. on Ethics and Prof'l Responsibility, Informal Op. 1373 (1976) (improper to mail plea to both opposing lawyer and client); ABA Comm. on Ethics and Prof'l Responsibility, Informal Op. 1348 (1975) (improper to send copy of settlement offer to opposing party despite belief that lawyer was not relaying offers); ABA Comm. on Prof'l Ethics, Informal Op. 1190 (1971) (negotiations with insurance adjuster permitted if lawyer's written consent provided); ABA Comm. on Professional Ethics and Grievances, Informal Op. 570 (1962) (lawyer's letter to insurance company and insured improper).

151. *See, e.g.,* People v. Selby, 156 Colo. 17, 396 P.2d 598 (1964) (defendant's lawyer prepared and filed motion on behalf of plaintiff, in which she "confessed marital guilt" and asked court to dismiss her complaint); *In re* Marietta, 223 Kan. 11, 569 P.2d 921 (1977) (lawyer caused client to communicate with opposing party by preparing release of liability for back child support and delivering it to client); State v. Thompson, 206 Kan. 326, 478 P.2d 208 (1970) (lawyer communicated with opposing party concerning child custody and disposition of certain property); Montgomery County Bar Ass'n v. Haupt, 277 Md. 326, 353 A.2d 629 (lawyer chased and confronted opposing party who took marital car), *cert. denied*, 429 U.S. 804 (1976); *In re* Wehringer, 135 A.2d 279, 525 N.Y.S.2d 604 (lawyer negotiated directly with opposing party), *cert. denied*, 488 U.S. 988 (1988); Tennessee Bar Ass'n v. Freemon, 50 Tenn. App. 567, 362 S.W.2d 828 (1961) (lawyer took pictures of opposing party in compromising position and talked with her in absence of counsel).

152. *See, e.g.,* Nai Cheng Chen v. Immigration and Naturalization Serv., 537 F.2d 566 (1st Cir. 1976) (questioning of represented alien by immigration officer permitted by immigration rules); New York State Ass'n for Retarded Children v. Carey, 706 F.2d 956 (2d Cir.) (balance struck in favor of allowing plaintiffs' counsel to interview state mental institution's employees outside presence of defendant's counsel), *cert. denied*, 464 U.S. 915 (1983); Vega v. Bloomsburgh, 427 F. Supp. 593 (D. Mass. 1977) (First Amendment interests outweighed state's interest in prohibiting opposing counsel from communicating with state employees likely to be called as witnesses against state); Frey v. Department of Health and Human Serv., 106 F.R.D. 32 (E.D.N.Y. 1985) (stronger reason to construe term "party" narrowly where the defendant is a government employer); Weinstein v. Rosengloom, 59 Ill.2d 475, 322 N.E.2d 20 (1974) (rule of Illinois Industrial Commission requiring

party continuing matter to notify adverse party personally by postcard not inconsistent with DR 7-104(A)); ABA Comm. on Ethics and Prof'l Responsibility, Informal Op. 83-1496 (1983) (government inspector/lawyer may conduct authorized inspection of regulated business without prior consent of lawyer for business); ABA Comm. on Prof'l Ethics, Informal Op. 985 (1967) (proper to serve formal offer of judgment directly on opposing party as expressly permitted by statute, provided copy is simultaneously served on lawyer and is not served for improper motive or purpose); *see also* C.W. WOLFRAM, MODERN LEGAL ETHICS § 11.6 at 614-15 (1986) (consent requirement particularly inappropriate when adversary is a government agency). But see ABA Comm. on Ethics and Prof'l Responsibility, Informal Op. 1377 (1976) (opposing counsel may not communicate with municipal employees with power to commit municipality unless authorized by law or consent of municipality's lawyer under predecessor Model Code).

153. *See e.g.,* United States v. Thomas, 474 F.2d 110 (10th Cir.) (immaterial whether agent knew defendant had counsel), *cert. denied,* 412 U.S. 932 (1973); United States v. Four Star, 428 F.2d 1406 (9th Cir.) (prosecutor's use of statement obtained in custodial interrogation by law enforcement agent constituted ethical violation), *cert. denied,* 400 U.S. 947 (1970); Schantz v. Eyman, 418 F.2d 11 (9th Cir. 1969) (after being refused psychiatric examination, prosecutor sent psychiatrist to defendant's home), *cert. denied,* 397 U.S. 1021 (1970); United States v. Batchelor, 484 F. Supp. 812 (E.D. Pa. 1980) (assistant district attorney may not interview defendant without consent of defendant's previously retained counsel). *But see* United States v. Cobbs, 481 F.2d 196 (3d Cir.) (custodial interrogation in absence of and without permission of retained or appointed counsel where accused deliberately and voluntarily chose to speak technically permissible but not commendable), *cert. denied,* 414 U.S. 980 (1973). It must further be noted that this prohibition applies even if the defendant initiates the communication. *See, e.g.,* People v. Green, 405 Mich. 273, 274 N.W.2d 448 (1979) (immaterial that defendant initiated interview and indicated he did not want attorney present); *see also* Note, *The Prosecutor's Dilemma: Can a Criminal Be Interviewed Outside the Presence of His Attorney?* 6 J. LEGAL PROF. 347 (1981).

154. *See, e.g.,* United States v. Schwimmer, 882 F.2d 22 (2d Cir. 1989) (prosecutor's lawful questioning of convicted criminal defendant before grand jury and outside presence of defendant's counsel was "authorized by law" and did not violate anti-contact rule), *cert. denied,* 110 S. Ct. 1114 (1990); United States v. Sutton, 801 F.2d 1346 (D.C. Cir. 1986) (Sixth Amendment and anti-contact rule do not apply to taping that occurred during investigation stage but before initiation of judicial proceedings, such as a formal charge or indictment); United States v. Dobbs, 711 F.2d 84 (8th Cir. 1983) (noncustodial interview with government agent prior to initiation of judicial proceedings does not raise ethical issues); United States v. Fitterer, 710 F.2d 1328 (8th Cir.) (ethics rules not intended to stymie undercover investigation when subject retains counsel even if retained as part of grand jury investigation), *cert. denied,* 464 U.S. 852 (1983); United States v. Jamil, 707 F.2d 638 (2d Cir. 1983) (government investigator who tape-recorded suspect in noncustodial setting prior to indictment was not acting as "alter ego" of prosecutor, who was not privy to arrangement); United States v. Kenny, 645 F.2d 1323 (9th Cir.) (noncustodial tape recording prior to charge, arrest or indictment does not implicate ethical problems addressed by disciplinary rules), *cert. denied,* 452 U.S. 920 (1981); United States v. Lemonakis, 485 F.2d 941 (D.C. Cir. 1973) (government instructions to informant provided by prosecutor were not such as to make informant "alter ego" of prosecutor), *cert. denied,* 415 U.S. 989 (1974). *But see* United States v. Hammad, 858 F.2d 834 (2d Cir. 1988) (informant was alter ego of prosecutor, communication improper), *cert. denied,* 111 S. Ct. 192 (1990).

155. 858 F.2d 834 (2d Cir. 1988), *cert. denied,* 111 S. Ct. 192 (1990).

156. Memorandum of Rich Thornburgh, June 6, 1989, "Communication with Persons Represented by Counsel." A thorough analysis of this policy may be found in *ABA/BNA Lawyers Manual on Prof'l. Conduct,* 5 CURRENT REP. 427-31 (Jan. 3, 1990).

157. ABA House of Delegates Report No. 301 (approved Feb. 12-13, 1990). *See generally* Norton, *Ethics and the Attorney General,* 74 JUDICATURE 203 (December-January 1991); Thornburgh, *Ethics*

and the Attorney General: The Attorney General Responds, 74 Judicature 290 (April-May 1991); *ABA/BNA Law. Manual on Prof. Conduct*, 6 Current Rep. 280 (Aug. 29, 1990); Glaberson, *Thornburgh Policy Leads to a Sharp Ethics Battle*, N.Y. Times, March 1, 1991, at B9.

158. United States v. Lopez, 765 F. Supp. 1433 (N.D. Cal. 1991), reported in the The New York Times, May 25, 1991 at 14, *U.S. Judge Assails Thornburgh Plan.*

159. *See, e.g.,* Mills Land and Walter v. Golden West Refining Corp., 186 Cal. App. 116, 230 Cal. Rptr. 461 (1986) (disqualification of lawyer who directly communicated with corporate directors appropriate; disqualification of lawyer's firm, however, improper); Shelton v. Hess, 599 F. Supp. 905 (S.D. Tex. 1984) (contacts by plaintiff's lawyer unfairly prejudiced defendant, disqualification appropriate); *but see* Ceramco Inc. v. Lee Pharmaceuticals, 510 F.2d 268 (2d Cir. 1975) (telephone call to corporate employees to secure information relating to venue question not commendable but disqualification not required); Meat Price Investigators Ass'n v. Iowa Beef Processors, Inc., 448 F. Supp. 1 (S.D. Iowa 1977) (while lawyer probably overstepped bounds of responsible conduct, insufficient showing of prejudice to warrant disqualification), *aff'd*, 572 F.2d (8th Cir. 1978).

160. *See also* Rule 4.2.

161. *See, e.g.*, Briggs v. McWeeny, 796 S.2d 516 (Conn. 2002) (lawyer attempted to alter, destroy, or conceal engineering report with potential evidentiary value in litigation—disqualification was imposed); *In re* Zeiger, 692 A.2d 1351 (D.C. 1997) (lawyer altered medical records and then submitted them to insurance carrier); *but see In re* Wilka, 638 N.W.2d 245 (S.D. 2001) (lawyer's use of incomplete drug report at visitation hearing did not violate Rule 3.4(a); lawyer censured under different rule for misleading response to question from judge regarding report).

162. *See, e.g., In re* Geisler, 614 N.E.2d 939 (Ind. 1993) (lawyer obstructed prosecutor's access to evidence by helping witness to become unavailable for service and trial); *Restatement (Third) of the Law Governing Lawyers,* § 116(3) (2000) (lawyer may not unlawfully induce or assist a prospective witness to evade or ignore process obliging the witness to appear to testify).

163. *See* Rule 1.13(d).

164. *See, e.g.*, Hopkins v. Troutner, 4 P.3d 557 (Idaho 2000) (court ordered relief from a settlement agreement where defendant's attorney told the unrepresented plaintiff the case was worth $3,000 to $4,000, without advising plaintiff to consult counsel); State *ex rel.* Oklahoma Bar Ass'n v. Berry, 969 P.2d 975 (Okla. 1998) (creditor's lawyer advised unrepresented bankruptcy petitioner that petition was not completed properly, and that she should convert from a Chapter 7 to a Chapter 13 proceeding).

165. 659 So. 2d 1156 (Fla. App. 1995).

166. *See also* Barfuss v. Diversicare Corp.. of America, 656 So. 2d 486 (Fla. App. 1995) (prohibiting contact with former employees).

167. *See* Rules 1.2 and 1.4.

168. 22 A.L.R. 2d 659; 85 A.L.R. 3d 1161; 55 A.L.R. 4th 336.

169. 76 A.L.R. 2d 262.

170. 64 A.L.R. 3d 385.

171. Dees v. Scott, 347 So. 2d 475 (Fla. App. 1977).

172. 4 A.L.R. 4th 765.

173. 42 A.L.R. 4th 1130.

174. 27 A.L.R. 4th 568—this privilege was terminated by statute relating to certain state agencies, such as in Fla. Stat. Ann. § 768.28.

175. 30 So. 2d 284 (Fla. 1947).

176. 41 A.L.R. Fed. 123.

177. Trilogy Communications Inc. v. Excom Realty, 279 N.J. Super, 442, 652 A.2d 1273.

178. *In re* Alfa Mutual Ins. Co., 631 So. 2d 858 (Ala. 1993).

179. 1995 WL 77870. (Ariz. App.).

180. *See also* Camwell v. District Court, 644 P.2d 26 (Colo. 1982).

181. Hollingsworth v. Essence Communications, Inc., 1977 WL 2585 (Del. Ch.), 4 Del. J. Corp. L. 567; United States v United Shoe Machinery Corp., 89 F. Supp. 357 (D. Mass. 1950) (landmark case by Judge Wyanski); Dean v. Dean, 607 So. 2d 494 (Fla. App. 1992) (it is enough for the privilege to be asserted if client merely consults an attorney about a legal question with a view to employing him professionally).

182. Seattle Northwest Securities Corp. v. SDG Holdings, 812 P.2d 488 (Wash. 1991).

183. International Entertainment Consultants Inc. v. Search Warrant by Arapahoe County Sheriff's Department, 647 P.2d 1215 (Colo. 1982), noting that seizure of client's records in the lawyer's office possibly implicates the privilege against self-incrimination, hence a hearing should have been held; *citing* Upjohn Co. v. United States, 449 U.S. 383 (1981).

184. Lemonik v. Eastern Airlines, Inc. 632 So. 2d 239 (Fla. App. 1994).

185. C. Eloin Feltner v. Internationale Nederlandeon Bank, N.V., 622 So. 2d 123 (Fla. App. 1993).

186. 31 A.L.R. 4th 458; 64 A.L.R. 3d 385.

187. Kent v. Maryland Cas. Co., 268 N.Y.S. 2d 461 (1966).

188. 56 A.L.R. Fed. 189; International Ass'n of Defense Counsel, Vol. 22, April 1996, *Switching Firms: Defendants to plaintiffs, what must be done to avoid disqualification?* Dworkin v. General Motors Corp., 906 F. Supp. 273 (E.D. Pa. 1995).

189. 33 A.L.R. 4th 539 § 4(a), 7; 38 A.L.R. 2d 670.

190. 347 So. 2d 475 (Fla. App. 1977).

191. FSA 473.011(1), 473.141.

192. *Citing* FSA 90.502 (attorney-client privilege).

193. *See, e.g.,* Rubin v. Katz, 347 F. Supp. 322 (E.D. Pa. 1972) (no privilege for an independent CPA).

194. 33 A.L.R. 4th 539, 4a, e.

195. 33 A.L.R. 4th 539, § 5.

196. 35 A.L.R. 4th 225.

197. 36 A.L.R. Fed. 686.

198. 33 A.L.R. 4th 539.

199. Kaiser Found. Hosps. v. Northstar Reinsurance Corp., 153 Cal. Rptr. 678 (Cal. App. 1979).

200. *Cf.* Safeco Ins. Co. v. Kartsone, 510 F. Supp. 856 (D. Cal. 1981).

201. Northwestern Mutual Ins. Co. v. Safeway Stores, 26 Cal. 3d 912, 164 Cal. Rptr. 709 (1980); Transit Casualty Co. v. Spink Corp., 94 Cal. App. 3d 124, 156 Cal. Rptr. 360 (1979) (disapproved on other grounds in Commercial Union Assurance Co. v. Safeway Stores, 26 Cal. 3d 912, 164 Cal. Rptr. 708 (1980)); Kaiser Found. Hosps. v. North Star Reinsurance Corp., 90 Cal. App. 3d 786, 153 Cal. Rptr. 678 (1979); Continental Casualty Co. v. United States Fidelity & Guaranty Co., 56 F. Supp. 384 (1981); Continental Casualty Co. v. Pacific Indemnity Co., 134 Cal. App. 3d 389, 184 Cal. Rptr. 583 (1982); Valentine v. Aetna Ins. Co., 375 F. Supp. 1347 (C.D. Cal. 1974).

202. *Kaiser Found., supra* note 199.

203. Northwestern Mutual Ins. Co. v. Farmers Ins. Group, 76 Cal. App. 3d 1031, 143 Cal. Rptr. 415 (1978) (primary carriers' bad-faith refusal to accept settlement offers within its policy limits necessitated payment by the excess carrier. Proceeding under the theory that the covenant of good faith and fair dealing had been breached, the excess carrier was then permitted to recover that payment from the primary carrier.).

204. 516 F. Supp. 384 (N.D. Cal. 1981).

205. See 47 A.L.R. 3d 676-741; *see also* FLA STAT. ANN. § 631.391 (affiliates defined).

206. 47 A.L.R. 3d 676.

207. 31 A.L.R. 3d 557.

208. 22 A.L.R. FED. 643.

209. Week v. Dist. Court of Second Judicial Dist., 422 P.2d 46 (Colo. 1967); 31 A.L.R. 3d 522.

210. 1 A.L.R. 4th 1124, 98 A.L.R. 2d 241; 9 A.L.R. Fed. 685.

211. *See* 9 A.L.R. Fed. 685.

212. *See* 96 A.L.R. 159.

213. 19 A.L.R. 3d 1134; *see* Fla Stat. Ann. § 631.391 (for insolvency court powers to obtain records of affiliates of the insolvent insurer).

214. 52 A.L.R. 3d 636.

215. 7 A.L.R. 4th 8.

216. Kentucky Central Life Ins. Co. v. Park Broadcasting, 913 S.W.2d 330 (Ky. App. 1996).

217. Consolidated Edison Co. of New York Inc. v. Ins. Dept. of the State of New York, 532 N.Y.S.2d 186 (N.Y. Sup. Ct. 1988). *But see* Allendale Mutual Ins. Co. v. Ball Data Systems Inc., 152 F.R.D. 132 (N.D. Ill. 1993) (documents relating to reinsurance were discoverable under Rule 26(b)(2)).

218. 98 A.L.R. 3d 561, versus privilege, 85 A.L.R. 3d 1161.

219. 19 A.L.R. 3d 1318.

220. 13 A.L.R. 3d 1025.

221. 22 A.L.R. 2d 659.

222. 5 U.S. Code Ann. § 552(B)(6).

223. § 552(b)(7)(D); 594 A.L.R. Fed. 550.

224. 5 USCA § 552(b)(5); 54 A.L.R. Fed. 280.

225. *See* 9 A.L.R. Fed. 970.

226. *See* 34 A.L.R. 3d 775 (ex-attorney-client privilege asserted, court to instruct that no adverse inference be drawn).

227. 58 A.L.R. 2d 1037.

228. *See Insurance—Bad Faith Penalty,* 33 A.L.R. 4th.

229. Tackert v. State Farm Fire and Cas. Ins. Co., 653 A.2d 254 (Del. 1995).

230. Fla. Stat. Ann. § 624.155

231. Doan v. John Hancock Mut. Life. Ins. Co., 727 So. 2d 40 (Fla. App. 1999) receding from Rubio v. State Farm Fire and Cas. Ins. Co., 662 So. 2d 956 (Fla. App. 1995).

232. *See, e.g.,* Auto-Owners. Ins. Co. v. Conquest, 658 So. 2d 928 (Fla. 1995).

233. Couch on Insurance, 2d, § 26.420-26.421, 443, 444.

234. *Id.,* §§ 79.43-79.46.

235. 96 A.L.R. 2d 320.

236. 23 A.L.R. 2d 862; 70 A.L.R. 2d 783.

237. 73 ALR.2d 146.

238. 44 A.L.R. 2d 127.

CHAPTER 10

Attorney-Client and Work-Product Doctrines in Environmental Coverage Litigation

MARGARET E. WETHERALD
DEBORAH DOWD

This article discusses the attorney-client privilege and the work-product doctrine in the context of environmental coverage actions. In 1991, the Illinois Supreme Court gave a narrow reading to both the attorney-client privilege and the work-product doctrine, allowing insurers wide-ranging access to the insured's communications and materials that were prepared for the underlying environmental liability litigation.[1] Since then, however, many courts have rejected the Illinois Supreme Court's approach, preferring, instead, to interpret both the attorney-client privilege and the work-product doctrine expansively. This more expansive or protective approach is typified by the California appellate court decision in *Rockwell Int'l Corp. v. Superior Ct. (Aetna Cas. & Sur. Co.)*.[2]

In general, the decisions depend to an extent on the wording of the particular court rule or statute that governs the privilege and work product. The decisions also depend on the way in which the court characterizes the relationship between the insurer and the insured when there is a dispute about coverage for the underlying environmental liability action.[3] In analyzing the attorney-client privilege and the work-product doctrine, the courts focus on three specific concepts: the "common interest" exception, the "at issue" exception, and the effect of the cooperation clause found in the insurance contract. The Illinois and California opinions supply the framework for discussing these three areas.

In the seminal case of *Waste Management, Inc. v. International Surplus Lines Ins. Co.*,[4] the insurance *policies* provided indemnification for defense costs. Under the policies, the insurers had the right but not the duty to defend. The insured owned and operated five hazardous waste disposal sites. The insured sought reimbursement from its insurers for defense costs expended in an environmental liability lawsuit in which the insured was sued for personal injury and property damage caused by the migration of toxic wastes with respect to one site (the Miller lawsuit). The insured retained counsel and eventually settled this lawsuit. In an unrelated lawsuit pertaining to a different site, the insured was sued by the prior owners of the hazardous waste disposal site; the insured won on its counterclaim for negligent design, construction, and operation of the site (the Nunn lawsuit). The insured then requested reimbursement for the defense costs it had expended in the Miller lawsuit, but it did not seek insurance coverage for the defense costs associated with the Nunn litigation. Nevertheless, in the subsequent coverage litigation, the Illinois Supreme Court required the insured to produce to its insurers defense counsel's files from both the Nunn and the Miller litigations.

Turning first to the attorney-client privilege, the *Waste Management, Inc.* court noted that the privilege was an exception to the Illinois policy favoring disclosure and was, therefore, to be interpreted narrowly. The court agreed with the insurers that the "at issue" exception would apply since the issue in the coverage litigation was defense counsel's conduct of the underlying environmental litigation. But, since no attorney-client privilege attached to the documents in the first place, the "at issue" exception was irrelevant. Instead, the court premised its disclosure decision on the "common interest" concept[5] and on the cooperation clause in the insurance contract,[6] reasoning that the insured could not have had an expectation of privacy since the contract required it to cooperate with its insurers.

The court paraphrased the policy's cooperation clause, which required the insured to assist the insurers in conducting suits and enforcing contribution or indemnity rights and to give the insurers information and assistance as required. The *Waste Management, Inc.* court concluded that because of the cooperation clause the insured could not have had any expectation of confidentiality—a root requirement for the attorney-client privilege. Moreover, in its supplemental opinion upon denial of rehearing, the court said that there was an implied duty to cooperate, even when the policy did not contain an explicit provision. And, the duty to cooperate required the insured to assist an insurer in gaining information and knowledge about the underlying matter so the insurer could assess coverage, even when the insurer was not required to defend.

The insurers also convinced the court that the "common interest" doctrine made the attorney-client privilege unavailable to the insureds. The doctrine applies when two parties that share a common interest communicate with the same attorney; in any subsequent dispute between the two parties, the communications with the attorney are not privileged. The insured argued that there was no common interest because the insurers had not provided a defense in the underlying environmental liability litigation and because the insureds were not seeking reimbursement for any costs associated with the Nunn litigation. Thus, the defense attorney had neither been retained by the insurers nor was in direct communication with the insurer, the accepted prerequisites for application of the common interest exception. The Illinois Supreme Court disagreed in a somewhat strained analysis, insisting that the insurers and the insured were in privity of contract and that the insurers' potential liability for defense costs created a common interest. With regard to the Nunn litigation, the court decided that the cooperation clause encompassed situations where the insured was not seeking indemnification for defense costs.

The *Waste Management, Inc.* court also rejected the insured's argument that the work-product doctrine protected the underlying defense files. The court ruled that the doctrine did not apply because the material was prepared for the mutual benefit of the insured and the insurer, not in an adversarial setting as contemplated by the work-product doctrine. Nonetheless, the court went on to say that the defense attorney's mental impressions and case assessment (classic opinion work product) were discoverable because they were not available from any other source. Disclosure was required because defense counsel's decisions about which parties to bring in for contribution and which parties to release affected the insurer's liability if any, for cleanup costs. Lastly, the court concluded that an emerging "at issue" exception to the work-product doctrine applied and supported disclosure because the sought-after material was the basis for the lawsuit or its defense. This holding on the work-product doctrine was modified in the supplemental opinion on denial of rehearing, the court explaining that the insured only had to produce defense litigation files once there had been a determination that the particular site was covered.

The California decision in *Rockwell Int'l Corp. v. Superior Ct. (Aetna Cas. & Sur. Co.)*[7] typifies the more expansive application of the attorney-client privilege and the work-product doctrine in environmental coverage litigation. Rockwell was sued in the 1980s in a number of environmental contamination lawsuits. Some of its insurers defended under a reservation of rights while others declined to defend. The policies included a standard cooperation clause that required Rockwell to "'cooperate with the Company . . . attend hearings and trials . . . assist in effecting settlements, securing and giving evidence, obtaining the attendance of witnesses and in the conduct of suits. . . .'"[8] During discovery in the subsequent coverage litigation, Rockwell withheld documents and consultants' reports, asserting the attorney-client privilege and the work-product doctrine. The insurers argued that the cooperation clause negated the insured's expectation of privacy and required full disclosure of documents generated in the underlying actions and of discussions with defense counsel. The California court described this argument as "fanciful."[9]

The *Rockwell* court began its analysis by quoting the California evidence statute, which established a presumption in favor of the attorney-client privilege and placed the burden of proof that the communication was not privileged on the party seeking disclosure. (In contrast, the Illinois court cited a general court rule regarding privilege that did not specify presumptions or burdens of proof.[10]) The California court then noted that the cooperation clause was designed to permit an insurer to present a complete defense and that the drafter never considered the clause to be a waiver of the attorney-client privilege. The language of the policy provision, itself, gave no indication that a waiver was intended. Finally, the *Rockwell* court explained that when the insurer disputes coverage and provides a defense while reserving its right to litigate the coverage dispute, the interests of the insurer and the insured are in conflict. In this situation, a California statute requires that the insured be given independent counsel who, by statute, is not required to disclose privileged material to the insurer. Allowing the standard cooperation clause to abrogate the attorney-client privilege would fly in the face of the California statutory scheme.

The California court also refused to apply the common interest exception. Pursuant to a California statute, the common interest or joint client exception applies only when two or more clients have consulted or retained a lawyer upon a matter of common interest. Here, the attorneys representing Rockwell were neither retained by nor consulted by the carriers, so the exception did not apply.

Lastly, the *Rockwell* court parted company with the *Waste Management* court on the "at issue" exception. This exception applies when the client puts at issue the substance or content of a protected communication. It does not apply when the communication is merely one form of indirect evidence in a coverage case, which really turns on the underlying facts. Since Rockwell had not put a confidential communication in issue, the insurers were not entitled to privileged material.

Common Interest Exception to Attorney-Client Privilege and Work-Product Doctrine

Some courts after *Waste Management, Inc.* and *Rockwell* decided that the insurer and the insured shared a common interest, for purposes of the attorney-client privilege and the work-product doctrine, in attempting to minimize liability in the underlying litigation while other courts decided that the brewing coverage dispute prevented a commonality of interest.[11]

"At Issue" Exception

The "at issue" exception to the attorney-client privilege applies when (1) by some affirmative act (2) a party makes the protected information relevant to the case and (3) the opposing party is thereby denied vital information. Information is not "vital" when it is available from another source.[12] After reciting the three prongs of the exception, the Massachusetts court refused to require an insured's assignee to produce investigative reports, attachments, and file memoranda regarding the insured's use of pollutants, its operations, and its concerns for groundwater contamination. The reports were prepared after the insured became the focus of investigative efforts. Rejecting the *Waste Management* court's decision, the Massachusetts court ruled that, although the insured could not use the privileges as a sword, the insurer had failed to show that the reports were vital because the information was unavailable from any other source.

The "at issue" exception followed by the *Waste Management* court was also recently rejected by the Florida appellate court in *Eastern Air Lines, Inc. v. United States Aviation Underwriters, Inc.*[13] Eastern entered into an agreement with the Dade County Department of Environmental Resources and the Dade County Aviation Department to clean up fuel spills that had contaminated soil and water. Eastern then sought coverage from its insurers. The trial court had ruled that, merely by suing its insurers, Eastern had waived the attorney-client privilege as to all information relating to the extent, timing, and manner of pollution events for which it sought coverage. The appellate court disagreed, ruling that the trial court's rule eviscerated the privilege entirely.[14]

The Wisconsin appellate court distinguished between the attorney-client privilege and the work-product doctrine in analyzing the "at issue" exception in an insurance coverage dispute over the costs of defending an action brought by the State against the policyholder.[15] With regard to the attorney-client privilege, the court ruled that documents were not discoverable merely because they were relevant and that instituting a lawsuit did not put the documents "at issue," based on the Wisconsin privilege statute. To obtain discovery of attorney-client privileged material, the insurers would have to show that the insured intended to disclose the privileged communications in proving its claim. However, with regard to the work-product doctrine, material is discoverable when it is not privileged, is relevant, and the party seeking it has a substantial need and cannot without undue hardship obtain equivalent information.

Cooperation Clause

The Florida appellate court in *Eastern Air Lines, Inc.*, supra, also rejected the *Waste Management* rule that the cooperation clause in the insurance policy operated as a contractual waiver of the attorney-client privilege. First, the Florida statute establishing the attorney-client privilege and its exceptions made no mention of a cooperation clause. Second, the clause was designed to prevent fraud and collusion in underlying liability proceedings. Third, the clause operates when the insurer and the insured are in a fiduciary relationship, not when they are in an adversarial coverage dispute. The Wisconsin court in *State v. Hydrite Chem. Co.*[16] joined the courts that have ruled that the cooperation clause did not operate as a contractual waiver of the attorney-client privilege.[17]

Notes

1. Waste Management, Inc. v. International Surplus Lines Ins. Co., 144 Ill. 2d 178, 161 Ill. Dec. 774, 579 N.E.2d 322 (1991).

2. 26 Cal. App. 4th 1255, 32 Cal. Rptr. 2d 153 (1994) (*review denied*, 1994).

3. *See* Karon O. Bowdre, *Enhanced Obligation of Good Faith*, 59 ALA. L. REV. 755, 798 (1999) (majority rule is that when insurer defends under reservation of rights, the insurer and the insured do not share a common interest; material that the insured discloses to defense counsel is not discoverable because the insurer-insured relationship is adversarial).

4. 144 Ill. 2d 178, 161 Ill. Dec. 774, 579 N.E.2d 322 (1991).

5. *See* P. Nicholas Gimbel & Elizabeth W. Fox, *Key Discovery Battlegrounds Regarding Coverage under Commercial General Liability Policies*, 598 PLI/LIT 305 at 385 (1999); LEE R. RUSS, COUCH ON INSURANCE 3d § 250:57 (2003).

6. *See* TOD ZUCKERMAN & MARK RASKOFF, ENVIRONMENTAL INS. LITIG.: LAW & PRACTICE § 14:11 (2003).

7. 26 Cal. App. 4th 1255, 32 Cal. Rptr. 2d 153 (1994) (*review denied*, 1994).

8. 26 Cal. App. 4th at 1259.

9. *Id*. at 1260.

10. 579 N.E.2d at 326.

11. *See* EDO Corp. v. Newark Ins. Co., 145 F.R.D.18, 23 (D. Conn. 1992) (work product does not apply in later coverage dispute if materials were prepared when insured and insurer shared common, nonadversarial interests, and insured was under duty to cooperate); Metro Wastewater Reclamation Dist. v. Continental Cas. Co., 142 F.R.D. 471, 476 (D. Colo. 1992) (common interest

between insurer and insured in preventing additional claims for environmental liability and in favorably resolving such claims; insurer entitled to correspondence between insured and its attorneys, between attorneys and consultants with regard to site, reports to insured from its consultants, and in-house memoranda relating to the site or to governmental PRP proceedings). *But see* Carey-Canada, Inc. v. Aetna Cas. & Sur. Co., 118 F.R.D. 250 (D.D.C. 1987) (common interest exception to attorney-client privilege or work-product doctrine does not apply where insured prepared settlement materials for underlying liability action at a time when coverage was uncertain); Bituminous Cas. Corp. v. Tonka Corp., 140 F.R.D. 382 (D. Minn. 1992) (when defense attorney never represented insurer seeking documents, common interest exception to attorney-client privilege does not apply); Pittston Co. v. Allianz Ins. Co., 143 F.R.D. 66 (D.N.J. 1992) (common interest exception would be distorted if insurer given access to attorney-client communications and work product after refusing to participate in underlying environmental liability action); Vermont Gas. Sys., Inc. v. USF&G, 151 F.R.D. 268 (D. Vt. 1993) (where insurer and insured are in adversarial relationship regarding coverage and they never shared counsel or litigation strategy, common interest exception unavailable); State v. Hydrite Chem. Co., 220 Wis.2d 51, 582 N.W.2d 411 (Ct. App. 1998) (attorney must be retained or consulted by two or more clients for exception to apply).

12. Dedham-Westwood Water Dist. v. National Union Fire Ins. Co., 2000 WL 33419021 (Mass. Super. Ct. 2/4/00; unpublished).

13. 716 So. 2d 340 (Fla. Ct. App. 1998).

14. *Accord,* Remington Arms Co. v. Liberty Mut. Ins. Co., 142 F.R.D. 408 (D. Del. 1992) (merely bringing coverage action does not satisfy "at issue" exception); Pittston Co. v. Allianz Ins. Co., 143 F.R.D. 66 (D.N.J. 1992) ("at issue" exception requires disclosure of attorney-client communications and work-product material only when insured injects privileged documents into claim or defense); Vermont Gas Sys., Inc. v. USF&G, 151 F.R.D. 268 (D. Vt. 1993) (exception does not apply when neither the costs nor the insured's strategy in responding to third-party claims are in issue). *But see* Metro Wastewater Reclamation Dist. v. Continental Cas. Co., 142 F.R.D. 471 (D. Colo. 1992) ("at issue" exception required disclosure of correspondence between insured and consultants or attorneys, consultant's reports, and in-house memoranda relating to site or PRP proceedings because coverage depended on whether and when insured knew of property damage and release of contaminants).

15. State v. Hydrite Chem. Co., 220 Wis. 2d 51, 582 N.W.2d 411 (Ct. App. 1998).

16. 220 Wis. 2d 51. 582 N.W. 2d 411 (Ct. App. 1998).

17. *See* Bituminous Cas. Corp. v. Tonka Corp., 140 F.R.D. at 386; *Remington Arms*, 142 F.R.D. at 417; *Pittston*, 143 F.R.D. at 72. *But see EDO Corp.*, 145 F.R.D. at 23 (explicit duty to cooperate allows insurer to discover communications with attorneys regarding underlying action brought by governmental authorities in subsequent coverage litigation).

CHAPTER 11

Preserving the Confidentiality of Investigations by In-House and Outside Counsel

AIMEE B. ANDERSON*

Introduction

A carefully planned and executed internal investigation can enable a corporate defendant to identify and evaluate evidence that may be used against it in litigation and to marshal the evidence that supports its position. The process of investigation frequently involves the identification and interviewing of current and former employees at various levels within the corporation and the identification and analysis of pertinent corporate records and documents.

The question of how to maintain the confidentiality of the materials generated in the course of such a review, including notes, drafts, interim or tentative findings, and investigative reports, is of critical importance. While the process of gathering, analyzing, and reporting upon the critical facts may prove extremely useful to the company in formulating and implementing an informed and effective defense strategy, if confidentiality is compromised, it can also provide one's adversaries with a detailed road map into the inner workings and vulnerabilities of the company. Indeed, it is not unlikely that such a report, and the underlying documentation, will be responsive to discovery requests or subpoenas served upon the corporation during litigation. Special precautions must, therefore, be taken before initiating such an investigation and at every stage thereafter to maximize the likelihood that the confidentiality of the fruits of the investigation will be preserved.

---

* The author wishes to acknowledge the assistance of Leslie Gogan, an associate at Wildman, Harrold, Allen & Dixon LLP, in the preparation of this chapter.

Application of the Privilege to the Corporate Client

In general, courts have developed the concept of the attorney-corporate client privilege by direct analogy to the privilege possessed by natural persons, but there are some important differences. The client interacts with his attorney through several functions: by communicating information, receiving advice, and acting upon that advice. These functions are united in the individual client. When the client is a corporation, however, those who possess pertinent information are not necessarily those who make the corporate decisions. Characteristically, modern corporations, especially large ones, are decentralized, with significant authority and information vested in middle management and lower echelon employees.[1]

The Scope of the Privilege before *Upjohn v. United States*:
The Control Group Test

One of the first federal courts to discuss the corporate attorney-client privilege at length was the district court in *United States v. United Shoe Mach. Corp.*[2] That court held that the privilege applies to "information furnished [to the attorney] by an officer or employee of the [corporation] in confidence and without the presence of third persons."[3] The court implicitly assumed that all communications between counsel and corporate personnel for the purpose of obtaining legal advice were privileged.

However, other courts found unacceptable a rule that so broadly protected the communication of any employee with the corporation's attorney.[4] Consequently, a debate over the appropriate scope of the attorney-corporate client privilege ensued, and two competing theories took center stage: (1) the "control group test" and (2) the "subject matter test."

The "control group" test was first articulated in *Philadelphia v. Westinghouse Elec. Corp.*[5] In analyzing the privilege issue, the court first noted that the attorney-client privilege applies only when the purpose of the communication is the securing of legal advice or assistance.[6] Further, the court pointed out, this advice must be sought on behalf of the one making the communication, not on behalf of someone else, who would be merely a witness.[7] The court framed the issue presented to it in the following question: "How are we going to determine whether the person making the communication is the client or is a witness?"[8] In responding, the court reviewed various test proposals and ultimately concluded:

> [I]f the employee making the communication, of whatever rank he may be, is in a position to control or even to take a substantial part in a decision about any action which the corporation may take upon the advice of the attorney, or if he is an authorized member of a body or group which has that authority, then, in effect, he is (or personifies) the corporation when he makes his disclosure to the lawyer and the privilege would apply. In all other cases the employee would be merely giving information to the lawyer to enable the latter to advise those in the corporation having the authority to act or refrain from acting on the advice.[9]

Many federal courts that subsequently considered the scope of the attorney-corporate client privilege over the next two decades followed the control group test.[10]

Upjohn v. United States: The Supreme Court Rejects the Control Group Test

The United States Supreme Court, however, specifically rejected the control group test in *Upjohn Co. v. United States*, finding that it "frustrates the very purpose of the privilege by discouraging the communication of relevant information by employees of the client to attorneys seeking to render legal advice to the client corporation."[11] Once again the scope of the attorney-corporate client privilege was raised, specifically, whether the privilege extended to communications between lower-level corporate employees and corporate attorneys.[12] The Court's rationale in considering the issue was its belief that the advice of counsel was typically more important to the non-control group employees and the restrictions of the control group test hindered corporate counsel's ability to fully advise the company.[13]

In *Upjohn* independent accountants conducted an audit of one of the pharmaceutical manufacturer's foreign subsidiaries and discovered evidence that it had improperly paid foreign government officials. The accountants reported the discovery to Upjohn's general counsel, who discussed the matter with the chairman of the board and outside counsel.

As a result of these discussions, the corporation began an internal investigation. Specifically, its general counsel, in consultation with outside counsel, sent a questionnaire to all of the company's overseas managers, soliciting information regarding the alleged payment. The managers were advised that the investigation was highly confidential, and they were directed to return their responses directly to the general counsel. The general counsel and outside counsel also interviewed the recipients of the questionnaires and a number of other current or former officers and employees as part of the investigation. The attorneys made handwritten notes during these interviews that reflected the content of the conversations and their impressions of them. Upjohn then disclosed the fact of the questionable payments to the IRS, which began an investigation into the tax consequences.

The IRS subsequently issued an administrative summons for the production of all documents gathered during Upjohn's investigation. The company, however, refused to comply on the grounds that the documents were protected from disclosure by either (1) the attorney-client privilege or (2) the work-product doctrine. The district court adopted the recommendation of the magistrate, who enforced the summons.

The Sixth Circuit agreed that the privilege did not apply to the employee responses, based on the trial court's finding that the executives responding to the questionnaire were not within the "control group" of senior executives entitled to "control or even to take a substantial part in a decision about any action which the corporation may take upon the advice of the attorney."[14]

The Supreme Court reversed that decision. Delivering the opinion of the Court, Justice Rehnquist wrote:

> In the corporate context, . . . it will frequently be employees beyond the
> control group as defined by the court below . . . who will possess the infor-

mation needed by the corporation's lawyers. Middle-level—and indeed lower-level— employees can, by actions within the scope of their employment, embroil the corporation in serious legal difficulties, and it is only natural that these employees would have the relevant information needed by corporate counsel if he is adequately to advise the client with respect to such actual or potential difficulties.

* * *

The control group test adopted by the court below thus frustrates the very purpose of the privilege by discouraging the communication of relevant information by employees of the client to attorneys seeking to render legal advice to the client corporation. The attorney's advice will also frequently be more significant to noncontrol group members than to those who officially sanction the advice, and the control group test makes it more difficult to convey full and frank legal advice to the employees who will put into effect the client corporation's policy.[15]

The Supreme Court thus concluded that the communications between Upjohn's employees and its counsel, including both the responses to questionnaires and the attorney notes reflecting the interview responses, were protected by the attorney-client privilege. In reaching its decision, the Court focused on several factors: (1) the purpose of the investigation permitted counsel "to be in a position to give legal advice to the company"; (2) the communications were considered "highly confidential" when made and had been kept confidential; (3) the communications between the employees of the corporation and counsel for the corporation, "acting as such," were at the direction of corporate superiors in order to secure legal advice from counsel; (4) the communications "concerned matters within the scope of the employees' corporate duties, and the employees themselves were sufficiently aware that they were being questioned in order that the corporation could obtain legal advice"; and (5) the information necessary to formulate a basis for legal advice was "not available from upper-echelon management."[16] By extending the attorney-client privilege to communications between counsel for the corporation and lower-echelon employees, *Upjohn* has become the gauge for every court's further consideration of this issue.

The Scope of the Privilege after *Upjohn*: The Subject Matter Test

Since *Upjohn*, the scope of the attorney-corporate client privilege still evokes considerable debate, and courts struggle to define an appropriate test.[17] The principal alternative formulated in direct response to the control group test (and advocated after *Upjohn*) is the "subject matter" or "scope of employment" test. The Seventh Circuit first enunciated this test in *Harper & Row Publishers v. Decker*.[18] Here the court examined "why an attorney was consulted rather than with whom he communicated."[19]

Harper & Row involved an antitrust action brought by plaintiffs (local governments, public schools, and libraries) against several defendants allegedly involved in a conspiracy to inflate the price of children's books. Employees of the defendant corporations testified before a grand jury and were debriefed by attorneys for the corporations. The plaintiffs then sought to discover the attorneys' notes on the debriefing sessions, but the defendants refused to supply them, claiming the protection of both the attorney-client privilege and the work-product doctrine.[20] Ruling that the control group test was inadequate, the Seventh Circuit concluded that a communication from a corporate employee is privileged "where the employee makes the communication at the direction of his superiors . . . and where the subject matter . . . dealt with in the communication is the performance by the employee of the duties of his employment."[21]

Today, most states have for all intents and purposes abandoned the strict control group test. These same courts, nevertheless, do not automatically invoke the subject matter test because they perceive it to be an imperfect fit between the purpose of the privilege and the actual functioning of the corporation.[22]

The *Samaritan* court, after reviewing the different privilege tests, found each of them, even the approach of *Upjohn*, to be unsuitable and formulated its own. The event at issue in that case was a surgical procedure at a hospital during which a child's heart stopped. Following the incident, several nurses and a scrub technician were interviewed by the nurse paralegal on behalf of the hospital's lawyer. At deposition, these witnesses could not remember what had occurred during the surgery, and the plaintiffs sought production of the record of the interviews.

Believing a "functional approach that focuses on the relationship between the communicator and the need for legal services" would better promote the underlying purposes of the attorney-client privilege, the *Samaritan* court held that any communication initiated by an employee that seeks legal advice from corporate counsel on behalf of the corporation is privileged.[23] The court also held the opposite situation to be privileged as well. "Where someone other than the employee initiates the communication, a factual communication by a corporate employee to corporate counsel is within the corporation's privilege if it concerns the employee's own conduct within the scope of his or her employment and is made to assist the lawyer in assessing or responding to the legal consequences of that conduct for the corporate client."[24]

The overwhelming majority of jurisdictions currently utilize one of the following privilege tests: (1) a modified version of the subject matter test; (2) a modified version of the control group test; or (3) some combination of both tests.[25]

It should be noted that the control group test, however, still has a small minority of adherents. The state courts of Illinois, Michigan, Minnesota, and Pennsylvania still use the control group test to determine whether a communication between a corporate employee and corporate counsel is privileged.[26]

In-House and Outside Counsel and the Distinction between Legal and Business Advice

The attorney-client privilege encompasses communications which seek or provide legal advice, that is, the attorney must be acting in his legal capacity at the time of the communication.[27] Ordinary business advice, however, is not protected.[28] The privilege applies to in-house counsel as well as outside counsel.[29] In fact, "in-house attorneys may constitute the 'client' for purposes of a corporation's communications with its outside counsel."[30]

Difficult questions can arise, however; when lawyers, particularly in-house counsel, undertake activities which involve mixed questions of business and law.[31] Soliciting or giving business advice along with legal advice does not automatically cast the privilege aside; it may still attach.[32] However, there is no bright line by which to determine whether in-house counsel is acting in a professional legal capacity for the purpose of the attorney-client privilege. Some courts have observed that the legal protection of the communication, for privilege purposes, will depend upon the context of the communication and the lawyer's activities.[33] "The key is that communications must be primarily legal [although] the privilege is not necessarily lost when non-legal information is part of a communication seeking or giving legal advice."[34]

Judge Leahy in the case of *Zenith Radio Corp. v. Radio Corp. of America*,[35] stated:

> Acting as a lawyer encompasses the whole orbit of legal functions. When he acts as an advisor, the attorney must give predominantly legal advice to retain his client's privilege of non-disclosure, not solely, or even largely, business advice.[36]

Matters that can be handled as easily by laymen as by lawyers may or may not be privileged; the analysis is situational.[37]

Rather than indiscriminately grouping all communications as either legal or non-legal, a court must scrutinize each communication individually, by analyzing the content and purpose of each, and not just cursorily looking to whether it contained business information or whether it was received by an attorney.[38] In *Diversified Indus. v. Meredith*,[39] the court upheld a corporation's claim of privilege for a report by outside counsel who had been retained to investigate bribery charges. The report of the investigation, based on interviews of employees and an analysis of data compiled by an accounting firm, evaluated the corporation's conduct and issued recommendations.

The court first noted that the fact that the matter had been referred by the corporation to a law firm was "prima facie so committed for the sake of the legal advice," "absent a clear showing to the contrary."[40] The outside firm had conducted a full "professional investigation," but more important, according to the court, the firm had been given the authority to analyze, evaluate, and draw conclusions regarding previous corporate conduct as well as to make recommendations regarding a future course of action.[41] The court also noted that although Diversified could have hired lay accountants and investigators to conduct the inquiry, "neither would have had the training, skills and background necessary to make the independent analysis and recommendations" that the company deemed necessary.[42] The dissent, however, focused on the corporation's minutes from its board meetings that stated that the law firm was being hired as an investigator, not as legal counsel.[43] It also emphasized the fact that the outside firm's report consisted primarily of a description of the investigation and recommendations, which, according to the dissent, "could have been made by any[one] . . . [an investigator, accountant, or banker alike] possessing ordinary common sense and business prudence."[44]

Thus, the courts examine whether counsel's activity involves the application of law to facts or the rendering of an opinion of law in response to the client's legal inquiries.[45] While there is no legal distinction between in-house and outside counsel for the purpose of the attorney-client privilege, the activities of in-house counsel will probably be subjected to closer scrutiny.[46] Accordingly, where in-house counsel performs all or part of the investigation or the preparation of the report, care should be taken to substantiate that he is acting in a legal, rather than a business capacity.

Dual Representation of the Corporation and the Employee

It may on occasion occur that the attorney-client privilege exists not only as to communications on behalf of the corporation but as to certain communications on behalf of an individual employee as well. As the court noted in *Diversified Indus. v. Meredith*:[47]

> Ordinarily, the privilege belongs to the corporation and an employee cannot himself claim the attorney-client privilege and prevent disclosure of communications between himself and the corporation's counsel if the corporation has waived the privilege. . . . However, circumstances may reveal that the employee sought legal advice from the corporation's counsel for himself or that counsel acted as a joint attorney. Under such circumstances, he may have a privilege.[48]

This is not the usual situation, however, and should not be presumed. In fact, "the default assumption is that the attorney only represents the corporate entity, not the individuals" therein.[49] Furthermore, it is the burden of the corporate individual to overcome this presumption.[50]

In *United States v. Martin*, a corporation's attorney handled a few isolated and relatively minor legal tasks for one of its officers personally. The attorney, however, believed he had been hired by and was working for the corporation.[51] Under these circumstances the district court found no basis for a personal privilege claim between the officer and the corporation's attorney, a finding which the circuit court upheld.[52]

Several jurisdictions, including the First, Second, Tenth, and D.C. Circuits have adopted a five-part test, formulated by the Third Circuit in *In re Bevill, Bresler & Schulman Asset Mgmt. Corp.*,[53] which corporate employees must satisfy in order to personally assert the attorney-client privilege.[54] Such an employee must show that: (1) he approached counsel for legal advice; (2) he clearly enunciated to corporate counsel his intent to seek advice in his individual capacity; (3) corporate counsel knew that a conflict could arise but communicated with the employee in an individual capacity anyway; (4) the conversation was confidential; and (5) the substantive nature of the conversation did not involve company affairs.[55]

A corporate officer, however, can still assert the attorney-client privilege personally between himself and the corporation's attorney even if their conversation substantively involved corporate affairs.[56] Only if the officer and attorney discussed the officer's "personal liability, legal rights, or actions," not just the corporation's "rights and responsibilities," will the officer have a legitimate expectation of confidentiality that could still protect the communication.[57] Attorneys and corporate employees alike must bear in mind that "blanket [privilege] assertions are extremely disfavored." Privilege claims must specifically identify each communication as well as its supporting basis.[58]

Communications with Former Employees
During the Course of the Investigation

The *Upjohn* Court declined to address the applicability of the attorney-client privilege to former employees.[59] However, the Ninth Circuit has observed that the privilege applies to communications with prior employees by extension of the *Upjohn* rationale. "Former employees, as well as current employees, may possess the relevant information needed by corporate counsel to advise the client with respect to actual or potential difficulties."[60]

In reviewing an unusual set of circumstances, the court in *Baxter Travenol Lab. v. Lemay*,[61] held that *Upjohn* protects communications "even if the information, therein, was originally obtained before the communicator became the corporate client's employee, as long as the communication is made by the client's employee, qua employee, at the client's behest, in order to secure legal advice, and such communication is intended by the client and participants to be confidential."[62]

In more recent years, however, some courts have expressed concern regarding the broad extension of the *Upjohn* rationale to former employees.[63]

Nevertheless, some courts have extended the privilege to former employees within two general situations: the privilege could extend "to communications between corporate counsel and a former employee" when the communications either (1) relate to the employee's knowledge or actions, acquired or conducted, during the former work relationship; or (2) were already privileged when first communicated during the past employment.[64]

Once communications are deemed privileged, they "should not automatically lose their protected status" just because the employee left the company.[65] Sometimes, however, to include activities or knowledge acquired during the past employment "sweeps too broadly" because "former employees are not the client . . . [t]hey share no identity of interest in the outcome of the litigation."[66] Some courts, therefore, will treat communications between current corporate counsel and a former employee "no differently from communications with any other third-party fact witness," unless a stronger connection to the former employee is demonstrated.[67]

Communication Between Corporate Counsel and Contract Employees

In today's economy, corporations frequently staff their workforces with contract employees, saving thousands of dollars in overhead costs like health and retirement benefits. Could this practice affect the assertion of the corporation's attorney-client privilege if it becomes embroiled in litigation that involves the contract employee as a witness? Does the attorney-client privilege exist between a corporation's counsel and its contract employees?

The relatively sparse case law addressing this issue is split. Most courts will extend the privilege, but a few decline, citing the importance of fact-finding on the outcome.[68]

In *Energy Capital*, the Federal Claims Court noted that including contract employees within a corporation's attorney-client privilege, although unusual, was not unprecedented. Not all contractors automatically qualify, however.[69] For the court to decide whether the contractor in question qualifies for protection, the proponent-corporation must present a "detailed factual showing" that "establish[es] the relationship between the client" and the contractor.[70] Because the proponent-corporation in *Energy Capital* failed to present any facts about its relationships with its contractors, the court could not rule as to whether they should be protected.[71] The corporation failed to meet its burden of proof, and its contractors were ordered to comply with discovery requests.

A court such as *Miramar* that declines to extend the attorney-client privilege to contract employees rationalizes that such an extension "would require stretching *Upjohn* one step further," and come one step closer to totally eroding the limits placed on the attorney-client privilege.[72] The *Miramar* court held that including contractors within a corporation's attorney-client privilege "would represent a tremendous expansion of the privilege beyond corporate employees to any individual contractually associated with a corporation on a full-time basis for some period of time."[73] Such an extension, according to *Miramar*, would overly encumber the judicial truth-seeking process.

Attorney-Client Privilege in the Parent/Subsidiary Relationship

In *Admiral Ins. Co. v. United States Dist. Court*,[74] the Ninth Circuit was faced with a claim of privilege on behalf of the subsidiary of a party. Noting that *Upjohn* had "rejected a mechanistic approach" to the corporate privilege issue, the court held that "communications between employees of a subsidiary corporation and counsel for the parent corporation . . . would be privileged if the employee possesses information critical to the representation of the parent company and the communications concern matters within the scope of employment."[75]

The court in *Bowne, Inc. v. AmBase Corp.*,[76] however, while remarking that some courts have recognized a privilege for communications of a parent corporation shared with its wholly-owned subsidiary, nevertheless found that "they have done so only upon a showing that a common attorney was representing both corporate entities or that the two corporations shared a common legal interest and thus came within the joint-client rule [citations omitted], or that the disclosure was made to an employee of the subsidiary for the principal or sole purpose of eliciting assistance to the attorney in rendering legal advice or other legal services."[77] Moreover, the court noted, "[t]he burden is on the corporation to provide information about its own internal security practices which would support a finding of confidentiality. If a corporation wants the benefit of the privilege it should enforce a fairly firm 'need to know' of the communication rule."[78]

After articulating both of the above standards, the court in *Edison Corp. v. Town of Secaucus*[79] applied both precedents and denied a motion to compel a deponent's answers as to questions regarding conversations between the deponent (an employee of the parent corporation) and an attorney for the subsidiary company. The court concluded that under both *Admiral* and *Bowne* "the lawyer-client privilege applie[d] to communications between . . . the attorney for the subsidiary, and . . . the employee of the parent." The court based its decision on the fact that: (1) the employee possessed information relevant to the litigation; and (2) the subsidiary and parent corporations possessed "a substantial community of legal interest" in the underlying litigation.[80] Only the subsidiary was embroiled in the litigation; however, a community of legal interest existed because the outcome of subsidiary's appeal directly impacted the parent corporation. Thus, the privilege extended between them.

Communications with Non-Lawyers Acting at the Direction of Lawyers

Generally, any communication between an attorney and a client that is assisted by a necessary facilitator, whether interpreter, messenger, paralegal, or agent of the client is considered a privileged communication.[81]

The pertinent consideration is whether the non-lawyer's assistance was necessary for the attorney to give legal advice.[82] The inquiry is narrow and avoids extending privilege unnecessarily[83] (holding that the trial court reasonably found the consultant was intimately connected to the giving of legal advice). Courts typically ask whether the information submitted by the non-lawyer was "made at the request of the attorney or the client" and whether the purpose of the assistance "was to put in usable form information obtained from the client."[84]

Finding that the accounting services procured by the attorneys were not necessary, the court in *United States v. Chevrontexaco*[85] held that the communications to, from, and between the accounting firm and corporate counsel were not privileged.[86] The proponent corporation unequivocally stated that "its in-house counsel had 'significant expertise,' [and] that its in-house counsel undertook legal analysis of the issues."[87] The court, therefore, deemed the accounting consultation as unnecessary because that firm neither acted as a necessary "translator" nor "put Chevron's communications or information 'into terms that [its in-house counsel] can use effectively.'"[88]

Exceptions to the Attorney-Client Privilege

The attorney-client privilege is not absolute but is subject to certain exceptions where the courts have determined that the privilege must give way to some other, competing policy.

The Fiduciary Exception

Exceptions to the privilege have been found in circumstances in which the stockholders of a company seek disclosure of materials which are claimed by the board of directors to be privileged.[89] In *Garner v. Wolfinbarger*,[90] the court explained: "[W]here the corporation is in suit against its stockholders on charges of acting inimically to stockholder interests, protection of those interests as well as those of the corporation and of the public require that the availability of the privilege be subject to the right of the stockholders to show cause why it should not be invoked in the particular instance."[91] The exception applies in both shareholder derivative suits and non-derivative suits such as a class action securities fraud litigation. The latter, however, should be subjected to a higher burden of proof before the court actually strips away the privilege.[92]

Not all state courts have formally adopted the *Garner* exception or the federal court's reasoning justifying it.[93]

The Crime-Fraud Exception

It is axiomatic that the privilege does not extend to otherwise protected communications between attorney and client in furtherance of ongoing or contemplated criminal or fraudulent conduct.[94]

The courts have developed a two-pronged test to determine whether the crime-fraud exception to the attorney-client privilege applies: "[T]he party opposing the privilege need make only a prima facie showing that the communications either (i) were made for an unlawful purpose or to further an illegal scheme or (ii) reflect an ongoing or future unlawful or illegal scheme or activity."[95]

"The purported crime or fraud need not be proved."[96] However, there must at least be a foundation of fact with which to support the exception; a "mere allegation" will not suffice.[97] Nevertheless, the crime-fraud need not be proved "beyond a reasonable doubt."[98] The exception applies even though the attorney is completely unaware of actual or contemplated improper uses of his or her advice.[99]

The "At-Issue" Exception

The "at-issue" exception comes into play by virtue of a party's reliance on a privileged communication as an essential part of its claim or defense.[100] Fairness requires such an exception.[101] However, "[a]dvice is not in issue merely because it is relevant, and does not necessarily become in issue merely because the attorney's advice might affect the client's state of mind in a relevant manner. The advice of counsel is placed in issue where the client asserts a claim or defense, and attempts to prove that claim or defense by disclosing or describing an attorney-client communication."[102]

The Public Policy Exception

A more nebulous exception to the attorney-client privilege is the "public policy" exception, under which some courts have ordered production of privileged materials under the theory that some overriding public policy requires disclosure despite a valid privilege.[103]

In *Leonen v. Johns-Manville*,[104] the court found that internal memoranda and other correspondence of the corporate defendant "may show if and when [it] became aware of the health dangers associated with asbestos. Plaintiffs have shown the need and relevancy of this material to their case. Moreover, these documents are unavailable from any less intrusive sources."[105]

Waiver of the Attorney-Client Privilege

The attorney-client privilege belongs to the client,[106] although his attorney may assert it for him. The option to waive the privilege belongs likewise to the client, although here, too, the attorney, as agent of the client, can effect a waiver.[107]

"As a general rule, the 'attorney-client privilege is waived by voluntary disclosure of private communications by an individual or corporation.'"[108] For example, waiver can occur when confidential information is discussed in the presence of a third party or published to the public.[109]

Disclosure of otherwise privileged materials, however, can also be inadvertent, and when litigation includes a large number of documents, "there is more likely to be an inadvertent disclosure [rather] than a knowing waiver."[110] Regrettably, there is no conformity regarding the effect of inadvertent disclosure across the jurisdictions.[111] Courts use three different approaches to determine whether an inadvertent disclosure constitutes a voluntary waiver.[112] The three prevailing views are: (1) the strict approach; (2) the balanced approach; and (3) the lenient approach.[113]

The "strict" theory holds that inadvertent disclosure always results in waiver since the effect of the disclosure cannot be reversed, whether such disclosure was voluntary or negligent.[114] This approach holds attorneys and clients accountable for any carelessness in handling privileged communications and provides certainty in results. However, this approach may also have a chilling effect on the communication that takes place when a client consults an attorney.[115]

At the other extreme the so-called "lenient" theory argues that inadvertent disclosure by the attorney cannot waive the privilege on behalf of the client who did not intend disclosure.[116] This approach "remains true to the core principle of attorney-client privilege, . . . [i.e.,] it exists to protect the client."[117] This approach, however, "creates little incentive for lawyers to maintain tight control over privileged material . . . [and] it ignores the importance of confidentiality."[118]

The approach at the mid-point applies a balancing test, which looks to five factors: "(1) the reasonableness of the precautions taken to prevent inadvertent disclosure in view of the extent of the document production, (2) the number of inadvertent disclosures, (3) the extent of the disclosure, (4) the promptness of measures taken to rectify the disclosure, and (5) whether the overriding interests of justice would or would not be served by relieving the party of its error."[119] The balancing test promotes the purpose of the privilege, assures the client its confidences will not be exposed due to "minor mistakes," and "creates an incentive for counsel to engage in" careful, thoughtful production due to the specter of waiver.[120]

In *Abamar Hous. & Dev. v. Lisa Daly Lady Decor*,[121] the court not only held that inadvertently disclosed yet still privileged documents could not be used to the disadvantage of the opposing party-sender, but even admonished counsel to remember the ethical dictate that obliges an adversary to promptly notify the sender of the mistaken disclosure.[122]

Nor is the scope of inadvertent waiver consistent among different jurisdictions. The Sixth Circuit summarized the state of affairs within the courts as follows: "the case law addressing the issue of limited waiver [is] in a state of 'hopeless confusion.'"[123]

Inadvertent disclosure in some jurisdictions may be held to waive the privilege as to that document.[124] On the other hand, the waiver may be interpreted to extend to all other communications on the same subject matter.[125] Waiver in the context of a particular lawsuit may even extend to subsequent litigation, despite a stipulation by the attorneys involved to restrict the waiver to the original litigation.[126]

In *In re John Doe Corp.*,[127] the court held that the disclosure of a business ethics review prepared by in-house counsel to counsel for an underwriter in connection with a public offering of the company's securities waived the privilege with respect to the review. The court rejected the client's arguments that it had been "coerced" to disclose the review "by the legal duty of due diligence and the millions of dollars riding on the public offering of registered securities." It held that regardless of "the economic imperatives, the privilege is lost, not because of voluntariness or involuntariness, but because the need for confidentiality served by the privilege is inconsistent with such disclosure."[128]

On the other hand, in *Leibel v. GMC*,[129] the court held that although a corporation had previously disclosed what was otherwise a privileged document in a separate case that had proceeded in a different jurisdiction, the disclosure did not automatically constitute waiver of the attorney-client privilege in the case at bar.[130] In *Leibel*, the court remanded the case for further consideration because it held that the district court must conduct a separate analysis of whether the corporation had waived the privilege, reasoning that to hold otherwise would allow a party to invade the privilege even if it obtained the communication inadvertently, fraudulently or in bad faith. Inadvertent waiver in the previous litigation did not necessarily extend to the current case.[131]

The attorney-client privilege is not waived by sharing a privileged communication with one who has a common legal interest concerning the subject matter of the document or who is involved in the "joint defense" of the litigation.[132] However, "the [common interest] must be identical, not similar, and be legal, not solely commercial."[133]

Two types of communications are protected by the attorney-client privilege in the context of a common legal interest: "(1) communications between co-defendants in actual litigation and their counsel; and (2) communications between potential co-defendants and their counsel."[134]

Finally, with regard to drafts of a final report, some courts have held that disclosure of a final report to a third party does not destroy the underlying privilege attached to the interim drafts of that report.[135]

Given the varying interpretations of the scope of waiver, it seems prudent to exercise caution in the disclosure of privileged materials and to assert the privilege as to all communications which may be privileged.

The Work-Product Doctrine in the Corporate Client Context

The work-product doctrine provides an important protection for materials prepared by in-house and outside counsel. It is recognized, by the Supreme Court, as being "distinct from and broader than the attorney-client privilege."[136] Certain materials not protected by the attorney-client privilege may, nevertheless, be protected under the work-product doctrine, at least during the discovery process.

The Distinction between the Attorney-Client Privilege and the Work-Product Doctrine

The attorney-client privilege and the work product doctrine are distinct theories of protection, and the purpose and requirements of each are different. In *In re Sealed Case*,[137] the D.C. Circuit explained:

> To the extent that they overlap, the work-product privilege is the broader of the two. The attorney-client privilege covers only confidential communications between attorney and client, and it focuses on the attorney-client relationship. Thus, information other than "communications," or communications that do not involve both attorney and client, are unprotected. . . . The work-product privilege, on the other hand, is not limited to communications. At the very least, it applies to material "obtained or prepared by an

adversary's counsel" in the course of his legal duties, provided that the work was done "with an eye toward litigation." The work-product privilege protects both the attorney-client relationship and a complex of individual interests particular to attorneys that their clients may not share.[138]

The Ninth Circuit, however, interpreted the attorney-client privilege to be the more absolute of the two, in that it cannot be abrogated on a showing of unavailability of the information through other means.[139] Having found the statement at issue to be protected by the attorney-client privilege, and faced with an argument that the privilege must give way in view of the witness's expressed intention to invoke the Fifth Amendment at his deposition, the court decided that "[a]n unavailability exception is . . . inconsistent with the nature and purpose of the privilege."[140] It found that, in ordering production of the privileged statement based on plaintiffs' claim that the information could not otherwise be obtained, the lower court had confused the notions of attorney-client privilege and work-product doctrine. It explained: "The principal difference between the attorney-client privilege and the work-product doctrine, in terms of the protections each provides, is that the privilege cannot be overcome by a showing of need, whereas a showing of need may justify discovery of an attorney's work product."[141]

Such necessity or justification, according to the present rule, may exist upon a showing that the materials are needed to prepare the case and that the materials or their substantial equivalent cannot otherwise be obtained without undue hardship via other means.[142]

The party requesting the otherwise privileged documents must "make a strong showing" of the materials' relevance, importance, and lack of attainability.[143]

Moreover, since the work-product doctrine is designed "to protect an attorney's work product from falling into the hands of an adversary," the effect of disclosure to a third party is different. "Most courts hold that to waive the protection of the work-product doctrine, the disclosure must enable an adversary to gain access to the information."[144]

The Application of the Work-Product Doctrine

The work-product doctrine is codified in Rule 26(b)(3) of the Federal Rules of Civil Procedure. In distinction to the attorney-client privilege, it is federal law which governs the application and interpretation of the work-product doctrine in federal court litigation, even in diversity cases.[145] In parallel with the privilege, the burden of demonstrating the applicability of the work-product doctrine falls upon the party seeking its protection.[146] The immunity only protects items produced or prepared for litigation; it does not protect against the disclosure of underlying facts.[147] Likewise, this immunity from discovery is inapplicable to business documents or those "'documents prepared in the ordinary course of business that would have been created in essentially similar form irrespective of the litigation' even if such documents would also be useful in the event of litigation."[148]

Although some documents included within an attorney's work product may not actually be prepared by counsel, this fact is not necessarily dispositive of whether the proponent has met the second element.[149] The doctrine itself expressly protects materials prepared by "a co-party or a representative of a party, including attorneys, consultants, agents, or investigators."[150] As the Supreme Court observed in *Nobles*, attorneys must rely, out of necessity, on the assistance of other people when preparing for trial; their materials are likewise protected.[151]

"Opinion work product" is almost absolutely protected against disclosure.[152] Only with an express waiver can opinion product become discoverable.[153] However, "ordinary or fact work product" is not; it retains limited protection and can be discoverable even absent a waiver.[154] Work-product protection is granted only until the adversary can demonstrate some necessity or justification for obtaining the materials.[155]

Materials Obtained or Prepared "In Anticipation of Litigation"

Only documents prepared "in anticipation of litigation" are protected under the work-product doctrine.[156] Thus, the application of the doctrine depends on how imminent the anticipated litigation is.

Materials prepared before and subsequently collected or used in anticipation of litigation are not work product, and documents prepared in the ordinary course of business, even if related to litigation, are not protected.[157] In *Bartley v. Isuzu Motors*,[158] the court held that prior depositions and other materials collected by plaintiff's attorney from other sources, including ATLA, had not been prepared in anticipation of the pending litigation and hence were not protected by the work-product doctrine.

In *United States v. Adlman*,[159] however, the court took a broad view of the timing requirement. Pointing out that specific circumstances may indicate a reasonable probability of future litigation, although no "event" has yet occurred,[160] the court reasoned that "there is no rule that bars application of work-product protection to documents created prior to the event giving rise to litigation. . . . In many instances, the expected litigation is quite concrete, notwithstanding that the events giving rise to it have not yet occurred."

Work-Product Protection in Subsequent Litigation

It has generally been held that work product from a prior action retains its qualified immunity from disclosure even in subsequent, unrelated litigation.[161] However, some courts have required that the two cases be related.[162] And in *Westinghouse Elec. Corp. v. Republic of Philippines*,[163] the court held that disclosure of work product in the context of SEC and DOJ investigations waived all work-product protection "as against all other adversaries."[164]

Conclusion

Given the judicially perceived tension between the protection of the attorney-client privilege and the avowed search for truth through the discovery process, it is impossible to guarantee the confidentiality of an internal investigative report. The law in this area is complex and subject to changing and developing interpretations. Nevertheless, certain measures can maximize the likelihood that confidentiality will be maintained. Well before embarking on an internal investigation or the preparation of an investigative report, one should identify and evaluate the affirmative steps that can be taken to substantiate the applicability of the attorney-client privilege and the work-product doctrine to the investigative process, any resulting report and underlying documentation, and the maintenance of the materials in a manner clearly designed to restrict access and to preserve confidentiality.

Notes

1. *See* Upjohn Co. v. United States, 449 U.S. 383, 391, 101 S. Ct. 677, 683 (1981); Diversified Industries v. Meredith, 572 F.2d 596, 608-09 (8th Cir. 1977) ("In a corporation, it may be necessary to glean information relevant to a legal problem from middle management and non-management personnel as well as from top executives."). Thus, the scope of the privilege in the corporate context is a recurrent, fact-intensive issue for the courts, one to be determined on a case-by-case basis. United States v. Edwards, 39 F. Supp. 2d 716, 731 (M.D. La. 1999), *citing* Upjohn v. United States, 449 U.S. at 396-7.

2. 89 F. Supp. 357 (D. Mass. 1950).

3. *Id.* at 359.

4. E.I. du Pont de Nemours & Co. v. Forma-Pack, Inc., 351 Md. 396, 418 (Md. 1998) (listing cases that questioned the broad scope that *United Shoe* gave the attorney-client privilege with regards to corporations); Philadelphia v. Westinghouse Elec. Corp., 210 F. Supp. 483, 485 (E.D. Pa. 1962) (suggesting that the *United Shoe* holding, which extended the attorney-client privilege to a broad class of corporate employees, conflicted with Hickman v. Taylor).

5. 210 F. Supp. 483 (E.D. Pa. 1962).

6. *Id.* at 484.

7. *Id.*

8. *Id.* at 485.

9. *Id.*

10. Consolidation Coal Co. v. Bucyrus-Erie Co., 432 N.E.2d 250, 257 (Ill. 1982) (holding that the control group test strikes a reasonable balance between competing policies); *In re* Grand Jury Investigation, 599 F.2d 1224, 1237 (3d Cir. 1979) (collecting cases).

11. 449 U.S. at 392, 101 S. Ct. at 684.

12. *Id.* at 383, 101 S. Ct. at 677.

13. *Id.* at 392, 101 S. Ct. at 684.

14. 449 U.S. at 390, 101 S. Ct. at 683.

15. 449 U.S. at 391-92, 101 S. Ct. at 683-84.

16. 449 U.S. at 394-95, 101 S. Ct. at 685.

17. Baisley v. Missisquoi Cemetery Ass'n, 708 A.2d 924, 929 (Vt. 1998).

18. 423 F.2d 487 (7th Cir. 1970), *aff'd*, 400 U.S. 348 (1971).

19. Consolidation Coal Co. v. Bucyrus-Erie Co., 432 N.E.2d 250, 255 (1982).

20. 423 F.2d at 490-91.

21. *Id.* at 491-92.

22. *See* Samaritan Found. v. Goodfarb, 862 P.2d 870 (Ariz. 1993) (although the control group test is underinclusive, the subject matter test can be overinclusive); Baisley v. Missisquoi Cemetery Ass'n, 708 A.2d 924, 929 (Vt. 1998) ("interpreted in its broadest sense, the attorney-client privilege would create a vast zone of silence around corporate affairs").

23. 862 P.2d at 876-78.

24. *Id.* at 880.

25. Blumenthal v. Kimber Mfg. Inc., 826 A.2d 1088 (Conn. 2003) (adopting a four-part test that resembles neither the control group nor the subject matter test); Doe *ex rel.* Doe v. Archdiocese of

the Catholic Church, 721 So. 2d 428, 429 (Fla. App. 1998) (using a test that combined the tests set forth in *Harper & Row* and *Diversified Industries*); Nat'l Converting & Fulfillment Corp. v. Bankers Trust Corp., 134 F. Supp. 2d 804, 805-06 (N.D. Tex. 2001) (holding that the Texas legislature adopted both the control group and subject matter tests within the language of its Rule of Evidence 503(a)(2)(A) and (B)).

26. *See, e.g.,* Sterling Fin. Mgt. L.P., v. UBS PaineWebber Inc., 782 N.E.2d 895, 448 (Ill. App. Ct. 2002); Land v. GMC, 2000 U.S. Dist. LEXIS 9809 *1, 3 (E.D. Pa. 2000) (collecting both Pennsylvania and Michigan cases that hold "an employee or agent must act in a representative capacity and be authorized to bind or act on behalf of the corporation regarding the subject matter at issue to qualify as a 'client' for purposes of the attorney-client privilege"); Leer v. Chicago, M., S. P. & P. R. Co., 308 N.W.2d 305, 309 (Minn. 1981) (if an employee is only a witness and not a party to a subsequent action, any communication he made in a general investigation does not create an attorney-client relationship).

27. Western Resources, Inc. v. Union Pac. R.R. Co., 2002 U.S. Dist. LEXIS 1911 *1, 25 (D. Kan. 2002).

28. *Id. See also* Teltron, Inc. v. Alexander, 132 F.R.D. 394 (E.D. Pa. 1990).

29. United States Postal Serv. v. Phelps Dodge Ref. Corp., 852 F. Supp. 156, 160 (E.D.N.Y. 1994). *See also* Caremark, Inc. v. Affiliated Computer Servs., Inc., 192 F.R.D. 263, 268 (N.D. Ill. 2000) (extending privilege to a legal team that consisted of in-house and outside counsel as well as an intermediary agent coordinating the legal strategy, "an example of the modern corporate reality").

30. United States v. Chevrontexaco Corp., 241 F. Supp. 2d 1065, 1076-1077 (N.D. Cal. 2002).

31. *See, e.g.,* Burroughs Wellcome Co. v. Barr Labs, Inc., 143 F.R.D. 611 (E.D.N.C. 1992).

32. *In re* Currency Conversion Fee Antitrust Litig., 2002 U.S. Dist. LEXIS 21196 *1, 6 (S.D.N.Y. 2002).

33. *See* Fleet Bus. Credit Corp. v. Hill City Oil Co., 2002 U.S. Dist. LEXIS 23896 (W.D. Tenn. 2002) (when deciding whether privilege exists, the determinative factors are the "who, when, and why involved" in the exchange of information).

34. Arcuri v. Trump Taj Mahal Assocs., 154 F.R.D. 97, 102 (D.N.J. 1994).

35. 121 F. Supp. 792, 794 (D. Del. 1954).

36. *Id.* at 794.

37. City of Springfield v. Rexnord Corp., 196 F.R.D. 7, 8-9 (D. Mass. 2000) (in-house counsel wears many hats and distinctions are difficult to make). *See* United States Postal Serv. v. Phelps Dodge Ref. Corp., 852 F. Supp. 156, 160 (E.D.N.Y. 1994) (privilege applied even though laymen could have performed the tasks counsel completed, "because the transaction was not a routine business matter and required considerable involvement with a state regulatory agency, . . . [therefore] the expectation of confidentiality [was] arguably greater").

38. Potter v. United States, 2002 U.S. Dist. LEXIS 20031 *1, 18 (S.D. Cal. 2002) (corporate officer who was corporate counsel wore two hats and acted as both but the court delineated between the roles and segregated privileged from non-privileged communication).

39. 572 F.2d 596 (8th Cir. 1978) (en banc).

40. *Id.* at 610.

41. *Id.*

42. *Id.*

43. *Id.* at 614.

44. *Id.* at 615.

45. *See* City of Springfield v. Rexnord Corp., 196 F.R.D. at 9.

46. Financial Technologies Int'l v. Smith, 2000 U.S. Dist. LEXIS 18220 *1, 20 (S.D.N.Y. 2000) (refusing to extend to corporations the "reasonable belief exception" afforded individuals and hold-

ing that corporate in-house counsel must actually be, not merely believed to be, a licensed attorney in order to be protected under the attorney-client privilege).

47.   572 F.2d 596, 611 n.5 (8th Cir. 1978).

48.   572 F.2d 611 n.5.

49.   *In re* Grand Jury Subpoena, 274 F.3d 563, 571 (1st Cir. 2001); *See* United States v. Martin, 278 F.3d 988, 1000 (9th Cir. 2002) ("corporation's privilege does not extend automatically to Defendant [officer] in his individual capacity").

50.   *In re* Grand Jury Subpoena, 274 F.3d at 571.

51.   *Id.* at 1000.

52.   *Id. See also* Philadelphia v. Westinghouse Elec. Corp., 210 F. Supp. 483, 484 (E.D. Pa. 1962) (individual employee's privilege claim rejected since employee had been specifically advised by attorney that if his disclosures revealed a violation of written company policies, the lawyer would report the violations to management).

53.   805 F.2d 120 (3d Cir. 1986).

54.   *See In re* Grand Jury Subpoena, 274 F.3d 563, 571 (1st Cir. 2001) (collecting cases).

55.   *Id.*

56.   Grand Jury Proceedings v. United States, 156 F.3d 1038, 1041-2 (10th Cir. 1998).

57.   *Id.* at 1041-2.

58.   United States v. Martin, 278 F.3d at 1000.

59.   449 U.S. at 394 n.3, 101 S. Ct. at 685 n.3.

60.   Admiral Ins. Co. v. United States Dist. Court, 881 F.2d 1486, 1493 (9th Cir. 1988), *quoting In re* Coordinated Pretrial Proceedings in Petroleum Products Antitrust Litig., 658 F.2d 1355, 1361 (9th Cir. 1981), *cert. denied*, 455 U.S. 990 (1982).

61.   89 F.R.D. 410, 414 (S.D. Ohio 1981).

62.   *Id.* at 414.

63.   Infosystems, Inc. v. Ceridian Corp., 197 F.R.D. 303, 305 (E.D. Mich. 2000) ("a close reading of Upjohn fails to support this extension"); Peralta v. Cendant Corp., 190 F.R.D. 38, 40 (D. Conn. 1999) ("wholesale application of the Upjohn principles to former employees . . . is not justified by the underlying reasoning of Upjohn").

64.   Peralta v. Cendant, 190 F.R.D at 39, 41. *See also* Infosystems, Inc. v. Ceridian Corp., 197 F.R.D at 305-6; Valassis v. Samelson, 143 F.R.D. 118, 124 (E.D. Mich. 1992) (privilege covers former employee who still had a present connection to the corporation or who still held confidential information unique to himself, which was discussed with current corporate counsel).

65.   Infosystems, Inc. v. Ceridian Corp., 197 F.R.D. at 305 (agreeing with the *Valassis* and *Peralta* courts).

66.   *Id.* at 305, *quoting* Clark Equip. Co. v. Lift Parts Mfg. Co., 1985 U.S. Dist. LEXIS 15457 *1, 5 (N.D. Ill. 1985).

67.   Infosystems, Inc. v. Ceridian Corp., 197 F.R.D. at 306. *See also* City of New York v. Coastal Oil N.Y., Inc., 2000 U.S. Dist. LEXIS 1010 *1, 6 (S.D.N.Y. 2000).

68.   *In re* Bieter Co., 16 F.3d 929, 937 (8th Cir. 1994) (no distinction between types of employees); Energy Capital Corp. v. United States, 45 Fed. Cl. 481, 491 (U.S. Claims 2000) (reviewing case law and treatise materials; concluding that theoretically an independent contractor could be treated as the client's agent and covered by the privilege); Alliance Constr. Solutions, Inc. v. Dep't of Corr., 54 P.3d 861, 869 (Colo. 2002) (certain circumstances warrant regarding communications between an independent contractor and the entity's counsel as privileged); John E. Sexton, *A Post-Upjohn Consideration of the Corporate Attorney-Client Privilege*, 57 N.Y.U. L. Rev. 443, 500 (1982) (explaining the rationale for the inclusion of independent contractors within the attorney-client privilege, a rationale approved by *In re* Bieter and Energy Capital); *but cf.* Miramar Constr. Co. v. Home Depot, Inc., 167 F. Supp. 2d 182, 185 (D. P.R. 2001) (declining to extend attorney-client privilege to a corporation's contract employee).

69. Energy Capital Corp. v. United States, 45 Fed. Cl. at 492.

70. *Id.*

71. *Id.*

72. Miramar Constr. Co. v. Home Depot, Inc., 167 F. Supp. 2d at 185.

73. *Id.*

74. 881 F.2d 1486 (9th Cir. 1988).

75. *Id.* at 1493.

76. 150 F.R.D. 465 (S.D.N.Y. 1993).

77. *Id.* at 491.

78. *Id. See also* Southern Air Transp., Inc. v. SAT Group, Inc., 255 B.R. 706, 711 (S.D. Ohio 2000) ("[p]arent and subsidiary corporations generally share a common interest, and may, in appropriate circumstances, be considered a single client for purposes of the attorney-client privilege"). *Cf.* Cary Oil Co. v. MG Ref. & Mktg., Inc., 2000 U.S. Dist. LEXIS 17587 (S.D.N.Y 2000) (defendant subsidiary corporation did not waive privilege when it disclosed information to the parent corporation, despite the parent's non-involvement with the litigation).

79. 17 N.J. Tax 178, 185 (N.J. Tax 1998).

80. *Id.*

81. *See* Financial Technologies Int'l v. Smith, 2000 U.S. Dist. LEXIS 18220, 15-16 (S.D.N.Y. 2000) (collecting cases); *In re* Bieter Co., 16 F.3d 929 (8th Cir. 1994) (privilege extended to consultant); McCaugherty v. Siffermann, 132 F.R.D. 234 (N.D. Cal. 1990) (under rationale of *Upjohn*, privilege extends to consultants).

82. Olson v. Accessory Controls & Equip. Corp., 254 Conn. 145, 160 (Conn. 2000).

83. *Id.*

84. *Id. See also* United States v. Chevrontexaco Corp., 241 F. Supp. 2d 1065, 1072 (N.D. Ca. 2002); United States v. Adlman, 68 F.3d 1495, 1499-1500 (2d Cir. 1995) ("What is vital to the privilege is that the communication be made in confidence for the purpose of obtaining legal advice from the lawyer. If what is sought is not legal advice but only accounting service . . . or if the advice sought is the accountant's rather than the lawyer's, no privilege exists," *quoting* United States v. Kovel, 296 F.2d 918, 922 (2d Cir. 1961)).

85. 241 F. Supp. 2d 1065 (N.D. Cal. 2002).

86. *Id.* at 1072.

87. *Id.*

88. *Id.* at 1072. *See also* Caremark, Inc. v. Affiliated Computer Servs., Inc., 192 F.R.D. 263, 269 (N.D. Ill. 2000) (whether privilege extends to communications with an agent of the corporation and the corporation's attorney depends on the service given by the agent). *Cf.* Viacom, Inc. v. Sumitomo Corp., 200 F.R.D. 213, 220 (S.D.N.Y. 2001) (extending privilege to a third party consultant, retained by defense counsel, because the court found the consultant to be the functional equivalent of an employee of defendant).

89. Garner v. Wolfinbarger, 430 F.2d 1093 (5th Cir. 1970) *cert. denied*, 401 U.S. 974 (1971).

90. 430 F.2d 1093 (5th Cir. 1970) *cert. denied*, 401 U.S. 974 (1971).

91. *Id.* at 1103-04. *See also In re* Dow Corning Corp., 261 F.3d 280, 286 (2d Cir. 2001); *In re* Occidental Petroleum Corp., 217 F.3d 293, 297-8 (5th Cir. 2000).

92. *See* Picard Chem. Profit Sharing Plan v. Perrigo Co., 951 F. Supp. 679, 686-7 (W.D. Mich. 1996).

93. *See* National Football League Properties, Inc. v. Superior Court, 65 Cal. App. 4th 100, 107 (Cal. App. 1998) (declining to adopt the federal exception set forth in *Garner*); Milroy v. Hanson, 875 F. Supp. 646, 651 (D. Neb. 1995) (same). United States v. Mett, 178 F.3d 1058, 1063 (9th Cir. 1999) (collecting cases) noted that various circuits recognize a genuine fiduciary exception to privilege in fiduciary relationships, as in the case before it, where an employer was acting as trustee in an ERISA matter.

94. Bairnco Corp. Securities Litig. v. Keene Corp., 148 F.R.D. 91 (S.D.N.Y. 1993); Gutter v. E.I. DuPont de Nemours, 124 F. Supp. 2d 1291, 1298 (S.D. Fla. 2000) (collecting cases).

95. X Corp. v. Doe, 805 F. Supp. 1298, 1307 (E.D. Va. 1992).

96. *Id.*

97. Gutter v. E.I. Dupont de Nemous, 124 F. Supp. 2d at 1299.

98. United States v. Braun, 2003 U.S. Dist. LEXIS 14340 *1, 12 (N.D. Cal. 2003). *See also* United States v. Barrier Indus., 1997 U.S. Dist. LEXIS 318 *1, (S.D.N.Y. 1997) (using a probable cause standard or equivalent).

99. *Braun*, 2003 U.S. Dist. LEXIS 14340 at 11.

100. *See* Rhone-Poulenc Rorer Inc. v. Home Indem. Co., 32 F.3d 851, 863 (3d Cir. 1994).

101. *In re* Grand Jury Proceedings v. United States, 2003 U.S. App. LEXIS 22396 *1, 6-8 (2d Cir. 2003).

102. *Id. See also* Fitzgerald v. Cantor, 1999 Del. Ch. LEXIS 10 (Del. Ch. 1999) (for the "at issue" exception to apply, the party requesting the privileged information must be placed at a disadvantage due to the inability to review the concealed information).

103. *See* Sackman v. Liggett Group, 920 F. Supp. 357, 365 (E.D.N.Y. 1996) (collecting cases that recognize an exception to the attorney-client privilege when "a compelling public policy . . . concern" exists such as "protecting the public health") (privilege decision vacated on other grounds).

104. 135 F.R.D. 94, 100 (D.N.J. 1990).

105. *Id.* at 100. *But see* Arcuri v. Trump Taj Mahal Assocs., 154 F.R.D. 97, 105 (D.N.J. 1994) ("The attorney-client privilege, if an[d] when attached to a communication (and excepting, of course, valid waiver), is absolute, and there is no 'balance' to be 'tested,' and no 'needs' test, as might be the case with a qualified privilege.").

106. X Corp. v. Doe, 805 F. Supp. 1298 (E.D. Va. 1992).

107. Hydraflow, Inc. v. Enidine Inc., 145 F.R.D. 626 (W.D.N.Y. 1993); Contra Fleet Bus. Credit Corp. v. Hill City Oil Co., 2002 U.S. Dist. LEXIS 23896 *1, 9 (W.D. Tenn. 2002) ("privilege 'belongs to the client' and only the client may waive it").

108. Tenn. Laborers Health & Welfare Fund v. Columbia/HCA Healthcare Corp., 293 F.3d 289, 294 (5th Cir. 2002).

109. Contra Fleet Bus. Credit Corp. v. Hill City Oil Co., 2002 U.S. Dist. LEXIS 23896 at 9.

110. Baker's Aid v. Hussmann Foodservice Co., 1988 U.S. Dist. LEXIS 14528 *1, 13 (E.D.N.Y. 1988). *See also* Lloyds Bank PLC v. Republic of Ecuador, 1997 U.S. Dist. LEXIS 2416 *1, 13 (S.D.N.Y. 1997).

111. Alldread v. Grenada, 988 F.2d 1425, 1434 (5th Cir. 1993).

112. Gray v. Bicknell, 86 F.3d 1472, 1483 (8th Cir. 1996).

113. *Id.*

114. New York v. Microsoft Corp., 2002 U.S. Dist. LEXIS 7684 *1, 9 (D.C. Cir. 2002) ("even where the disclosure was inadvertent," waiver exists; and "[s]hort of court-compelled disclosure or other equally extraordinary circumstances, [the D.C. Circuit] will not distinguish between various degrees of 'voluntariness' in waivers of the attorney-client privilege").

115. *Gray, supra* note 112 at 1483.

116. *Id.*

117. *Id.*

118. *Id. See also Hydraflow*, 145 F.R.D. 626 (W.D.N.Y. 1993); *Gray*, 86 F.3d 1472, 1483 (8th Cir. 1996).

119. *Hydraflow,* 145 F.R.D. at 637 (W.D.N.Y. 1993). *See also Gray*, 86 F.3d at 1483 (8th Cir. 1996).

120. Lloyds Bank PLC v. Republic of Ecuador, 1997 U.S. Dist. LEXIS 2416 at 10-11. *See also* Abamar Hous. & Dev. v. Lisa Daly Lady Decor, 698 So. 2d 279 (Fla. App. 1997).

121. 698 So. 2d 279 (Fla. App. 1997).

122. *Id.* at 276, 278. *See also* United States *ex rel.* Bagley v. TRW, Inc., 204 F.R.D. 170, 183 (C.D. Cal. 2001) (although no formal ethical rules required the recipient of documents that were obviously privileged to return them, "many authorities supported such an approach.")

123. Tenn. Laborers Health & Welfare Fund v. Columbia/HCA Healthcare Corp., 293 F.3d at 294-95.

124. *See, e.g.,* Smith v. Armour Pharmaceutical Co., 838 F. Supp. 1573, 1575 (S.D. Fla. 1993); Hechinger Inv. Co. v. Fleet Retail Fin. Group, 2003 U.S. Dist. LEXIS 22402 (D. Del. 2003) ("[t]he general rule that a disclosure waives not only the specific communication but also the subject matter of it in other communications is not appropriate in the case of inadvertent disclosure. . . . In a proper case of inadvertent disclosure, the waiver should cover only the specific document in issue.").

125. *In re* Grand Jury Proceedings October 12, 1995, 78 F.3d 251 (6th Cir. 1996) (defining subject matter narrowly); Texaco P. R. v. Department of Consumer Affairs, 60 F.3d 867 (1st Cir. 1995); (applying the principles to the litigation generally, Westinghouse Elec. Corp. v. Republic of Philippines, 951 F.2d 1414 (3d Cir. 1991); Bowne, Inc. v. AmBase Corp., 150 F.R.D. 465, 479 (S.D.N.Y. 1993) ("waiver will be found even if the disclosure took place in a forum other than the lawsuit in which the waiver issue is raised, and even if the disclosure was made for a proper purpose to a person with an interest that is common to him and the privilege holder, unless that common interest is the receipt of legal services by an attorney").

126. 150 F.R.D. at 485 (S.D.N.Y. 1993) ("disclosure in the context of litigation—whether by trial or deposition testimony or by production of documents—will result in an implied waiver broader than the original disclosure itself").

127. 675 F.2d 482 (2d Cir. 1982).

128. *Id.* at 489.

129. 646 N.W.2d 179 (Mich. Ct. App. 2002).

130. *Id.* at 187.

131. *Id.*

132. Graco Children's Prods. v. Dressler, 1995 U.S. Dist. LEXIS 8157 *1, 14 (N.D. Ill. 1995).

133. *Id. See also* Westinghouse Elec. Corp. v. Republic of Philippines, 951 F.2d 1414 (3d Cir. 1991).

134. *In re* Santa Fe Int'l Corp., 272 F.3d 705, 710 (5th Cir. 2001).

135. *In re* Air Crash Disaster at Sioux City, Iowa on July 19, 1989, 133 F.R.D. 515, 518 (N.D. Ill. 1990).

136. S. Scrap Material Co. v. Fleming, 2003 U.S. Dist. LEXIS 10815 *1, 21 (E.D. La. 2003) (*citing* Hickman v. Taylor, 329 U.S. 495, 508 (1947) and United States v. Nobles, 422 U.S. 225, 238 (1975)).

137. 676 F.2d 793 (D.C. App. 1982).

138. 676 F.2d at 808-09.

139. Admiral Ins. Co. v. United States Dist. Court, 881 F.2d 1486 (9th Cir. 1988).

140. *Id.* at 1494.

141. *Id. See also* Westinghouse Elec. Corp. v. Republic of Philippines, 951 F.2d 1414, 1428 (3d Cir. 1991).

142. *See* Fed. R. Civ. P. 26(b)(3); National Union Fire Ins. Co. v. Murray Sheet Metal Co., 967 F.2d 980, 984-85 (4th Cir. 1992).

143. United States v. Duke Energy Corp., 208 F.R.D. 553, 556 (M.D.N.C. 2002). *See also* Prebena Wire Bending Mach. Co. v. Transit Worldwide Corp, 1999 U.S. Dist. LEXIS 18035, *12-13 (S.D.N.Y. 1999) (holding that e-mail documents that addressed testimony, which contained significant probative value regarding a possible admission against interest that a witness could no longer recall, established a substantial need for the e-mails, and prevailed over the work-product doctrine); City of Springfield v. Rexnord Corp., 196 F.R.D. 7, 10 (D. Mass. 2000) (holding that a substantial need existed mandating production of otherwise privileged documents because the material was 20 years old and contained facts given by participants whose current whereabouts were unknown).

144. Westinghouse Elec. Corp. v. Republic of Philippines, 951 F.2d at 1428 (holding that the SEC and the DOJ, in investigating Westinghouse, were in fact adversaries). *See also* Bank Brussels Lambert v. Credit Lyonnais Suisse, 160 F.R.D. 437 (S.D.N.Y. 1995).

145. Remington Arms Co. v. Liberty Mutual Ins. Co., 142 F.R.D. 408, 418 (D. Del. 1992).

146. Leonen v. Johns-Manville, 135 F.R.D. 94, 96 (D.N.J. 1990).

147. Blockbuster Entertainment Corp. v. McComb Video, Inc., 145 F.R.D. 402, 403 (M.D. La. 1992).

148. Long-Term Capital Holdings v. United States, 2002 U.S. Dist. LEXIS 23224 (D. Conn. 2002), *quoting* U.S. v. Adlman, 134 F.3d 1194, 1196 (2d Cir. 1998).

149. S. Scrap Material Co. v. Fleming, 2003 U.S. Dist. LEXIS 10815 at 20.

150. *Id. See also* Rule 26(b)(3); *Prebena*, 1999 U.S. Dist. LEXIS 18035 at *7 (including work compiled by consultants, sureties, indemnitors, insurers, or other agents as well).

151. *Nobles, supra* note 136 at 225, 238-39 (1975).

152. *Hickman, supra* note 136 at 511-12.

153. Tenn. Laborers Health & Welfare Fund v. Columbia/HCA Healthcare Corp., 293 F.3d at 294.

154. *Id.*; Remington Arms Co. v. Liberty Mutual Insurance Co., 142 F.R.D. 408, 419 (D. Del. 1992).

155. *Id.*

156. Leonen v. Johns-Manville, 135 F.R.D. 94, 97 (D.N.J. 1990) ("there must have been an identifiable specific claim or impending litigation when the materials were prepared").

157. *See, e.g.,* Bank Brussels Lambert, 160 F.R.D. 437, 449 (S.D.N.Y. 1995).

158. 158 F.R.D. 165 (D. Colo. 1994).

159. 68 F.3d 1495, 1501 (2d Cir. 1995).

160. "If, for example, a party expects to be sued by a particular adverse claimant in the event it undertakes to trade under a disputed mark or publishes a book the copyright of which is contested, we see no reason why work-product protection should not apply to preparatory litigation studies undertaken by the party (or its representatives) before it begins to trade under the contested mark or publishes the book. Nor should the answer be different for a party that prepares to initiate the lawsuit in the expectation that another is about to begin trade under the party's mark, or about to publish a work to which the party claims the copyright." 68 F.3d at 1501.

161. Shipes v. BIC Corp., 154 F.R.D. 301, 305 (M.D. Ga. 1994); S. Scrap Material Co. v. Fleming, 2003 U.S. Dist. LEXIS 10815 at 23 (the work product privilege "does not evaporate . . . when the litigation for which the document was prepared has ended").

162. Leonen v. Johns-Manville, 135 F.R.D. 94, 97 (D.N.J. 1990) (requiring a "close connection in parties or subject matter between the two matters").

163. 951 F. 2d 1414, 1429 (3d Cir. 1991).

164. *See also In re* Worlds of Wonder Securities Litig., 147 F.R.D. 208 (N.D. Cal. 1992).

CHAPTER 12

Applying the Attorney-Client Privilege to Investigations Involving Attorneys: What Is Fair Game in Discovery?

DAVID E. BLAND
SCOTT G. JOHNSON
ELISABETH M. WILL

Introduction

Clients often retain attorneys to conduct investigations in a myriad of different factual settings. Examples include an investigation of potential medical malpractice on behalf of a hospital,[1] an investigation of sexual discrimination complaints on behalf of an employer,[2] an investigation on behalf of a factory owner of a factory explosion that killed and injured several on-site contractors,[3] an investigation of potential arson on behalf of a property insurance carrier,[4] an investigation of potential fraud and other improprieties on behalf of a bank,[5] an investigation on behalf of a multinational corporation of questionable payments to a foreign governmental official to secure government business,[6] and an investigation into the insurance aspects surrounding the World Trade Center attack.[7] Attorneys then communicate the results of their investigations to their clients.[8]

When the client's adversary seeks discovery of the communications between the client and the attorney investigator, the following question arises: What documents or information are fair game in discovery? Generally, the attorney-client privilege protects only those communications between attorney and client where the attorney is acting in his or her capacity as an attorney and not in some other capacity. Similarly, the attorney-client privilege applies only to those communications between attorneys and clients made for the purpose of obtaining or giving legal advice.[9]

Therefore, to determine whether the attorney-client privilege shields production of the documents and information relating to an attorney's investigation, one must first ascertain whether the attorney was acting in his or her capacity as an attorney and, if so, whether the attorney-client communication containing the results of the investigation was made with the purpose of giving legal advice. The scope of the attorney-client privilege also may depend upon whether the client is a corporation or an individual and whether the attorney's advice is based on information from non-clients. The work-product doctrine also may protect written documents containing the attorney's investigative results if the investigation was performed "in anticipation of litigation." This chapter will address these issues as well as others that arise as a result of an attorney's investigation.

The Attorney-Client Privilege Defined

The attorney-client privilege is the "oldest of the privileges for confidential communications known to the common law."[10] Its purpose is to "encourage full and frank communication between attorneys and their clients and thereby promote broader public interests in the observance of law and administration of justice."[11] Thus, it affords complete protection from disclosure to confidential communications between attorney and client, but is subject to several exceptions.[12] The "privilege protects both client communications to their attorneys and communications from the attorney to the client that include legal advice or reflect information provided by the client in confidence."[13] But since the privilege hinders full discovery of the truth, it is sometimes narrowly construed.[14]

The following criteria are typical of the requirements most jurisdictions have established to determine whether the attorney-client privilege applies: (1) the person claiming the privilege either is or seeks to be a client; (2) the person to whom the communication was made is an attorney acting as such; (3) the communication relates to matters conveyed by the client to the attorney in confidence for the purpose of obtaining a legal opinion, or legal services, or for assistance in legal proceedings; and (4) the privilege has been claimed and not waived by the client.[15]

While the attorney-client privilege protects the disclosure of confidential information communicated between a client and an attorney for the purpose of obtaining or giving legal advice or assistance,[16] the attorney-client privilege does not prevent the disclosure of facts, documents, or other matters not privileged.[17] Thus, during discovery, a client must disclose the facts of which he is aware, whether or not he disclosed them to his attorney, but neither he nor his attorney can be questioned about whether those facts were disclosed and what advice was given.[18] Similarly, documents supplied to an attorney are not protected from disclosure in discovery, but whether or not they were provided to the attorney is a privileged matter.[19] Documents created by virtue of the attorney-client relationship may be protected from disclosure by the work-product doctrine.[20]

The attorney-client privilege applies not only to communications made directly to attorneys, but also to communications made to the subordinates or employees of attorneys, such as investigators, paralegals, law clerks, secretaries, or other persons acting as agents of the attorney.[21] Thus, statements made by the client to a private investigator employed by the client's attorney are protected by the attorney-client privilege to the same extent as if made directly to the attorney.[22]

Is the Attorney Investigator Acting as an Attorney?

The attorney-client privilege attaches only to communications made to an attorney acting in his or her "capacity as such."[23] Thus, the first issue addressed is whether an attorney hired to conduct an investigation is acting in his or her capacity as an attorney. Generally, an attorney is acting in the capacity of an attorney when he or she is being consulted by a client for the purpose of obtaining legal services or advice.[24] The privilege will not apply to attorney-client communications in cases where the client hires the attorney for business or personal advice or to perform the work of a non-lawyer.[25] Many courts dealing with attorney investigations in the insurance context, however, have had great difficulty in drawing the line between attorneys who are rendering legal advice and those who are merely performing the ordinary business of claims investigation for their clients.[26]

Attorney Investigator Acting in Capacity of Attorney

The New York Court of Appeals provided an excellent analysis of the "acting as such" requirement in *Spectrum Systems International Corp. v. Chemical Bank.*[27] There, Chemical Bank retained a law firm to "perform an investigation and render legal advice to Chemical regarding possible fraud by its employees and outside vendors, and to counsel Chemical with respect to litigation options."[28] The law firm interviewed Chemical's employees, a former Chemical officer, and representatives of Spectrum itself.[29] The law firm then prepared a report of the results of its investigation. The "Spectrum" section of the report consisted of a three-page narrative describing the problem and the facts, and a final paragraph containing the firm's opinion as to the possible claims, an estimate of Chemical's damages, the weaknesses of such a claim, and the firm's view that there was insufficient proof to establish particular matters described in the letter.[30] After Spectrum sued Chemical and learned about the report, Spectrum requested it in discovery. Chemical moved for a protective order. The Supreme Court, without ever viewing the documents, ordered the documents produced.[31] On appeal, the appellate division modified the order, requiring the trial court to conduct an in camera inspection to determine materiality and necessity.[32] The appellate division, having itself reviewed the documents, concluded that the documents were not privileged because, as the purpose of the investigation was to obtain business, rather than legal, advice, Chemical had not met its burden of proving that the investigation was done by lawyers acting as lawyers:

> The communications pertain to an investigation of the plaintiff corporation and its employees, and suggest corruption prevention measures to be employed in the future. The records do not focus on any imminent litigation, nor on the parties' legal rights or obligations. There is no indication that legal research was performed in order to reach any conclusion with regard to the parties' legal positions. The outside law firm's final report, instead, reveals that meetings were to be held at some future date to discuss the course of action to be taken.
>
> The information requested was assembled to aid defendant in the operation of its business and as such is not exempt from disclosure. . . .

[D]efendant's own affirmation attests to the fact that the material was not prepared primarily for litigation and that, in fact, there were other motivating forces behind its preparation.[33]

The appellate division, nonetheless, granted leave to appeal to the court of appeals, certifying one question: Was its order properly made?[34]

The court of appeals answered this question in the negative.[35] Unlike the appellate division, the court of appeals found that the purpose of the attorney's investigation was to render legal advice to the client:

[T]he privilege is not narrowly confined to the repetition of confidences that were supplied to the lawyer by the client. That cramped view of the attorney-client privilege is at odds with the underlying policy of encouraging open communication; it poses inordinate practical difficulties in making surgical separations so as not to risk revealing client confidences; and it denies that an attorney can have *any* role in fact-gathering incident to the rendition of legal advice and services. The memorandum in *Rossi* included the lawyer's conversations with plaintiff's counsel and with third parties, as well as the lawyer's opinion and advice. Yet we determined, from reviewing the full content and context of the communication, that its purpose was to convey legal advice to the client, and we held the entire document exempt from discovery. We reach the same conclusion here.[36]

[A]n investigative report does not become privileged merely because it was sent to an attorney. Nor is such a report privileged merely because an investigation was conducted by an attorney; a lawyer's communication is not cloaked with privilege when the lawyer is hired for business or personal advice, or to do the work of a non-lawyer. Yet it is also the case that, while information received from third persons may not itself be privileged, a lawyer's communication to a client that includes such information in its legal analysis and advice may stand on different footing. The critical inquiry is whether, viewing the lawyer's communication in its full content and context, it was made in order to render legal advice or services to the client.[37]

Here we conclude that the facts were selected and presented in the [law firm's] report as the foundation for the law firm's advice, and that the communication was primarily and predominantly of a legal character.[38]

The court rejected any requirements that litigation be contemplated or that the attorney's investigative report contain legal research in order to be privileged:

The prospect of litigation may be relevant to the subject of work-product and trial preparation materials, but the attorney-client privilege is not tied to the contemplation of litigation.

. . .

Similarly, the absence of legal research in an attorney's communication is not determinative of privilege, so long as the communication reflects the attorney's professional skills and judgments. Legal advice may be grounded in experience as well as research.[39]

The court reached a similar conclusion in *Leucadia, Inc. v. Reliance Insurance Co.*,[40] where a subsidiary retained outside counsel to draft a company policy on conflicts of interest and to thereafter investigate past conduct to determine whether it complied with the newly drafted policy. Leucadia then filed suit under a bond issued by Reliance, and Reliance sought production of the outside counsel's 65-page report analyzing a series of past transactions on the basis that the information was gathered as part of a factual investigation, not for the rendition of legal services.[41] The court rejected this argument, holding: "Here counsel were engaged to determine whether plaintiff had legally enforceable rights against its employees or its insurer, and the privilege extends to factual matter given to counsel to enable them to render such an opinion."[42]

Courts in other cases have also found that an attorney investigator was acting in his or her capacity as an attorney. For example, in *State ex rel. United States Fidelity & Guaranty Co. v. Canady*[43] and *Dunn v. State Farm Fire & Casualty Co.*,[44] the courts concluded that an attorney retained by the insurer to investigate a suspicious fire was acting as an attorney, not an investigator, and his reports to the insurer were protected communications.[45] Similarly, in *In re State Commission of Investigation Subpoena Number 5441*,[46] the court found that an attorney hired by a school board association was acting in the capacity of a lawyer during his investigation of alleged improprieties in an investment program run by an insurance group of which the school board association was a member.[47] Also, in *Carte Blanche (Singapore) PTE., Ltd. v. Diners Club International, Inc.*,[48] the court found that an attorney investigating a proposed transaction in connection with an existing franchise agreement acted in his capacity as a lawyer in doing so.[49] Finally, the Fourth Circuit, in *In re Allen*, held that an attorney hired to investigate possible document mismanagement and breaches of confidentiality in an Attorney General's office was acting in her capacity as an attorney and that reports relating to her investigation were privileged because they were connected to the furnishing of legal advice.[50]

Attorney Investigator Not Acting in Capacity of Attorney

Courts have not permitted clients to cloak a routine business investigation with attorney-client privilege protection simply by retaining an attorney to conduct that investigation.[51] Most of these cases have arisen in the context of an insurance company client where the courts have found that the attorney's investigation was part of the insurer's ordinary business of claims investigation.[52]

Mission National Insurance Co. v. Lilly[53] is a good example. There, Mission insured a nightclub in northern Minnesota that was destroyed by fire. Because Mission retained the Cozen & O'Connor law firm "as a matter of course to conduct its claims adjustment investigations in a geographic area including Minnesota for all claims exceeding $25,000,"[54] the Cozen firm investigated the loss and corresponded with Mission. After Mission sued for declaratory relief, the insured sought production of Mission's claim file, including correspondence from Cozen's office.[55] The court concluded that the Cozen firm was not acting as counsel, but was performing a business function of Mission, thereby rendering the results of Cozen's investigation discoverable:

> It is not the precepts of law that give rise to the difficulty in this case; instead, the difficulty exists because of plaintiffs [sic] decision, immediately upon receiving notice of the fire, to employ attorneys to fulfill its ordinary business function of claims investigation. Counsel for plaintiff agrees that Cozen & O'Connor was the only party responsible for performing that pure, ordinary business function.
>
> . . .
>
> To the extent that Cozen & O'Connor acted as claims adjusters, then, their work-product, communications to client, and impressions about the facts will be treated herein as the ordinary business of plaintiff, outside the scope of the asserted privileges. This approach results in the majority of the file being discoverable.[56]

A similar result can be seen in *St. Paul Reinsurance Co. v. Commercial Financial Corp.*[57] There, St. Paul Reinsurance Co. and Zurich Reinsurance (London) Ltd. ("the insurers") provided employment practice liability coverage to Commercial Financial Corp. ("CFC").[58] The insurers filed a declaratory judgment action, claiming that CFC made material misrepresentations in its application for coverage.[59] On that basis, they denied CFC's claims for coverage of employment discrimination claims by employees and sought rescission of the policy. CFC filed a counterclaim arguing that the insurers acted in bad faith by denying the claims.[60] To support its defense and counterclaims, CFC sought discovery of certain claim investigations undertaken by the insurers, which the insurers attempted to shield on the grounds of attorney-client privilege.[61] The insurers had hired an attorney to conduct an investigation into CFC's claims. CFC argued that the insurers had an existing obligation in the ordinary course of business to investigate and adjust CFC's claims; thus, the insurers could not shield the claims investigation documents produced by the attorney under the attorney-client privilege.[62] The insurers responded that the documents generated after they began to consider rescission of the policy were privileged, since, at that point, they ceased to be normal business functions.[63]

The court agreed with CFC, rejecting the insurers' argument that the claims investigation files should be shielded from discovery because they were prepared by an attorney.[64] Specifically, the court held that even when the insurers and their attorney began to consider rescission on the grounds of nondisclosure, that consideration was part of the investigation of the availability of coverage, and, therefore, part of an insurer's normal business processes.[65]

While *Lilly* and *St. Paul Reinsurance* present fairly clear examples of an attorney performing an investigation that is part of the client's ordinary business, *National Farmers Union Property & Casualty Co. v. District Court*[66] demonstrates that the line between an ordinary business investigation and an investigation to provide legal advice is not always clear.

In *National Farmers Union*, the court held that communications between the attorneys and their insurance company client that described a factual investigation were not protected by the attorney-client privilege. National Farmers Union ("NFU") provided lease guaranty insurance to its insured, Tenneco, whereby NFU guaranteed payment of rents which came due under a sublease during the policy period in the event of a default. Following a default on the sublease payments, Tenneco made a claim under the NFU policy.[67] NFU referred the matter to its general counsel, who in turn contacted outside counsel to investigate whether the claim was covered under the policy. Outside counsel submitted a lengthy memorandum to NFU's general counsel relating the results of the investigation.[68] NFU subsequently denied Tenneco's claim. Tenneco sued and later filed a motion to compel production of certain documents, including the memorandum from the outside counsel to NFU's general counsel. Following in camera review, the trial court ruled that the first 27 pages of the memorandum were discoverable as ordinary business records.[69]

On appeal, NFU argued that the memorandum was prepared by outside counsel in response to a request for legal advice relating to an investigation of the origination of the policy and the validity of the claim. The Colorado Supreme Court, however, rejected this argument. First, the court reasoned that the attorneys interviewed various officers and employees to determine the factual circumstances concerning the issuance of the policy and were acting more in the role of claims investigators than legal counsel for NFU. Second, the court reasoned that the dominant purpose of the interviews was to provide NFU with the factual circumstances underlying the issuance of the policy. Third, the court noted that there was no showing that the persons interviewed by the attorneys were ever informed that the attorneys were acting as company counsel or that the purpose of the investigation was to allow the company to obtain legal advice. Finally, the court stated that there was no indication that the employees were ever told that the investigation was confidential.[70] The court held that the attorney-client privilege did not protect the first 27 pages of the memorandum because the information was not legal advice but the result of a factual investigation relating to the issuance of the policy.[71] The remainder of the memorandum contained legal conclusions and was not discoverable.[72]

In his dissent, Justice Rovira focused on the role of the attorneys hired by NFU, noting that, upon receiving the insured's demand for payment, NFU referred the matter to its general counsel who, in turn, retained outside attorneys to investigate the circumstances under which the policy was issued and determine whether the insured's claim should be denied.[73] The outside attorneys then initiated the investigation and submitted a memorandum to NFU, which provided information concerning the facts and circumstances surrounding the issuance of the policy and counsel's recommendation regarding whether the insured's claim should be paid.[74] The dissent concluded: "Where, as here, the client seeks the assistance of counsel to determine the operative facts and obtain legal advice based on those facts, I would, consistent with the purposes of the privilege, protect the memorandum against compelled disclosure."[75]

In essence, the Colorado Supreme Court relied on the premise that the attorneys hired by NFU were not acting as attorneys, but rather were acting in another capacity—as claims investigators. *National Farmers Union*, however, appears wrongly decided. The court failed to focus on the real reason the attorneys were retained—to render an opinion concerning whether the insured's claims should be denied. The attorneys had to investigate the facts to determine the circumstances under which the policy was issued before they could render their opinion on the denial of the claim. The attorneys were not acting as claims investigators, but rather as attorneys hired to investigate the factual circumstances and render a legal opinion accordingly.[76]

Investigations conducted by attorneys hired by insureds may also be discoverable as illustrated by the recent decision in *SR International Business Insurance Co. v. World Trade Center Properties LLC,*[77] which arose out of the September 11, 2001 attack on the World Trade Center. There, a lender for World Trade Center leaseholders retained an insurance advisor in July 2001 to help determine the amount of insurance coverage that the leaseholders should obtain.[78] After the September 11 attack, the lender's employees and the insurance advisor conducted an investigation to gather information regarding the available insurance.[79] In the subsequent suit by the lease-holders for insurance coverage, SR International moved for an order compelling pro-duction of the documents resulting from the post-September 11 investigation.[80] The lender, however, claimed that the information-gathering activities were protected by the attorney-client privilege, since the employees of the insurance advisor were acting as litigation consultants to the lender's in-house counsel in the investigation following the September 11 attack.[81]

The United States District Court for the Southern District of New York held that the communications with investors after the terrorist attack were performed in the normal course of business and were, therefore, not protected.[82] The court found that the purpose of the investor meetings was to provide information in response to the investors' inquiries and not to provide legal advice. The court also found that notes documenting facts were not protected because the attorney-client privilege does not protect underlying facts.[83] The court did find, however, that some meetings between the lender's employees and the lender's in-house counsel were privileged, since those communications sought legal advice.[84]

Summary

The *Spectrum Systems* and *Leucadia* cases illustrate that the communications between attorney and client relating to the attorney's investigation will be protected by the attorney-client privilege as long as the attorney is acting in his or her capacity as an attorney. The *National Farmers Union, Lilly, St. Paul Reinsurance,* and *SR International* cases, however, demonstrate that not all attorneys conducting investigations on behalf of clients are acting in the capacity of an attorney. Where, as in *Lilly, St. Paul Reinsurance,* and *SR International,* the attorney is performing an investigation that can be generally considered part of the client's ordinary business practices, a client cannot shield the results of that investigation simply by having an attorney conduct the investigation. *National Farmers Union* illustrates that the line between an ordinary business investigation and an investigation for purposes of obtaining legal advice is not always clear. To obtain attorney-client privilege protection of attorney-client in-vestigative communications, the party seeking to invoke the privilege must carry the burden of establishing that the attorney's investigation was conducted to render legal advice to the client. *Spectrum Systems* correctly notes that the prospect of litigation is irrelevant to a determination of whether the client is seeking legal advice and that an attorney-investigator is acting in her capacity as an attorney where the attorney's report integrates the factual results of the investigation with the attorney's assessment of the client's legal position or options.

Special Problems Facing Corporations That Retain Counsel to Investigate

Corporations face a special problem when they hire attorneys to investigate and provide legal advice—which employees can the attorney talk to and keep the communications within the attorney-client privilege? The first case to establish guidelines in these situations was *City of Philadelphia v. Westinghouse Electric Corp.*[85] The court there determined that those employees in the "control group" would be covered by the privilege.[86] The control group included only those members of senior management who may be in a position to control or take action on the advice of the attorney.[87] While some courts followed the control group approach,[88] other courts developed a "subject matter" test, which required application of several factors to determine if the subject matter of a communication was attorney-client privileged.[89]

Supreme Court Rejects Control Group Test

In *Upjohn Co. v. United States,*[90] the Supreme Court directly addressed a factual situation where an attorney conducted an investigation and interviewed numerous corporate employees, many of whom were not within the control group. In *Upjohn*, the attorney's investigation commenced after independent accountants conducting an audit of one of Upjohn's foreign subsidiaries discovered that improper payments had been made to foreign government officials in order to secure government business. After the accountants informed Upjohn's general counsel, Gerard Thomas, of the bribes, Thomas consulted with outside counsel and decided to enlist the aid of outside counsel in investigating the questionable payments.[91] Outside counsel prepared a letter containing a questionnaire that was sent by Upjohn's chairman to various Upjohn employees, including those outside the control group. The letter, which included an admonition that the investigation was "highly confidential," specified that the purpose of the investigation was to determine the nature and magnitude of any payments made by Upjohn to any foreign government officials, and stated that management needed full information concerning any such payments.[92] The responses were sent directly to Thomas. Thomas and outside counsel also interviewed the recipients of the questionnaires and 33 other Upjohn employees, and took notes during these interviews.[93]

The IRS thereafter began an investigation to determine the tax consequences of the alleged payments after receiving a report about them from Upjohn.[94] In the course of the investigation, the IRS subpoenaed all of Thomas' investigative files, including the questionnaires, memoranda, and notes of the interviews. After Upjohn refused to produce the questionnaires and notes, the IRS sought enforcement from the district court, which ordered their production. The Third Circuit upheld this decision.[95]

On further appeal, the Supreme Court held that the communications made by the employees (and the responses to the questionnaires) were protected by the attorney-client privilege.[96] The Court rejected the application of the control group test because it discouraged the communication of relevant information by the client's employees to the attorneys seeking to render legal advice to the corporation.[97] The Court recognized that because lower echelon corporate employees often embroil a corporation in serious legal difficulties, these employees often have the only relevant information needed by counsel to render legal advice to the corporation. If the communications with these employees are not privileged, the Court reasoned that the attorney faced a "Hobson's choice"—interview employees without the protection of the attorney-client privilege or forego those interviews and render advice to the corporation based on incomplete information.[98] Because the control group test too narrowly protected what the Court believed was privileged information, the Court rejected it in favor of the subject matter approach.[99]

Upjohn, which arose from an investigation by the United States Internal Revenue Service, addressed the federal common law attorney-client privilege[100] and, thus, is not binding on state courts[101] or on federal courts in diversity cases.[102] Some state courts have followed the *Upjohn* approach,[103] while others have modified the *Upjohn* test. For example, in *Southern Bell Telephone & Telegraph Co. v. Deason*,[104] the Florida Supreme Court had to determine the extent of the attorney-client privilege when a regulated utility with a duty to disclose investigates its own conduct through counsel.[105] The Florida Public Services Commission ("PSC") argued that, because Southern Bell was regulated by state statute, the *Upjohn* rule did not apply, and the information it sought was not protected by the attorney-client privilege.[106] The court first rejected the control group test because it failed to recognize the "crucial role [that] middle and lower-level employees play in the corporation's activities."[107] The court then rejected the PSC's argument that the rules of privilege should be applied differently because Southern Bell was a regulated industry.[108] The court adopted the subject matter test,[109] relying principally on the rule developed in *Harper & Row Publishers, Inc. v. Decker*[110] as modified by *Diversified Industries, Inc. v. Meredith*.[111] The court then applied the rule it had announced to the information Southern Bell claimed was privileged, allowing the PSC to discover some of it, and protecting some from discovery.[112]

The Control Group Theory Remains Viable

The control group theory continues to be applied by some state courts, even in light of *Upjohn*. For example, in *Consolidation Coal Co. v. Bucyrus-Erie Co.*,[113] the Illinois Supreme Court rejected the *Upjohn* approach in favor of the control group test.[114] The Illinois Supreme Court reasoned that the control group test struck a reasonable balance between protecting corporate decision makers' consultations with counsel and minimizing the amount of factual information that is immune from discovery.[115] Under this theory, however, communications to and from the person whose conduct gave rise to the potential corporate liability are protected, whether or not that person is part of the control group.[116]

The Texas Supreme Court endorsed the control group approach in *National Tank Co. v. Brotherton*,[117] relying principally on a state rule of evidence enacted by the Texas Legislature two years after the *Upjohn* decision.[118] In *National Tank*, an explosion in one of National's plants critically injured a National employee, who later died from his injuries, and two employees of a subcontractor.[119] National's general counsel dispatched Townsend, National's safety and risk control coordinator who normally reported directly to counsel, to the plant to interview four National employees.[120] Precht, a representative of National's liability insurer, also interviewed nine National employees and prepared three accident reports that he sent directly to National's general counsel.[121] In subsequent litigation, the plaintiff requested all reports prepared in connection with the accident investigation.[122] The trial court ordered the documents produced.[123] National appealed, and the court of civil appeals affirmed in an unpublished decision.[124] National sought mandamus from the supreme court.[125]

The Texas Supreme Court interpreted the recently promulgated rule of evidence as adopting the control group test and refused to protect the statements taken by Townsend on behalf of National's general counsel under the attorney-client privilege. The court ruled that the employees that Townsend interviewed were not "representatives" of National for the purposes of the Texas rule, and therefore, communications from those employees to Townsend were not privileged.[126] Even though the employees "may have been speaking with management's blessing," they had not been authorized to seek legal advice on National's behalf, and thus fell outside the group of employees whose communications with counsel would be privileged.[127] Because Precht was not within the defined "control group" under Texas law, his reports to general counsel were likewise not privileged.[128]

Arizona Adopts a Third Approach

In *Samaritan Foundation v. Goodfarb*,[129] the Arizona Supreme Court rejected both the control group test and the subject matter test in favor of the "functional approach." In *Samaritan*, a child's heart stopped during surgery and the hospital's lawyer investigated the incident. The lawyer directed a nurse paralegal to interview three nurses and a scrub technician who were present during the surgery. The paralegal summarized the interviews in a memorandum that she submitted to the hospital's corporate counsel.[130]

The child sued, and when the employees were unable to remember what happened in the operating room during their depositions, she sought production of the summaries prepared by the paralegal.[131] The trial court rejected the hospital's argument that the summaries were protected by the attorney-client privilege, but gave them limited protection under the work-product doctrine.[132] The hospital appealed, and the appellate court upheld the trial court's ruling, adopting a modified form of the control group test for application of the attorney-client privilege.[133] The appellate court found that the requisite showing of need for the information had been made and upheld the trial court's decision that the summaries were discoverable.[134]

The Arizona Supreme Court rejected the court of appeals' "qualified privilege" approach,[135] opting instead for the "functional approach," which focuses on the relationship between the communicator and the need for legal services.[136] The court rejected both *Upjohn*'s subject matter test and the control group test for the same reason—both would protect communications made by employees of a corporation in their capacity as witnesses to an event in which they were uninvolved from a liability perspective.[137] In the court's view, any privilege that attaches to communications between corporate employees and the corporation's attorneys must protect the legitimate needs of the corporation to obtain legal advice, yet not be so broad as to encompass statements made by mere witnesses to an event. The court held that:

> [W]here someone other than the employee initiates the communication, a factual communication by a corporate employee to corporate counsel is within the corporation's privilege if it concerns the employee's own conduct within the scope of his or her employment and is made to assist the lawyer in assessing or responding to the legal consequences of that conduct for the corporate client. This excludes from the privilege communications from those who, but for their status as officers, agents, or employees, are witnesses.[138]

Because the statements of the employees in this case were not of the kind described, the court ruled that the paralegal's summaries were discoverable.[139]

In response to the *Samaritan* decision, the Arizona Legislature enacted Section 12-2234 of the Arizona Statutes,[140] which modifies the *Samaritan* decision and codifies the attorney-client privilege applicable not just to corporations, but to all business entities.[141] This statute protects communications with any employee of an entity and counsel if the communication is either (1) for the purpose of providing legal advice to the entity or (2) for the purpose of obtaining information in order to provide such advice.[142] The statute also provides that the employee is not relieved of a duty to disclose facts by virtue of the statute.[143] Accordingly, the witness statements the court viewed as not privileged in *Samaritan* would have been privileged under the statute.

Recently, the Arizona Court of Appeals was called upon to interpret and extend the legislative modification of *Samaritan*. In *Roman Catholic Diocese v. Superior Court*,[144] the State of Arizona requested various documents from the Diocese, which the Diocese withheld based on the corporate attorney-client privilege as enunciated in *Samaritan* and codified in Arizona Statute Section 12-2234. Specifically, the Diocese asked the court to interpret Arizona Statute Section 13-4062(2), the codification of the attorney-client privilege in criminal cases, in such a way as to incorporate the amendment to Section 12-2234, which protects any communications between an attorney and a corporate employee to provide or obtain legal advice.[145]

The appellate court, however, rejected the Diocese's interpretation. The court observed that the civil and criminal attorney-client statutes were very similar when *Samaritan* was decided.[146] But after the *Samaritan* decision, the legislature amended the civil attorney-client privilege statute in an effort to broaden the privilege afforded to corporations in civil cases.[147] The Arizona Legislature, however, did not modify the criminal attorney-client privilege statute—a fact that was critical to the court's decision to reject the Diocese's argument to extend the civil amendment to the criminal statute.[148]

Summary

As the foregoing cases demonstrate, the fact that a lawyer investigates in her capacity as a lawyer for a corporate client does not necessarily mean that the communications to or from that lawyer will be protected. In those jurisdictions that follow *Upjohn*, an attorney can be more confident that the communications with the client's employees will be protected. In a control group jurisdiction, the communications will not be protected by the attorney-client privilege unless the communicator or recipient of the communication from the attorney is within the narrowly defined control group or is the person whose conduct gave rise to the potential liability. In states that follow Arizona's functional approach, communications to or from an employee whose conduct may give rise to liability of the corporation are protected; communications to or from mere witnesses to an event are not.

Information from Non-Clients: Is It Protected?

Another issue that arises in cases where attorneys conduct investigations is the scope of protection for information supplied by non-clients. Indeed, in some investigations, much of the information will be supplied by non-clients. The attorney transmits the information to his or her client, and it forms the basis of counsel's legal advice and recommendations.

Application of the Attorney-Client Privilege

Under Professor Wigmore's approach, the attorney-client privilege does not apply if the attorney's legal advice to the client is based on information obtained from third parties.[149] This rule, if accurately stated, directly affects communications between attorneys and clients in a variety of contexts.[150] In fact, many courts hold that there is no attorney-client privilege for documents relating to factual information obtained from non-client sources.[151]

The court in *United States v. United Shoe Machinery Corp.*[152] followed the Wigmore approach. There, the government brought a civil antitrust action against United Shoe and sought to introduce numerous exhibits that United claimed were attorney-client privileged.[153] The first category of exhibits included letters to or from outside attorneys.[154] At the time of the communications, "each of the law partnerships was counsel for United, its subsidiaries and affiliates."[155] The court found that the privilege did not apply when the legal advice is based on "facts disclosed to the attorney by a person outside the organization of defendant and its affiliates. . . ."[156]

United Shoe is not simply an archaic decision with no recent support. Its support, however, appears limited to the federal courts. In *Merrin Jewelry Co. v. St. Paul Fire & Marine Insurance Co.*,[157] the court held that the report of an attorney hired by St. Paul to conduct an examination under oath in response to a theft claim was not privileged because it was based on information obtained from a non-client during the examination.[158] Similarly, in *J.P. Foley & Co. v. Vanderbilt*,[159] the court ordered production of communications from attorney to client because they were based on information from third parties.[160]

While not going as far as *United Shoe*, other courts have ordered parties to produce facts that the party's attorney discovered from non-client sources. In *Carte Blanche (Singapore) PTE., Ltd. v. Diners Club International, Inc.*,[161] for example, the court ordered the client to produce its attorney's letter containing the results of an investigation from various non-client sources.[162] Finally, in *Allen v. West Point-Pepperell, Inc.*,[163] the court found that "plaintiffs and [counsel] must disclose to defendants all facts of which they were aware at all times relevant to this action, whether or not those facts were communicated by plaintiffs to [counsel] and whether or not those facts were learned by plaintiffs from [counsel]."[164] But the written communications between plaintiffs and counsel were deemed privileged and not discoverable.[165]

In contrast, the Missouri Supreme Court considered and rejected the Wigmore approach in *State ex rel. Great American Insurance Co. v. Smith*.[166] There, Great American insured Cannova, who reported a fire loss and made claim for the damage. Great American hired an attorney, Risjord, to investigate the loss. At the conclusion of Risjord's investigation, Great American denied Cannova's claim on the grounds of arson, and Cannova sued.[167] Great American's claim files were produced, except for three letters from Risjord to Great American, which Great American claimed were privileged.[168] After the trial court ordered production of the letters, Great American sought prohibition, and the supreme court ordered the trial court to conduct an *in* camera review of the letters pursuant to the direction set forth in the opinion, which approximated the Wigmore approach.[169] The trial court reviewed the letters in camera and again ordered their production.[170]

Great American appealed again, and this time the supreme court rejected the Wigmore approach it had adopted in the earlier decision and reversed the trial court's order.[171] The court's rationale is instructive. First, the court determined that Wigmore's view was a narrow one, directed toward limiting the scope of protected information.[172] The court found that society's interests were better served by protecting communication between attorney and client beyond that suggested by Wigmore.[173] Second, the court found the rule proposed by the American Law Institute[174] better reflected the reality of an attorney-client relationship today.[175] The court then adopted a two-part test to determine whether the privilege applies:

> There is no question but that the three letters Risjord wrote to relators pertained to these matters in which he had been employed. Risjord so stated and the court's findings as set out in the letter of April 21, 1977, so show. If this were not so, we would direct the court to conduct a hearing and examine representatives of relators or Risjord or both to determine whether at the time the letters were written, the relation of attorney and client regarding the insurance claims existed, and whether the letters pertained to the matters for which Risjord had been employed. If either answer were in the negative, the privilege would not apply.[176]

When comparing the Wigmore view to that of the court in *Great American*, the better reasoned view is that of the Missouri Supreme Court, keeping in mind the scope of the privilege—communications are protected, but facts are not.[177] The *Great American* court emphasized the protective scope of the attorney-client privilege as it applies to investigative reports:

> When a client goes to an attorney and asks him to represent him on a claim which he believes he has against someone or which is being asserted against him, even if he as yet has no knowledge or information about the claim, subsequent communications by the attorney to the client should be privileged. Some of the advice given by the attorney may be based on informa-

tion obtained from sources other than the client. Some of what the attorney says will not actually be advice as to a course of conduct to be followed. Part may be analysis of what is known to date of the situation. Part may be a discussion of additional avenues to be pursued. Part may be keeping the client advised of things done or opinions formed to date. All of these communications, not just the advice, are essential elements of attorney-client consultation. All should be protected.[178]

But the court also distinguishes information that is not protected by the attorney-client privilege and, thus, is discoverable:

> This does not mean that discoverable factual information can be made privileged by being recited by the attorney or the client in their confidential communications. Only the actual attorney-client communications are privileged. . . . If [the investigative report documents prepared by investigators who were hired by the attorney or client] had been attached to or discussed in the letters from Risjord to relators [client], the fact that the attorney's letters would be privileged would not cause the GAB reports or the FBI letter to become protected by the attorney-client privilege.[179]

Are Former Employees Clients or Third Parties?

One question left open in *Upjohn* is whether communications with a corporation's former employees are protected by the attorney-client privilege.[180] Because this issue had not been addressed in the courts below, the *Upjohn* Court declined to opine on it.[181]

But in *In re Coordinated Pretrial Proceedings*,[182] the court applied the *Upjohn* rule in the context of former employees. The trial court disqualified defense counsel from representing present employees (other than corporate executives) and former employees in discovery depositions[183] because the court wanted to allow the plaintiffs to fully inquire into the communications made at "orientation" sessions between the witnesses and defense counsel.[184] On appeal, the court applied the principles of *Upjohn*, which had been decided after the trial court ruled, and concluded that the trial court's ruling would have been different.[185] The court concluded that the *Upjohn* rationale applied with equal force to former employees:

> Although *Upjohn* was specifically limited to current employees, the same rationale applies to the ex-employees (and current employees) involved in this case. Former employees, as well as current employees, may possess the relevant information needed by corporate counsel to advise the client with respect to actual or potential difficulties. Again, the attorney-client privilege is served by the certainty that conversations between the attorney and client will remain privileged after the employee leaves.[186]

Other federal and state courts have reached the same conclusion.[187] Furthermore, the Fourth Circuit noted, in *In re Allen*,[188] that courts that have declined to apply the attor-

ney-client privilege to communications between the client's attorney and former employees have done so because they were following state law or because the former
employee was not an employee when the relevant conduct occurred.[189]

What Must Be Disclosed?

Even if attorney-client privileged communications contain discoverable factual information, it does not necessarily mean that communications containing those facts "are
fair game in discovery."[190] Some courts hold that the written communications do not
have to be produced, but rather, the client must, in either depositions or interrogatory
responses, disclose the discoverable factual information.[191] Other courts require the
written communication to be produced with the exception of any redacted portions
relating to legal advice.[192]

If the Court's admonition in *Upjohn* that the protection of the attorney-client privilege applies only to communications and not facts is correct, then the obvious answer
is that the communication should never be produced, but the party must always provide requested information in response to interrogatories or in depositions. The *Upjohn*
Court clearly stated that the witnesses interviewed by counsel could be deposed and
had to answer questions; what the government could not obtain were the questionnaires those witnesses filled out. In *Samaritan*, for example, the hospital should have
disclosed all of the *facts* the nurses knew in response to well-crafted interrogatories,
even when the nurses could not recall those facts in their depositions.

Additional Attorney-Client Privilege Issues

Who Is the Client?

In some cases, an attorney may actually have two clients, even though only one client
is or will be named as a party in litigation. An attorney representing both the insurer
and the insured in a subrogation suit and an attorney representing a liability insurer
and the insured in a casualty defense matter are just two examples.[193] The attorney-
client privilege should apply whether or not the person asserting the privilege is named
as a party. In *United Coal Cos. v. Powell Construction Co.*,[194] for example, the court
held that communications between United Coal's property insurance carrier and an
attorney it retained to file a subrogation action on its behalf but in the name of the
insured, which also retained the attorney to recover its uninsured loss, were privileged.[195]

Other courts, however, have taken a more restrictive view. In *Sterling Drilling Co.
v. Spector*,[196] the court found that an attorney hired by an insured's insurer to defend
the insured in subsequent litigation represented only the insurer. *Sterling Drilling* involved the death of a worker in an industrial accident. The employer's insurer hired an
attorney to conduct an investigation into the insured's punitive damages exposure and
to provide legal advice regarding those damages.[197] While the *Sterling* court implicitly
found that the insurer shared an attorney-client privilege with the investigating attorney, the court refused to extend this protection to the employer because there was "no
evidence that [the investigating attorney] had any real contact with [the employer]
concerning the conduct of the investigation including the taking of the statements."[198]

When Is the Client a Client?

The attorney-client privilege also applies to communications between an attorney and a prospective client.[199] The privilege will be inapplicable, however, where there is no clear prospective attorney-client relationship[200] as the case *Poluch v. American Fan Co.*[201] illustrates. There, Poluch was injured at work, and his employer's workers' compensation carrier retained Creative Services, an investigative agency, to determine the nature and extent of Poluch's injuries and the potential financial exposure of the workers' compensation carrier.[202] Poluch hired her own attorney to pursue legal action against the manufacturer of the equipment allegedly responsible for Poluch's injury. After Creative Services completed its investigation, but before Poluch initiated a products liability action against the manufacturer, Poluch's attorney was also retained by the workers' compensation carrier to represent its subrogated interest. The workers' compensation carrier then turned over the entire workers' compensation file to Poluch's attorney.[203]

In discovery, the manufacturer requested production of the entire workers' compensation file. Poluch turned over certain portions of the file, but withheld the investigation report. Poluch's counsel argued that the workers' compensation carrier was always in some sense "a de facto client."[204] Poluch's attorney argued that the prospect of subrogation was a matter always considered by the insurer, and, therefore, the information obtained by the carrier's investigator was protected by the attorney-client privilege or the work-product doctrine.[205] The court disagreed, holding that no attorney-client relationship existed between Poluch's attorney and the workers' compensation carrier at the time of the investigation, and, therefore, the attorney-client privilege did not apply.[206] The court also found that the work-product doctrine did not apply because of the lack of an attorney-client relationship at the time of the investigation.[207]

Two recent cases have analyzed the attorney-client privilege as it applies to situations involving prospective clients. In a case involving a dispute surrounding a tax strategy, *Diversified Group, Inc. v. Daugerdas,*[208] the United States District Court for the Southern District of New York held that communications predating the attorney engagement agreement were not privileged because there was no indication that the client intended to obtain legal advice from the communication. In fact, the court stated that there was "strong evidence" that the client sought business, not legal, advice from the attorney.[209] Although the communications here did not fall within the purview of a prospective attorney-client relationship, the court noted that "[c]ommunications with an attorney that predate formal retention may be privileged 'if the party divulging [the] confidences and secrets to [the] attorney believes that he is approaching the attorney in a professional capacity with the intent to secure legal advice.'"[210]

The court in *Auscape International v. National Geographic Society*[211] focused on letters sent to prospective class action participants. There, the court held that the letters were not privileged, even if the sending of the letters was intended to further the interests of existing clients, because they constituted a form of "direct mail advertising."[212] The court analogized the letters to radio commercials advising potential plaintiffs that they may have a claim for asbestos exposure.[213] One form of advertising (direct mail) should not be considered privileged, while another (radio broadcast) is not, the court reasoned. Application of the privilege in this context, the court said, "would take the attorney-client privilege to a galaxy far, far away from its roots and one that it is unnecessary to visit."[214]

Has the Privilege Been Waived?

The attorney-client privilege, of course, is waived when the communications have been revealed to third parties.[215] Courts have developed a limited exception to this rule where the parties have a common legal interest.[216] While known as the "joint defense privilege," some courts have held that the same privilege applies to cooperating plaintiffs.[217] Generally, to establish the existence of a joint defense privilege, the party asserting the privilege must show that (1) the communications were made in the course of a joint defense effort, (2) the statements were designed to further the effort, and (3) the privilege has not otherwise been waived.[218] Courts analyze several factors when determining whether parties qualify for the joint defense privilege, such as the method of payment, allocation of decision-making roles, requests for advice, presence at meetings, and frequency and content of correspondence.[219]

In cases involving an attorney's investigation, the attorney-client privilege is also waived when the substance of the attorney's investigation has been placed "at issue"—as a defense or claim—in litigation. Under the "at issue" doctrine, a party may be deemed to have waived the privilege where:

> (1) assertion of the privilege was a result of some affirmative act, such as filing suit, by the asserting party; (2) through this affirmative act, the asserting party put the protected information at issue by making it relevant to the case; and (3) application of the privilege would have denied the opposing party access to information vital to his defense.[220]

Courts have narrowly construed the "at issue" waiver, limiting it to situations where the party puts the contents of an attorney-client communication at issue by asserting a claim or defense it intends to prove through disclosure of that communication.[221] For example, in *Harding v. Dana Transport, Inc.*,[222] the defendant hired outside counsel to perform an investigation after two employees filed an administrative complaint for sexual harassment. In defense of the administrative action, Dana asserted that it had "fully investigated" plaintiffs' complaint and "found that there is no supporting evidence" that the acts complained of occurred.[223] In a later Title VII proceeding in federal court, the defendant sought to introduce evidence of the investigation as a defense to the plaintiffs' claim, because proof of "sufficiently effective" procedures for investigating and remediating alleged discrimination is a valid defense.[224] At the same time, however, Dana resisted attempts by plaintiffs' counsel to inquire into the substance of the investigation by invoking the attorney-client privilege.[225] The court found that the defendant had waived the privilege by raising the investigation as a defense to the plaintiffs' Title VII and New Jersey state claims.[226] The court's rationale, in part, was that "[w]ithout such information, the plaintiffs cannot determine the seriousness of Dana's investigation into the plaintiffs' allegations of sexual harassment."[227] Because "the investigation, itself, provides a defense to liability," plaintiffs must be permitted to probe the substance of the investigation, not merely the fact that it occurred.[228] Other jurisdictions faced with similar situations have adopted the *Harding* rationale.[229]

The Connecticut Supreme Court, in *Metropolitan Life Insurance Co. v. Aetna Casualty and Surety Co.*,[230] established limits on the at issue doctrine. In *Metropolitan Life*, the insured, who sued the excess liability insurer to recover the cost of settling asbestos tort cases after the insurer refused to defend the insured, sought to prevent disclosure of documents containing communications with other attorneys regarding the settlement of the tort cases.[231] The court held that the documents were protected by the attorney-client privilege. Although the insured's senior officials had relied on counsel's advice to settle the asbestos tort actions, the insured was not relying on those privileged communications to prove the reasonableness of the settlements.[232] The court stated the following:

> Merely because the communications are relevant does not place them at issue. . . . If admitting that one relied on legal advice in making a decision put the communications relating to the advice at issue, such advice would be at issue whenever the legal decision was litigated. If that were true, the at issue doctrine would severely erode the attorney-client privilege and undermine the public policy considerations upon which it is based.[233]

Work-Product Issues

Even if attorney-client communications from attorney to client reflecting factual information or information received from non-clients are not protected by the attorney-client privilege, the work-product doctrine may preclude discovery in some cases. Work-product issues arise frequently in litigation involving insurance investigations.[234]

The work-product doctrine was first recognized by the United States Supreme Court in *Hickman v. Taylor*.[235] In *Hickman*, the Court addressed the discoverability of statements taken by a lawyer representing a tugboat company. The statements had been taken from several witnesses to a tugboat accident that killed five crew members and were recorded in memoranda prepared by the attorney.[236] The Court held that the attorney-client privilege was inapplicable, but also held that the memoranda were not discoverable based on an immunity for materials prepared by attorneys in anticipation of litigation.[237] The Court indicated that the statements might be discoverable upon a sufficient showing of need, but that it would be nearly impossible to discover information containing the attorney's mental impressions.[238]

The *Hickman* decision was essentially codified in a 1970 amendment to Rule 26 of the Federal Rules of Civil Procedure.[239] Rule 26(b)(3) of the Federal Rules of Civil Procedure protects from disclosure documents and materials otherwise discoverable that were prepared in anticipation of litigation or for trial by or for another party or by or for the other party's representative, including an attorney, consultant, insurer, or agent, except upon a showing that the party seeking discovery has substantial need for the materials in the preparation of his case and is unable, without undue hardship, to obtain the substantial equivalent of the materials by other means.[240] Rule 26(b)(3), however, provides virtually absolute protection to work-product materials that contain the mental impressions, conclusions, opinions, or legal theories of an attorney or other representative of a party concerning the litigation.[241] The reasoning behind the nearly unconditional protection of opinion work product was described by the Fourth Circuit in *Chaudhry v. Gallerizzo*:[242]

> [C]ourts should proceed cautiously when requested to adopt a rule that would have an inhibitive effect on an attorney's freedom to express and record his mental impressions and opinions without fear of having these impressions and opinions used against the client." As a result, "opinion work product enjoys a nearly absolute immunity and can be discovered only in very rare and extraordinary circumstances.[243]

Most states have similar, if not identical, rules providing strong protection to work-product materials.[244]

Assuming the documents are relevant, courts generally use a two-step analysis to determine whether the work-product doctrine provides protection to the disclosure of the documents: Were they compiled in anticipation of litigation or trial, and if so, has the party seeking discovery shown substantial need and undue hardship?[245]

In Anticipation of Litigation

The first step in the analysis—whether the document was prepared "in anticipation of litigation"—is the one most often addressed by the courts. This issue arises most often because the line between documents prepared in the ordinary course of business and those prepared in anticipation of litigation is not always clear. Generally, courts ask not whether litigation was a certainty but rather whether the document was prepared "with an eye toward litigation."[246]

Courts have taken differing views as to the meaning of the phrase "in anticipation of litigation." For example, the Fifth Circuit requires that a document be prepared "primarily to assist in litigation" for work-product protection to apply. In *United States v. Davis*,[247] the Fifth Circuit held that documents prepared in conjunction with a tax return were not protected by the work-product doctrine. In so holding, the court held that work-product protection applies to a document only if the "primary motivating purpose behind the creation of the document was to aid in possible future litigation."[248] Thus, under the Fifth Circuit's standard, a document is protected by the work-product doctrine only if the party invoking the doctrine establishes that the document was created *primarily* to assist in possible future litigation; if the document was created primarily to aid in a business decision and secondarily to aid in future litigation, the document is not protected by the work-product doctrine.

The more common standard for defining "in anticipation of litigation" is set out in the Second Circuit's decision in *United States v. Adlman*.[249] There, an aerospace manufacturer considered merging with its subsidiaries. The merger was designed to produce a loss and corresponding tax refund; therefore, the manufacturer expected an IRS challenge that would result in litigation. Litigation with the IRS did ensue, and the IRS moved to compel production of a legal memorandum prepared by the manufacturer's accountant/lawyer.[250]

The *Adlman* court framed the issue as follows: "[W]hether Rule 26(b)(3) is inapplicable to a litigation analysis prepared by a party or its representative in order to inform a business decision which turns on the party's assessment of the likely outcome of litigation expected to result from the transaction."[251] Use of the "primary motivating purpose" test that was endorsed by the Fifth Circuit would not protect the present document, the court reasoned, because the document's primary purpose was to "inform a business decision," not to aid in possible future litigation.[252] This scenario forced the court to undertake a critical analysis of the "primary motivating purpose" test, since, in the *Adlman* court's opinion, use of the "primary motivating purpose" test would impede business transactions and access to information needed to make sound decisions. Furthermore, the use of the "primary motivating purpose" test in these circumstances would offend the very purpose of the work-product doctrine and leave no "zone of privacy" for companies to obtain an assessment of how litigation may affect their business decisions.[253]

Based on the foregoing analysis, the *Adlman* court adopted a "because of" standard—a document prepared "because of" anticipated litigation will be protected by the work-product doctrine:

> A document created because of anticipated litigation, which tends to reveal mental impressions, conclusions, opinions, or theories concerning the litigation, does not lose work-product protection merely because it is intended to assist in the making of a business decision influenced by the likely outcome of the anticipated litigation. Where a document was created because of anticipated litigation, and would not have been prepared in substantially similar form but for the prospect of litigation, it falls within Rule 26(b)(3).[254]

Recently, the United States District Court for the Northern District of California promulgated a third standard for determining whether a document is prepared "in anticipation of litigation." In *Jumpsport, Inc. v. Jumpking, Inc.*,[255] the court concluded that deciding whether a document was prepared in anticipation of litigation requires a two-prong test. The first prong considers "whether the party trying to invoke work-product protection has shown that the prospect of litigation was a substantial factor in the mix of considerations, purposes, or forces that led to the preparation of the document."[256] If this prong is satisfied, the court must ask a second question: whether denying protection to the document would harm the policy objectives underlying the work product doctrine (or, conversely, whether granting work-product protection would advance the policy objectives surrounding the work-product doctrine).[257] A document is granted protection only if it meets both requirements, which the document at issue in *Jumpsport*—a draft report prepared by an accounting and consulting firm that contained a description of the U.S. economy and the sporting goods market, a company overview, a valuation of invested capital and intellectual property, and a valuation synthesis and conclusion—did not.[258]

No matter which test the court employs, the "in anticipation of litigation" requirement does not include documents prepared merely to avoid litigation. As the court in *In re Grand Jury Proceedings* stated, "to find that 'avoidance of litigation' without more constitutes 'in anticipation of litigation' would 'represent an insurmountable barrier to normal discovery' and could subsume all compliance activities by a company as protected from discovery."[259] Because of the divergent views as to what constitutes "in anticipation of litigation," courts have looked at whether an attorney's investigation was conducted in the ordinary course of business or whether it was conducted in anticipation of litigation on a case-by-case basis. For example, in *Ryall v. Appleton Electric Co.*,[260] the court found that notes of interviews by the client's chief employment counsel in a sexual harassment investigation commenced in response to contact by an employee's attorney, which indicated that litigation was imminent, were protected by the work-product doctrine.[261] Similarly, in *Arkwright Mutual Insurance Co. v. National Union Fire Insurance Co.*,[262] the court determined that a subrogation investigation undertaken by counsel for a property insurer was not within the normal business activities of the insurer and was therefore protected by the work-product doctrine.[263] In contrast, the court in *In re Leslie Fay Companies, Inc. Securities Litigation*[264] held that the work-product doctrine did not protect documents relating to an attorney's investigation of a client's publicly alleged accounting irregularities.[265] The investigation was conducted primarily for business purposes because the client used the investigation results to make decisions on firing responsible personnel, to implement a new financial structure, organization, and internal control systems, and to reassure creditors and lenders that the culpable parties and suspect internal policies "were being vigorously sought and rooted out."[266] And, in a recent case, *City of Springfield v. Rexnord Corp.*, the court held that documents that might have been prepared in anticipation of possible litigation with the Massachusetts Department of Environmental Quality Engineering were not protected by the work-product privilege, since they were prepared primarily for media inquiries and represented the corporation's public statements.[267]

Substantial Need

The final step in the analysis is determining whether materials and documents prepared in anticipation of litigation may still be discoverable because the requesting party can establish that it has a substantial need for the materials and is unable, without undue hardship, to obtain the substantial equivalent of the materials by other means. Courts generally find such a need where a witness, for example, is unavailable, hostile, or has difficulty recalling information previously given to an attorney.[268] Some courts also find such a need when bad faith allegations are made.[269] While factual materials may be discovered upon a showing of "substantial need," the attorney's mental impressions, conclusions, opinions, or legal theories are not discoverable.[270]

In sum, there is nothing attorneys can do to absolutely insure that the results of their investigation will be protected by the work-product doctrine. There are, however, steps attorney can take to help establish that investigation materials were prepared in anticipation of litigation. For example, the attorney can, upon receiving a request to evaluate and investigate on behalf of a client, send a confirming letter to the client which notes that the attorney is investigating and evaluating the matter in anticipation of litigation, specifying the precise claims the attorney "anticipates." The attorney can make sure she is not performing a task that the client would perform as a regular part of its business if it had not hired the attorney, especially if the client is an insurance company. The lawyer can also make sure that any related claims are considered to protect the work product of all of those involved. Finally, while the work-product doctrine may shield *documents* from discovery, most courts hold that an opposing party can, by interrogatories or by deposition, discover factual information learned during an investigation.[271]

Conclusion

The attorney who conducts a factual investigation for the purpose of providing legal advice to her client should be able to communicate those facts to her client within the purview of the attorney-client privilege. This is clearly the majority rule, but it has not garnered a universal following. An attorney undertaking an investigation for a corporation may not be able to speak with employees at every level within the company under the cloak of the privilege, although the majority rule protects communications by corporate employees with knowledge no matter what position they hold in the company. When the facts are gleaned from third parties, the better reasoned rule protects the communication of them under the attorney-client privilege, at least where such facts were necessary to the rendering of the requested legal advice. Again, this rule is not universally followed. Even in those jurisdictions that may not recognize a privilege as to third-party facts, absent extraordinary circumstances, the work-product doctrine should shield the communications from discovery.

Notes

1. Samaritan Found. v. Goodfarb, 862 P.2d 870 (Ariz. 1993); Hyams v. Evanston Hosp., 587 N.E.2d 1127 (Ill. App. Ct. 1992).

2. Harding v. Dana Transp. Inc., 914 F. Supp. 1084 (D.N.J. 1996).

3. Nat'l Tank Co. v. Brotherton, 851 S.W.2d 193 (Tex. 1993).

4. Dunn v. State Farm Fire & Cas. Co., 927 F.2d 869 (5th Cir. 1991); Burr v. United Farm Bureau Mut. Ins. Co., 560 N.E.2d 1250 (Ind. Ct. App. 1990); State *ex rel.* United States Fid. & Guar. Co. v. Canady, 460 S.E.2d 677 (W. Va. 1995).

5. Spectrum Sys. Int'l Corp. v. Chem. Bank, 581 N.E.2d 1055 (N.Y. 1991).

6. Upjohn Co. v. United States, 449 U.S. 383 (1981).

7. SR Int'l Bus. Ins. Co. v. World Trade Ctr. Props. LLC, No. 01 Civ. 9291 (JSM), 2002 U.S. Dist. LEXIS 11949 (S.D.N.Y. July 3, 2002).

8. *See In re* Allen, 106 F.3d 582, 602 (4th Cir. 1997) (noting that "[c]ourts have consistently recognized that investigation may be an important part of an attorney's legal services to a client").

9. *See infra* notes 23-84 and accompanying text.

10. *Upjohn, supra* note 6 at 389.

11. *Id.*

12. Ohio courts have recognized a "bad faith" exception to the general rule. *See* Garg v. State Auto. Mut. Ins. Co., C.A. Case No. 2003 CA 12, 2003 Ohio App. LEXIS 5297, at *16 (Ohio Ct. App. Nov. 7, 2003) (holding that the attorney-client privilege did not protect materials in a claims file created prior to the denial of the claim that would provide insight into whether the insurer acted in bad faith in handling the insured's claims); Boone v. Vanliner Ins. Co., 744 N.E.2d 154, 158 (Ohio 2001) (holding that "in an action alleging bad faith denial of insurance coverage, the insured is entitled to discover claims file materials containing attorney-client communications related to the issue of coverage that were created prior to the denial of coverage"); Moskovitz v. Mt. Sinai Med. Ctr., 635 N.E.2d 331, 349 (Ohio 1994) ("[D]ocuments and other things showing the lack of a good

faith effort to settle by a party or the attorneys acting on his or her behalf are wholly unworthy of the protections afforded by any claimed privilege.").

A similar exception to the general rule, the "crime-fraud" exception, applies if the client communicates with its attorney to obtain advice or assistance while committing what the client knows is a crime or fraud. The Florida Court of Appeals recently rejected an insured's attempt to use the crime-fraud exception to discover attorney-client privileged information from its insurer in a suit following the denial of an insurance claim. In Butler, Pappas, Weihmuller, Katz, Craig v. Coral Reef of Key Biscayne Developers, Inc., Case Nos. 3DO3-1987 & 3DO3-1975, 2003 Fla. App. LEXIS 18093 (Fla. Dist. Ct. App. Nov. 26, 2003), the court rejected the insured's argument that the insurer had committed fraud in denying the insured's claim because the insurer had a reasonable basis for the denial. *Id.* at *10. Thus, all attorney-client conversations between the insurer and its counsel were privileged and not subject to discovery. *Id.* at *12.

13. Fine v. Facet Aerospace Prods. Co., 133 F.R.D. 439, 444 (S.D.N.Y. 1990); *see, e.g.*, *In re* Grand Jury Subpoena Bierman, 765 F.2d 1014 (11th Cir. 1985), *vacated in part*, 788 F.2d 1511 (11th Cir. 1986); Colton v. United States, 306 F.2d 633, 636-37 (2d Cir. 1962), *cert. denied*, 371 U.S. 951 (1963); Tisby v. Buffalo Gen. Hosp., 157 F.R.D. 157, 168 (W.D.N.Y. 1994); Spectrum Sys. Int'l Corp. v. Chem. Bank, 581 N.E.2d 1055, 1060 (N.Y. 1991); Victor v. Fanning Starkey Co., 486 P.2d 323, 324 (Wash. Ct. App. 1971).

14. *See, e.g.*, *In re* Grand Jury Subpoena, 204 F.3d 516, 519-20 (4th Cir. 2000).

15. United States v. Mobil Corp., 149 F.R.D. 533, 536 (N.D. Tex. 1993); Henson v. Wyeth Labs., Inc., 118 F.R.D. 584, 587 (W.D. Va. 1987); United States v. United Shoe Mach. Corp., 89 F. Supp. 357, 358-59 (D. Mass. 1950). Wigmore further separates these factors into eight:

> (1) Where legal advice of any kind is sought (2) from a professional legal adviser in his capacity as such, (3) the communications relating to that purpose, (4) made in confidence (5) by the client, (6) are at his instance permanently protected (7) from disclosure by himself or by the legal adviser, (8) except the protection be waived.

8 James H. Wigmore, Evidence In Trials at Common Law § 2292 at 554 (James McNaughton rev. ed. 1961 & Supp. 1996).

16. *See generally* James W. Strong, et al., McCormick on Evidence §§ 87-97 (4th ed. 1992); Wigmore, *supra* note 15, §§ 2290-2329. The privilege also protects an attorney's communications to a client if those communications would reveal either confidential client communications or legal advice or opinions of the attorney. *See, e.g.*, Schenet v. Anderson, 678 F. Supp. 1280, 1281 (E.D. Mich. 1988); Potts v. Allis-Chalmers Corp., 118 F.R.D. 597, 602 (N.D. Ind. 1987); Henson v. Wyeth Lab., Inc. 118 F.R.D. 584, 587 (W.D. Va. 1987).

17. Upjohn Co. v. United States, 449 U.S. 383, 395-96 (1981). Quoting from *Philadelphia v. Westinghouse Electrical Corp.*, 205 F. Supp. 830, 831 (E.D. Pa. 1962), the Court stated:

> [The] protection of the privilege extends only to *communications* and not facts. A fact is one thing and a communication concerning that fact is an entirely different thing. The client cannot be compelled to answer the question, "What did you say or write to the attorney?" but may not refuse to disclose any relevant fact within his knowledge merely because he incorporated a statement of such fact into his communication to his attorney.

Id. (emphasis added by *Upjohn* Court); *see also* Pippenger v. Gruppe, 883 F. Supp. 1201, 1208 (S.D. Ind. 1994) ("It is beyond question that the attorney-client privilege does not preclude discovery of factual information."); Spectrum Sys. Int'l Corp. v. Chem. Bank, 581 N.E.2d 1055, 1060 (N.Y. 1991) ("The privilege is of course limited to communications—not underlying facts."). *See generally* Wigmore, *supra* note 15, §§ 2306-2311.

18. *See, e.g.*, Hardy v. N.Y. News, Inc., 114 F.R.D. 633, 644 (S.D.N.Y. 1987); Byers v. Burleson, 100 F.R.D. 436, 438 (D.D.C. 1983).

19. *See, e.g.*, Sneider v. Kimberly-Clark Corp., 91 F.R.D. 1, 4 (N.D. Ill. 1980); *In re* Ampicillin Antitrust Litig., 81 F.R.D. 377, 385 n.9 (D.D.C. 1978).

20. *See infra* notes 234-71 and accompanying text.

21. *See* Tyne v. Time Warner Entm't Co., 212 F.R.D. 596 (M.D. Fla. 2002) (holding that attorney-client privilege applied to documents prepared by witness who, although not an attorney, acted as an extension or agent of legal department of corporation); Dabney v. Inv. Corp. of Am., 82 F.R.D. 464, 465 (E.D. Pa. 1979). *But see* Reed Dairy Farm v. Consumers Power Co., 576 N.W.2d 709 (Mich. Ct. App. 1998) (holding that the attorney-client privilege did not attach to attorney's paralegal, because, even though an employee of the attorney, he was not acting as an agent of the attorney, and the information sought was not the type that the attorney-client privilege was designed to protect).

22. Clark v. City of Munster, 115 F.R.D. 609, 613 (N.D. Ind. 1987); Am. Nat'l Watermattress Corp. v. Manville, 642 P.2d 1330, 1333-34 (Alaska 1982). It makes no difference whether the investigator is an employee of the attorney or is hired by the attorney to conduct the investigation.

23. *See supra* note 15 and accompanying text.

24. *See* Westinghouse Elec. Corp. v. Kerr-McGee Corp., 580 F.2d 1311, 1319-20 (7th Cir. 1978), *cert. denied*, 439 U.S. 955 (1978); Henson v. Wyeth Lab., Inc., 118 F.R.D. 584, 587 (W.D. Va. 1987); Heathcoat v. Sante Fe Int'l Corp., 532 F. Supp. 961, 964 (E.D. Ark. 1982); *see also* Boca Investerings P'ship v. United States, 31 F. Supp. 2d 9 (D.D.C. 1998), *reversed in part*, 314 F.3d 625 (D.C. Cir. 2003) (holding that communications with in-house counsel concerning legal advice were protected by attorney-client privilege, but communications made by and to the same in-house lawyer with respect to business matters, management decisions, and business advice were not protected by privilege).

25. *See, e.g.*, *Westinghouse*, 580 F.2d at 1320; Smithkline Beecham Corp. v. Apotex Corp., 194 F.R.D. 624 (N.D. Ill. 2000) (holding that attorney-authored meeting agendas were not protected by the attorney-client privilege in patent infringement suit, since it was unlikely that legal advice was involved); *Henson*, 118 F.R.D. at 587. *See generally* WIGMORE, *supra* note 15, §§ 2296-2299.

26. *See, e.g.*, Goodyear Tire & Rubber Co. v. Chiles Power Supply, Inc., 190 F.R.D. 532, 535 (S.D. Ind. 1999) (noting that there is no bright-line rule for courts deciding whether an attorney is acting in his or her capacity as such).

27. 581 N.E.2d 1055 (N.Y. 1991).

28. *Id.* at 1058.

29. *Id.*

30. *Id.*

31. *Id.* at 1059.

32. Spectrum Sys. Int'l Corp. v. Chem. Bank, 558 N.Y.S.2d 486 (N.Y. App. Div. 1990), *modified*, 581 N.E.2d 1055 (N.Y. 1991).

33. *Id.* at 488.

34. *Spectrum Systems,* 581 N.E.2d at 1059.

35. *Id.* at 1059, 1062.

36. *Id.* at 1060-61 (citations omitted).

37. *Id.* at 1061 (citations omitted).

38. *Id.*

39. *Id.* at 1061-62.

40. 101 F.R.D. 674 (S.D.N.Y. 1983).

41. *Id.* at 676-77.

42. *Id.* at 678; *see also* State v. von Bulow, 475 A.2d 995, 1005 (R.I. 1984) (finding that an attorney hired to investigate the circumstances surrounding Martha von Bulow's comatose condition was acting as an attorney during his investigation).

43. 460 S.E.2d 677 (W. Va. 1995).

44. 927 F.2d 869 (5th Cir. 1991).

45. *Id.* at 875 ("The privilege is not waived if the attorneys perform investigative tasks provided that these investigative tasks are related to the rendition of legal services."); *Canady*, 460 S.E.2d at 689-90, 692. Because of the absence of crucial factual findings, however, the *Canady* court remanded the issue to the trial court for further consideration in light of the court's opinion. The *Canady* court also refused, however, to "adopt a *per se* rule making ordinary investigative employees, who hold licenses to practice law, attorneys for purposes of the attorney-client privilege." *Id.* at 690. In the insurance industry context, such a decision "would shield from discovery documents that otherwise would not be entitled to any protection if written by an employee who holds no law license but who performs the same investigation and duties." *Id.*

46. 544 A.2d 893 (N.J. Super. Ct. App. Div. 1988).

47. *Id.* at 895.

48. 130 F.R.D. 28 (S.D.N.Y. 1990).

49. *Id.* at 31-32.

50. 106 F.3d 582, 602-03 (4th Cir. 1997).

51. *See, e.g.*, Reichhold Chems. v. Hartford Accident & Indem. Co., No. XO CV 880160018S, 2000 Conn. Super. LEXIS 2164 (Conn. Super. Ct. Aug. 15, 2000) (holding that, since the insurers had merely assigned their investigations to attorneys, the information obtained was discoverable).

52. California has recognized the importance of files created in the investigation of a claim filed by an insured by promulgating regulations that require insurance companies to investigate every filed claim and maintain claims files containing all documents, notes, and workpapers relevant to each claim. *See* 2,002 Ranch, L.L.C. v. Superior Court, No. D042323, 2003 Cal. App. LEXIS 1804, at *37-38 (Cal. Ct. App. Dec. 5, 2003) (citing CAL. CODE REGS. tit. 10, § 2695.5, subd. (e)(3) & § 2695.3 subds. (a) & (b)). *2,002 Ranch* noted, however, that the entirety of the claims file is not discoverable—attorney-client protected communications are exempt from discovery. *See id.* at *39.

53. 112 F.R.D. 160 (D. Minn. 1986).

54. *Id.* at 162.

55. *Id.* at 162-63.

56. *Id.* at 163. The court also relied on the fact that Mission retained other counsel to handle the lawsuit that Lilly filed. *Id.*

57. 197 F.R.D. 620 (N.D. Iowa 2000).

58. *Id.* at 623.

59. *Id.*

60. *Id.* at 624.

61. *Id.* at 626.

62. *Id.*

63. *Id.* at 637.

64. *Id.* at 641.

65. *Id.* at 638.

66. 718 P.2d 1044 (Colo. 1986).

67. *Id.* at 1046.

68. There is no indication that the key factor here was that the investigative work was performed by outside counsel and not in-house counsel.

69. 718 P.2d at 1046, 1048.

70. *Id.* at 1049.

71. *Id.*

72. *Id.*

73. *Id.* at 1050 (Rovira, J., dissenting).

74. *Id.*

75. *Id.*

76. *National Farmers Union* has been criticized by commentators. *See* Kenneth A. Hindman & Paul W. Burke, *A Frightening Discovery*, THE BRIEF, Spring 1988, at 18.

77. No. 01 Civ. 9290 (JSM), 2002 U.S. Dist. LEXIS 11949 (S.D.N.Y. July 3, 2002).

78. *Id.* at *2.

79. *Id.*

80. *Id.* at *1.

81. *Id.* at *2-3.

82. *Id.* at *13.

83. *Id.* at *12.

84. *Id.*

85. 210 F. Supp. 483 (E.D. Pa. 1962), *mandamus denied sub nom.,* Gen. Elec. Co. v. Kirkpatrick, 312 F.2d 742 (3d Cir. 1962), *cert. denied,* 372 U.S. 943 (1963).

86. *Id.* at 485.

87. *Id. See generally In re* Grand Jury Investigation, 599 F.2d 1224 (3d Cir. 1979) (adopting control group approach).

88. *See, e.g.,* Natta v. Hogan, 392 F.2d 686 (10th Cir. 1968).

89. Diversified Indus., Inc. v. Meredith, 572 F.2d 596 (8th Cir. 1977) (en banc); Harper & Row Publishers, Inc. v. Decker, 423 F.2d 487 (7th Cir. 1970), *aff'd per curium without opinion by an equally divided Court,* 400 U.S. 348 (1971). In *Harper & Row,* the court held that employee communications are privileged when: (1) The employee makes the communications at the direction of the employee's superior; and (2) the subject matter upon which the attorney's advice is sought by the corporation and dealt with in the communication is the performance by the employee of the duties of his or her employment. *Harper & Row,* 423 F.2d at 491-92. *Meredith* expanded the second *Harper & Row* factor and added three additional factors:

> (1) The communication was made for the purpose of securing legal advice; (2) the employee making the communication did so at the direction of his corporate superior; (3) the superior made the request so the corporation could secure legal advice; (4) the subject matter of the communication is within the scope of the employee's corporate duties; and (5) the communication is not disseminated beyond those persons who, because of the corporate structure, need to know its contents.

Meredith, 572 F.2d at 609.

90. 449 U.S. 383 (1981).

91. *Id.* at 386.

92. *Id.* at 387.

93. *Id.*

94. *Id.* Upjohn simultaneously sent the report to the SEC and to the IRS.

95. United States v. Upjohn Co., 600 F.2d 1223 (6th Cir. 1979), *rev'd,* 449 U.S. 383 (1981).

96. *Upjohn,* 449 U.S. at 390-91. Because the Court viewed investigative activities as a necessary predicate to the rendering of legal advice, the Court determined that the activities of Mr. Thomas and outside counsel were done in the capacity of lawyers:

> The communications at issue were made by Upjohn employees to counsel for Upjohn acting as such, at the direction of corporate superiors in order to secure legal advice from counsel. As the magistrate found, "Mr. Thomas consulted with the Chairman of the Board and outside counsel and thereafter conducted a factual investigation to determine the nature and extent of the questionable payments and to be in a position to give legal advice to the company with respect to the payments." . . . Information, not available from upper-echelon management, was needed to supply a basis for legal advice concerning compliance with securities and tax laws, foreign laws, currency regulations, duties to shareholders, and potential litigation in each of these areas.

Id. at 394.

97. *Id.* at 392.

98. *Id.* at 391-92. The Court quoted in part from *Diversified Industries, Inc. v. Meredith,* 572 F.2d 596 (8th Cir. 1978), which highlighted the scope of the "Hobson's choice" inherent in adopting the subject-matter test.

99. *Upjohn,* 449 U.S. at 397.

100. Some courts have applied *Upjohn* to cases interpreting ethical rules barring *ex parte* contact with represented parties when the party is an organization, of which a detailed discussion is outside the scope of this article. *See* Palmer v. Pioneer Inn Assocs., Ltd., 59 P.3d 1237 (Nev. 2002) (the no-contact rule restricts contact with only those employees whose actions are legally binding upon the organization); *see also* Chancellor v. Boeing Co., 678 F. Supp. 250 (D. Kan. 1988) (citing *Upjohn* in support of its rejection of the control group test for determining whether a witness was a party under the no-contact rule). *But see* Capital Cities/ABC, Inc., 52 Fair Empl. Prac. Cas. (BNA) 1842 (S.D.N.Y. 1990) (holding that the *Upjohn* decision should not be extended to *ex parte* contact cases).

101. FED. R. EVID. 501 ("[I]n civil actions and proceedings, with respect to an element of a claim or defense as to which State law supplies the rule of decision, the privilege of a witness, person, government, State, or political subdivision thereof shall be determined in accordance with State law."); *see, e.g.,* Samaritan Found. v. Goodfarb, 862 P.2d 870, 873-76 (Ariz. 1993); Consolidation Coal Co. v. Bucyrus-Erie Co., 432 N.E.2d 250, 254-57 (Ill. 1982).

102. Under the Federal Rules of Evidence, *Upjohn* will govern in any case in federal court where there is federal question jurisdiction, but state law will control in those federal cases where there is diversity jurisdiction. *See* FED. R. EVID. 501; *see, e.g.,* Nakajima v. Gen. Motors Corp., 857 F. Supp. 100, 104 (D.D.C. 1994); Barrett Indus. Trucks, Inc. v. Old Republic Ins. Co., 129 F.R.D. 515, 516-17 (N.D. Ill. 1990); Command Transp., Inc. v. Y.S. Line (USA) Corp., 116 F.R.D. 94, 95, 97 n.10 (D. Mass. 1987).

103. *See, e.g.,* Lexington Pub. Library v. Clark, 90 S.W.3d 53, 59 (Ky. 2002); Wardleigh v. Dist. Court, 891 P.2d 1180 (Nev. 1995).

104. 632 So. 2d 1377 (Fla. 1994).

105. *Id.* at 1379-80, 1384-89. The court identified a number of different kinds of information claimed to be privileged, including audits, interviews between security personnel and employees, notes of interviews of employees by counsel, and statistical analyses. *Id.*

106. *Id.* at 1381-82.

107. *Id.* at 1381. The court explained:

> Although upper-echelon management may be responsible for making decisions on be-half of the corporation, the non-control group employees are frequently the ones responsible for implementing those decisions. Thus, an attorney representing the corporation is charged with gathering facts from employees with information relevant to the corporation's legal problems, regardless of their rank.

Id.

108. *Id.* at 1382.

109. *Id.* at 1383. Under the *Southern Bell* test, a corporation's communications with counsel are protected by the attorney-client privilege if (1) the communication would not have been made but for the contemplation of legal services; (2) the employee making the communication was directed to do so by his or her corporate superior; (3) the superior made the request of the employee as part of the corporation's efforts to secure legal services or advice; (4) the content of the communication relates to the legal services being rendered to the corporation, and the subject matter is within the scope of the employee's duties at the corporation, and (5) the communication is not disseminated beyond those persons, who, because of the corporation's structure, need to know its contents. *Id.*; *see also* Tyne v. Time Warner Entm't Co., 212 F.R.D. 596 (M.D. Fla. 2002) (noting that Florida has rejected the control group test in favor of the subject matter test).

110. 423 F.2d 487 (7th Cir. 1970), *aff'd per curium without opinion by an equally divided Court*, 400 U.S. 348 (1971).

111. 572 F.2d 596 (8th Cir. 1977). The *Harper & Row/Meredith* subject matter test can be found *supra* at note 89.

112. 632 So. 2d at 1384-89.

113. 432 N.E.2d 250 (Ill. 1982).

114. *Id.* at 256-57. There, Bucyrus-Erie's counsel conducted an investigation into the failure of equipment manufactured by Bucyrus-Erie that damaged Consolidation's coal mine. *Id.* at 251. At issue were Bucyrus-Erie's attorney's notes and a metallurgical report of Bucyrus-Erie employees. *Id.* The notes in question were made by in-house counsel of interviews with numerous Bucyrus-Erie employees. *Id.* The report was described as a notebook containing objective information, mathematical computations, formulae, tables, charts, drawings, photographs, industry specifications, and handwritten notes. *Id.* at 254. The trial court rejected Bucyrus-Erie's objections to discovery of these documents, and the court of appeals essentially affirmed the trial court's decision. *Id.* at 253-54.

115. *Id.* at 257. The court defined a member of the control group as one "whose advisory role to top management in a particular area is such that a decision would not normally be made without his advice or opinion, and whose opinion in fact forms the basis of any final decision by those with actual authority. . . ." *Id.* at 258. If the individual merely supplies information to those on whom top management relies, that individual is not within the control group. *Id.* Because Sailors was not in the control group, his report was not protected. *Id.*

116. Golminas v. Fred Teitelbaum Constr. Co., 251 N.E.2d 314 (Ill. App. Ct. 1969). The court stated the following:

> [T]he principle underlying the attorney-client privilege would demand that an employee's communications should be privileged when the employee of the defendant corporation is also a defendant or is a person who may be charged with liability and makes statements regarding facts with which he or his employer may be charged, which statements are given or delivered to the attorney who represents either or both of them.

Id. at 318.

117. 851 S.W.2d 193 (Tex. 1993).

118. Tex. R. Civ. Evid. 503.

119. 851 S.W.2d at 195.

120. *Id.* at 195-96.

121. *Id.* at 196. National's general counsel immediately notified the liability insurer and encouraged the liability insurer to conduct an investigation of the explosion. *Id.* at 195.

122. *Id.*

123. *Id.* at 196.

124. *Id.*

125. *Id.* Under Texas law, National was entitled to relief only if the discovery order constituted a clear abuse of discretion and the aggrieved party had no adequate remedy by an ordinary appeal. *Id.* at 207.

126. *Id.* at 197.

127. *Id.* at 199.

128. *Id.* at 199-200.

129. 862 P.2d 870 (Ariz. 1993).

130. *Id.* at 873.

131. *Id.*

132. *Id.* The trial court ordered *in camera* inspection of the documents, and all protected information would be redacted before the summaries—the "functional equivalent of a witness statement"—were turned over to plaintiffs. *See* Samaritan Found. v. Superior Court, 844 P.2d 593, 596 (Ariz. Ct. App. 1992), *vacated in part*, 862 P.2d 870 (Ariz. 1993).

133. *Samaritan*, 844 P.2d at 605. The traditional control group test was modified by the court in these respects: (1) management must direct a corporate employee to communicate in confidence with the corporation's legal staff about matters within the scope of the employment; (2) no requirement of "anticipation of litigation" applies; (3) the qualified privilege can be overcome in the same way as the work-product doctrine—proof of substantial need and the inability to obtain the substantial equivalent by other means; and (4) the party seeking discovery must show its substantial need outweighs the corporation's interest in maintaining confidentiality. *Id.* at 605-06.

134. *Id.* at 607.

135. The court noted that a qualified privilege "is an uncertain privilege, and an uncertain privilege is tantamount to no privilege at all." *Samaritan*, 862 P.2d at 879.

136. *Id.*

137. *Id.*

138. *Id.* at 880.

139. *Id.* at 880-81. The court commented on one other fact that appears to have had some impact on the court's decision. At the time of the interviews, each of the witnesses signed a form consenting to representation by Samaritan if a claim was filed against her. *Samaritan*, 844 P.2d at 596. The Arizona Supreme Court viewed this as an "acknowledgment that the corporation was not satisfied that the employee statements were within the corporation's privilege. . . . [I]t is difficult to see what these forms intended to accomplish other than to silence the employees by shielding their communications in the cloak of the attorney-client privilege." *Samaritan*, 862 P.2d at 880-81.

140. ARIZ. REV. STAT. ANN. § 12-2234 (1996). For a review of the legislative history and a commentary on the statute generally, *see* W. Todd Coleman, Note, *Arizona's Attorney-Client Communications Privilege for Corporations*, 27 ARIZ. ST. L.J. 335 (1995). The author concludes that the legislative history suggests that the statute was intended to be a codification of *Upjohn. See id.* at 351-53.

141. ARIZ. REV. STAT. ANN. § 12-2234(B) (1996). The statute applies to an employee of a "corporation, governmental entity, partnership, business, association, or other similar entity or an employer. . . ." *Id.*

142. *Id.* § 12-2234(B.1), (B.2).

143. *Id.* § 12-2234(C).

144. 62 P.3d 970 (Ariz. Ct. App. 2003).

145. *Id.* at 972.

146. *Id.* at 971.

147. *Id.*

148. *Id.* at 975.

149. WIGMORE, *supra* note 15, § 2320, at 628. Professor Wigmore states: "That the *attorney's communications* to the client are also within the privilege was always assumed in the earlier cases and has seldom been brought into question." *Id.* (emphasis in original). The supporting footnote cites to one early case, *United States v. United Shoe Machinery Corp.*, 89 F. Supp. 357 (D. Mass. 1950), for the proposition that legal advice based on information from third parties is not privileged.

150. The rule would not protect communications in virtually every area of litigation for it is truly the rare case that does not involve facts obtained from non-client third parties.

151. *See, e.g.*, Dombrowski v. Bell Atl. Corp., 128 F. Supp. 2d 216, 219 (E.D. Pa. 2000); Standard Chartered Bank PLC v. Ayala Int'l Holdings (U.S.) Inc., 111 F.R.D. 76, 80 (S.D.N.Y. 1986); *see also* Kenford Co. v. County of Erie, 390 N.Y.S.2d 715, 719 (N.Y. App. Div. 1977) ("[I]n this respect, the attorney serves as fact-gathering agent for the client.").

152. 89 F. Supp. 357 (D. Mass. 1950).

153. Defendant produced these documents to the government in response to a subpoena subject to agreement from the government that all privilege objections would be preserved and were not waived. *Id.* at 359. This fact was not raised by the court as a factor in its decision. *Id.*

154. *Id.* It is not clear who within the company communicated with outside counsel, but this fact is unimportant to the result ultimately reached.

155. *Id.*

156. *Id.*

157. 49 F.R.D. 54 (S.D.N.Y. 1970).

158. *Id.* at 57. The court held that, because the policy allowed the examination under oath to be conducted by "any person" designated by the insurer, the fact that the insurer chose an attorney should not allow the insurer to protect the attorney's report. *Id.* After *in camera* review, the court commented: "The [*in camera*] study discloses that the report consists almost *in toto* of an analysis of the sworn testimony such as 'any person' (lawyer or not) might have made. The facts are summarized; credibility is appraised; inferences are proposed—all tasks we entrust daily to lay jurors." *Id.* This kind of information would likely be protected from discovery by FED. R. CIV. P. 26(b) (3) as the "mental impressions, conclusions, [or] opinions" of an attorney or other representative of a party. *See infra* notes 239-40 and accompanying text.

159. 65 F.R.D. 523 (S.D.N.Y. 1974).

160. *Id.* at 526.

161. 130 F.R.D. 28 (S.D.N.Y. 1990).

162. *Id.* at 33. The Magistrate Judge reviewed the attorney's letter *in camera* and "found them to be communicating factual information, not legal advice." *Id.* The Magistrate Judge ordered the letter to be produced, with the exception of redacted portions relating to legal advice. The district court upheld the Magistrate Judge's ruling. *Id.*

163. 848 F. Supp. 423 (S.D.N.Y. 1994).

164. *Id.* at 428.

165. *Id.*

166. 574 S.W.2d 379 (Mo. 1978), *rev'g*, 563 S.W.2d 62 (Mo. 1978).

167. *Id.* at 380.

168. *Id.* at 380-81.

169. *Id.*

170. *Id.* at 382.

171. *Id.*

172. *Id.* at 382-83. The court found the Wigmore approach would only protect (1) advice from the lawyer concerning a communication from his client, (2) anything the lawyer said that could be an admission of the client, and (3) anything the lawyer said that would lead to an inference about what the client may have said to the lawyer. The court found this insufficient "to accomplish the objective for which the privilege was created and now exists." *Id.* at 384.

173. *Id.* at 383.

174. ALI MODEL CODE OF EVIDENCE, Rule 209(d) (1942) (defining a "confidential communication between client and lawyer" as "information transmitted by a voluntary act of disclosure between a client and his lawyer in confidence"; this definition includes information transmitted voluntarily by any means).

175. *Id.* The court stated:

> The nature and complexity of our present system of justice and the relationships among people and between the people and their government make the preservation and protection of the attorney-client privilege even more essential. If this is to be accomplished, when one undertakes to confer in confidence with an attorney whom he employs in connection with a particular matter at hand, it is vital that all of what the client says to the lawyer and what the lawyer says to the client to be treated as confidential and protected by the attorney-client privilege. This is what the client expects.

Id.

176. *Id.* at 386.

177. *Id.* at 385.

178. *Id.* at 384-85 (footnotes omitted).

179. *Id.* at 385; *see also In re* Bd. of Registration for the Healing Arts v. Spinden, 798 S.W.2d 472, 476 (Mo. Ct. App. 1990) (holding that investigative reports prepared by state medical board investigators acting at direction of board's general counsel were discoverable by doctor in administrative action). The New York Court of Appeals reached a similar conclusion in *Rossi v. Blue Cross & Blue Shield of Greater N.Y.*, 540 N.E.2d 703 (N.Y. 1989). There, in-house counsel wrote a memorandum to Blue Cross's medical director, describing the results of an investigation counsel had undertaken, including conversations with plaintiff's attorney, conversations with the FDA, an analysis of a Blue Cross reimbursement policy, and his opinion and advice regarding a form used to reject certain kinds of medical charges. *Id.* at 704. The court decided that the entire memorandum was protected by the attorney-client privilege, stating:

> So long as the communication is primarily or predominately of a legal character, the privilege is not lost merely by reason of the fact that it also refers to certain non-legal matters. Indeed, the nature of a lawyer's role is such that legal advice may often include reference to other relevant considerations. Here, it is plain from the content and context of the communication that it was for the purpose of facilitating the lawyer's rendition of legal advice to his client.

Id. at 706 (citations omitted).

180. The *Upjohn* Court noted that 7 of the 86 employees interviewed by counsel had terminated their employment by the time they were interviewed. Upjohn Co. v. United States, 449 U.S. 383, 394 n.3 (1981).

181. In a concurring opinion, Chief Justice Burger suggested that the *Upjohn* rule should apply to communications otherwise falling within the framework of *Upjohn*. *See id.* at 402-03.

182. 658 F.2d 1355 (9th Cir. 1981), *cert. denied*, 455 U.S. 990 (1982).

183. *Id.* at 1356.

184. *Id.* at 1359.

185. *Id.* at 1361.

186. *Id.* at 1361 n.7 (citations omitted). This opinion remains as recognized authority in the Ninth Circuit. *See* Admiral Ins. Co. v. Dist. Court, 881 F.2d 1486, 1493 (9th Cir. 1989).

187. *See, e.g.*, Command Transp., Inc. v. Y.S. Line (USA) Corp., 116 F.R.D. 94, 96-97 (D. Mass. 1987); Porter v. Arco Metals Co., 642 F. Supp. 1116, 1118 (D. Mont. 1986); Denver Post Corp. v. Univ. of Colo., 739 P.2d 874, 880 (Colo. Ct. App. 1987). *But see* Infosystems, Inc. v. Ceridian Corp., 197 F.R.D. 303, 305-06 (E.D. Mich. 2000) (holding that no privilege can attach to communications with former employees absent special circumstances); Clark Equip. Co. v. Lift Parts Mfg. Co., No. 82 C 4585, 1985 U.S. Dist. LEXIS 15457, at *14 (N.D. Ill. Oct. 1, 1985) ("[T]his Court holds that post-employment communications with former employees are not within the scope of the attorney-client privilege."). For cases reaching similar conclusions, but in different contexts, *see* Peralta v. Cendant Corp., 190 F.R.D. 38 (D. Conn. 1999) (holding that the attorney-client privilege attaches to communications with former employees only if the communications relate to knowledge obtained during employment or the communications were held with the employee prior to termination and were privileged at that time); Camden v. State of Md., 910 F. Supp. 1115 (D. Md. 1996); Fruehauf Trailer Corp. v. Hagelthorn, 528 N.W.2d 778 (Mich. Ct. App. 1995).

188. 106 F.3d 582 (4th Cir. 1997).

189. *Id.* at 606 (citing Nakajima v. Gen. Motors, 857 F. Supp. 100, 104 (D.D.C. 1994) (D.C. law); Barrett Indus. Trucks v. Old Republic Ins. Co., 129 F.R.D. 515, 517-18 (N.D. Ill. 1990) (Illinois law); Connolly Data Sys. v. Victor Techs., 114 F.R.D. 89, 93-94 (S.D. Cal. 1987) (California law)).

190. Documents in a party's counsel's files are within the scope of documents that must be

produced in response to a discovery request directed to that party. Rule 34 of the Federal Rules of Civil Procedure, for example, requires parties to produce requested documents that are within their possession, custody, or control. *See* FED. R. CIV. P. 34. "Control" is broadly construed to mean not only physical possession but the legal or practical right to obtain them from another source on demand. *See, e.g.,* Golden Trade v. Lee Apparel Co., 143 F.R.D. 514, 525 (S.D.N.Y. 1992); M.L.C., Inc. v. N. Am. Philips Corp., 109 F.R.D. 134, 136 (S.D.N.Y. 1986). Thus, "documents in the possession of a party's counsel are deemed within the control of the party, regardless of the origin of the documents." Arkwright Mut. Ins. Co. v. Nat'l Union Fire Ins. Co., No. 90 Civ. 7811, 1994 WL 510043, at *3 (S.D.N.Y. Sept. 16, 1994); *see also* Hanson v. Gartland S.S. Co., 34 F.R.D. 493, 496 (N.D. Ohio 1964).

191. *See, e.g.,* Arkwright Mut. Ins. Co. v. Nat'l Union Fire Ins. Co., No. 90 Civ. 7811, 1994 WL 510043 (S.D.N.Y. Sept. 16, 1994). In *Arkwright*, National Union sought production of documents in the possession of Arkwright's counsel in prior litigation and in possession of counsel hired by Arkwright to conduct a subrogation investigation. National Union argued that some of the claimed attorney-client privileged documents lost their privilege because they contain discoverable factual information. The court rejected National Union's argument, noting "[t]hat principle simply means that Arkwright must, in either depositions or interrogatory responses, disclose relevant facts if National Union inquires, not that any privileged communications containing facts are fair game in discovery." *Id.* at *8.

192. *See, e.g.,* Carte Blanche (Singapore) PTE, Ltd. v. Diners Club Int'l, Inc., 130 F.R.D. 28, 31 (S.D.N.Y. 1990) (information the court called "factual" obtained from third parties must be disclosed).

193. *See, e.g.,* Port Auth. of N.Y. v. Arcadian Corp., Civ. No. 96-1635, 1996 U.S. Dist. LEXIS 22038 (D.N.J. Sept. 30, 1996) (holding that an attorney who represents an insurer in a subrogation action also owes a fiduciary duty to the insured); Doctors' Co. Ins. Servs. v. Superior Court, 275 Cal. Rptr. 674, 680-81 (Cal. Ct. App. 1990) (holding that an attorney employed by an insurance company to defend an action against an insured represents both the insurer and the insured). *But see* Pine Island Farmers Coop v. Erstad & Riemer, P.A., 649 N.W.2d 444 (Minn. 2002) (holding that defense counsel did not represent both the insured and the insurer in an action brought against the insured, because defense counsel did not consult with or obtain the express consent of the insured to engage in the dual representation).

194. 839 F.2d 958 (3d Cir. 1988).

195. *Id.* at 965. In this case, United Coal Companies owned a coal mine and processing plant, and operated an aerial tramway to transport coal refuse from one of its processing facilities. *Id.* at 960. United sustained a loss when a haul rope broke, causing 62 cars on the aerial tramway to fall to the ground. United's property insurers paid United $1.5 million, thereby becoming subrogated to United's rights against the manufacturer and installer. *Id.* The subrogation receipts authorized the insurers to sue in United's name. The insurers retained attorneys to pursue subrogation. United also retained the same attorneys to recover its uninsured loss. The attorneys filed suit in United's name against the manufacturer and installer for the entire loss, including United's uninsured loss. *Id.* During the course of discovery, defendants filed discovery requests seeking the production of two letters from the attorneys to the property insurers. *Id.* at 961. United withheld these documents from production as privileged, and defendants moved to compel. *Id.* at 960-61. The trial court granted the motion to compel because the insurers were not named plaintiffs in the action. The reported colloquy between the court and counsel for the plaintiff is instructive:

> Ms. MacKarey: Your Honor, I think the problem is the insurance companies are our clients. You know, if I could just have a moment to address this.
> The Court: Not according to the caption of the case.
> Ms. MacKarey: They may not be named plaintiff. They are our clients. We were re-

tained by them. They have an interest in this action.

> The Court: If those documents are not in the hands of these defendants by Monday at noon, this case will be dismissed.

Id. at 964.

On appeal, the Third Circuit, recognizing the true nature of a subrogation action, determined that the trial court had erred:

> It is undisputed that the correspondence in issue is between attorneys and insurance companies which retained them to prosecute this action.
>
> . . . Where, as here, an attorney represents two clients, the privilege applies to those clients as against a common adversary. . . . Thus the district court committed legal error when it ruled that the non-party status of the insurers was dispositive on their claim of attorney-client privilege. They were clients, and no more was required to support their assertion of the privilege.

Id. at 965.

196. 761 S.W.2d 74 (Tex. App. 1988).

197. *Id.* at 76.

198. *Id.* In many jurisdictions, communications made by an insured to his liability insurance company, concerning an event which may be made the basis of a claim against him covered by the policy, is a privileged attorney-client communication if the policy requires the liability insurer to defend the insured through its attorney and the communication is intended for the information or assistance of the attorney hired by the liability insurer to defend the insured. *See, e.g.*, State Farm Fire & Cas. Co. v. Superior Court, 254 Cal. Rptr. 543 (Cal. Ct. App. 1988); Hyams v. Evanston Hosp., 587 N.E.2d 1127 (Ill. App. Ct. 1992). Other courts have explicitly refused to apply the attorney-client privilege to insured-insurer communications. *See, e.g.*, Linde Thomson Langworthy Kohn & Van Dyke v. Resolution Trust Corp., 5 F.3d 1508, 1515 (D.C. Cir. 1993).

199. *In re* Bevill, Bresler & Schulman Asset Mgmt. Corp., 805 F.2d 120, 124 n.1 (3d Cir. 1986); Moore v. Tri-City Hosp. Auth., 118 F.R.D. 646, 648 (N.D. Ga. 1988); Am. Nat'l Watermattress Corp. v. Manville, 642 P.2d 1330, 1333 (Alaska 1982) ; Nat'l W. Life Ins. Co. v. Walters, 216 So. 2d 485, 486 (Fla. Dist. Ct. App. 1968).

200. Potential clients are increasingly requesting that firms engage in competitive interviewing processes in which a client (usually a large corporation) interviews several different law firms for the same assignment. Participating in such a process can raise several ethical issues, including the creation of an attorney-client relationship between the law firm and the prospective client even when the law firm did not intend such a relationship to exist, the concomitant creation of a duty to maintain confidences of that "client," and disqualification of the firm from representing another party in the same or a substantially related matter, even though the law firm was not retained. *See, e.g.*, B.F. Goodrich Co. v. Formosa Plastics Corp., 638 F. Supp. 1050 (S.D. Tex. 1986) (holding that no attorney-client relationship had been created during one-day interview, because firm had not actually received confidential information); Bridge Prods., Inc. v. Quantum Chem. Corp., 20 Envtl. L. Rep. (Envtl. L. Inst.) 20,940 (N.D. Ill. Apr. 27, 1990) (disqualifying firm based on a prior interview attended by the corporation's CEO, its general counsel, and two lawyers from the firm, since the corporation had shared confidences with the firm and had reasonably believed that the firm was acting as its attorney); Kenneth D. Agran, *The Treacherous Path to the Diamond-Studded Tiara: Ethical Dilemmas in Legal Beauty Contests*, 9 Geo. J. Legal Ethics 1307 (1996) (recommending presumption of lawyer-client relationship in initial consultation, rebuttable only by written waiver from prospective client); Debra Bassett Perschbacher & Rex R. Perschbacher, *Enter at Your Own Risk: The Initial Consultation & Conflicts of Interest*, 3 Geo. J. Legal Ethics 689, 704-05 (1990) (arguing that the lawyer must make it clear to the prospective client that no attorney-client relationship is being created by the consultation).

201. 119 F.R.D. 621 (D. Mass. 1988).

202. *Id.* at 622.

203. *Id.*

204. *Id.*

205. *Id.* at 621-22.

206. *Id.* at 622.

207. *Id.*

208. Diversified Group, Inc. v. Daugerdas, Nos. 00 Civ. 0771 (SAS), 00 Civ. 6484 (SAS), 2003 U.S. Dist. LEXIS 16284 (S.D.N.Y. Sept. 5, 2003).

209. *Id.* at *11.

210. *Id.* at *10-11 (quoting Bennet Silvershein Assoc. v. Furman, 776 F. Supp. 800, 803 (S.D.N.Y. 1991) (internal quotation marks and citation omitted)).

211. No. 02 Civ. 6441 (LAK), 2002 U.S. Dist. LEXIS 26318 (S.D.N.Y. Oct. 8, 2002).

212. *Id.* at *3.

213. *Id.*

214. *Id.*

215. *See, e.g., In re* Subpoenas Duces Tecum, 738 F.2d 1367, 1369 (D.C. Cir. 1984); *In re* Grand Jury Proceedings, 727 F. 2d 1352, 1356 (4th Cir. 1984). As a general rule, only the client, and not its counsel, may waive the attorney-client privilege. *See, e.g.,* United States v. AT&T, 642 F.2d 1285, 1299 (D.C. Cir. 1980); Carte Blanche (Singapore) PTE., Ltd. v. Diners Club Int'l, Inc., 130 F.R.D. 28, 31 (S.D.N.Y. 1990); Leibel v. Gen. Motors Corp., 646 N.W.2d 179, 185 (Mich. Ct. App. 2002) ("The attorney-client privilege is personal to the client, and only the client can waive it."). However, the attorney may waive the attorney-client privilege on behalf of his client where the client voluntarily discloses or voluntarily consents to disclosure of the privileged communication. *See, e.g.,* Perrignon v. Bergen Brunswig Corp., 77 F.R.D. 455, 460 (N.D. Cal. 1978).

216. *See, e.g., In re* Grand Jury Subpoenas, 902 F.2d 244, 248-49 (4th Cir. 1990); Waller v. Fin. Corp. of Am., 828 F.2d 579, 583 n.7 (9th Cir. 1987); *In re* Bevill, Bresler & Schulman Asset Mgmt. Corp., 805 F.2d 120, 126 (3d Cir. 1986); Weil Ceramics & Glass, Inc. v. Work, 110 F.R.D. 500, 502-03 (E.D.N.Y. 1986); *In re* Bairnco Corp. Sec. Litig., 148 F.R.D. 91, 102 (S.D.N.Y. 1993).

217. *See, e.g,* Loustalet v. Refco, Inc., 154 F.R.D. 243, 247 (C.D. Cal. 1993).

218. *In re* Bevill, Bresler & Schulman Asset Mgmt. Corp., 805 F.2d 120, 126 (3d Cir. 1986); *see also* United States v. Evans, 113 F.3d 1457, 1467 (7th Cir. 1997) (quoting United States v. Schwimmer, 892 F.2d 237, 243-44 (2d Cir. 1989) (noting that the "joint defense privilege" is also referred to as the "common interest rule")).

219. FDIC v. Ogden Corp., 202 F.3d 454, 461 (1st Cir. 2000) (citing McMorgan & Co. v. First Cal. Mortgage Co., 931 F. Supp. 699, 702 (N.D. Cal. 1996).

220. Hearn v. Rhay, 68 F.R.D. 574, 581 (E.D. Wash. 1975). Many courts applying the at-issue waiver follow *Hearn*'s three-factor test. *See, e.g.,* Conkling v. Turner, 883 F.2d 431, 434 (5th Cir. 1989) (citing cases); Remington Arms Co. v. Liberty Mut. Ins. Co., 142 F.R.D. 408, 413 (D. Del. 1992). Other courts follow a variation of *Hearn*'s three-factor test. *See, e.g.,* Koppers Co. v. Aetna Cas. & Sur. Co., 847 F. Supp. 360, 363 (W.D. Pa. 1994). In *Koppers*, for example, the court adopted the first two *Hearn* factors but replaced the third factor with a balancing test—"the likelihood of chilling the type of ordinarily-privileged communication is outweighed by the unfairness to the seeking party if privilege is found." *Id.* at 363-64.

221. *See, e.g.,* N. River Ins. Co. v. Phila. Reinsurance Corp., 797 F. Supp. 363, 370 (D.N.J. 1992); Fox v. Cal. Sierra Fin. Serv., 120 F.R.D. 520 (N.D.Cal. 1988).

222. 914 F. Supp. 1084 (D.N.J. 1996).

223. *Id.* at 1093.

224. *Id.* at 1094.

225. *Id.* at 1088.

226. *Id.* at 1091-92.

227. *Id.* at 1094.

228. *Id.* at 1096.

229. *See, e.g.,* Brownell v. Roadway Package Sys., Inc., 185 F.R.D. 19, 25 (N.D.N.Y. 1999); Peterson v. Wallace Computer Servs., Inc., 984 F. Supp. 821, 825 (D. Vt. 1997); Johnson v. Rauland-Borg Corp., 961 F. Supp. 208, 211 (N.D. Ill. 1997); Wellpoint Health Networks, Inc. v. Superior Court, 68 Cal. Rptr. 2d 844, 855-56 (Cal. Ct. App. 1997).

230. 730 A.2d 51 (Conn. 1999).

231. *Id.* at 53.

232. *Id.* at 61.

233. *Id.*

234. *See, e.g.,* St. Paul Reinsurance Co. v. Commercial Fin. Corp., 197 F.R.D. 620, 630 (N.D. Iowa 2000) ("Numerous courts have noted the difficulty of determining the scope of work-product privilege as it applies to insurance claims files or records from an insurer's investigation of an insured's claim . . ."); Goodyear Tire & Rubber Co. v. Chiles Power Supply, Inc., 190 F.R.D. 532, 535 (S.D. Ind. 1999) ("Because an insurer's business is to investigate claims that may or may not result in litigation, application of the work-product privilege to insurance claims investigations has been frequently litigated.").

235. 329 U.S. 495 (1947).

236. *Id.* at 498.

237. *Id.* at 510.

238. *Id.* at 509-12.

239. FED. R. CIV. P. 26, Advisory Committee Notes; *see also* United Steelworks of Am. v. Ivaco, Inc., No. 1:01-CV-0426-CAP, 2003 U.S. Dist. LEXIS 10008, at *9-10 (N.D. Ga. Jan. 13, 2003) (noting that the work-product doctrine, established by Hickman v. Taylor, 329 U.S. 495 (1947), is codified in FED. R. CIV. P. 26(b)(3)).

240. FED. R. CIV. P. 26(b)(3).

241. Upjohn Co. v. United States, 449 U.S. 383, 397-402 (1981). While the Court stopped short of adopting an absolute rule because the issue had not been directly decided below, the Court held that the notes prepared by the attorneys during conversations were likely not discoverable. *Id.* at 401-02. The Court stated:

> [S]uch work product [the notes] cannot be disclosed simply on a showing of substantial need and inability to obtain the equivalent without undue hardship.
>
> While we are not prepared at this juncture to say that such material is always protected by the work-product rule, we think a far stronger showing of necessity and unavailability by other means than was made by the Government or applied by the Magistrate in this case would be necessary to compel disclosure.

Id.

242. 174 F.3d 394 (4th Cir. 1999).

243. *Id.* at 403 (quoting *In re* Grand Jury Proceedings, 33 F.3d 342, 348 (4th Cir. 1994)) (internal citations omitted); *see also* Conn. Indem. Co. v. Carrier Haulers, Inc., 197 F.R.D. 564, 570 (W.D.N.C. 2000) ("The work-product privilege is intended to prevent a litigant from taking a free ride on the research and thinking of his opponent's lawyer and to avoid the resulting deterrent to a lawyer's committing his thoughts to paper.").

244. *See, e.g.,* ARIZ. R. CIV. P. 26(b)(3); CAL. CIV. PROC. CODE § 2018 (West Supp. 1996); MICH. CT. R. 2.302(B)(3); MINN. R. CIV. P. 26.02(3).

245. Taroli v. Gen. Elec. Co., 114 F.R.D. 97, 98 (N.D. Ind. 1987), *aff'd*, 840 F.2d 920 (7th Cir. 1988); State Farm Fire & Cas. Co. v. Perrigan, 102 F.R.D. 235, 237 (W.D. Va. 1984).

246. Hickman v. Taylor, 329 U.S. 495, 511 (1947). *Compare* United States v. Adlman, 68 F.3d 1495 (2d Cir. 1995) (holding that the work-product protection can apply even when the event giv-

ing rise to the litigation has not yet occurred), *and* A. Michael's Piano, Inc. v. Fed. Trade Comm'n, 18 F.3d 138, 146 (2d Cir. 1994) (holding that documents prepared during close out of an investigation by employees who believed litigation would never occur are protected), *with* Binks Mfg. Co. v. Nat'l Presto Indus., Inc., 709 F.2d 1109, 1120 (7th Cir. 1983) (holding that an investigation performed while settlement discussions were ongoing was not in anticipation of litigation).

247. 636 F.2d 1028 (5th Cir. 1981).

248. *Id.* at 1040.

249. 134 F.3d 1194 (2d Cir. 1998).

250. *Id.* at 1195.

251. *Id.* at 1197.

252. *Id.* at 1198.

253. *Id.* at 1201-02.

254. *Id.* at 1195; *see also In re* Grand Jury Proceedings, No. M-11-189, 2001 U.S. Dist. LEXIS 15646, at *49 (S.D.N.Y. Oct. 3, 2001) ("It is not enough that the document was created after the threat of litigation is real, but it is also necessary that the motivation for creating that document be the litigation.").

255. 213 F.R.D. 329 (N.D. Cal. 2003).

256. *Id.* at 330-31.

257. *Id.* at 331.

258. *Id.*

259. *In re* Grand Jury Proceedings, 2001 U.S. Dist. LEXIS 15646, at *52 (quoting *In re* William L. Derienzo, No. 5-96-01186, 1998 Bankr. LEXIS 635, at *15 (Bankr. M.D. Pa. Apr. 28, 1998)).

260. 153 F.R.D. 660 (D. Colo. 1994).

261. *Id.* at 662-63; *see also In re* Grand Jury Subpoena, 599 F.2d 504, 511 (2d Cir. 1979) (holding that questionnaire prepared and sent by attorney to 71 employees of corporate client and the employees' replies and memoranda containing results of interviews with 39 of the employees were prepared in anticipation of litigation).

262. No. 90 Civ. 7811, 1994 WL 510043 (S.D.N.Y. Sept. 16, 1994).

263. *Id.* at *9.

Because insurers investigate claims in the ordinary course of business, courts have struggled to apply the work-product doctrine in insurance cases. There appears to be three different approaches to the question of whether documents compiled by an attorney or insurer after an insurance loss have been prepared in anticipation of litigation. The first approach generally denies protection to insurance reports prepared after a loss that may generate a potential claim. *See, e.g.,* Thomas Organ Co. v. Jadranska Slobodna Plovidba, 54 F.R.D. 367, 374 (N.D. Ill. 1972).

The second view provides the work-product protection to documents if they were generated after a loss which likely will be litigated. *See, e.g.,* Basinger v. Glacial Carriers, Inc., 107 F.R.D. 771, 773-74 (M.D. Pa. 1985).

The final approach is a case-by-case analysis which considers the unique factual context of the given factual situation. This is the approach taken by most courts today. *See, e.g.,* McNulty v. Bally's Park Place, Inc., 120 F.R.D. 27 (E.D. Pa. 1988) (statement taken by insurance adjuster from witness at the request of insured's legal department was prepared in anticipation of litigation but statement was discoverable because of substantial need of plaintiff in view of fact that witness was the only eyewitness to the incident in question, and was not located); Taroli v. Gen. Elec. Co., 114 F.R.D. 97 (N.D. Ind. 1987) (defendant failed to demonstrate that its investigation following injury caused by explosion of fluorescent lightbulb manufactured by defendant was conducted in anticipation of litigation, even where defendant received subrogation notice from plaintiff's workers' compensation carrier); W. Nat'l. Bank of Denver v. Employers Ins. of Wausau, 109 F.R.D. 55 (D. Colo. 1985) (holding that investigation by law firm hired by liability insurer was not work product, but rather the investigative file of the insurer prepared in the ordinary course of business); State Farm

Fire & Cas. Co. v. Perrigan, 102 F.R.D. 235 (W.D. Va. 1984) (investigative report prepared by independent investigator hired by insurer was not work product but rather prepared during the ordinary course of investigating a fire); Fine v. Bellefonte Underwriters Ins. Co., 91 F.R.D. 420 (S.D.N.Y. 1981) (holding that investigation by insurer was routine investigation of possibly resistible claim and reports generated during such investigation held discoverable).

264.   161 F.R.D. 274 (S.D.N.Y. 1995).

265.   *Id.* at 280-81.

266.   *Id.*; *see also* Phillips Elecs. N. Am. Corp. v. Universal Elecs. Inc., 892 F. Supp. 108, 110 (D. Del. 1995) (documents relating to patent infringement investigations, tests, and analyses performed by plaintiff's employees for its in-house counsel were prepared in the ordinary course of business).

267.   196 F.R.D. 7 (D. Mass. 2000).

268.   Holton v. S.W. Marine, Inc., No. 00-1427 Section "L" (5), 2000 U.S. Dist. LEXIS 16604 (E.D. La. Nov. 9, 2000); McNulty v. Bally's Park Place, Inc., 120 F.R.D. 27, 30 (E.D. Pa. 1988); Long's Drug Stores v. Howe, 657 P.2d 412, 417 (Ariz. 1983).

269.   *See, e.g.*, Brown v. Superior Court, 670 P.2d 725 (Ariz. 1983) (complete file of insurer subject to discovery on ground that substantial equivalent not obtainable; no attorney-client privilege asserted). *But see* Aetna Cas. & Sur. Co. v. Superior Court, 200 Cal. Rptr. 471 (Cal. Ct. App. 1984) (communications between attorney and insurer not discoverable in bad faith action when insurer's representatives can articulate insurer's reasons for denying claim).

270.   FED. R. CIV. P. 26(b)(3); Upjohn Co. v United States, 449 U.S. 383 (1981); *In re* Leslie Fay Cos. Sec. Litig., 161 F.R.D. 274, 279 (S.D.N.Y. 1995). The U.S. Supreme Court has said that "[a]t its core, the work-product doctrine shelters the mental processes of the attorney, providing a privileged area within which he can analyze and prepare his client's case." United States v. Nobles, 422 U.S. 225, 238 (1975).

271.   *See, e.g.*, Raso v. CMC Equip. Rental, Inc., 154 F.R.D. 126, 128 (E.D. Pa. 1994); Eoppolo v. Nat'l R.R. Passenger Corp., 108 F.R.D. 292, 294 (E.D. Pa. 1985).

CHAPTER 13

Conflict Between the Permissive Scope of Fact Witness Investigation and Protection of Attorney-Client Communication[*]

VINCENT S. WALKOWIAK

Definition of the Problem

Whether in-house counsel, plaintiff or defendant, the issue of proper investigation of a claim or defense inevitably involves interviewing persons with knowledge. Certain potential witnesses cannot be interviewed without the permission of the opposing party, and no attorney would consider contacting a party without first contacting the attorney representing that party. The issue of which witnesses can and which witnesses cannot be interviewed without first contacting opposing counsel, however, becomes clouded in litigation involving corporations. Limitations on contacting parties become more difficult to apply with clarity when the potential witness is a current employee, or more typically, a former disgruntled employee. This chapter will address the problems associated with witness contact in those circumstances where the witness may have some current or former affiliation with a party, but whose position does not clearly indicate that they are a current or former client represented by opposing counsel.

---

[*] This chapter is an update and rewrite of *"Who Can I Talk to?" Scaling the Wall of the Attorney-Client Privilege in Contacting Witnesses,* by Alan F. Wagner, published in the Second Edition of THE ATTORNEY CLIENT PRIVILEGE UNDER SIEGE.

There are few clear solutions to this problem, and the answers that the courts have provided are nearly as varied as the factual circumstances in which these issues were presented to the courts. Regrettably, the courts even seem to disagree on the underlying purposes of the rules involved, and their interpretations have produced widely disparate results. Few common themes or bright line tests have emerged beyond the obvious restriction against communicating directly with a represented individual or in some instances the managerial level of a corporate party. Under these circumstances, there is little for counsel to rely upon in making strategic litigation decision that they can be confident will not be criticized later as unethical and improper.

All states have adopted ethical rules that preclude ex parte communication with parties represented by counsel.[1]

Rule 4.2 of the American Bar Association Model Rules of Professional Conduct, entitled "Communication with Person Represented by Counsel," addresses the prohibition of speaking with opposing parties in the following manner:

> In representing a client, a lawyer shall not communicate about the subject of the representation with a person the lawyer knows to be represented by another lawyer in the matter, unless the lawyer has the consent of the other lawyer or is authorized by law to do so.[2]

This rule is clear enough when the parties are individuals.[3] A lawyer shall not communicate with a represented party, however that communication comes about. In *Faison v. Thornton*,[4] the defendant himself contacted the plaintiffs' counsel directly, without knowledge of his attorney, and discussed the litigation with plaintiffs' counsel. In disqualifying the plaintiffs' counsel for the contact, the court noted that the rule does not permit the client to waive the requirements of this ethical rule and that counsel, if contacted by an adverse party, is obliged to terminate the communication and contact opposing counsel in order to continue any communication with the represented party.[5] However, as the attorney-client privilege itself is subject to interpretation when the client is a corporation involving control group or subject matter tests to determine who is entitled to assert the attorney-client privilege, which employees may invoke it, or which may waive it, this rule was also not so clear when the other party was a corporation or other business entity and even less so, prior to the 1995 amendment which substituted the word "person" for "party." The comment to the predecessor to the current rule as well as the current comment provide minimal guidance:

> In the case of an organization, this rule prohibits communications by a lawyer for one party concerning the matter in representation with persons having a managerial responsibility on behalf of the organization, and with any other person whose act or omission in connection with that matter may be imputed to the organization for purposes of civil or criminal liability or whose statement may constitute admission on the part of the organization.[6]

Thus, while courts regularly found that corporate organizations were included as parties under this rule, the principle issue in contention was and is which employees or agents of that corporate organization could be approached ex parte.[7]

The ABA rules and comment were and are substantially similar to the rules adopted by the states, but they were and are not identical.[8] For example, in Florida, prior to the 1995 amendment, the rule, by appearance, was clearer and broader than the ABA counterpart. It was rules such as Florida's that attempted to make the restriction of witness contact apparently more clear that encouraged the 1995 amendment to the ABA rule. The Florida rule attempted to make the obligation under the rule clearer by the substitution of person for party—a change that was subsequently adopted by the ABA in 1995.[9]

Unfortunately, neither the Florida version nor the ABA amendment has sufficiently removed all ambiguity. Courts have continued to struggle when determining the scope of whether a particular employee falls within the class protected by this rule of ethics.

Current Employees

Courts have articulated a number of tests to determine whether a current employee falls within a protected category including: the control group test, the binding admission test, the balancing test, the blanket test, the managing-speaking test, the scope of employment test, and the alter ego test.[10] These various tests have, in part, been incorporated into the Comment to the ABA Rule. The categories of witnesses who cannot be contacted by opposing counsel are those "having managerial responsibility on behalf of the organization," those "whose act or omission in connection with that matter may be imputed to the organization for purposes of civil or criminal liability," and those "whose statement may constitute an admission on the part of the organization."[11]

At a minimum, however, all of these tests recognize that there are key individuals in every corporation who cannot be contacted by plaintiff's counsel without the permission of the company's attorney. This key group includes "those top management persons who had the responsibility of making final decisions and those employees whose advisory role to top management form the basis of any final decision by top management."[12] It also includes "those employees who have the legal authority to 'bind' the corporation in a legal evidentiary sense, that is, those employees who have 'speaking authority' for the corporation."[13] One of the broader tests applied is the so-called scope-of-employment test, which precludes ex parte interviews with employees about "matters within the scope of the employee's employment."[14]

An employee who serves as an internal technical expert may be neither part of the control group nor one whose conduct may establish the company's liability. Nevertheless, the public policy underlying the need to protect an in-house expert's work has been recognized. Protection should be afforded the information of such an in-house expert so that the expert's role in evaluating and improving company products can proceed without fear that such actions will later be used against the company in lawsuits.[15]

Combining many of the above factors, the New Jersey Supreme Court articulated the following standards of conduct under New Jersey's Professional Rule of Conduct 4.2:

[W]e shall for the present limit the application of RPC 4.2 in the organizational context to (a) the control group, which for now, we interpret to mean those employees of the organization entrusted with the management of the case or matter in question, and (b) the employee or employees whose conduct, in and of itself, establishes the organization's liability. With respect to that latter class of employees, we interpret the RPC to require notice of, rather than consent from, the organization's attorney and to be in effect after filing of an indictment or civil complaint. Any deliberate delay in filing to circumvent the ethical restraints of the RPC will not be countenanced. For now, these ethical restraints apply to the interview of present and former employees in the two classes.[16]

Thus, "for now" plaintiff's counsel would be barred from any ex parte contact with present or former management employees within the "control group," but permitted, with notice, to pursue contacts with even present employees who are distinct from the control group.[17]

One of the broadest tests prohibiting contact of employees is that articulated by the California Appellate Court in *Mills Land & Water Co. v. Golden W. Ref. Co.*,[18] which held that Rule 4.2 is best read as precluding contact with all current employees of the corporate party: "[I]t is best to draw a clear and unequivocal line—opposing counsel should not have ex parte contacts concerning a subject of controversy with the employees of a corporate party to the controversy."[19] This decision was based, in large part, on the United States Supreme Court's discussion of the attorney-client privilege in *Upjohn Co. v. United States*,[20] in which the court rejected the narrow "control group" test because it "discourage[d] the communication of relevant information by employees of the client to attorneys seeking to render legal advice to the client corporation." Two California city bar associations have likewise banned all contact with current employees of corporate parties.[21]

Former Employees

Generally, ex parte contacts with former employees by plaintiff's counsel are not barred by Rule 4.2. Although there is some authority to the contrary,[22] the majority of courts have ruled that Rule 4.2 does not govern communication with former employees.[23] Moreover the ABA itself has taken this position:

[I]t is the opinion of the Committee that a lawyer representing a client in a matter adverse to a corporate party that is represented by another lawyer may, without violating Model Rule 4.2, communicate about the subject of the representation with an unrepresented former employee of the corporate party without the consent of the corporation's lawyer.[24]

As explained by the court in *Hanntz v. Shiley, Inc., Div. of Pfizer, Inc.*,[25] a product liability action involving allegedly defective artificial heart valves in which the court permitted plaintiff's counsel to interview, ex parte, employees familiar with how heart valves are handled during the manufacturing process, applying Rule 4.2 to former employees does not serve the primary purposes of the rule of preventing "represented party from being overwhelmed by opposing counsel in the absence of friendly counsel" and preventing "the disruption of the attorney-client relationship by opposing counsel."[26] Former employees, even managerial employees, the court maintained, cannot bind the corporation once their agency relationship with the corporation is terminated.[27] In addition, the testimony of such employees cannot be imputed to the corporation as an admission, as least under the Federal Rules of Evidence, because the employee is not acting within the scope of his or her employment.[28] That contact is not without limitation, however, as the plaintiffs' counsel learned in *Rentclub, Inc. v. Transamerica Rental Finance Corp.*[29]

In *Rentclub,* a case from the Federal Court of the Middle District of Pennsylvania, a party retained their opponents' former chief financial officer. The former financial officer was then retained by counsel for that party as a "trial consultant" in a contract dispute litigation with the former CFO's former employer. The law firm later paid the former chief financial officer and, five days later, he executed an affidavit adverse to his former employer. This prompted a motion to disqualify the firm for its communication with the former chief financial officer and the alleged appearance of professional impropriety.[30]

In deciding to disqualify counsel, the trial court first held that a former employee may be considered a "party" for purposes of the ethical constraint in contacting an opposing party and then looked to the rule's comments to define "party" as including: (1) managerial employees, (2) any other person whose acts or omissions in connection with the matter at issue may be imputed to the corporation for liability, and (3) persons whose statements constitute admissions by the corporation.[31] Noting that the first and third categories "are clearly limited to current employees," the court nonetheless determined that the second category would include a former employee who possessed privileged or confidential information or materials.

> [A] former employee who is a "party" because of his position and knowledge will remain a party even after he leaves the corporation because that employee has a memory. The corporation continues to have a vital interest in the employee's knowledge of privileged information and its potential release to opposing counsel in litigation after the employee leaves.[32]

Extending the definition of "party" to include former managerial employees possessing privileged information and ruling that the former chief financial officer fell within the rule, the district court disqualified the firm that had retained him as a trial consultant and required their client to obtain substitute counsel.[33]

The court that decided the *Rentclub, Inc. v. Transamerica Rental Finance Corp.* case was faced with a similar but not identical problem in *Browning v. AT&T Paradyne.*[34] In *Browning*, a supervisory employee of a corporate defendant became involved in evaluating and terminating fellow employees in a corporate reduction in force. Soon thereafter, the supervisor himself was terminated. When the terminated supervisor joined as a plaintiff with the former employees who he had helped terminate from the company and brought an age discrimination suit, the corporate defendant moved to disqualify plaintiff's counsel by virtue of his communication with the company's former supervisor.

Not surprisingly, the court was unwilling to give the *Rentclub* decision such reach, noting that to do so would place the former employee in an untenable predicament because he could not be represented by defendant's counsel since their interest are in conflict as evidenced by the age discrimination suit and the defendant's counterclaim. The court found, therefore, that the plaintiffs' counsel could not logically be accused of having ex parte communications with their own client.[35]

The *Rentclub* decision which applied the prohibition of communications with a party to former managerial employees has not been more broadly interpreted at least within the same federal district. In *Lang v. Reedy Creek Improvement District,*[36] the court refused to expand the scope of the *Rentclub* decision and allowed plaintiffs' counsel to conduct ex parte communications with former firefighters in their investigation of a sex discrimination suit brought by other former female firefighters.

Recognizing that the *Rentclub* decision focused on high-level employees who were privy to substantial privileged or confidential information, the *Lang* court weighed the conflicting need of the parties by weighing their conflicts needs:

> . . . the Plaintiffs' need for informal discovery and the Defendants' need for effective legal representation and to avoid both unnecessary impediments to informal discovery and inadequate protection of corporate interests.[37]

Balancing these interests, the court noted that "[p]roof of wrongdoing, and especially of discrimination is difficult to establish and Plaintiffs must be afforded the opportunities to discover all factual information pertinent to their case."[38] The *Lang* court, however, did not give plaintiffs' counsel carte blanche to interview everyone with such information and precluded contact with current employees. It stated that:

> [I]t would be difficult to conceive of a scenario in which Plaintiffs could contact current employees . . . without risking violation of the ethical rules. . . . Because of the increased risks of prejudice to the defendants that would arise from ex parte communications with current employees, the plain language of the ethical rules, and defendants' opposition to such contact, the court is unwilling to give plaintiffs the "'green light for such discovery." [39]

In addition, the court set strict guidelines for the proposed contact by the plaintiff's counsel. It required that plaintiff's counsel immediately identify herself as the attorney representing the plaintiff and specify the purpose of the contact and advise the former employee that she need not participate in any interview. The court also cautioned that plaintiff's counsel should avoid any disclosure of privileged materials. In contacting former employees, plaintiff's counsel was directed to create a list of all persons contacted and preserve any and all statements or notes resulting from the contact. These lists and notes were subject to review by defense counsel subject to the protection afforded by the attorney work-product privilege.[40]

Decisions are also divided on the issue of the permissible scope of contact for former employees. In *Barfuss v. Diversicare Corporation of America*[41] and *Reynoso v. Grenald's Park Manor, Inc.,*[42] two Florida state courts charted two very different paths regarding the scope of communications permitted with former employees. In *Barfuss,* the court ruled that plaintiff's counsel was not permitted to have communications with former nursing home employees who had participated in the plaintiff's care. On the other hand, the court permitted counsel to speak with former employees who did not provide any care to the plaintiff—characterizing these employees as "merely witnesses" to the plaintiff's care, and thus, not likely to possess privileged information.[43]

Another Florida District Court provided a more liberal view of the rule.[44] In *Reynoso v. Granald's Park Manor, Inc.,*[45] the court held that Rule 4-4.2 did not prevent the plaintiff from conducting ex parte interviews—either directly or through investigators—with 60 former employees of the defendant nursing home who had formerly worked in the plaintiff's ward. In doing so, the court was quick to counsel that "no inquiry can be made into any matters that are the subject of attorney/client privilege, and the requirements of Rule 4-4.3, entitled *"Dealing with Unrepresented Persons"* must be scrupulously observed."[46] The *Reynoso* decision was followed by yet another court in *Estate of Schwartz v. H.B.A. Management,*[47] which permitted contact with former nursing home employees.

The American Bar Association has issued a formal ethical opinion in agreement with the more liberal view that an attorney may speak with former employees, seemingly without regard to the position previously held by the employees. The ABA Opinion points out that:

> [N]either the rule nor its comment purport to deal with former employees of a corporate party. Because an organizational party (as contrasted to an individual party) necessarily acts through others, however, the concerns reflected in the comment to Rule 4-4.2 may survive the termination of the employment relationship.
>
> [A] lawyer representing a client in a matter adverse to a corporate party that is represented by another attorney may, without violating Model Rule 4.2, communicate about the subject of the representation with an unrepresented former employee of the corporate party without the consent of the corporation's lawyer.[48]

The Florida Bar reached the same result in its analysis of the rule, finding that "former managers and other former employees are not within the scope of the rule of ex parte context." As comforting as these decisions might seem, they are not binding on any court including those courts in Florida that may be called upon to review the matter.

The court in *Lang* was not alone in its approach to permitting contact with former employees only after the establishment of a strict protocol for the contact itself—often providing to the opposing parties the fruits of the interview itself as a condition of the sought-after ex parte communication.[49]

Some courts, however, have taken a less restrictive view and permit contact with former employees unrestricted by considerations other than the applicable ethical rules regulating contact with an unrepresented person. In *Rewis v. FMC Corporation,*[50] the court took yet another approach to the ex parte communication issue—holding that the ethical rule did not reach former employees, even managerial employees, with whom counsel is free to communicate. Of course, the court noted that contact with former employees who were in fact represented by the company's counsel would be impermissible and proscribed inquiry into privileged matters.

A number of other courts have given counsel permission to contact any former employee. In doing so, these courts often explained their decision by the purpose of the rule itself. The rule, it is said, presumes that persons contacted by counsel may be susceptible to manipulation by opposing counsel and is thereby designed to prevent unrepresented persons from being overwhelmed in the absence of friendly counsel and to protect the attorney-client privilege.[51]

In *Hanntz v. Shiley, Inc., a Division of Pfizer, Inc.,*[52] the court acknowledged these concerns but held that they were only "remotely, if ever, implicated in the situation of a former employee" and that other ethical restrictions would protect inquiry into privileged matters and unfair communication with the unrepresented. While nothing in the rule or the comment limits the categories of persons with whom communication is prohibited to current employees, it is likewise true that they do not indicate that the rule reaches beyond the binds of employment.[53]

There appears to be a majority of courts which interpret the rule to permit contact with former employees, although in doing so frequently point out other ethical constraints in dealing with unrepresented persons and impermissibly acquiring privileged information.[54]

Some courts have permitted contact with former employees, but prohibited contact with former managerial employees whose acts are the subject of the litigation or who took some part in the alleged wrongful acts.[55]

The price for guessing wrong about how a particular judge will feel about the particular communication with former or current employees can be stiff. The question of who counsel may speak to, on occasion presents itself in the context of a motion to disqualify, for fees, or other sanctions. On occasion, counsel will find themselves fighting an ethical war on which their ability to remain in the case turns. Sometimes those battles are lost altogether and sometimes less onerous sanctions are levied— such as the exclusion of testimony or fines.[56]

The Attorney-Client Privilege Affords the Most Effective Protection Against Exploitation of a Turncoat Former Employee

The attorney-client privilege covering a communication between a former employee and an organization's counsel "belongs to the organization, and can only be waived by the organization."[57]

Thus, where a former employee has information that is protected by the corporation's attorney-client privilege, the scope of inquiry is severely limited and effectively makes such an employee off limits.[58] A similar caution was expressed by the court in *Dubois v. Gradco Sys., Inc.,* in which the court stated, "with respect to any unrepresented former employee, plaintiff's counsel must take care not to seek to include or listen to disclosures by the former employees of any privileged attorney-client communications to which the employee was privy."[59] Thus, the court's opinion in *Rentclub, Inc. v. Transamerica Rental Finance Corp.*, is entirely consistent with this line of decisions.[60] The ABA has taken a similar position:

> With respect to *any* unrepresented former employee, of course, the potentially-communicating adversary attorney must be careful not to seek to induce the former employee to violate the privilege attaching to attorney-client communications to the extent that his or her communications as a former employee with his or her former employer's counsel are protected by the privilege (a privilege not belonging to or for the benefit of the former employee, by the former employer). Such an attempt could violate Rule 4.4 (requiring respect for the rights of third persons).[61]

A corporation faced with the testimony of a former employee therefore has the right to aggressively protect privileged information from disclosure, particularly when the employee is playing a role in litigation against the company. Employers can also take comfort in knowing that a plaintiff's attorney giving consideration to exploitation of the former employee may be given pause by the risk of violating Rule 4.4 of the Code of Professional Responsibility and the fallout from such a violation which might include disciplinary proceedings, disqualification as counsel, or exclusion of testimony. The message in such circumstances to former employees' and plaintiffs' counsel alike should be that the privilege and all communications that are encompassed by it will be maintained and defended by the corporation by whatever means are necessary.

Creation of Attorney-Client Relationships

It should be noted that the the attorney-client relationship must be legitimate and cannot be created ex parte.

In *Brown v. St. Joseph's County,*[62] the defendant argued that its insurance carrier provided coverage for current and former employees and had provided counsel to its former employees. Therefore, the argument went, communication with former employees was prohibited because they were represented. The court noting that the attorney-client relationship was generally determined by principles of agency and contract held that it could not be unilaterally created without the "client's" consent and refused to permit the assertion of the privilege.[63]

Strategies to Prevent Access to Key People and Access to Information

Identify Key People

Within a large organization, there is no way that every individual who could potentially become a witness can be identified. However, recent history suggests that the most likely candidates are either within the group of those involved in policy decisions or those who are or were part of the litigation defense team. These individuals can be identified on a "short list." Management should be aware that employees in these areas are in possession of information which is capable of being distorted by an adversary and used as a powerful weapon against the company. With respect to such persons there must be during employment and particularly at termination, a conscious effort to minimize the risk that they will testify against the corporation. Addressing any "personnel problems" in a timely fashion by the employee's supervisor and the company's human resources department may be the best way to prevent future litigation problems.

When the names of former employees have to be disclosed in discovery, the company or its counsel should contact them to alert them of this fact and let them know that they may be contacted by plaintiff's counsel. Obviously, ethical considerations must be honored. Whereas a present employee may be advised to refrain from giving information to another party, the same is not true with respect to former employees. However, it is permissible to suggest to ex-employees that in view of possible obligations arising out of the past employment, they might prefer to refer plaintiff's counsel either to their own attorney or to the company's counsel. In any event, a serious effort should be made to build a positive relationship with the ex-employee, possibly utilizing the good offices of a present employee friendly to the former colleague.

Confidentiality Agreements

Confidentiality agreements can also be an effective method of protecting confidential business information and trade secrets. Although strictly speaking, written agreements are not necessary to enforce non-disclosure of trade secrets, they are evidence that the employee was aware that the company deemed the information confidential and proprietary. Courts have routinely upheld employment agreements containing non-competition agreements and confidentiality agreements which do not overreach.[64] As with any contract, confidentiality agreements require consideration to be enforceable. It is best to include any such agreement in the initial agreements at the beginning of employment. A confidentiality agreement signed at termination as a condition of obtaining the final paycheck may not reflect sufficient consideration and be unenforceable.

Enjoin the Former Employee

Breach of a valid confidentiality agreement provides a legal basis to enjoin a former employee from working with plaintiff's counsel. In *Uniroyal Goodrich Tire Co. v. Hudson*,[65] for example, the court refused to dissolve an injunction it issued on November 4, 1993, precluding William Hudson, a former Uniroyal employee, from giving expert testimony in a product liability action pending in state court in Georgia. Uniroyal successfully argued that the agreement signed by Mr. Hudson, which prohibited him from disclosing or using Uniroyal trade secrets and confidential or proprietary information, was a valid and enforceable contract, and that Mr. Hudson's testimony would conflict with the secrecy agreement.

In addition, there are common law and statutory prohibitions in many states against the disclosure of confidential business information.[66] These prohibitions are perhaps strongest and most likely to be enforced with respect to those whose work was predominantly and intimately integrated with legal counsel.[67] Defense counsel should be able to enjoin a former employee in this category from consulting and testifying for parties adverse to his or her former employer.

In *American Motors Corp. v. Huffstutler*,[68] the Ohio Supreme Court reinstated AMC's permanent injunction preventing one of AMC's former employees from testifying and consulting with attorneys in product liability litigation involving AMC without AMC's consent or an order of the court. The employee, Rahn Huffstutler, had worked for AMC as an engineer. While employed by AMC, he attended law school and, after graduation, was admitted to the Ohio bar. Huffstutler subsequently became manager of a product-design study group and worked closely with both in-house and private outside counsel on product liability cases. Later, he became a technical specialist, responsible for new vehicle model and production analysis, and thereafter, became AMC's manager of quality services. Huffstutler was terminated by AMC, and soon began marketing himself as an expert witness against AMC.[69] In upholding the permanent injunction the Ohio State Court wrote:

> Huffstutler was an agent of AMC Jeep's Legal Department and frequently gave legal advice and performed legal analysis; that he served from 1981 to 1982 as an important member of the product liability defense team; that he represented AMC Jeep as counsel in product liability matters and routinely consulted with AMC Jeep's legal staff and retained counsel; that he assisted AMC Jeep's legal staff in retaining expert witnesses and met with experts to prepare strategy for defense; that he recommended outside counsel; that he suggested lines of testimony and cross-examination; and that he gave generously of his engineering judgment and legal training to assist counsel in the preparation of defenses.[70]

The court viewed Huffstutler, at a minimum, as an agent of AMC's legal counsel and, as such, held him subject to all of the restrictions of the attorney-client privilege and work-product doctrine.[71] In so doing, the court also explained that "[t]he attorney-client privilege . . . protects against any dissemination of information obtained in the confidential relationship. Thus, allowing consultation and discussion (even without testifying) of privileged information would effectively emasculate the privilege."[72]

Similarly, in *Elwell v. General Motors*,[73] General Motors successfully obtained a permanent injunction precluding Ronald Elwell, a former GM engineer who worked as a member of GM's in-house litigation defense team, from:

> . . . consulting or discussing with or disclosing to any person any of General Motors Corporation's trade secrets, confidential information or matters of attorney-client work product relating in any manner to the subject matter of any product liability litigation whether already filed or filed in the future which Ronald Elwell received, had knowledge of, or was entrusted with during his employment with General Motors Corporation.[74]

Elwell's duties as an in-house litigation expert included, among other things, interpreting technical information made available to GM's legal staff and outside counsel; consulting with GM's engineers in connection with product liability litigation; advising GM's lawyers on strategic litigation issues and responding to counsel's inquiries before, during, and after trial; developing demonstrative evidence to be used at trial, including laboratory testing of components and crash testing of vehicles; and testifying as an expert witness for GM in cases challenging the fuel systems of GM vehicles. Elwell was also enjoined from "testifying, without the prior written consent of General Motors Corporation, either upon deposition or at trial, as an expert witness, or as a witness of any kind, and from consulting with attorneys or their agents in any litigation already filed or to be filed in the future, involving General Motors Corporation as an owner, seller, manufacturer, and/or designer of the product(s) in issue." The court's order, however, expressly exempted Mr. Elwell's activity in connection with the Moseley litigation, in which he had already provided deposition testimony. In so doing, the court concluded that GM had met its burden of establishing that (1) it would be irreparably harmed if Elwell disclosed privileged information in his possession; (2) GM had no adequate remedy at law; and (3) that the public interest weighed in favor of granting the permanent injunction. *Elwell* illustrates the advisability of choosing a forum for injunction proceedings apart from the jurisdiction in which a product liability case involving the former employee is pending.

Quashing Third-Party Subpoenas

Through discovery or investigation, a plaintiff may identify a pertinent former employee who is not interested in being a turncoat. This has not deterred plaintiff's counsel on occasion from noticing such an individual for a deposition and having a subpoena served to enforce the former employee's presence. The plaintiff's attorney may not be seeking to elicit new information to help his case, but may be attempting to put words into the witness's mouth using leading questions and documents already in his possession. The former employee could be faced with responding to questions beginning with "Isn't it true that . . ." followed by the extract sought to be memorialized by the witness's sworn testimony. Under the Federal Rules of Civil Procedure, there is a mechanism for preventing this "back door" approach.

Rule 45, which governs third-party subpoenas, enables an employee to move to quash the subpoena if it "requires disclosure of privileged or other protected matter and that no exception or waiver applies. . . ."[75] The same tactic can be taken if the subpoena "requires disclosure of a trade secret or other confidential research, development, or commercial information. . . ."[76] It would be appropriate to furnish counsel to the former employee for this purpose. Furthermore, the defendant company itself should have standing to seek, on behalf of a former employee, an order to protect the company's rights and privileges with respect to the information sought by way of deposition pursuant to Federal Rule 45.[77]

Trial Strategies

Move to Disqualify

A motion to disqualify former employees and experts can be used at trial. In *Lumber & Cedar Co. v. Norton Co.*,[78] involving a product defect claim by a window manufacturer against a window sealant manufacturer, the plaintiff window manufacturer successfully moved to disqualify the defendant's expert on the ground that the expert had previously been engaged as a consulting engineer for the plaintiff. In granting this motion, the court noted that the matters involved in the pending litigation were "substantially related" to the matters worked on by the expert, in which he obtained a "basic understanding of . . . modus operandi, patterns of operation, decision-making process, and the like."[79] In some jurisdictions, a motion in limine may be the preferred vehicle to disqualify a former employee from testifying at trial, or at least to bar testimony of privileged or other confidential information.[80]

In a particularly egregious case, it may also be possible to move to disqualify the attorney or firm that improperly obtains privileged information. The oft-cited case of *Williams v. Trans World Airlines. Inc.,*[81] involving a former TWA employee who had assisted attorneys in investigating employment discrimination charges, provides a good example of a plaintiff's law firm being disqualified for using the former employee. In so doing, the court wrote:

> Non-lawyer personnel are widely used by lawyers to assist in rendering legal services. Paralegals, investigators, and secretaries must have ready access to client confidences in order to assist their attorney employers. If information provided by a client in confidence to an attorney for the purpose of obtaining legal advice could be used against the client because a member of the attorney's non-lawyer support staff left the attorney's employment, it would have a devastating effect both on the free flow of information between client and attorney and on the cost and quality of the legal services rendered by an attorney. Every departing secretary, investigator, or paralegal would be free to impart confidential information to the opposition without effective restraint. The only practical way to assure that this will not happen and to preserve public trust in the scrupulous administration of justice is to subject these "agents" of lawyers to the same disability lawyers have when they leave legal employment with confidential information.[82]

Sizing Up the Hostile Ex-Employee Witness

The ex-employee with a grudge against the former employer is an old story and probably dates back to the beginnings of master-servant relationships. The causes are not infinite but are so numerous that there is no point in trying to list them. Events in our economy in recent years, for example, downsizing, restructuring, etc., have the potential fallout of creating ex-employees who feel, rightly or wrongly, that their loyalties have been betrayed. Such ex-employees may be ripe prospects for a retaliatory strike delivered by testifying against their old employer in the context of a products claim.

While one should not become lost in amateur psychological analyses of such individuals, some consideration of the background of their feelings of antagonism may be helpful in developing an approach for cross-examination. The antagonism may not be universal. The employee may have fond relationships with former co-workers, even supervisors. With some individuals, bitter feelings may be overridden by appealing to the individual's own sense of integrity or professionalism. There may be, in many cases, the opportunity for defense counsel to induce the ex-employee to soften the effect of anticipated adverse testimony.

The Former Witness at Trial

There always will be cases in which, for whatever reason, a former employee will show up as a witness and will be permitted a great deal of freedom by the court to testify. The gravamen of the testimony of such a witness is generally not the merits of the case, but establishment of the defendant as a corporate rogue routinely making decisions exalting profits over safety, and systematically destroying or concealing unfavorable documents.

Any discussion of strategy on dealing with the former employee on cross-examination must start with a disclaimer: every case and every witness is different. Each defense lawyer will have a personal method and style which will be right for him or her. Even though we are in a highly subjective area, there are a few observations which might be helpful. It goes without saying that once the former employee's role has been established, a searing and perhaps exhaustive deposition should be scheduled as promptly as possible. Limitations of the former employee's knowledge and role in past decisions and events can be identified. Also, concessions may be obtained including the former employee's observations of responsible conduct on the part of the corporation which might undercut the theme of the rogue corporation.

As noted above, the former employee is invariably, although not necessarily universally, hostile. If possible this hostility should be used to attack the credibility of the testimony. Merely establishing that the witness bears animosity against the former employer is seldom enough because the jury may view the animosity as justified. Unless the circumstances giving rise to the animosity weigh heavily against the former employee, it is probably best to establish the existence of hostility, and not attempt to establish the reason for the hostility. The cross-examination of the former employee, once hostility has been established, can set the stage for affirmative evidence presented by the corporate defendant in its own case to refute the substance of the former employee's claims.

The ultimate goal, with a concerted strategy incorporating defense witnesses and documents along with the former employee's cross-examination, should be to demonstrate that the subject ex-employee is a bitter individual who will exaggerate his importance, fill in the great gaps of his firsthand knowledge with raw speculation, and take great liberties with the truth in seeking revenge on his former employer. This may not always be possible, and it never will be easy to accomplish, but it just might make the plaintiff's attorney regret that he ever recruited the former employee.

Conclusion

As previously discussed, the former employee witness is not in court to testify on the merits. His or her role is to poison the atmosphere so the defendant will not get a fair trial. The problem this creates is not one which can be ignored. Wherever possible it should be anticipated and efforts made to minimize its insertion into litigation. Where the law permits the availability of such a witness to a plaintiff, the turncoat issue should be attacked. At trial, the problem must be addressed in the opening statement and put into context right at the beginning. Once the evidence is completed, there should be no loose ends that have not been attended to either in cross-examination or in the defendant's case. If things have gone right, the plaintiff's use of the turncoat may be the most effective argument of all in demonstrating the lack of merit of the claim.

Notes

1. *See* ABA, ANNOTATED MODEL RULES OF PROF'L CONDUCT (4th ed. 1999).

2. ABA, MODEL RULES OF PROF'L CONDUCT, Rule 4.2 (1999).

3. *See generally* Sinaiko, *Ex Parte Communication and the Corporate Adversary: A New Approach*, 66 N.Y.U.L. REV. 1456, 1463-75 (1991) for a discussion of the purposes underlying the prohibition of ex parte communication of represented parties.

4. 863 F. Supp. 1204 (D. Nev. 1993).

5. *Id.* at 1213.

6. Comment, ABA, MODEL RULES OF PROF'L CONDUCT, Rule 4.2 (1983). The current comment adds little to the attorney. *See* ABA, ANNOTATED MODEL RULES OF PROF'L CONDUCT, Comment 4, Rule 4.2 (4th ed. 1999).

7. *See generally* Krulewitch, *Ex Parte Communication with Corporate Parties: The Communication with One of Adverse Interest*, 82 N.W.U. L. REV. (1988).

8. *See, e.g.,* Rule 44.2 of the Rules regulating the Florida Bar, 494 So. 2d 977, 1065 (Fla. 1986).

9. ABA, ANNOTATED MODEL RULES OF PROF'L CONDUCT, Rule 4.2 (4th ed. 1999).

10. *See* Sinaiko, note 3, *supra* at 1482; *see also* Annot., *Right of Attorney to Conduct Ex Parte Interviews with Corporate Party's Non-management Employees*, 50 A.L.R. 4th 652, 656-57 (1985).

11. ABA, MODEL RULES OF PROF'L CONDUCT, comment, Rule 4.2 (1999).

12. Fair Automotive Repair, Inc. v. Car-X Serv. Sys. Inc., 128 Ill. App. 3d 763, 471 N.E.2d 554, 560 (Ill. App. 1984) (articulating the control group test); Messing, Rudovsky & Waliky, P.C. v. President and Fellows of Harvard College, 436 Mass. 347, 764 N.E.2d 825 (2002). *See also In re* Investigation of FMC Corp., 430 F. Supp. 1108 (D. W.Va. 1977) (applying West Virginia law to preclude interviews of only the president, chairman of the board, and select plant managers).

13. Wright by Wright v. Group Health Hosp., 103 Wash. 2d 192, 691 P.2d 564, 569 (1984) (setting forth the binding admission test). *See also* Niesig v. Team I, 76 N.Y.2d 363, 558 N.E.2d 1030, 1035, 559 N.Y.S.2d 493 (1990) (precluding ex parte communication with "corporate employees whose acts or omissions in the matter under inquiry are binding on the corporation," that is, "employees with 'speaking authority' for the corporation," "employees who are so closely identified with the interests of the corporate party as to be indistinguishable from it," and those "actually effectuating the advice of counsel in the matter"); and agents of a party who can bind the party in litigation or settle controversies on its behalf. Frey v. Department of Health & Human Servs., 106 F.R.D. 32, 37-38 (E.D.N.Y. 1985); Chancellor v. Boeing Co., 678 F. Supp. 250 (D. Kan. 1988); State v. Ciba-Geigy Corp., 247 N.J. Super. Ct. 314, 589 A.2d 180 (App. 1991).

14. Massachusetts Bar Ass'n., Formal Op. 7, at 1 (1982). Of course, the broadest test is a blanket prohibition against contacting any employees. *See* Mills Land & Water Co. v. Golden W. Ref. Co., 186 Cal. App. 3d 116, 230 Cal. Rptr. 461 (1986); *see also* New York County Lawyer's Ass'n. Op. 528 (1965).

15. *See, e.g.,* Adams v. Shell Oil Co. (*In re* Shell Oil Refinery), 132 F.R.D. 437, 441 (E.D. La. 1990) (noting that the protection of in-house expert's work "supports improved public safety and other social benefits of self-analysis"); Hermsdorfter v. American Motors Corp., 96 F.R.D. 13, 15 (W.D.N.Y. 1982).

16. *In re* Opinion 668 of the Advisory Comm. on Professional Ethics, 134 N.J. 284, 303, 633 A.2d 959, 964 (1993).

17. *Id.*

18. 186 Cal. App. 3d 116, 230 Cal. Rptr. 461, 467 (1986).

19. *Id.*

20. 449 U.S. 383, 392 (1981).

21. Los Angeles County Bar Ass'n., Formal Op. 410 (Mar. 24, 1983); Santiago Bar Ass'n., Ethics Comm. Op. 1984-5 (1984). *See* note 13, *supra.*

22. A few courts have read 4.2 as prohibiting ex parte communication with former employees of a corporate party "if there is the possibility of the witnesses' testimony being imputed [to the company]," Public Serv. Elec. & Gas Co. v. Associated Elec. & Gas Ins. Servs., Ltd., 745 F. Supp. 1037, 1042 (D.N.J. 1990), a position which effectively precludes ex parte contact with all former employees who may have any information about the events in litigation. The Ninth Circuit has rules that ex parte communication with a former employee should be prohibited because such employees "may possess the relevant information needed by corporate counsel to advise the client with respect to actual or potential difficulties. Again, the attorney-client privilege is served by the certainty that conversations between the attorney and client will remain privileged after the employee leaves." *In re* Coordinated Pretrial Proceedings in Petroleum Prods. Antitrust Litig., 658 F.2d 1355, 1361 n.7 (9th Cir. 1981) (finding that the relationale of *Upjohn* applies with equal vigor to ex-employees), *cert. denied*, 455 U.S. 990 (1982) (citation omitted).

23. *See, e.g.,* Sherrod v. Furniture Ctr., 769 F. Supp. 1021, 1022 (W.D. Tenn. 1991); Hanntz v. Shiley, Inc., Div. of Pfizer, Inc., 766 F. Supp. 258, 263 (D.N.J. 1991); Dillon Co., Inc. v. SICO Co., No. 92-1512, 1993 U.S. Dist. LEXIS 17450, at *11 (E.D. Pa. Nov. 24, 1993). In *Dillon Co.*, the court articulated the following test to determine when Rule 4.2 should be applied to former employees:

> [A] rational approach should be employed whereby the propriety of the ex parte contact is determined by assessing the actual likelihood of disclosure of privileged materials, not a nebulous fear that such disclosure might occur. That assessment would depend upon weighing such factors as the positions of the former employees in relation to the issues in the suit; whether they were privy to communication between the former employer and its counsel concerning the subject matter of the litigation, or otherwise; the nature of the inquiry by opposing counsel; and how much time had elapsed between the end of the employment relationship and the questioning by opposing counsel. When such factors point to the conclusion that there is a substantial risk of disclosure of privileged matters, as opposed to the risk of the adverse party learning information which might be damaging to the former employer's litigation position, then appropriate notice should be given to the former employees concerning the former employer and, perhaps, the former employer's counsel should be notified prior to any ex parte interview. Any question concerning the appropriateness of the adversary's decision to proceed with ex parte contact with specific former employees can be resolved by determining whether any information gathered by the opponent actually intrudes upon privileged matters. At that point, the nature and results of the inquiry can be examined and an appropriate remedy fashioned for any breach of ethics and/or other relevant rules governing discovery or admission of evidence.

24. ABA Comm. on Ethics and Prof'l Responsibility, Formal Op. 91-1991. A Connecticut District Court, partly relying on the ABA's formal opinion, concluded that Connecticut's analogue to Rule 4.2 does not prohibit ex parte contact with former employees. Dubois v. Gradco Sys., Inc., 136 F.R.D. 341, 345 (D. Conn. 1991). In so doing, the court reasoned that if the drafters of Model Rule 4.2 meant "other person" to include former employees, they easily could have done so explicitly: there seems little doubt that the drafters would have been explicit had they intended, as defendants claim they did intend, to overturn the traditional view the former employees are not encompassed within the term some "party." *In re* Domestic Air Transp. Antitrust Litig., 141 F.R.D. 556, 561 (N.D. Ga. 1992) ("Rule 4.2 does not prohibit communications with former employees of a defen-

dant corporation as long as the former employees are not in fact represented by the corporation's attorney."). *But see* Lang v. Superior Court, 170 Ariz. 602, 826 P.2d 1228 (1992) (refusing to follow the ABA's formal opinion because former employees may be persons whose acts or omissions in connection with the matter in litigation might be imputed to the corporate defendant).

25. 766 F. Supp. 258 (D.N.J. 1991).

26. *Id.* at 265.

27. *Id.* at 266.

28. *Id.*

29. 811 F. Supp. 651 (M.D. Fla. 1992, *aff'd*, 43 F.3d 1439 (11th Cir. 1995).

30. As the *Rentclub* court noted, Florida's Code of Professional Responsibility does not note an express provision including conduct having the appearance of impropriety, but Florida case law unquestionably retains the requirement. State Farm Mutual Auto. Co. v. K.A.W., etc., et al., 575 So. 2d 630 (Fla. 1991) even the appearance of impropriety may, under the appropriate circumstances, require prompt remedial action. . . . Consequently, any doubt is to be resolved in favor of disqualification." *Id.* at 633.

31. 811 F. Supp. at 657. *See* Polycast Technology Corp. v. Uniroyal, Inc., 129 F.R.D. 621, 625 (S.D.N.Y 1990).

32. 811 F. Supp. at 658.

33. The court seemed to be particularly troubled by the firm for having paid the witness for factual testimony and not "trial consultation." The court thus applied a two-prong test to determine whether the appearance of impropriety warranted disqualification:

> First, although proof of actual wrongdoing is not required, there must exist a reasonable possibility that some specific identifiable impropriety did in fact occur. Second, the likelihood of public suspicion or obloquy must outweigh the social interests that will be served by the attorney's continued participation in the case.

811 F. Supp. at 64, *citing* Norton v. Tallahassee Mem. Hosp., 689 F.2d 938 (11th Cir. 1982).

34. 838 F. Supp. 1564 (M.D. Fla. 1993)

35. 838 F. Supp at 1567-68.

36. 888 F. Supp. 1143 (M.D. Fla. 1995).

37. 888 F. Supp. at 1145.

38. *Id*. at 1148.

39. 888 F. Supp. at 1148. *See* Polycast Technology Corp. v. Uniroyal, Inc., 129 F.R.D. 621, 625 (S.D.N.Y 1990).

40. *Id.* at 1148-49.

41. 656 So. 2d 486 (Fla. Ct. App. 1995).

42. 659 So. 2d 1156 (Fla. Ct. App. 1995).

43. 656 So. 2d at 1156 (Fla. Ct. App. 1995).

44. *See* Manor Care of Dunedin, Inc. v. Keiser, 611 So. 2d 1305 (Fla. Ct. App. 1992) (permitting contact with all former nursing home employees).

45. 659 So. 2d 1156 (Fla. Ct. App. 1995).

46. 659 So. 2d at 1158.

47. 673 So. 2d 116 (Fla. 4th DCA 1996).

48. ABA Committee on Professional Ethics and Professional Responsibility, Formal Opinion 91-359 (1991).

49. Curley v. Cumberland Farms, Inc., 134 F.R.D. 77, 92 (D.N.J. 1991) (permitting contact with non-managerial, former employees); *In re* Home Shopping Network, 1989 WL 201085 (M.D. Fla. 1989); Suggs v. Capital Cities/ABC, Inc., 1990 WL 182314 (S.D.N.Y. 1990); *In re* Environmental Insurance Declaratory Judgment Action, 252 N.J. Super. 510, 600 A.2d 165 (1993); Monsanto Co. v. Aetna Casualty and Surety Co., 593 A.2d 1013 (Del. 1990); Barfuss v. Diversicare Corp. of America, 656 So. 2d 486, 489 (Fla. Ct. App. 1995).

50. Case No. 88-47-CIV-T-10(C) (M.D. Fla. 1989).

51. Frey v. Department of Health and Human Services, 106 F.R.D. 32, 34 (E.D.N.Y. 1985); Valassis v. Samelson, 143 F.R.D. 118, 120 (E.D. Mich. 1992); Curley v. Cumberland Farms, Inc., 134 F.R.D. 77, 87 (D.N.J. 1991); Sherrod v. The Furniture Center, 769 F. Supp. 1021, 1022 (W.D. Tenn. 1991).

52. 766 F. Supp 258, 265 (D.N.J. 1991).

53. *See also* Centennial Management Services, Inc. v. AXA Re Vie, 193 F.R.D. 671 (D. Kan. 2000) (former employees who no longer have an employment relationship are not included within the meaning of the term "party" for purposes of the rule prohibiting lawyer contact with a party).

54. Cram v. Lamson & Sessions Co., Carlon Division, 148 F.R.D. 259 (S.D. Iowa 1993); Wright v. Wright, 691 P.2d 564 (Wash. 1984); United States v. Western Electric, 1990-1 Trade Cases, X68, 939, 190 WL 39129 (D.C. Cir. 1990); Siguel v. Trustees of Tufts College, 1990 WL 29199 (D. Mass. 1990); Niesig v. Team I, 76 N.Y.2d 363, 369, 559 N.Y.S. 493, 558 N.E.2d 1030 (1990); DiOssi v. Edison, 583 A.2d 1343, 1345 (Del. 1990); Goff v. Wheaton Industries, 145 F.R.D. 351, 356 (D.N.J. 1992); Polycast Technology Corporation v. Uniroyal, Inc., 129 F.R.D. 621, 629 (S.D.N.Y. 1990); Hanntz v. Shiley, Inc., a Division of Pfizer, Inc., 766 F. Supp 258 (D.N.J. 1991); Action Air Freight, Inc. v. Pilot Air Freight Corp., 769 F. Supp. 899, 904 (E.D. Pa. 1991), appeal dismissed, 961 F.2d 207 (3d Cir. 1992); Shearson Lehman Bros. v. Wasatch Bank, 139 F.R.D. 412, 418 (D. Utah 1991); Dubois v. Gradco Systems, Inc., 136 F.R.D. 341, 345-47 (D. Conn. 1991); Valassis v. Samelson, 143 F.R.D. 118, 120 (E.D. Mich. 1992); *In re* Domestic Air Transp. Antitrust Litig., 141 F.R.D. 556, 564 (M.D. Ga. 1992); *Strawser Exxon*, 843 P.2d 613, 621 (Wyo. 1992); State v. CIBA-GEIGY Corp., 247 N.J. Super. 314, 589 A.2d 180 (1991); McCallum v. CSY Transp., 149 F.R.D. 104, 110 (M.D. Ga. 1993); Brown v. St. Joseph's County, 148 F.R.D. 246 (N.D. Ind. 1993).

55. Chancellor v. Boeing Co., 678 F. Supp. 250 (D. Kan. 1988); Porter v. Arco Metals Div. of Atlantic Richfield, 642 F. Supp. 1116, 1118 (D. Mont. 1986); Amarin Plastics, Inc. v. Maryland Cup Corp., 116 F.R.D. 36, 39-40 (D. Mass. 1987); Frey v. Dep't of Health and Human Services, 106 F.R.D. 32, 36 (E.D.N.Y. 1985); University Patents, Inc. v. Kligman, 737 F. Supp. 325, 328 (E.D. Pa. 1990); PPG Indus, Inc. v. BASF Corp., 134 F.R.D. 118, 121 (W.D. Pa. 1990); Bobele v. Superior Court, 199 Cal. App. 3d 708, 245 Cal Rptr. 144, 147 (1988).

56. Rentclub, Inc. v. Transamerica Rental Finance Corp., 811 F. Supp. 651 (M.D. Fla. 1992, *aff'd*, 43 F.3d 1439 (11th Cir. 1995); Faison v. Thornton, 863 F. Supp. 1204 (D. Nev. 1993); Cagguila v. Wythe Laboratories, 127 F.R.D. 653 (E.D. Pa. 1989); University Patents, Inc. v. Kligman, 737 F. Supp. 325, 328 (E.D. Pa. 1990); Cronin v. Eighth Judicial Dist. Court, 781 P.2d 1150, 1153 (Nev. 1989); Sheldon v. Hess, 599 F. Supp. 905 (S.D. Tex. 1984); American Protection Ins. Co. v. MGM Grand Hotel, No. CV-L V-82-26 HDM (D. Nev. Mar. 13, 1986); Camden v. The State of Maryland, No. PJM 93-1854 (D. Ma. 1996, Jan. 24, 1996); Noorily v. Thomas Betts Corp., No. 93-2227 (D.N.J. Aug. 17, 1995).

57. *E.g.*, Cram v. Lamson & Sessions Co., 148 F.R.D. 259, 266 (S.D. Iowa 1993) (*quoting* Sequa Corp. v. Lititech, Inc., 807 F. Supp. 653, 668 (D. Colo. 1992).

58. Thus, the court in Breedlove v. Tele-Trip Co., No. 91C5702, 1992 WL 202147, *2 (N.D. Ill. Aug. 14, 1992) concluded that no formal order barring communication with former employees who may be privy to privileged conversation or information is necessary because plaintiff's counsel, an officer of the court, "are, of course, barred from exploring these communications or other privileged matters with the witnesses").

59. 136 F.R.D. at 347.

60. 811 F. Supp. 651 (N.D. Fla. 1992).

61. ABA Comm. on Ethics and Prof'l Responsibility, Formal Op. 91-359 (1991).

62. 148 F. Supp. 246 (N.D. Ind. 1993).

63. *Id.* at 250; *see* United States v. Keplinger, 766 F. Supp. 678, 701-02 (7th Cir. 1985).

64. *See. e.g.,* Basicomputer Corp. v. Scott, 973 F.2d 507, 511-12 (6th Cir. 1992) (indicating that Ohio law recognizes the enforceability of non-disclosure agreements between employers and employees); Uniroyal Goodrich Tire Co. v. Hudson, No. 93-CV-74346-DI, 1994 WL 289000, at *3 (E.D. Mich. June 28, 1994) (enforcing an agreement signed by a former employee of Uniroyal prohibiting him from disclosing or using Uniroyal trade secrets and confidential or proprietary information after he left the company).

65. No. 93-CV-74346-D1, 1994 WL 289000 (E.D. Mich. June 28, 1994).

66. *See. e.g.,* Ohio Rev. Code Ann. § 1333.81 ("No employee of another, who in the course and within the scope of his employment receives any confidential matter or information, shall knowingly, without the consent of his employer, furnish or disclose such matter or information to any person not privileged to acquire it."); Valises v. Samilson, 143 F.R.D., 118, 124 (E.D. Mich. 1992) (noting that individuals who become privy to privileged information during their employment remain precluded from disclosing that information even after they end their employment).

67. Valises v. Samilson, 143 F.R.D. 118, 124; Palmer v. Zobec, 144 F.R.D. 66, 67 (D. Md. 1992); Mayer v. Dell, 139 F.R.D. 1, 3 (D.D.C. 1991); Marvin Lumber & Cedar Co. v. Norton Co., 113 F.R.D. 588, 590-91 (D. Minn. 1986); Conforti & Eisele, Inc. v. Division of Building and Construction, 170 N.J. Super. 64, 405 A.2d 487, 492 (1979); United States v. Kovel, 296 F.2d 918, 921 (2d Cir. 1961); Williams v. Trans World Airlines. Inc., 588 F. Supp. 1037, 1044 (W.D. Mo. 1984).

68. 61 Ohio St. 3d 343, 575 N.E.2d 116 (Ohio 1991).

69. 575 N.E.2d at 119.

70. *Id.* at 118.

71. *Id.* at 119.

72. *Id.* at 120-21; *see also* People v. Marcy, 91 Mich. App. 399, 283 N.W.2d 754, 757 (1979) ("Although decisions vary from one jurisdiction to another, the attorney-client privilege has been extended to cover, inter alia, an accountant, investigator, engineer . . . employed by either the client or the attorney to assist the attorney. . . ."); D.I. Chadborne. Inc. v. Superior Court, 60 Cal. 2d 723, 36 Cal. Rptr. 468, 388 P.2d 700, 709 (1964); *see generally* Annotation. *Persons Other than Client or Attorney Affected By, or Included Within, Attorney-Client Privilege,* 96 A.L.R. 2d 125 (1964).

73. No. 91-115946NZ (Mich. Cir. Ct. 1992).

74. Elwell's duties as an in-house litigation expert included, among other things, interpreting technical information made available to GM's legal staff and outside counsel; consulting with GM's engineers in connection with product liability litigation; advising GM's lawyers on strategic litigation issues and responding to counsel's inquiries before, during, and after trial; developing demonstrative evidence to be used at trial, including laboratory testing of components and crash testing of vehicles; and testifying as an expert witness for GM in cases challenging the fuel systems of GM vehicles.

75. Fed. R. Civ. P. 45(c)(3)(A)(iii).

76. Fed. R. Civ. P. 45(c)(3)(13)(i).

77. *See* David D. Siegel, *Practice Commentaries,* 28 U.S.C.A. at 391, Fed. R. Civ. P. 38-50, C45-22 (West 1992) (the adverse party may move to quash a non-party subpoena "if that party has its own rights to assert in suppressing the subpoena, as where the subpoena seeks materials that would fall under one of the privileged categories (involving the party's privilege, of course")).

78. 113 F.R.D. 588 (D. Minn. 1986).

79. *Id.* at 591. Although *Marvin Lumber* involved a turncoat expert, as opposed to a turncoat employee, the case is still instructive. *See generally* Michael Hoening, *The "Turncoat" Expert,* N.Y. L. J. Sept. 9, 1991, at 3; Richard A. Saloman & Charles F. Regan, Jr., *Dealing with the Turncoat Expert,* Prod. Safety & Liab. Rep. (BNA) 644 (May 31, 1991).

80. *See* Dillon Cos. v. SICO, *supra.*

81. 588 F. Supp. 1037 (W.D. Mo. 1984).

82.   588 F. Supp. at 1044. *See also* Rentclub. Inc. v. Transamerica Rental Finance Corp., 811 F. Supp. 651 (M.D. Fla. 1992), (disqualifying attorney who hired former CFO of defendant as a "trial consultant" because the former executive was privy to relevant confidential and proprietary information); University Patents. Inc. v. Kligman, 737 F. Supp. 325 (E.D. Pa. 1990) (denying plaintiffs' motion for disqualification because defendant's attorneys had conducted ex parte interviews with plaintiffs' employees, but precluding the use of the information obtained from the employees (a) who were officers, directors, or managers; (b) whose acts or omissions could bind or impute liability to the plaintiffs; and (c) whose statements could be used as admissions against the plaintiffs).

CHAPTER 14

Discovery of the In-House Expert Assigned to Litigation

JOSEPH C. KEARFOTT

Introduction

The train left your client's plant 36 hours earlier. As it passed through a small Midwest town during the morning rush hour, a coupling failed, causing a derailment. Your client's tank car was one of those that overturned and spilled its contents.

As fate would have it, the car contained a highly caustic agent used in manufacturing. A number of railroad workers and townspeople were exposed to the chemical and taken ill. Fortunately, none of their illnesses was serious, and all were released from the local hospital within 48 hours.

The inevitable complaint on behalf of 300 plaintiffs is served on your client two months later. The allegations are not limited to the minor injuries that were apparent at the time of the derailment. They instead charge that exposure to your client's chemical has caused diffuse organic brain damage and has permanently injured the plaintiffs' peripheral nervous systems, immune systems, livers, kidneys, and other body organs. The complaint also contends that the plaintiffs' risk of developing cancer has been substantially enhanced as a result of the exposure and seeks an award for medical monitoring.

You are hired to defend the company's interests. You consult with your client and quickly learn that your client has employees who are extremely knowledgeable on the toxicity of the spilled chemical. Both because of their expertise and for financial reasons, you want to use these employees as consultants rather than hire outside experts. These "employee" or "in-house" experts have not been participants in the events giving rise to the lawsuit. They will be specially assigned to the case for trial preparation and will not be trial witnesses. They may become privy to highly sensitive information.

You face one of the first questions of the representation: can you use these in-house experts and at the same time protect their findings and conclusions from discovery?

Protecting the Non-Testifying In-House Expert's Work from Discovery

Rule 26(b)(4) of the Federal Rules of Civil Procedure governs the discovery of experts and expert information.[1] Subsection (A) of this rule provides liberal discovery of an expert whom a party expects to call as a trial witness. After making the mandatory disclosures of Rule 26(a)(2), a party may, under Rule 26(b)(4)(A), depose another party's expert witness.

In contrast, Rule 26(b)(4)(B) severely curtails the discovery of non-testifying experts "who ha[ve] been retained or specially employed . . . in anticipation of litigation or preparation for trial." Facts known or opinions held by such experts may be obtained by an opponent only "upon a showing of exceptional circumstances." Discoverability under this subsection usually turns on whether a party possesses factual information which the opposing party cannot obtain through the exercise of ordinary diligence. Courts generally find "exceptional circumstances" warranting discovery of non-testifying experts in either of two situations: (1) where a condition observed by the expert is no longer observable; or (2) where the condition is subject to replication, but the costs of replication would be prohibitive.[2]

Rule 26(b)(4)(B) does not mention specifically employee or in-house experts. If the in-house expert is going to be a trial witness, the facts and opinions known by him of course may be discovered under subsection (A) of this rule. Further, if he was a participant in the events which gave rise to the lawsuit, it is clear that discovery is available, limited only by the relevancy standard of Rule 26(b)(1) and any applicable privileges.[3] On the other hand, if the in-house expert is specially assigned to a matter for trial preparation and will not be a trial witness, courts and commentators disagree over whether his work is protected from discovery.[4] There are three views.[5]

The Three Views

Total Protection

One view is that the non-testifying in-house expert is totally immune from discovery.[6] This view is based on the former introductory language of Rule 26(b)(4) (deleted in the 1993 amendments), which stated that discovery of experts who acquired information in anticipation of litigation or for trial "may be obtained *only* as follows."[7] Because non-testifying in-house experts may acquire information for the first time in preparation for trial and they are not specifically mentioned in the subsections of the rule that follow, the argument was that no discovery of these experts is permitted.

This view is not as far-fetched as it may first seem. It finds some support in the 1970 Advisory Committee Note.[8] The note states that because subsection (B) of the rule does not mention experts "informally consulted in preparation for trial," it precludes discovery of these experts.[9] Since non-testifying in-house experts also are not expressly mentioned in this subsection, a consistent interpretation of the rule requires that they also would be immune from discovery.[10]

To date, there has been no reported federal decision in which a court has adopted this blanket view. In fact, at least one court has held that while experts "informally consulted" cannot be deposed or discovered under Rule 26(b)(4), "they are discoverable by independent investigative methods and subject to [discovery under] Rule 45."[11] To the extent that this rationale likewise is applicable to non-testifying in-house experts, the view that such experts enjoy complete immunity from discovery appears unlikely to attract much support in the future.

No Protection

A second view is that no protection is afforded to the non-testifying in-house expert and that he should be treated as an ordinary witness. Under this view, an in-house expert and his work are subject to the lenient relevancy discovery standard of Rule 26(b)(1). As with any witness, the in-house expert could still avail himself of the protections offered by the attorney-client privilege and the work-product rule. The difference, according to the view adopted by several courts and commentators, is that the in-house expert enjoys no presumption of immunity from deposition.

In *Virginia Electric & Power Company v. Sun Shipbuilding & Dry Dock Co.*,[12] plaintiff, Vepco, brought an action against Sun Shipbuilding for breach of contract. Vepco sought to compel production of certain reports which Sun Shipbuilding's employees had prepared. Sun Shipbuilding objected to discovery on the ground, among others, that the reports were prepared in anticipation of litigation by employees who were experts and who were protected by Rule 26(b)(4)(B). The trial court rejected this argument for several reasons.

First, the court reasoned that an employee, even if qualified as an expert, could not be considered an expert within the meaning of the rule because of his inability to "see all sides of the issue."[13] Second, the court defined "specially employed" as an "expert [who] is put on the payroll for the specific purpose of deriving facts and opinions for use in trial preparation or anticipated litigation."[14] Third, it noted that Rule 26(b)(4)(C), requiring payment of fees and expenses to the opposing party's experts, was not meant to apply to a master-servant relationship.[15] Finally, the court concluded that the rule would have been drafted using "specially assigned" in place of "specially employed" if it had been meant to apply to an ordinary employee assigned for trial preparation.[16]

In *Clark v. General Motors Corp.*,[17] a federal magistrate also rejected the argument that discovery of a non-testifying in-house expert was limited by Rule 26(b)(4)(B). He noted that the expert was a regular employee and that this fact "makes all the difference in the world."[18] The magistrate apparently concluded that all regular employees are outside of the rule's protection.[19] Other cases suggest a similar result.[20]

The cases holding that in-house experts are not entitled to protection under Rule 26(b)(4)(B) were decided before the 1993 amendments to Rule 26. Rule 26(a)(2) now requires that the identity of experts be disclosed and that the disclosure be accompanied by a written report prepared and signed by the witness. These requirements apply both to witnesses who are "retained or specially employed to provide expert testimony" and to those "whose duties as an employee of the party regularly involve giving expert testimony."

The 1993 amendments thus make clear that corporate employees can be expert witnesses within the meaning of Rule 26. To the extent that earlier cases provided no protection on the grounds that they were not, such reasoning should no longer apply. The flip side of this coin, however, is that Rule 26(b)(4)(B) was not amended to refer specifically to employees assigned to litigation. Creative minds can argue from this failure to amend either total protection from discovery or no protection beyond that available to an ordinary witness. To date, however, it appears that no court has specifically addressed either side of this argument.

Some Protection

A third and better reasoned view is that an in-house expert can be "specially employed" within the meaning of Rule 26(b)(4)(B).[21] Under this view, a regular employee is specially employed when he has not been an actor or viewer of the events giving rise to the lawsuit and he is assigned by a party to a particular matter in anticipation of litigation or for trial preparation.

An early case that adopted this approach was *Seiffer v. Topsy's International Inc.*[22] In this securities law case, third-party defendant Touche Ross had prepared audits of Topsy's engagements. Touche's counsel later asked one of Touche's new partners, Van Camp, to assist with any litigation arising out of these audits. Van Camp reviewed the audit papers at counsel's request and made a report to counsel.

The underwriters sought to depose Van Camp. Touche argued that Van Camp's deposition could not be taken because he was an expert who had been "retained or specially employed" within the meaning of Rule 26(b)(4)(A). The underwriters countered by suggesting that since Van Camp was a partner in Touche, a party to the action, he was "clearly deposable."[23]

The court did not allow the deposition. It concluded that Van Camp was within the protection of Rule 26(b)(4)(B) and that the underwriters had failed to show exceptional circumstances.[24] It based its decision on four factors. First, Van Camp was not "simply a general employee"; he had been asked to assist with the litigation at counsel's request.[25] Second, he had had no prior involvement in the audits that gave rise to the lawsuit. Third, he had reviewed the audits in question and had prepared a report only at counsel's request. Fourth, he would not be called as a witness.[26] The court also noted that parenthetical language of the Advisory Committee Note, by strong negative implication, supported the view that "an in-house expert may be specially employed as well as an expert drawn from personnel other than the party's own."[27]

Perhaps the most thoroughly reasoned case reaching this same conclusion was *In re Shell Oil Refinery.*[28] This was a class action arising out of an explosion at an oil refinery. Plaintiffs sought the testimony of two employees of defendant who had conducted an investigation of the accident under the direction of legal counsel. Defendant had originally designated these employees as expert witnesses, but later withdrew the designation. The court held that defendant was entitled to withdraw the designation, making the employees non-testifying experts.[29] The court analyzed various cases and commentary on whether any in-house experts could be "retained or specially employed" within the meaning of Rule 26(b)(4)(B). It concluded that they can be:

> The court finds that the persuasive authority favors application of Rule 26(b)(4)(B) to non-testifying in-house experts. To rule otherwise would encourage economic waste by requiring an employer to hire independent experts to obtain the protection of Rule 26(b)(4). Protection of an in-house expert's opinion's [sic] supports improved public safety and other social benefits of self-analysis. That the work of an in-house expert is used not only to defend a lawsuit but also to improve a company's operations or product design does not remove him from the parameters of Rule 26(b)(4)(B).[30]

The court concluded that a case-by-case approach was necessary.[31] It found that Shell's employees were specially employed in preparation for litigation. The fact that they were not paid additional compensation for the work or assigned exclusively to the litigation was not conclusive.[32]

A more recent case adopting a case-by-case approach was *Kiser v. General Motors Corp.*[33] The plaintiff in this product liability suit alleged that a defect in the driver's seat of her car caused it to recline when the car was struck from behind. GMC sent an in-house product analysis engineer to participate in an inspection of plaintiff's wrecked vehicle conducted by plaintiff's expert.[34] When plaintiff sought to depose GMC's in-house expert, GMC refused to make him available on the ground that he was a nontestifying expert immune from discovery under Rule 26(b)(4)(B). Specifically, GMC noted that it employed its engineer "to provide preliminary technical analysis as a consulting expert on product liability claims and lawsuits."[35] Following the case-by-case approach set forth in *In re Shell Oil Refinery*, the court found GMC's in-house engineer, Confer, "clearly within the ambit of Rule 26(b)(4)(B)."[36] In doing so, it observed:

> It is of no moment that Confer has not been assigned to work exclusively on this litigation or that he did not receive additional compensation for work on this case. Confer was not merely conducting normal business activities. He was specifically employed for litigation assistance.[37]

Affording in-house experts the protection of Rule 26(b)(4)(B) passes the ultimate litmus test: it makes sense. The older *Vepco* and *Clark* approach requires a party to hire outside experts in order to gain protection under Rule 26(b)(4)(B) even when perfectly competent in-house experts are available. This only adds to the already high cost of complex litigation. It also flies in the face of one of the fundamental goals of the Federal Rules of Civil Procedure, namely, "to secure the just, speedy, and inexpensive determination of every action."[38] Some states have addressed expressly the *Vepco-Clark* position by amending their rules to protect in-house experts.[39]

Caveats/Limits on Protection

Even where it is recognized, the protection afforded to non-testifying in-house experts under Rule 26(b)(4)(B) is subject to several important caveats. First, such experts are not immunized against discovery of their preexisting knowledge. It has long been recognized "that one may simultaneously be a litigational expert with Rule

26(b)(4) protection as to some matters and simply an unprotected actor or witness as to others."[40] The rule clearly applies to in-house experts. In *Dallas v. Marion Power Shovel Co.*,[41] for example, plaintiff sought to elicit expert opinions from defendant's vice president of marketing and engineering regarding the design of the product at issue in the case. Because defendant made no showing that the vice president's opinions had been developed in anticipation of the litigation, the court ruled that Rule 26(b)(4)(B) did not bar plaintiff from discovery of those opinions.[42]

Second, interaction between the non-testifying in-house expert and a testifying expert can jeopardize the protection otherwise afforded to the former. At the very least, materials generated by the in-house expert are subject to discovery under Rule 26(a)(2)(B) to the extent that they are "considered by" a testifying expert in forming any of his opinions.[43] The in-house expert runs the risk of waiving the protection of Rule 26(b)(4)(B) altogether where he actually collaborates with a testifying expert in preparation of the latter's expert report.[44]

Finally, the burden is on the party seeking the protection of Rule 26(b)(4)(B) to establish the prerequisites for its application. In *Shipes v. BIC Corp.*,[45] a case arising out of an allegedly defective disposable lighter, plaintiff sought discovery of opinions held by one of BIC's in-house experts, who had not been identified as a trial witness. Following *In re Shell Oil Refinery*,[46] the court observed that Rule 26(b)(4)(B) "does not deny protection to the opinions of all in-house experts. . . . Rather, the party seeking protection of the opinions must establish that the expert was retained in anticipation of litigation."[47] Because BIC had not asserted that the expert was specially retained for litigation, but had only described him as a "quality assurance manager," plaintiff was entitled to depose him on his expert opinions.[48]

Suggestions to Minimize Risk of Discovery

Because of the uncertainty in the law, there is no guarantee that an individual judge will prohibit a deposition of the non-testifying in-house expert. Nevertheless, certain steps by defense counsel can reduce the risk that sensitive information will be discovered from his client's employees.[49] These steps include:

1. Draft a consulting agreement for the employee by which he is specifically assigned to work on the litigation under the direction of counsel. It would be ideal for the litigation to be his only job responsibility.
2. Be certain that the employee was not an "actor or viewer" of the events giving rise to the litigation.
3. Have the employee prepare written reports only upon request of counsel. Be certain that he does not share these reports or his findings with other, non-expert employees.
4. Do not use the employee to "ghostwrite" the report of a testifying expert. The more contact the employee has with the testifying expert, the more likely it is that discovery of the employee will be allowed.
5. Have the employee keep all of his reports and correspondence with defense counsel in a separate file away from records kept in the ordinary course of business.

6. Consider increasing the salary of the employee to buttress further the argument of his "special employment."
7. Make certain that the company has another witness capable of responding to a Rule 30(b)(6) notice to take depositions if one is filed relating to the specialty area of your in-house expert.

In the absence of a rule or clear precedent in defense counsel's jurisdiction that protects in-house experts from discovery, these steps may persuade a court that the in-house expert has been "specially employed" within the meaning of Rule 26(b)(4).

Conclusion

The view adopted by the courts in *Seiffer, In re Shell Oil Refinery,* and *Kiser,* and a clear majority of the commentators, is consistent with Rule 26 and the policies underlying the discovery rules. In-house experts who have not been "viewers or actors" should be treated as "retained or specially employed" whenever they are specially assigned to a matter in anticipation of litigation or for trial preparation.

The current state of the law on the use of non-testifying in-house experts requires defense counsel to consider carefully the benefits and risks associated with their use. If defense counsel finds himself in a situation where he wants to use his client's regular employees as consultants, he should with careful planning be successful in securing the protection of Rule 26(b)(4)(B).

Notes

1. This paper concentrates primarily on Federal Rule of Civil Procedure 26(b)(4) and federal cases interpreting it. Since many states have adopted rules of procedure identical or similar to the Federal Rules, these cases also may be followed by courts in those states. *See, e.g.,* General Accident Fire & Life Assurance Corp. v. Cohen, 203 Va. 810, 127 S.E.2d 399, 401 (1962) (since Virginia rule of procedure was taken verbatim from Fed. R. Civ. P. 36, Virginia legislature is presumed to have adopted the construction of the statute by the federal courts).

Federal Rule of Civil Procedure 26(b)(4) provides in pertinent part:

(4) Trial Preparation: Experts.

(A) A party may depose any person who has been identified as an expert whose opinions may be presented at trial. If a report from the expert is required under subdivision (a)(2)(B), the deposition shall not be conducted until after the report is provided.

(B) A party may, through interrogatories or by deposition, discover facts known or opinions held by an expert who has been retained or specially employed by another party in anticipation of litigation or preparation for trial and who is not expected to be called as a witness at trial, only as provided in Rule 35(b) or upon a showing of exceptional circumstances under which it is impracticable for the party seeking discovery to obtain facts or opinions on the same subject by other means.

(C) Unless manifest injustice would result, (i) the court shall require that the party seeking discovery pay the expert a reasonable fee for time spent in responding to discovery under this subdivision; and (ii) with respect to discovery obtained under subdivision (b)(4)(B) of this rule the court shall require the party seeking discovery to pay the other party a fair portion of the fees and expenses reasonably incurred by the latter party in obtaining facts and opinions from the expert.

Most of the cases addressing discovery of in-house experts under Rule 26(b)(4) were decided under the rule as it existed before the December 1993 amendments. The few reported decisions to date applying the amended rule have not based their reasoning upon the distinctions between the former and current versions of the rule. *See, e.g.,* Kiser v. General Motors Corp., 2000 WL 1006239 (E.D. La. 2000).

2. *See* Braun v. Lorillard, Inc., 84 F.3d 230, 236 (7th Cir. 1996); *see also* Delcastor, Inc. v. Vail Associates Inc., 108 F.R.D. 405, 408 (D. Colo. 1985) ("exceptional circumstances" test met where defendant's engineering consultant was only expert to have made observations of mudslide site before its condition changed).

3. *See* Advisory Comm. Note, 48 F.R.D. 487, 503 (1970) ("expert whose information was not acquired in preparation for trial but rather because he was an actor or viewer with respect to transactions or occurrences that are part of the subject matter of the lawsuit should be treated as an ordinary witness"); *see also* Note, *Rule 26(b)(4) of the Federal Rules of Civil Procedure; Discovery of Expert Information,* 42 U. MIAMI L. REV. 1101, 1168 (1988) [hereinafter Note, *Discovery of Expert Information*].

A plaintiff's request for injunctive relief or allegation of ongoing matters also has been held to be reason to deny a non-testifying in-house expert protection under Rule 26(b)(4)(B). *See* Kansas-Neb. Natural Gas v. Marathon Oil Co., 109 F.R.D. 12, 16 (D. Neb. 1985). Similarly, if there is a question about the extent of a corporate defendant's knowledge about the harmfulness of a product, protection under Rule 26(b)(4) also may be denied. *See* Roesburg v. Johns-Manville Corp., 85 F.R.D. 292, 303 (E.D. Pa. 1980) (plaintiff would be able to discover facts known and opinions held by defendant's non-witness experts, since discovery was directed at learning extent of defendant's knowledge of asbestos and asbestos-related diseases).

4. Indeed, as one treatise has noted: "The problem area that has arisen is whether a regular employee of a party can ever be considered to be 'specially employed' within the meaning of Rule 26(b)(4)(B). It may be that no parsing of the rule and Advisory Committee Note will afford a fully satisfactory answer to that question." 8 Charles Alan Wright & Arthur R. Miller, *Federal Practice and Procedure* § 2033 (2d ed. 1994 & Supp. 2003).

5. For a more detailed analysis of the three views and the theories and policy reasons that underlie each, *see generally* Pielemeier, *Discovery of Non-Testifying "In-House" Experts Under Federal Rule of Civil Procedure 26,* 58 IND. L.J. 597 (1983); Note, *The In-House Expert Witness: Discovery Under The Federal Rules of Civil Procedure,* 33 S.D. L. REV. 283 (1988) [hereinafter Note, *The In-House Expert Witness*]; *see also* Note, *Discovery of Expert Information, supra* note 3, at 1168-1172.

6. *See* Comment, *Ambiguities After the 1970 Amendments to the Federal Rules of Civil Procedure Relating to Discovery of Experts and Attorney's Work Product,* 17 WAYNE L. REV. 1145, 1167 (1971) [hereinafter Comment, *Ambiguities*].

7. Fed. R. Civ. P. 26(b)(4) (revised 1993) (emphasis added).

8. Advisory Comm. Note, *supra* note 3, at 504; *see also* Comment, *Ambiguities, supra* note 6, at 1167.

9. Advisory Comm. Note, *supra* note 3, at 504; *see also* USM Corp. v. American Aerosols, Inc., 631 F.2d 420, 424-25 (6th Cir. 1980) ("Since discovery of expert information acquired in anticipation of litigation can only be had in accordance with Rule 26(b)(4), if no provision is made for experts informally consulted in anticipation of litigation, no discovery concerning them is permissible.").

10. *See* Comment, *Ambiguities, supra* note 6, at 1167; Note, *The In-House Expert Witness, supra* note 5, at 293.

11. Procter & Gamble Co. v. Haugen, 184 F.R.D. 410, 413 (D. Utah 1999).

12. 68 F.R.D. 397 (E.D. Va. 1975).

13. *Id.* at 407.

14. *Id.*

15. *Id.*

16. *Id.* at 408.

17. 20 Fed. R. Serv. 2d 679 (D. Mass. 1975).

18. *Id.* at 687.

19. *Id.*

20. *See* NEC America Inc. v. United States, 636 F. Supp. 476, 480 (C.I.T. 1986) (since expert witness was employee of plaintiff, he was not entitled to any protection under Rule 26(b)(4)), *aff'd*, 857 F.2d 787 (Fed. Cir. 1988), *cert. denied*, 489 U.S. 1017 (1989); Kansas-Neb. Natural Gas v. Marathon Oil Co., 109 F.R.D. 12, 16 (D. Neb. 1985) ("the use of the terms 'retained or specially employed' implies something more than simply the assignment of a current employee to a particular problem raised by current litigation"); *cf.,* U.S. Energy Corp. v. Nukem, Inc., 163 F.R.D. 344, 347-48 (D. Colo. 1995) (plaintiffs' chief financial officer was not entitled to be paid for his deposition time under the parties' agreement for payment of experts' fees; in-house experts are to be treated as ordinary witnesses for discovery purposes).

21. *See* Graham, *Discovery of Experts Under Rule 26(b)(4) of the Federal Rules of Civil Procedure Part One: An Analytical Study*, U. ILL. L.F. 895, 942 (1976); Pielemeier, *supra* note 5, at 597; Note, *Discovery of Expert Information, supra* note 3, at 1172; Note, *The In-House Expert Witness, supra* note 5, at 302.

22. 69 F.R.D. 69 (D. Kan. 1975).

23. *Id.* at 72.

24. *Id.*

25. *Id.*

26. *Id.*

27. *Id.* at 73 n.3; *see* Advisory Comm. Note, *supra* note 3, at 503 ("Subdivision (b)(4)(B) deals with an expert who has been retained or specially employed by a party in anticipation of litigation or preparation for trial (thus excluding an expert who is simply a general employee of the party not specially employed on the case), . . ."). *See also In re* Sinking of Barge Ranger I, 92 F.R.D. 486, 489 n.5 (S.D. Tex. 1981) ("It may be possible for a party's regular employees to be specifically employed in anticipation of litigation or preparation for trial") (dictum).

28. 132 F.R.D. 437 (E.D. La. 1990).

29. *See id.* at 440.

30. *Id.* at 441.

31. *See id.* at 442.

32. *See id.* In a later opinion, the court ruled that these two employees, as well as eight others who had been specially employed in preparation for trial, could be deposed about their knowledge of defendant's refining activities that they gained in their regular employment outside of litigation assistance. *See In re* Shell Oil Refinery, 134 F.R.D. 148, 150 (E.D. La. 1990).

33. 2000 WL 1006239 (E.D. La. 2000).

34. *Id.* at *1.

35. *Id.* at *2.

36. *Id.*

37. *Id.*

38. FED. R. CIV. P. 1; *see* Note, *Discovery of Expert Information, supra* note 3, at 1172.

39. Note, *Discovery of Expert Information, supra* note 3, at n.496 (noting that Alabama adopted Rule 26(b) verbatim from the federal rule but later added the words "or assigned" to expand protection of rule to in-house experts); *see also* ILL. ANN. STAT. ch. 110A, para. 220 (Smith-Hurd 1985) (defining an expert witness as "an employee of a party, a party, or an independent contractor").

40. Marine Petroleum Co. v. Champlin Petroleum Co., 641 F.2d 984, 992 (D.C. Cir. 1979).

41. 126 F.R.D. 539 (S.D. Ill. 1989).

42. *See id.* at 540-42.

43. *See* Fed. R. Civ. P. 26(a)(2)(B) (requiring report of testifying expert to include, *inter alia*, "the data or other information considered by the witness in forming the opinions"); *see also* Kiser v. General Motors Corp., 2000 WL 1006239 (E.D. La. 2000) (preliminary report of non-testifying in-house expert produced pursuant to Rule 26(a)(2)(B) because it had been reviewed by testifying experts).

44. *See, e.g.,* Herman v. Marine Midland Bank, 207 F.R.D. 26 (W.D.N.Y. 2002) (defendant entitled to depose purported non-testifying expert who provided substantial assistance to plaintiff's expert in preparing expert report, where non-testifying expert performed more than half of total hours required to generate report, and he accounted for more than half of fee paid for production of report).

45. 154 F.R.D. 301 (M.D. Ga. 1994).

46. The court also cited Taroli v. General Elec. Co., 114 F.R.D. 97, 98 (N.D. Ind. 1987), *aff'd without opinion*, 840 F.2d 920 (7th Cir. 1988).

47. 154 F.R.D. at 308.

48. *See id.*

49. *See* Note, *The In-House Expert Witness, supra* note 5, at 302.

CHAPTER 15

Loss of Attorney-Client Privilege Through Inadvertent Disclosure of Privileged Documents[*]

VINCENT S. WALKOWIAK
SARAH E. LEMONS
PROF. THOMAS J. LEACH

Introduction

There is no doubt that every attorney makes mistakes. Some mistakes are serious; while others are not. Some mistakes are correctable; others are not. While not every document within the attorney-client privilege has great significance, as a general matter an attorney's inadvertent disclosure of privileged documents must undoubtedly be regarded as a very serious mistake. Thus, the issue becomes whether such a mistake is correctable or irrevocable.

While the problem of inadvertent disclosure of privileged documents can arise in a variety of ways,[1] it most commonly arises in the context of pretrial production of documents. Although the common occurrence of inadvertent disclosure may occur during pretrial production of documents, the reliance upon the fax machine and more significantly, electronic mail have changed the landscape of pretrial production and have created more concern for inadvertent disclosure. Regardless of the manner of the inadvertent disclosure, however, pretrial production within document intensive litigation remains the paradigm case.

Although a unique case in many respects, *Transamerica Computer Co. v. IBM Corp.*[2] illustrates the problem. IBM was a defendant in an antitrust case brought by Control Data Corporation. The district judge overseeing the litigation issued a pretrial order dramatically accelerating the document inspection that had been in progress. The Court of Appeals described the effect of this order as:

---

* This updated chapter was originally published in the Second Edition of *The Attorney-Client Privilege*.

[R]equir[ing] IBM to produce within a three-month period for inspection and for adversary copying approximately 17 million pages of documents. To say the least, the logistical problems confronting IBM were monumental and were exacerbated by a number of factors. For example, the documents which CDC sought to have IBM produce for inspection had not been produced during any previous litigation and they were not grouped or batched together so as to be readily accessible. Most of the documents were particularly difficult to screen for privilege, for they were letters and memoranda contained in myriad headquarters-type files randomly strewn throughout various IBM branches and divisional headquarters.[3]

As a result of herculean efforts, IBM succeeded in screening each of the more than 17 million pages of documents and meeting the discovery deadline. About 491,000 pages were withheld under a claim of privilege. However, it was discovered that some 1,138 privileged documents (consisting of about 5,800 pages) were inadvertently disclosed. Because of the special circumstances involved, it was ultimately found that the privilege was not lost as a result of this inadvertent production of privileged materials.[4]

Along with the production of millions of documents, like that in *Transamerica*, comes the newly discoverable electronic mail, or e-mail. This addition to discoverable information makes protection of the attorney-client privilege much more significant and difficult. There are numerous advantages to e-mail such as cost, efficiency, speed, and versatility; thus, more and more attorneys and law firms are relying on this form of communication with clients and outside counsel.[5] However, while paper documents can be destroyed or returned, erasing or retrieving an e-mail is altogether more difficult.[6] Even if the attorney or client deletes an e-mail message from his computer, most of this electronic information is still stored on a back-up system file.[7] Further, courts have expressed their opinions that e-mail is not secure[8] and some commentators have compared e-mail to sending a postcard through the mail.[9]

Imagine a case wherein the attorney drafts a highly confidential document and wants to send the document to outside co-counsel so that co-counsel may express his opinion on the document. The attorney knows that the most efficient way to send the document is through e-mail because co-counsel can receive it in seconds and can make suggestions and return it with the same ease.[10] The attorney types the e-mail and hits send, but immediately realizes that she has inadvertently sent the document to opposing counsel rather than co-counsel.[11] There may be nothing that she can do to cancel this e-mail. She now faces the issue of waiver of the attorney-client privilege through her mistaken e-mail of her client's highly confidential document.[12] And although courts have yet to comprehensively address the issue of the inadvertent disclosure of privileged information through electronic mail, they have addressed inadvertent disclosure of privileged material during pretrial production and from the situations important rules have been set and trends have been disclosed.

At least one jurisdiction has addressed the issue of inadvertent waiver by procedural rule.[13] By virtue of this rule-oriented approach, Texas has eliminated the need for the application of a case law determined test to establish whether there has been a waiver of privilege.[14] The majority of jurisdictions have, however, not taken this approach.

In those jurisdictions which still decide the issue by case law, there are essentially three different tests employed to determine whether production of privileged documents results in a loss of the privilege. The different tests reflect a long-standing ambivalence about the attorney-client privilege and, in our view, some confusion about the concept of waiver. Accordingly, before considering the several tests it is helpful to address the core concepts of privilege and waiver.

Attorney-Client Privilege and Waiver

The attorney-client privilege is the oldest of all privileges protecting confidential communications known to the common law.[15] The privilege is generally regarded as an essential component of the adversary system and thought to uphold the honor of the profession.[16] As the Supreme Court has explained: "Its purpose is to encourage full and frank communication between attorneys and their clients and thereby promote broader public interests in the observance of law and administration of justice. The privilege recognizes that sound legal advice or advocacy serves public ends and that such advice or advocacy depends upon the lawyer's being fully informed by the client."[17] In the absence of the privilege, clients would be dissuaded from seeking legal advice or hesitant to reveal adverse information that might not remain confidential.[18] Therefore, the privilege must be so highly valued that one judge has described it as "sacred."[19]

On the other hand, the adversary system is, fundamentally, a truth-seeking process. Because the attorney-client privilege (like all privileges) may suppress relevant information, it in a sense hampers the search for the truth by forcing the courts to exclude otherwise relevant evidence.[20] Wigmore observes that the privilege "is worth preserving for the sake of a general policy but it is nonetheless an obstacle to the investigation of the truth. It ought to be strictly confined within the narrowest possible limits consistent with the logic of its principle."[21] Or, as Professor Hazard says, though regarded as indispensable to the lawyer's role as advocate and counselor, "the attorney-client privilege has its victims . . ." because it is "not only a principle of privacy, but also a device for cover-ups."[22] Reflecting this ambivalence are opinions from some courts stressing on some occasions the need for a liberal construction of the privilege[23] and on others a strict construction.[24] It is also reflected in the several tests propounded for determining whether the inadvertent disclosure of privileged documents results in loss of the privilege.

The loss of privilege as a result of inadvertent production of privileged materials is almost universally regarded as a "waiver" issue.[25] Though it may ultimately be necessary to apply this label to the conclusion that the privilege has been lost (for example, to place the conclusion within the scope of the governing statutory scheme), it is dangerous to try to use the waiver concept as a means of reaching that conclusion, at least without being aware of how dramatically this approach skews analysis.

"Waiver" is traditionally defined as "an intentional relinquishment or abandonment of a known right or privilege."[26] This definition makes the client's intention virtually conclusive of the matter, regardless of the objective failure to take any reasonable steps to preserve the privilege, or, indeed, even affirmative conduct placing privileged communications in issue.

However, on a more practical level, the demands of society require an assessment of the action or inaction in terms broader than merely the actor's intent. Thus, when the conduct of the privilege-holder is objectively inconsistent with upholding the privilege, the conduct is said to result in an "implied waiver."[27] But to say there is an implied waiver despite the privilege-holder's insistence that he did not intend to waive the privilege requires that "waiver" means something other than the intentional relinquishment of a known right.

This apparent paradox can be resolved by undertaking a functional analysis of the waiver concept. In reality the operative concept of waiver incorporates the reasonable expectations of society and the judicial system. A person who intends privileged matters to remain privileged must act accordingly. Therefore, at any stage of legal proceedings, failure to claim attorney-client privilege constitutes waiver.[28] Nevertheless, because of the appearance of the inconsistent application of the waiver doctrine, it seems fair to say that "waiver" is a shorthand term used to cover several distinct situations in which the courts refuse, for one reason or another, to recognize the privilege.[29] This being so, use of the term does not advance analysis of any given privilege question. The traditional concept of waiver focuses on the intent of the privilege-holder. Intent may be more or less important in any given case. Its significance, however, should be addressed directly, not assumed by knee-jerk application of the waiver rubric.

The possible risk of losing privilege through inadvertent disclosure is a major issue to be addressed. With respect to the loss of privilege through inadvertent disclosure, the courts do not agree on one approach to determine whether the privilege is lost.[30] The answer is found on a continuum of tests.[31] Presently, with each of the three tests, the holder of the privilege will possibly find three different results with respect to inadvertent disclosure. Therefore, the courts' failure to follow a uniform approach creates much confusion and uncertainty among lawyers who face issues of inadvertent disclosure.[32]

The Strict Approach: Privilege Automatically Lost by Disclosure

The traditional test for determining whether production of privileged documents to a litigation adversary results in loss of the privilege is extraordinarily simple: disclosure automatically means the end of the privilege. Wigmore, the leading proponent of this "strict responsibility" test, explains that the attorney and client have the means, and therefore must bear the risk of failure, to preserve the confidentiality of their communications. "The risk of insufficient precautions is on the client."[33]

Those advocating this view stress that the privilege acts as an obstacle to discovery of the truth;[34] that disclosure of privileged materials makes it impossible to achieve the benefits of the privilege, i.e., secrecy;[35] and that "when the policy underlying the rule can no longer be served, it would amount to no more than mechanical obedience to a formula to continue to recognize it."[36]

Additionally, some courts favor the strict test because "mistake or inadvertence is, after all, merely a euphemism for negligence, and, certainly . . . one is expected to pay a price for one's negligence."[37] And one court specifically rejected the "middle ground" test because "the opinions of the courts in these cases, after a substantial amount of verbiage, can be reduced to a bottom line to the effect that the precautions were inadequate because they were not effective in preventing the disclosure of privileged documents."[38]

Another rationale for the strict approach centers on the unfairness to the party seeking to use the inadvertently disclosed communication. Once a party adopts the disclosed information into its case preparation, "fairness requires that [the] privilege cease whether [the opponent] intended the result or not."[39] In *Suburban Sew 'N Sweep, Inc. v. Swiss-Bernina, Inc.*,[40] because the information in the documents obtained formed the basis of the lawsuit, plaintiff would have been unable to proceed if it were not allowed to use the communications. The court recognized the issue of privilege to be a "close question," but, adopting the strict approach, ruled the communications admissible. The court was persuaded that, due to the unusual circumstances, the policy of encouraging open communication between attorneys and their clients would not be served by recognizing the privilege.

Finally, some courts are attracted to the strict approach because it forces self-regulatory behavior. In *In re Sealed Case*,[41] the court explained that the strict approach creates a strong incentive for careful document management, stating, "the courts will grant no greater protection to those who assert the privilege than their own precautions warrant."[42] If an attorney wants to keep the privilege, it is completely within her and her client's power to retain the confidentiality. "In other words, if a client wishes to preserve the privilege, it must treat the confidentiality of attorney-client communications like jewels—if not crown jewels."[43]

An attorney arguing against a claim of privilege for inadvertently disclosed documents can invoke significant practical advantages in support of the strict responsibility test: It is exceptionally predictable and easy to apply, thus minimizing litigation over the issue and encouraging the greatest possible diligence in protection of the privilege. Moreover, although the point is often overlooked, this approach is most consistent with the waiver rules typically applied during trial. If an attorney's client is asked a question that would invade the privilege, the attorney's failure to object timely results in a loss of the privilege.[44] If the privilege is lost for failure to object timely under circumstances where a split-second decision must be made, it seems appropriate to apply at least an equally strict rule to pretrial discovery, where there is far greater opportunity and time to analyze the situation and exercise an informed judgment as to whether or not to invoke the privilege.

A good example of the application of this rationale is found in *In re Grand Jury Investigation of Ocean Transportation*.[45] Defendant's original counsel turned over to opposing counsel a group of documents marked with a "P." After inspection, opposing counsel asked if these specific documents were intended to be privileged. Defendant's counsel, after investigating, replied that they were not intended to be privileged. Six months later, new counsel discovered the error. The court noted that "perhaps this latter rule should not be strictly applied to all cases of unknown or inadvertent disclosure; this, however, is not a case where any such exception would be appropriate. Here, the disclosure cannot be viewed as having been inadvertent in all respects. Original counsel knew that some papers marked "P" had been divulged. This production was brought to their attention on at least one occasion; each time, however, counsel declined to assert the privilege."[46]

Where the question is unsettled, as it is in many jurisdictions, a party contending against a claim of privilege for inadvertently disclosed documents should consider urging the strict responsibility rule.[47] However, many courts have expressed that the strict approach is too harsh.[48] They argue that the strict approach sacrifices the value of protecting the client for the sake of certainty of results.[49] Although this approach may have some appeal because it most certainly makes attorneys and clients accountable for their carelessness in handling privileged matters, it has been rejected by many jurisdictions because of its pronounced inflexibility and significant intrusion on the attorney-client relationship.[50] Therefore, counsel should not be surprised if a court says, "The automatic waiver rule is too harsh, depriving the client of protection against the use of the privileged communication in court. An error quickly discovered could not be corrected under this approach once the documents had been trotted over, even if the opposing party had little opportunity to view the documents."[51] While actual cases are not decided by trends, they are often influenced by them, and "[t]he modern trend is away from the strict responsibility approach."[52]

The Lenient Approach: Client's Subjective Intent to Waive

Competing with the strict responsibility test is its polar opposite—the client's subjective intent test. Although there are differing formulations of the test, its central focus is on the client's intent to waive the privilege. Stated in basic terms, the subjective intent test holds that as long as the client did not intend to waive the privilege, the privilege remains intact, despite disclosure of the client's confidences to her adversary.[53]

While a client's lack of intent to preserve the privilege may be sufficient reason to hold that it has been waived, it is difficult to see why the converse should be true. One of the few cases adopting this approach is *Mendenhall v. Barber-Greene Co.*[54] According to the *Mendenhall* court, "the better-reasoned rule is that mere inadvertent production does not waive the privilege."[55] The court reasoned that "inadvertent production is the antithesis" of an intentional relinquishment of a known right and, if the privilege is for the welfare of the *client*, more than the *attorney's* negligence should be required before the *client* loses the privilege (emphasis in original).[56]

There are very serious problems with every step of this analysis. First, the authorities cited as representing the "better-reasoned rule"[57] contain little analysis and, ultimately, involve application of a New York statute that was construed to require that a waiver under the statute be made in open court. Commenting on *Mendenhall,* another district court observed that the cited cases have "limited precedential value."[58]

Mendenhall's rationale is as weak as its cited authority. As noted above, to define waiver as intentional relinquishment of a known right is to beg the question whether the privilege should be upheld or not. And the court's suggestion that a distinction should be drawn between the client and his attorney ignores the basic rule charging a client with the conduct of his lawyer.[59]

Although one court reasoned that the *Mendenhall* approach is preferable to the strict approach when dealing with discovery situations involving the production of thousands of documents,[60] Mendenhall is not generally followed.[61] The primary objection to its approach is that it exalts subjective considerations over objective ones, such as whether the client and his attorney have taken reasonable efforts to protect the privilege, and the effects on the opposing party and the litigation process of trying to resurrect the privilege after disclosure. Further, the courts have expressed that this approach gives little incentive for attorneys to maintain tight control over privileged documents.[62]

This approach has the same practical advantages as the strict responsibility test— predictability and ease of application so as to minimize litigation. This approach clearly fits true to the core of the attorney-client privilege which can only be waived by the holder of the privilege, the client.[63] It may be objected, however, that with its focus on subjective intent, this approach does nothing to encourage care to preserve confidences. Some commentators urge a modified form of this test requiring both objective and subjective manifestations of intent, which may meet some of the objections to the pure subjective intent approach.[64]

The Middle Ground: Evaluation of the Circumstances Test

Rejecting both extremes, most courts in recent years have used a balancing test to determine whether inadvertent production of privileged documents forfeits the privilege. Although it has been called by several different names, this approach "is one under which the courts make a decision based on an evaluation of the circumstances, rather than automatically finding a waiver or a retention of the privilege."[65] Its proponents generally agree that "[a]lthough a more difficult approach to employ, ultimately this approach is fairer to both parties and the policy of preserving the privilege for confidential communications as it focuses on the confidentiality aspect of the privilege."[66]

This approach weighs the surrounding circumstances to determine whether production of the privileged documents should result in a loss of privilege. Under the middle ground approach, the court will undertake a five-step analysis of the inadvertent disclosure to determine whether the privilege should remain intact.[67] The court will consider the following five factors: (1) the reasonableness of the precautions taken to prevent inadvertent disclosure; (2) the time taken to rectify the error; (3) the scope of the discovery; (4) the extent of the disclosure; and (5) the "overreaching issue of fairness." [68]

In *Lois Sportswear, U.S.A., Inc. v. Levi*, the court narrowly upheld the privilege as against a demand for production after plaintiff's counsel had inadvertently been allowed to review 22 privileged documents out of 16,000 inspected and 3,000 pages requested to be produced.[69] Because the documents had been seen by but not delivered to opposing counsel, element (2) (time to rectify) inherently weighed in defendant's favor. The rather extensive discovery demand, the comparatively small number of privileged documents disclosed, and the fact they had been subject to only visual inspection all similarly weighed in defendant's favor.

Nevertheless, Levi almost lost because "[a]s to the reasonableness of the precautions, Levi only just adequately protected its privilege."[70] Among the criticisms of Levi's precautions were: (1) Levi apparently had no practice of designating documents as confidential at the time of origination; (2) there was no specific description of the screening instructions given by Levi's Deputy General Counsel to the paralegal actually doing the screening; and (3) there was no specific evidence that the procedures actually followed had screened out any privileged documents.

An illustration of this test's flexibility is found in *Hydraflow, Inc. v. Enidine Inc.*,[71] where plaintiff's local counsel, when delivering documents to the court for an *in camera* inspection, accidentally delivered copies also to opposing counsel. The court emphasized that the delivery was clearly a mistake, and that the overreaching issue of fairness weighed heavily in plaintiff's favor.[72]

Another court has stated that the "middle of the road" approach is to be favored because, as to the consideration of fairness, it takes into account the special problems that arise during discovery.[73]

An extensive discussion of the law in this area is set forth in *Kanter v. Superior Court*.[74] Although *Kanter* has been ordered not published in the official *California Reporter* pursuant to Rule 976 of the California Rules of Court, and the opinion withdrawn, the court's analysis and the approach which it took to this difficult situation is worth considering. In *Kanter*, defendants' counsel had sent documents to a copy service with instructions to copy them all, but noting that "privileged docs (yellowed pages) are to be kept in our office." The copied documents were returned to defendants' counsel in a single box. He forwarded them to plaintiff's attorney. The box contained copies of the entire litigation file from the underlying case, including some 160 privileged documents.

Approximately 15 months later, plaintiff's counsel deposed one Edelstein, who had been the defense lawyer in the underlying case. Plaintiff's counsel referred to certain documents that defendants' counsel claimed were privileged and had been inadvertently produced.

Defendants moved for a protective order and for return of the privileged documents. Plaintiff's attorney moved to compel answers to the questions Edelstein had refused to answer regarding these documents. The trial court ruled for defendants. The Court of Appeal issued a peremptory writ overturning the order.

Kanter was a case of first impression in California. After discussing the various possible approaches the court adopted the multifactor balancing approach.[75] The court concluded that every factor weighed against sustaining the claim of privilege. As noted, this opinion was subsequently withdrawn by the court and ordered not published by the court which rendered it.

The case law does not permit meaningful generalization on the weighing of the different factors. For example, in *Lois Sportswear*, substantially all the factors pointed in one direction. In *Hartford Fire Ins. Co. v. Garvey*,[76] the court found a waiver where the error was rectified quickly but reasonable precaution had not been taken, the scope of discovery was limited, and disclosure was complete. In *Parkway Gallery v. Kittinger/ Pennsylvania House Group*,[77] the court started with a presumption that disclosure equaled waiver of privilege and then reviewed the various factors. The requested discovery was extensive but the court did not count this as favoring defendants because they were not operating under severe time constraints. Defendants did react quickly when the error was discovered. The court was not convinced the screening precautions were sufficient, and the court also stressed that when disclosure is complete, a court cannot restore confidentiality but "can only attempt to restrain further erosion."[78]

Given this fact, the court observed that to grant a protective order would require "a very strong showing with respect to the other factors."[79] The privilege was held to be waived. Lastly, in *Gray v. Bicknell*, Bicknell inadvertently disclosed two letters between Bicknell and his attorney which addressed a wide range of matters relating to the litigation.[80] The court undertook a brief analysis of each of the approaches, finding the middle ground test to be the best approach.[81] The court upheld the district court by finding no waiver of the privilege, since the litigation involved a vast number of documents, and in the course of production, the paralegal inadvertently included the two letters.[82] Further, the court stated the middle ground approach was the best approach because it struck the appropriate balance between protecting the privilege and, under certain circumstances, allowing unprotected disclosure to waive the privilege.[83]

Although consistently presented as a multifactor test, upon reflection this approach appears really to concentrate primarily on two considerations—the conduct of the client and lawyer claiming the privilege, and the prejudice to the party to whom the privileged material was disclosed should the court uphold the privilege despite disclosure. Thus, "reasonable precautions" is really an umbrella concept that embraces time taken to rectify the error, scope of discovery, and special circumstances. All these considerations point to the same question: did the lawyer/client invoking the privilege really act in the careful manner we expect from someone truly concerned with guarding a confidence, both before and after the inadvertent disclosure?

The other umbrella concept is that of fairness, which embraces the extent of disclosure and special circumstances. The time taken to rectify the error must also be included here, as it affects prejudice. The basic question is: Would it be fair to the person who has received the privileged information to try to make her expunge his knowledge of it from the litigation?[84] If a party receives privileged documents and integrates them into her trial preparation, the efforts to "restore" the privilege may place her at a permanent disadvantage. In *Kanter,* for example, the court agreed that "given the time that the documents were in the hands of plaintiff's counsel, the information gleaned from the documents has saturated counsel's mind, thereby presenting the old dilemma of 'unringing the bell.'"[85]

Like the previous two approaches, the middle ground test is criticized for its uncertainty and wide discretion given to judges. Nevertheless, this approach accounts for the inevitable error in the modern, extremely document intensive litigation, but continues to treat carelessness and negligence of the attorney as an indication of waiver.[86] As the *Gray* court pointed out, the middle ground test is the most thoughtful approach because it gives the courts broader discretion to determine whether waiver occurred through inadvertent disclosure and if so, the scope of that waiver.[87]

How to Protect the Privilege—Avoiding Production and Retrieving Privileged Materials

As the preceding discussion demonstrates, inadvertent disclosure of privileged documents does not necessarily mean the end of the privilege. Nevertheless, both lawyer and client should assume that it will, and plan accordingly. This will minimize the risk of inadvertent disclosure and maximize the chance that if such disclosure occurs it will not be held fatal to the privilege. With the increasing technological advances and great reliance upon e-mail communication, there must be greater protection and attention to the issue of inadvertent disclosure.

Both attorney and client should make a practice of identifying privileged communications as such and keeping them segregated from unprivileged documents, as well as, when applicable, placing such notation in the subject line of e-mail communication. For example, many attorneys stamp or type "Privileged Attorney-Client Communication" on documents. Even if such a document is not kept apart from unprivileged communication, it will be easier to spot by anyone who screens the documents. A sophisticated client could color-code or otherwise mark different types of communications.

When a document production request is made, an attorney should carefully oversee the process and create a record that demonstrates the care taken to prevent disclosure of privileged documents. First, counsel should obtain from her client an estimate on how long it will take the client to compile documents and to make a preliminary segregation of privileged documents. To this estimate should be added the time necessary for a second review by the attorney or someone directly under her supervision. If production has been demanded before this two-step review can be accomplished, counsel should make an effort to obtain additional time either by agreement or by court order. If time pressure necessitates a compromise of the screening procedures, this should be reflected in the record. Moreover, while a stipulation that production of privileged documents will not constitute a waiver of the privilege may not be accepted by all courts,[88] it should certainly be obtained if possible. In addition, or (where no stipulation is possible) instead, every effort should be made to obtain a court order to the effect that inadvertent disclosure will not result in loss of the privilege.[89] Further, with respect to e-mail communication, a confidential attorney-client privilege paragraph should be included on all potentially protected e-mails. Although this paragraph may not guarantee the protection of privilege and prevent waiver,[90] it is a necessary step in protecting one's client.

Time permitting, a two-stage screening process should be used. Screening instructions should be given by the lawyer to the client in such a form that the instructions can be used as a self-serving exhibit if need be. The attorney should briefly explain attorney-client privilege and identify by category materials falling (or likely to fall) within the privilege, e.g., all correspondence to or from counsel, incident reports, legal memoranda. Initial screening ideally should be done by someone with legal training under the supervision of in-house counsel. As a general matter, the screener should be instructed to err on the side of privilege.

During initial screening separate lists of privileged and unprivileged documents should be prepared. For each document, the authors and recipients should be identified by name and position (e.g., John Jones, Risk Manager, to Richard Smith, General Counsel), date, and general subject matter.

Counsel must be responsible for the next level of review. At a minimum, counsel must personally review the lists of documents. Any which, on their face, appear to be wrongly categorized should be inspected by counsel. Beyond this, someone with legal training no less than that of a paralegal should do a complete review of all documents. Again, a self-serving screening instruction should be put in writing. Uncertainty about whether a document is privileged or not must be resolved by counsel. Once all privileged documents have been identified, they should be marked as such and segregated. If copies are made, they should not be made at the same time the unprivileged materials are copied.

All documents sent or otherwise disclosed to opposing counsel should be marked in a way that will make it possible to tell after the fact exactly what was disclosed. Counsel should retain an exact duplicate set of anything disclosed. Immediately after disclosure, someone who has participated in the screening process should review the duplicate set to see if anything was inadvertently disclosed. All these efforts should be documented.

When production is actually made, counsel should consider sending a letter explaining that every effort has been made to produce all requested documents that are not privileged, and that if any privileged documents were produced it was inadvertent and not intended as a waiver. Often, identification of any documents claimed to be privileged must be made.[91] The list of privileged documents can be used to inform opposing counsel that no document on the list was intended to be disclosed.

As soon as counsel has reason to believe any privileged document has been disclosed, she must immediately act to protect the privilege.[92] First, a demand for return of the documents must be made. Second, the attorney must then follow with a motion for protective order seeking return of the documents, all copies, notes, etc., and prohibiting any disclosure of, use of, or reference to the documents. If opposing counsel will not agree to treat the documents as privileged pending resolution of the motion, these efforts should proceed on an emergency basis.[93]

If the jurisdiction appears to follow the traditional test of automatic loss of privilege through disclosure, a full-scale attack should be mounted against this test. If the jurisdiction is not already committed to the evaluation of the circumstances approach, counsel should consider advocating the subjective intent approach as a first line of attack. Under the evaluation of the circumstances approach, all favorable criteria should be emphasized, but in particular the efforts made to protect the privilege and the lack of prejudice to the other side.[94]

A careful, conscientious attorney will not necessarily always succeed in curing any mistaken disclosure of privileged documents, but she has by far the best chance of doing so.

Notes

1. *See, e.g.,* Suburban Sew 'N Sweep, Inc. v. Swiss-Bernina, Inc., 91 F.R.D. 254 (N.D. Ill. 1981) (privileged documents culled from a trash container).

2. 573 F.2d 646 (9th Cir. 1978).

3. *Id.* at 648.

4. *Id.* at 651-52.

5. Amy M. Fulmer Stevenson, Comment: *Making a Wrong Turn on the Information Superhighway: Electronic Mail, the Attorney-Client Privilege and Inadvertent Disclosure,* 26 CAP. U.L. REV. 347, 350 (1997).

6. *Id.*

7. *Id.*

8. *See* American Civil Liberties Union v. Reno, 929 F. Supp. 824 (E.D. Pa. 1996).

9. Stevenson, 26 CAP. U.L. REV. at 353.

10. *Id.* at 357.

11. *Id.*

12. *Id.*

13. Tex. R. Civ. P. 193.3(d) states:

> (d) *Privilege not waived by production.* A party who produces material or information without intending to waive a claim of privilege does not waive that claim under these rules or the Rules of Evidence if—within ten days or a short time ordered by the court, after the producing party actually discovers that such production was made—the producing party amends the response, identifying the material or information produced and stating the privilege asserted. If the producing party thus amends the response to assert a privilege, the requesting party must promptly return the specified material or information and any copies pending any ruling by the court denying the privilege.

14. *Id.*

15. *See* 8 JOHN H. WIGMORE, EVIDENCE § 2290, at 542 (McNaughton rev. ed. 1961). For an interesting qualification of this general proposition, *see* Geoffrey C. Hazard, Jr., *An Historical Perspective on the Attorney-Client Privilege*, 66 CALIF. L. REV. 1061 (1978).

16. Robert A. Pikowsky, *Privilege and Confidentiality of Attorney-Client Communication Via E-mail*, 51 BAYLOR L. REV. 483, 489 (Summer 1999).

17. Upjohn Co. v. United States, 449 U.S. 383, 389 (1981); Trammel v. United States, 445 U.S. 40, 51 (1980) ("The lawyer-client privilege rests on the need for the advocate and counselor to know all that relates to the client's reasons for seeking representation if the professional mission is to be carried out."); Hunt v. Blackburn, 128 U.S. 464, 470 (1888) ("The rule . . . is founded upon the necessity, in the interest and administration of justice, of the aid of persons having knowledge of the law and skilled in its practice, which assistance can only be safely and readily availed of when free from the consequences or the apprehension of disclosure.").

18. Pikowsky, note 16, *supra.*

19. People v. Kor, 246 P.2d 94, 100 (Cal. Ct. App. 1954) (Shinn, J., concurring).

20. Pikowsky, note 16, *supra.*

21. 8 WIGMORE, note 15, *supra*, § 2291, at 554.

22. Hazard, note 15, *supra*, at 1062.

23. *E.g.*, People v. Flores, 139 Cal. Rptr. 546, 549 (Ct. App. 1977).

24. *E.g.,* Gonzales v. Municipal Court., 136 Cal. Rptr. 475, 481 (Ct. App. 1977).

25. *See, e.g.,* Goldsborough v. Eagle Crest Partners, Ltd., 105 Or. App. 499, 805 P.2d 723 (1991), *aff'd,* 314 Or. 336, 838 P.2d 1069 (1992). *See generally* George A. Davidson & William H. Voth, *Waiver of the Attorney-Client Privilege*, 64 OR. L. REV. 637 (1986); Wesley M. Ayres, *Comment, Attorney-Client Privilege: The Necessity of Intent to Waive the Privilege in Inadvertent Disclosure Cases*, 18 PAC. L.J. 59 (1986); James M. Grippando, *Attorney-Client Privilege: Implied Waiver Through Inadvertent Disclosure of Documents*, 39 U. MIAMI L. REV. 511 (1985); Note, *Inadvertent Disclosure of Documents Subject to the Attorney-Client Privilege*, 82 MICH. L. REV. 598 (1983). *See, however,* Comment 4 to Tex. R. of Civ. Proc. R. 193.3(d), in which the question of whether waiver principles should apply to inadvertent disclosure is squarely addressed by rule and rejected.

> d. Rule 193.3(d) is a new provision that allows a party to assert a claim of privilege to material or information produced inadvertently without intending to waive the privilege. The provision is commonly used in complex cases to reduce costs and risks to large document productions. The focus is on the intent to waive the privilege, not the intent to produce the material or information. A party who fails to diligently screen documents before producing them does not waive a claim of privilege. This rule is thus broader than TRE 511 and overturns Granada Corp. v. First Court of Appeals, 844 S.W.2d 223 (Tex. 1992), to the extent the two conflict. The ten-day period (which may be shortened by the court) allowed for an amended response does not run from the production of the material or information but from the party's first awareness of the mistake. To avoid complications at trial, a party may identify prior to trial the documents intended to be offered,

thereby triggering the obligation to assert any overlooked privilege under this rule. A trial court may also order this procedure.

26. Johnson v. Zerbst, 304 U.S. 458, 464 (1938).

27. *See, e.g.*, Chicago Title Ins. Co. v. Superior Court, 220 Cal. Rptr. 507, 512 (Ct. App. 1985).

28. Pikowsky, note 16, *supra*, at 494.

29. Davidson & Voth, note 25, *supra*, at 639; Pikowsky, note 16, *supra*, at 494.

30. Stevenson, note 5, *supra*, at 359.

31. *Id.*

32. *See id.*

33. 8 WIGMORE, note 15, *supra*, § 2325, at 633.

34. *See, e.g., In re* Grand Jury Investigation of Ocean Transp., 604 F.2d 672, 675 (D.C. Cir.), *cert. denied,* 444 U.S. 915 (1979); Underwater Storage. Inc. v. United States Rubber Co., 314 F. Supp. 546, 547 (D.D.C. 1970); United States v. Kelsey-Hayes Wheel Co., 15 F.R.D. 461, 465 (E.D. Mich. 1954).

35. United States v. Kelsey-Hayes Wheel Co., *supra* note 32, at 465; W.R. Grace & Co. v. Pullman, Inc., 446 F. Supp. 771, 775 (W.D. Okla. 1976).

36. United States v. Kelsey-Hayes Wheel Co., 15 F.R.D. at 465.

37. *In re* Standard Fin. Mgmt. Corp., 77 Bankr. 324, 330 (D. Mass. 1987).

38. International Digital Sys. Corp. v. Digital Equip. Corp., 120 F.R.D. 445, 449 (D. Mass. 1988).

39. 8 WIGMORE, *supra* note 15, § 2327, at 636.

40. *Supra,* note 1.

41. 877 F.2d 976 (D.C. Cir. 1989).

42. *In re* Sealed Case, 877 F.2d. 976, 980 (D.C. Cir. 1989).

43. *Id.*

44. *E.g.,* Julrik Prods., Inc. v. Chester, 113 Cal. Rptr. 527, 530 (Ct. App. 1974); Mize v. Atchison. T. & S.F. Ry. Co., 120 Cal. Rptr. 787, 795 (Ct. App. 1975).

45. 604 F.2d 672 (D.C. Cir.), *cert. denied*, 444 U.S. 915 (1979).

46. *Id.* at 675.

47. In its modern enlightened form, only voluntary disclosure would automatically result in loss of privilege, eliminating the extreme claim that documents lose their privilege when they are stolen. *See* Note, *Inadvertent Disclosure of Documents Subject to the Attorney-Client Privilege,* note 25, *supra,* at 612-16.

48. *See* Gray v. Bicknell, 86 F.3d 1472, 1483 (8th Cir. 1996).

49. *Id.*

50. *Id.*

51. Although ordered not citable and not published in the official reports, the court's rationale in Kanter v. Superior Court, 253 Cal. Rptr. 810, 816-17 (Ct. App. 1988) is quite enlightening.

52. Ayres, note 25, *supra* at 74.

53. *Id.* at 81-82; Gray v. Bicknell, 86 F.3d 1472 (8th Cir. 1996). Compare this approach with the Texas approach, which does not inquire into intent at all.

54. 531 F. Supp. 951 (N.D. Ill. 1982).

55. *Id.* at 954.

56. *Id.* at 955. *See also,* Farm Credit Bank v. Huether, 454 N.W.2d 710 (N.D. 1998).

57. Dunn Chemical Co. v. Sybron Corp., 1975-2 Trade Cas. ¶ 60,561 at 67,463 (S.D.N.Y. 1975); Conn. Mut. Life Ins. Co. v. Shields, 18 F.R.D. 448, 451 (S.D.N.Y. 1955).

58. Hartford Fire Ins. Co. v. Garvey, 109 F.R.D. 323, 329 (N.D. Cal. 1985). *See also* Kanter v. Superior Court, 253 Cal. Rptr. at 814.

59. *See In re* Grand Jury Investigation of Ocean Transp., *supra* note 32, at 675. *See generally* Carroll v. Abbott Labs., Inc., 187 Cal. Rptr. 592, 595 (Ct. App. 1982).

60. Kansas-Neb. Natural Gas v. Marathon Oil, 109 F.R.D. 12 (D. Neb. 1985).

61. Michigan appears to have a similar rule. Sterling v. Keidan, 162 Mich. App. 88, 412 N.W.2d 255 (1987). In contrast, *see, e.g.,* Hartford Fire Ins. Co. v. Garvey, 109 F.R.D. at 331-32; Chubb Integrated Sys. v. Nat'l Bank of Washington, 103 F.R.D. 52, 66 (D.D.C. 1984); United States v. Willis, 565 F.Supp. 1186, 1204 (S.D. Iowa 1983); Champion Int'l Corp. v. Int'l Paper Co., 486 F. Supp. 1328, 1332 (N.D. Ga. 1980); Duplan Corp. v. Deering Milliken, Inc., 397 F. Supp. 1146, 1162 (D.S.C. 1974).

62. Gray v. Bicknell, 86 F.2d 1472 (8th Cir. 1996).

63. *Id.*

64. *See* Note, *Inadvertent Disclosure of Documents Subject to the Attorney-Client Privilege,* note 25, *supra* note 23, at 610.

65. Kanter v. Superior Court, 253 Cal. Rptr. at 815 (*see* note 51, *supra*).

66. *Id.* One advocate of this approach even claims it "is more understandable and easier to apply than the strict responsibility standard." Grippando, *supra* note 25, at 527. This is a difficult position to sustain for a multifactor balancing test. *See* Ayres, *supra* note 25, at 79-80.

67. *See* Gray v. Bicknell, 86 F.3d at 1483-84.

68. Gray v. Bicknell, 86 F.3d at 1484; Alldread v. City of Grenada, 988 F.2d 1425, 1433 (5th Cir. 1993); Lois Sportswear, U.S.A. Inc. v. Levi Strauss & Co., 104 F.R.D. 103 (S.D.N.Y. 1985).

69. 104 F.R.D. 103.

70. *Id.* at 105.

71. 145 F.R.D. 626 (W.D.N.Y. 1993).

72. *Id.* at 638. It may be surmised the court took this view in part because the error was local counsel's, not supervising counsel's.

73. *See* Gray v. Bicknell, 86 F.3d at 1484 ("The middle test is best suited to achieving a fair result. It accounts for the errors that inevitably occur in modern, document-intensive litigation. . . .").

74. 253 Cal. Rptr. 810 (Ct. App. 1988).

75. *Id.*

76. 109 F.R.D. 323 (N.D. Cal. 1985).

77. 116 F.R.D. 363 (M.D.N.C. 1987).

78. *Id.* at 52.

79. *Id.*

80. Gray v. Bicknell, 86 F.3d at 1482.

81. *Id.* at 1484.

82. *Id.* at 1482.

83. *Id.* at 1484.

84. *But see* U.S. v. Pepper's Steel and Alloys, Inc., 742 F. Supp. 641, 645 (S.D. Fla. 1990) (calling receipt of documents a "windfall").

85. 253 Cal. Rptr. at 820. One article on the subject suggests that, as an analytical tool, estoppel may be the more appropriate rubric under which to test the correct result of one party's inadvertent production of privileged information to its opponent. John T. Hundley, *"Inadvertent Waiver" of Evidentiary Privileges: Can Reformulating the Issue Lead to More Sensible Decisions?* 19 S. ILL. U. L. J. 263 (1995). While the notion of estoppel seems to underlie the discussions of "fairness" in many of the cases, it is also true that the opinions do not directly frame the question as one of estoppel *vel non.* When we consider that the negligence concept is used to support both the strict and middle-ground tests—under the strict test if you make the mistake you lose; under the middle-ground test you may lose, and you probably have an uphill battle to win—it seems correct to rate harm to the non-producing party as a crucial, and perhaps the most important, factor. Given that, in normal negligence settings, even when it has been found that a duty owed has been breached, no liability attaches unless harm is shown, it may be logically argued that the same standard should apply when the question is the "liability" of a negligent document producer. To be sure, it may be only the rare case in which no harm can be demonstrated, but that rarity does not render the estoppel factor inappropriate.

86. *See* Gray v. Bicknell, 86 F.3d at 1484.

87. *Id.*

88. *See* Permian Corp. v. United States, 665 F.2d 1214, 1216 (D.C. Cir. 1981); *Chubb Integrated Sys.*, 103 F.R.D. at 67-68.

89. *See* Transamerica Computer Co. v. IBM Corp., 573 F.2d at 649-50.

90. *See* Data Gen. Corp. v. Grumman Sys. Support Corp., 139 F.R.D. 556, 561 (D. Mass. 1991) (The court found the several documents' privilege as waived even though they were marked "Confidential," declaring that "merely marking the documents in such a manner does not constitute the requisite protection required.").

91. *See, e.g.*, FED. R. CIV. P. 26(b)(5).

92. Some jurisdictions dictate the time period in which the attorney has to respond to the inadvertent production. For example, in Texas, the producing party has 10 days (or a shorter period ordered by the court) to amend its production responses and assert privilege. *See* TEX. R. CIV. P. 193.3(d). The benefits of the Texas approach are obvious, however, since it does not require any evaluation of the production to determine if the waiver has occurred and a request requires return of the allegedly privileged document.

93. While it can be argued that the party denying the claim of privilege for facially privileged materials should have the burden of proving waiver, where the documents have been produced courts typically place the burden of establishing a non-waiver on the party claiming privilege. *E.g.*, Weil v. Investment/Indicators, Research & Management, 647 F.2d 18, 25 (9th Cir. 1981); Kanter v. Superior Court, 253 Cal. Rptr. at 811.

94. Counsel should also be prepared to do damage control in the event the privilege is held to be lost. Unlike the case of a voluntary waiver, courts are less inclined to hold that disclosure of some privileged documents results in a waiver with respect to all other communications on the same subject matter. *See, e.g.* Weil v. Investment/Indicators Research & Management, 647 F.2d at 25; Parkway Gallery v. Kittinger/Pennsylvania House Group, 116 F.R.D. at 52.

Moreover, a court might be persuaded to grant a protective order and to modify trial procedures to limit the disclosure of the materials to the case in which the error occurred.

CHAPTER 16

Putting Attorneys on the Witness Stand and Their Advice at Issue: The Perils of Selective Waiver of Privilege[*]

ALAN J. MARTIN
DEMETRIOS G. METROPOULOS
VERONICA L. SPICER

Introduction

What would possess a litigant to put his attorney on the witness stand or his advice at issue? At first glance, many tactical considerations weigh in favor of such efforts. For example, in today's environment of complex litigation—inside and outside of the insurance area—a litigant's attorney typically has the best command of the facts. Unlike other witnesses who may only be privy to pieces of the puzzle, the attorney is uniquely situated to be a "big picture" person as a result of having gathered and marshaled the facts.

A closely related consideration is the continuity represented by the attorney. Large companies frequently have employee turnover commensurate to their size, and large cases frequently wind their way through pretrial discovery for an extended period of time. The one constant may be the attorney.

Training can also hold a lawyer in good stead to be a witness. Attorneys tend to be authoritative and articulate speakers. Trial attorneys have years of experience presenting complex legal issues to a jury in layman's terms. Knowing the goals of cross-examination, they also possess the wherewithal to anticipate and avoid pitfalls that often trap the uninitiated. As zealous advocates, attorneys can go a long way toward articulating facts in a manner consistent with the "company line."

The strategy of reliance on either the testimony or advice of counsel also comports with commercial reality. Facing an increasingly complex web of laws and regulations on the one hand and an increasingly litigious society on the other, corporations

---

[*] This chapter is an updated version of the chapter originally co-authored by Alan J. Martin and Nancy K. Linnerooth in the 1989 edition of this publication.

and business people have given attorneys a correspondingly greater role in everyday decision making. Should litigation nonetheless arise from those decisions, a natural response is to turn to the same attorneys, who not only have firsthand knowledge of the challenged decision but also are most familiar with the legal process.

In the insurance coverage area, the temptation to use attorney witnesses can be great. For example, a company confronted with a rash of product liability cases can be expected to turn to its trusted attorneys to handle the defense. If the number of cases is large, the resulting discovery almost certainly will touch upon the inner workings of the company. A long-standing relationship with a given law firm can go a long way toward the recognition and careful handling of sensitive areas. At the same time, a dispute may arise with the company's insurer as to coverage for costs allegedly related to the defense. Given the sensitivity of the issues and the potential for overlap, the company may determine to use the same law firm to defend the underlying cases and to press the insurance coverage claims. If so, a very dangerous die may have been cast.

Under the scenario outlined, the same law firm handling the underlying defense is also arguing for insurance coverage. As a result, the law firm is in a unique position to structure the underlying defense in such a manner as to give the appearance of insurance coverage and, thereby, to reinforce its client's claims. Because insurance carriers and their policyholders usually make every effort to avoid trial among themselves until the underlying crisis has passed, the policyholder's attorneys can represent their client on both fronts until just before the trial of the coverage dispute. At that time, with the underlying cases all but history, the attorneys can withdraw as counsel for the insured in the coverage litigation in order to act as trial witnesses regarding the defense of the underlying cases.

Once the attorneys withdraw and are designated as witnesses, however, the question immediately becomes: "To what extent has privilege been waived?" The classic "sword and shield" scenario arises. On the one hand, the insured seeks to use the attorneys' testimony and advice regarding the structure of the underlying defense as a sword at trial while, on the other hand, it invokes the attorney-client privilege and the work-product immunity to shield previous communications regarding coverage issues. As is discussed below, the potential for waiver of privilege dramatically alters the attractiveness of an attorney as a witness—so much so that many civil litigants are unwilling to risk the consequences of such actions. While it is not completely uncommon for attorneys to be called as witnesses in criminal matters (see Part B.1, *infra*), there are a limited number of civil cases considering the issue. This case law suggests, however, that the perils are very real and that one is well advised to think carefully before reaching for this particular sword.

The Attorney as Witness

The few civil cases on the subject of attorney witnesses make it clear that a party who names retained counsel as a witness risks waiver of both the privilege for attorney-client communications and the work-product immunity on communications that relate to the subject of the attorney's testimony.[1] Furthermore, courts have been willing to interpret the waiver as having a long reach into otherwise privileged communications and immune documents. The following sections describe this area of the law, beginning with the early cases, particularly in the patent area, and following its evolution through the decisions in *Northbrook Excess & Surplus Ins. Co. v. Procter & Gamble Co.*,[2] a case much like that hypothesized in the introduction, and into its most recent applications.

Handgards

A leading case on the issue of attorney witnesses is *Handgards, Inc. v. Johnson & Johnson*.[3] Handgards alleged that Johnson & Johnson brought a series of patent infringement suits against it in bad faith as part of a conspiracy to eliminate competition. In order to rebut assertions that its attorneys knew the patents were invalid at the time they filed suit, Johnson & Johnson planned to call as witnesses three of its lawyers, who were primarily responsible for the prior patent cases, to testify as to legal advice they gave Johnson & Johnson.

The court found that Johnson & Johnson's "deliberate injection of the advice of counsel into a case waives the attorney-client privilege as to communications and documents relating to the advice."[4] This waiver encompassed not only the advice about which the attorneys would testify, but also their entire litigation files, which the court ordered to be submitted for an in camera inspection to determine which documents fell within Handgards' production request.

Underlying Considerations

The reasoning of the court in *Handgards* is followed by most courts faced with similar circumstances. The main justification for finding that Johnson & Johnson waived its attorney-client privilege, according to the court, was that it would be unfair to Handgards to allow Johnson & Johnson to disclose self-serving communications at the same time that it withheld damaging ones on the same subject. Other courts have analogized such a tactic to using the privilege as both a sword and a shield. If a party uses part of his privileged communications with his lawyer as a "sword" to support his position in litigation, he may not shield unfavorable communications on the same issue from his opponent with a claim of privilege.[5]

Necessity is another theme to which courts return in justifying a finding of waiver of the privilege. For example, in *Leybold-Heraeus Technologies, Inc. v. Midwest Instrument Co.*,[6] the court found persuasive the argument that waiver was mandated by the opposing party's need to ascertain the basis of opinions in order to cross-examine effectively two attorneys who had been designated as trial witnesses. There, as in *Handgards*, a patentee (LHT) named its attorneys as witnesses to testify as to their asserted good faith in filing suit against an alleged infringer (Minco). In an opinion adopting *Handgards*, the court found that LHT waived its privilege because of the necessity that Minco have all communications on the same subjects on which the attorneys would testify in order to perform an adequate cross-examination.[7]

Work-Product Immunity

Courts have taken pains to point out that work product has a source of immunity from discovery independent of the attorney-client privilege.[8] The attorney-client privilege is intended "to encourage full and frank communication between attorneys and their clients."[9] The work-product doctrine was developed to protect the lawyer's privacy, allowing case development without fear of an adversary later looking over his shoulder or raiding the fruits of his efforts.[10] Indeed, the "mental impressions, conclusions, opinions, or legal theories of an attorney"—more commonly known as "opinion" work product—enjoy heightened protection,[11] which some courts have even deemed "nearly absolute."[12] In theory, then, a waiver of the attorney-client privilege does not necessarily result in a breach of the work-product immunity.

Once a court has found that a party needs information in the hands of the opposing party and counsel in order to effectively cross-examine an attorney witness, the logical (and sometimes only) place to find such information is in the attorney's work product. So, with a nod to the distinctiveness of the two doctrines, the courts nevertheless open discovery on work product after the client waives the attorney-client privilege by calling counsel as a witness. Thus, the court in *Handgards* ordered the attorney witnesses to produce "a wide range of materials, including all relevant records, opinion letters, interviews of witnesses, internal files, memoranda, and notes" related to the attorneys' opinions of the merits of their client's patents and the related infringement suits.[13] Similarly, in *Leybold-Heraeus*, the opposing party gained access to documents in which the attorney witnesses participated, either as authors or as recipients, and which related to the issue of their good faith in conducting the underlying patent lawsuits.

The Attorney as an Expert Witness

Recent variations on this theme involves the use of attorneys as "expert" witnesses. The added twist: Discovery rules require an expert to disclose information considered in forming an opinion—even privileged information.[14] The question now is how much—not whether—information must be disclosed. Some courts have adopted a bright-line rule that Federal Rule of Civil Procedure 26 mandates disclosure of all information shared with a testifying expert, including an attorney's mental impressions and opinions. Other courts have ruled that "core attorney work product" is protected from discovery.[15] The principle of fundamental fairness still comes into play for many courts.[16]

Once again, the intellectual property context has provided fertile ground for these discovery disputes. This is perhaps understandable: A patent or copyright attorney often possesses an extensive and uniquely specialized technical and professional background, combined with knowledge gained through the patent or copyright application process or through trial preparation. The latter source of knowledge, however—which would otherwise be protected under the work-product doctrine—often becomes fair game when the attorney seeks to become a testifying expert. Perhaps of most concern to the litigant, the attorney expert may be required to disclose *all* information relevant to an opinion—including trial strategy, as well as theories that had been *rejected*. In other words, the party seeking to offer an attorney expert must first turn over sensitive work product and legal theories, and then watch its attorney critique (or even reject) those theories on the stand.

Vaughan Furniture Co. v. Featureline Mfg. Inc.[17] presents a useful illustration of these concerns. The plaintiff in *Vaughan Furniture* listed one of its attorneys (who had been involved in the suit from the start) as an expert on its copyright and patent claims, but sought to withhold work product materials documenting trial strategy discussions between the prospective expert and its other attorneys. Observing that the documents would be "necessary for appropriate cross-examination," the court curtly rejected plaintiff's work-product objections: "A party waives the opinion work product protection of its attorney by naming its attorney as an expert witness."[18]

The court then outlined the broad scope of its ruling, stating that the waiver applied "to those documents which the expert reviewed at any time and which would be relevant to the formulation of [the attorney's] expert opinion."[19] The relevant documents included those "discussing trial strategy," and included opinions "even if the opinions were rejected as a basis for the expert opinion."[20] As the court put it, "[a] change of opinion by the expert can be an important fact." *Id.* As a result, the sole limitation on disclosure would be items "completely unrelated to the subject matter of [the expert's] opinion."[21]

In a related vein, attorneys who hold multiple roles in a company and then serve as the company's representative under Federal Rule of Civil Procedure 30(b)(6) may also face these issues. In *Adler v. Wallace Computer Serv., Inc.,*[22] Wallace's general counsel—and vice president—served as the company's Rule 30(b)(6) representative. The court held that in this second role the attorney waived Wallace's attorney-client privilege by answering deposition questions based on privileged information. Due to those disclosures, the court granted the plaintiff's motion to compel answers to questions that the attorney had declined to respond to on the basis of attorney-client privilege.

While privileged material may be deemed discoverable, counsel may still be able to avoid being deposed—if someone else can provide the requested information. The seminal case for deposing counsel is *Shelton v. American Motors Corp.*[23] In *Shelton,* the Eighth Circuit formulated a three-part test for determining when opposing counsel may be deposed. A party must show that (1) no other means exist to obtain the information; (2) the information is relevant and nonprivileged; and (3) the information is crucial to the case.[24] Importantly, *Shelton* may only protect counsel from questions about a current case; the attorney may still have to answer questions about actions in a prior, completed case.[25]

Pretrial Procedure

As should be apparent, courts do not find it necessary to wait until a party's lawyer has actually been placed on the witness stand before allowing discovery of privileged material. To do so would defeat the purpose of discovery. Once a party indicates that counsel may testify, the opposing party is entitled to pretrial discovery of the issues related to the attorney's proposed testimony.[26]

If an attorney witness refuses to answer questions or turn over documents after a client waives the attorney-client privilege, courts are prepared to bar the attorney's testimony on any issue related to the privilege.[27] The plaintiff in *Torres v. 100 North LaSalle Partnership* intended to call as a witness her former lawyer, who claimed privilege in refusing to answer 12 questions at his deposition. The court gave the plaintiff a choice: If she allowed the deposition to be reopened and directed the lawyer to answer questions, he could testify without restriction at trial; otherwise he would be barred from testifying on any issue to which he had asserted the privilege.

Northbrook v. Procter & Gamble

It is against this backdrop of case law that the Northern District of Illinois rendered a series of decisions in the case of *Northbrook Excess & Surplus Ins. Co. v. Procter & Gamble Co.*[28] *Northbrook* involved a declaratory judgment action by certain excess insurers of Procter & Gamble (P&G) to determine their coverage obligations as a result of toxic shock syndrome litigation against P&G and its tampon product "Rely." On January 14, 1988, the magistrate rendered the first decision relating to attorney-client privilege and work-product immunity that, among other issues, considered the status of *in-house* P&G attorneys designated as trial witnesses. The magistrate was unequivocal in finding a complete subject matter waiver for P&G's claims of attorney-client privilege and work product:

> P&G attorneys . . . who have been designated as trial witnesses, are ordered to testify in full in deposition as to matters on which they are to testify at trial and without regard to any claim of attorney-client or work product privilege. By designating those attorneys as trial witnesses, P&G has waived both privileges, but only with respect to the subjects on which they will testify at trial. [29]

P&G did not appeal the decision to the district judge.

The parties' focus then shifted to P&G's outside counsel, Dinsmore & Shohl ("Dinsmore"). The relationship between the Dinsmore firm and P&G went back to the turn of the century, and Dinsmore had served as P&G's national coordinating counsel in the toxic shock litigation. Dinsmore also represented P&G in the insurance coverage litigation. Thus, in the early days of the coverage suit, the insurers had moved to disqualify Dinsmore on the grounds that its attorneys would be required as trial witnesses. P&G persuaded the court that, for the time being at least, Dinsmore testimony would not be required, and the district judge denied the insurers' motion without prejudice.

Just days before the close of discovery—and following close on the heels of the magistrate's January 14 ruling as to P&G's in-house attorneys—Dinsmore withdrew as trial counsel on grounds that its attorneys would testify at trial after all, on the handling of the underlying Rely defense. The insurers in turn protested P&G's last-minute reversal and moved to exclude any such testimony.[30] P&G vigorously opposed the motion, criticizing the proposed exclusion as "drastic" and "potentially outcome determinative."[31] The magistrate agreed—but also allowed the insurers to reopen discovery on a limited basis.[32] In so doing, the magistrate nonetheless acknowledged that "[j]ust what additional discovery the insurers wish to undertake is not clear."[33]

With discovery reopened, the insurers played their hole card—serving a subpoena on Dinsmore that called not only for documents related to the underlying Rely defense efforts (which P&G conceded were discoverable) but for "[a]ll documents relating to the present insurance coverage dispute between [P&G] and the Insurers."[34] P&G filed for a protective order, contending that its attorneys would testify only on defense issues, not on coverage issues, and that the latter subjects remained privileged from discovery.

In an opinion dated July 8, 1988, the magistrate ruled on P&G's objections. Framing the insurers' arguments in favor of a wholesale waiver, the magistrate stated:

> The insurers argue that from the inception of the Rely litigation, insurance coverage issues were inextricably intertwined with decisions by P&G and Dinsmore regarding the Rely defense effort and that Dinsmore was involved in structuring that defense effort and various defense activities for which P&G claims insurance coverage so as to give an untrue appearance that they were defense-oriented. The insurers say that those expenditures and activities were not matters on which P&G initially expected insurance coverage, but their true purpose was to create an appearance which would support insurance claims rather than to conduct a reasonable and efficient defense. The insurers also maintain that they are entitled to use the involvement of Dinsmore attorneys in coverage issues to impeach the testimony of those witnesses relating to the Rely defense effort.[35]

The magistrate agreed with this assessment, noting that deposition excerpts and documents showed that from the beginning P&G and Dinsmore perceived a close relationship between insurance coverage issues and various Rely defense activities. Accordingly, he concluded that "P&G has waived its attorney-client privilege as to insurance coverage questions relating to Rely defense activities."[36]

As regards work-product immunity, the magistrate found a corresponding waiver on two grounds. First, to the extent that a showing of "compelling need" was necessary, he found that it had been made.[37] The magistrate noted that "[d]ocuments relating to Dinsmore's treatment of the insurance coverage issues in relation to its conduct of the underlying product liability litigation may bear on central issues in this case and are not available from any other source." Second, he reasoned that "[w]ork product immunity may also be waived by the appearance of the attorney as a witness."[38]

The magistrate's decision left open the possibility of some limitation on the waiver if P&G could demonstrate that it completed its basic decisions relating to the conduct of Rely defense efforts at a given point in time and then subsequently focused on the prosecution of the coverage litigation.[39] The burden of establishing this limitation, however, fell squarely on P&G.[40] The magistrate also cautioned P&G—twice—that failure to provide the requested discovery would lead him to reconsider his ruling allowing Dinsmore attorneys to testify at trial.[41]

Naturally, P&G appealed to the district court judge. On December 28, 1988, the district court affirmed the magistrate's ruling.[42] While reassuring P&G that the ruling did not give the insurers authority to "root around through all the Dinsmore files," the judge accepted the magistrate's central premise that privilege claims were waived "as to insurance coverage questions relating to Rely defense activities."[43]

In the court's view, because Dinsmore attorneys were supposed to testify on "what" was done to defend the Rely cases and "why," documents relevant to these considerations were discoverable even if they contained otherwise privileged information regarding policy coverage considerations.[44] As the court stressed in the closing paragraph of its opinion, "[t]o the extent that 'what' and 'why' involve policy coverage considerations, so be it."[45]

One can only assume that when P&G first considered designating Dinsmore attorneys as witnesses in the coverage action, and then fought tooth and nail to persuade the court to go along, it did not contemplate having to produce to the insurers documents relating to that very litigation.

Putting the Advice of Counsel at Issue

Although the emergence of attorneys as witnesses is relatively recent, courts have long found implied waivers of the attorney-client privilege where a party puts the advice of his attorney "at issue" in litigation. Yet, in recent years, courts have expanded the scope of the circumstances that constitute such a waiver to include, for example, situations in which a party puts his state of mind at issue and the court finds privileged matter to be the best evidence of the party's state of mind. Thus, in addition to the danger that the *scope* of a waiver may exceed expectations, a litigant must face the possibility that its pleadings and strategies might implicitly—even unintentionally—effect a waiver of privilege where none had been foreseen at all.

Criminal Cases

The theory of implied waiver of the attorney-client privilege has some of its early roots in criminal cases. The most clear-cut and uncontroversial of the decisions involve prisoners who move to set aside their convictions on the grounds that they received ineffective assistance of counsel. Courts have routinely held that this waives the attorney-client privilege.[46] In *Johnson v. Alabama,*[47] the Eleventh Circuit held that "there should be no confusion that a habeas petitioner alleging that his counsel made unreasonable strategic decisions waives any claim of privilege over the contents of communications with counsel relevant to assessing the reasonableness of those decisions in the circumstances."[48]

In a case more closely related to the civil context, the defendant in a prosecution for tax evasion alleged that he amended his returns on the advice of his former attorney. He was held to have waived the attorney-client privilege with respect to evidence about his former attorney's advocacy of his interest.[49]

Civil Cases: The General Rule

The holding is the same in civil cases: Where a party relies on the advice of counsel as a defense, the opposing party can explore privileged matters to see if the advice was given and taken.[50]

Panter v. Marshall Field & Co.[51] arose out of Marshall Field's successful opposition to a takeover bid. As part of that opposition, Marshall Field had filed an antitrust suit against the prospective bidder. After the takeover fizzled, certain Marshall Field's shareholders filed a class action against the company, its officers, and directors (collectively, "Marshall Field"), alleging violations of the securities laws. Marshall Field sought to "rely heavily" on an "advice of counsel" defense,[52] but also claimed protection for certain documents under the attorney-client privilege and work product doctrine.

The district court first rejected Marshall Field's claim of privilege: "Where, as here, a party asserts as an essential element of his defense reliance upon the advice of counsel, we believe the party waives the attorney-client privilege with respect to all communications, whether written or oral, to or from counsel concerning the transactions for which counsel's advice was sought."[53]

The *Panter* court then turned its attention to the assertion of "work product." There, despite acknowledging (in a footnote) the different scope and purposes of the attorney-client privilege and work-product doctrine, the court reached the same conclusion:

> Whether styled as a showing of a sufficiently compelling need or as a waiver of the work-product privilege, we find that the defendants' reliance in this litigation upon the advice of counsel as a major justification for their actions . . . and as a defense to these shareholders' suits renders the advice and actions of counsel a central issue, and as such overcomes the attorneys' work-product privilege . . . .[54]

Hearn and Progeny—the State of Mind Exception

By pleading reliance on the advice of counsel as a defense, a party typically seeks to disprove the alleged existence of a culpable "state of mind"—whether it be the intent to commit a crime or the existence of "bad faith" in handling an insurance claim. But, as the preceding discussion makes clear, the party who employs such a strategy risks losing the protection afforded by the attorney-client privilege and work-product doctrine.

The next logical question is whether a party can base a defense, or even an affirmative claim for relief, on its state of mind alone, and thus stop short of an implied privilege waiver. This is the question faced in *Hearn v. Rhay*,[55] a particularly influential case on this subject. *Hearn* helped open the floodgates of implied waiver and has been relied upon by some courts to vitiate the attorney-client privilege on even slight pretexts.

Hearn *and the Qualified Immunity Defense*

Hearn was a civil rights action brought against prison officials by an inmate who alleged that his confinement in a mental health unit constituted "cruel and unusual punishment" and violated his right to due process. Defendants asserted the affirmative defense of "qualified immunity"—in other words, they contended that they acted in good faith, pursuant to their understanding of the law, and were therefore immune from the suit for damages. The plaintiff sought discovery of all the legal advice the defendants received on the legality of his confinement in the mental health unit. The court agreed with the plaintiff's contention that the defendants waived their attorney-client privilege by asserting their qualified immunity as a defense.

In an oft-quoted passage, the *Hearn* court analyzed several cases where the privilege was held to be waived and drew the following conclusions:

> All of these established exceptions to the rules of privilege have a common denominator; in each instance, the party asserting the privilege placed information protected by it in issue through some affirmative act for his own benefit, and to allow the privilege to protect against disclosure of such

information would have been *manifestly unfair* to the opposing party. The factors common to each exception may be summarized as follows: (1) assertion of the privilege was a result of some affirmative act, such as filing suit, by the asserting party; (2) through this affirmative act, the asserting party put the protected information at issue by making it relevant to the case; and (3) application of the privilege would have denied the opposing party access to information *vital* to his defense. Thus, where these three conditions exist, a court should find that the party asserting a privilege has impliedly waived it through his own affirmative conduct.[56]

The *Hearn* court found all three elements present in the case before it. Concluding that the content of the assertedly privileged communications was "inextricably merged with the elements of plaintiff's case and defendants' affirmative defense," the court allowed discovery of any legal advice and confidential communications between the defendants and the state attorney general that related to the issues of malice toward the plaintiff or knowledge of plaintiff's constitutional rights.[57]

The holding in *Hearn* has considerable emotional appeal: In making his case, the plaintiff prisoner had presented substantial evidence showing that the conditions of his confinement were "deplorable" and that those conditions persisted even after the attorney general notified one of the defendants that such confinement violated the plaintiff's constitutional rights. In addition, the court's logic—particularly its consideration of the "manifest[ ] unfair[ness]" of the defendants' partial disclosure and its reference to the plaintiff's "vital" need for the allegedly protected communications—parallels the "fairness" and "necessity" considerations underlying the more traditional implied waiver decisions described above. Finally, even though the *Hearn* defendants neither put their attorney on the stand nor directly pled reliance on his advice, they did plead "state of mind" as a defense—and, as the court found, the circumstances of the case "inextricably merged" attorney-client communications with that "state of mind."[58]

As the ensuing discussion shows, subsequent decisions have applied the *Hearn* court's broad language, and its flexible three-part test, in a wide array of settings.[59] As a result, today's litigant must consider the risk that a proposed claim or defense might put the legal advice and work product of its attorneys "at issue."

The "Good Faith" Defense

"Good faith" is a common defense to numerous torts outside the civil rights context. These cases represent the simplest, and shortest, extension of *Hearn*'s reasoning. For example, in *McLaughlin v. Lunde Truck Sales, Inc.*,[60] a suit by the Department of Labor to enjoin alleged violations of federal minimum wage laws, the defendants argued that they acted in good-faith reliance on representations by Department officials, and offered an affidavit by their former attorney to support that position. The Department argued, and the court held, that the defendants waived their attorney-client privilege by asserting "good faith" and by "injecting their former counsel's affidavit in support of their good faith defense."[61]

Similarly, the defendants in *Dawson v. New York Life Ins. Co.*[62] asserted a qualified privilege to justify their allegedly defamatory speeches. "Good faith" was an element of this defense; and because the defendants had used information obtained from their attorneys to help write their speeches, the court held that any applicable privilege had been waived.

In some circumstances, a careful attorney may be able to craft a good-faith defense and not waive attorney-client privilege.[63] An example of care in pleading is *Cardtoons, L.C. v. Major League Baseball Players Ass'n.*[64] In *Cardtoons*, the plaintiff planned to print parody baseball cards—sparking a cease and desist letter from the defendant. Plaintiff responded with a suit alleging a potpourri of claims, including several that required proof of defendant's intent. While the court warned that the issue of waiver could be teed up again if the defendant relied on attorney work product at trial in support of its good-faith argument, it found that the defendant's assertion of good faith, when plaintiff had the burden of proving bad faith, was insufficient in and of itself to waive the attorney-client privilege. The mere fact that privileged communications would make it easier for the plaintiff to prove its case was not enough to waive the defendant's attorney-client privilege.

Cardtoons is distinguishable from *McLaughlin* and *Dawson* in two important ways. First, the good-faith defense in *Cardtoons* simply denied an element of the plaintiff's claim. It was not an affirmative defense that was voluntarily injected into the case. In *McLaughlin*, by contrast, good faith was part of a qualified privilege defense to a defamation claim. Similarly, in *Dawson,* good faith was asserted as an affirmative defense to a Fair Labor Standards Act claim. Second, the defendant in *Cardtoons* did not claim or imply that attorney work product was the primary support for its good-faith claim. Reliance on attorney work product only came up in response to plaintiff's request for admissions, depositions of defendant's attorney, and oral argument on plaintiff's motion to compel. Even then, defendant showed that the attorney work product was, at best, one factor among several and not necessary to support its case. Despite the plaintiff's questions about attorney work product, the court did not consider the material "at issue" without some affirmative act or representation from the defendant that it was going to rely on the substance of the material. By contrast, in *McLaughlin*, the defendant voluntarily submitted an affidavit from its counsel regarding his interpretation of events—implying that it relied upon that information in making its good-faith determination.[65] It is important to note that a party can, in essence, volunteer reliance on attorney advice when that is the only logical support for its position. For example, potentially protected information was central to supporting (and refuting) the qualified privilege claim in *Dawson*. Although the defendant did not explicitly volunteer that it would rely on attorney-client information, that reliance was implied when all of the relevant deponents (defendant's employees) stated that they either (1) directly relied on attorney information to prepare allegedly defamatory statements, or (2) knew of the attorney information before making such statements. Thus, while courts clearly consider whether reliance on an attorney is volunteered, a party should be careful to not implicitly "volunteer" such reliance.

Equitable Estoppel

A party may also make "state of mind" an issue by trying to toll a statute of limitations. Adopting the reasoning of *Hearn*, a district court found the privilege was waived where the plaintiff buyers of securities claimed that the defendant underwriters were estopped to assert the statutory bar, as they had convinced the plaintiffs to withhold suit while they tried to save the corporation. In *Connell v. Bernstein-Macaulay, Inc.*,[66] the court found that the plaintiffs had waived the privilege on the issue of whether or not they had withheld suit solely or principally because of the defendants' persuasion. In broad language, the court stated that:

> . . . where a litigant seeks to avoid a statutory protection which has been established for the benefit of his adversary [by a claim of estoppel]; and where it appears that there is a good faith basis for believing that invasion of the attorney-client privilege would shed light on the validity of such claim of estoppel; the party making such assertion must be deemed to have waived the privilege.[67]

Clearly, the *Connell* court was reluctant to permit an assertion of attorney-client privilege to defeat the public policy reflected in the tolling statute. In using such broad language, however, the court ignored its implications: Invasion of the attorney-client privilege would "shed light" on the validity of virtually *any* claim.[68]

Courts have also found waiver as a result of estoppel claims in other, more generic contexts. For example, when the defendant in a patent infringement action claimed that the plaintiff was estopped from enforcing its patent because of the defendant's detrimental reliance on the plaintiff's previous inaction, the court found a waiver as to any documents that tended to show the defendant had instead relied on the advice of its lawyers that the patent was invalid in *Southwire Co. v. Essex Group, Inc.*[69] Although there was some objective evidence available showing reliance on inaction, the *Southwire* court found that, in fairness, the plaintiff should be permitted discovery of privileged documents to show the defendant's subjective intent. The court found the claim of waiver particularly compelling in view of the defendant's reliance on the opinions of its lawyers as a defense to a different claim, that of willful infringement. This alternative theory gave some credence to the plaintiff's claim that the defendant relied on something other than the plaintiff's inaction.

Fraud

The issue of reliance is also present in cases of alleged fraud. Accordingly, as one might expect, the issue of implied waiver has arisen as well. In *Sedco Int'l, S.A. v. Cory*,[70] the Eighth Circuit held that an investor, by asserting fraudulent inducement, "at most, waived his right to assert the privilege to prevent disclosure of communications which might have proven he did not rely on [his opponent's] statements or that such reliance was unreasonable."[71] However, the court refused to compel disclosure of privileged communications, finding that none of those communications could possibly show that the investor relied on anything other than the alleged misstatements.

Some later opinions have followed *Sedco*'s legal conclusion, finding that allegations of fraud constitute an implied waiver of privilege.[72] Other courts have adopted *Sedco*'s factual finding that privileged matters were not relevant to the issue of reliance, and thus have allowed disclosure only from the alleged victim itself (i.e., what it knew, why it acted).[73]

Contractual Intent

"State of mind" issues also arise in connection with contract disputes. In many cases, one party will try to go beyond the four corners of its agreement and introduce extrinsic evidence of its underlying understanding or intent. Because attorneys often play a role in contract negotiation, their advice is arguably "intertwined" with the client's contractual intent. Thus, it should come as no surprise that several courts have found the party employing such a strategy to have waived its attorney-client privilege.[74]

Back-to-back decisions by a Massachusetts federal district court in the case of *Sax v. Sax*[75] provide a useful illustration of this principle at work. *Sax* involved a "Memorandum Agreement" between Lawrence and John Sax. Both parties were represented by counsel during the lengthy negotiations that preceded the Agreement. Lawrence Sax sued to enforce the Agreement; John Sax alleged, among other things, that the Agreement was invalid because it was vague and the parties did not have a mutual understanding of its terms.

In an opinion filed March 15, 1991, the district court observed that "John Sax has raised an issue of his lack of understanding of the Memorandum Agreement in circumstances in which perhaps the only person who would have explained the agreement to him was his attorney."[76] As a result, the court held that he had implicitly waived his attorney-client privilege.

Apparently believing that turnabout would be fair play, John Sax then filed a motion challenging Lawrence Sax's privilege claims. This time, the district judge ruled differently: Finding that Lawrence Sax had simply sought a declaration that the Agreement, as written, was valid—without relying on extrinsic evidence, his attorney's advice or his own "state of mind"—the court upheld his privilege claims.[77]

Beyond "State of Mind"

As the preceding section describes, *Hearn* itself, and much of its progeny, focus on a party's allegations as to its state of mind. Yet *Hearn*'s underlying rationales—fairness and necessity—are not logically confined to "state of mind" issues. Thus, some decisions hold that a party loses privilege by making other factual allegations that implicitly put attorney advice or work product "at issue."

In *United States v. Exxon Corp.*,[78] the government accused Exxon of overcharging its customers. As a defense, Exxon asserted that it had relied, in good faith, on representations by the Department of Energy. The court found that Exxon had accordingly waived attorney-client privilege, reasoning that "[t]here is no other reasonable way for plaintiff to explore Exxon's corporate state of mind, a consideration now central to this suit."[79]

Thus far, then, the *Exxon* decision simply tracked previous case law in finding a waiver based on the assertion of an affirmative "state of mind" defense. At that point, however, the court went on to consider Exxon's motion to dismiss for lack of indispensable parties, in which Exxon alleged that it did not cause overcharges by other owners of oil interests. As with Exxon's good-faith defense, the court held that the defense of causation effected a waiver of privilege. As the court explained matters, "[w]hether Exxon had an overall scheme to pressure other interest owners to adopt certain pricing policies can only be effectively determined by exploring attorney-client discussions wherein such a scheme *may* have been concocted."[80]

The Delaware Supreme Court took a similar view of an insurance company's "causation" defense in *Tackett v. State Farm Fire & Casualty Ins. Co.*[81] The policyholders in *Tackett* sued State Farm for its alleged "bad faith" delay in processing a claim. State Farm, perhaps leery of the consequences of an "advice-of-counsel" or "good faith" defense, alleged instead that it had processed the claim in "routine" fashion, and that any delay had been caused by its policyholders' lack of cooperation. The court had no trouble finding that State Farm's allegations implicated its communications with counsel and thus waived privilege as to *any* legal advice received during the claims-handling process. Observing that "[f]airness requires that assertions of fact be tested by disclosure," the court held that "where, as here, an insurer makes factual representations which implicitly rely upon legal advice as justification for non-payment of claims, the insurer cannot shield itself from disclosure of the *complete advice of counsel* relevant to the handling of the claim."[82]

Damages claims may also put attorney advice or work product at issue. In *Rutgard v. Haynes*,[83] a legal malpractice case, the court noted that a party does not waive attorney-client privilege simply by including attorneys' fees in a damages claim. But in *Rutgard*, the plaintiff also claimed damages for a settlement negotiated by another attorney. In those circumstances, the court found that the reasonableness of the attorney's actions in negotiating the settlement was at issue and privileged information was discoverable.

Further Extensions of the Implied Waiver Doctrine

Refusal of Advice-of-Counsel Defense

Hearn addressed the situation where a party implicitly places attorney advice at issue without affirmatively pleading an advice-of-counsel defense. Later decisions suggest that a waiver may be possible even when that party expressly *refuses* to rely on an advice-of-counsel defense. In *In re Consolidated Litigation Concerning International Harvester's Disposition of Wisconsin Steel*,[84] International Harvester (IH) sold the assets of a subsidiary to a buyer who not long thereafter filed for bankruptcy. The buyer, who had assumed responsibility for the subsidiary's pension liabilities, joined the pension guaranty company and the subsidiary's employees in an action against IH. They claimed that IH knew the buyer was doomed to fail and that the sale was merely a sham to avoid pension liabilities.

International Harvester specifically disclaimed any intention of relying on an advice-of-counsel defense. However, IH's defense position was that it acted *reasonably* on the basis of information known to it. The court said that it "would be reluctant" to grant a discovery motion if IH could present its proposed defense without disclosing any attorney-client communications. The court warned that if IH relied on any attorney-client communications to show that it acted reasonably, it would waive the privilege as to those communications and all others that pertained to the same subject matter.[85]

The Second Circuit's decision in the criminal securities-fraud case *United States v. Bilzerian*[86] takes this analysis one step further. The defendant in *Bilzerian* sought to testify that he had made a good-faith attempt to comply with the securities laws in certain investment transactions, which were later found illegal. Bilzerian did not plan to assert an advice-of-counsel defense; indeed, he did not plan to disclose the content or even the existence of any privileged communications. Nonetheless, the trial court held—and the Second Circuit agreed—that the proposed defense would result in a waiver of attorney-client privilege.[87] Citing *Hearn* and *Exxon*, the appellate court explained that Bilzerian's "good faith" testimony "would have put his knowledge of the law and the basis for his understanding of what the law required in issue," and that otherwise privileged communications "would have been directly relevant in determining the extent of his knowledge and, as a result, his intent."[88]

As previously described, decisions in the criminal arena laid some of the early foundations of the "at issue" doctrine, while civil cases like *Hearn* expanded that doctrine to create a wide-ranging "state of mind" exception. *Bilzerian* shows that principles developed in the civil context are now, in turn, influencing decisions in criminal cases. The doctrine of implied waiver has come full circle.

Pleading by Opponent

Not only may a litigant put his own attorney's advice at issue—both affirmatively or implicitly—but the *opposing* party may also place this advice at issue through its pleadings. In *Bird v. Penn Central Co.*,[89] plaintiffs sued to rescind certain insurance policies. The policyholders raised the defense of laches, claiming that the plaintiffs knew or should have known of the grounds for rescission long before they brought suit, since their counsel had investigated prior claims that the defendants had made under the policies. The court found a crucial issue to be what the plaintiffs knew or should have known, and therefore it held that the relevant work product of plaintiffs' attorneys, including legal theories and conclusions, was discoverable:

> Because the nature of [the opposing party's] defense concerns knowledge, legal theories and conclusions of plaintiffs' attorneys charged with claim investigation, such "advice of counsel" evidenced in these documents is discoverable when it is directly relevant to a possible rescission action or suggests reasons to indicate the propriety of such an action.[90]

Likewise, in *AM Int'l, Inc. v. Eastman Kodak Co.*,[91] the court was persuaded that, because *Kodak* alleged that *AMI* knowingly filed suit based on invalid patents, discovery from *AMI* was appropriate. Since this allegation put the opinions of AMI's attorneys directly at issue, and Kodak's need was "compelling," the court ordered the relevant work product produced. In a nutshell, "[a]n attorney's work product is discoverable where such information is directly at issue and the need for production is compelling."[92]

The Scope of an Implied Privilege Waiver

Most courts agree that an implied waiver of attorney-client privilege, once established, extends to all communications on the applicable "subject matter." Their application of this test, however, can be as elusive, as expansive, and as unpredictable as the concepts of "fairness" and "necessity" on which the doctrine of implied waiver rests.

These variations begin with the allocation of the initial burden of proof between the opposing parties. In some jurisdictions, the party seeking to limit the scope of a waiver faces an uphill battle. Courts generally disfavor privileges and construe them narrowly.[93] Moreover, a finding of implied waiver is made more likely because courts generally place the burden of establishing privilege on the claimant.[94] The party asserting the attorney-client privilege has the burden of proving not only that the communications at issue are privileged, but also that the privilege has not been waived,[95] and that the scope of such waiver can be limited.[96] This does not mean, however, that the party asserting the attorney-client privilege need both make and refute the opposing party's case for waiver. As described in *First Federal Savings Bank of Hegewisch v. United States*,[97] the party asserting the privilege has the initial burden of establishing the elements of the privilege, but the burden then shifts to the party opposing the privilege to establish a prima facie case of waiver. If that case is made, the burden shifts back to the party asserting the privilege to rebut the prima facie case by demonstrating that the privilege is still viable.

Another issue is the scope of waiver. Since the waiver doctrine is designed to *prevent* a party from selective (and possibly distorted) disclosure of privileged communications, these courts naturally take a skeptical look at attempted subject matter limitations.[98]

Conversely, however, some decisions give priority to the interests served by the attorney-client privilege and narrowly construe the scope of its waiver.[99] In such cases, "[i]f a discernible line exists between the information withheld and the information disclosed, the line should be maintained."[100] In justifying a narrow construction of the scope of implied waiver, the Ninth Circuit described the doctrine as "striking a bargain with the holder of the privilege by letting him know how much of the privilege he must waive to proceed with his claim."[101] Under this philosophy, (1) waiver should be no broader than necessary to ensure the fairness of the proceedings, (2) the holder of the privilege has the option of preserving the confidentiality of the privileged communications by abandoning his claim, and (3) the party turning over protective materials is entitled to rely on the limits of the waiver as described by the court.[102] Thus, such cases acknowledge that in some circumstances, limits on waiver can be discerned and realistically applied. By doing so, they give the party opposing discovery more of an opportunity to lessen the scope and consequences of waiver.

Further complicating the issues is the disparity in factual situations, both in the context from which privileged communications spring and in the type and subject of the communications themselves. For obvious reasons, courts do not explain in detail the nature of documents that they find privileged. Indeed, many decisions simply record the results of a document-by-document in camera review, and thus have little general applicability.

The variations in philosophy and results continue even on appellate review.[103] Appellate courts differ in the degree of deference they are willing to give a trial judge in assessing the scope of a privilege waiver. The U.S. Court of Appeals for the D.C. Circuit, for instance, applies the deferential "abuse of discretion" standard.[104] On the other hand, the Sixth Circuit uses the nondeferential "de novo" standard that generally applies to a trial court's legal conclusions.[105]

Within the broad confines set by these competing trial court philosophies and appellate standards, there are specific recurring issues that warrant attention in litigation planning. For example, where a party attempts to rely on the advice or opinions of counsel, most courts find—and many litigants concede—that its opponent is entitled to discover the communications and analyses underlying that opinion.[106] In addition, however, the opposing party might also gain access to the advice and opinions of *other* attorneys consulted by that client, and to communications and analyses dated *after* the opinion on which the client relies.[107] Once again, the rationale is fairness—courts find that the jury, in assessing whether a party was "reasonable" in relying on one attorney's advice, is entitled to know if the client received overwhelming advice to the contrary from other attorneys,[108] or if the client subsequently learned that this original advice was wrong.[109]

Given the wide variety of decisions in this area, however, the most important lesson for the litigant lies not as much in attempting to discern or construct a clear-cut legal standard, but in recognizing that there might not be one. In assessing a litigation strategy that risks an implied waiver of privilege, one should carefully consider the scope of that waiver: more specifically, (1) whether the magistrate or judge with jurisdiction over the case takes a broad or narrow view on such issues, (2) whether the party can draw a defensible boundary on discovery, and (3) whether and how it can handle a "worst case," broad-scope waiver.

Conclusion

Throughout the course of a lawsuit, attorneys and their clients are concerned about pursuing, and preserving, every available theory of defense or relief. The prevailing standards of liberal "notice" pleading and free-form discovery facilitate, and thus reinforce, such an approach. There is, however, always a danger that some theories may prove counterproductive in the context of the case as a whole.

The very real possibility that a certain theory may force its proponent to put his attorneys on the stand, or to put their advice at issue, significantly raises the stakes. As the preceding analysis makes clear, a party may studiously avoid any reliance on the advice of counsel, but still implicitly (albeit inadvertently) open the door to otherwise privileged matters. Alternatively, that party may voluntarily put its attorneys on the stand, fully expecting to waive privilege on certain communications—only to find, as in *Northbrook*, that the scope of its waiver far exceeds expectations.

True, a litigant may find he has no choice but to press a certain claim and risk a "subject matter" waiver. Also, a party may find that privileged communications are, on balance, favorable or even critical to his case. The instinctive reaction to jealously guard privileged materials may not always be the right one. The important lesson is that attorney and client should anticipate the inevitable discovery battles and make an informed decision to risk or not risk a waiver of privilege—before a court, with help from the opposing party, makes that decision for them.

Notes

1. This chapter does not address the issue of waiver of the attorney-client privilege by failure to object when an opponent questions a party's attorney in the same case, *Young v. Taylor*, 466 F.2d

1329 (10th Cir. 1972) (failure to object during examination of defendant attorney waived privilege as to testimony of attorney's secretary regarding privileged conversation she heard between two defendants), or in a related case, *Drimmer v. Appleton*, 628 F. Supp. 1249 (S.D.N.Y. 1986) (failure to object to testimony at hearing on motion in Nevada to enforce settlement agreement waived privilege in subsequent New York trial on settlement agreement), or by disclosure to a governmental agency, *Westinghouse Elec. Corp. v. Republic of the Philippines*, 951 F.2d 1414 (3d Cir. 1991) (by voluntarily disclosing results of outside counsel's investigation to the SEC and to the Department of Justice, client waived attorney-client privilege and work-product immunity in subsequent action brought by Philippine government).

2. No. 83 C 3150 (N.D. Ill. 1988).

3. 413 F. Supp. 926 (N.D. Cal. 1976).

4. 413 F. Supp. at 929.

5. Chevron Corp. v. Pennzoil Co., 974 F.2d 1156 (9th Cir. 1992); *see also* SNK Corp. of America v. Atlus Dream Entm't Co., Ltd., 188 F.R.D. 566, 573 (N.D. Cal. 1999).

6. 118 F.R.D. 609 (E.D. Wis. 1987).

7. Note that, just as one can waive the attorney-client privilege by putting his lawyer on the stand, one can also waive the privilege by calling as a witness some third party, like an investigator hired by the attorney, whose communications are otherwise protected by the attorney-client privilege. *See* Clark v. City of Munster, 115 F.R.D. 609 (N.D. Ind. 1987) (if plaintiff was to call private investigators hired by attorney to assist in defense of criminal proceeding as witnesses in subsequent civil action, plaintiff would waive attorney-client privilege and would have to produce investigators' files to defendants); Brown v. Trigg, 791 F.2d 598 (7th Cir. 1986) (defendant in adult trial for felony-murder waived attorney-client privilege and work-product protection by having administrator of polygraph test testify at juvenile court waiver hearing).

8. Handgards v. Johnson & Johnson, 413 F. Supp. at 929; Vilastor-Kent Theatre Corp. v. Brandt, 19 F.R.D. 522, 524 (S.D.N.Y. 1956).

9. Upjohn Co. v. United States, 449 U.S. 383, 389 (1981).

10. *See* Hickman v. Taylor, 329 U.S. 495 (1947).

11. *See* Fed. R. Civ. P. 26(b)(3).

12. *In re* Allen, 106 F.3d 582, 607 (4th Cir. 1997) (quotations and citations omitted); *but see* Rutgard v. Haynes, 185 F.R.D. 596, 601 (S.D. Cal. 1999) (opinion work product is discoverable when information is directly at issue and need is compelling).

13. 413 F. Supp. at 928.

14. *See* 1993 Committee Notes to Fed. R. Civ. P. 26(a)(2).

15. Mfr. Admin. and Mgmt Sys., Inc. v. ICT Group, Inc., 212 F.R.D. 110, 114 (E.D.N.Y. 2002).

16. *See In re* Pioneer Hi-Bred Int'l, Inc., 238 F.3d 1370, 1375 (Fed. Cir. 2001) ("fundamental fairness requires disclosure of all information supplied to a testifying expert in connection with his testimony"); *see also* Herman v. Marine Midland Bank, 207 F.R.D. 26, 29 (W.D.N.Y. 2002) ("expert disclosure requirement of Rule 26(a)(2)(B) trumps the substantial protection otherwise accorded opinion work product under Rule 26(b)(3)").

17. 56 F.R.D. 123 (M.D.N.C. 1994).

18. *Id.* at 128.

19. *Id.*

20. *Id.*

21. *Id.* at 128-29. Additional decisions in this area, which reach similar results, include *Bio-Rad Lab., Inc. v. Pharmacia, Inc.*, 130 F.R.D. 116 (N.D. Cal. 1990), and *Mushroom Assocs. v. Monterey Mushrooms, Inc.*, 25 U.S.P.Q.2d 1304 (N.D. Cal. 1992).

22. 202 F.R.D. 666 (N.D. Ga. 2001).

23. 805 F.2d 1323 (8th Cir. 1986). *See* Simmons Foods, Inc. v. Willis, 191 F.R.D. 625, 630 (D. Kan. 2000) (noting that *Shelton* test is majority rule).

24. Pamida, Inc. v. E.S. Originals, Inc., 281 F.3d 726, 729 (8th Cir. 2002) (applying *Shelton* factors); *see also* Nguyen v. Excel Corp., 197 F.3d 200, 208-09 (5th Cir. 1999) (counsel deposed when executives were unable to respond to queries without stating reliance on counsel or consulting with counsel).

25. *See* Pamida v. E.S. Originals, Inc., 281 F.3d at 730-31; *see also* United States v. Titchell, 261 F.3d 348, 351-52 (3d Cir. 2001) (since attorney had previously testified for client at workers' compensation hearing, privilege was waived, at least as to the testimony in the prior proceeding); GFI, Inc. v. Franklin Corp., 60 U.S.P.Q.2d 1141, 1143 (Fed. Cir. 2001) (party waived its attorney-client privilege by allowing its attorney to testify about privileged matters in an earlier case).

26. *Handgards*, 413 F. Supp. at 929.

27. Torres v. 100 North LaSalle Partnership, No. 80 C 6454 (N.D. Ill. Dec. 29, 1983). If a party refuses *all* discovery, of course, the court would likely refuse to allow the attorney to take the stand at all. *Cf.* Int'l Tel. & Tel. Corp. v. United Tel. of Fla., 60 F.R.D. 177, 186 (M.D. Fla. 1973) (failure of party to allow pretrial discovery of privileged matter that party intends to introduce at trial will preclude introduction of that evidence).

28. No. 83 C 3150 (N.D. Ill. 1988).

29. Northbrook Excess & Surplus Ins. Co. v. Procter & Gamble Co., No. 83 C 3150, 1988 WL 5027, at *1 (N.D. Ill. Jan. 14, 1988) (citing *Handgards*).

30. Northbrook Excess & Surplus Ins. Co. v. Procter & Gamble Co., No. 83 C 3150, 1988 WL 28753 (N.D. Ill. Mar. 21, 1988).

31. *Id.* at *2.

32. *Id.*

33. *Id.*

34. Northbrook Excess & Surplus Ins. Co. v. Procter & Gamble Co., No. 83 C 3150, 1988 WL 74462, at *1 (N.D. Ill. July 8, 1988).

35. *Id.* at *2.

36. *Id.*

37. *Id.* at *3.

38. *Id.* (citing Brown v. Trigg, 791 F.2d 598, 601 (7th Cir. 1986)).

39. *Id.* at *2.

40. *Id.*

41. *Id.* at *1, *3.

42. Northbrook Excess & Surplus Ins. Co. v. Procter & Gamble Co., No. 83 C 3150, 1988 WL 142218 (N.D. Ill. Dec. 28, 1988).

43. *Id.* at *2.

44. *Id.*

45. *Id.*

46. *See* Johnson v. Alabama, 256 F.3d 1156, 1179 (11th Cir. 2001) (state prisoner filed a federal habeas corpus petition based on, among other things, the allegedly unreasonable trial strategy selected by counsel).

47. *Id.*

48. *Id.* at 1179; *see also* United States v. Woodall, 438 F.2d 1317 (5th Cir. 1970) (defendant waived privilege by seeking to withdraw guilty pleas on basis that he lacked knowledge of their consequences and by filing affidavit that coercion from former counsel voided pleas). These holdings are akin to the general principle that the attorney-client privilege does not apply in a dispute between the attorney and client.

49. United States v. Mierzwicki, 500 F. Supp. 1331 (D. Md. 1980).

50. *See* Panter v. Marshall Field & Co., 80 F.R.D. 718 (N.D. Ill. 1978) (reliance on advice of counsel asserted as defense to alleged violations of securities laws); *see also* Minnesota Specialty Crops, Inc. v. Minnesota Wild Hockey Club, L.P., 210 F.R.D. 673, 675 (D. Minn. 2002); Wender v.

United Servs. Auto. Ass'n, 434 A.2d 1372 (D.C. 1981) (reliance on advice of counsel asserted by insurance company as defense to alleged bad-faith failure to settle underlying lawsuit).

51. 80 F.R.D. at 718 (N.D. Ill. 1978).

52. 80 F.R.D. at 720.

53. *Id.* at 721.

54. *Id.* at 725 (footnote omitted).

55. 68 F.R.D. 574 (E.D. Wash. 1975).

56. 68 F.R.D. at 581 (emphasis added).

57. *Id.* at 582-83.

58. *Id.* at 581-82.

59. *Hearn* is a middle ground between (1) the "automatic waiver" rule, which provides that "a litigant automatically waives the privilege upon assertion of a claim, counterclaim, or affirmative defense that raises as an issue a matter to which otherwise privileged material is relevant" and (2) the more deferential standard that "a litigant waives the attorney-client privilege if, and only if, the litigant directly puts the attorney's advice at issue in the litigation." Frontier Refining, Inc. v. Gorman-Rupp Co., Inc., 136 F.3d 695, 699-700 (10th Cir. 1998).

60. 714 F. Supp. 916 (N.D. Ill. 1989).

61. 714 F. Supp. at 919.

62. 901 F. Supp. 1362 (N.D. Ill. 1995).

63. *See* United States v. Newell, 315 F.3d 510, 525 (5th Cir. 2002) (attorney-client privilege not waived when party showed that good-faith defense "was not based on advice of counsel, but rather on a simple lack of knowledge of the wrongdoing and absence of intent to participate in it").

64. 199 F.R.D. 677, 681-82 (N.D. Okla. 2001).

65. *See* Trouble v. Wet Seal, Inc., 179 F. Supp. 2d 291, 303-04 (S.D.N.Y. 2001) (party can protect attorney-client privilege as long as it does not rely on advice of counsel for defense of good faith).

66. 407 F. Supp. 420 (S.D.N.Y. 1976).

67. 407 F. Supp. at 423 (footnote omitted).

68. Other cases involving tolling provisions include *Conkling v. Turner*, 883 F.2d 431 (5th Cir. 1989) (by claiming that statute was tolled until his attorney informed him of defendant's alleged fraud, plaintiff waived privilege); *Russell v. Curtin Matheson Scientific, Inc.,* 493 F. Supp. 456 (S.D. Tex. 1980) (by claiming that 180-day notice requirement was tolled because the Department of Labor affirmatively misled them as to that requirement, plaintiffs waived the privilege for communications that occurred more than 180 days prior to actual filing of notice); and *Byers v. Burleson,* 100 F.R.D. 436 (D.D.C. 1983) (by claiming that statute was tolled while he was allegedly unaware of grounds for legal malpractice action, plaintiff waived privilege).

69. 570 F. Supp. 643 (N.D. Ill. 1983).

70. 683 F.2d 1201, 1206 (8th Cir.), *cert. denied*, 459 U.S. 1017 (1982).

71. *Id.* at 1206.

72. *See, e.g.,* Synalloy Corp. v. Gray, 142 F.R.D. 266 (D. Del. 1992); FDIC v. Wise, 139 F.R.D. 168 (D. Colo. 1991).

73. *See, e.g.,* Pippenger v. Gruppe, 883 F. Supp. 1201 (S.D. Ind. 1994).

74 *See, e.g.,* Pitney-Bowes, Inc. v. Mestre, 86 F.R.D. 444 (S.D. Fla. 1980); *see also* Medtronic, Inc. v. Intermedics, Inc., 162 F.R.D. 133 (D. Minn. 1995) (holding that defendant's potential use of extrinsic evidence would effect a waiver of attorney-client privilege, and giving defendant ten days to notify plaintiff whether it would use such evidence at trial). Indeed, where the contract in question is a settlement agreement, the scope of this waiver may extend to attorney work product. *See* Coleco Indus., Inc. v. Universal City Studios, Inc., 110 F.R.D. 688, 691-92 (S.D.N.Y. 1986).

75. 136 F.R.D. 542 (D. Mass. 1991).

76. *Id.* at 544.

77. *Id.*

78. 94 F.R.D. 246 (D.D.C. 1981).

79. 94 F.R.D. at 249.

80. *Id.* (emphasis added). One commentator has described this facet of the *Exxon* decision as "outrageous." Note, *Developments in the Law—Privileged Communications*, 98 Harv. L. Rev. 1450, 1642 (1985). It bears noting that, had the government instead tried to use the more traditional "crime-fraud" exception to pierce privileged communications relating to Exxon's purported pricing "scheme," it would have had to make a preliminary showing that the scheme *had* been "concocted." *See* United States v. Zolin, 491 U.S. 554, 570-72 (1989).

81. 653 A.2d 254 (Del. 1995).

82. *Id.* at 260 (emphasis added).

83. 185 F.R.D. 596, 599 (S.D. Cal. 1999).

84. 666 F. Supp. 1148 (N.D. Ill. 1987).

85. *Id.* at 1151.

86. 926 F.2d 1285 (2d Cir.), *cert. denied*, 502 U.S. 813 (1991).

87. In the same vein, several litigants have tried to avoid a waiver by relying only on the fact that they *consulted* counsel, without disclosing or relying on any specific communications or opinions. For the most part, these efforts have proved unsuccessful. *See, e.g.,* Dorr-Oliver Inc. v. Fluid-Quip, Inc., 834 F. Supp. 1008, 1012 (N.D. Ill. 1993) ("Defendants cannot have it both ways; they cannot seek refuge in consultation with counsel as evidence of their good faith yet prevent [plaintiff] from discovering the contents of the communication.").

88. 926 F.2d at 1292.

89. 61 F.R.D. 43 (E.D. Pa. 1973).

90. 61 F.R.D. at 47.

91. 35 Fed. R. Serv. 2d (Callaghan) 311 (N.D. Ill. 1982),

92. *Id.* at 314.

93. *See* Radiant Burners, Inc. v. American Gas Ass'n, 320 F.2d 314, 323 (7th Cir.) (citing 8 Wigmore § 2291), *cert. denied*, 375 U.S. 929 (1963).

94. FTC v. Shaffner, 626 F.2d 32, 37 (7th Cir. 1980); Schachar v. American Acad. of Ophthalmology, Inc., 106 F.R.D. 187, 191 (N.D. Ill. 1985). As always, counsel should research the law of his or her jurisdiction. Under state law, presumptions may differ. *See* Murray v. Gemplus Intern., S.A., 217 F.R.D. 362, 366 n.5 (E.D. Pa. 2003) ("Unlike federal common law, Pennsylvania places the burden of proof on the party which asserts that the privilege has been waived.") (quotations and citations omitted); *see also* Black v. Southwestern Water Conserv. Dist., 74 P.3d 462, 467 (Colo. Ct. App. 2003).

Another point to note is that there is some disagreement about the burden for proving waiver of work-product immunity. *See* S.E.C. v. Buntrock, 217 F.R.D. 441, 447 (N.D. Ill. 2003) ("The burden is on the party asserting a waiver of work-product immunity to establish the waiver."); *but see* Bank of America, N.A. v. Terra Nova Ins. Co., 212 F.R.D. 166, 169 (S.D.N.Y. 2002) ("The party asserting the protection afforded by the work product doctrine has the burden of showing both that the protection exists and that it has not been waived.").

95. *In re* Consolidated Litig. Concerning Int'l Harvester's Disposition of Wisconsin Steel, 666 F. Supp. 1148, 1157 (N.D. Ill. 1987).

96. *See* Fujisawa Pharmaceutical Co., Ltd. v. Kapoor, 162 F.R.D. 539, 541 (N.D. Ill. 1995).

97. 55 Fed. Cl. 263, 267 (Fed. Cl. 2003).

98. *See* Glenmede Trust Co. v. Thompson, 56 F.3d 476, 486 (3d Cir. 1995) ("There is an inherent risk in permitting the party asserting a defense of its reliance on advice of counsel to define the parameters of the waiver of the attorney-client privilege as to that advice.").

99. *See, e.g.,* Starsight Telecast, Inc. v. Gemstar Dev. Corp., 158 F.R.D. 650, 655 (N.D. Cal. 1994).

100. *Id.* (quotation omitted).

101. Bittaker v. Woodford, 331 F.3d 715, 720 (9th Cir. 2003).

102. *Id.* at 702-21; *see also* Atlantic Inv. Mgmt., LLC v. Millennium Fund I, Ltd., 212 F.R.D. 395, 398-99 (N.D. Ill 2002) (waiver limited to communications relevant to defense based on privilege).

103. Although we do not address this issue, there is some disagreement as to when a party can appeal a court's privilege ruling. In *United States v. Philip Morris Inc.,* 314 F.3d 612 (D.C. Cir. 2003), the D.C. Circuit discussed the importance of the attorney-client privilege and agreed to hear an interlocutory appeal involving the attorney-client privilege under the collateral order doctrine. Rejecting holdings from other circuits that a party could obtain effective review of an adverse privilege ruling by refusing to release material, standing in contempt, and then appealing the contempt order, the D.C. Circuit stated that it did not consider civil contempt an appealable order and that a party might decide not to risk sanctions—even to preserve a clearly meritorious privilege claim. *Id.* at 179.

104. *See In re* Sealed Case, 877 F.2d 976, 981 (D.C. Cir. 1989). *See also* Motley v. Marathon Oil Co., 71 F.3d 1547, 1550 (10th Cir. 1995), *cert. denied,* 116 S. Ct. 1678 (1996).

105. *In re* Grand Jury Proceedings, 78 F.3d 251, 253-54 (6th Cir. 1996).

106. *See* Garfinkle v. Arcata Nat'l Corp., 64 F.R.D. 688, 689 (S.D.N.Y. 1974) (holding that defendant's reliance on attorney's opinion letter entitled plaintiff to examine the surrounding circumstances: "[Plaintiff] cannot be limited to the letter itself—the finished product. He is entitled to know how the letter came into being.").

107. *See, e.g.,* Micron Separations, Inc. v. Pall Corp., 159 F.R.D. 361, 363-65 (D. Mass. 1995).

108. *See, e.g.,* SEC v. Forma, 117 F.R.D. 516, 523 n.5 (S.D.N.Y. 1987).

109. *See, e.g.,* Micron Separations v. Pell Corp., 159 F.R.D. at 363.

Appendix 1
Risk-of-Waiver Continuum

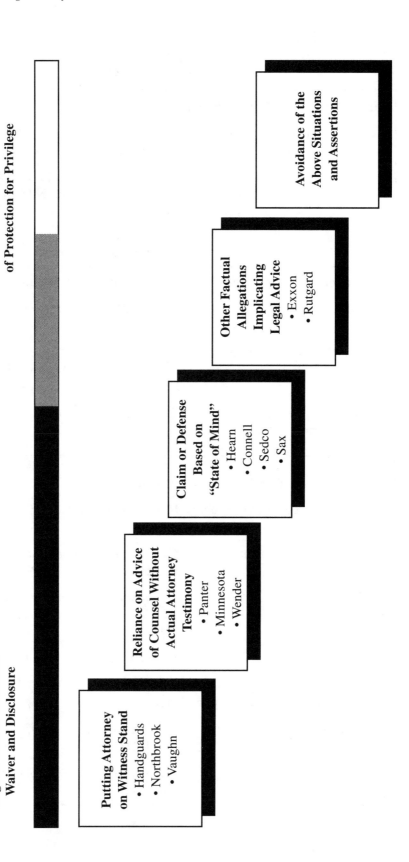

Highest Risk of Wholesale Waiver and Disclosure

Greatest Likelihood of Protection for Privilege

Putting Attorney on Witness Stand
- Handguards
- Northbrook
- Vaughn

Reliance on Advice of Counsel Without Actual Attorney Testimony
- Panter
- Minnesota
- Wender

Claim or Defense Based on "State of Mind"
- Hearn
- Connell
- Sedco
- Sax

Other Factual Allegations Implicating Legal Advice
- Exxon
- Rutgard

Avoidance of the Above Situations and Assertions

Appendix 2
Case Summary Chart

Putting Attorney on Witness Stand	
1. Good faith in bringing suit	*Handgards, Inc. v. Johnson & Johnson,* 413 F. Supp. 926 (N.D. Cal. 1976)
2. Insurance coverage of defense costs	*Northbrook Excess & Surplus Ins. Co. v. Procter & Gamble Co.* (N.D. Ill. 1988) (several decisions)
3. Expert witness	*Vaughan Furniture Co. v. Featureline Mfg., Inc.,* 156 F.R.D. 123 (M.D.N.C. 1994)
Reliance on Advice of Counsel Without Actual Attorney Testimony	
1. Good faith in bringing suit	*Panter v. Marshall Field & Co.,* 80 F.R.D. 718 (N.D. Ill. 1978)
2. Good faith in adopting trademark	*Minnesota Specialty Crops, Inc. v. Minnesota Wild Hockey Club, L.P.,* 210 F.R.D. 673 (D. Minn. 2002)
3. Good faith in refusing to settle insurance claim	*Wender v. United Servs. Auto. Ass'n,* 434 A.2d 1372 (D.C. 1981)
Claim or Defense Based on "State Of Mind"	
1. Good faith (qualified immunity)	*Hearn v. Rhay,* 68 F.R.D. 574 (E.D. Wash. 1975)
2. Estoppel (tolling statute of limitations)	*Connell v. Bernstein-Macaulay, Inc.,* 407 F. Supp. 420) (S.D.N.Y. 1976)
3. Fraud	*Sedco Int'l S.A. v. Cory,* 683 F.2d 1201 (8th Cir.), *cert. denied,* 459 U.S. 1017 (1982)
4. Contractual intent	*Sax v. Sax,* 136 F.R.D. 542 (D. Mass. 1991)
Other Factual Allegations Implicating Attorney Advice	
1. Causation	*United States v. Exxon Corp.,* 94 F.R.D. 246 (D.D.C. 1981)
2. Damages	*Rutgard v. Haynes,* 185 F.R.D. 596 (S.D. Cal. 1999)

CHAPTER 17

Preserving Candor:
The Hidden Danger from "Exceptions"
to the Attorney-Client Privilege[*]

KENNETH A. HINDMAN
STEVEN A. WAGNER

What Lawyers and Clients Understand
About the Attorney-Client Privilege

Most lawyers believe that their communications to their clients, and those from their clients to them, are protected from disclosure by the attorney-client privilege, with only very limited exceptions.[1] It is virtually certain that clients also believe that this is so, without concern about whether the existence of the privilege depends on the subject matter being discussed, or on the type of work being performed by the lawyer. Their conception of the attorney-client privilege would probably resemble this statement by the Supreme Court of Missouri:

> When a client goes to an attorney and asks him to represent him on a claim which he believes he has against someone or which is being asserted against him, even if he as yet has no knowledge or information about the claim, subsequent communications by the attorney to the client should be privileged. Some of the advice given by the attorney may be based on informa-

---

  * This chapter is an outgrowth of articles published in earlier editions of this compilation: Hindman & Burke, "The Attorney-Client Privilege in the 'Bad Faith' Case: Does It Still Protect Anything?" published in THE ATTORNEY-CLIENT PRIVILEGE UNDER SIEGE (ABA 1989); and Burke & Hindman, "The Attorney-Client Privilege in the 'Bad Faith' Case: Does It Still Protect Anything?" published in ATTORNEY-CLIENT PRIVILEGE IN CIVIL LITIGATION, 2d ed. (ABA 1997).

tion obtained from sources other than the client. Some of what the attorney says will not actually be advice as to a course of conduct to be followed. Part may be an analysis of what is known to date of the situation. Part may be a discussion of additional avenues to be pursued. Part may be keeping the client advised of things done or opinions formed to date. All of these communications, not just the advice, are essential elements of attorney-client consultation. All should be protected.[2]

This charter will suggest, however, that lawyers and clients who hold to this "traditional" view of the attorney-client privilege are likely to be mistaken, in that their communications are almost certainly at some risk of disclosure, even if those communications are kept strictly confidential.[3]

There is a real danger that expansion of the exceptions to the attorney-client privilege will destroy the basic understanding between lawyers and clients that their communications are confidential. Further, expansion of the exceptions and resultant loss of trust between lawyers and clients could well destroy the ability of lawyers to assess the merits of their clients' cases based upon full information. In turn, lawyers would lose their ability to resolve their clients' matters informally, which would cause grave harm to the legal system as a whole. To avoid these serious consequences, the courts should construe exceptions to the attorney-client privilege narrowly and should punish severely those who attempt to manipulate the attorney-client privilege to conceal evidence.

The Unspoken Understanding Between Lawyers and Clients

As the United States Supreme Court has recognized, clients tell their lawyers things about which they are ashamed, embarrassed, or fearful.[4] Clients do not typically know exactly what information is legally pertinent, and they therefore disclose a range of information that, in most cases, they earnestly desire to keep private.[5] It is common sense that, if clients believed that lawyers would be forced to disclose what clients said to them, candid attorney-client communications would cease.[6] This is perhaps more clearly the case with individual clients than with corporate/business clients, but it is true in both settings.

For example, lawyers who have practiced in Europe, where there is no privilege, have reported that the absence of the privilege had an inhibiting effect on communications; while oral communications continued to be candid to some extent, written communications became sanitized, and much more circumspect, against the possibility of their being disclosed.[7] The effect of such loss of candor is not only that clients will not tell their lawyers the (potentially embarrassing or dangerous) truth, but also that lawyers will no longer give clients clear, unequivocal advice.[8]

Only by free communication can a lawyer assess the merits of a client's position, talk frankly with the opposing party or lawyer, and reach a fair resolution of the client's problem. This is the process by which nearly all cases are resolved. If the lawyer does not know the truth, he cannot discuss cases frankly enough to resolve them. Similarly, if lawyers cannot give their clients advice clearly and confidentially, the process will not work, because clients will not understand proposed resolutions and the reasons for them, and will therefore be unlikely to agree to those resolutions.

Substantive Law

The danger to the attorney-client privilege arises from the modern trend to base some types of liability on the opposing party's state of mind, the "reasonableness" of his actions, or similar subjective considerations. That is, liability in such cases is based not only on whether a party adhered to a standard of conduct, or fulfilled the terms of a contract, but also on *how* the party did so. When a party's state of mind is placed at issue, it is easy to argue that what the party told his lawyer, and any advice the party received from his lawyer, are relevant evidence. There are many different contexts in which the law now allows liability to be based on "intent" or "state of mind": the most obvious are claims against insurers based on allegations of "bad faith." Liability under state "abusive litigation" statutes and under Federal Rule 11 also turns, at least in part, on whether the defending party had a "good-faith basis" for its actions.

There is no way to avoid the conflict between claims of "need for" discovery of attorney-client communications in such cases and the "normal" assumption that such communications are privileged.[9] The substantive law has jumped ahead of clear thinking about its effect on the privilege, so that determining when and to what extent "bad-faith" claims[10] affect the attorney-client privilege has become wildly unpredictable and uncertain.

Procedural and Process Considerations

The proliferation of substantive bad-faith claims has coincided with acceptance by some courts and scholars of the "Wigmore view" of a tightly restricted attorney-client privilege. In that view:

> Its benefits are all indirect and speculative; its obstruction is plain and concrete . . . . It is worth preserving for the sake of a general policy, but it is nonetheless an obstacle to the investigation of the truth. It ought to be strictly confined within the narrowest possible limits consistent with the logic of its principle.[11]

That is, the privilege is a necessary evil, to be restricted to its narrowest bounds. Therefore, under the Wigmore view, (1) the privilege is the exception rather than the rule, and (2) exceptions to the privilege are to be interpreted broadly. This point of view is contrary to the "traditional view" and to the expectations of most attorneys and their clients.[12]

Courts attempting to apply a "restricted" privilege have created a bewildering group of criteria and explanations for how and when the privilege applies; for example:

- [T]he Court should recognize a privilege only where the *injury* that would inure to the relation by the disclosure of the communications [is] *greater than the benefit* thereby gained for a correct disposal of litigation.[13]

- [C]ommunications are shielded only if they rest on confidential information obtained from the client . . . . The attorney-client privilege, therefore,
  does not protect an attorney's opinion or advice, but only the secrecy of the
  underlying facts obtained from the client.[14]
- [T]he privilege should attach only where extending its protection would
  foster more forthright and complete communication between the attorney
  and her client about the client's legal dilemma.[15]
- The information-holder's motive for the communication, to the extent that
  it can be discerned from the document, thus is an important consideration.
  If the information-holder will communicate with the attorney even if the
  privilege does not exist, or if a nonlegal objective is sufficient to stimulate
  communication with the attorney, then there is no reason for the privilege
  to attach.[16]

Formulations of the privilege such as these make it difficult for lawyers and clients "to predict with some degree of certainty whether particular discussions will be
protected," as the United States Supreme Court has said that they should be able to
do.[17] The Court's concern was that "an uncertain privilege, or one which purports to
be certain but results in widely varying applications by the Courts, is little better than
no privilege at all."[18]

The problem of uncertainty has been made worse by the willingness of some
courts to remove the privilege from otherwise protected communications, based on
bad-faith allegations in later litigation. Attorneys and their clients cannot anticipate
whether a court will determine after the fact that a confidential communication has
become "at issue."[19]

Removing the privilege because a communication is "at issue" makes application
of the privilege uncertain because the communication is placed "at issue" by allegations made by the opposing party, rather than by any action of the privilege holder.
Some courts recognized early on that allowing privileges to be "waived" because of
the other party's allegations would quickly make any privilege useless. For example,
the Texas Supreme Court accurately observed that:

> [I]f a plaintiff attempting to prove the validity of a claim against an insurer
> could obtain the insurer's investigative files merely by alleging the insurer
> acted in bad faith, all insurance claims would contain such allegations.[20]

One court has held that attorney-client communications were placed at issue by a
counterclaim contending that the plaintiff filed suit on patents it knew were invalid.[21]
Other courts have held that the privilege is lost where a party responds to an allegation
of knowingly wrongful action by explaining why it believed that its actions were justified.[22] The court held that the defending party could avoid losing the privilege by
simply denying allegations of wrongdoing, but would lose the privilege if it "advances
its own interpretation of the law as a defense."[23] The defending party disavowed any
reliance on advice of its counsel, stating that it was relying on the objective merits of
its legal position, but it was held to have "thrust" its lawyer's knowledge into the
litigation and to have waived the privilege.[24] Not surprisingly, this holding was criti-

cized as introducing "intolerable uncertainty into the question whether attorneys and their clients can regard communications as privileged."[25]

While a few courts have refused to allow such "after the fact" privilege determinations,[26] many more appear willing to permit them, creating real practical problems for attorneys and clients, and ignoring the U.S. Supreme Court's admonition that:

> Balancing *ex post* the importance of the information against client interest
> . . . introduces substantial uncertainty into the privilege's application. For
> just that reason, we have rejected use of a balancing test in defining the
> contours of the privilege.[27]

Loose and undefined standards not only make the privilege "uncertain" for attorneys and clients to apply, they also create problems for the courts themselves. As one federal district court judge observed:

> Lawyers love to know the secret communications between opposing par-
> ties and their counsel. And some lawyers love to strike fear into hearts of
> opponents by attempting to discover those communications. Motions to
> penetrate clearly applicable privileges can be tools for harassment. . . . The
> looser the standard [for the privilege], the greater the risk that it will be
> abused for such tactical purposes. . . . If . . . relatively soft showings were
> sufficient both to generate substantial adversarial proceedings and to shift
> the risk of nonpersuasion to the holder of the privilege, the temptation to
> initiate such challenges would be considerable. . . . Using a less substan-
> tial, poorly defined, and only vaguely understood standard also makes rul-
> ings on challenges to the privilege less predictable. When the rulings are
> less predictable, the incentives to launch challenges increase—as do the
> burdens on the courts.[28]

The problems caused by this lack of standards can be seen in how the exceptions to the privilege are applied.

How Restricting the Scope of the Privilege Expands Exceptions to the Privilege

Three general types of exceptions to the privilege have developed: (1) the exception for "non-legal" work performed by a lawyer; (2) the "at issue"/"bad faith" exception; and (3) the "crime-fraud" exception. Restricting the scope of the privilege and qualifying its applicability makes each type of exception broader and more difficult to apply, and creates conflicts with the traditional practices of attorneys and clients.

Exception for "Non-Legal" Work

This exception removes the privilege from work which, although performed by lawyer, is not viewed as "legal work." That means either that (a) the work is seen as not involving "lawyering" skills (i.e., not applying legal principles to solving a problem), or (b) the work is of the type that would otherwise be classified as "legal," but the privilege is removed because the lawyer's work is part of the "normal course of business" of his client.

Removing the privilege under this type of exception necessarily conflicts with the desire of clients to hire lawyers to perform a variety of tasks, some of which could very well be performed by non-lawyers. For example, some courts have denied the privilege where lawyers performed fact investigations for their clients.[29]

As the United States Supreme Court recognized in *Upjohn*, however: "The first step in the resolution of any legal problem is ascertaining the factual background, and sifting through the facts with an eye to the legally relevant."[30] The Supreme Court's reasoning has been followed in many cases, acknowledging that clients often want to have a lawyer investigate a matter, regardless of whether a non-lawyer could also do so. As one federal circuit court observed, if a party simply needed a lay investigator to collect and summarize information, it could have used its own staff and avoided the expense of hiring counsel; however " . . . clients often do retain lawyers to perform investigative work because they want the benefit of a lawyer's expertise and judgment"; in that particular case, for example, the court emphasized that "[the lawyer's] interview memoranda evidenced that her understanding of the underlying *legal* issues dictated the direction of the interviews."[31]

The privilege applies in such a traditional view simply because the lawyer's work "pertains to a matter on which the attorney was consulted for his professional advice."[32]

Other courts have denied protection to a lawyer's work which, from the client's point of view, was done pursuant to a request for legal advice, because the work was characterized as part of the client's "normal course of business."[33] In some cases, the courts make rough assumptions as to whether lawyers' work is protected based more on whether the lawyers were outside or in-house counsel, or on their positions in the client's business organization, than on the specifics of their clients' requests for legal assistance.[34]

In some cases, a lawyer's work is seen as part of the normal course of business of his client because the lawyer actually makes management decisions, or performs work that is required of the client by law or by contract. Removing the privilege in such situations likely does not conflict with most clients' concept of the privilege, since the lawyer in that type of setting is participating in a business decision or transaction rather than acting as an advisor to the client.[35]

Even determining whether a lawyer is performing "business" or "legal" work creates practical problems for the courts. In any such case, applying the exception requires the type of fact-based analysis performed by the district court in the *ChevronTexaco* case; that court determined that:

> These communications were not made primarily, if at all, for the purpose of seeking legal advice. The contents of these communications are purely financial. They reflect factual information used to implement the transaction.[36]

Obviously, coming to such a conclusion required that the court read the documents involved in detail and determine where each fit into the overall series of events. If nothing else, the court's conclusion that the contents of the particular set of e-mails at issue was "purely financial" shows that the court read the entire set of documents.

"Bad Faith"/"At Issue" Exception

Clients can avoid losing the privilege under the "non-lawyer work" exception by having their lawyers act as advisors, rather than as participants, or by being prepared to present independent evidence as to a matter "investigated" by lawyers. Most clients, the authors believe, would readily accept that a lawyer's participation in the actual events at issue (e.g., having voted to terminate an employee in a wrongful discharge case) means that his "work" would not be privileged. Clients would probably also accept that, for example, they could not legitimately refuse to disclose facts discovered by a lawyer on the grounds of privilege.

The authors believe that clients understand that the lawyer's role is to be "outside" the client's decisions, and that that separation is necessary to maintain the right to consider the lawyer's advice privileged. That conception of the roles of attorneys and clients worked well enough when the "operative facts" of cases were what the client did, and whether the client's actions met the terms of a contract or a tort standard of duty. In such an earlier view of things, whether the client received legal advice or the content of that advice was beside the point.

As discussed above, however, the advent of bad-faith causes of action has led to placing the decision-making process behind any client action "at issue." The bad-faith causes of action that underlie the exception are now part of our substantive law, and will remain so. The courts have struggled to allow the privilege to coexist with them, without being destroyed by them, but the inherent nature of bad-faith claims makes that difficult.

A bad-faith case[37] is resolved under legal principles such as: ". . . whether an insurer has acted in bad faith towards its insured depends on the reasonableness of its conduct . . . [W]hether the insurer knew that its conduct was unreasonable. . . ." A finding of bad faith "is predicated precisely on the *manner* in which [Defendant] reached its decision."[38]

Such a determination requires inquiries into:

> Any investigations conducted by the [Defendant], the information available to the company at the time its decision was made, and the manner in which the company arrived at its decision, including reliance on advice of counsel.[39]

That is, the "operative facts" in a bad-faith case include all steps the client took to reach the decision in question.[40]

In turn, the courts have held that "bad faith actions . . . can only be proved by showing exactly how the company processed the claim, how thoroughly it was considered and why the company took the action it did."[41] From that, it followed that documents held by the accused party were freely discoverable.[42] Some courts have dismissed out of hand claims of privilege in bad-faith cases, even where part of the materials in question were attorney-client letters: "[T]he time-worn claims of . . . attorney-client privilege cannot be invoked to the [Defendant's] benefit where the only issue in the case is whether the company breached its duty of good faith in processing the insured's claim"[43]

A client may carefully use his lawyer as an "advisor" rather than having him "participate" in the client's decisions, but the lawyer's advice may nevertheless be put at issue by bad-faith allegations. In bad-faith situations, the lawyer's "advice" becomes as much of an issue as the client's decision in the underlying dispute. In fact, the underlying dispute (breach of contract, commission of a tort) may become irrelevant, because the client may be held independently liable for the breach of an "implied covenant of good faith and fair dealing"[44] or an "abusive litigation" statute.

By placing virtually any attorney-client communication at risk of disclosure on bad-faith grounds, however, the courts have made it risky for clients to consult attorneys for guidance, where they fear that they may be "doing wrong." Those, of course, are the very situations in which clients are most likely to consult lawyers. One of the principal bases for the United States Supreme Court's approval of a broad corporate attorney-client privilege in *Upjohn* was that:

> The narrow scope given the attorney-client privilege by the court below not only makes it difficult for corporate attorneys to formulate sound advice when their client is faced with a specific legal problem, but also threatens the valuable efforts of corporate counsel to insure their client's compliance with the law.[45]

That is, if clients are afraid to disclose their concerns about the lawfulness of their planned actions, lawyers cannot fulfill their roles as counselors to guide their clients' actions to conform to the law.

The bad-faith exception may negate the privilege entirely, or at least the uncertainty as to when the exception might apply will have that effect. This consequence can be avoided (1) if the courts recognize that clients have the right to be advised by lawyers, and (2) if lawyers and clients recognize that the substantive law now requires that they carefully consider how lawyers are used, in light of potential bad-faith liability.

In dealing with this problem, the courts have acknowledged that "it would be a rare confidential communication that would not satisfy the relevancy test."[46] Also, attorney-client communications have "pragmatic importance," but if the privilege could be abrogated on that ground, "the privilege would have little meaning."[47]

Avoiding the loss of the privilege requires that the courts restrict the situations in which an opposing party can force abrogation of the privilege by way of its allegations against the privilege holder. For example, the advice of counsel is not necessarily "interjected into" a case by a responding party's denial of allegations where the responding party may have had legal advice regarding those allegations.[48]

Courts also should be wary of allowing essentially legal arguments to form the basis for waiver of the privilege (e.g., they should determine the legitimacy of legal positions on the merits of those positions, rather than allowing discovery of attorney opinions as to the strength of those positions).

Lawyers and clients in this era, however, also have to recognize that the decision-making process as to any act by a client may be placed at issue. The client, therefore, cannot ignore the fact that *he* must be able to explain the bases for his decision, since the substantive law has made those relevant to liability.

Clients, therefore, must either participate themselves, for example, in investigations undertaken by lawyers, or must have an independent basis (aside from advice, facts, or conclusions conveyed by a lawyer) for any decisions that rest on information provided by lawyers. This approach would require clients who now simply "turn over" matters to lawyers, then sign off on a course of action recommended by the lawyers, to become more personally involved in those matters. Only by truly being able to provide evidence as to how and why decisions were reached can clients expect the courts to uphold the privilege for lawyers' advice. That is, the reasoning behind decisions must be the client's rather than the lawyer's.

If clients do not undertake this responsibility, they may well have to choose between having a lawyer with knowledge of the decision-making process testify, or being precluded from offering evidence to explain the conduct, if that information is with the lawyer, but is not produced on grounds of privilege.[49]

Courts thus must respect the legitimacy of clients' consulting with lawyers and avoiding disclosure of such communications by simple allegations of bad faith. These considerations also have caused increasing and similar problems for the courts in interpreting the "crime-fraud" exception to the privilege.

The "Crime-Fraud" Exception

The "crime-fraud" exception developed to prevent clients from profiting from abuse of the attorney-client relationship. For example, one court found evidence of "an ongoing or imminent crime or fraud" in a "pervasive and systematic scheme to destroy or alter subpoenaed evidence," coupled with "routinely perjured testimony by the party's archivist," "all with the knowledge and participation of [party's] legal department."[50] In another case, the exception applied where fiduciaries accused of creating false financial statements sought legal assistance in rescinding a sale "for their own personal benefit," in conflict with the interests of the company's shareholders.[51]

The exception, however, has increasingly been applied not in cases of real abuse, but to simple allegations of tort. At the same time, the showing required to invoke the exception has become increasingly minimal.

Without much apparent hesitation, some courts have leaped from applying the exception to cases of "crime" or "fraud" to allegations of tortious conduct. As one court put it: "We are convinced that the consideration underlying the firmly established denial of the privilege for communications and furtherance of crime or fraud . . . is equally compelling with regard to communications in furtherance of the intentional tort [emotional distress] of which plaintiffs herein complain."[52]

The crime-fraud exception has become increasingly difficult to apply consistently because the showing required to invoke the exception has decreased, just as the breadth of its coverage has increased. For example, one court held that the "prima facie case" required to defeat the privilege consisted of "requiring that the evidence in favor of [the] proposition be sufficient to support a finding in its favor, if all of the evidence to the contrary be disregarded."[53] In other words, the privilege could be done away with by meeting the "motion to dismiss" standard, without necessarily proving any facts, and without considering any evidence to the contrary. Another court required only that there be a showing of "some foundation in fact" to constitute a prima facie case to abrogate the privilege.[54]

With "tort" or "bad faith" allegations becoming a common adjunct to any litigation, the danger is apparent that even minimal accusations of such conduct will abrogate the privilege on "crime-fraud" grounds. The courts have therefore been forced to confront the danger that this exception, like the bad-faith exception, will destroy the ability of clients to consult attorneys about potentially problematic conduct. As one court put it:

> Good-faith consultations with attorneys by clients who are uncertain about the legal implications of a proposed course of conduct are entitled to the privilege, even if that action should later be held improper.[55]

Similarly,

> If legal advice loses its privileged status merely because the opponent claims that the advice was sought to conceal a fraud, the privilege quickly evaporates. If that were the law, few clients would dare talk to lawyers, because the privilege would disappear the moment their opponent charged a cover-up.[56]

In order to preserve the predominant place of the privilege in relation to the crime-fraud exception, the courts should return to applying the exception only to cases to which it clearly applies. For example, most jurisdictions require that fraud be pleaded "with specificity." The courts should refuse to apply the exception when a proponent has not set out supporting facts under such pleading rules.

Similarly, the courts should reject attempts to use "tort" allegations as "crimes" or "frauds"; for example, a defendant's delays in responding to a plaintiff's insurance claim, and other investigatory activity, could not legitimately be described as "crimes."[57] Another court explained the "fundamental differences between fraud and bad faith" as follows:

> Bad faith denial of insurance means simply that the insurer breached an implied contractual agreement . . . . This need not implicate false or misleading statements by the insurer. For example, an insurer may act in bad faith if it simply denies coverage without any explanation. The gravamen of fraud, however, is falsity. . . . [58]

The court went on to point out that "even courts that find bad faith within the crime-fraud exception have difficulty equating bad faith with fraud. Ultimately, these courts simply make a policy decision that bad faith should not be protected by the lawyer-client privilege."[59]

Other courts have refused to draw strained inferences of criminal or fraudulent conduct as bases for invoking the exception (e.g., court refused to infer that legal advice was sought in order to further illegal conduct from fact that client discussed campaign finance laws with counsel, then "within weeks" violated those laws).[60] Other courts have required more convincing circumstantial evidence to support the exception (e.g., client knew when he consulted attorney that his intended conduct was unlawful, because he had surreptitiously created corporations to receive funds from his employer, he immediately received "substantial funds" following initial payments by his employer, and he had agreed in writing to abide by his employer's policy against self-dealing).[61]

Judicial self-restraint of this type is especially necessary to avoid overburdening the courts with fact-intensive "privilege" determinations.

Why the Courts Are Not the Answer

Reported cases increasingly reveal that proponents of the exceptions discussed above believe that the courts can ensure that the exceptions are applied fairly and consistently. The authors believe that the courts cannot begin to ensure such results, and that to expect them to do so would damage their ability to handle the cases before them.

Proponents of the exceptions appear also to believe that, upon a minimal showing that an exception may apply to a group of documents, they should be able to have a court physically review the documents in camera. Advocates of in camera inspections rarely, however, acknowledge the degree to which such inspections interfere with the normal work of the courts.

In the *St. John's Law Review* article cited earlier, several magistrates and judges "volunteered that when corporate parties were involved," in camera reviews could be "time-consuming, tedious, or unpleasant task[s] to be avoided whenever possible."[62] One federal magistrate commented, along the same lines:

> The larger the volume of documents reviewed in camera, the greater the potential harm to the privilege and the greater burden on the courts. These kinds of burdens consume finite judicial resources. . . . In other words, large-scale inspections of the kind that would be involved here impose real and substantial costs on the administration of justice.[63]

In addition, it is difficult for judges to conduct such reviews during the pretrial discovery stage of cases (when, however, most such reviews appear to occur). Most judges have no reason to learn the details of a case at the discovery stage; that usually occurs, at the earliest, when a motion for summary judgment is filed. Not surprisingly, one magistrate commented that "it is especially difficult during the early stages of pretrial discovery to know whether particular facts are even relevant to the litigation."[64]

Perhaps because they dislike conducting in camera reviews themselves, judges often delegate those reviews to their law clerks. The clerks, however, are often less capable than the parties or the judge of competently resolving such disputes, since they typically lack trial or general practice experience.[65]

The burden that in camera inspections impose on the courts is made worse by the fact that, under the current very loose and unspecific standards for applying the privilege, such inspections may routinely be required. That is so because, under many newer formulations of the privilege, it is not possible to determine that a communication is or is not "privileged" based on the fact that it is an attorney-client communication. Rather, the context of the communication and the intent of the parties may have to be ascertained. Under such standards, there are few obvious answers to questions of privilege.

Loose and vague standards also virtually ensure that when a court conducts an in camera review, the court will have to read each document in full and analyze it in reference both to other documents reviewed and to several external factors.

The need for in camera reviews whenever a party argues that the privilege should not apply and the depth of treatment required in any review can easily be seen, while the decision as to whether the privilege applies must turn on factors such as:

- The degree of injury that disclosure would cause to the attorney-client relationship;[66]
- Whether a communication "rests on" or "discloses" client confidences;[67]
- The effect upholding the privilege would have on fostering "more forthright and complete communication" between lawyer and client;[68] and
- Whether a "nonlegal objective" would have been sufficient to stimulate communication with the lawyer.[69]

Especially considering the increasing caseloads and cuts in resources that confront almost all courts, it is absolutely unrealistic to expect the courts to give in camera reviews the time and attention their theoretical purpose would require.

Perhaps the worst aspect of emphasizing the courts' role in resolving privilege questions is that emphasis is thereby drawn away from attorney-client relationships outside litigation; it is there that the most serious harm from the expansion of the exceptions will occur.

Why Litigation-Based Rules Should Not Define the Privilege

Those favoring the expansion of exceptions to the attorney-client privilege are concerned with what evidence will be available in discovery or admissible at trial. They argue that putting all relevant evidence before the fact-finder will increase the likelihood of a just result. The authors believe, however, that defining the scope of the privilege and its exceptions according to such "litigation" considerations is both shortsighted and foolish.

Litigated cases make up an insignificant fraction of all matters about which clients consult attorneys, yet virtually no attention is given to the effect "litigation-based" rules would have on the vast majority of non-litigated matters. It is obvious, however, from the discussion above that a qualified, uncertain privilege, subject to "exceptions," would have the general effect of discouraging clients from consulting lawyers.

This is the primary reason why vaguely defined exceptions are dangerous to the legal system: They will potentially make the overall legal system unworkable in the interest of satisfying largely theoretical concerns of academics and of the parties in a tiny number of cases in litigation.

Full disclosure of the facts does increase the likelihood of a "just result" in any given case, but the legal system should be more concerned with whether that information is conveyed by clients to their lawyers in everyday consultations than with whether such information is presented in court.

It is our observation that lawyers "resolve" virtually all cases that pass through our legal system; the number of matters adjudicated in courts is minuscule by comparison. It is clear that lawyers have to know the facts from their clients, "warts and all."[70] Lawyers resolve cases by making judgments about the merits and equities of their clients' cases, talking frankly with opposing lawyers to find a fair resolution of the problem, and convincing their clients that the recommended resolution should be accepted. Each stage of the process requires that the lawyer and client know all of the facts and be able to speak frankly to each other. For example, one way lawyers establish trust in negotiations is by acknowledging the weaknesses in their clients' cases. Lawyers also must be able to convey to their clients conclusions that the clients "may not want to hear," such as why a seemingly unsatisfactory settlement is fair, given the deficiencies in the client's case.[71]

The process described occurs constantly; in some cases the lawyer may even advise his client not to pursue a matter at all, based on the client's frank disclosures. That, too, is a "resolution" of a case.

Clearly, if the process described becomes impossible because clients are afraid that their communications will be disclosed, the legal system will quickly become overloaded; many otherwise quickly resolved cases will either be litigated or will be resolved outside the legal system. On the other hand, if the privilege were circumscribed as suggested, the effect on the legal system as a whole would be negligible.

Conclusion

A primary concern is that courts and commentators have lost sight of the larger picture, in their efforts to manipulate the attorney-client privilege in discovery and evidentiary matters. Once the privilege has become "uncertain," the potential for harm to the overall legal system is quite real.

Such harm is particularly hard to justify where the attempt to expand the use of privileged material in court is both impractical and unlikely, in any event, to yield evidence of any real importance.

Ultimately, preserving the privilege requires that the system as a whole trusts lawyers not to abuse the privilege.[72] Some abuse will undoubtedly occur under this recommended scheme for the privilege; it would be naive to pretend otherwise after the revelations of lawyer misconduct in cases such as the Enron debacle.[73]

There is no doubt, however, that a certain number of lawyers who want to abuse the privilege will "get away with it," in any event, simply because there is no way to know what transpires in the millions of attorney-client communications that occur every day. This will be so no matter how severe the rules regarding exceptions to the privilege become, simply because only a minor fraction of any abuses will come to light.

Furthermore, as the United States Supreme Court has observed in *Upjohn*, denying disclosure of privileged documents "puts the adversary in no worse position than if the communications had never taken place."[74] Correspondingly, if the exceptions overcome the privilege, the "good stuff" (written attorney-client communications) will simply cease to exist.[75] Moreover, the judges in the *St. John's Law Review* study found that the privileged information at issue in litigated cases turned out to be "necessary" (i.e., crucial or highly significant) to proving a claim or a defense only "rarely."[76]

The courts do, however, have a significant responsibility in preserving the privilege. While it is clear that the courts cannot, and should not, monitor the relations between lawyers and clients in general, they should vigorously impose sanctions against lawyers and clients who set up systems to abuse the privilege. Published examples include (1) an insurer that retained a particular law firm "as a matter of course" to investigate all claims over $25,000 (thereby attempting to make its whole investigation "privileged");[77] (2) an insurer that realized its policies did not contain exclusions barring serious environmental claims, then "referred" all such claims to a law firm, bypassing its own adjusters and conducting no adjustment activities, in an effort to preclude discovery;[78] and (3) a hospital that routinely "signed up" any hospital employee who witnessed an accident as an "individual client," interviewed the "client," then refused to allow the "client" to see a summary of his interview when he was unable, at his deposition two years later, to recall the events surrounding the accident.[79]

We believe that the courts are well able to recognize such tactics, and that they have the ability to determine if this type of abuse is occurring (e.g., by questioning the attorneys and clients involved in camera). Behavior such as that mentioned makes it appear to the public that the privilege is simply another means of "hiding information"; it should therefore be punished with severity in order to preserve public support for the privilege and its many other benefits.

The general public's ability in the future to consult lawyers confidentially without fear that those discussions will be disclosed, and the enormously beneficial practical consequences that flow from that ability, will be damaged unless the courts are mindful of the danger posed by expanding exceptions to the attorney-client privilege.

Notes

1. An example of such exception might be where no effort was made to keep communications confidential; e.g., publishing advice in newsletter. Southern Guaranty Ins. Co. v. Ash, 383 S.E.2d 579, 583-84 (Ga. App. 1989) (conducting conference in presence of a third party, sending attorney-client letter to third party).

2. State *ex rel*. Great American Ins. Co. v. Smith, 574 S.W.2d 379, 384-85 (Mo. 1978) (footnotes omitted).

3. *See, e.g.*, State Farm Mut. Auto. Ins. Co. v. Lee, 13 P.3d 1169, 1176 n.4 (Ariz. 2000) (Even conduct that in no way "evinces" an intention to waive the privilege may nevertheless cause a waiver ". . . when the conduct . . . places the claimant in such a position, with reference to the

evidence, that it would be unfair and inconsistent to permit the retention of the privilege. . . .") (quoting 8 WIGMORE, § 2388, p. 855).

4. Swidler & Berlin v. United States, 524 U.S. 399, 407-08 (1998).

5. *Id.*, 524 U.S. at 407-08 (attorneys act as counselors on personal and family matters; ". . . confidences about family matters or financial problems must be revealed . . . . The same is true of owners of small businesses . . .").

6. *See generally* Vincent C. Alexander, *The Corporate Attorney-Client Privilege: A Study of the Participants*, 63 ST. JOHN'S L. REV. 191, 269 n.247 (1989) (suggesting that, even if clients do not know the exact terms of the privilege, they would surely know it if there were no privilege).

7. *Id.* at 255 (speculating that oral communications are affected less because there is no written evidence of their content).

8. *Id.* at 274 (the danger of such sanitized advice is that ". . . instead of condemning proposed illegal conduct in no uncertain terms, the lawyer's legal opinion might be framed in an ambiguous manner, perhaps leading the client to take action that would violate the law or result in litigation").

9. *Compare* Great American, *supra* note 2 at 383 (noting Dean Wigmore's emphasis on the fundamental societal need to have all evidence having a rational probative value placed before the trier of fact in a lawsuit) *with* Wesp v. Everson, 33 P.3d 191, 197 (Colo. 2001) ("Because the attorney-client privilege may frustrate the fact-finding process, it exists in constant tension with the judicial system's truth-seeking goals. However, that tension is the price that society must pay for the availability of justice to every citizen, which is the value that the privilege is designed to ensure.") (citations and internal punctuation omitted).

10. "Bad faith" is a term of art encompassing the types of cases mentioned above.

11. Coleman v. Am. Broadcasting Cos., 106 F.R.D. 201, 205 n.2 (D.D.C. 1985).

12. Great American, *supra* note 2 at 383 (noting that some commentators "view confidentiality of communications between attorney and client as the more fundamental policy, to which disclosure is the exception").

13. Dinkins v. State of Ohio, 116 F.R.D. 270, 272-73 (N.D. Ohio 1987) (case involving a claimed investigatory privilege) (emphasis in the original) (internal punctuation omitted).

14. Alexander v. Federal Bureau of Investigation, 193 F.R.D. 1, 5 (D.D.C. 2000) (internal punctuation omitted). Similarly, *see* Loftis v. Amica Mut. Ins. Co., 175 F.R.D. 5, 7, 10 (D. Conn. 1997) (attorney letter containing legal advice on exposure to bad-faith claim was not within privilege because it did not disclose any client confidences).

15. United States v. ChevronTexaco Corp., 241 F. Supp. 2d 1065, 1070 (N.D. Cal. 2002) (emphasis omitted).

16. Robinson v. Texas Auto. Dealers Ass'n, 214 F.R.D. 432, 439-40 (E.D. Tex. 2003) (internal quotation marks omitted), *rev'd on other grounds, In re* Texas Auto. Dealers Ass'n, 2003 WL 21911333 (5th Cir. 2003).

17. Upjohn Co. v. United States, 449 U.S. 383, 393 (1981).

18. *Id.* at 393; *see also* Samaritan Found. v. Goodfarb, 862 P.2d 870, 879 (Ariz. 1993) (". . . an uncertain privilege has the potential of achieving the worst possible result: it could harm the truth-seeking process without a corresponding increase in candor . . . . [A] narrow but absolute privilege is preferable to a broad but amorphous one.").

19. As they can more likely anticipate the loss of the privilege if they do not keep communications confidential, or if they discuss an ongoing crime or fraud.

20. Maryland Am. Gen. Ins. Co. v. Blackmon, 639 S.W.2d 455, 458 (Tex. 1982) (case involving the work-product privilege).

21. Kockums Indus. Ltd. v. Salem Equip., Inc., 561 F. Supp. 168, 172 (D. Ore. 1983).

22. *Lee, supra* note 3 at 1175.

23. *Id.* at 1178, 1179.

24. *Id.* at 1180, 1184.

25. *Id.* at 1186 (McGregor, J., dissenting).

26. *See, e.g.,* Dixie Mill Supply Co., Inc. v. Continental Casualty Co., 168 F.R.D. 554, 556-57 (E.D. La. 1996) ("[Plaintiff] insists that defendants have affirmatively placed at issue their state of mind and their knowledge of Louisiana law, which must have come from their attorneys, by asserting that they acted in good faith in compliance with the insurance policies and their legal obligations. . . . Such a rule would permit a plaintiff to force a defendant to abrogate its privileges simply by asserting in the complaint that the defendant acted in bad faith, which the defendant then denies and says that, to the contrary, it acted in good faith. . . . [A]ttorney advice is not in issue because it is relevant, and does not necessarily become an issue merely because the attorney's advice might affect the client's state of mind in a relevant manner.) (internal quotation marks omitted).

27. *Swidler, supra* note 4 (citing *Upjohn, supra* note 17 at 393).

28. Laser Indus., Ltd. v. Reliant Technologies, Inc., 167 F.R.D. 417, 424, 433, 441 (N.D. Cal. 1996) (applying crime-fraud exception to privilege).

29. *See, e.g.,* National Farmers Union Property and Casualty Co. v. District Court, 718 P.2d 1044, 1049 (Colo. 1986) (en banc) (denying privilege for portion of attorney's memorandum summarizing "the results of a factual investigation").

30. *Upjohn, supra* note 17 at 390-91.

31. *In re* Allen, 106 F.R.D. 582, 602 n.19, 604, 605 (4th Cir. 1997) (emphasis in original); *see also* Dunn v. State Farm Fire & Casualty Co., 122 F.R.D. 507, 509 (N.D. Miss. 1988), *aff'd,* 927 F.2d 869 (5th Cir. 1991) (a lawyer brings to bear the ". . . training, skills, and background necessary to make the professional independent analysis and legal recommendations sought by [the client]"); *see also* Lipton Realty, Inc. v. St. Louis Hous. Auth., 705 S.W.2d 565, 570 (Mo. Ct. App. 1986) (lawyer's letter to client, detailing his on-site observations of condition of buildings and recommending settlement negotiations, was privileged).

32. *Lipton, supra* note 31 at 570.

33. Some courts have held that certain types of tasks, even if performed by lawyers, are not within the privilege; *e.g.,* preparing tax returns is viewed as primarily an accounting function, even though it may require some knowledge of law. *See* United States v. Davis, 636 F.2d 1028, 1043 (5th Cir. 1981).

34. *See, e.g., ChevronTexaco, supra* note 15 at 1076 (communications between a corporation and its outside legal counsel are presumed to be made in order to seek legal advice, but that presumption does not extend to communications with in-house counsel); *see also, e.g.,* Boca Investerings Partnership v. United States, 31 F. Supp. 2d 9, 12 (D.D.C. 1998) ("One important indicator of whether a lawyer is involved in giving legal advice . . . is his or her place in the corporation's organizational chart." There is a presumption that a lawyer in the legal department is giving legal advice, but an opposite presumption where a lawyer " . . . works for the Financial Group or some other seemingly management or business side of the house.").

35. *See e.g.,* City of Elmira v. Larry Walter, Inc., 453 N.Y.S.2d 259, 260 (N.Y. App. Div. 1982) (lawyer also made business decision responding to request that surety complete construction project); Marten v. Yellow Freight Sys., Inc., 1998 WL 13244, *9 (D. Kan. 1998) (lawyer who was required to serve on "employment review committee," and who voted to terminate employee); Mission Nat'l Ins. Co. v. Lilly, 112 F.R.D. 160, 164 (D. Minn. 1986) (factual investigation by lawyers that was required by terms of insurance policy); Sanders v. Alabama State Bar, 161 F.R.D. 470, 473 (M.D. Ala. 1995) (recommendation by Bar counsel not privileged because investigating complaints and making recommendations was normal business of Bar).

36. *ChevronTexaco,* 241 F. Supp. 2d at 1078.

37. *See* note 11.

38. Deese v. State Farm Mut. Auto. Ins. Co., 838 P.2d 1265, 1268, 1270 (Ariz. 1992) (emphasis in original).

39. *In re* Bergeson, 112 F.R.D. 692, 697 (D. Mont. 1986).

40. *City of Elmira, supra* note 35 at 260.

41. Brown v. Superior Court, 670 P.2d 725, 734 (Ariz. 1983) (en banc) (construing work-product privilege).

42. *Id.* at 734.

43. Silva v. Fire Ins. Exch., 112 F.R.D. 699, 700 (D. Mont. 1986).

44. *Deese, supra* note 38 at 1270 (". . . absence of a breach of an express term of the policy is not fatal to a bad faith claim where the plaintiff can prove a breach of the implied covenant of good faith and fair dealing.").

45. *Upjohn, supra* note 17 at 392. The authors suggest that the Supreme Court's statements apply with even greater force to the behavior of individual clients and the benefit of their lawyers' actions.

46. Dontzin v. Myer, 694 A.2d 264, 268 (N.J. Super. App. Div. 1997).

47. Twin City Fire Ins. Co. v. Burke, 63 P.3d 282, 287 (Ariz. 2003) (en banc).

48. *Id.* at 286. Note, however, that the conduct of the defendant in this case was not directly at issue.

49. *See, e.g.*, United Technologies Corp. v. Am. Home Assurance Co., 118 F. Supp. 2d 174, 178 n.2 (D. Conn. 2000) (where discovery concerning communications with lawyers assigned to handle claims was withheld as privileged, "there could be no explanatory testimony from those attorneys to dispel the clear negative inferences that no good faith claims settlement practice was under way . . . .").

50. *In re* Sealed Case, 754 F.2d 395, 399, 400 (D.C. Cir. 1985).

51. *In re* Diasonics Securities Litig., 110 F.R.D. 570, 575 (D. Colo. 1986).

52. Diamond v. Stratton, 95 F.R.D. 503, 505 (S.D.N.Y. 1982); *see Coleman, supra* note 11 at 207 (listing other decisions applying the exception to tort allegations).

53. United Services Auto. Ass'n. v. Werley, 526 P.2d 28, 32 n.15 (Alaska 1974); *cf. Laser Indus., Ltd.,* 167 F.R.D. at 425 (courts would reason unreliably if they were permitted to consider only the evidence of the party trying to penetrate the privilege, without regard to the opposing party's evidence).

54. Caldwell v. District Court, 644 P.2d 26, 32 (Colo. 1982).

55. State *ex rel.* North Pacific Lumber Co. v. Unis, 579 P.2d 1291, 1295 (Ore. 1978), quoted in *Caldwell, supra* note 54 at 32.

56. Nesse v. Pittman, 202 F.R.D. 344, 351 (D.D.C. 2001).

57. Ferrara & DiMercurio, Inc. v. St. Paul Mercury Ins. Co., 173 F.R.D. 7, 12 (D. Mass. 1997).

58. Freedom Trust v. Chubb Group of Ins. Cos., 38 F. Supp. 2d 1170, 1172-73 (C.D. Cal. 1999).

59. *Id.* at 1173 n.3 (citing *Werley,* 526 P.2d 28, as an example of such a court).

60. *In re* Sealed Case, 107 F.3d 46, 50 (D.C. Cir. 1997).

61. United States v. Skeddle, 989 F. Supp. 890, 901-02 (N.D. Ohio 1997).

62. 63 St. John's L. Rev. at 256-57 (internal quotation marks omitted).

63. *Laser, supra* note 28 at 421.

64. 63 St. John's L. Rev. at 260; *see also Laser, supra* note 28 at 436 (". . . judges should exercise considerable caution when they are pressed during the discovery stage of complex litigation to find that a showing of crime or fraud that is sufficient to justify penetrating the privilege has been made.").

65. One of the authors served with great satisfaction as a judge's law clerk, but found conducting in camera document reviews extremely difficult and time-consuming, for the reasons stated.

66. *See* note 14.

67. *See* note 15.

68. *See* note 16.

69. *See* note 17.

70. *See* 63 St. John's L. Rev. at 396 n.733 (one in-house lawyer "said that the principal value of the attorney-client privilege . . . is the protection it offers to 'the mistakes, speculations, opinions, theories, ideas, and inferences' that clients communicate to lawyers").

71. *See, e.g.,* State *ex rel.* United States Fidelity & Guar. Co. v. Montana Second Judicial District Court, 783 P.2d 911, 915-16 (Mont. 1989) (privilege "allows for an honest, careful and prompt analysis by qualified persons. . . . The free flow of information between attorney and client equally benefits the claimant because it is this kind of communication which results in the settlement of most insurance claims.").

72. As one judge put it: "If the majority does not believe that corporations can be trusted with a meaningful attorney-client privilege, they should say so and attempt to justify such a conclusion." *Samaritan Found.*, 844 P.2d (Voss, P.J., dissenting), *rev'd, Samaritan Found.*, 862 P.2d 870.

73. The authors suggest that the risk of harm from abuse of the privilege may be lessened by the fact that areas where such conduct might affect large numbers of people are often strictly regulated outside the court system (e.g., Securities and Exchange Commission, Sarbanes-Oxley Act).

74. *Upjohn, supra* note 17 at 395.

75. *See* notes 8 & 9.

76. 63 St. John's L. Rev. at 259 n.190.

77. *Mission, supra* note 35 at 162.

78. *United Technologies, supra* note 49 at 176.

79. *Samaritan Found., supra* note 18 at 873, 880.

CHAPTER 18

The Self-Defense Exception to the Attorney's Ethical Obligation to Maintain Client Confidences

MICHAEL F. PEZZULLI

Attorneys operate under a broad ethical mandate not to disclose client confidences. This ethical obligation can apply to communications made before the establishment of an attorney-client relationship and survives the death of the client.[1] It is broader than the attorney-client evidentiary privilege. But virtually all codes of professional responsibility recognize the "self-defense exception" to the rule prohibiting an attorney from disclosing client confidences. The self-defense exception is the focus of this chapter.

Rule 1.6 of the ABA Model Rules of Professional Conduct

The ethical duty to maintain confidences and the attorney-client privilege, while often overlapping, are different in a number of respects. The attorney-client privilege is an evidentiary privilege applicable primarily in judicial proceedings. The generally recognized purpose of the attorney-client privilege is to:

> . . . encourage full and frank communication between attorneys and their clients and thereby promote broader public interests in the observance of law and administration of justice. The privilege recognizes that sound legal advice or advocacy serves public ends and that such advice or advocacy depends upon the lawyer's being fully informed by the client.[2]

Generally, the attorney-client privilege is narrowly construed and applies "only to those situations in which the party invoking the privilege consulted an attorney for the purpose of securing a legal opinion or services and in connection with that consultation communicated information that was intended to be kept confidential."[3] The attorney-client privilege protects only the communications themselves, not the underlying facts, the disclosure of which may be compelled from those who communicated them to the attorney.[4] This means that a client may be asked about the underlying facts of an occurrence or transaction (unless able to refuse under the Fifth Amendment), but not whether those facts were related to the client's lawyer.[5]

The ethical obligation to preserve client confidences arises from broader policy and ethical considerations.

> The obligation of an attorney not to misuse information acquired in the course of representation serves to vindicate the trust and reliance that clients place in their attorneys. A client would feel wronged if an opponent prevailed against him with the aid of an attorney who formerly represented the client in the same matter. . . . This would undermine public confidence in the legal system as a means for adjudicating disputes. We recognize that this concern implicates the principle embodied in Canon 9 that attorneys "should avoid even the appearance of professional impropriety."[6]

The duty of confidentiality is directed toward attorneys and provides that attorneys may not disclose, even voluntarily, what he or she has learned about a client, no matter where or how it was learned. For example, if an attorney learns information about a client from a third party, that material is not within the attorney-client privilege (because it is not a communication from the client). However, such information, provided it is related to representation of the client or is acquired in the course of representing the client, is covered by the duty of confidentiality.[7]

While the attorney-client privilege can be waived through disclosure to third parties, the duty of confidentiality is not waived under such circumstances. An attorney is still ethically obligated to maintain the confidences.

Since the ABA Model Rules of Professional Conduct were adopted in 1983, a majority of states adopted rules similar to the Model Rules. Rule 1.6 of the Model Rules of Professional Conduct is broader than its predecessor, DR 4-101(A) of the Model Code of Professional Responsibility. DR 4-101 provides:

> (A) "Confidence" refers to information protected by the attorney-client privilege under applicable law, and "secret" refers to other information gained in the professional relationship that the client has requested be held inviolate or the disclosure of which would be embarrassing or would be likely to be detrimental to the client.
> (B) Except when permitted under DR 4-101(C), a lawyer shall not knowingly:
>
>> (1) Reveal a confidence or secret of his client.
>> (2) Use a confidence or secret of his client to the disadvantage of the client.
>> (3) Use a confidence or secret of his client for the advantage of himself or of a third person, unless the client consents after full disclosure.

(C) A lawyer may reveal:

(1) Confidences or secrets with the consent of the client or clients affected, but only after a full disclosure to them.
(2) Confidences or secrets when permitted under Disciplinary Rules or required by law or court order.
(3) The intention of his client to commit a crime and the information necessary to prevent the crime.
(4) Confidences or secrets necessary to establish or collect his fee or to defend himself or his employees or associates against an accusation of wrongful conduct.

(D) A lawyer shall exercise reasonable care to prevent his employees, associates, and others whose services are utilized by him from disclosing or using confidences or secrets of a client, except that a lawyer may reveal the information allowed by DR 4-101(C) through an employee.[8]

The version of Model Rule 1.6 adopted in 1983 provided:

(a) A lawyer shall not reveal information relating to representation of a client unless the client consents after consultation, except for disclosures that are impliedly authorized in order to carry out the representation and except as stated in paragraph (b).
(b) A lawyer may reveal such information to the extent the lawyer reasonably believes necessary:

(1) to prevent the client from committing a criminal act that the lawyer believes is likely to result in imminent death or substantial bodily harm; or
(2) to establish a claim or defense on behalf of the lawyer in a controversy between the lawyer and the client, to establish a defense to a criminal charge or civil claim against the lawyer based upon conduct in which the client was involved, or to respond to allegations in any proceedings concerning the lawyer's representation of the client.[9]

In contrast with the Model Code, old Rule 1.6 applies to information relating to the representation of the client even if it is acquired before or after the relationship existed. Further, it does not require the client to specify the information to be kept confidential or allow the attorney to speculate as to whether the information might be embarrassing or detrimental.[10] Further, the Model Rule is broader in that it allows revelation of confidences to support any "claim or defense" against the client, as opposed to just a claim to collect a fee.

In the spring of 1997, the American Bar Association Commission on Evaluation of the Rules of Professional Conduct (the "Ethics 2000 Commission") undertook a comprehensive study and evaluation of the ABA Model Rules in light of developments in the law and in the legal profession.[11] The Commission recommended several substantive changes to the rule, but most were rejected by the House of Delegates for the American Bar Association.[12]

As approved by the House, new Rule 1.6(b)(1) provides the lawyer with discretion to reveal a client confidence if the lawyer believes it "necessary to prevent reasonably certain death or substantial bodily harm."[13] The new rule changed "imminent" to "reasonably certain" and eliminated the requirement that the client's crime be the cause of the problem. Disclosure is permissible whether or not the act in question is a crime or the act of the lawyer's client. The House rejected, however, the Commission's proposed 1.6(b)(2), which would have permitted, but not required, the disclosure of information to the extent the lawyer reasonably believes necessary to prevent client crimes or frauds that are reasonably certain to provide substantial economic injury.[14]

Although no changes were made to the language of the self-defense exception, new commentary directs that "a disclosure adverse to the client's interest should be no greater than the lawyer reasonably believes necessary to accomplish this purpose."[15] Also, a new commentary instructs that a lawyer has a duty to make non-frivolous legal challenges to disclosure requirements external to the rules.[16]

The Self-Defense Exception

Rule 1.6 "is not intended to disarm an attorney from protecting his rights and reputation as against a former client."[17] The self-defense exception set forth in Rule 1.6(b)(2) applies in five principal situations: (1) in defense of lawsuits brought by clients;[18] (2) in fee disputes with clients; (3) when an attorney may be implicated or accused of criminal misconduct relating to representation of a client; (4) to defend charges of professional misconduct; and (5) in habeas corpus proceedings where the client is asserting ineffective assistance of counsel.[19] And, although some commentators have asserted that this provision merely allows lawyers to use confidential information in fee-collection disputes, the plain language of the rule is broader than this.[20] Revealing a client confidence should not be treated lightly, even if the disclosure is authorized by Rule 1.6. "The general ethical norm that information acquired in the course of representation of a client not be disclosed to the client's disadvantage nor revealed without the client's consent . . . should serve as a warning to lawyers that an exception founded upon self-defense ought to be invoked gingerly, after careful study and deliberation."[21] Any disclosures made under the aegis of Rule 1.6(b)(2) must be strictly limited so that (1) only necessary information or communications are disclosed and (2) the disclosure is to persons or entities that must have access to the information.[22]

To ensure that attorney disclosures are reasonable and as narrow as possible, some courts have held that the party seeking the lawyer's testimony must submit proposed questions and responses for in camera review.[23] Whether required or not, however, it would be prudent to seek court approval before disclosing confidences.

The comments to the Model Rules make it clear that attorneys need not wait for formal charges or a lawsuit to be filed before they are allowed to disclose confidences in self-defense.

> The lawyer's right to respond arises when an assertion of such complicity
> has been made. Paragraph (b)(2) does not require the lawyer to await the
> commencement of an action or proceeding that charges such complicity,
> so that the defense may be established by responding directly to a third
> party who has made such an assertion. The right to defend, of course, ap-
> plies where a proceeding has been commenced. Where practicable and not
> prejudicial to the lawyer's ability to establish a defense, the lawyer should
> advise the client of the third party's assertion and request that the client
> respond appropriately. In any event, disclosure should be no greater than
> the lawyer reasonably believes is necessary to vindicate innocence, the
> disclosure should be made in a manner which limits access to the informa-
> tion to the tribunal or other persons having a need to know it, and appropri-
> ate protective orders or other arrangements should be sought by the lawyer
> to the fullest extent practicable.[24]

The comment allows for prophylactic or "offensive" use of disclosure to protect the
attorney's reputation and financial interests to the extent that extended litigation is
expensive. It remains to be seen how "offensively" courts will allow attorneys to use
confidential information.[25]

Another problematic situation arises when an attorney discovers that he has un-
knowingly assisted in an illegal transaction. Generally, disclosure could not be justified under Rule 1.6(b)(1), as it allows for disclosure only where death or serious bodily
injury is in issue and where the offense has not yet been committed. However, to the
extent that the lawyer believes that he could be exposed to criminal or civil liability, he
might be justified in offensively disclosing confidential information under Rule
1.6(b)(2).

The Model Rule is also silent on whether disclosure is authorized when a lawyer
seeks advice from other professionals about how to comply with the lawyer codes or
other aspects of the law governing lawyers. In some circumstances, the lawyer may
not know about or understand a professional rule or fiduciary duty that clearly dictates
a course of action. In others, the lawyer may be faced with conflicting duties and need
advice about how to proceed. At least one commentator has suggested that the lawyer
seek advice using only hypotheticals, unless a more detailed discussion of the facts is
necessary to obtain proper counsel.[26]

Finally, a corporate attorney who represents a public company may have affirmative duties to disclose information under Section 307 of the Sarbanes-Oxley Act[27] that
conflict with Model Rule 1.6. The interaction between Sarbanes-Oxley and Model
Rule 1.6 is beyond the scope of this chapter; however, it should be noted that at least
41 states have adopted rules, similar to the proposed Rule 1.6 that was rejected by the
House, which either authorize or require disclosure to prevent a client from perpetrat-
ing a fraud that constitutes a crime.[28]

Illustrative Cases

One of the classic cases on offensive use of disclosure of client confidences is
Meyerhofer v. Empire Fire & Marine Ins. Co.[29] Goldberg was an associate working on

a securities disclosure statement, and he took the position that certain matters should be included in the statement. His superiors apparently disagreed, and Goldberg left the firm as a result. Goldberg learned that "he was to be included as a defendant in the impending action."[30] Investors brought a securities fraud claim and included Goldberg and Goldberg's former firm as defendants. Goldberg met with plaintiffs' counsel twice and provided them with evidence regarding his nonparticipation in the wrongful conduct: the affidavit and attachments he had given the Securities and Exchange Commission several months earlier.

> He hoped that [the affidavit and attachments] would verify his nonparticipation in the finder's fee omission and convince the [plaintiffs'] firm that he should not be a defendant. The [plaintiffs'] firm was satisfied with Goldberg's explanations and, upon their motion, granted by the court, he was dropped as a defendant. After receiving Goldberg's affidavit, the [plaintiffs'] firm amended plaintiffs' complaint. The amendments added more specific facts but did not change the theory or substance of the original complaint.[31]

The court concluded that even though Goldberg's disclosure was arguably broader than necessary, he had not violated the applicable Code of Professional Responsibility.[32]

The United States District Court for the Eastern District of Virginia has held that a former in-house counsel could not disclose the confidences of his former employer in an effort to recover in a qui tam action.[33]

> Nothing in the False Claims Act preempts state statutes and rules that regulate an attorney's disclosure of client confidences. The Act permits "a person" to file a *qui tam* suit; it does not require him to do so. Nor does the Act immunize a relator for actions taken that violate state law. Therefore, where an attorney's disclosure of client confidences is prohibited by state law in a given circumstance, that attorney risks subjecting himself to corresponding state disciplinary proceedings should he attempt to make the disclosure in a *qui tam* suit.[34]

Ultimately, the district court held that the former employee could not recover as a relator because a previously entered permanent injunction prevented him from making the necessary disclosures of client confidences to satisfy the requirements of the False Claims Act.[35] ("[The former employee] cannot be a relator in this action for the sole reason that he does not possess enough information that he may legally disclose to form the basis of a valid complaint against X Corp.").

A law firm that formerly represented a bankruptcy debtor and drafted a creditor plan did not violate the duty to maintain client confidences according to the dicta of a U.S. bankruptcy court.[36]

> This Court finds that [the law firm] did not use client confidences to draft is Disclosure Statement or Plan of Reorganization. If it had, however, the

rules of ethics would not necessarily have been violated. To hold otherwise would prevent a law firm from ever collecting its fee in a former client's bankruptcy. Accordingly, the Creditor Plan has been proposed in good faith and should be confirmed.[37]

In *Eckhaus v. Alfa-Laval, Inc.*, the United States District Court for the Southern District of New York examined whether a former in-house counsel could disclose his former employer's confidences while pursuing a defamation claim against the employer.[38] Eckhaus, the in-house counsel, asserted that he was defamed by false statements contained in a performance review. The performance review asserted that Eckhaus's performance was deficient with respect to a number of litigation matters. The employer moved for summary judgment, arguing that Eckhaus would have to violate the applicable Code of Professional Responsibility in order to maintain his claim. The district court agreed with the employer.

> Although plaintiff's complaint states a cause of action for defamation, the law strikes the appropriate balance between the rights of an attorney to seek compensation for injuries suffered at the hand of a client and the right of the client not to be held hostage to an attorney's threat to reveal confidential information.
>
> . . .
>
> Plaintiff justifies his revelations by relying on the exception to the general rule set forth in DR 4-101(C)(4). By raising wholly new issues, plaintiff has exceeded the scope of DR 4-101(C)(4). Furthermore, the cases applying DR 4-101(C)(4) are cases in which the client initiated the lawsuit and where the "accusation of wrongful conduct" is asserted as a formal claim against the attorney. . . . Informal charges made during a performance review of an in-house attorney specifically contemplated by his employment contract do not amount to an "accusation of wrongful conduct" [as that term is used in DR 4-101(C)(4)].[39]

The *Eckhaus* court went on to note that Eckhaus could disclose the confidence to defend against his employer's claim of breach of fiduciary duty.[40]

Depending on the context of the disclosure, some courts have allowed in-house counsel to disclose confidential information if necessary to support a wrongful discharge claim.

In *Browning v. AT&T Paradyne*, the question was whether it was a violation of the duty to maintain client confidences for an attorney to represent an employee in a suit against his former employer where the employee might have confidential information relevant to other lawsuits against the employer in which the attorney was participating.[41] Luedecke was an employee of AT&T Paradyne and participated in decision-making regarding reductions in AT&T Paradyne's workforce. Luedecke reviewed the terminations of a number of employees and assisted in evaluations of a number of other employees. Several of the terminated and demoted employees brought suit against AT&T Paradyne alleging age discrimination. Luedecke was also terminated. Luedecke filed a complaint with the EEOC and was later joined as a plaintiff in the suit brought by the other employees. AT&T Paradyne sought to disqualify Luedecke's attorney on a number of grounds. One of the grounds was that the attorney improperly induced Luedecke to divulge AT&T Paradyne's confidences in violation of Florida's version of Rule 1.6. The district court rejected AT&T Paradyne's argument.

> Defendant's assertion that Plaintiffs' counsel have violated [Rule 1.6] is unfounded. [Rule 1.6] requires attorneys to maintain confidentiality and imposes upon attorneys a correlative duty to refrain from inducing others to disclose confidential matters. It is necessary that Plaintiff Luedecke disclose pertinent matters to his counsel in furtherance of the case in which he is a party. This does not fall within the realm of improperly inducing Plaintiff Luedecke to disclose confidential matters. In fact, Defendant has recognized that the information that Plaintiff Luedecke is privy to is not considered privileged and does not suggest that Plaintiffs may not obtain it through proper discovery. Defendant is concerned by the fact that Plaintiffs will have access to this information outside the bounds of traditional discovery. This particular concern is not within the scope of [Rule 1.6].[42]

In *Burkhart*, the plaintiff was a junior patent attorney who believed his boss had ordered him to prepare fraudulent patent applications. The plaintiff was fired after he refused to file the applications. The district court granted summary judgment to the employer, ruling that his claim could not proceed if he needed to use confidential information to support his claims. The Montana Supreme Court reversed summary judgment in favor of the employer, holding that Rule 1.6(b) authorized using the information to establish a claim against the employer. The Montana Court relied heavily on the fact that the plain language of Rule 1.6(b) was broader than the previous version of DR 4-101(C) of the Model Code, which permitted disclosure only to "establish or collect his fee or to defend himself or his employees or associates against an accusation of wrongful conduct."[43]

The court in *Crews* went even further. In that case, in-house counsel reported her boss—corporate general counsel—to the state bar because she was not a licensed attorney. Subsequently, the plaintiff alleged she was constructively discharged in violation of public policy. The Tennessee Supreme Court allowed the suit to proceed, holding that the plaintiff had a "permissive duty" to report the unauthorized practice of law, even if that duty was in conflict with the duty to maintain confidences.[44]

But in *In re McLane*, the Kansas Supreme Court publicly censured an attorney who threatened a previous client—by way of a letter to her new attorney—with disclosure of embarrassing facts he learned during both his private and professional relationship with the client.[45] The Kansas Court rejected the argument that the disclosures to the new attorney where authorized by Kansas Rule of Professional Conduct 1.6(b), because the disclosures were not made to establish a claim or defense and there was no current proceeding, but merely to harass and embarrass the former client.[46]

In *United States v. Cavin*, the Fifth Circuit examined the question of whether it was error to exclude an attorney's proffered evidence regarding the ethical constraints he operated under in rendering legal services to a client who "is using or has used his services to accomplish a fraud."[47] The court set forth an excellent analysis of the conflicting ethical norms an attorney must balance in such a situation.

> The black-letter rule is that the lawyer must disclose a material fact when disclosure is necessary to avoid assisting a criminal or fraudulent act by a client, unless disclosure is prohibited by the rule against revealing client confidences. Because such disclosure would consist of client confidences, it would seem that disclosure is prohibited, leaving the lawyer in the position of an accomplice. But that is not the rule; a lawyer may not commit a fraud. The parameters of his obligations, however, depend on the circumstances. How active a role does the lawyer play in the reporting process: is he a background advisor or the spokesperson? Is the content such that the agency likely would be misled without disclosure of the damaging fact? Would the omission mislead because of a statement by the lawyer or because of an oversight by the agency? Finally, what if the lawyer reasonably believes that the legal significance of the undisclosed information is such that the agency's reporting requirements do not call for disclosure, but the lawyer suspects that the agency would disagree? One authority holds that disclosure is not required [citing ABA Formal Ethics Opinion 93-375]. If disclosure is not required, arguably it is forbidden.
>
> These are some of the complex considerations facing a lawyer whose client is using or has used his services to accomplish a fraud. To the extent that they guide his conduct, they are directly relevant to his intent. We therefore join our Eleventh Circuit colleagues [*United States v. Kelly*, 888 F.2d 732 (11th Cir. 1989)] in holding that a lawyer accused of participating in his client's fraud is entitled to present evidence of his professional, including ethical, responsibilities, and the manner in which they influenced him. Exclusion of such evidence prevents the lawyer from effectively presenting his defense. [48]

The Fifth Circuit also held that the attorney was entitled to instructions in the charge detailing the relevant ethical responsibilities.[49]

The case of *Grassmuek v. Ogden Murphy Wallace, P.L.L.C.*, illustrates how complex the issues can become when multiple interests are involved.[50] In *Grassmuek*, several individuals where indicted on multiple counts of mail fraud, wire fraud, securities fraud, money laundering, and conspiracy to commit these offenses. The plaintiff was a court-appointed receiver, acting on behalf of the corporate entities alleged to have taken part in the crimes through their agents. Both before and after the indictments, the government in the criminal action sought and collected a vast amount of documentary evidence through the use of warrants, grand jury subpoenas and various cooperating sources, both private and governmental. The government was seeking to compel production of documents from the receiver; the receiver was seeking to use the documents against the attorneys who represented the criminal defendant and the corporate entities; the criminal defendant was seeking to protect disclosure based on the attorney-client privilege; and the civil-defendant law firm was seeking disclosure of all documents, but noted that a small subset of the documents were generated in representation of the criminal defendant in his individual—as opposed to corporate—capacity.[51]

To resolve the issues, the court first applied the five-part test articulated in *In re Grand Jury Subpoena*[52] to determine whether a person who was represented in both his or her corporate and individual capacities may personally assert the attorney-client privilege over a document.

Under the five-part test, parties asserting the privilege must show: (1) they approached counsel for the purpose of seeking legal advice; (2) when they approached counsel they made it clear they were seeking advice in their individual rather than in their representative capacity; (3) the attorney saw fit to communicate with the individual in his individual capacity; (4) the substance of their conversations were confidential; and (5) the substance of their conversations did not concern matters within the company or the general affairs of the company.[53] A client represented both as an individual and as an agent of a corporation may assert an individual privilege only to the extent the communications regarding individual acts and liabilities are segregable from discussions about the corporation.[54] After resolving the five-part test against the individual criminal defendant, the court also noted that, even if he could have asserted an individual privilege, the documents were subject to disclosure to allow the law firm to defend itself under the self-defense exception contained in the Washington Rules of Professional Conduct.[55]

Notes

1. *See* Commonwealth v. Mrozek, 657 A.2d 997, 998-1000 (Pa. 1995) (holding that statement made by client in the course of seeking legal representation to secretary was confidential); *In re* John Doe Grand Jury Investigation, 562 N.E.2d 69, 72 (Mass. 1990) (upholding attorney's refusal to testify before grand jury regarding statements deceased client made to him regarding murder); State v. Macumber, 544 P.2d 1084, 1086 (Ariz. 1976) (en banc) (holding that attorney could not testify as a defense witness in the criminal trial of another that his deceased client confessed to the murder).

2. Upjohn Co. v. United States, 449 U.S. 383, 389 (1981).

3. *In re* Grand Jury Proceedings, 727 F.2d 1352, 1355 (4th Cir. 1984); X Corp. v. Doe, 805 F. Supp. 1298, 1305 (E.D. Va. 1992).

4. *Upjohn Co.*, *supra* note 2 at 395.

5. *See id.*

6. Brennan's Inc. v. Brennan's Restaurants, Inc., 590 F.2d 168, 172 (5th Cir. 1979).

7. MODEL RULES OF PROF'L CONDUCT R. 1.6 cmt. 1.

8. MODEL CODE OF PROF'L RESPONSIBILITY DR 4-101 (1980).

9. MODEL RULES OF PROF'L CONDUCT R. 1.6 (1993).

10. *See* MODEL RULES OF PROF'L CONDUCT R. 1.6 cmt. 1.

11. Margaret Colgate Love, *The Revised ABA Model Rules of Professional Conduct: Summary of the Work of Ethics* 2000, 15 GEO. J. LEGAL ETHICS 441 (2002). Margaret Love is a member of the Ethics 2000 Commission. This article provides a comprehensive summary of the work of the Ethics 2000 Commission and the proposed changes to the Model Rules. She notes that as of 1997, 39 states and the District of Columbia had adopted some version of the Model Rules, but that there were significant variations in particular rules from jurisdiction to jurisdiction.

12. *Id.* at 450-51.

13. *See* E. Norman Veasey, *Ethics 2000: Thoughts and Comments on Key Issues of Professional Responsibility in the Twenty-First Century*, 5 DEL. L. REV. 1, 8-9 (2002). E. Norman Veasey is Chief Justice of Delaware and Chair of the Ethics 2000 Commission.

14. *Id.*

15. Margaret Colgate Love, *The Revised ABA Model Rules of Professional Conduct: Summary of the Work of Ethics 2000*, 15 GEO. J. LEGAL ETHICS 441, 450-52 (2002).

16. *Id.*

17. *In re* McLaren, 115 B.R. 922, 927 (Bankr. N.D. Ohio 1990).

18. *See* Heartbreak Cabaret Corp. v. Cruz & Toledo Restaurant Corp., 699 F. Supp. 1066, 1070 (S.D.N.Y. 1988); *In re* Nat'l Mortgage Equity Corp. Mortgage Pool Certificates Sec. Litig., 120 F.R.D. 687, 691-92 (C.D. Cal. 1988).

> In the case at bar, Zuckerman and Birnbaum, confronted with serious charges, wish to retain the Friedman firm to defend against those charges; and, in order that counsel may be properly instructed, Zuckerman and Birnbaum obviously require the ability to talk to their attorneys about their perceptions of the facts. It matters not that in doing so, Zuckerman and Birnbaum may reveal communications with former clients which would be confidential. As a matter of common sense, when a former client sues his former attorney, the client places the attorney in a position where previously confidential communications must be revealed to trial counsel defending the attorney in the suit.

Heartbreak Cabaret Corp., 699 F. Supp. at 1070.

19. *See* Euell v. Rosemeyer, 153 F.R.D. 576 (W.D. Pa. 1993).

> Rule 1.6 provides that while an attorney is prohibited from revealing information relating to representation of the client even after the lawyer-client relationship is terminated, an attorney may reveal such information to respond to allegations concerning the lawyer's representation of the client. Therefore, attorney Vogel is expressly permitted to disclose information regarding his representation of petitioner in any proceeding regarding the effectiveness of that representation.

Euell, 153 F.R.D. at 578.

20. *See, e.g.*, Crews v. Buckman Labs Int'l, Inc., 78 S.W.3d 852, 863-64 (Tenn. 2002) (interpreting authorization of the use of confidences to establish a "claim or defense" literally and authorizing in-house counsel to use confidential information to establish retaliatory discharge claim); Burkhart v. Semitool, Inc., 5 P.3d 1031, 1041 (Mont. 2000) (stating that a lawyer "does not forfeit his rights simply because to prove them he must utilize confidential information. Nor does the client gain a right to cheat the lawyer by imparting confidences to him."); *but see* Douglas v. DynMcDermott Petroleum Operations Co., 144 F.3d 364 (5th Cir. 1998) (holding that while in-house counsel disclosing informally to third parties information relating to interoffice complaints of discrimination may constitute opposition to practices made unlawful by Title VII, such conduct is nevertheless unprotected under Title VII as a matter of law because such disclosure constitutes an ethical violation of her duty of loyalty and confidentiality).

21. Morin v. Turpin, 728 F. Supp. 952, 957 (S.D.N.Y. 1989) (interpreting the Model Code and holding that attorney breached his ethical obligations because the situation was not "urgent" enough to warrant disclosure of confidences without first seeking the consent of the client).

22. MODEL RULES OF PROF'L CONDUCT R. 1.6 cmt. 1.

23. *See* First Fed. Sav. & Loan Ass'n v. Oppenheim, Appel, Dixon & Co., 110 F.R.D. 557 (S.D.N.Y. 1986); United States v. Omni Int'l Corp., 634 F. Supp. 1414 (D. Md. 1986).

24. MODEL RULES OF PROF'L CONDUCT R. 1.6 cmt. 1.

25. *See* United States v. Monnat, 853 F. Supp. 1301 (D. Kan. 1994) (discussing the ethical problems confronting an attorney by IRS Form 8300 and 26 U.S.C. § 60501(a)).

26. Susan R. Martin, *Nebraska and the Model Rules of Professional Conduct: In Defense of Client Lawyer Confidentiality . . . and its Exceptions*, 81 NEB. L. REV. 1320, 1343 (2003). Susan R. Martin is a professor of law and values at the University of Toledo College of Law. She served as an advisor to the America Law Institute's RESTATEMENT (THIRD) OF THE LAW GOVERNING LAWYERS from 1988 to 2000, and as a member of the Ethics 2000 Commission from 1987 to 2002.

27. *See* Sarbanes-Oxley Act of 2002 § 307, 116 Stat. at 784, 15 U.S.C. § 7245 (describing the rules of professional responsibility for attorneys).

28. *See* E. Norman Veasey, *Ethics 2000: Thoughts and Comments on Key Issues of Professional Responsibility in the Twenty-First Century*, 5 DEL. L. REV. 1, 9-10 (2002).

29. 497 F.2d 1190 (2d Cir. N.Y. 1974).

30. *Meyerhofer*, 497 F.2d at 1193.

31. *Id.*

32. *Id.* at 1196.

33. United States v. X Corp., 862 F. Supp. 1502, 1507 (E.D. Va. 1994).

34. *Id.* at 1507.

35. *Id.* at 1510.

36. *In re* Burton Securities, S.A., 148 B.R. 478, 480 (Bankr. S.D. Tex. 1992).

37. *Id.* at 480.

38. Eckhaus v. Alfa-Laval, Inc., 764 F. Supp. 34 (S.D.N.Y. 1991).

39. *Id.* at 38. *Eckhaus* was decided under provisions of the New York laws of professional conduct similar to the Model Code. As the Model Rules allow for disclosure "to establish a claim or defense on behalf of the lawyer in a controversy between the lawyer and the client," a different holding would probably result under the Model Rules.

40. *Id.*

41. Browning v. AT&T Paradyne Corp., 838 F. Supp. 1564 (M.D. Fla. 1993).

42. *Id.* at 1568.

43. *Burkhart, supra* note 20, at 1041.

44. *Crews, supra* note 20, at 865.

45. *In re* Bryan, 275 Kan. 202, 61 P.3d 641, 643 (Kan. 2003). The stipulated facts indicate that the attorney and client became romantically involved during the course of representation.

46. *Id.* at 214.

47. United States v. Cavin, 39 F.3d 1299, 1309 (5th Cir. La. 1994).

48. *Id.* at 1308-09 (footnotes omitted).

49. *Id.* at 1310.

50. 213 F.R.D. 567, 570 (W.D. Wash. 2003).

51. *Id.* at 568-69.

52. Podewils v. NLRB, 274 F.3d 536, 571 (1st Cir. 2001) (adopting the five-part test of *In re* Bevill, Bresler & Schulman Asset Mgmt. Corp., 805 F.2d 120, 123 (3d Cir. 1986)).

53. *Id.*

54. *Id.*

55. *Grassmueck, supra* note 50 at 571.

CHAPTER 19

Perspectives on the Attorney-Client Privilege and the Work-Product Doctrine

ALLAN KANNER
TIBOR NAGY

Introduction

Privileges limit the obligations of a party or non-party to produce otherwise proper discovery. Two of the oldest and most universally accepted privileges are the attorney-client privilege and the work-product doctrine. Historically, these privileges have reflected a balance between the goal of full disclosure at trial[1] and the facilitation of our adversary system of justice, in particular the need for unfettered communication with counsel and the protection of attorney work product.

As times change, however, greater importance is being placed on judicial management, particularly in complex cases. Concerns about efficiency and fair results have led courts to seek the truth as directly as possible, pushing the discovery-privilege balance toward greater disclosure. The balance has been further pushed by increasing efforts by industry to involve attorneys in managing risk,[2] on the one hand, and by government to regulate with greater disclosure and reporting requirements, on the other.[3] Cultural aversion to lawyer secrecy and lawyer complicity in client wrongdoing no doubt has also had an impact.[4] This chapter explores the changes driven by these phenomena. We focus on three particular privilege contexts: (1) the evolving role of corporate counsel and changing conceptions of secrecy; (2) the use of the crime-fraud exception to the attorney-client privilege and work-product doctrine; and (3) attorney contact with former corporate employees. In each context, new problems have pushed courts to seek answers by falling back on the policy underlying the privileges, which, in turn, has led to a trend of greater disclosure in discovery.

The Attorney-Client Privilege and the Work-Product Doctrine

Privileges exist to promote social policy. If the privilege is abused, there ceases to be a justification for it.[5] The modern justification for the husband-wife privilege, for example, "is its perceived role in fostering the harmony and sanctity of the marriage relation-ship."[6] If, however, this justification does not actually apply in a given case—if, for example, the marriage is a sham or the contested testimony concerns spousal abuse—the privilege gives way, "in the light of reason and experience," to the general rule of full disclosure.[7]

Similarly, the attorney-client privilege and the work-product doctrine are not abso-lute privileges. Unlike the husband-wife privilege or the physician-patient privilege, the attorney-client privilege and the work-product doctrine serve the specific purpose of facilitating the proper functioning of our civil and criminal justice systems, and not some purpose independent of the law. Thus, when applying either the attorney-client privilege or the work-product doctrine would not actually further the legitimate ends of our justice system, courts should and have recognized exceptions.

The Attorney-Client Privilege

A classic statement of the reason for the attorney-client privilege appears in *Swidler & Berlin v. United States*:

> The attorney-client privilege is one of the oldest recognized privileges for confidential communications. The privilege is intended to encourage "full and frank communications between attorneys and their clients and thereby promote broader public interests in the observance of law and the adminis-tration of justice."[8]

Given this purpose, the primary factual question relative to the application of the attor-ney-client privilege is, why did the attorney and client communicate? Generally, if the communication was the result of the client's lawfully seeking and the attorney's law-fully rendering legal services, the privilege applies. If, however, the communication was the result of the client's seeking to conceal a past crime or to perpetrate a future one, protecting the confidentiality of the communication no longer serves the purpose of the attorney-client privilege and the privilege does not apply.[9] Other exceptions to the privi-lege have been similarly developed by the courts in a purposive fashion.[10]

In keeping with this approach, the party asserting the attorney-client privilege has the burden of proving its existence—blanket claims of privilege will not suffice.[11] The elements of the privilege under federal law are as follows:

(1) the asserted holder of the privilege is or sought to become a client; and
(2) the person to whom the communication was made
    (a) is a member of a bar or a court, or his agent / subordinate, and
    (b) in connection with this communication is acting as a lawyer or assisting communication between the attorney and client; and
(3) the communication relates to a fact of which the attorney was informed
    (a) by his client, and
    (b) without the presence of strangers, and
    (c) for the purpose of securing primarily either
        (i) an opinion on law or
        (ii) legal services or
        (iii) assistance in some legal proceeding, and

(iv) not for the purpose of committing a crime or tort; and
(4) the privilege has been
(a) claimed and
(b) not waived by the client[12]

As these elements make clear, the attorney-client privilege applies not only to statements made to the attorney, but also to statements made to the attorney's agents in the course of the representation.[13] If the privilege applies, furthermore, the communications are rendered *inadmissible*, and not simply undiscoverable.[14]

The traditional rule regarding the privilege when the client is a corporation was stated in *Philadelphia v. Westinghouse Elec. Corp.*: an employee's statement to corporate counsel is not privileged unless the employee "is in a position to control or even to take a substantial part in a decision about any action which the corporation may take upon the advice of an attorney, or he is an authorized member of a body or group which has that authority."[15] In *Upjohn v. United States,* the Supreme Court rejected this so-called control group test and held that the attorney-client privilege could apply to lower-level employees.[16] The attorney-client privilege belongs to the client, however, and the corporate attorney-client privilege is no different: it can be asserted or waived only by an authorized corporate representative.[17] It therefore also extends to communications with former employees.[18]

The attorney-client privilege does not apply when the client puts an otherwise protected communication "at issue." One version of the "at issue" exception states that a party may be deemed to have waived the privilege where:

(1) assertion of privilege was a result of some affirmative act, such as filing suit;
(2) through this affirmative act, the asserting party put protected information at issue by making it relevant to the case; and
(3) application of privilege would deny the opposing party access to information vital to its defense.[19]

Thus, under this version of the exception, the mere placing of a party's state of mind at issue in litigation results in waiver. For example, prison officials who raise the affirmative defense of immunity waive the attorney-client privilege with respect to communications bearing on their knowledge of prisoners' constitutional rights.[20] Another version of the "at issue" exception requires a showing of overt and explicit reliance on the advice of counsel to trigger waiver. Thus, for example, an insured consumer product manufacturer does not necessarily waive the attorney-client privilege with respect to advice from its counsel simply by bringing a declaratory action for coverage, even though its state of mind is in issue and the contested communications are highly relevant.[21]

The Work-Product Doctrine

The work-product doctrine affords protection to materials prepared by an attorney or her agent in anticipation of litigation or for use in trial.[22] It is therefore distinct from and broader than the attorney-client privilege. In the civil context, the doctrine is codified in Federal Rule of Civil Procedure 26(b)(3), which provides that "the court shall protect against disclosure of the mental impressions, conclusions, opinions, or legal theories of an attorney or other representative of a party concerning the litigation."

In contrast to the confidentiality rationale underlying the attorney-client privilege, the work-product doctrine is based primarily on an anti-freeloader principle. The Advisory Committee for the 1970 amendments to Rule 26(b), for example, noted that each side to litigation "should be encouraged to prepare independently" and that "one side should not automatically have the benefit of the detailed preparatory work of the other side."[23] As one court has put it, "[t]he immunity for this class of document is little more than an 'anti-freeloader' rule designed to prohibit one adverse party from riding to court on the enterprise of the other."[24] One way to think of the distinction between the two privileges is to consider the following. If the attorney-client privilege applies, the relevant information is rendered *inadmissible*, in keeping with the need to preserve the confidentiality of attorney-client communications. If, on the other hand, the work-product doctrine and not the attorney-client privilege applies, the relevant information is not necessarily inadmissible at all—indeed, it may be centrally relevant and very much admissible at trial. It would, however, generally not be subject to *discovery*. The adverse party would have to do its own work to obtain the information.

Furthermore, in order to be protected by the work-product doctrine, the documents or items must have been prepared "in anticipation of litigation or for trial."[25] Where documents are prepared with more than one purpose in mind, it will be considered work product only if "the primary motivating purpose" behind its preparation was "to aid in possible future litigation."[26] Controversy arises when the privilege is invoked for something done, arguably, in anticipation of litigation and not involving the skills of an attorney preparing for trial. For example, many businesses are increasingly subject to government reporting requirements, or routinely receive reports in the course of business.[27] These matters almost certainly are not privileged, despite the fact that in-house counsel are typically involved.[28] Likewise, the fact that a corporation sought an expert's opinion about the safety of a device does not in itself make that opinion work product. If the opinion was obtained prior to any particular litigation being anticipated, the work-product objection is not proper.

An early recognition of this is found in *Moran v. Pittsburgh-Des Moines Steel Co.*,[29] a wrongful death action arising out of the explosion of a liquified gas tank constructed by the defendants. The plaintiff in that case encountered objections when her attorney tried, during a deposition, to probe the thought processes of the employee responsible for the final approval of the design and materials used in building the tank. Overruling these objections, the court stressed that this expert was not someone specially retained to form an opinion on a given set of facts, but rather was the one "who decided all matters for the adverse party in the creation of the object from which the cause of action arises."[30] In the setting of this lawsuit, the expert's opinion was actually an ingredient of the events giving rise to the litigation.

> Although the answers to these [deposition] questions will carry the opinion of the witness, it will amount to a statement of facts as to why certain things were done, or not done, by the defendants. Unless this information is made available, and this is the one person who knows, a full and complete picture will not be presented when consideration is given as to whether negligence or lack of care existed in the construction of said tank.[31]

Material that is prepared or knowledge that is obtained as part of any organization's normal course of business is not work product because it cannot be said to have been prepared "primarily" to aid in possible future litigation.[32] The work-product objection is not proper, and should not be asserted, where the discovery requested asks for underlying factual information in the defendant's possession.[33]

The Evolving Role of Corporate Counsel

The growing practice of risk management and the increasingly important role of counsel in the everyday life of corporations in highly regulated industries appears to blur the already vague conception of what it means to say something is being done "in anticipation of trial." Some defendants are attempting to argue that the product of such self-analysis—which has been called the "Pinto privilege," since it would protect documents akin to those in the famous *Pinto* case—should be privileged in order to encourage such socially beneficial contemplation. This increased reliance upon the services of in-house counsel has caused courts to reevaluate the scope of the attorney-client and work-product privileges in this area. Initially, it is recognized that no legal difference exists between the application of these privileges to in-house and outside counsel.[34] Nevertheless, as the tasks of in-house counsel grow more diversified, parties seeking full disclosure of the allegedly protected information have sought to distinguish the applicability of the privileges to the various roles played by counsel. At one extreme, for example, is the in-house litigator doing a job not unlike his or her outside colleague, such as trial preparation in a matter in litigation. At the other extreme is the individual who has a law degree but is essentially doing a business job that could be accomplished by an MBA graduate. Clearly, communications with the in-house litigator are easily evaluated under the traditional attorney-client privilege. Similarly, the business work of a corporate employee who happens to have a law degree is easily determined not to be privileged. The difficult question is how, if at all, should the attorney-client privilege apply when the employee's role is part lawyer, part business executive?

The traditional law-business dichotomy has eroded substantially in regulated fields. For example, a business team in a regulated telecommunications company may include a lawyer who is giving strategic advice one moment and legal advice the next. Similarly, an attorney may be in the environmental department of a manufacturing concern as part of a compliance team as opposed to the general counsel's office. Is such an attorney an environmental professional or counselor, or both? The process has come to be much less formal than the traditional image of getting an opinion from counsel.

The Changing Role of In-House Counsel

The role of in-house counsel is undergoing a radical transformation that warrants reexamination of certain traditional ideas about the proper application of the attorney-client privilege. In short, the factual underpinnings of *Upjohn Co. v. United States*[35] may no longer exist in all cases. Consider, for example, the roles played by Mr. Stephen D. Ramsey, an attorney who is employed as vice president of corporate environmental programs for General Electric. Mr. Ramsey is not only an attorney, but also both the most knowledgeable person at GE regarding the company's environmental hazardous substances and cleanup policies and the head of GE personnel responsible for executing those policies. In May 1990, the *American Lawyer* interviewed GE's general counsel, Benjamin Heinman, who said that he lured Ramsey in-house for what he described as "not just a legal job. . . . He'll be running a whole environmental area." The *American Lawyer* also interviewed Mr. Ramsey himself and reported that his job entailed

> ". . . creating, developing, and managing environmental programs. He'll over-see 30 people, including engineers, technicians, and ten lawyers. 'I'll be ensuring that GE *at a corporate and business level* is doing everything they can to comply with existing laws and governmental regulations and [where possible] *to go beyond that'*. . . .
>
> Ramsey says he plans to help craft policies to govern waste management and pollutant levels at GE's numerous facilities abroad."[36]

In fact, GE's own press release of April 3, 1990 quoted GE Chairman John F. Welch, Jr. as saying, "Steve Ramsey's strong environmental background and proven track record will be extremely valuable in leading an environmental effort that *will involve all employees at every level of the company.*" The press release also said: "He will be responsible for ensuring consistent state-of-the-art environmental practices across the company's 13 key businesses in both the U.S. and abroad and for public policy issues involving the environment."[37]

Mr. Ramsey's job, and those of an increasing number of executives, clearly involve an intimately interwoven set of issues. In some cases, it is possible to distinguish an in-house counsel's attorney responsibilities from his or her business or administrative ones. For example, in *United States v. Lipshy,*[38] the defendant was both senior vice president and acting general counsel of the Zale Corporation. In response to allegations of misconduct made by a previous officer of Zale, the corporation requested that Lipshy serve as counsel to an ad hoc committee formed to investigate the allegations. In this capacity, Lipshy conducted interviews of company officers and employees. The court noted that although Lipshy signed the investigative report he submitted to Zale's Board of Directors as "Senior Vice President," such a title was not descriptive of his function in conducting the examination. Rather, the court analyzed Lipshy's investigation in the context in which it was performed—for the "purpose of obtaining information needed to advise the Committee in the legal implication of charges of misconduct"—and found it to be privileged.[39]

Nevertheless, courts have experienced some difficulty in determining whether communications sought to be shielded by the privilege involve business or legal advice. The task becomes particularly problematic when business and legal considerations are intertwined. While this factor will not destroy the privilege, commingling of legal and business advice provokes closer scrutiny of the communications. For example, in *SCM Corporation v. Xerox Corp.,*[40] the chief executive officer and president of Xerox Corporation, in response to questions concerning the business reasons for granting or refusing to grant licenses, testified that the reasons were so intertwined with legal advice that he could not answer without disclosing privileged communications. This tactic did not thwart the court's inquiry, however. While recognizing that the "mere mention" of business considerations was not sufficient to compel disclosure of otherwise privileged communications, the court noted that when the ultimate decisions required exercise of business judgment, the "relevant nonlegal considerations incidental to the formulation of legal advice were business reasons and not privileged."[41] The court reasoned that such considerations:

> ... are like any other business evaluations and motivations and do not enjoy protection because they are alluded to by conscientious counsel. To protect the business components in the decisional process would be a distortion of the privilege. The attorney-client privilege was not intended to encourage businessmen to discuss basic reasons for a particular course of action.[42]

Because the witness could not isolate the separate business and legal aspects, he was ordered to answer the objectionable questions in an affidavit to be submitted for in camera inspection, and he was further ordered to describe in the affidavit his decision-making process in order to enable the court to determine whether the business considerations were incidental to the legal consultation. Thus, although business interests might be influenced by legal considerations, the business concerns were subject to disclosure, even though the legal advice from counsel was protected.

Not all courts have required the production of mixed legal and business communications, however. In *Ohio-Sealy Mattress Co. v. Sealy, Inc.*,[43] defendants sought the return of a letter authored by counsel for defendant and inadvertently produced during expedited discovery. The court, while recognizing plaintiff's claim that the letter contained business advice which was not privileged, nonetheless stated:

> [T]he January 6, 1987 letter contains an admixture of business and legal advice that is not readily divisible into separate categories. Indeed, any effort to parse the advice which is "legal" from that which is "business" would be hazardous at best. Accordingly, the letter must be treated as one to which the privilege would attach, subject, of course, to any exceptions to the attorney-client privilege that may apply.

Thus, while the entire document would not be within the scope of the attorney-client privilege under *SCM Corp.* because it contained a mixture of business and legal advice, it would be within the attorney-client privilege under *Ohio-Sealy*.

The Use of Outside Counsel in Internal Investigations

One way to increase the likelihood that communications conveyed during an internal investigation will be protected by the attorney-client privilege is to use outside counsel. *Diversified Industries, Inc. v. Meredith*[44] illustrates the point. In that case the court upheld a corporation's claim of privilege for a report by outside counsel who had been retained to investigate bribery charges. The report of the investigation, which was based on interviews of employees and an analysis of data compiled by an accounting firm, evaluated the corporation's conduct and issued recommendations.

The court first noted that the fact that the matter was referred by the corporation to a law firm was prima facie evidence for the purpose of obtaining legal advice, "absent a clear showing to the contrary."[45] The court noted that the mandate of the firm was to conduct a full "professional investigation."[46] For example, the firm was authorized to interview any employee of the corporation who might have knowledge of the facts. "Perhaps most importantly, it was given the authority to analyze the accounting data, to evaluate and draw conclusions as to the propriety of past actions and to make recommendations for possible future courses of action."[47] The court also noted that, although "[a]ccountants could have been hired by Diversified to audit the books and lay investigators could have been employed to interview employees . . . neither could have had the training, skills and background necessary to make the independent analysis and recommendations which the Board felt was essential to the future welfare of the corporation."[48]

For the purpose of planning such investigations, furthermore, the dissent in this case is instructive. The dissent focused on the minutes of board meetings at which the law firm was hired as an investigator, not as a legal counsel, and the fact that the report consisted primarily of a description of the investigation. It was also noted that the "recommendations could have been made by any firm of private investigators, or by accountants, or by bankers, or, for that matter, by any person possessing ordinary common sense and business prudence."[49]

Thus, courts are likely to examine whether the information sought and acted upon by counsel involved the application of law to facts or the rendering of an opinion of law in response to the client's legal inquiries. While there is formally no legal distinction between in-house and outside counsel for the purpose of the attorney-client privilege, the activities of in-house counsel will probably be subjected to closer scrutiny. Accordingly, where in-house counsel performs all or part of the investigation or the preparation of the report, care should be taken to substantiate that he is acting in a legal, rather than a business, capacity. If outside counsel are retained, it should be made clear that *legal* services are an integral part of their duties.

Changing Conceptions of Secrecy

Although courts have traditionally espoused doctrines averse to secrecy,[50] recent trends have increased this aversion and have led to the creation of new rules governing confidentiality and the lawyer-client relationship. For example, in *Pansy v. Borough of Stroudsburg,* the Third Circuit held that local newspapers had standing to intervene and challenge a confidentiality order entered by the district court in facilitating a settlement in an employment discrimination suit.[51] After commenting on "the widespread and increasing use by district courts of confidentiality orders to facilitate settlements, and the consequential sacrifice of public access to the information deemed confidential by such orders," the court held that the district court had abused its discretion in granting and maintaining the order of confidentiality:

> [S]imply because courts have the power to grant orders of confidentiality does not mean that such orders may be granted arbitrarily. Disturbingly, some courts routinely sign orders which contain confidentiality clauses without considering the propriety of such orders, or the countervailing public interests which are sacrificed by the orders. Because defendants request orders of confidentiality as a condition of settlement, courts are willing to grant these requests in an effort to facilitate settlement without sufficiently inquiring into the potential public interest in obtaining information concerning the settlement agreement.[52]

Every circuit court that has considered the question has come to the conclusion that nonparties may permissively intervene for the purpose of challenging confidentiality orders.[53] Furthermore, the indiscriminate issuance of confidentiality orders and the resulting secrecy of information generated through judicial proceedings has become increasingly disfavored in the courts.[54]

The recent wave of corporate scandals and the resulting backlash has added to this anti-secrecy trend, and it is now clear that new rules are likely to govern the confidentiality of communications between attorneys and clients. On August 11, 2003, the American Bar Association voted to adopt amendments to its Model Rules of Professional Conduct, including amendments to Model Rule 1.6, Confidentiality of Information, and Model Rule 1.13, Organization as Client.[55] As amended, Rule 1.6 permits an attorney to release information to enable affected persons or authorities "to prevent the client from committing a crime or fraud that is reasonably certain to result in substantial injury to the financial interests or property of another and in furtherance of which the client has used or is using the lawyer's services." Previously the rule allowed lawyers to reveal information related to the representation of a client only if such a disclosure was believed necessary to prevent "reasonably certain death or substantial bodily harm." The amended rule thus brings lawyers' duty of confidentiality into conformance with the prevailing scope of the attorney-client privilege.[56]

Model Rule 1.13, which governs attorneys' duties of confidentiality with respect to organizational clients, now provides that if a lawyer representing a corporation or other organization "knows" that a corporate officer or employee is engaged in a violation of law that is likely to result in "substantial injury" to the organization, "then the lawyer shall proceed as is reasonably necessary in the best interest of the organization." In addition, unless the lawyer "reasonably believes that it is not necessary in the best interest of the organization to do so, the lawyer shall refer the matter to higher authority in the organization, including, if warranted by the circumstances, to the highest authority that can act on behalf of the organization as determined by applicable law."

Amended Model Rule 1.13(c) further provides that if internal up-the-ladder reporting fails to elicit an appropriate response to the violation, "then the lawyer may reveal information relating to the representation whether or not Rule 1.6 permits such disclosure, but only if and to the extent the lawyer reasonably believes necessary to prevent substantial injury to the organization." The new rule thus allows disclosure of confidential information to *outsiders* in appropriate circumstances. The old rule allowed lawyers to resign from the representation, but stopped short of allowing them to report the wrongdoing to outsiders. Significantly, Rule 1.13(d) makes clear that permission to report wrongdoing outside the organization does not apply when a lawyer has been engaged to investigate an alleged violation of law or to defend an organization or corporate officer accused of violating the law.

Although the practical effect of the amendments is yet to be seen, they clearly respond to the increasing aversion to lawyer secrecy and perceived complicity in corporate client wrongdoing. Courts applying rules modeled after Rule 1.13(d), centrally important to internal investigations, are likely to have to confront the issues raised earlier.

The Crime-Fraud Exception

Regardless of whether in-house or outside counsel are involved, there has been a pronounced trend toward utilizing an exception to the attorney-client privilege and the work-product doctrine that is recognized both under federal law and in all 50 states: the crime-fraud exception. The crime-fraud exception has played a critical role in tobacco litigation,[57] and, in the wake of an atmosphere of corporate scandals, the doctrine was recently given new force in the amendments to the Model Rules of Professional Conduct discussed above.[58] Perhaps most significantly, courts have increasingly adopted evidentiary standards that give more meaningful effect to this exception to the attorney-client privilege.

Origin and Purpose

It has often been noted that the attorney-client privilege is the oldest and most universally accepted privilege recognized by the common law.[59] The crime-fraud exception, in turn, is perhaps the oldest and most universally accepted exception to the privilege. Wigmore's treatise begins its discussion of the crime-fraud exception with the following:

> It has been agreed from the beginning that the privilege cannot avail to protect the client in concerting with the attorney a crime or other evil enterprise. This is for the logically sufficient reason that no such enterprise falls within the just scope of the relation between adviser and client.[60]

The purpose of the crime-fraud exception, then, is straightforward: clients should not be able to use legal advice to perpetrate or plan unlawful activity and then use the privilege as a shield from disclosure.[61] In the words of the leading Supreme Court opinion, "[T]he purpose of the crime-fraud exception [is] to assure that the 'seal of secrecy' between lawyer and client does not extend to communications made for the purpose of getting advice for the commission of a fraud or crime."[62]

Scope of the Exception

While the purpose of the exception is straightforward, its precise scope is not. As a general rule, otherwise privileged communications are not protected if they are meant to further future or ongoing criminal or fraudulent conduct, including other wrongful conduct such as intentional torts.[63] There are, furthermore, several well-established principles regarding the exception's application. Communications regarding *past* crime or fraud are within the attorney-client privilege.[64] The attorney-client privilege, furthermore, "is strongest where a client seeks counsel's advice to determine the legality of conduct before taking action."[65] When, however, a client seeks advice for the purpose of furthering a *present* or *future* crime or fraud, or for the purpose of *concealing* a past crime or fraud, the exception applies and the communications are not privileged.[66] Finally, it is well established that the attorney's innocence is irrelevant when applying the crime-fraud exception. The focus is on the client's conduct and intentions.[67]

A significant difference, however, can be found among jurisdictions as to what conduct falls within the exception. Several courts have adopted a strict, technical version of the exception: the conduct in question must satisfy statutorily or judicially recognized elements of a particular crime or fraud.[68] Under this view, for example, a client who sought advice for the purpose of engaging in "inequitable conduct" in the course of prosecuting a patent application—which, under the substantive patent law, would mean the client forfeits the right to enforce the patent—would still receive the benefit of the attorney-client privilege, so long as the conduct did not meet all of the technical elements of common-law fraud (for example, the privilege challenger can prove scienter but cannot prove reliance by the Patent and Trademark Office [PTO]).[69]

Most courts today, however, apply a broader view of the crime-fraud exception.[70] Thus, in these jurisdictions, legal advice sought with fraudulent intent does not receive the benefit of the attorney-client privilege, regardless of whether the client happens to succeed in inducing reliance. In the patent application scenario discussed above, for example, the party who had engaged in inequitable conduct before the PTO would not receive the benefit of the privilege, even if the privilege challenger could not prove reliance.

Similarly, the existence of potential defenses to criminal or tortious conduct does not necessarily preclude application of the crime-fraud exception, as illustrated by a recent case from the Fifth Circuit.[71] In *In re Grand Jury Subpoena,* the government argued that certain documents, which had been inadvertently disclosed, revealed that the defendant corporation had used its counsel to help it conceal the extent of its noncompliance with environmental regulations from state and federal regulators. In response, the corporation argued that the existence of potential defenses to the alleged violations precluded application of the crime-fraud exception to its claim of attorney-client privilege.[72] After considering both claims, Judge Robert Parker noted:

> While the targets of this investigation may have valid defenses that preclude indictment or conviction for fraud or criminal environmental violations, the existence of a potential defense does not mean that the district court reversibly erred. . . . [A]ppellants' argument that they complied with one potentially valid interpretation of the regulations does not speak to whether the Government made out a prima facie case of fraud. . . . Therefore, we find no error in the district court's denial of Appellants' motion to quash subpoenas.[73]

This broader view of the crime-fraud exception is much more consistent with the policies on which the attorney-client privilege is based. As the Supreme Court has noted: "The attorney-client privilege is not without its costs. Since the privilege has the effect of withholding relevant information from the factfinder, it applies only where necessary to achieve its purpose."[74] The scope of the attorney-client privilege, then, is not appropriately determined by technicalities but by considerations of substantive justice. Courts should not limit the exception to conduct that consists of statutorily or judicially defined elements of a particular crime or fraud. While such formal, legal notice of wrongful conduct is relevant to whether conduct can be held criminal, it plainly goes beyond what is required to achieve the purpose of the attorney-client privilege.

Evidentiary Standards

Another question that courts must confront in applying the crime-fraud exception is what evidentiary standards should be used. While courts have not adopted a single definitive procedure for making crime-fraud exception determinations, there appears to be a well-established consensus that the parties seeking discovery need only meet a burden of making out a prima facie case of the underlying crime or fraud. Several courts, however, have adopted a rule that requires parties to show by a preponderance of the evidence that the exception applies. The policies underlying the crime-fraud exception and the leading case law strongly suggest that the preponderance standard is the wrong rule and should not be followed.

In the federal courts, any consideration of the proper procedure for determining whether the crime-fraud exception applies must begin with *Zolin v. United States.*[75] Prior to the Supreme Court's opinion in *Zolin,* there was considerable controversy among the circuits about what evidence courts could consider in making a crime-fraud exception determination. The rule finally established in *Zolin* was clear: courts could consider "any relevant evidence, lawfully obtained, that has not been adjudicated to be privileged."[76] This, of course, includes the contested communications themselves, which are often the best evidence of their own true nature. Thus *Zolin* clearly established the propriety of in camera review of allegedly privileged communications.[77] Furthermore, the *Zolin* Court specified that the party contesting the claim of privilege "must present evidence sufficient to support a reasonable belief that in camera review may yield evidence that establishes the exception's applicability."[78] Once this showing is made, however, the contested communications themselves "may provide the evidentiary basis for the ultimate showing that the crime-fraud exception applies."[79] That is, the Court held that independent evidence of the crime or fraud was not required to apply the exception.

While *Zolin* established the requirement for obtaining in camera review of contested communications, it did not resolve the question of ultimate burden of proof, and different standards have emerged in the courts.[80] The most troubling of these standards holds that the party contesting the privilege must establish by a preponderance of the evidence that the crime-fraud exception applies. For example, in *Laser Industries, Ltd. v. Reliant Technologies, Inc.,* the district court recognized that the question of the burden of proof to be applied in making a crime-fraud exception determination "remains open."[81] The court, in a lengthy opinion that ruminates on the policies underlying the attorney-client privilege and the crime-fraud exception, held that in addition to the initial evidentiary showing described in *Zolin,* the party contesting the privilege should bear the ultimate burden of proof on the issue, that burden being a preponderance of the evidence.[82] This was the right decision, according to the court, for two reasons. First, placing the burden of proof on the alleged privilege holder would "impose unjustifiable burdens on courts," since shifting the burden of persuasion would make "the temptation to initiate such challenges . . . considerable."[83] Second, this latter rule would "jeopardize" the attorney-client privilege because "counsel might feel pressured to disclose considerable information about those communications and the circumstances in which they were made in order to reduce the likelihood that the court would not find their explanations satisfactory."[84]

The *Laser Industries* court is wrong on both points. First, it is not at all clear that parties who have a good-faith belief that the crime-fraud exception applies will not, even if they bear the ultimate burden of proof, move ahead with their prima facie showing and request for in camera inspection under *Zolin*—at the very least they would be bringing the issue to the court's attention. Second, far from jeopardizing the attorney-client privilege, placing the burden of persuasion on the alleged privilege holder ensures that the privilege is not abused. This is so for at least two reasons. First, the general rule is and always has been that the party claiming the privilege has the burden of proving its existence.[85] That burden should include persuading the court that, after an opponent has made a prima facie showing of crime or fraud, the attorney-client communications were not made for unlawful purposes. Second, from a truth-seeking perspective it is plainly more efficient to place the burden of persuasion on the alleged privilege-holder, since that party (1) has superior information on the nature of the communications and (2) is asking the court to prevent disclosure of relevant evidence precisely because of its nature. Finally, there is no merit to the *Laser Industries* court's concern that "counsel might feel pressured to disclose considerable information" about the communications: if the party seeking discovery can make the prima facie showing under *Zolin*, the alleged privilege holder is already required to disclose the most confidential information to the court—the statements themselves.

A better approach, and one much more consistent with the policies behind the attorney-client privilege and the crime-fraud exception, is the procedure used by the court in *Gutter v. E.I. DuPont de Nemours*.[86] In *Gutter*, a securities class action, the court held that the plaintiffs had established a prima facie case of fraud and then addressed the question of the appropriate burden of proof. After recognizing that "many courts have struggled with questions such as . . . the ultimate burden of proof,"[87] the court concluded that the appropriate procedure is as follows:

> [T]he party opposing the privilege on the crime-fraud exception has the initial burden of producing evidence which, if unexplained, would be *prima facie* proof of the existence of the exception. The burden of persuasion then shifts to the party asserting the privilege to give a reasonable explanation of its conduct.[88]

As discussed above, placing the burden of persuasion on the party claiming the privilege is more consistent with the truth-seeking function of the civil justice system. If the contested communications in *Gutter* really deserved the "seal of secrecy" of the attorney-client privilege, the defendants were clearly in the better position to so convince the court. Furthermore, as the *Gutter* court noted, the rule it adopted was "consistent with the general rule that the burden of proof to establish the existence of the attorney-client privilege rests on the party who claims the privilege."[89] In other words, the *Gutter* rule and not the rule in *Laser Industries* works to preserve the policy underlying the attorney-client privilege.

Building a Crime-Fraud Exception Argument in Mass Disaster Cases

As discussed above, the party seeking disclosure bears at least the burden of establishing a prima facie case that the crime-fraud exception applies. Because this entails demonstrating that communications or work product that have not even been disclosed were used for a particular purpose, the burden can be a difficult one, and the type of evidence that can be used is of particular interest. This is particularly so in the mass disaster context, where defendants' incentives to engage in cover-ups involving counsel, and to ensure that these cover-ups never come to light, are particularly high.

Perhaps the leading opinion on this issue is *In re A.H. Robins Co., Inc., "Dalkon Shield" IUD Products Liability Litigation.*[90] During the multidistrict litigation involving A.H. Robins's infamous intrauterine device, plaintiffs' counsel moved to compel production of five memoranda, known as the "Burke memoranda," that Robins claimed were protected by both the attorney-client privilege and the work-product doctrine. The "Burke memoranda" were drafted by Robins attorneys, addressed to regional and district managers and sales representatives, and signed by one of Robins's vice presidents and, in one case, its general counsel. Robins claimed that all five memoranda requested information needed by counsel to defend it in litigation. Plaintiffs' counsel argued that the crime-fraud exception should be applied to Robins's claims of attorney-client privilege and work-product doctrine protection. In writing the order ultimately compelling production, Judge Theis noted: "The focal issue is whether the record reflects sufficient evidence to invoke the crime or fraud exception. The Court does not offer any opinion as to the truth of the facts asserted in the pleadings. At this juncture, the Court is concerned solely with applying the known facts to the plaintiffs' burden of establishing only a prima facie showing of crime or fraud."[91] The court applied Kansas law on the crime-fraud exception, which did not allow using the contested documents themselves as evidence that the exception should apply. The court was thus concerned solely with independent evidence of crime or fraud.

Plaintiffs sought first to establish that Robins had engaged in the fraud of misrepresenting the safety of its products to consumers and second to establish that Robins had used its counsel in furtherance of that fraud. The single most comprehensive piece of evidence offered by the plaintiffs was the report issued by the Special Masters who had been appointed to monitor and assist with discovery in related Dalkon litigation in the District of Minnesota. The Masters had examined over 15,000 pages of documents that had been produced for in camera inspection. Over Robins's objections, Judge Theis took judicial notice of the report's conclusions, including the Masters' determination that Robins had knowingly misrepresented the safety of its product and that a prima facie case of fraud had been established. As to the involvement of Robins's counsel, the Masters reasoned as follows:

> Plaintiffs maintain that the ongoing scheme to misrepresent to the public the nature and efficacy of the Dalkon Shield was perpetuated in a cover-up phase at the direction of William A. Forest, Jr., Secretary and General Counsel. It is clear from the various depositions and exhibits that the legal department was closely involved in questions of labeling, marketing, product characteristics, and dealings with the FDA, as well as litigation about the Dalkon Shield. Thus, it is a reasonable inference that corporate counsel was aware of the facts giving rise to the ongoing fraudulent scheme discussed above.[92]

The second piece of evidence, relied upon both in the Masters' report and independently by Judge Theis, was Robins's conduct in other Dalkon Shield cases. The Masters, for example, pointed to the decision in *Harre v. A.H. Robins*, in which the Eleventh Circuit concluded that a Robins expert witness had committed perjury with the complicity of counsel.[93] The Masters stated, "We obviously do not rely on these decisions for our factual determinations in this matter, but they do tend to corroborate our finding of at least a prima facie case of a massive fraudulent scheme perpetrated on the public with the knowing assistance of members of the professional bar."[94] Similarly, Judge Theis concluded that:

> Although Robins complains about the use of other proceedings as evidence of crime or fraud in the instant case, the Court finds Robins procedural conduct in other cases to be relevant to the present motion. When the issue is whether Robins perpetrated a massive fraud to deceive the public, the cases across the country cannot be viewed as discrete and isolated instances.[95]

Accordingly, the court reviewed several cases from around the country in which plaintiffs had requested the same "secret" documents relating to Robins's testing of its product. The review revealed a pattern of settling cases to avoid production of the documents; engaging in stalling tactics, including motions for reconsideration, motions for stay pending appeal, and petitions for writ of mandamus; and of outright refusal to comply with orders for production. Judge Theis stated:

> While the Court recognizes that Robins has an absolute duty to protect its client's interests, and although the various steps of defense may appear innocuous in isolation, when viewed collectively and in tandem with the evidence contained in the Masters' Report, the repeated delays and instances of nonproduction provide support for the application of the crime or fraud exception.[96]

Proceedings in other cases thus formed a critical part of the plaintiffs' prima facie case that the crime-fraud exception should apply, and there is no doubt that they heavily if not decisively influenced Judge Theis's ruling. A favorable report by a Special Master is obviously good evidence to have in making out a case for applying the crime-fraud exception. Plaintiffs' counsel, however, should also be sure to monitor and record the relevant activity of defendants' attorneys in other cases. To that end, litigation groups could prove especially helpful in winning the crime-fraud exception argument in mass disaster cases.

Communications with Former Employees

Modern courts have generally forbidden attorneys from communicating with represented persons outside the presence of their counsel. An issue that has received recent attention is how this general rule applies in the context of ex parte contact with a corporation's former employees. The rule most courts apply to this issue is Rule 4.2 of the ABA Model Rules of Professional Conduct:

> In representing a client, a lawyer shall not communicate about the subject of the representation with a party the lawyer knows to be represented by another lawyer in the matter, unless the lawyer has the consent of the other lawyer or is authorized by law to do so. A lawyer shall not effect the prohibited communication through a third person, including the lawyer's client (emphasis supplied).[97]

As is readily apparent, Rule 4.2 was created to protect the attorney-client relationship and privileged information which stems therefrom.[98] Neither the rule nor the official comments to it, however, specifically address the question of ex parte contacts with former employees, and in fact a majority of courts have held that Rule 4.2 does not generally prohibit this type of contact. Where, however, privileged or otherwise confidential information is clearly implicated, courts have held that the rule bars ex parte contact with former employees. The extent to which such contact is barred, and the specific scenarios that trigger the bar, differ widely among the states.[99] Generally, typical scenarios in which ex parte contact would be barred include those in which the former employee had been in a managerial position or belonged to the control group during his employment; where the former employee had participated in the litigation or was otherwise exposed to relevant privileged or confidential information; or where the former employee's acts or omissions could be imputed to the organization for liability purposes.

One case that squarely addresses the issue of ex parte contacts with former employees and the application of Rule 4.2 is *In re Shell Oil Refinery*.[100] The case involved a plaintiff's attorney's ex parte contact with an employee of Shell. In addition to providing general information, the employee secreted proprietary documents from Shell and gave them to the attorney.

In issuing a protective order prohibiting the plaintiff's attorney from using documents obtained outside normal discovery channels and prohibiting further ex parte contact with this employee, the court noted the three categories of persons enumerated in the comment to Model Rule 4.2 that an attorney should treat as "parties" for the purpose of the rule:

1. persons with managerial responsibility;
2. any other person whose acts or omissions concerning the subject of the representation may be imputed to the organization for liability purposes; or,
3. whose statements may constitute admissions on the part of the organization.[101]

The court further stated that "[i]nformal interviews with employees of a corporate party can in certain circumstances be entirely appropriate. For example, under Rule 4.2 a low-level employee whose conduct or scope of employment was not involved in the disputed events could be interviewed ex parte by adverse counsel." The court noted that if the communication had merely been an interview with the employee, the question would focus on whether or not the communication was with a "party."

Subsequent to the order issued above, Shell discovered the name of the employee who had secreted the information and thus terminated his employment. The court then amended the order to prohibit any ex parte communication with the now ex-employee, stating that the order should apply to him regardless of his status because although he presumably no longer had access to Shell documents, he was still able to convey proprietary information to the attorney.

The *Shell Oil* court's amendment to its ex parte communication order is indicative of courts' concern with preventing "disclosure of privileged information by the former employee."[102] Courts generally reason that because "[a]ny privilege existing between the former employee and the organization's counsel belongs to the organization, [the privilege] can only be waived by the organization."[103] That is, the attorney-client privilege operates to prevent disclosure of privileged information by former employees, and courts prohibit ex parte contacts with former employees to serve that end.[104] Whether or not the former employee possesses privileged material, however, is dealt with on a case-by-case basis.[105] If there is no risk of inappropriate disclosure or if the former employee can longer bind the corporation, ex parte contact with the former employee should not be prohibited.

In *Wright by Wright v. Group Health Hospital*, for example, the Washington Supreme Court held that since the former employees could no longer bind the corporation, they were entirely outside the restrictions on ex parte contact imposed by the state's version of Model Rule 4.2.[106] In *Wright*, an injured child and his parents had sued a hospital and doctor, alleging that they committed malpractice in the mother's labor and delivery of the child. The family's lawyer asked for and received a list of nurses involved in caring for the mother, but counsel for the hospital advised the family's lawyer that he considered the nurses to be his clients and that the family's lawyer was to make no efforts to contact them. The family's lawyer disagreed and moved for a protective order confirming his right to conduct ex parte interviews of current and former employees as long as they were not managerial. Reversing a trial court order denying the motion, the Washington Supreme Court noted that the family's lawyer intended to interview nurses who, unlike the doctor, were not formally parties to the pending litigation, even though they were or had been employees of a party. The court observed that the issue presented a policy conflict between the need of the adverse attorney for information that might be in the corporation's exclusive possession but too expensive or impractical to obtain through formal discovery and the need of the corporation to protect itself. After reviewing a range of decisions on the topic, the court concluded that the best test was one that interpreted "party" to mean those employees with legal authority to speak for and bind the corporation. The court stated that, because former employees cannot possibly speak for a corporation, the general rule against ex parte contacts with represented parties did not apply to them.

Where the relevant concern for the organization is not that its former employees' statements can be imputed to it but rather the disclosure of information protected by the attorney-client privilege, courts have to balance the need for informal discovery in the civil justice system against the risk of violating the attorney-client privilege. In *G-I Holdings, Inc. v. Baron & Budd*, for example, the plaintiff, a holding company for former asbestos manufacturers, brought a civil RICO suit against a leading asbestos plaintiff's law firm.[107] The holding company hired investigators to conduct ex parte interviews with the law firm's current and former employees, including paralegals and word processors. The law firm sought a protective order from the court, claiming that the interviews threatened to invade the attorney-client privilege between the firm and its clients. The court noted that:

> It is consistent with time-honored and decision-honored principles that counsel for all parties have a right to interview an adverse party's witnesses (the witness willing) in private, without the presence or consent of opposing counsel and without a transcript being made. This principle applies to former employees of an adverse party. Indeed, *ex parte* interviews with such persons have been recognized as having an important role in information gathering in that former employees often have emotional or economic ties to their former employer and would sometimes be reluctant to come forward

with potentially damaging information if they could only do so in the presence of the corporation's attorney.[108]

The court thus recognized both the legitimacy and the importance of ex parte contacts with former employees. Nevertheless, the court also recognized the countervailing interests:

> However, former employees who possess knowledge regarding privileged communications do present a "distinct problem" where *ex parte* interviews are concerned. One aspect of this problem is that, where the former employee is a lay person, it is unrealistic to think that he will know what information or communications are privileged, so that even where disclosure of such matters is not intended it may well occur inadvertently.[109]

The court then balanced the hardships and concluded that a protective order was required. Two factors were particularly significant: the former employees had been "extensively" exposed to privileged information, and "the investigators are themselves lay persons and, thus, are in little better position than the interviewees to assess whether privileged material is being disclosed."[110] Finally, the court considered the appropriate nature and scope of the protective order. It concluded that the parties had a choice: (1) no ex parte interviews could take place, and instead notice would have to be given to the defendant law firm, so that its counsel could be present during the interviews; or (2) the interviews would take place before a special master, who would monitor the interviews with respect to the issue of privilege.[111] The *G-I Holdings* court thus gave adequate consideration to the concerns on both sides of the ex parte contacts dispute.

The opinion illustrates two important points that must be considered when conducting ex parte interviews. First, interviews conducted by lay persons such as investigators are likely to be seen as posing a greater threat to privileged communications than those conducted by counsel. Second, courts are not likely to find the use of form questions or form warnings during such interviews to be adequate protection of privileged communications, particularly when the former employees are lay people.[112] When ex parte interviews with former employees are necessary, attorneys should conduct the interviews themselves whenever possible. Furthermore, because former employees are often lay people, adequate precautions must be taken to protect privileged information. Rather than using form questions, counsel should identify easily discernible *topics* and determine whether discussion of these topics threatens the asserted privilege. If not, ex parte interviews limited to these topics are entirely appropriate.

Conclusion

In the landmark case of *United States v. Nixon*, the Supreme Court stated that "exceptions to the demand for every man's evidence are not lightly created nor expansively construed, for they are in derogation of the search for truth."[113] The attorney-client privilege and the work-product doctrine are two well-established exceptions to the demand for every man's evidence, exceptions considered essential to the proper functioning of our legal system. As our society changes, however, our legal system and the values that shape it change as well. Courts have reexamined the roles played by corporate attorneys; the propriety of keeping information generated through judicial proceedings secret; and the proper procedure for determining whether attorney-client communications occurred in furtherance of a crime or fraud. As this chapter has shown, courts have typically dealt with these issues by taking a purposive approach to the attorney-client privilege and the work-product doctrine. The conclusions they have reached indicate a trend toward greater disclosure and toward narrowing the exceptions to the demand for every man's evidence.

Notes

1. Stated another way, the emphasis is on avoiding trial by ambush. *E.g.,* Herbert v. Lando, 441 U.S. 153, 177 (1979) ("the deposition-discovery rules are to be accorded a broad and liberal treatment to effect their purpose of adequately informing the litigants in civil trials").

2. *See, e.g.,* D.M. Osborne, *The Sidley-Heineman Connection,* THE AMERICAN LAWYER (May 1990), discussed *infra.*

3. *See generally* Lance Cole, *Revoking Our Privileges: Federal Law Enforcement's Multi-Front Assault on the Attorney-Client Privilege (And Why It Is Misguided),* 48 VILL. L. REV. 469 (2003).

4. *See, e.g., Attorneys Face New Rules on Secrets,* CHRISTIAN SCIENCE MONITOR, Aug. 13, 2003, *available at* http://www.csmonitor.com/2003/0813/p02s01-usju.html.

5. 8 J. WIGMORE ON EVIDENCE, § 2298 at 5777 (McNaughton, rev. 1961) ("[I]t is difficult to see how . . . the law can protect a deliberate plan to defy the law and oust another person of his rights whatever the precise nature of those rights might be.").

6. Trammel v. United States, 445 U.S. 40, 44 (1980).

7. FED. R. EVID. 501.

8. 524 U.S. 399 (1998).

9. *See infra* discussion of the crime-fraud exception in Part IV.

10. *See, e.g.,* Trammel v. United States, 445 U.S. 40, 44 (1980) (discussing development of spousal privilege).

11. United States v. Munoz, 233 F.3d 1117, 1128 (9th Cir. 2000).

12. Rhone-Poulenc Rorer, Inc. v. Home Indemnity Co., 32 F.3d 851, 862 (3d Cir. 1994).

13. *Id.; see also* Advanced Tech. Assoc., Inc. v. Herley Indus., Inc., 1996 WL 711018, *5 (E.D. Pa. 1996); United States v. Kovel, 296 F.2d 918 (2d Cir. 1961) (communications to accountant that enabled attorney to prepare defense in tax fraud case were protected by privilege).

14. In contrast, if a communication is protected by the work-product doctrine it is not necessarily inadmissible, but rather is rendered generally undiscoverable. See *infra* discussion in § II.B.

15. Philadelphia v. Westinghouse Elec. Corp., 210 F. Supp. 483, 485 (E.D. Pa. 1962).

16. Upjohn v. United States, 449 U.S. 383 (1981).

17. Commodity Futures Trading Comm'n v. Weintraub, 471 U.S. 343, 348 (1985).

18. Union Pacific Ry. Co. v. Mower, 219 F.3d 1069, 1072 n.2 (9th Cir. 2000); *see also infra* discussion of communications with former employees in Part V.

19. Hearn v. Rhay, 68 F.R.D. 574, 581 (E.D. Wash. 1975).

20. *Id.*

21. Rhone-Poulenc Rorer Inc. v. Home Indemnity Co., 32 F.3d 851 (3d Cir. 1994) (requiring overt and explicit reliance on advice of counsel to trigger waiver).

22. Hickman v. Taylor, 329 U.S. 495 (1947).

23. FED. R. CIV. P. 26, Advisory Committee Notes, 1970 amend., *reprinted in* 48 F.R.D. 487, 501 (1970).

24. National Union Fire Ins. v. Murray Sheet Metal, 967 F.2d 980, 985 (4th Cir. 1992).

25. A main feature of the 1970 amendments to the Federal Rules of Civil Procedure was the inclusion of explicit regulations where disclosures of work product are involved. Rule 26(b)(3) provides that even though "documents and tangible things" may be "otherwise discoverable" in that they are "relevant to the subject matter," where they were "prepared in anticipation of litigation or for trial,"

then discovery may be obtained "only upon a showing that the party seeking discovery has substantial need of the materials in the preparation of the party's case and that the party is unable without undue hardship to obtain the substantial equivalent of the materials by other means." Rule 26(b)(3) eschews the phrase "work product" and uses somewhat different phraseology in its description of the showing that must be made to obtain discovery in this area. The rule extends its protection to the product of the preparation activities not only of the party but also to any representative of the party, such as "[the party's] attorney, consultant, surety, indemnitor, insurer, or agent."

26. *See* Binks Mfg. Co. v. National Presto Indus., Inc., 709 F.2d 1109, 1119 (7th Cir. 1983); *In re Leslie Fay Cos. Secs. Litig.*, 161 F.R.D. 274 (S.D.N.Y. 1995) (foreseeing litigation and conducting an internal investigation does not automatically qualify the investigative materials as work product), *citing* 8 CHARLES A. WRIGHT, ET AL., FEDERAL PRACTICE AND PROCEDURE § 2024 (2d ed. 1994).

27. *E.g., Kanner, Superfund and the Future of Toxic Tort Litigation*, 2 TXLR 671 (Nov. 11, 1987).

28. *E.g., National Union Fire Ins. Co. v. Murray Sheet Metal Co.*, 967 F.2d 980, 984 (4th Cir. 1992); *see also* Burden-Meeks v. Welch, 319 F.3d 897, 899 (7th Cir. 2003) ("Federal law extends the privilege to communications about legal subjects, and it is hard to see why a business evaluation meets that description. Hiring lawyers to do consultants' work does not bring a privilege into play.").

29. Moran v. Pittsburgh-Des Moines Steel Co., 6 F.R.D. 594 (D.C. Pa. 1947).

30. *Id.*

31. *Id.* at 596.

32. *See* FED. R. CIV. PROC. 26(b)(4); *see also In re* United Telecommunications, Inc., 151 F.R.D. 127 (D. Kan. 1993); American Bankers Insurance Co. v. Colorado Flying Academy, 97 F.R.D. 515, 517 (D. Colo. 1983); Fine v. Bellefonte Underwriters Insurance Company, 91 F.R.D. 420, 423 (S.D.N.Y. 1981); APL Corp. v. Aetna Casualty & Surety Co., 91 F.R.D. 10, 13 (D. Md. 1980).

33. *See* Hickman v. Taylor, 329 U.S. 495, 508-09 (1947). To some extent, counsel on both sides must have an appreciation of an organization's business, including applicable regulations and regulatory schemes, in order to deal effectively with work-product concerns.

34. *See* United States v. Davis, *infra*.

35. 449 U.S. 383 (1981).

36. AMERICAN LAWYER (May 1990).

37. *Id.*

38. United States v. Lipshy, 492 F. Supp. 35 (N.D. Tex. 1979).

39. *Id.*

40. SCM Corp. v. Xerox Corp., 70 F.R.D. 508 (D. Ct. 1976).

41. *Id.* at 517. *See also* United States v. Davis, *supra* (The mere fact that business advice is given or solicited does not automatically render the privilege lost; where the advice is prominently legal as opposed to business in nature, the privilege will still attach.).

42. *Id.* (citations omitted).

43. Ohio-Sealy Mattress Co. v. Sealy, Inc., No. 8853, slip op. (Del. Ch. 1987).

44. Diversified Indus., Inc. v. Meredith, 572 F.2d 596 (8th Cir. 1978) (en banc).

45. *Id.* at 610.

46. *Id.* at 609.

47. *Id.* at 610.

48. *Id.*

49. *Id.* at 615.

50. *See, e.g.*, United States v. Nixon, 418 U.S. 683, 710 (1974) ("[E]xceptions to the demand for every man's evidence are not lightly created nor expansively construed, for they are in derogation of the search for truth."); Littlejohn v. Bic Corp., 851 F.2d 673 (newspaper's "motions for intervention and access were based, in part, on the public's common law right of access to judicial proceedings and records. The existence of such a right is beyond dispute.").

51. 23 F.3d 772 (3d Cir. 1994).

52. *Id.* at 785-86.

53. E.E.O.C. v. National Children's Center, Inc., 146 F.3d 1042, 1045 (D.C. Cir. 1998).

54. *Id.*; *see also* Ford v. City of Huntsville, 242 F.3d 235 (5th Cir. 2001) (district court abused its discretion in entering confidentiality order without adequately identifying compelling reason for it).

55. *See generally ABA Section of Business Law eSource* (August 2003), *available at* http://www.abanet.org/buslaw/newsletter/0015/.

56. See *infra* discussion of the crime-fraud exception to the attorney-client privilege, which holds that otherwise privileged communications are not protected if they are meant to further future or ongoing criminal or fraudulent conduct, including other wrongful conduct such as intentional torts.

57. *See generally* Ronald Motley & Tucker Player, *Issues in "Crime-Fraud" Practice and Procedure: The Tobacco Litigation Experience*, 49 S.C. L. REV. 187 (1998); *and* Christine Hatfield, Comment, *The Privilege Doctrines—Are They Just Another Discovery Tool Utilized by the Tobacco Industry to Conceal Damaging Information?*, 16 PACE L. REV. 525 (1996).

58. *See* MODEL RULES OF PROF'L CONDUCT 1.13 & 1.6 (as amended).

59. Upjohn Co. v. United States, 449 U.S. 383, 389 (1981).

60. 8 WIGMORE ON EVIDENCE § 2298 (John T. McNaughton, rev. 1961).

61. The same rationale applies to the work-product doctrine. *See, e.g.*, *In re* International Sys. & Controls Corp. Sec. Litig., 693 F.2d 1235, 1242 (5th Cir. 1982).

62. United States v. Zolin, 491 U.S. 554, 563 (1989) (citations omitted).

63. *In re* Grand Jury Subpoena, 223 F.3d 213, 217 (3d Cir. 2000); *In re* Sealed Case, 754 F.2d 395, 399 (D.C. Cir. 1985).

64. Zolin v. United States, 491 U.S. 554, 562 (1989).

65. United States v. Jacobs, 117 F.3d 82, 88 (2d Cir. 1997).

66. *In re* Sealed Case, 754 F.2d 395, 399 (D.C. Cir.1985); *In re* John Doe Corp., 675 F.2d 482, 491 (2d Cir. 1982).

67. *In re* BankAmerica Corp. Sec. Litig., 270 F.3d 639, 642 (8th Cir. 2001); United States v. Chen, 99 F.3d 1495, 1504 (9th Cir. 1996); *In re* Grand Jury Proceedings v. (Under Seal), 102 F.3d 748, 750-51 (4th Cir. 1996); *In re* Grand Jury Proceedings, 680 F.2d 1026, 1028 (5th Cir. 1982).

68. *See, e.g.*, Union Carbide Corp. v. Dow Chem. Co., 619 F. Supp. 1036, 1051 (D. Del. 1985); Research Corp. v. Gourmet's Delight Mushroom Co., 560 F. Supp. 811, 820 (E.D. Pa. 1983).

69. Laser Indus., Ltd. v. Reliant Techs., Inc., 167 F.R.D. 417, 423 (N.D. Cal. 1996).

70. *See, e.g.*, Sandberg v. Virginia Bankshares, Inc., 979 F.2d 332, 353-54 (4th Cir. 1992) (finding that "improprieties, breaches of fiduciary duties, and violations of securities laws" are sufficient to deny application of the attorney-client privilege); *In re* Sealed Case, 754 F.2d 395, 399 (D.C. Cir. 1985) (extending the exception to "crime, fraud or other misconduct"); Cooksey v. Hilton Int'l Co., 863 F. Supp. 150, 151 (S.D.N.Y. 1994) (applying the exception to "intentional torts moored in fraud"); Volcanic Gardens Mgmt. Co. v. Paxson, 847 S.W.2d 343, 347 (Tex. Ct. App. 1993) (refusing to limit the application of the exception only in cases of common law or criminal fraud); *In re* Callan, 300 A.2d 868, 877 (N.J. Super. Ct. Ch. Div. 1973).

71. *In re* Grand Jury Subpoena, 220 F.3d 406 (5th Cir. 2000).

72. *Id.* at 410.

73. *Id.*

74. United States v. Zolin, 491 U.S. 554, 562 (1989) (citations omitted).

75. *Id.*

76. *Id.* at 575.

77. *See, e.g.*, *In re* BankAmerica Corp. Sec. Litig., 270 F.3d 639, 644 (8th Cir. 2001) ("We have found no case in which this court affirmed an order to produce documents under the crime-fraud exception where the district court did not first review the documents in camera.").

78. 491 U.S. at 574-75.

79. *Id.* at 574 n.12.

80. *See, e.g.*, United States v. Jacobs, 117 F.3d 82, 87 (2d Cir. 1997) (parties must "demonstrate that there is a factual basis for a showing of probable cause to believe that crime or fraud has been

committed and that the communications in question were in furtherance of the fraud or crime," after which decision regarding exception is left to discretion of the trial court); *In re* Sealed Case, 107 F.3d 46, 50 (D.C. Cir. 1997) (party "offers evidence that if believed by the trier of fact would establish the elements of an ongoing or imminent crime or fraud," then decision is left to trial court's discretion); United States v. Martin, 278 F.3d 988, 1001 (9th Cir. 2001) (parties "must present the district court with sufficient evidence to make its prima facie case . . . [and] must persuade the court to find that the communications with the lawyer were in furtherance of an intended or present illegality and that there is some relationship between the communications and the illegality").

81.   167 F.R.D 417, 432 (N.D. Cal. 1996).

82.   *Id.* at 433.

83.   *Id.*

84.   *Id.*

85.   *See* United States v. Rodriguez, 948 F.2d 914, 916 (5th Cir. 1991).

86.   124 F. Supp. 2d 1291 (S.D. Fla. 2000).

87.   *Id.* at 1305. The court cited as an example but did not discuss *Laser Industries.*

88.   *Id.* at 1307.

89.   *Id.*

90.   107 F.R.D. 2 (D. Kan. 1985).

91.   *Id.* at *9.

92.   *Id.* at *11.

93.   *See* 750 F.2d 1501 (11th Cir. 1985).

94.   107 F.R.D. at *11.

95.   *Id.* at 13.

96.   *Id.* at *14.

97.   Most states have adopted the Model Rule or the functional equivalent. *See generally* Benjamin J. Vernia, *Right of Attorney to Conduct* Ex parte *Interviews with Former Corporate Employees*, 57 A.L.R. 5th 633 (1998).

98.   Dubois v. Gradco Systems, Inc., 136 F.R.D. 341, 344 (D. Conn. 1991), *citing* G. HAZARD & W. HODES, THE LAW OF LAWYERING: A HANDBOOK ON THE MODEL RULES OF PROFESSIONAL CONDUCT 436 (1988 Supp.).

99.   *See* Benjamin J. Vernia, *Right of Attorney to Conduct* Ex parte *Interviews with Former Corporate Employees*, 57 A.L.R. 5th 633 §§ 3 & 5 (1998).

100.   143 F.R.D. 105 (E.D. La. 1992).

101.   Comment to MODEL RULES OF PROF'L CONDUCT R. 4.2.

102.   Cram v. Lamson & Sessions Co. Carlon Div., 148 F.R.D. 259, 261 (S.D. Iowa 1993); Polycast Technology Corp. v. Uniroyal, Inc., 129 F.R.D. 621 (S.D.N.Y. 1990).

103.   Sequa Corp. v. Lititech, Inc., 807 F. Supp. 653, 668 (D. Colo. 1992); *Cram,* 148 F.R.D. at 266.

104.   Valassis v. Samelson, 143 F.R.D. 118, 124 (E.D. Mich. 1992).

105.   *Polycast,* F.R.D. at 628; Browning v. AT&T Paradyne, 838 F. Supp. 1564, 1567 (M.D. Fla. 1993).

106.   691 P.2d 564 (Wash. 1984).

107.   199 F.R.D. 529 (S.D.N.Y. 2001).

108.   *Id.* at 533, *citing* Polycast Technology Corp. v. Uniroyal, Inc., 129 F.R.D. 621 (S.D.N.Y. 1990).

109.   *Id.*

110.   *Id.* at 535.

111.   *Id.* at 536.

112.   *See, e.g.*, Benjamin J. Vernia, *Right of Attorney to Conduct* Ex parte *Interviews with Former Corporate Employees*, 57 A.L.R. 5th 633 (1998) (suggesting that attorneys should "establish a script of statements and questions to be followed in all initial contacts with former employees").

113.   United States v. Nixon, 418 U.S. 683, 710 (1974)

CHAPTER 20

The Joint Defense Privilege:
An Illusion or a Magic Wand?

JEFFERY J. CARLSON

Introduction

The plaintiff in a toxic tort action often brings suit against several parties, and accordingly the defendants should examine the benefits of entering into a joint defense or cost-sharing agreement. Besides the obvious cost savings and strategic advantages of undertaking some form of coordinated defense, the joint defense arrangement may also minimize the potential for friction and discord among defendants (which often plays a major role in assisting the plaintiff in establishing his case) and may serve to discourage piecemeal settlements (which helps to finance the plaintiff's action against the remaining defendants). These cost-sharing arrangements may range from the engagement of a single defense counsel for all purposes to the establishment of a defense committee, which assigns the lead role on particular projects to a particular defendant or defendants. While the extent to which a joint or coordinated defense is feasible will depend on the facts in each case, it is important to recognize that such arrangements can offer significant benefits and advantages to all parties and can offer flexibility in the process.

Courts have generally recognized the "joint defense" or "common interest" doctrine in applying the attorney-client privilege and work-product doctrine to multi-defendant cases.[1] Under the "joint defense" or "common interest" doctrine, a privilege is not waived upon disclosure to a third party where the third party "shares a common interest with the disclosing party which is adverse to that of the party seeking discovery."[2] However, the determination of a privilege in a toxic tort litigation case, as in any case, is made on a case-by-case basis; therefore, it is important to understand exactly what each privilege seeks to protect before attempting to predict whether a specific communication will be afforded protection.

Basic Overview of the Attorney-Client and Work-Product Privileges

Attorney-Client Privilege

In federal cases, there is no uniform federal standard defining the attorney-client privilege; therefore, the law of the forum state applies.[3]

The attorney-client privilege exists to protect confidential communications between a client and his attorney—in effect, to protect the attorney-client relationship. Its purpose is to protect not only the giving of professional advice to those who can act upon it,[4] but also the giving of information to the lawyer to enable him to give sound advice.[5] In general, "the underlying rationale for the attorney-client privilege is to encourage free communication between client and attorney."[6] At the insistence of the client, these communications are permanently protected.[7]

Work-Product Privilege

In federal courts, the work-product privilege, unlike the attorney-client privilege, is governed by the uniform federal standard embodied in Federal Rule of Civil Procedure 26(b)(3). Rule 26(b)(3) provides, in part, that:

> [A] party may obtain discovery of documents and tangible things otherwise discoverable . . . and prepared in anticipation of litigation or for trial by or for another party or by or for that other party's representative . . . only upon a showing that the party seeking discovery has substantial need of the materials in the preparation of the party's case and that the party is unable without undue hardship to obtain the substantial equivalent of the materials by other means. In ordering discovery of such materials when the required showing has been made, the court shall protect against disclosure of the mental impressions, conclusions, opinions, or legal theories of an attorney or other representative of a party concerning the litigation.[8]

The application of the work-product doctrine to specific documents is guided by the seminal case of *Hickman v. Taylor*.[9] In *Hickman,* the Supreme Court undertook the difficult task of reconciling the competing interests of liberalized discovery and the privacy of an attorney's files. The court recognized that an attorney, engaged in the representation of his client, must be allowed a certain degree of privacy so as to be able to discharge his duties to his client responsibly and effectively. To this end, the Supreme Court stated that an attorney's "proper preparation of a client's case demands that he assemble information, sift what he considers to be the relevant from the irrelevant facts, prepare his legal theories and plan his strategy without undue and needless interference."[10]

Since *Hickman,* courts have made a distinction between "ordinary" work product and "opinion" work product. Generally, courts have described "ordinary" work product as those facts and materials gathered by counsel during an investigation of a matter, whereas "opinion" work product consists of the mental impressions and thought process employed by counsel in formulating strategy.[11]

There is a split among the federal courts as to when, if ever, opinion work product may be produced. The leading case denying all discovery of opinion work product is *Duplan Corp. v. Moulinage et Retorderie de Chavanoz.*[12] In *Duplan,* the Fourth Circuit reasoned that "no showing of relevance, substantial need or undue hardship should justify compelling disclosure of an attorney's mental impressions, conclusions, opinions or legal theories. This is made clear by the rule's use of the term 'shall' as opposed to 'may.'"[13] *Accord Board of Trustees v. Coulter Corp.,* 118 F.R.D. 532 (S.D. Fla. 1987).

Other courts, however, take the position that a party seeking opinion work product must make a showing beyond the substantial need/undue hardship test enunciated in Federal Rule of Civil Procedure 26(b)(3).[14] Cases requiring a heightened showing, beyond the substantial need/undue hardship test, reason that an ad hoc denial of discovery of all opinion work product ignores the advisory committee notes to the 1970 amendment to Rule 26(b)(3), which state that the rule "conform[s] to the holdings of the cases, when viewed in light of their facts. In *Hickman,* the Court stated that 'if there should be a rare situation justifying production of [work-product], petitioner's case is not of that type.'"[15] So far, the Supreme Court has declined to decide whether "opinion" work product is absolutely protected from discovery.[16]

The Applicability of the Attorney-Client Privilege and the Work-Product Privilege in the Context of a Joint Defense Arrangement

Attorney-Client Privilege

Issues involving the attorney-client and work-product privilege naturally arise out of the use of shared counsel. In this respect, the question becomes whether the otherwise applicable privilege is waived as a consequence of disclosure either to a common attorney or to counsel for co-defendants.

It is long settled in all American jurisdictions that where two or more parties employ a lawyer as their common counsel, communications to that attorney are confidential and privileged as against all common adversaries.[17]

Where the defendants choose to have their independent counsel work together in a shared defense arrangement, information passed between them is privileged to the extent that it is part of an ongoing and joint effort to set up a common defense strategy. In a joint defense arrangement, the attorney-client privilege protects communications by a client to his own lawyer, even though the lawyer may subsequently share that information with co-defendants.[18]

Similarly, the attorney-client privilege protects information communicated by a client to counsel for co-defendants.[19] In *Eisenberg v. Gagnon,*[20] the three different defendants were represented by three different law firms but were undertaking the coordination of a joint defense. A principal of one of the defendants corresponded with one of the other defendants' lawyer regarding information that one of the other defendants knew and should have disclosed and the trial strategy that the defendant should adopt in connection therewith. The court held that this communication was protected by the attorney-client privilege, reasoning that the shared information was at best viewed as part of an ongoing and joint effort to set up a common defense strategy between a defendant and the attorney responsible for coordinating a common defense position. The court determined that communications to an attorney to establish a common defense strategy are privileged, even though the attorney represents a different client who may have some adverse interests.[21]

Generally, to establish the joint defense privilege, courts require the parties to demonstrate that the communications (1) were intended to be kept confidential, (2) were made in the pursuit of a joint legal effort, and (3) were intended to advance a common interest.[22]

It must also be noted that the terms "joint defense privilege" and "common interest doctrine" have been used interchangeably. On the one hand, it has been stated that:

> Where the third party shares a common interest with the disclosing party which is adverse to the party seeking discovery, any existing privilege is not waived. This is known as the common interest or joint defense doctrine.[23]

Conversely, other courts have distinguished between the two terms; the joint defense privilege has been described as "protect[ing] communications between two or more parties and their respective counsel if they are engaged in a joint defense effort."[24] In contrast, the common interest doctrine "protects communications between a lawyer and two or more clients regarding a matter of common interest."[25] However, review of the cases discussing these terms shows the distinctions are more form than substance; both describe the same concept of maintaining the attorney-client privilege in a joint defense situation.

A thorough analysis and application of the joint defense privilege was seen in the Eighth Circuit case *John Morrell & Co. v. Local Union 304A.*[26] In *Morrell,* unions representing workers at the plaintiff's meat-packing plant in South Dakota had a judgment entered against them following an illegal strike by the union's members at the plant. On appeal, the union contended the trial court erred in finding that an internal memorandum written by the plaintiff's general counsel, which came into the union's possession due to another pending lawsuit, was protected by the attorney-client joint defense privilege. Prior to the matter at issue, a group of employees at Morrell's Iowa plant brought an action against Morrell and a union involved in the instant appeal regarding the Iowa plant's closing. The union cross-complained against Morrell. Morrell reached a settlement with the workers and entered into a joint defense agreement with the workers, allowing them access to privileged Morrell documents for use in their case against the union. These privileged documents came into the union's hands when the employees' expert witness inadvertently produced them at his deposition. The union later sought to use these documents in defending the *Morrell v. Local Union 304A* action regarding the illegal strike in South Dakota. The district court barred the use of the documents obtained by the union, citing the attorney-client privilege.

The Eighth Circuit affirmed. The court held that in the previous case (regarding the Iowa plant's closure), "[t]he . . . employees and Morrell shared a joint defense privilege by virtue of being aligned on the same side following their settlement and the international union's cross-claims."[27] In finding the joint defense privilege applicable, the court reasoned that "when information is exchanged between various co-defendants and their attorneys, . . . this exchange is not made for the purpose of allowing unlimited publication and use, but rather, the exchange is made for the limited purpose of assisting in their common cause."[28] Finding no waiver by the previous inadvertent production of the document, the court found that the joint defense privilege was a bar to the document's introduction.[29]

Work-Product Privilege

It is stated that information shared among defendants participating in a joint-defense arrangement "operates only within narrow confines . . . the principal restriction is that the material in question must have been prepared in anticipation of litigation."[30] The determination of whether documents were prepared in anticipation of litigation is clearly a factual determination.[31] Many courts use the imminence of litigation as a measuring stick for determining whether the documents were actually prepared in anticipation of litigation. The cases are not entirely clear as to how imminent the litigation must be, or whether it must be imminent at all, in order for the privilege to apply. One aspect which is clear in determining the imminence of litigation, and thus whether the documents were prepared "in anticipation of litigation," is that in multiparty situations that arise in the context of toxic tort litigation, the courts usually require some sort of nexus between consultations with lawyers and "representation and possible subsequent proceedings."[32]

A question that will often arise in toxic tort litigation is whether documents that have been afforded the work-product privilege in a previous case continue to be protected by that privilege beyond the termination of the litigation. The split of authority among the courts in this area is clear.[33] Three divergent views have been followed by the courts. Some courts adhere to the view that the work-product privilege applies only if the materials were prepared in anticipation of the present litigation before the court. Thus, documents prepared for one case are freely discoverable in a subsequent case.[34]

At the other extreme, some courts have held that "what is needed, if we are to remain faithful to the articulated policies of *Hickman,* is a perpetual protection for work product, one that extends beyond the termination of the litigation for which the documents were prepared."[35]

Finding neither of these extreme options useful, some courts have taken a third, intermediate approach under which the extension of the work-product privilege from one case to a subsequent case depends upon "whether the first action was complete, and upon the relationship between the first and second actions."[36] Following this approach, a substantial body of federal case law supports the conclusion that the work-product privilege extends to subsequent cases only when those cases are related.[37]

Waiver

Both the attorney-client and work-product privileges may be deemed waived upon the disclosure of relevant information to third parties, on the theory that disclosure is incompatible with keeping information privileged. However, in the context of a joint defense arrangement, there should be no waiver where the information is passed to a third party who shares a common interest in the litigation. A substantial amount of case law establishes that attorneys aligned in a joint defense posture "may exchange privileged communications and attorney work-product in order to prepare a common defense without waiving either privilege."[38]

Attorney-Client Privilege

As stated, there is no waiver of the attorney-client privilege where the client or client's attorney discloses information to counsel for co-defendants when a joint defense has been undertaken.[39] In this scenario, in order to preserve the attorney-client privilege, an attorney must be careful to share only that information which relates to issues presented in the common defense. When such information is shared among joint defense counsel, it can be inferred that the disclosure was made under the expectation that the communication was confidential and shall remain private. Thus, the information retains its privileged nature because it has remained within the confidential relationship developed and shared by the parties with a common interest in the litigation. It may also be inferred that those parties with common interests on a particular issue against a common adversary share information for the limited and restricted purpose of assisting in asserting their common claims. As such, the transferee is not at all likely to disclose the information to the adversary.[40] In sum, the joint defense privilege is meant to recognize "the advantages of, and even the necessity for, an exchange or pooling of information between attorneys representing parties sharing such a common interest in litigation, actual or prospective."[41]

It bears repeating that in order for the applicable joint defense privileges to remain viable, the information must only be shared among those parties sharing a common interest in the litigation; the joint defense privilege may be waived where privileged communications are disclosed to third parties. The analysis usually hinges on whether the disclosure was inadvertent or knowing.[42] Three distinct lines of authority have arisen in determining whether a disclosed privileged communication to a third party waives the joint defense privilege.[43]

The first position taken by the courts on this issue would automatically waive any applicable joint defense privilege upon *any* disclosure of privileged information. To this end, it has been stated that "[t]he rule in this circuit is plain. Disclosure of otherwise privileged material, even where disclosure was inadvertent, serves as a waiver of the privilege."[44] A second view would preclude waiver of a joint defense privilege following the inadvertent production of otherwise privileged material during the course of discovery. This view is grounded on the theory that waiver of a privilege may only occur if the holder of the privilege has knowingly sanctioned the waiver. On this point, it has been stated that "we are taught from first-year law school that waiver imports the 'intentional relinquishment or abandonment of a known right'. . . [i]nadvertent production is the antithesis of that concept."[45]

A third position followed by various courts in determining whether waiver of a privilege has taken place through inadvertent production of privileged documents recognizes the burdens of discovery and realizes that an unintended error in some instances may waive a privilege. Courts following this intermediate approach often take into account a number of factors to determine whether waiver has taken place. Often, the decision regarding whether waiver has taken place turns on the precautions taken by the disclosing party to prevent the disclosure, the number of privileged documents which have been disclosed, the extent of the disclosure, the promptness of measures taken to rectify the disclosure, and whether the interests of justice would be served in finding a waiver of the privilege.[46]

At least one court has taken the position that the determination of inadvertent versus knowing disclosure of privileged material, and the resulting question of waiver, may be avoided by entering into a pre-discovery order. It has been suggested that in a document-intensive case, the parties may enter into a pre-discovery order stating that unintended disclosure of privileged material will not operate as a waiver of any privilege. Under such facts, the Ninth Circuit concluded that it was "obvious" no such waiver had occurred after the parties had entered into, and the court had approved, such an order.[47]

It has also been held that "the joint defense privilege cannot be waived without the consent of all parties to the defense, except in the situation where one of the joint defendants becomes an adverse party in litigation."[48] For example, the Fifth Circuit in *Wilson P. Abraham Constr. Corp. v. Armco Steel Corp.*[49] held that where information is exchanged between co-defendants and attorneys in a joint defense setting, "this exchange is not made for the purpose of allowing unlimited publication and use, but rather, the exchange is made for the limited purpose of assisting in their common cause. In such a situation, an attorney who is the recipient of such information breaches his fiduciary duty if he later, in his representation of another client, is able to use this information to the detriment of one of the co-defendants."[50]

Similarly, it has been held that a subsidiary could not later waive a joint defense privilege without the consent of its former parent.[51]

Many courts take the position that the joint defense privilege is waived if the co-defendants later litigate against each other.[52] The justification for this rule was discussed in *In re Matter of Grand Jury Subpoena Duces Tecum,* wherein the court stated that once the co-defendants take action against each other, neither "can reasonably be allowed to deny to the other the use of information which he already has by virtue of the former's known disclosure."[53] Under the joint defense privilege, communications between co-defendants are only privileged as to third parties. Once co-defendants reposition themselves to take action against each other, there is a restructuring of the parties' rights to make their interests adverse and any information exchanged between them in a previous litigation no longer privileged. This rule can prove to be very damaging in a toxic tort case where a joint defense has been undertaken and one or several co-defendants subsequently take action against each other in the form of indemnity claims and the like. For this reason, this waiver rule should always be considered when drafting a joint defense agreement, and the necessary precautions should be taken in the form of a confidentiality clause. Without this limitation, a joint defense would become impractical, as no defendant would be protected against a co-defendant trading a waiver in order to obtain a separate settlement.[54]

Work-Product Privilege

Similarly, the work-product privilege is not considered waived where counsel presenting a joint defense share information relating to their common interests.[55] Again, the scope of the work-product privilege is defined by the purpose of the privilege itself: to promote the adversarial system by safeguarding the fruits of an attorney's trial preparation from the discovery attempts of his opponent.[56] The rationale behind the privilege is that information is to be protected against opposing parties, rather than against all others outside a particular confidential relationship. Thus, communications in the joint defense scenario will lose their work-product protection only to the extent that the information is either unrelated to the common interests of the parties or is transferred to someone outside of the confidential relationship, thereby waiving the privilege.

In *D'Ippolito v. Cities Service Co.*,[57] the plaintiff in a private suit raised the work-product privilege to prevent disclosure of an exhibit, but conceded that he had voluntarily disclosed the exhibit to attorneys in the antitrust division of the Department of Justice. Observing that the government was not a party to the lawsuit, the court found that "the disclosure of the document cannot be termed as an interchange of information between counsel on the same side of the litigation."[58] Consequently, the court held the privilege to be waived. This holding illustrates a narrow interpretation of "common interest," which limits it to co-parties.

In contrast to *D'Ippolito,* a subsequent case by the same court (the Southern District of New York) held the work-product privilege was not waived by disclosure of trial preparation documents by a private antitrust plaintiff to the government. The court in *G.A.F. Corp. v. Eastman Kodak Co.*[59] found that despite voluntary disclosure of the subject documents to persons not on the same side of the litigation, the privilege remained intact. Rejecting the standard announced by the court *in D'Ippolito,* the court held that waiver would occur, if at all, only if the disclosure "substantially increased" the possibility of an opposing party obtaining the information.[60] Since the disclosure in *G.A.F.* had occurred under a statutory guarantee of confidentiality on the part of the government, the court held the conditions of waiver were not satisfied.

In settling the issue for the Second Circuit, the appellate court declined to adopt a "per se" rule regarding whether all voluntary disclosures to the government operate to waive the protections of the work-product rule. *In re Steinhardt Partners, L.P.*[61] followed widely publicized allegations of wrongdoing in the market for treasury notes during 1991. Following these allegations, the Securities and Exchange Commission began an informal investigation of Steinhardt Partners and others. As part of the investigation, the SEC's enforcement division requested that Steinhardt's counsel prepare a memoranda addressing various legal issues arising during the investigation. Steinhardt prepared the memo and submitted it to the SEC, requesting that it remain confidential.

Following these events, various civil suits were initiated by private parties against Steinhardt and others, alleging manipulations of the treasury note markets. During discovery, plaintiffs requested all documents previously produced by Steinhardt to any investigating government agency. Steinhardt identified the memo it had drafted for the SEC, but declined to provide it, citing work-product protection. The district court granted plaintiffs' motion to compel. Steinhardt appealed for a writ of mandamus. The Second Circuit denied the writ, reasoning that "[o]nce a party allows an adversary to share the otherwise privileged thought processes of counsel, the need for the privilege disappears."[62] The court further held that a client cannot be permitted to pick and choose among third parties for whom the work-product protection is waived and to whom it applies.[63] However, the Second Circuit took pains to emphasize that the ruling declined to adopt a per se rule that all voluntary disclosures to the government waive work-product protection, choosing instead to declare that "[c]rafting rules relating to privilege in matters of government investigations must be done on a case-by-case basis."[64]

In still another case, the court in *United States v. American Tel. & Tel. Co.*[65] adopted the *G.A.F.* standard of waiver, reasoning that the purpose of the work-product privilege is to protect information from opponents—not necessarily all other parties. In this light, the court held that "[a] disclosure made in the pursuit of such trial preparation, and not inconsistent with maintaining secrecy against opponents, should be allowed without waiver of the privilege."[66]

The court recognized that the existence of common interests between a transferor and transferee is relevant to deciding whether the disclosure is consistent with the nature of the work-product privilege. However, the court explained that while the *G.A.F.* standard should not be read so broadly as to allow confidential disclosure to *any* person without waiver of the work-product privilege, at the same time the existence of "common interests" should not be interpreted as narrowly limiting the privilege to co-parties. The court thus laid down a new standard in defining the boundaries of the work-product privilege: as long as the transferor and the transferee anticipate litigation against a common adversary on the same issue or issues, they have strong common interests in sharing the fruits of their trial preparation efforts.[67]

United States v. American Tel. & Tel. Co. expanded the circle within which information retains its work-product protection. Not only did the court broaden the definition of "common interests," but it also recognized an expansive definition of the type of document afforded the work-product privilege. The court held that documents can come within this privilege if they were prepared in anticipation of litigation, or for trial by or for another party, or by or for that other party's representative (including his attorney, consultant, surety, indemnitor, insurer or agent).[68] Thus, documents prepared by the attorneys for the intervenor specifically in anticipation of litigation in a previous case were protected against discovery in the present case.

The Use of a Confidential Clause as a Precautionary Measure

As a precautionary measure, attorneys participating in a shared joint defense arrangement should always consider including a confidentiality clause in the joint defense contract. The inclusion of such a clause may serve to bolster the claim of privilege. When the transfer of information to parties with common interests is conducted under a guarantee of confidentiality, the case against waiver is strengthened.[69] This is so, another court reasoned, because common interests may be seen among parties having the strong incentive "in sharing the fruit of trial preparation efforts."[70] As such, having a signed non-disclosure waiver was described by the court as "a guarantee of confidentiality."[71]

The Crime-Fraud Exception

Despite the otherwise rigid protection accorded privileged materials, the immunity granted these documents may be waived by a showing that the documents claimed to be protected under the attorney-client or work-product privileges were prepared in furtherance of a crime or fraud.[72] To this end, it is stated that "[the] privilege serves the purpose of promoting broader public interests in the observance of law and administration of justice. However, it is not an absolute privilege. It applies only where necessary to achieve its purpose and protects only those communications necessary to obtain legal advice."[73]

Generally speaking, documents will lose their privileged nature where the attorney has been used in his professional capacity to facilitate or promote criminal activity.[74] This "crime-fraud" exception to the attorney-client and work-product privileges applies even where the attorney is unaware that his advice is sought to further an illegal purpose.[75] As cogently stated by the Sixth Circuit, "All reasons for the attorney-client privilege are completely eviscerated when a client consults an attorney not for advice on past misconduct, but for legal assistance in carrying out a contemplated or ongoing crime or fraud."[76]

Issues Concerning Insurance Coverage Groups

The Privileged Nature of Communications Shared with Insurer

In environmental and toxic tort litigation cases, insurers are usually always involved in one form or another. Sometimes they may be involved as parties to the action, but in many cases they may not be named parties. One question that must be addressed is to what extent the information shared with the insurer is protected by the work-product privilege.

The work-product privilege is not restricted to documents containing the mental impressions of an attorney.[77] The federal rule itself states that the court shall "protect against disclosure of the mental impressions, conclusions, opinions or legal theories of an attorney or other representative of a party concerning the litigation."[78] Therefore, any ruling that the work-product privilege is inapplicable to documents containing mental impressions of anyone other than a lawyer is inconsistent with the plain language of the rule. In the context of a criminal case, the Supreme Court has observed that while the rule shelters the mental processes of an attorney, it is not restricted to attorneys. Rather:

> The doctrine is an intensely practical one, grounded in the realities of litigation in our adversary system. One of those realities is that attorneys often must rely on the assistance of investigators and other agents in the compilation of materials and preparation for trial. It is therefore necessary that the doctrine protect materials prepared by agents for the attorney as well as those prepared by the attorney himself.[79]

Accordingly, federal courts have consistently ruled that the work-product doctrine is not inapplicable merely because the material was prepared by or for a party's insurer or agents of the insurer.[80] In *Home Ins. Co. v. Ballenger Corp.*,[81] the defendant sought discovery of a report to the plaintiff insurer's home office made by the plaintiff's regional claims supervisor. The document apparently contained evaluations and opinions of Home's agents as to certain insurance files. The court held that this information was protected by the work-product privilege and thus not discoverable by the defendant.[82]

Material prepared by or for a party's insurer or agents of the insurer have been accorded work-product protection even where the insurer is not a named party in the action. In *Basinger v. Glacier Carriers, Inc.*,[83] defendants served a deposition subpoena upon the assistant claims manager for REMCO Insurance Company, strangers to the litigation, commanding that the claims manager produce for them REMCO's claim file on the motor vehicle accident giving rise to the action. The court noted that if a party to a litigation is partially protected by Federal Rule of Civil Procedure 26(b)(3) from having to disclose certain information to an opposing party, it would be unjust to require a non-party to deliver the same kind of information to a party who may subsequently join the non-party in the litigation. In holding that the files were protected by the work-product privilege, the court held:

> REMCO's file contains internal memoranda reflecting the mental impressions, conclusions, opinions and theories of its agents regarding the value of a potential claim against (its insured). Rule 26(b)(3) prohibits their discovery since they concern the litigation.[84]

Federal courts, however, are not in agreement as to whether an insurer's claim file, prepared after an accident that may generate a potential claim, can be protected from discovery under Rule 26(b)(3). Three approaches have been taken by the federal courts in determining whether work-product protection applies. Under one approach, courts deny work-product protection to insurance reports prepared after accidents that may generate a claim. The leading case illustrating this position is *Thomas Organ Co. v. Jadranska Slobodna Plovidba.*[85] *Thomas Organ* was an admiralty matter arising from cargo loss aboard a vessel, wherein the court found that:

> [A] report or statement made by or to a party's agent (other than to any attorney acting in the role of counselor), which has not been requested by nor prepared for an attorney's legal expertise, must be conclusively presumed to have been made in the ordinary course of business and thus not within the purview of the limited privilege of . . . Rule 26(b)(3) and (b)(4). . . . An insurance company by the nature of its business is not called into action until one of its insureds has suffered some form of injury and has a potential claim . . . . We do not believe that Rule 26(b)(3) was designed to so insulate insurance companies merely because they always deal with potential claims.[86]

The *Thomas Organ* view has been rejected by many courts and treatise writers as contrary to the intent of Rule 26(b). Courts disagreeing with the restrictive view expressed in *Thomas Organ* have adopted one of two other positions. A liberal view would greatly expand the protection of the work-product privilege to insurance reports prepared following incidents.[87] Other courts, rejecting the extreme liberal and rigid positions enunciated by the *Fontaine* and *Thomas Organs* courts, respectively, have chosen to employ a case-by-case approach.[88]

Again, to be protected under the work-product privilege, the documents must have been prepared in anticipation of litigation. In *Simon v. G.D. Searle & Co.*,[89] the court held that corporate risk management documents that were prepared by non-lawyer corporate officials were not prepared in anticipation of litigation and thus were not protected from discovery.[90] This inquiry is fact-intensive. It must be shown that in light of the document and the factual situation of the case, it can fairly be said that the document was prepared because of the prospect of litigation. Even though litigation is already a prospect, there is no work-product immunity for documents prepared in the regular course of business that are not for the purposes of litigation.[91]

The court in *State Farm Fire & Casualty Co. v. Perrigan*[92] held that an investigator's report was prepared in the ordinary course of business and not in anticipation of trial, and thus was discoverable despite the work-product claim. The investigator's report, which was relevant to discover evidence leading to the cause and the motive for a fire, was prepared during the course of performing an investigation approximately nine days after the fire occurred. Moreover, the court noted that the report was prepared while the insurer was in the process of adjusting the claim and before the insurer had decided whether to pay the loss or become involved in litigation. The report was thus held discoverable.

Western Nat'l Bank of Denver v. Employers Ins. of Wausau[93] also illustrates a narrow interpretation of when a document is "prepared in anticipation of litigation." In *Western Nat'l Bank,* an insured had brought an action against its insurer alleging bad faith on the part of the insurer for failure to pay a claim. The court held that the insured was entitled to obtain discovery of letters from the law firm retained by the insurer, since the test for recovery was whether a reasonable insurer would have denied the claim under similar facts and circumstances. The insured was also allowed to obtain discovery of the law firm's file when the court determined that the file was an investigative file of the insurer prepared in the ordinary course of business, rather than work product.

Some courts have given the "in anticipation of litigation" requirement a broader interpretation. In *Janicker v. George Washington Univ.,*[94] the investigative file of an insurer was held to be work product, immunized from pretrial discovery, as it was prepared in anticipation of claims. These claims, if denied, would have clearly led to suits. Litigation and investigative material generated or produced by counsel after filing of the suit were also deemed to be work product. Similarly, a broad interpretation of the "in anticipation of litigation" requirement is found in *Catino v. Travelers Ins. Co. Inc.*[95] In *Catino,* the plaintiff won a judgment against the defendant's insured, which went unpaid. The insured later assigned his claims against the insurer to the judgment plaintiff, who thereupon filed suit against the insurer for negligence in failing to settle the original action. However, months prior to filing his action against the insurer, the judgment plaintiff sent a demand letter outlining his requirements for settling the case to the insurer. Following the demand letter, the insurer prepared various documents, which were later sought during discovery. The court determined that despite the fact that the third-party suit against the insurer had not yet been filed, the documents were clearly work product, as they were drafted in anticipation of litigation.[96]

And, an insurer's disclosure of work-product information to its reinsurers did not waive the protection where the insurer intended that the communications would remain confidential and protected from their common adversaries.[97]

Privileges Afforded Plaintiffs in Joint Prosecution Against Insurer

In some cases, multiple plaintiffs may wish to join in an action against one or more insurers. In this scenario, it can be reasoned that the privileges afforded the plaintiffs in their joint prosecution will be determined in much the same manner as they are for the joint defense privilege. As long as the plaintiffs have a strong common interest in sharing the fruits of their trial preparation efforts, it would be difficult to argue that privileges attaching to certain confidential documents have been waived. It is settled law that where two or more parties employ a lawyer as their common attorney, their communications to the attorney are confidential and privileged as against a common adversary.[98] This is true whether the parties are defendants or plaintiffs.

As stated, as a general rule there is no waiver of the attorney-client privilege where the client or the client's attorney discloses information to counsel for co-defendants after a joint defense has been undertaken.[99] It seems logical that this same general principle will apply where the privilege is asserted by the plaintiffs in a joint prosecution arrangement, since the same rationale and justifications apply.[100]

Similarly, the work-product privilege afforded to documents shared among joint defendants would also apply to protect communications shared among plaintiffs in a joint prosecution scenario. Again, as long as the transferor and transferee anticipate litigation against a common adversary on the same issue or issues, they have a strong common interest in sharing the results of their efforts.[101] This logic applies whether the privilege is asserted on the defense side or the prosecution side. In both situations the disclosure is not inconsistent with maintaining secrecy against deponents.

Conclusion

The "joint-defense" privilege can continue to protect otherwise privileged communication if handled properly. For the attorney-client privilege to apply, the communication between the attorney and client must be for the purpose of giving and receiving legal advice. Similarly, the work-product privilege protects documents containing the thoughts, impressions, and strategy of the attorney or his agent, prepared in anticipation of litigation. These privileges are often not waived by the communication of such privileged information to co-parties who have aligned themselves in a "joint defense."

Notes

1. *See, e.g.,* Wilson P. Abraham Constr. Corp. v. Armco Steel Corp., 559 F.2d 250, 253 (5th Cir. 1977).
2. Allendale Mut. Ins. Co. v. Bull Data Sys., Inc., 152 F.R.D. 132, 140 (M.D. Ill. 1993).
3. United Coal Cos. v. Powell Constr. Co., 839 F.2d 958 (3d Cir. 1988); Samuelson v. Susen, 576 F.2d 546 (3d Cir. 1978); Fed. R. Evid. R. 501.
4. *In re* L.T.V. Securities Litig., 89 F.R.D. 595 (N.D. Tex. 1981).
5. Upjohn Co. v. United States, 449 U.S. 383 (1981).
6. Fromson v. Anitec Printing Plates, Inc., 152 F.R.D. 2, 3 (D. Mass. 1993).
7. Diversified Indus., Inc. v. Meredith, 572 F.2d 596 (8th Cir. 1977).
8. Fed. R. Civ. Proc. R. 26(b)(3).
9. 329 U.S. 495 (1947).

10. *Id.* at 511.

11. *See* Duplan Corp. v. Moulinage et Retorderie de Chavanoz, 509 F.2d 730 (4th Cir. 1974).

12. *Id.*

13. *Id.* at 734.

14. Holmgren v. State Farm Mut. Auto. Ins. Co., 976 F.2d 573 (9th Cir. 1992).

15. *Id.* at 577 (citing *Hickman,* 329 U.S. 495, 511). *Accord, In re* Minebea Co., Ltd., 143 F.R.D. 494 (S.D.N.Y. 1992).

16. Upjohn Co. v. United States, 449 U.S. 383, 401 (1981).

17. 2 WEINSTEIN & BERGER, WEINSTEIN'S EVIDENCE § 503(b)[06] (1991); John Morrell & Co. v. Local Union 304A, 913 F.2d 544 (8th Cir. 1990), *cert. denied,* 500 U.S. 905 (1991).

18. Waller v. Financial Corp. of America, 828 F.2d 579 (9th Cir. 1987); United States v. McPartlin, 595 F.2d 1321 (7th Cir. 1979), *cert. denied,* 444 U.S. 833 (1979); Sedalcek v. Morgan Whitney Trading Group, 795 F. Supp. 329 (C.D. Cal. 1992).

19. Eisenberg v. Gagnon, 766 F.2d 770 (3d Cir. 1985).

20. *Id.*

21. *Id.* at 787-88. *See also* Haines v. Liggett Group, Inc., 975 F.2d 81 (3d Cir. 1992) (tobacco company defendants exchanged information among various attorneys representing them in order to adequately prepare a joint defense) *and* United States v. Schwimmer, 892 F.2d 237 (2d Cir. 1989) (protecting communications made to an accountant aiding attorneys conducting a joint defense).

22. *See* United States v. Bay State Ambulance & Hosp. Rental Serv., Inc., 874 F.2d 20 (1st Cir. 1989).

23. Allendale Mut. Ins. Co. v. Bull Data Systems, Inc., 152 F.R.D. 132, 140 (N.D. Ill. 1993) (citations omitted).

24. *In re* Sealed Case, 29 F.3d 715, 719 n.5 (D.C. Cir. 1994).

25. *Id.* at 719; Boyd v. Comdata Network, Inc., 88 S.W.3d 203 (Tenn. 2002).

26. 913 F.2d 544 (8th Cir. 1990).

27. *Id.* at 555-56.

28. *Id.* (quoting Wilson P. Abraham Constr. Corp. v. Armco Steel Corp., 559 F.2d 250 (5th Cir. 1977)).

29. *Id. See also In re* L.T.V. Securities Litig., 89 F.R.D. 595 (N.D. Tex. 1981).

30. Allendale Mut. Ins. Co. v. Bull Data Systems, Inc., 152 F.R.D. 132, 135-36 (N.D. Ill. 1993).

31. *In re* Grand Jury Subpoena, 784 F.2d 857 (8th Cir. 1986).

32. Hunydee v. United States, 355 F.2d 183, 185 (9th Cir. 1965).

33. Doubleday v. Ruh, 149 F.R.D. 601 n.4 (E.D. Cal. 1993).

34. United States v. IBM, 66 F.R.D. 154 (S.D.N.Y. 1974). *See also* Hanover Shoe, Inc. v. United Shoe Mach. Corp., 207 F. Supp. 407 (N.D. Pa. 1962) (materials must be prepared for the case at bar).

35. *In re* Murphy, 560 F.2d 326, 334 (8th Cir. 1977). *See also* Duplan Corp. v. Moulinage Retorderie de Chavanoz, 487 F.2d 480 (4th Cir. 1973).

36. Levingston v. Allis-Chalmers Corp., 109 F.R.D. 546 (S.D. Miss. 1985).

37. *Id. See also* 8 WRIGHT & MILLER, FEDERAL PRACTICE AND PROCEDURE § 2024 (2d ed. 1994).

38. Schachar v. American Acad. of Ophthalmology, Inc., 106 F.RD. 187, 191 (N.D. Ill. 1985).

39. *Id.* at 191.

40. Continental Oil Co. v. United States, 330 F.2d 347 (9th Cir. 1964).

41. 106 F.R.D. at 192 (quoting Transmirra Prod. Corp. v. Monsanto Chem. Co., 26 F.R.D. 572, 579 (S.D.N.Y. 1960)).

42. *See* 8 WRIGHT & MILLER, FEDERAL PRACTICE AND PROCEDURE § 2016.2 (2d ed. 1994).

43. FDIC v. Singh, 140 F.R.D. 252 (D. Me. 1992).

44. Wichita Land and Cattle Co. v. American Fed. Bank, 148 F.R.D. 456, 457 (D.D.C. 1992).

45. Mendenhall v. Barber-Greene Co., 531 F. Supp. 951, 955 (N.D. Ill. 1982). *See also* Berg Electronics, Inc. v. Molex, Inc., 875 F. Supp. 261 (D. Del. 1995), Redland Soccer Club v. Department of the Army, 55 F.3d 827 (3d Cir. 1995) (inadvertent disclosure of documents does not qualify as a voluntary waiver).

46. Edwards v. Whitaker, 868 F. Supp. 226 (M.D. Tenn. 1994).

47. Transamerica Computer Co. v. IBM, 573 F.2d 646 (9th Cir. 1978).

48. Ohio-Sealy Mattress Mfg. Co. v. Kaplan, 90 F.R.D. 21 (N.D. Ill. 1980) (citing *In re* Grand Jury Subpoena Duces Tecum, 406 F. Supp. 381, 393-94 (S.D.N.Y. 1975)).

49. 559 F.2d 250 (5th Cir. 1977).

50. *Id.* at 253.

51. Medcom Holding Co. v. Baxter Travenol Labs., Inc., 689 F. Supp. 841 (N.D. Ill. 1988).

52. United States v. Moscony, 697 F. Supp. 888 (E.D. Pa. 1988).

53. *Id.* at 394.

54. *In re* Sealed Case, 120 F.R.D. 66 (N.D. Ill. 1988).

55. United States v. American Tel. & Tel. Co., 642 F.2d 1285 (D.C. Cir. 1980).

56. *See* Hickman v. Taylor, 329 U.S. 495 (1947).

57. 39 F.R.D. 610 (S.D.N.Y. 1965).

58. *Id.*

59. 85 F.R.D. 46 (S.D.N.Y. 1979).

60. *Id.* at 72.

61. 9 F.3d 230 (2d Cir. 1993).

62. *Id.* at 235.

63. *Id. But see Diversified, supra* note 7 (no waiver of privilege under similar circumstances).

64. 9 F.3d at 236.

65. 642 F.2d 1285 (D.C. Cir. 1980).

66. United States v. American Tel. & Tel. Co., 642 F.2d 1285, 1299 (D.C. Cir. 1980).

67. *Id.* at 1299.

68. *Id.* at 1297-98.

69. United States v. American Tel. & Tel. Co., *supra* note 55 at 1299-1300.

70. United States v. Gulf Oil Corp., 760 F.2d 292 (Temp. Emer. Ct. App. 1985).

71. *Id.*

72. *See generally* Fausek v. White, 965 F.2d 126 (6th Cir. 1992).

73. *In re* Antitrust Grand Jury, 805 F.2d 155, 162 (6th Cir. 1986).

74. Loustalet v. Refco, Inc., 154 F.R.D. 243 (C.D. Cal. 1993).

75. *Id.* at 245.

76. *In re* Antitrust Grand Jury, *supra* note 73.

77. United States v. Nobles, 422 U.S. 225 (1975).

78. Fed. R. Civ. Proc. R. 26(b)(3).

79. United States v. Nobles, 422 U.S. 225, 238-39.

80. *See* Railroad Salvage of Conn., Inc. v. Japan Freight Consolidators (USA), Inc., 97 F.R.D. 37 (E.D.N.Y. 1983), *aff'd,* 779 F.2d 38 (2d Cir. 1985) (correspondence between the defendant and its liability insurance carriers protected).

81. 74 F.R.D. 93 (N.D. Ga. 1977).

82. *Compare* Holmgren v. State Farm Mut. Auto Ins. Co., 976 F.2d 573 (9th Cir. 1992) (finding work-product doctrine applicable, but allowing discovery due to compelling need).

83. 107 F.R.D. 771 (N.D. Pa. 1985).

84. *Id.* at 775.

85. 54 F.R.D. 367 (N.D. Ill. 1972).

86. *Id.* at 372-73.

87. Fontaine v. Sunflower Beef Carrier, 87 F.R.D. 89 (E.D. Mo. 1980).

88. *See* Airheart v. Chicago & Northwestern Transp. Co., 128 F.R.D. 669 (D.S.D. 1989).

89. 816 F.2d 397 (8th Cir. 1987).

90. *See also* Banks v. Wilson, 151 F.R.D. 109 (D. Minn. 1993).

91. *Id.* at 112.

92. 102 F.R.D. 235 (D. Va. 1984).

93. 109 F.R.D. 55 (D. Colo. 1985).

94. 94 F.R.D. 648 (D.D.C. 1982).

95. 136 F.R.D. 534 (D. Mass. 1991).

96. *Id.*

97. Minn. School Board's Assn. Ins. Trust v. Employer's Ins. Co. of Wausau, 183 F.R.D. 627 (N.D. Ill. 1999).

98. United Coal Cos. v. Powell Constr. Co., 839 F.2d 958 (3d Cir. 1988).

99. *See* Haines v. Liggett Group, Inc., 975 F.2d 81 (3d Cir. 1992).

100. *See, e.g.,* Schachar v. American Acad. of Ophthalmology, Inc., 106 F.R.D. 187 (N.D. Ill. 1985).

101. *Id.*

CHAPTER 21

Duties of Emergency Disclosure to the Government Under CERCLA, EPCRA, and the Clean Air Act

NEAL A. HUESKE
BRIEN J. FLANAGAN

Introduction

As federal, state, and local agencies have refined and added to the panoply of environmental regulations facing industry and the regulated sector, much of the focus in recent years has shifted from "command and control" regulation toward programs aimed at identifying potential sources of pollution and evaluating the risks associated with those sources. These programs have been developed with the goal of educating the public and allowing the local community to become involved in a facility's pollution prevention efforts and planning. The benefits of such programs are obvious: a well-informed public will more realistically understand the risks (or lack of risk) of a facility's operations, while such public scrutiny usually encourages a facility to improve its processes and minimize the chance for a catastrophic release.

Virtually every major environmental statute contains provisions aimed at emergency notification and disclosure to the government. The primary disclosure statutes are the Comprehensive Environmental Response, Compensation and Liability Act (CERCLA)[1] and the Emergency Planning and Community Right to Know Act (EPCRA),[2] both of which give the government broad authority to obtain information from regulated industries. Both statutes require regulated facilities to compile, store, and report specific data concerning the existence or release of hazardous substances. The provisions of these statutes mandate a variety of different types of monitoring, record keeping, and reporting schemes. CERCLA also authorizes the EPA to enter the premises of a facility to collect information and review records addressing the environmental and health aspects of the entity's activities.

Similarly, both the Clean Water Act (CWA)[3] and the Clean Air Act (CAA) contain provisions that require the compilation and disclosure of information aimed at identifying sources of pollutant emissions to water resources and to the air.[4] Specifically, Congress added a comprehensive Accidental Release Prevention program to the Clean Air Act during substantial revisions in 1990. Like the planning and reporting requirements of EPCRA, the Accidental Release Prevention program of the CAA requires a facility to disclose the exact types and quantities of certain toxic chemicals stored, processed, or used at the facility.

From an industry standpoint, there are obvious risks in disclosing this type of information. The reports produced under the CERCLA, EPCRA, and CAA mandates will contain accurate and verifiable information describing a business's environmental control efforts. As a result, the EPA or other governmental agencies may attempt to use such information to build an enforcement case against the reporting business, despite recent efforts to quell such enforcement through the implementation of voluntary audit privileges.[5] The information required to be disclosed under the statutes may be used to prove knowledge on the part of corporate officers of environmental violations. The comprehensive reporting schemes established by CERCLA and EPCRA may also encompass information concerning confidential production processes or sensitive trade secrets of the corporation.

More important, once this information finds its way into government files, it becomes easily accessible to the public through the express terms of the statutes or the federal Freedom of Information Act.[6] Possession of this sensitive information by the public may cause damage, often unfairly, to the business reputation of the industry, provide advantages to a competitor, or encourage a citizens' suit under various pollution control laws.

This chapter examines the obligations of a business under CERCLA, EPCRA, and the CAA to record and report environmental compliance data and related information to the EPA and other governmental entities. The nature of the rights of a regulated industry to withhold certain kinds of information is also examined. Finally, this chapter discusses government obligations to disclose or protect such information under the terms of the statutes and regulations, as well as under the Freedom of Information Act.

Notifying Government Agencies

Notification Requirements Under CERCLA and EPCRA

A government agency may receive its first information regarding the environmental affairs of an industry if a release occurs from a facility. Section 103 of CERCLA and Section 304 of EPCRA impose an affirmative duty on the person in charge of a facility to report any release of a hazardous substance into the environment.[7] Determining whether an occurrence constitutes a reportable release is one of the more important legal decisions facing lawyers who provide advice to industrial clients.

What Is a Reportable Release?

Generally speaking, federal laws mandate that a report be filed immediately following a release of a hazardous substance into the environment.[8] A "release" is defined broadly to include any spilling, leaking, pumping, pouring, emitting, emptying, discharging, injecting, escaping, leaching, dumping, or disposing into the environment.[9] Even spills or discharges that remain on the facility or installation grounds must be reported unless they are successfully contained. The EPA has explained that "examples of such releases are spills from tanks or valves onto concrete pads or into lined ditches open to the outside air, releases from pipes into open lagoons or ponds, or any other discharges that are not wholly contained within buildings or structures."[10] Releases that are wholly contained within buildings or structures do not require notification.[11]

What Is a Hazardous Substance?

A "hazardous substance" is defined to include substances deemed hazardous by other federal environmental statutes, by reference to general hazard criteria, or by EPA determination that a substance is a threat to public health or welfare.[12] The current list of hazardous substances is found at 40 Code of Federal Regulations (C.F.R.) section 302.4.

"Extremely hazardous substances" (EHS) under EPCRA are some 400 substances contained in a list published by EPA at 40 C.F.R. Part 355, Appendix A.[13] This list includes a "threshold planning quantity" (TPQ) and a "reportable quantity" (RQ) for each EHS.[14]

At What Volume Does a Release Become Reportable?

Notification must only be given if a substance qualifying as "hazardous" under CERCLA or "extremely hazardous" under EPCRA is released in quantities equal to or greater than the reportable quantity set by EPA regulations. The RQs for hazardous substances are listed in 40 C.F.R. section 302.4. The list of RQs for extremely hazardous substances can be found at 40 C.F.R. section 355, Appendix A. If the EPA has not determined the reportable quantity of a substance, CERCLA provides that the reportable quantity will be one pound.[15] The reportable quantity is calculated by totaling the emissions over a 24-hour period.[16]

What to Report

The notification required under EPCRA section 304 for releases to the environment of "hazardous substances" or "extremely hazardous substances" must contain the following information: (1) the chemical name or identity of the substance involved; (2) an indication of whether the substance is on the EPA list of extremely hazardous substances; (3) an estimate of the quantity of any such substance released; (4) the time, duration, and location of the release; (5) the medium into which the release occurred; (6) any known or anticipated health risks associated with the release; (7) proper precautions to be taken as a result of the release; and (8) the name and telephone number of the person or persons to be contacted for further information. *See* EPCRA §

304(b)(2). As soon as practicable after a release that requires emergency notification under EPCRA, a facility shall provide to the relevant state or local entities a written follow-up notice setting forth and updating the information required to be communicated orally.[17]

Section 111(g) of CERCLA imposes a second reporting requirement on owners and operators of vessels or facilities from which a hazardous substance has been released. Under this provision, such owners and operators must provide reasonable notice to potential injured parties by publication in local newspapers serving the area affected by each release.

Exemptions from Notification

Under the express terms of CERCLA and EPCRA, certain types of releases are exempted from the emergency reporting requirements. Specifically, a facility need not report (1) federally permitted releases; (2) certain continuous releases; (3) pesticide applications; and (4) releases that result in exposure only to persons within the workplace and that do not reach the environment. Also, as mentioned above, a release that does not exceed the appropriate reportable quantity in any 24-hour period is exempt from reporting.[18] These exceptions apply both to notification for releases of hazardous substances under CERCLA section 103 and releases of extremely hazardous substances under EPCRA section 304.

Federally Permitted Releases

The most important exclusion from the CERCLA and EPCRA reporting requirement is the exception for "federally permitted releases." A federally permitted release is any discharge that is in compliance with a permit issued under the Clean Water Act, the Resource Conservation and Recovery Act (RCRA), any Clean Air Act permit or State Implementation Plan, the Underground Injection Control Program established under the Safe Drinking Water Act, and other similar federally permitted activities.[19] This exemption applies whether federal, state, or local authority issues the permit.[20] EPA has also construed a "federally permitted release" to include the disposal of hazardous substances at both interim status and permitted treatment, storage, and disposal (TSD) facilities under RCRA.[21]

The federally permitted release exemption has been narrowly construed to mean that only chemicals specifically listed in an air or water discharge permit may be released into the environment without notification to the appropriate agency.[22] In other words, a facility's air emissions or water discharges must be reported if they are not subject to or in compliance with an applicable permit, even if the permit is silent as to the particular discharges.

Continuous Releases[23]

Section 103(f)(2) of CERCLA also exempts from the reporting requirements any releases that are: "continuous . . . , stable in quantity and rate" and (1) that are from a facility that notified EPA by mid-June 1981 under CERCLA section 103(c) that it handled hazardous substances, or (2) for which notification has been given under CERCLA section 103 for a period sufficient to establish the continuity, quantity, and regularity of such releases. Notification of continuous releases must be given annually or whenever there is a "statistically significant increase" in the release of hazardous substances. In 1990, EPA promulgated its interpretation of CERCLA section 103(f)(2) reporting requirements. 55 Fed. Reg. 30166 (July 24, 1990).[24]

Normal Application of Fertilizers and Pesticides

Section 103(e) of CERCLA provides an exemption for the "application" of a pesticide registered under Federal Insecticide, Fungicide, and Rodenticide Act (FIFRA), provided that application is consistent with the pesticide's registration and labelling requirements. Thus, this exemption would not cover accidental leaks or spills of pesticides, nor any releases of pesticide ingredients.

Releases to the Workplace

Finally, releases that result in exposure only to persons within the workplace and do not reach the environment need not be reported.[25] CERCLA defines "release" as the emission of a substance "into the environment." Thus, a spill of a liquid substance onto the concrete floor of an enclosed manufacturing plant that remained entirely within the facility would not be a release into the environment. In contrast, EPA has stated that a spill on the grounds outside the facility of the plant could be a release into the environment, even if wholly contained within the boundaries of the property on which the facility is located.[26] EPCRA's reporting requirements also contain an exemption for releases that result in exposure to persons solely within the boundaries of the facility.[27]

EPA Investigations and Inspections Under CERCLA

Under certain circumstances, EPA is given broad authority by CERCLA to initiate investigations, monitoring, and testing at privately owned facilities. EPA may also require facility owners to produce a wide range of documents and information concerning the presence of hazardous substances at the facility. Finally, CERCLA gives EPA power to enter private premises to gather information or copy documents.[28] EPA may use the information acquired from these inspections to determine appropriate responses to releases at the site or as a basis for an enforcement action.[29] However, the Federal District Court from the Western District of Virginia has greatly limited EPA's ability to inspect and take soil or groundwater samples from private property.[30] These opinions recognize strict limits on the EPA's ability to inspect and take soil or groundwater samples from private property. The court relied heavily on Fourth Amendment limitations to unreasonable searches. It appears that as long as a private property owner exhibits an actual expectation of privacy in things buried or otherwise contained in the property, EPA cannot constitutionally search without a warrant or consent.

EPA Investigations, Monitoring, and Testing

The EPA is given authority to "undertake . . . investigations, monitoring, surveying, testing, and other information gathering . . ." at a privately owned facility.[31] These investigations may be initiated in a variety of circumstances. Specifically, investigations may be undertaken whenever (1) the EPA is authorized to provide for a remedial action at the site; (2) the EPA has reason to believe that a release has occurred or is about to occur; and (3) the EPA has reason to believe that illness, disease, or complaints may be attributable to exposure to a hazardous substance, pollutant, or contaminant.[32] Similarly, the scope of the investigation or testing warranted under this provision is extremely broad. Under the terms of the statute, the EPA may investigate to determine the source and nature of the hazardous substance, pollutant, or contaminant involved, the extent of the release or threat of release, and the extent of the danger to public health, welfare, or the environment.[33]

EPA Inspection and Requests to Produce Information

In addition to its authority to investigate, test, and monitor a site, the EPA may request the production of relevant documents or may enter the premises in order to inspect and copy the same.[34]

Whenever the EPA has a reasonable basis to believe that there may be a release or threat of release of a hazardous substance, pollutant, or contaminant, it may require the site owner to produce a broad range of information. Specifically, under CERCLA section 104(e)(2), the EPA may require any person to produce information relating to (1) the identification, nature, and quantity of materials that have been or are generated, treated, stored, or disposed of at a facility or transported to the facility; (2) the nature or extent of a release or threatened release of a hazardous substance at or from a facility; and (3) the ability of a person to pay for or to perform a cleanup.

Any person must grant access to EPA, and EPA has authority to enter the facility premises at any reasonable time in order to "inspect and copy all documents or records relating to such matters."[35] In the alternative, the person having such information may copy and furnish it to the EPA at his or her expense.[36]

The EPA's request for information regarding hazardous substances will generally be upheld where (1) the investigation is within the agency's authority; (2) the request is not too indefinite; and (3) the information requested is reasonably relevant.[37] The courts have, however, put some restraints on EPA's information-gathering activities pursuant to CERCLA section 104(e). In *Bunker Limited Partnership v. United States*,[38] the court ruled that an EPA inspection warrant "does not authorize the EPA to review all documents to determine which it feels fall within the parameters of the warrant." The court held that the site owner, not the EPA, is responsible for searching its own documents and producing only those which are responsive to the warrant.[39] The arguments advanced by counsel and the court's reasoning provide fabric to weave arguments against blanket disclosure requests.

In the event that a site owner withholds consent to any EPA request for information or any EPA entry and inspection under CERCLA section 104(e), the EPA is given the authority to issue a compliance order.[40] These compliance orders may be enforced in a civil action where fines and penalties may be assessed for inadequate responses.[41] Furthermore, the courts are directed to enjoin interference with such information requests unless "under the circumstances of the case the demand for information or documents is arbitrary and capricious, an abuse of discretion, or otherwise not in accordance with law."[42]

Reporting Requirements Under EPCRA

EPCRA was adopted as part of the Superfund Amendment and Reauthorization Act of 1986 (known as SARA).[43] EPCRA established requirements for emergency planning, notification of chemical usages, and hazardous or toxic chemical reporting aimed at informing the local community of potentially hazardous substances present at a facility. These *community's* right-to-know provisions are distinct from an *employee's* right-to-know laws which are covered under Occupational Safety and Health Administration (OSHA) and are directed to informing employees of the hazardous chemicals with which they might come into contact.

In addition to the federal EPCRA, many states have enacted their own emergency planning and community-right-to-know laws and regulations. The federal EPCRA includes three major components aimed at enumerating the chemicals stored, used, or released at certain qualifying facilities.

Material Safety Data Sheets

EPCRA section 311 requires facilities that must prepare material safety data sheets (MSDS) for a hazardous chemical under OSHA regulations to submit either copies of their MSDS or a list of MSDS chemicals to the local Emergency Planning Committee, the State Emergency Response Commission, and the local fire department. The EPA has established minimum threshold quantities for hazardous chemicals below which a facility is not required to report its MSDS. These are:

1. For "hazardous chemicals" as defined in OSHA,[44] a quantity present at the facility at any one time in an amount exceeding 10,000 pounds; and
2. For "extremely hazardous substances" (EHS) listed under EPCRA, a quantity exceeding the TPQ or 500 pounds, whichever is less.

The MSDS must be made available by the local Emergency Planning Committee upon request by any member of the public.[45] Furthermore, an MSDS or a revised list must be provided when new hazardous chemicals become present at a facility or significant new information is discovered about the hazardous chemical.[46]

Emergency and Hazardous Chemical Inventory Forms

EPCRA section 312 requires a facility to submit annually a hazardous chemical inventory form to the local Emergency Planning Committee, the State Emergency Response Commission, and the local fire department.[47] The hazardous chemicals covered by this section are those for which facilities are required to prepare an MSDS under OSHA's regulations and that were present at the facility at any time during the previous calendar year above the same minimum thresholds applicable to MSDS.

EPCRA establishes a two-tier reporting scheme. Under Tier I, facilities must submit an aggregate of all hazardous chemicals by each applicable hazard category.[48] The facility must also prepare and maintain more extensive Tier II information, but must only submit it upon request by a local committee, state commission, or local fire department. The Tier II information that a facility must maintain and keep available includes: (1) the chemical name or the common name as indicated on the MSDS; (2) an estimate of the maximum amount of the chemical present at any time during the preceding calendar year; (3) a brief description of the manner of storage of the chemical; and (4) the location of the chemical at the facility.[49] The public may also request Tier II information from the State Commission or the local committee.[50]

Toxic Chemical Release Reports

Section 313 of EPCRA requires that certain facilities "submit annually, no later than July 1 of each year, a Toxic Chemical Release Inventory Reporting Form ('Form R') for each Toxic Chemical listed under 40 C.F.R. § 372.65 that was manufactured, imported, processed, or otherwise used during the preceding calendar year in quantities exceeding established chemical thresholds."[51] The Form R's document the facility's use of certain listed toxic chemicals and all releases (including routine emissions) of those chemicals into the environment.[52]

EPCRA section 313 covers over 600 chemicals and chemical categories specifically listed at 40 C.F.R. section 372.65. The list is changed and updated frequently. EPA must maintain a national toxic chemical inventory (the toxic release inventory, or TRI) based on the data submitted, which is available to the public.[53]

Designated facilities are required to report on releases of toxic chemicals into the air, water, and land.[54] In addition, they need to report off-site transfers—a transfer of wastes for chemical recycling, treatment, or disposal at a separate facility. Industries required to report include manufacturing; metal mining; coal mining; electrical utilities; treatment, storage, and disposal facilities; solvent recovery services; petroleum bulk terminals; and all federal facilities owned or operated by executive branch agencies.[55]

Facilities to whom the section 313 reporting obligations apply are those that have 10 or more full-time employees and meet the established thresholds for manufacture, processing, or "otherwise use" of listed chemicals (i.e., manufactures or processes over 25,000 pounds of the approximately 600 designated chemicals or 28 chemical categories specified in the regulations, or uses more than 10,000 pounds of any designated chemical or category). These facilities must report their releases and other waste management quantities (including quantities transferred off-site for further waste management). Once the applicable threshold is surpassed, every activity involving that chemical must be reported on the Form R. Typically, in an EPA action to enforce EPCRA section 313, the crucial determination is whether the facility "otherwise used" a chemical for which the reporting requirements apply.[56]

Small-source facilities may avoid filing Form R's and instead file an "alternate threshold reporting form" pursuant to an EPA rule promulgated in November 1994. This rule allows a facility to file a short-form certification statement if it manufactures, processes, or otherwise uses a TRI chemical in an amount less than one million pounds, if the facility releases, disposes of, or treats less than 500 pounds of the chemical during the year.[57] The "release" quantity is taken from section 8 of the Form R and includes material released into the environment, material used for energy recovery on- and off-site, material recycled on- and off-site, and material treated on- and off-site.[58] If a facility uses the alternate threshold form, it must maintain documentation supporting its use and release calculations for three years after submission of the certification statement.[59]

Additionally, certain exemptions to the EPCRA section 313 requirements may be applicable.[60]

1. **Mixtures**: Toxic chemicals present at the facility in a mixture below a de minimis concentration (one percent; or 0.1 percent for carcinogens) is not included in the threshold calculations, and the appropriate MSDS and inventory forms may be filed for the mixture itself.[61]

2. **Labs**: Toxic chemicals present in a laboratory are not included in threshold calculations.

3. **Articles**: Toxic chemicals present in "articles" are exempt from the threshold calculations and from Form R reporting. An article is a manufactured item, formed to shape during manufacture, which has end-use functions dependent on its shape and does not release a toxic chemical under normal conditions.

4. **Exemptions**: Routine maintenance, structural components of a facility, personal use of chemicals by employees, operation of motor vehicles, and other such uses are exempt from EPCRA reporting requirements.

5. **Leased Premises**: An owner of leased premises is not required to report; however, the operator or lessee of that establishment may be subject to the reporting requirements and is solely responsible for meeting all reporting requirements.[62]

6. **Business Parks**: Within business or industrial parks, owners of separate establishments with no common corporate or business interests must treat their own establishment separately for purposes of section 313.[63]

Reporting Requirements Under the Clean Air Act

In addition to the monitoring, record keeping, and reporting requirements of the Clean Air Act federal operating permit program (and any state permit programs),[64] the act provides for an Accidental Release Prevention and Risk Management program. Like EPCRA, this part of the CAA forces a facility to identify the *potential* for a catastrophic release before it happens and put in place an appropriate emergency response plan.

On June 20, 1996, EPA promulgated final rules to implement the requirements of CAA section 112(r), which are contained at 40 C.F.R. Part 68. Basically, if a facility maintains processes that contain more than a threshold quantity of a regulated substance, it is subject to the rule.

The list of regulated substances and threshold quantities is at 40 C.F.R. section 68.130. Currently, the list includes 77 regulated toxic substances and 63 regulated flammable substances. As of August, 1996, the list also includes all Division 1.1 high-explosive substances as listed by the U.S. Department of Transportation in 49 C.F.R. section 172.101, but EPA has delisted explosives for the reason that they are adequately regulated under other programs by other agencies.[65]

If a facility contains over a threshold quantity of a regulated substance, the regulation prescribes requirements according to which one of three "programs" a facility's processes fall into. Eligibility for a particular program is based on "process" criteria, which can be less than the entire source. Program 1 is available to any process that has not had an accidental release with off-site consequences in five years and has no public receptors within the distance specified in a worst-case release scenario. Program 3 applies to processes in nine listed SIC codes[66] and also to all processes subject to OSHA's Process Safety Management Standard found at 29 C.F.R. section 1910.119. Program 2 sources are any sources that are not Program 1 or 3.

While there are some differences, most affected sources will need to prepare a worst-case scenario with off-site consequence analysis, an alternate release scenario, a five-year accident history, a hazard assessment, and, most important, a Risk Management Plan (RMP). The RMP is the backbone of the Accidental Release Prevention program and will require the source to gather significant data, perform detailed modeling of release scenarios, and put in place an emergency response plan. Also, the source will be required to perform a compliance audit at least every three years and certify its compliance to the implementing agency. In addition, there are registration and certification requirements. Because this is a new program, it remains to be seen what the relative costs of compliance will be.

The effective date for the regulations is August 16, 1996. The owner or operator of an affected source must comply no later than June 21, 1999: three years after the date on which a regulated substance is first listed, or the date on which a regulated substance is first present in more than a threshold quantity in a process, whichever is later.

All of the information submitted by a facility as part of a RMP is available for public review, subject to limitations under 42 U.S.C. section 7414(c).

Protection from Disclosure as a Result of Voluntary Audit Privilege

Although not an actual reporting requirement, a voluntary environmental audit may allow for disclosure while affording some protection to the disclosing entity. In late 1995, the EPA issued its final policy on environmental audits.[67] This final policy offers penalty reductions for certain violations discovered through companies' audits and reported to EPA, but does not extend a "privilege" to audit documents. To qualify for any of the penalty breaks offered by EPA's final policy, a company must discover a violation systematically, confess the transgression to EPA promptly, and correct the problem quickly.

Specifically, to qualify under EPA's policy, the particular violation and the company's response to its discovery must meet all of the following nine conditions:

1. **Systematic discovery**. The company must discover the violation through a formal audit process or through some other systematic management program to prevent, detect, and correct violations.
2. **Voluntary discovery**. Discovery of the violation cannot result from monitoring that the company is legally required to perform, such as sampling required by a permit.
3. **Prompt disclosure to EPA**. The company must disclose a violation in writing to EPA, not just to the relevant state or local agency, within 10 days of discovery. The clock starts ticking when the company discovers that a violation may have occurred.

4. **Not in anticipation of enforcement**. The discovery and disclosure of the violation cannot be a reaction to knowledge of a pending inspection, enforcement action, or third-party complaint.

5. **Correction and remediation**. The company must correct the problem within 60 days, fix any harm, and certify in writing to the appropriate local and state agencies and EPA that it has done so.

6. **Prevention of recurrence**. The company must agree in writing with EPA to take any steps required to prevent a recurrence of the violation.

7. **Not a repeat violation**. The company may not have recently received clear notice of similar violations and had an opportunity to correct and prevent them.

8. **Not a significant violation**. The violation may not have caused serious harm or imminent and substantial endangerment. Also, the violation may not be of a specific term of judicial or administrative order or consent agreement.

9. **Cooperation**. The company must assist EPA's investigation of the violation and related violations.

If a company qualifies for a penalty break under EPA's audit policy, EPA will not refer violations to the Department of Justice for criminal prosecution. Secondly, EPA will reduce civil penalties and will waive all "gravity-based" or punitive aspects of the civil penalty. For violations that a company discovers in good faith but not through a systematic audit process, and which meet Conditions 2 through 9, EPA will reduce the gravity-based component by 75 percent. EPA may still seek to recover the "economic benefit" component of civil penalties, even for violations that meet all nine conditions.

The final policy reaffirms EPA's opposition to protecting a company's environmental audit documents from disclosure through "privilege." The most that EPA promises is to refrain from routinely requesting or using an audit report to *initiate* an investigation. In other words, EPA maintains that it still may utilize the raw numbers and factual observations generated by an audit in its ongoing oversight of the facility.[68] While the EPA has pushed for federal audit privilege legislation, the Clinton administration has repeatedly voiced its opposition to such laws and the legislation was not enacted.

The proliferation of statutorily mandated audit privileges at the state level has been a source of controversy for EPA, which has publicly expressed concern that many state programs go too far in hindering the enforcement of federal environmental laws. For instance, EPA only conditionally approved the Title V air permit programs for Texas and Idaho because those states enacted audit privileges that, EPA argued, interfered with its ability to rigorously enforce the Clean Air Act through penalties and injunctive relief.[69] Also, EPA claimed that Texas's audit privilege statute conflicted with the Clean Air Act's protection for whistle-blowers because it limited disclosure of audit information by employees of the company.

EPA Disclosure of Information to the Public

This section examines EPA's statutory duty to provide public disclosure or to protect from public access information obtained from a regulated facility. Under both the Freedom of Information Act (FOIA)[70] and the provisions of CERCLA, EPCRA, and the CAA, EPA is obligated to disclose to the public much of the information it receives from regulated industries. The statutes do, however, contain some restrictions on this disclosure.

Public Access to Information Under FOIA

The Freedom of Information Act was enacted by Congress in order to encourage the establishment of a general policy of "full agency disclosure" of policies, rules, factual data, and similar records.[71] Under the FOIA, every federal agency is required to disclose a wide range of information to the public upon request. The statute was designed "to pierce the veil of administrative secrecy and to open agency action to the light of public scrutiny."[72] The strong presumption in favor of disclosure places the burden on the agency to justify the withholding of any requested documents.[73]

Congress did, however, recognize the need to limit the scope of agency disclosure in certain circumstances. As a result, the FOIA contains nine specific exemptions in section 552(b). The nine exemptions of the FOIA ordinarily provide the only basis for nondisclosure and are generally discretionary, not mandatory, in nature.[74] Moreover, FOIA does not provide a private party a right of action to enjoin agency disclosure.[75]

Disclosure of Information by the EPA Under FOIA

The EPA, as a federal agency, is required to disclose records to any person pursuant to a request for "agency records which (A) reasonably describes such records and (B) is made in accordance with published rules stating the time, place, fees (if any) and procedures to be followed . . . ."[76] The EPA's FOIA regulations are published at 40 C.F.R. Part 2.[77]

The EPA's regulations regarding implementation of the FOIA adopt a policy of the fullest possible disclosure of records to the public, consistent with the rights of individuals to privacy, the duty to keep confidential business information secret, and the need for EPA to promote frank policy deliberations and to pursue its official activities without undue disruption.[78]

Under the FOIA, the EPA must disclose agency records in response to properly prepared requests unless the information falls within one of the nine FOIA exemptions. Courts have generally construed the FOIA to require a very narrow interpretation of each exemption.[79] Even if the requested information is exempt from disclosure under the FOIA, agencies may release the records where there is no compelling reason for withholding the information.[80]

In most situations, only three of the FOIA exemptions from disclosure will impact an agency's decision with regard to the release of environmental data. Specifically, 5 U.S.C. section 552 provides that no records will be disclosed which contain:

> b(3) information that is specifically exempted from disclosure by other statutes ("Exemption 3");
> b(4) trade secret information ("Exemption 4"); and
> b(7) information compiled as investigatory records for enforcement purposes ("Exemption 7").

Each of these exemptions will be examined in detail.

Information Exempted by Statute

Under Exemption 3, documents "specifically exempted from disclosure by statute . . . [need not be disclosed] provided that such statute (A) requires that matters be withheld from the public in such a manner as to leave no discretion on the issue or (B) establishes particular criteria for withholding or refers to particular matters to be withheld."[81] Thus, the exemption applies only if the federal statute at issue specifically exempts matters from disclosure and the records are covered by the particular nondisclosure statute at issue.

Court have required that the federal statute at issue specifically exempts matters from public disclosure before records may be withheld under this exemption.[82] In *Reporters Commission for Freedom of the Press v. United States Department of Justice,*[83] the court held that records may be withheld under the authority of another statute pursuant to Exemption 3 "if and only if that statute meets the requirements of exemption 3, including the threshold requirement that it specifically exempt matters from disclosure."[84] The court reasoned that there must be a clear congressional purpose in the actual words of the statute to be exempt from disclosure.[85]

Once it is established that a statute is a nondisclosure statute and that it meets at least one of the requirements of Exemption 3, an agency must also establish that the records in question fall within the withholding provision of the nondisclosure statute.[86]

CERCLA section 104(e)(7) provides that records, reports, or information obtained by the EPA shall be disclosed to the public:

> except that upon a showing satisfactory to the President . . . by any person that records, reports, or information, or particular part thereof . . . if made public would divulge information entitled to protection under § 1905 of Title 18, such information or particular portion thereof shall be considered confidential . . . .

18 U.S.C. section 1905 establishes criminal penalties for agency employees who disclose confidential information that:

> concerns or relates to the secrets, processes, operations, style of work, or apparatus, or to the identity, confidential statistical data, amount or source of any income, profits, losses, or expenditures of any person, firm, partnership, corporation or association.

In the case of *Guerra v. Guajardo,*[87] the term "confidential" was construed to apply only to information which, if released, is likely (1) to impair the government's ability to obtain necessary information in the future, or (2) to cause substantial harm to the competitive position of the person from whom the information was obtained. Furthermore, a person who is claiming that information is confidential under CERCLA must comply with the provisions of section 104(e)(7)(E). Information will not be deemed confidential under CERCLA unless (1) such person has not disclosed the information to any other person, other than specified government officials; (2) the information is not required to be disclosed to the public under any other federal or state law; (3) disclosure of the information is likely to cause substantial harm to the competitive position of such person; and (4) the specific chemical identity is not readily discoverable through reverse engineering.[88]

Trade Secrets

Section 552(b)(4) of the FOIA exempts from disclosure "trade secrets and commercial or financial information obtained from a person and is privileged or confidential." This exemption is interpreted by courts to apply to a more narrowly defined set of information than that which qualifies as confidential under 18 U.S.C. section 1905. Exemption 4 applies if a three-part test is satisfied: (1) The information for which exemption is sought must be a "trade secret[]" or "commercial or financial" in character; (2) it must be "obtained from a person";[89] and (3) it must be "privileged or confidential."[90] This exemption is intended to protect the interests of both the government and submitters of information. Its existence encourages submitters to voluntarily furnish useful commercial or financial information to the government, and it correspondingly provides the government with an assurance that such information will be reliable. In addition, the exemption affords protection to those submitters who are required to furnish commercial or financial information to the government by safeguarding them from competitive disadvantages that could result from the disclosure.

Courts have adopted a narrow "common law" definition of the term "trade secret" that differs from the broad definition used in the *Restatement of Torts*. In *Public Citizen Health Research Group v. FDA*,[91] the term "trade secret" was narrowly defined as "a secret, commercially valuable plan, formula, process, or device that is used for the making, preparing, compounding or processing of trade commodities and that could be said to be the end product of either innovation or substantial effort."[92] This definition requires that there be a "direct relationship" between the trade secret and the productive process.[93] The language of 18 U.S.C. section 1905 encompasses not only trade secrets but other types of information relevant to process, operation, and style of work.

Investigatory Records

Section 552(b)(7) of the FOIA exempts from disclosure "investigatory records compiled for law enforcement purposes, but only to the extent that the production of such records would (A) interfere with enforcement proceedings . . . ." FOIA lessened the showing of harm required from a demonstration that release "would interfere with" to "could reasonably be expected to interfere with" enforcement proceedings.[94] Determining the applicability of this exemption requires a two-step analysis focusing on (1) whether a law enforcement proceeding is pending or prospective, and (2) whether release of information about it could reasonably be expected to cause some articulable harm.[95]

In *Gregory v. Federal Deposit Insurance Corp.*, the court narrowly construed this exception to encompass only documents "which focus with special intensity on specific alleged illegal acts and particular parties."[96] The court specifically held that this exemption does not apply to documents prepared as "routine administration, surveillance or oversight of federal programs."[97] Under this analysis, records and reports required to be disclosed under CERCLA or EPCRA probably are not protected from disclosure as investigatory in nature. This type of information arguably is collected or reported to the EPA as part of its routine administration and surveillance of the CERCLA and EPCRA programs. Information or records obtained during EPA investigations and inspections for enforcement purposes, however, or information obtained from a facility as a result of a compliance order will fit the definition of "investigatory records compiled for law enforcement purposes." As such, this information will most likely be protected from disclosure by the EPA pursuant to Section 552(b)(7) of the FOIA.

Trade Secret Protection Under EPCRA

Under the terms of EPCRA, a regulated facility is given explicit protection from disclosure of trade secrets. This provision does not, however, give facilities blanket authority to withhold any information which they consider sensitive or confidential. Section 322 of EPCRA provides that a person required to submit reports under sections 302, 303, 311, 312, or 313 "may withhold from such submittal the specific chemical identity" of any hazardous substance if the identity of the chemical is *in fact* a trade secret. EPA has promulgated administrative rules to guide its implementation of this section.[98] These rules provide detailed procedures that a submitter must follow in order to file a trade secrecy claim.[99] In addition, the regulations outline the analysis that the EPA must undertake in making a determination as to whether any trade secrecy claim is valid.[100] Finally, the regulations contain the procedures to be used by the public for requesting disclosure of chemical identities claimed as trade secrets.[101]

A "trade secret" is defined as:

> Any confidential formula, pattern, process, device, information or compilation of information that is used in a submitter's business, and that gives the submitter an opportunity to obtain an advantage over competitors who do not know or use it. EPA intends to be guided by the Restatement of Torts, § 757, Comment b.[102]

If a facility wishes to invoke trade secrecy protection for a chemical, it must submit to EPA an unsanitized version of the required report, including the specific chemical identity claimed to be protected, along with a sanitized version containing only the generic class or category of the chemical.[103] The sanitized report must be accompanied by a document that substantiates the trade secrecy claim in accordance with the provisions of 40 C.F.R. section 350.7.[104] Specifically, no person can claim protection as a trade secret unless:

1. Such person has not disclosed the information to any other person . . . and such person has taken reasonable measures to protect the confidentiality of such information and intends to continue to take such measures.
2. The information is not required to be disclosed, or otherwise made available, to the public under any other federal or state law.

3. Disclosure of the information is likely to cause substantial harm to the competitive position of such person.
4. The chemical identity is not readily discoverable through reverse engineering.

If the trade secrecy claim is determined by the EPA to be valid under the rules, only the sanitized version of the report will be disclosed to the public and local governments.[105] However, even if chemical identity information can be withheld from the public under these provisions, section 323 of EPCRA provides for disclosure to health professionals who need the information for diagnostic and treatment purposes.

Notably, 40 C.F.R. section 350.3(c)(2) states that any public request for access to chemical identities withheld as trade secrets are to be evaluated solely under the promulgated rules, and not the FOIA. Frivolous trade secret claims can subject the claimant to significant civil penalties of up to $25,000 per claim. Any person who knowingly and willfully divulges trade secret information can be fined up to $20,000 and subject to one year's imprisonment.

The EPA has recognized that when facilities explain why the chemical is a trade secret, they may need to cite other confidential business information in the substantiation.[106] FOIA section 322(f) and the applicable rules allow facilities to make claims of confidentiality for information they provide on their substantiations accompanying claims of trade secrecy. Under the rules, however, evaluation of these confidentiality claims and their disclosure to the public will be governed by the FOIA.[107]

Enforcement and Citizens' Suits

Failure to comply with any of the above-referenced requirements can subject the facility to significant civil or criminal penalties in an enforcement action by EPA or by the appropriate state agency. Penalties can be as high as $25,000 a day per day of violation.

The facility may also be subject to enforcement through a citizens' suit by neighbors or by interested environmental organizations. Under EPCRA, for instance, citizens' groups may sue a facility for failing to make the proper emergency notification and failing to submit the required MSDS under section 311, inventory forms under section 312, or Form R's under section 313. EPCRA § 326.[108]

Conclusion

CERCLA, EPCRA, and the Clean Air Act provide for comprehensive disclosure of information to the government. Under certain circumstances, disclosing this type of information may prove damaging to the regulated industry. However, free access to government records is the rule and not the exception. There are few protections from disclosure by the government, and these are narrowly construed. In light of this policy, businesses required to disclose information should be careful to release only that information specifically mandated by the statutes and which is not exempt from disclosure. Businesses that use, process, manufacture, store, or distribute hazardous substances and chemicals need an in-depth knowledge of the disclosure requirements surveyed above, as well as the requirements of other applicable state and federal statutes. The government's policy is to know and tell; sound business policy should be to know "when to hold 'em" and "when to show 'em."

Notes

1. 42 U.S.C. § 9601 *et seq.*
2. 42 U.S.C. § 11001 *et seq.*
3. 33 U.S.C. § 1251 *et seq.*
4. Several federal environmental statutes, including both the Clean Air Act and the Clean Water Act, mandate comprehensive permitting programs to regulate discharges of air pollution and water pollution to the environment; to manage the treatment, storage, and disposal of solid and hazardous wastes; and to address other environmental risks. Examples are the National Pollutant Discharge Elimination System (NPDES) permits for water discharges and Title V permits for air emissions. While these permitting programs contain significant monitoring, reporting, and record-keeping requirements, the extent of these requirements is beyond the scope of this article.
5. EPA's final audit policy can be found at 60 Fed. Reg. 66706 (Dec. 22, 1995). The audit policy is intended to eliminate or significantly reduce civil and criminal penalties for companies that voluntarily investigate and disclose violations that are promptly corrected. Practitioners should also check individual state regulations as many states have adopted their own audit policies. *See infra* Part VI.
6. 5 U.S.C. § 552.
7. Again, while this article will not explore the myriad of reporting and monitoring requirements under pollution control permit statutes, virtually every air and water discharge permit contains a requirement that the permitted facility report any unplanned discharges which exceed the permitted levels. *See, e.g.,* 40 C.F.R. § 970.6(a)(3)(iii)(B).
8. CERCLA § 103(a) and (b) expressly require any person in charge of a vessel, an offshore facility, or an onshore facility to immediately notify the National Response Center whenever there is release in a "reportable quantity" of any "hazardous substance" into the environment. 42 U.S.C. § 9603(a), (b).

In addition, EPCRA § 304 requires that the owner or operator of a facility report the release of any "extremely hazardous substance" from the facility. Under EPCRA, releases of a "hazardous substance" which require notification under CERCLA and any release of an "extremely hazardous substance" must be reported not only to the National Response Center, but also to the appropriate State Emergency Planning Commission and the local Emergency Planning Committee. These reporting obligations arise immediately after a person has actual knowledge of such a release.
9. *See* CERCLA § 101(22).
10. 50 Fed. Reg. 13456, 13462 (Apr. 4, 1985).
11. *See infra* Part II.
12. *See* CERCLA §§ 101(14) and 102; 42 U.S.C. §§ 9601(14) and 9602.
13. This list is also available on the EPA Web site at http://www.epa.gov.
14. A facility is subject to EPCRA's emergency planning requirements if a substance on the EHS list is present at any time in an amount greater than the TPQ. 40 C.F.R. § 355.30. These requirements include the development of an emergency response plan and participation in the local emergency planning committee.
15. *See also* EPCRA § 304(a)(3)(B)(ii).
16. 50 Fed. Reg. 13463 (Apr. 4, 1985).
17. *See* EPCRA § 304(c).
18. CERCLA § 103(a); EPCRA § 304(a).
19. *See* CERCLA §§ 103(a) and 101(10). (*See* 67 Fed. Reg. 18899 (Apr. 17, 2002).).

20. *See* CERCLA § 101(10).

21. *See* 50 Fed. Reg. 13462 (Apr. 4, 1985).

22. *See* United States v. Iron Mountain Mines, Inc., 812 F. Supp. 1528 (E.D. Cal. 1992); United States v. United Nuclear Corp., 814 F. Supp. 1552 (D.C.N.M. 1992); Idaho v. Bunker Hill Co., 635 F. Supp. 665 (D. Idaho 1986); *In re* Mobil Oil Corp., EPCRA App. No. 94-2, 5 EAD 490, 1994 WL 544260 (Env. App. Bd.).

23. A more thorough definition of "continuous release" is located at 55 Fed. Reg. 30166.

24. 55 Fed. Reg. 30166 (July 24, 1990). This has been codified at 40 C.F.R. § 302.8 and 40 C.F.R. § 355.40(a)(2)(iii).

25. 40 C.F.R. § 355.40(a)(2).

26. 50 Fed. Reg. 13462 (Apr. 4, 1985).

27. *See* EPCRA § 304(a)(4); *see also In re* Genicom Corp., 4 E.A.D. 426, 437 (E.P.A. 1992) ("If the release does not extend off-site, and thus the only persons potentially exposed were on-site, the reporting requirement does not apply."). Under the Occupational Safety and Health Act (Federal OSHA), spills within the workplace may still have to be reported. Any incident involving a fatality or the hospitalization of three or more employees must be reported immediately. *See* 27 C.F.R. § 1904.8. States may administer safety and health regulations as long as their regulations are "at least as effective as" federal OSHA's. 29 U.S.C. § 667(c) and (f).

28. *See* CERCLA § 104.

29. While this article discusses only EPA's authority to investigate and inspect, most state environmental regulatory agencies have also been granted such powers through the implementing legislation at the state level. A practitioner in this area should always refer to the state legislation to determine the state's police powers in this area.

30. *See* Reeves Bros. v. EPA, 956 F. Supp. 665 (W.D. Va. 1995), 956 F. Supp. 676 (W.D. Va. 1996).

31. CERCLA § 104(b)(1).

32. *Id.*

33. *Id.*

34. *See* CERCLA § 104(e).

35. CERCLA § 104(e)(2).

36. CERCLA § 104(e)(2)(ii).

37. *See* United States v. Gurley, 235 F. Supp. 2d 797 (W.D. Tenn. 2002); United States v. Liviola, 605 F. Supp. 96 (N.D. Ohio 1985).

38. 1985 WL 6037 (D. Idaho 1985) [unpublished].

39. Decision vacated as moot in *In re* Bunker Ltd. P'ship, 820 F.2d 308 (9th Cir. 1987).

40. CERCLA § 104(e)(5).

41. CERCLA § 104(e)(5)(B). *See also* United States v. Crown Roll Leaf Inc., 29 Env't Rep. Cas. (BNA) 2025 (D.N.J. 1989) (assessing fines where defendant failed to supply responses to an EPA information request); United States v. Charles George Trucking Co., 823 F.2d 685 (1st Cir. 1987).

42. CERCLA § 104(e)(5)(B)(ii).

43. EPCRA is also referred to at times as "SARA Title III." 42 U.S.C. §§ 11001 through 11050.

44. OSHA defines "hazardous chemical" to mean any substance that presents a physical or health hazard. 29 C.F.R. § 1910.1200(c). This covers just about everything—the federal government estimates that there are between 575,000 and 650,000 hazardous chemicals. 59 Fed. Reg. 6126 (Feb. 9, 1994).

45. EPCRA § 311(c)(2).

46. EPCRA § 311(d)(2).

47. Section 312 inventories are due each year on March 1 for the preceding calendar year. EPCRA 312(a)(2).

48. EPCRA § 312(d)(2).

49. *Id.*

50. EPCRA § 312(e)(3)(A).

51. *In re* K.O. Mfg., Inc., 5 E.A.D. 798, 800 (EAB 1995).

52. The following information is required on the Form R: (1) the name, location, and type of business; (2) off-site locations to which the facility transfers toxic chemicals; (3) whether the chemical is manufactured, processed, or otherwise used and the general categories of use of the chemical; (4) an estimate of the maximum amounts of the toxic chemical present at the facility at any time during the preceding year; (5) the quantity of the chemical entering each medium annually; and (6) waste treatment/disposal methods for each waste stream. Reports are sent to EPA and designated state agencies.

53. EPCRA § 313(j). The TRI list is available on the EPA Web site at http://www.epa.gov/tri.

54. 40 C.F.R. § 372.

55. *See* Executive Order 12856. *See* 62 Fed. Reg. 23834.

56. *See In re* Spang & Co., 1995 EPCRA LEXIS 8 (Oct. 1995).

57. 40 C.F.R. § 372.27.

58. *Id.*

59. 40 C.F.R. § 372.10.

60. *See* 40 C.F.R. § 372.38(a).

61. 40 C.F.R. § 372.38.

62. *See* 40 C.F.R. § 372.38(e).

63. *See id.*

64. C.A.A. § 112(r).

65. Explosives are subject to federal regulation by the Bureau of Alcohol, Tobacco and Firearms, the Mine Safety and Health Act, the Occupational Safety and Health Act, the Department of Defense, the Department of Transportation, and various state and local agencies. 61 Fed. Reg. 16598, 16599 (Apr. 15, 1996). *See* 61 Fed. Reg. 3170 (June 20, 1996). Threshold quantities for toxic and flammable substances range from 500 pounds to 20,000 pounds.

66. The Program 3 SIC codes are: 2611 (pulp mills), 2812 (chlor-alkali), 2819 (industrial inorganics), 2821 (plastics and resins), 2865 (cyclic crudes), 2869 (industrial organics), 2873 (nitrogen fertilizers), 2879 (agricultural chemicals), and 2911 (petroleum refineries).

67. 60 Fed. Reg. 66706 (Dec. 22, 1995).

68. Many states have adopted their own audit provisions and policies. At least some of these states have included formal privileges for environmental audit documents in their policies. A practitioner in this area should pay close attention to individual state law and policy regarding formal privileges. For example, Oregon has adopted a formal privilege for audit documents. *See* O.R.S. 469.963, *et seq.*

69. *See* 61 Fed. Reg. 30570 (June 17, 1996).

70. 5 U.S.C. § 552.

71. S. Rep. No. 813, 89th Congress, 1st Session (1965).

72. United States Dep't of State v. Ray, 425 U.S. 352, 361 (1976).

73. United States Dep't of State v. Ray, 502 U.S. 164, 173-74 (1991); *see also* Ethyl Corp. v. United States Envt'l Protection Agency, 25 F.3d 1241 (4th Cir. 1994).

74. *See* 5 U.S.C. § 552(d); Chrysler Corp. v. Brown, 441 U.S. 281, 293 (1979); Doe v. Veneman, 230 F. Supp. 2d 739 (W.D. Tex. 2002).

75. Chrysler Corp v. Brown, 441 U.S. 281 (1979).

76. Freedom of Information Act § 552(a)(3).

77. EPA's Public Information Rules can be found online at http://www.epa.gov/foia/foiaregs.htm.

78. 40 C.F.R. §§ 2.101-2.309; N.L.R.B. v. Robbins Tire & Rubber Co., 437 U.S. 214, 242 (1978).

79. Air Force v. Rose, 425 U.S. 352, 361 (1976); Welford v. Hardin, 444 F.2d 21 (4th Cir. 1971); Public Citizen Health Research Group v. FDA, 704 F.2d 1280 (D.C. Cir. 1983).

80. Chrysler Corp. v. Brown, 441 U.S. 281, 285 (1979); Charles River Park "A" Inc. v. HUD, 519 F.2d 935 (D.C. Cir. 1975).

81. Section 552(b)(3); Dayton Newspapers, Inc. v. United States Federal Bureau of Information, 1993 U.S. Dist. LEXIS at *9 (S.D. Ohio Feb. 9, 1993).

82. Schrecker v. United States Dep't of Justice, 74 F. Supp. 2d 26, 32 (D.D.C. 1999); *Dayton Newspapers, Inc.*, 1993 U.S. Dist. LEXIS at *9.

83. 816 F.2d 730 (D.C. Cir.).

84. *Id.* at 730, 734 (D.C. Cir.), *modified on other grounds*, 831 F.2d 1124 (D.C. Cir. 1987), *reversed on other grounds*, 489 U.S. 749 (1989).

85. *Id.* at 735; *Schrecker, supra* note 82.

86. Michaels Piano, Inc. v. FTC, 18 F.3d 138, 143 (3d Cir.), *cert. denied*, 115 S. Ct. 574 (1994).

87. 466 F. Supp. 1046 (D.C. Tex. 1978), *aff'd*, 597 F.2d 769 (5th Cir. 1978).

88. CERCLA § 104(e)(7)(E).

89. *Id.*

90. Section 552(b)(4); *see also* GC Micro Corp. v. Defense Logistics Agency, 33 F.3d 1109, 1112 (9th Cir. 1994); Continental Stock Transfer & Trust Co. v. SEC, 566 F.2d 373, 375 (2d Cir. 1977) (per curiam); Gulf & Western Industries, Inc. v. United States, 615 F.2d 527, 529 (D.C. Cir. 1979); Consumers Union v. VA, 301 F. Supp. 796, 802 (S.D.N.Y. 1969).

91. 704 F.2d 1280, 1288-89 (D.C. Cir. 1983).

92. *Id.* at 1288.

93. *Id.*

94. *See* Pub. L. No. 99-570, § 1802, 100 S. Tat. 3207-48.

95. *See* N.L.R.B. v. Robbins Tire & Rubber Co., 437 U.S. 214, 224 (1978).

96. *Id.*

97. *Id.* at 1334.

98. 40 C.F.R. Part 350.

99. 40 C.F.R. §§ 350.5-350.7.

100. 40 C.F.R. §§ 350.9-350.13.

101. 40 C.F.R. § 350.15.

102. 40 C.F.R. § 350.1.

103. 40 C.F.R. § 350.5(a) and § 350.5(b)(2).

104. *See also* § 322(b).

105. If the EPA does not grant the trade secret status, the facility may ask for a court to review the matter.

106. 53 Fed. Reg. 28772, 28774 (July 29, 1988).

107. 40 C.F.R. § 350.3(c)(3).

108. *See generally* Atlantic States Legal Found. v. United Musical Instruments, U.S.A., Inc., 61 F.3d 473 (6th Cir. 1995).

CHAPTER 22

Beyond the Labor and Employment Lawyer's Looking Glass: Who Is My Client?

JEFFREY S. GOLDMAN
PHILIP F. ACKERMAN

Introduction

To provide the best legal advice, an attorney must be fully informed of all the facts and evidence and must be able to discuss those facts and evidence openly with a client. Open communication between attorneys and clients is thus the cornerstone of sound legal advice. The privilege that protects that cornerstone is designed to foster full and frank disclosure of facts, possibilities, and reactions that are both helpful and harmful, without fear that those communications will be used to harm the client's interests.

The ultimate application of the privilege is a delicate balancing of two sometimes conflicting interests: the interest in allowing clients to get the best legal advice and the interest in ascertaining the truth. Changing the balance between these interests by expanding or narrowing the scope of the privilege will, in the long run, affect society's trust in lawyers and the entire legal profession.

The institutional client, like individual clients, requires confidence in the protections offered by the privilege to provide its attorney with as much information as possible. Unlike an individual, however, the corporate client's facts and evidence are usually in the possession of its numerous managers, supervisors, and employees. Accommodating the two conflicting interests of the privilege is therefore more difficult in the corporate context. That difficulty has only been exacerbated by the various definitions of the privilege in the corporate setting.

The labor and employment lawyer is particular prey to the dynamics of those variations. Historically, because of the framework of the National Labor Relations Act, labor lawyers viewed the businesses they either represented or attacked as divided into two forces: management and employees. Union attorneys spoke in confidence with not only their institutional clients, but also individual employees who were their clients' members. Alternatively, management lawyers felt they represented and could speak in confidence to any manager or supervisor.

This otherwise clean dividing line became blurred, if not obliterated, by two forces. First, the work of attorneys specializing in labor relations grew, as both the common law and the legislatures expanded the rights of employees. Common law tort and contract actions in state court have become commonplace, while statutory discrimination actions and other employment-related questions in both federal and state courts are one of the most rapidly rising sources of litigation today. Second, the institutional interest of unions and their employee-members has become far less significant. Hence, in addition to operating in their own insulated administrative world, labor and employment lawyers perform the great majority of their work in the state and federal courts.

To represent their clients effectively, labor and employment lawyers must therefore familiarize themselves with the various standards for privileged communications. They must also be familiar with the application of the privilege to communications with ERISA fiduciaries. Moreover, the existence of problems specific to labor and employment lawyers, such as the need to conduct investigations into ever-increasing harassment claims or to provide joint defense to supervisors and corporations, requires additional familiarity with the waiver rules.

The privilege law varies from state to state, and between state and federal courts. Although the Supreme Court's decision in *Upjohn*[1] provided guidance in the federal court system, mandates from the various states' courts have created disparate standards *and* definitions for the corporate client and its employees. The lack of predictable standards both between the states and at the state and federal levels creates an "Alice in Wonderland" climate. An attorney and his or her corporate client step through the looking glass when trying to determine "who is the client," whether a communication is privileged, and if actions desired to provide the best possible defense could result in a waiver of the privilege. This chapter will examine the dilemmas faced by courts, attorneys, and clients when attempting to ascertain the identity of the corporate client and the scope of the privilege afforded it.[2]

Background of the Attorney-Client Privilege

The attorney-client privilege is designed to encourage full and frank communication between attorneys and their clients in order to ensure effective representation.[3] Although the privilege shields the disclosure of the contents of a communication to the attorney, it does not insulate from disclosure the underlying facts communicated to an attorney or attorneys. Accordingly, while a client cannot typically be compelled to answer "what did you say to your attorney?," a client may not refuse to disclose relevant facts merely because those same facts were communicated to attorneys.[4]

At the inception of the privilege, clients were individuals. The advent of the corporation as a distinct legal entity, however, created difficulties applying the privilege that attorneys, clients, and the courts are still grappling with today. A corporation is a legal fiction, and as a purely legal entity has no existence apart from the law. The non-corporeal nature of the corporate client makes the application of the attorney-client privilege unpredictable; the corporation is the holder of the privilege and the attorney owes his allegiance to the corporation—not to the corporation's officers, directors, and employees. Yet, the attorney and corporate client may only communicate with each other through its officers, directors, and employees.[5]

Courts have come up with different solutions to identify the client for purposes of this privilege. Because of the lack of uniform standards, the answer to the question "Who is my client?" may vary depending upon whether an action is brought in state or federal court, and will vary depending upon in which state's court the case is brought. This lack of predictability creates a potential quagmire for the unsuspecting corporate client. The uncertainty of the scope of the privilege makes it crucial for the attorney and client to examine the law of the forum and to formulate procedures to maximize the applicability of the privilege.

The Attorney-Client Privilege in Federal Courts

The attorney-client privilege dates back to the sixteenth century and is believed to be the oldest of the confidential privileges known to the common law.[6] The most widely cited general statement of the privilege is that it applies only if: (1) the asserted holder of the privilege is or sought to become a client; (2) the person to whom the communication was made (a) is a member of the bar of a court or a subordinate thereof, and (b) in connection with this communication is acting as a lawyer; (3) the communication relates to a fact of which the attorney was informed (a) by the client (b) without the presence of strangers (c) for the purposes of securing primarily either (i) an opinion on law or (ii) legal services or (iii) assistance in some legal proceeding, and not (d) for the purpose of committing a crime or tort; and (4) the privilege has been (a) claimed and (b) not waived by the client.[7]

Because corporations were initially treated like other principals with agents,[8] the client was originally defined to include "any authorized representatives."[9] All communications between an agent of the client and the client's attorney were deemed privileged.[10] This view, however, was radically altered by *Radiant Burners Inc. v. American Gas Association*,[11] in which the attorney-client privilege was held not to extend to corporations. Although *Radiant Burners* was later reversed, its original holding caused courts to create numerous tests limiting and defining the previously unquestioned parameters of the privilege.

The first test to emerge was the control group test. Under the control group test, the privilege extended only to an employee, usually an officer or director, who was "in a position to control or even to take a substantial part in a decision about any action which the corporation may take upon the advice of the attorney . . . then, in effect, he is (or personifies) the corporation when he makes his disclosure to the lawyer."[12] This test generally protects only statements made by the upper echelon of corporate management and reflects the distinction between the corporation as an entity and the non-control group employees as individuals. It is based on the premise that only an employee who controls the actions of the corporation can personify the corporation.[13]

While the majority of the circuits adopted the control group test, other circuits rejected the test as unrealistically narrow and inadequate in considering the practicalities of the daily operations of a corporation. Instead, these circuits focused on the purpose of the communication rather than the communication's maker.[14] This focus led to the subject matter test. Under the subject matter test, an employee's communication was deemed that of the corporation and therefore privileged if the communication was made at the direction of the employee's corporate superior and the subject matter related to the performance of the employee's corporate duties.[15]

A third test also arose, a modified subject matter test. Under this test, a limited dissemination requirement was added. The privilege applied only if "(1) the communication was made for the purpose of securing legal advice; (2) the employee making the communication did so at the direction of his corporate superior; (3) the superior made the request so that the corporation could secure legal advice; (4) the subject matter of the communication was within the scope of the employee's corporate duties; and (5) the communication was not disseminated beyond those persons who, because of the corporate structure, needed to know its contents."[16]

The United States Supreme Court resolved the conflict among the circuits in *Upjohn Co. v. United States*[17] by rejecting the control group test. As the *Upjohn* Court explained, the control group test ignored the realities of the workplace:

> In the corporate context, however, it will frequently be employees beyond the control group . . . who will possess the information needed by the corporation's lawyers. Middle-level and indeed lower-level employees can, by actions within the scope of their employment, embroil the corporation in serious legal difficulties, and it is only natural that these employees would have the relevant information needed by corporate counsel if he is adequately to advise the client with respect to such actual or potential difficulties.[18]

The *Upjohn* Court noted the control group test frustrated "the very purpose of the privilege by discouraging the communication of relevant information by employees of the client to attorneys seeking to render legal advice to the client corporation."[19]

Rather than adopting a specific alternate test, however, the *Upjohn* Court set forth several factors on which the scope of the corporate attorney-client privilege should be developed on a case-by-case basis:

1. Whether the communications were made by corporate employees to corporate counsel at the direction of corporate superiors in order to secure legal advice from counsel;
2. Whether the information needed by corporate counsel to formulate the advice was unavailable to upper-level management;
3. Whether the communication concerned matters within the scope of the employee's corporate duties;
4. Whether the employees were aware that the communications were made in order to allow the corporation to obtain legal advice; and

5. Whether the communications were ordered to be kept confidential and had been kept confidential by the corporation.[20]

The *Upjohn* Court's unequivocal rejection of the control group test and adoption of a flexible approach focusing on the subject matter and function of the communications broadened the scope of the privilege. This flexibility, however, raised new questions as to the application of the factors: Were the factors enunciated by the court the only factors? Were some factors entitled to more weight than others? And must all factors be present in order to invoke the privilege? The new unpredictability of *Upjohn*'s case-by-case analysis did little to instill confidence in corporate clients and attorneys that their communications would indeed be confidential and privileged.

The risk of unevenness of the application of the factors is seen in the cases subsequent to *Upjohn*. In *Baxter Travenol Laboratories. Inc. v. LeMay*,[21] the court applied *Upjohn* and found that most of the factors favored the invocation of the privilege. The employee, however, also communicated matters outside the scope of his corporate duties to counsel. Applying the totality of the circumstances, the *LeMay* court determined that the existence of one negative factor was not significant. Rather, *LeMay* held that in order to foster uninhibited client communication, it would be improper to place emphasis on either the status or the content of the communication. By drawing an analogy to the individual client who retains the protection of the privilege when speaking to his or her attorney about information developed by others, the court held that "[t]he privilege should not be denied simply because the corporation must act, obtain knowledge, and communicate with counsel through other, natural persons."[22]

Conversely, in *Leer v. Chicago, Milwaukee, St. Paul & Pacific Railroad Co.*[23] the court, applying *Upjohn*, found that an employee's communications concerning an accident he witnessed were not privileged because they did not arise within the scope of the employee's job duties.

These holdings suggest that regardless of his or her position in the corporation, an employee may be entitled to assert the privilege if the communication, whether based on first- or secondhand information, centers on work-related matters. On the other hand, when the communications involve matters outside the scope of the employee's position, the employee is not sufficiently identified with the corporation to be deemed the "corporate client." Instead, the employee's status is like that of any third-party witness. As a practical matter, because courts are likely to find the totality of the circumstances more important than the absence or presence of any of the individual factors, a corporate client should assert the privilege in the absence of one or more of the *Upjohn* factors.

The Attorney-Client Privilege in State Courts

While federal courts now uniformly apply the *Upjohn* factors, albeit by assigning the different factors differing weight, some state courts do not follow *Upjohn*. As a result, in non-*Upjohn* states like Illinois, a different privilege test may be applied in the state and federal court systems. The inconsistent application of privilege tests is especially troublesome for employment lawyers who, because of the trend toward combining state tort actions with federal discrimination claims, face removal decisions in formulating defense strategies. A decision as to whether or not attorney-client privilege concerns should govern strategic decisions relating to removal or possible remand will, of course, depend upon the need to protect specific communications and the applicable standards. As the following survey of five states indicates, however, the lack of uniformity creates more uncertainty in determining the proper standard for the assertion of the corporate client's privilege.

California

California utilizes a factor analysis, similar to the *Upjohn* approach, to determine the applicability of its privilege.[24] In *D.I. Chadbourne, Inc. v. Superior Court*, the court sought to provide corporate clients the same opportunity as individuals to conduct privileged communications with their attorney, but held that the corporations should not receive greater privileges than individuals simply because it must utilize another entity or agent to communicate.[25] According to *Chadbourne*, the desired equity is achieved by conducting an inquiry similar to that later utilized by *Upjohn*—a corporate communication would be privileged only if the person from whom the information emanates reasonably intends the information to be confidential.[26] In other words, if the information is obtained by an employee in his or her corporate capacity from either the corporation or his or her on-the-job observance, and the corporation and/or the individual desires confidentiality, the disclosure of that information to the corporate attorney is privileged. If, on the other hand, the corporate employee is merely a witness to facts, such as a janitor witnessing sexual harassment or an industrial accident, his or her disclosure of those facts is not privileged.[27]

Illinois

While California is in accordance with *Upjohn*, Illinois is dramatically inapposite. In *Consolidated Coal Co. v. Bucyrus-Erie Co.*,[28] the Illinois Supreme Court expressly rejected *Upjohn* and adopted the control group test. After balancing the countervailing principles of privilege and liberal discovery, the court held that the balance favored broad discovery.[29] The *Consolidated Coal* court muddied the waters even further, however, when it modified the control group test. According to the Illinois Supreme Court, a particular employee's title or position is not determinative of inclusion in the control group. Rather, evidence is required that the employee whose communications are sought to be protected possesses actual authority to make or contribute to a judgment or decision.[30] For example, in *Claxton v. Thackston*,[31] a member of the board of directors who possessed sole corporate authority over manufacturing was denied control group status, and his communications therefore denied privilege status, because the record did not reflect that the director played any actual role in the corporate decision making at issue.[32] Conversely, *Consolidated Coal* left open the possibility of including within the control group an employee who, on the particular topic at issue, was ordinarily consulted or who provided opinions on which the final decision makers based their decision.[33] Illinois' modified control group test is yet another hybrid test to be considered in determining who is the corporate client.

Texas

In 1998, the Texas legislature amended its Rule of Civil Evidence codifying the privilege to change from the control group test to the subject-matter test.[34] In its codified rule, Texas clearly establishes that the subject matter group test will be utilized to determine who is a representative of the client for privilege purposes.[35]

Florida

After conducting a thorough analysis of *Upjohn*, Florida, in *Southern Bell Tel. & Tel. Co. v. Deason*,[36] adopted the previously described modified subject matter test. As the *Deason* court explained, the modified subject matter test best struck a balance between encouraging corporations to seek and receive effective legal advice and preventing corporate attorneys from being used as shields to thwart discovery. "[W]e set forth the following criteria to judge whether a corporation's communications are protected by the attorney-client privilege":

1. The communication would not have been made but for the contemplation of legal services;
2. The employee making the communication did so at the direction of his or her corporate superior;
3. The superior made the request of the employee as part of the corporation's effort to secure legal advice or services;
4. The content of the communication relates to the legal services being rendered, and the subject matter of the communication is within the scope of the employee's duties; and
5. The communication is not disseminated beyond those persons who, because of the corporate structure, need to know its contents.[37]

New York

Finally, although the varying privilege tests to be followed in the above-described state and federal jurisdictions engender confusion, those states have, at least, established the test to be utilized. New York, however, has not. While the New York Court of Appeals hinted an *Upjohn* standard may be applied,[38] no New York court has expressly adopted or rejected any approach.[39]

Because of the varied state and federal holdings, invocation of the attorney-client privilege may be a little like playing Russian roulette. Usually, by the onset of litigation, the attorney and client have communicated about the litigation. Yet, until an action is filed in either state or federal court, and remains there, the controlling privilege standard (including choice of law) is unknown. Accordingly, until an action comes to rest in a particular jurisdiction, the identity of the corporate client for privilege purposes is also unknown.

The Special Problem of Client Identity in ERISA Cases

The foregoing highlights the issue of whether a particular employee can be considered representative of the corporate client so that communications between that employee and a lawyer are protected by the attorney-client privilege. A somewhat different issue arises in ERISA benefits litigation, where an individual employee argues that the attorney-client privilege cannot be asserted to him for communications between ERISA fiduciaries and their lawyers. This argument is based on the so-called "fiduciary exception" doctrine, as discussed in *Garner v. Wolfinbarger*[40] and its progeny.

In the ERISA context, the argument goes that plan fiduciaries cannot assert the attorney-client privilege against the plan beneficiaries, since "the beneficiaries, not the plan trustee, are the clients of the attorney who provides legal advice for the administration of the plan."[41]

Even where applicable, this exception only applies to legal advice that relates to administration of the ERISA plan. In *Geissal v. Moore Medical Corp.*, a plan beneficiary claimed that he was wrongly denied health plan coverage and brought an ERISA claim against both the ERISA plan itself and his former employer as the administrator of the plan. The plan beneficiary sought to depose two lawyers who had advised the defendants regarding the plan's decision to terminate the beneficiary's coverage.

The court, after reviewing the case law, held that due to the fiduciary exception doctrine, the beneficiary was entitled to discover the basis upon which the plan terminated his coverage, including any communications with counsel related to that determination. The court rejected the argument that the determination of the beneficiary's claim did not relate to plan administration "[b]ecause the denial of claims is as much a part of the administration of a plan as the decision-making which results in no unhappy beneficiary."[42]

The court did not, however, allow the beneficiary to inquire into communications with counsel after the plan decided to terminate the beneficiary's coverage. For those communications, the record indicated that shortly after denial of the beneficiary's claims, the beneficiary retained counsel who suggested to the defendants that litigation was likely unless the defendants reversed their termination of coverage. "Those communications evidence that the interests of Mr. Geissal as a beneficiary of the plan and the interests of the plan administrator in justifying and protecting the decision to terminate sufficiently diverged and differed to warrant the plan administrator in obtaining confidential legal advice on the matter."[43]

A labor and employment lawyer, therefore, needs to be aware and cognizant of the potential non-application of the attorney-client privilege when a client asks for advice regarding ERISA coverage determinations. When a lawyer is consulted in such a situation, the client should be immediately alerted to the potential for disclosure to the beneficiary. On the flip side, lawyers representing ERISA beneficiaries need to be aware of this potentially outcome-determinative source of discovery.

Waiver

Otherwise privileged attorney client communications will no longer be protected if a client expressly or impliedly waives the privilege. Waiver usually occurs through excessive disclosure of documents or communications to either the government or private parties outside the corporation, or by failing to maintain the necessary confidentiality within the corporation. Disclosures such as the examples listed above are inconsistent with the purpose behind the privilege of protecting the confidentiality of a document or communication. In addition to the most common type of waiver—a simple inadvertent disclosure of an otherwise privileged document or communication—labor and employment attorneys are often presented with two scenarios that are fraught with waiver risk.

The first scenario arises in the defense of sexual or racial harassment allegations. Because corporate liability for harassment arises when the defendant-corporation knew or should have known of the harassment and failed to take prompt remedial action,[44] it is imperative that corporations immediately investigate and remediate the slightest valid allegation of harassment. When determining the adequacy and effectiveness of an employer's response to such claims or allegations, courts will consider, inter alia, the type of investigation conducted.[45]

Oftentimes, a corporation will contact counsel upon receiving harassment allegations, and oftentimes counsel, whether in-house or outside, will conduct the investigation. Although allowing corporate counsel to conduct an investigation seems to satisfy two objectives—one, demonstrating that the corporation engaged in the proper investigatory and remedial action, and two, allowing counsel to obtain the necessary information to defend the matter should it proceed to litigation—in all likelihood, the facts uncovered in the course of the investigation, as well as the actual investigatory contacts and steps, will not be privileged. As the United States District Court for New Jersey held, because the investigation itself provides a defense to liability, the corporation cannot argue that its investigatory process should be shielded from discovery.[46]

> Consistent with the doctrine of fairness, the plaintiffs must be permitted to probe the substance of [defendant's] alleged investigation to determine its sufficiency. Without having evidence of the actual content of the investigation, neither the plaintiff nor the factfinder at trial can discern the adequacy. Consequently, this court finds that [the corporation] has waived its attorney-client privilege with respect to the content of [its attorney's] investigation of the plaintiffs' allegations.[47]

In such a situation, corporate counsel's ability to learn the relevant facts in an otherwise privileged investigation should not be compromised by requiring him or her to perform the prophylactic investigatory function.

The second common waiver situation faced by labor and employment attorneys occurs when a discrimination or harassment plaintiff names both the supervisor and the corporate employer as defendants. While dual representation with a waiver of conflicts is a possibility, the likelihood that the interests of the supervisor and the corporation will, at some point, become adverse makes separate individual representation a better alternative.[48] In the separate representation context, however, how can corporate counsel conduct the necessary conversations with the key witness, the separately represented individual supervisor, and maintain the confidentiality of those communications? The answer is a joint defense agreement.

A joint defense privilege covers conversations between actual and potential co-defendants and their attorney or attorneys for any common defense purpose; significantly, the content of such communications may not be disclosed without the consent of all co-defendants.[49] To establish the existence of a joint defense privilege, the party asserting the privilege must show that (1) the communications were made in the course of an agreed-upon joint defense effort; (2) the communications were designed to further the effort; (3) at the time of the communication, litigation, or at least a strong possibility of future litigation, existed; and (4) the privilege was not previously waived.[50]

Once the attorney-client privilege is established, great care must be exercised to prevent an unintentional waiver of the privilege, especially in the common situations explained above. While the area of waiver provides more predictability than the establishment of the privilege, corporate waiver is always a risk. In addition to familiarity with the two examples, the need for establishing and following a prophylactic procedure when disclosing any documents or information cannot be overstated.

Procedures to Maximize Protection of the Confidentiality of Communications

To maximize the protection of the privilege and confidential communications, and to forestall the detrimental effects of an opposing counsel's ex parte contact, it is imperative to formulate prophylactic procedures for communication between the corporate client and its counsel.

1. Discuss the privilege and the necessity of formulating consistent procedures to ensure the maintenance of the confidentiality of the communications with the directors, officers, and managing agents of the corporate client.
2. Advise the directors, officers and managing agents that these procedures should be explained to and implemented by any employee who contacts corporate counsel for legal advice on behalf of the corporate client.
3. To the extent possible, put all communications between the attorney and corporate client in writing.
   a. A written request for legal advice should be made prior to communications with counsel.
   b. All written privileged communications should be clearly marked "Confidential—Attorney-Client Privilege."
4. Any communication with counsel by a mid- or low-level employee should occur at the direction of a corporate superior.
5. Clarify, either in writing or otherwise, that the purpose of communication is for legal advice on behalf of the corporation.
6. Provide the employee authority to contact counsel.
7. Ensure that a corporate superior directs, preferably in writing, that the communication be confidential and be confidentially maintained.
8. The confidentiality of the communications should be maintained internally. Procedures for restricting access to privileged communications should be formulated and implemented.
9. Do not utilize corporate counsel to conduct internal harassment investigations. The investigator, or an uninvolved supervisor or manager, should be in constant contact with the corporate attorney so as to provide the attorney assistance in conducting his or her own separate, privileged investigation "in anticipation of litigation."

10. Utilize explicit written joint defense agreements whenever a supervisor and the corporation are both named as parties.

Conclusion

The lack of predictable standards in the application of the attorney-client privilege and the prohibition against ex parte contact with a represented party creates a potential minefield through which an attorney must guide a corporate client. The various standards applied by the individual state and federal courts could force a corporate client seeking the protections offered by the privilege and rule to obtain legal advice under different formulations of the privilege in each state in which it does business. Moreover, depending on the cause of action, there is no guarantee whether an action will be filed in state or federal court. Thus, depending upon the jurisdiction, two identical communications may or may not be privileged.

Effective representation requires the confidentiality of attorney and client communications. Lack of certainty as to the confidentiality of the communications makes a client disinclined to communicate openly and fully with its attorney. Courts must recognize that the nature of a corporate client is unique from that of the individual client and must fashion standards to meet those needs. Crucial to this process is the development of uniform, predictable standards providing the attorney with the knowledge who his or her client is, and providing the corporate client the certainty that its communications with counsel will be privileged. Until such standards are established, attorneys and corporations alike will be forced to operate in this privileged wonderland.

Notes

1. Upjohn Co. v. United States, 449 U.S. 383, 389 (1984).
2. This paper confronts the identification problems in the private civil area only. The application of the privilege in the criminal context or with the government as a party is beyond the scope of this chapter.
3. *Upjohn, supra* note 1.
4. *Id.* at 395-96.
5. Jonas, *Who Is the Client? The Corporate Lawyer's Dilemma,* 39 HASTINGS L.J. 617 (1988).
6. *See* 8 WIGMORE ON EVIDENCE § 2290 (McNaughton, rev. 1961).
7. United States v. United Shoe Machinery Corp., 89 F. Supp. 357 (D. Mass. 1950), *as cited in* 27 A.L.R. 5th 76, 95 (1995).
8. Stern, *Attorney-Client Privilege: Supreme Court Repudiates the Control Group Test,* 67 A.B.A. J. 1142 (1981).
9. *Id.* The privilege extended only to communications by an officer, director or employee of the corporation.
10. *Id.*
11. 207 F. Supp. 771 (N.D. Ill. 1962).
12. Philadelphia v. Westinghouse Elec. Corp., 210 F. Supp. 483, 485 (E.D. Pa. 1962), *cert. denied*, General Electric Co. v. Kirkpatrick, 372 U.S. 943 (1963).
13. National Tank Co. v. Brotherton, 851 S.W.2d 193 (Tex. 1993).
14. Harper & Row Publishers, Inc. v. Decker, 423 F.2d 487, 491-92 (7th Cir.), *aff'd by an equally divided court*, 400 U.S. 348, *reh'g den.*, 401 U.S. 950 (1970).

15. *Id.*

16. Diversified Indus, Inc. v. Meredith, 572 F.2d 596 (8th Cir. 1977).

17. 449 U.S. 383.

18. *Upjohn*, 449 U.S. 383, 391.

19. *Id.* at 392; 4 MOORE'S FEDERAL PRACTICE 26-183 (2d ed. 1996).

20. *Upjohn,* 449 U.S. 383, 394-95; Gergacz, *Attorney-Corporate Client Privilege*, 37 BUS. LAW-YER 461 (1982).

21. 89 F.R.D. 410 (S.D. Ohio 1981).

22. *Id.* at 414.

23. 308 N.W.2d 305 (Minn. 1981), *cert. denied*, 455 U.S. 939 (1982).

24. D.I. Chadbourne, Inc. v. Superior Court, 60 Cal. 2d 723, 36 Cal. Rptr. 468, 388 P.2d 700 (1964).

25. *Id.*

26. *Id.*; 27 A.L.R. 5th 76 (1995).

27. *Id.*

28. 432 N.E.2d 250 (Ill. 1982).

29. *Id.* at 257.

30. *Id.*

31. 201 Ill. App. 3d 232, 147 Ill. Dec. 82, 559 N.E.2d 82 (1st Dist. 1990).

32. *Id.*; 27 A.L.R. 5th 76, 104 (1995).

33. *Id.* at 258.

34. TEX. R. CIV. EVID. 503(a)(2).

35. TEX. R. CIV. EVID. 503 cmt. to 1998 change, as explained in *In re* Monsanto Co., 998 S.W.2d 917, 922 (Tex. App. 1999).

36. 632 So. 2d 1377 (Fla. 1994).

37. *Id.* at 1383.

38. *Cf.* Niesig v. Team I, 76 N.Y.S.2d 363, 559 N.Y.S.2d 493, 558 N.E.2d 1030 (Ct. App. 1990).

39. *See* N.Y. JURIS. 2d § 867 n.94 and accompanying text (2003).

40. 430 F.2d 1093 (5th Cir. 1970).

41. Geissal v. Moore Med. Corp., 192 F.R.D. 620, 624 (E.D. Mo. 2000) (collecting cases).

42. 192 F.R.D. at 625.

43. *Id.* at 625-26.

44. *See* Meritor Sav. Bank FSB v. Vinson, 477 U.S. 57 (1986) and its progeny.

45. *Id.*

46. Harding v. Dana Transport, Inc., 914 F. Supp. 1084, 1096 (D.N.J. 1996); *see also* Brownell v. Roadway Package Sys., Inc., 185 F.R.D. 19, 24-25 (N.D.N.Y. 1999) (collecting cases).

47. 914 F. Supp. at 1096.

48. Dual representation raises possible common interest problems. As explained in Waste Management, Inc. v. Int'l Surplus Lines Ins. Co., 144 Ill. 2d 178, 579 N.E.2d 322, 338 (1991),

> Under the common interest doctrine, when an attorney acts for two different parties who each have a common interest, communications by either party to the attorney are not necessarily privileged in a subsequent controversy between the two parties.

49. *In re* Grand Jury Subpoenas, 902 F.2d 244 (4th Cir. 1990); Polycast Technology Corp. v. Uniroyal, Inc., 125 F.R.D. 47 (S.D.N.Y. 1989).

50. Haines v. Liggett Group, Inc., 975 F.2d 81, 94 (3d Cir. 1992); Metro Wastewater Reclamation Dist. v. Continental Casualty Co., 142 F.R.D. 471, 478 (D. Colo. 1992); Medcom Holding Co. v. Baxter Travenol Labs., 689 F. Supp. 841 (N.D. Ill. 1988).

Index